Sir Philip Sidney

Selected Prose and Poetry

Sir Philip Sidney
Selected Prose and Poetry

Edited by ROBERT KIMBROUGH

Second Edition

The University of Wisconsin Press

Published 1983

The University of Wisconsin Press
114 North Murray Street
Madison, Wisconsin 53715

The University of Wisconsin Press, Ltd.
1 Gower Street
London WC1E 6HA, England

The first edition *Sir Philip Sidney: Selected Prose and Poetry* was published by Holt, Rinehart and Winston, Inc., in 1969.

Printed in the United States of America

ISBN 0-299-09130-9 (cloth)
     0-299-09134-1 (paper)

CONTENTS

v

PREFACE

I N JANUARY 1969, opening the Preface to the first edition of *Sir Philip Sidney: Selected Prose and Poetry*, I wrote:

Sir Philip Sidney has long been recognized as a central figure in the English literary Renaissance. Yet, because of the breadth of his achievement as a writer, and because of the fascinating nature of his life as an Elizabethan, full and balanced attention has not always been paid to his writing. At present, there is, however, a renaissance of interest in Sidney the writer— the number of books, articles, and dissertations appearing in the last decade alone outweigh in quantity and quality the output of the rest of the century.

What I then called "this burst of interest" became an explosion in the next decade, and the percussions continue into the 80s. That Sidney has indeed been enshrined in scholardom is attested by the fact that now he even has his own *Newsletter*!

When the present anthology was first published, there were few Sidney texts available. Albert Feuillerat had edited the complete works in the twenties, but not in an entirely reliable manner, and his volumes were out of print for a long time, until the Cambridge University Press reprinted the prose parts of that edition in 1962. The year 1962 saw also the first important modern edition of Sidney—William Ringler's magnificent edition of the poems. That volume from the Oxford University Press was followed in 1973 by the *Old Arcadia* and *Miscellaneous Prose*; the *New Arcadia* and the *Correspondence* have yet to appear.

Sir Philip Sidney: Selected Prose and Poetry went through three printings before the original publisher, Holt, Rinehart and Winston, discontinued publication. The decision of the University of Wisconsin Press to issue this second edition pleases me for two reasons. Professionally, my colleagues and I across the country and in Canada have missed this most useful text in our Renaissance courses. But, selfishly, I welcome the opportunity to emend the text. More than 100 corrections have been made, most of them to rectify errors resulting from the first printer's failure to follow my typescript.

The Introduction places Sidney in the context of his time, both historically and aesthetically, and suggests the nature of his personal and literary achievements. The Chronology which follows the Introduction is a kind of summary, for it contains biographical, historical, and literary dates and data. In bringing the Selected Bibliography up to date for this edition I have included only seventeen new items, these just books and no articles. I have retained most of the earlier items so that someone coming to Sidney for the first time can get a sense of the essential scholarship and criticism which led to the proliferation of Sidney studies in the last twenty years. Thus it must be emphasized that the present bibliography is highly "selected."

The actual works of Sidney presented here are divided into four groups: Early Prose, Poetry, and Criticism; *The Defence of Poesy*; *Astrophel and Stella*; and the *New Arcadia*. Although each section has a separate Introduction, this arrangement should not discourage the reader from making correlations. For example, Book I of the *Old Arcadia* and Book I of the *New Arcadia* are each included in entirety in order to facilitate comparisons. Furthermore, the reader interested in *Astrophel and Stella* should look at Sidney's earlier verse in order to measure the achievement of the sonnet sequence. And, Sidney's *Defence* sheds light on both his fiction and his poetry.

All of the texts have been modernized in conformity with modern American English spelling and punctuation, except that obsolete words have not been transliterated and old spellings have been retained when essential for rhyme. Although in his Oxford edition Ringler tried to reconstruct the peculiarities of Sidney's spelling, there is in fact no holograph manuscript of any of Sidney's literary works, nor is there any printed text which has the ultimate authority of Sidney himself. To preserve, then, the vagaries of scribes and the inconsistencies of Elizabethan printing houses merely out of antiquarian bias is pointless: what Elizabethans saw in print they surely thought of as "modern."

Although the original texts which I have used as the basis for each of the texts presented here are noted in the separate Introductions, I should like to make some general acknowledgments. For permission to print a poem from *The Lady of May* as preserved in the Helmingham Hall manuscript (Hm), I am grateful to its then owner, Arthur Houghton. Hm has since been sold to the British Library. For their permission to print selections from the *Old Arcadia* from the St. John's manuscript (St), I should like to thank the Master and Fellows of St. John's College, Cambridge University. I also should like to thank Jean Robertson, editor of the Oxford Press *Old Arcadia* (1973), for generously lending me her film of St. The Cambridge University Press granted permission to print parts of a letter from Sidney to his brother Robert which appears in the *Complete Prose Works*. Finally, I owe a special kind of debt to William Ringler, who was generously willing to allow me to reprint poems from his edition; I was unable to use his text, however, because the Oxford University Press would not grant permission. In freshly editing the poems for this volume, then, I found that I have established a text that is somewhat more conservative than Ringler's. For example, I have not adopted his emendation of "Astrophel" as "Astrophil" not only because there is little justification—there is no need. Nevertheless, I have relied heavily on Ringler's critical apparatus and have adopted his abbreviated titles for the various poems (for example, OA 3 is the third poem appearing in context in the *Old Arcadia*, even though it reappears in the *New Arcadia*).

Working on the first edition of this volume, I received particular help from Alice Patricia Hogan and Gail White, who helped prepare the text, and from Margaret Callahan Neville and Roberta Gordon Amundson, who typed the entire text. To lay the way to a second edition, my students over the years collectively isolated most of the errors in the first edition. Various colleagues donated their copies of that edition so that preparation of this one could be carried out. Working on this second edition I have been assisted by Elizabeth Steinberg, who checked the classical languages, Andrew Weiner, who made suggestions for the bibliography, and Deanna Briley, who did the typing.

Madison, Wisconsin   Robert Kimbrough
June 1982

INTRODUCTION

THE LIFE, ART, AND CRITICISM of Sir Philip Sidney are marked by a search for wholeness, a pursuit of sincerity, and a plea for integrity. This closeness in relationship between the life and the creative and critical endeavors does not come about because Sidney was a man of letters. He was a courtier. As such, writing was part of his education, an education guided by "Art, Imitation, and Exercise," to use Sidney's casual phrase from the *Defence*.

For a life to be whole or a poem engaging, the three elements of this program each had to be developed, yet all kept in balance. Art had to do with personal skills and abilities, but skills and abilities constantly increasing in scope through learning the rules of conduct needed either to court an emperor or a lady, to pen a forensic oration or an epigram. Imitation was a call to follow the leads of the great men and writers, past as well as present, either in the ways they had lived or written, or in what they had achieved in life or art. And Exercise meant practice, in school and out—the maintenance of an active intercourse with the world, academic and nonacademic.

Although Sidney's generation was among the first to be brought up under the radical new humanism espoused by Thomas Elyot which held that those of gentle birth ought to undergo the exercise of formal education to make them fit to take their appropriate places in government, most sons of Elizabethan gentry and nobility still received their major education from exercise with nonacademic worlds—familial, social, courtly, national, and international—but worlds, unlike medieval ones, now in seeming total flux. Indeed, the influence of the revolutionary Tudor world on personality was direct. Gunpowder was too new to fear, but the new nation founded by Henry VII and the new religion started by Luther, and tentatively established by Henry VIII in the 1530s, created an explosive enough atmosphere to make all noblemen wonder how long their worlds, large and small, would hold together. Tudor materialism and love of ritual were sublimations of this anxiety, but the new learning established by Thomas Lynacre, William Grocyn, and Sir Thomas More, and implemented by Sir John Cheke, Roger Ascham, and Thomas Wilson provided an approach to life capable of stabilizing and directing the emergent nationalism and Protestantism by making all aware of their common heritage, shared nature, and collective destiny, as well as making each aware of inherent human power, individual responsibility, and glorious potential. The humanists' conception of Art as skill, a technical proficiency which could be taught through Imitation, and developed through Exercise was at the same time progressive and conservative. Sir Philip Sidney's education is a case in point.

The curious paradox of simultaneous turbulence and continuity, of chaos and calm, that marks sixteenth-century England can be seen in the details surrounding Philip Sidney's birth and baptism in 1554. He was born on November 30th at Penshurst, that famous thirteenth-century castle in Kent which symbolized to Ben Jonson the stability of England, but which in reality seemed to change hands with the accession of each new monarch from the time of Henry III. In fact, only in 1552 had Sidney's grandfather, Sir William, received it from Edward VI. Sir William's son Henry had been the boyhood companion and adult counsellor of Protestant Edward and was the son-in-law of the recently executed rebel, the Earl of Northumberland; still, just before the birth of Philip, Henry had been sent by Catholic Queen Mary to escort to England her husband-to-be, the King of Spain. Philip's mother, the former Mary Dudley, had been, ever since childhood, the friend and companion of Princess Elizabeth, and had helped her father Northumberland in his plot to put his son Guilford and Lady Jane Grey on the throne in 1553. Philip's Dudley uncles, to become under Elizabeth the powerful Earls of Leicester and Warwick, also had taken part in this Protestant plot, and had just been released from prison by Mary. But all along, his Sidney aunts had been lifelong, devoutly Catholic companions of Queen Mary. The Sidneys were either naively daring or coolly diplomatic; for Philip's godparents they picked the widowed Duchess of Northumberland and King Philip. The ultimate irony of this complex situation is that as Philip Sidney grew up, Philip of Spain became more and more the target of his political and religious anger.

In addition to the new nation and the new religion, Sidney was exposed from birth through his parents to the new learning of the humanists. Sir Henry, who had attended Oxford, while companion to Prince Edward must have conversed with Cheke and Ascham; and among his last efforts before being recalled as Lord Deputy of Ireland in 1571, were to found a number of grammar schools in which he was successful, and a university in Dublin in which he was not. Lady Mary (along with Princess Elizabeth and Lady Jane Grey) was one of the first ladies for whom tutors and formal education were provided. Thus, even though her husband was away on crown business during most of the first ten years of Philip's life, she was amply trained to oversee and even conduct his elementary education.

In 1564, the grammar school at Shrewsbury was a logical choice for the continuation of Philip's education because it was only thirty miles from Ludlow, where Sir Henry sat as President of Wales. But more important, under the headmastership of Thomas Ashton, Shrewsbury was fast becoming one of the most respected preparatory schools for Oxford and Cambridge, where (especially at Oxford) the curriculum was still founded squarely upon the trivium: grammar, rhetoric, and logic.

In the trivium, the main emphasis fell on rhetoric because it exploited grammar and employed logic. Furthermore, because rhetoric offered a means of amassing knowledge and cultivating skill through an exposure to tradition and a utilization of individual talent in order to prepare one to cope with the world, it was the main instrument of Art, Imitation, and Exercise. To shift the focus, the "3 Rs" of Elizabethan education were—Reason, Rhetoric, and Religion. The first was assumed, for it defined man's unique nature—a rational animal. The last was the end, for it provided the context for comprehending all of life. The burden on rhetoric, then, was immense: it was the means by which man cultivated his reason in order to prepare his soul for heaven.

Although it was variously analyzed and described, rhetoric consisted basically of invention, disposition, and eloquence, or to use rough modern equivalents, having something to say, figuring out how best to put it across, and saying it effectively. Because invention is the key to, or root of, the other two, the basis of effective rhetoric, and engaging art, was the discovery amid the flux and data of life of something significant to say in order to say it well. As George Gascoigne so emphatically put the case for invention: "I mean some good and fine device showing the quick capacity of a writer; and where I say good and fine invention, I mean that I would have it both fine and good."

Within the framework of Art, Imitation, and Exercise, a fine and good invention was achieved only if one knew the rules of art, studied the great masterworks of art, and practiced constantly in order to present one's own discoveries in recognizable ways and forms. Such an approach to writing is, of course, circumscribed and outdated (even though not much different from Eliot's theory of "tradition and individual talent"), and much Elizabethan art is "stuffy," in both senses, is merely "rhetoric." But when an artist realized that the ultimate rules were the rules of nature, the largest work to imitate was Dame Nature, and the most significant exercise was complete personal dedication to observation and reporting of life, then fine and good art was possible. Still, the first steps were taken in school.

Although Sidney went on to Oxford in 1568 and stayed through 1571, he did not take a degree. As nephew and favorite of the Earl of Leicester (also the Chancellor of Oxford) and as son of the President of Wales and Lord Deputy of Ireland, Sidney was sufficiently well placed that to do so would have been beneath the dignity of his position—the B.A. and M.A. still smacked of being trade degrees. As a potential courtier, one who would serve in national and international affairs, his education was to be crowned by a "grand tour."

The Exercise of the grand tour developed Sidney amazingly. He left, in the words of Leicester, "young and raw," but after his return in 1575, Elizabeth employed him on an important diplomatic mission. Part of the reason for this development can be attributed to the good luck of Sidney's falling into the hands of Hubert Languet—distinguished scholar (educated at Padua), fervent Protestant (converted by Melancthon), and trusted diplomat (the representative of the Elector of Saxony and a close consultant to the Prince of Orange)—whom he met upon arriving in Paris at the court of Charles IX in June 1572, when he stayed with Languet's friend, the English Ambassador and his own future father-in-law, Sir Francis Walsingham. King Charles was so taken by Sidney that he created him a Baron, an example of how Sidney was to be continually welcomed in the highest circles. He surely met as well the dowager Catherine de'Medici and her other Valois children: the Duke of Anjou, former suitor to Queen Elizabeth and soon to succeed his brother as Henry III; the Duke of Alençon, soon to succeed his brother as suitor and as Anjou; and Margaret, whose forced marriage to Henry of Navarre he witnessed on 18 August. This marriage was intended to bring the same kind of peace to France as Henry Tudor's marriage to Anne, daughter of Edward IV, had brought to England, but it was followed instead by the death of the Huguenot leader, the Admiral de Coligny, and the resultant massacre on St. Bartholomew's Day.

After the massacre, but before letters from England came asking for Sidney's return home, Walsingham decided that Sidney should leave Paris and sent him after Languet and Andreas Wechel, the printer, who had fled to Frankfort. There Sidney had the leisure to study firsthand the frictions and nascent alliances among the emerging Protestant states within the old Holy Roman Empire, and met some of the famous humanist printers and scholars, most notably Henri Estienne (Henry Stephens) in Heidelberg and Johan Sturm (friend of Ascham, admired by Burghley) in Strasburg. But then, as today, no matter what other countries one visited, Italy had to be included if the grand tour was to be complete—but not because of her antiquities. Then, Italy was the center of all that was new, fashionable, creative, and modern. Because Italy was as well the center of "immoral" Mediterranean society and "atheistical" Roman Catholicism, Ascham and Burghley both recommended against such trips. But

Sidney, brought up on the literature of ancient Italy, and coming from a country which he had been taught to believe was barren of letters, after a summer travelling in Austria and Hungary, must have looked forward in the fall of 1573 to the journey into Italy.

Learned and native drama were flourishing, Petrarch had taught the Italian language how to sing, Ariosto (not Dante) had proved that one could attain the heroic even in the vernacular, the academies and presses were pouring forth the wisdom of the ancients and commentaries of the moderns, and the arts were everywhere to be seen. In Venice during Sidney's stay Palladio was designing, Palestrina composing, and Titian still painting. When Languet asked for a portrait Sidney favored Veronese over Tinteretto. Although we do not know whether he met Tasso during his residence in Padua, or whom he may have met in Florence, from the Languet correspondence we do know something of his study: beside satisfying his thirst for political, military, economic, and geographical information, he added fluency in Italian to his French, learned some Spanish, began to pursue Greek beyond rudimentary grammar in order to read Aristotle at firsthand, and continued his study of Latin. Sketchy though they are, these few details indicate a full exposure to the high Renaissance in Northern Italy.

Sidney returned to Vienna in November 1574 where, after a trip to Poland, he spent the winter at the court of Maximillian. At this time, as we are reminded by the delightful opening of *The Defence of Poesy*, Sidney met Edward Wotton, who was to remain his close friend. We have no letters giving details concerning his stay, for he was with Languet, but his experience was such that Elizabeth asked him to return as her personal representative when the Emperor died within two years after Sidney returned to England, in the spring of 1575.

These two years were among the most exciting of Sidney's life, for, his education complete, he was ready to lead the full life of the courtier. As soon as he returned he was caught up in the whirl of court life, accompanying the Queen on her stately summer progress (during which the most notable entertainment was presented by Leicester at Kenilworth), seeking state employment, and taking part in tournaments and festivities. His attractive presence was rewarded in the spring of 1576 when the Queen made him her Cupbearer.

During this time, Walter Devereux, the Earl of Essex, at Court trying to refurbish his tarnished fortunes, real and political, was much drawn to Sidney and part of his plans for stabilizing his future seems to have been the negotiation of a marriage between Philip and his then eleven-year-old daughter Penelope. When Essex returned to Ireland in the summer as head of the army, Sidney went along in order to join his father campaigning in the field. During August Essex fell mortally ill in Dublin, put his affairs in order, and sent for Philip in order to urge the marriage contract. Although Essex died before he could return from the field, Sidney did accompany the body back to England in November and helped with the funeral arrangements. Sir Henry had never been fond of Essex. He was not tempted by a deathbed plea to carry through a contract which would only mean a further drain on his already meager wealth, and the marriage negotiations were broken in November.

In December the Queen called upon Philip to undertake that kind of mission he had been eager for when she named him head of the embassy to the Empire in order to send the Queen's sympathies for the death of Maximillian and congratulations for the election of his son Rudolph as successor. A similar mission to the Palatine was incorporated, for the Elector also had recently died, being replaced by his son Lewis. Naturally, the real purpose of the embassy was to find out the new Emperor's inclinations with regard to England specifically and Protestantism in general. In this latter regard the trip to the Palatine was especially important, for Lewis' brother Count Casimir was known to be, literally, a militant Protestant. Sidney was openly enthusiastic concerning the possibilities of a "Protestant League" that would be powerful enough to ignore France and mount direct force against Spain, hence, Rome. The initial point of attack would be the Low Countries now under the governorship of the fiery Spaniard, Don John of Austria, hero against the Turks at Lepanto, whom Sidney had met previously in Vienna. Hence, Sidney was also anxious to include a visit to William of Orange on his trip, and fortunately on his homeward progress, Edward Dyer came bringing, with the Queen's permission, Leicester's request that Sidney stand in as godfather to William's new daughter. Their conversations were such that William found Sidney so attractive and promising that he attempted to tie the Protestant hopes of the Low Countries (Holland and Zeeland) to England through a marriage between Sidney and his sister.

Ironically, because Sidney returned in the summer of 1577 in personal triumph, the Queen gave him no official position in the court or council, and not until the fall of 1585 did she call on him directly to undertake any crown business other than minor escort duty. Specifically, Sidney, in his enthusiastic support of the Protestant "cause," seems to have implied to Casimir that Elizabeth was more interested in a League than she was, for she immediately sent an ambassador to counteract any such implication. Sidney was a high-minded, quick-tempered activist—a combination of qualities entirely antithetic to the Queen's mode of operation. He was attractive enough to help swell a progress, and clever enough to stage and take part in a tournament, but too much of his own mind (as can be seen in the 1579 challenge to Oxford and the letter to the Queen opposing the Anjou marriage) to be trusted with serious business. Frustrated in his main endeavors, Sidney turned, during this period from 1577 to 1584, more and more to literature.

Sidney's first work, *The Lady of May*, bridges both worlds, courtly and literary, because it was an "entertainment" (a cross between a pageant and a masque) offered for Queen Elizabeth's flattery and enjoyment during a visit in May of 1578 to Wanstead, a gift of hers to Leicester, as was Kenilworth as well. Slight though it is, *The Lady of May* contains poetry and prose which point to Sidney's later art. As would be expected, it is an imitation, of the Italian May plays and folk debates, but has Sidney's hallmark—a particular concern with the differentiated "voices" of his characters, from the pompous pedagogue Rombus to the naturally sophisticated and innocent Lady of May. The manipulation of voice remains almost totally in the realm of diction and syntax, but in his next work, the addition of a narrator's voice added depth to the presentation.

The *Old Arcadia,* or the first version of *The Countess of Pembroke's Arcadia* as it must formally be described, is also an imitation, here of prose romance treated as if it were a five-act academic comedy (with the added innovation of four interludes of pastoral song, dance, and dialogue). Sidney emphasizes in his letter of presentation to his sister that the work was done casually, sometimes in her presence and sometimes sent to her as parts were finished, and without what Arnold would call "high seriousness." Much of this disclaimer, of course, betrays an artistic self-consciousness, but what is more revealing concerning the nature of Sidney's attitude is that the tone of each "Book," or "Act" is distinct from the other because Sidney gradually "writes out" the role and voice of the informal, urbane, ironic narrator so that by Book V he has reached the impersonal kind of narration which can be experienced in the first book of the *New Arcadia.*

A further indication of developing artistic seriousness on Sidney's part is that during the writing of the *Old Arcadia (c.* 1578–1580), Sidney became the center of a growing circle of literary friends concerned with the possibilities for a vernacular literature in England. The most notable member of the group was Edmund Spenser, and its most notable product was *The Shepherd's Calendar,* published in December 1579, dedicated to Sidney; but also in 1579, Stephen Gosson dedicated, for no good reason, his philistine *School of Abuse* to Sidney. The triple impetus of his own work, his speculative conversations with other men of letters, and his concern over the climate in England for literary art or "poesy," led naturally to his work on *The Defence of Poesy* (begun sometime after the fall of 1580 and probably completed by 1582), in which Sidney reveals his concern for the nature and role of both poetry and the poet, and his specific concern for the fate of vernacular letters in England.

For any nation to arrive at artistic maturity, it had to produce a native epic, and a native epic demanded a heroic meter. Naturally, then, a major concern of Sidney's group was prosody, as we know from the Spenser-Harvey correspondence of 1579, and as we can observe in Sidney's own early poetry, which is in a variety of forms, from loose native accentual-syllabic verse to rigid (as in his *Psalms*), from iambic quantitative verse to highly patterned correlative. Of all of the kinds of verse he tried, he found that none could make English sing except iambic, accentual-syllabic, and that best when carried out over five feet, but with metrical substitutions allowed and with flowing patterns of speech superimposed over the basic regularity of the meter. Such poetry created "voice."

To exploit this discovery of full "voice," Sidney invented Astrophel, his platonic-poetic-petrarchan persona whose beloved but unloving Stella forced through all the expected poses, postures, and philosophical positions of Petrarchan love in the first English sonnet sequence, *Astrophel and Stella* (written 1581–1582). Such was Sidney's achievement that the world has long taken the voice of Astrophel for Sidney's personal voice, whereas it is Sidney's personal voice and more—in short, it is his artistic voice.

When Sidney returned to *The Countess of Pembroke's Arcadia* to revise it, he brought with him the artistic seriousness displayed in the *Defence* and the artistic lessons learned from writing *Astrophel,* for his intention was to turn it into an epic poem in prose. Only he discovered after completing nearly three books that he had failed to determine whether the epic prose-poem was to be comic or tragic, and sometime in 1583 or 1584 he simply quit writing. Sidney did not leave the *New Arcadia* because he was called away to war. What he discovered in Book III was that his writing was taking on a kind of independent realism and significance which was no longer contained within his esthetic of Art, Imitation, and Exercise.

The shock of this recognition seems to have killed Sidney's endeavors of art: he left no indication whatsoever that he intended to pick up his pen again. The notes which Greville mentioned in November 1586 to Walsingham clearly refer to what Sidney wanted to amend in the *Old Arcadia;* Greville had heard that William Ponsonby wished to print "Sir Philip Sidney's Old Arcadia" but said that he had "a correction of that old one done four or five years since, which he left in trust with me, whereof there is no more copies, and fitter to be printed than the first one, which is so common, notwithstanding even that to be amended by a direction set down under his own hand how and why." To be sure, when he had started the *New Arcadia,* it was this never-revised version of the *Old* which he had in the back of his mind. But as the existing three books demonstrate, the *Old Arcadia* faded further from his attention, so much so that Basilius' arrival on the scene in Book III must have—to paraphrase Robert Frost—surprised Sidney as much as it surprises the reader. Sidney seems to have left off because he discovered that his art could no longer be considered a mere courtly "pass-time," but was a mistress as serious and demanding as Elizabeth, and he chose the Queen. His discipline was to be the cause of England against Spain, first by helping in the defensive arming of the channel coast, then by planning global, diversionary strategy, and at last by direct confrontation in the Netherlands.

Even though the Queen was not to employ him directly until late in 1585, Sidney was able to find occupation in state affairs, for in 1583 he was appointed as assistant to his uncle the Earl of Warwick, the Master of Ordinance (a kind of "Secretary of Defense") and he married the daughter of Sir Francis Walsingham, Elizabeth's "Secretary of State." As, so-to-speak, the assistant Secretary of Defense, Sidney's main duty was to oversee the arming of the Cinque Ports against probable Spanish invasion; as assistant Secretary of State, his "desk" was Scotland; and as a personal extension of both jobs was the planning of global strategy against Spain, his never-realized idea being to develop Naval piracy in the new world into full-scale amphibious raids against the diverse Spanish holdings. Furthermore, with Raleigh and others, he saw that England had a chance to strengthen her position in Europe through American colonization, a proposition which struck most Elizabethans as nonsense. But Sidney had in mind a plan much more bold and far-reaching than the Queen's policy of balancing off her enemies one against another, a policy she finally had to put aside after the shocking assassination of William in 1584 and the fall of Antwerp in 1585.

Elizabeth wisely withheld her now-called-for direct intervention in the Netherlands until the rebel states agreed to grant her the port cities of Flushing and Brill. Warwick had warned that these cities would most logically be used by Parma as bases for his planned invasion of England. Furthermore, they were the main ports of supply for the states of Zeeland and Holland, and controlled the main riverways into the Brabant and Flanders.

Thus, one can sense the significance of Sidney's appointment in September 1585 to the position of Governor-General at Flushing. Arriving in November, Sidney at long last was in the front lines, defending Queen and country in open warfare against Philip and Rome. His being in this important position fortunately brought a great deal of his correspondence into the official records, for his letters come as close as is historically possible to giving us the essential man: intelligent, good-hearted, principled, and, above all, energetic. Here we can feel Sidney's simple, but not fundamentalist or simplistic, faith, as well as his philosophical turn of mind, as can be seen in a letter to his father-in-law, 24 March 1586. The Queen has been reluctant to send her part of the soldiers' pay; Sidney knows that "I am called very ambitious and proud at home," and realizes from experience "how apt the Queen is to interpret every thing to my disadvantage." But Sidney does not whine, "For methinks I see the great work indeed in hand against the abusers of the world, wherein it is no greater fault to have confidence in man's power, then it is too hastily to despair of God's work. I think a wise and constant man ought never to grieve while he doth play, as a man may say, his own part truly, though others be out. But if himself leave his hold because other mariners will be idle, he will hardly forgive himself his own fault. For me, I cannot promise of my own course; no,— because I know there is a higher power that must uphold me, or else I shall fall. But certainly, I trust, I shall not by other men's wants be drawn from myself." Still, matters were sufficiently chaotic that he despaired of success in the coming campaigns: "We shall have a sore war upon us this summer, wherein if appointment had been kept and these disgraces forborn, which have greatly weakened us, we had been victorious."

Sidney was much in the field during the late spring and summer of 1586, for, in addition to the garrison of Flushing and a company of horses he had recruited in England, he had command of a regiment from Zeeland. That he rallied the morale of his city and its garrison, had the loyal backing of all of his men, and was being considered as the governor of Zeeland is proof that he carried out all of his responsibilities with success. In fact, at his death, it was generally assumed that he would soon replace his aging and none-too-popular uncle, Leicester, as overall military and political advisor to the Low Countries. There is no direct evidence that the Queen would have agreed, but two bits of evidence point the other way. Sidney's continued insistence that the English troops must get their pay finally seems to have reached her ears, for after Leicester had established himself "in-country," her instructions to him begin to take up Sidney's refrain: attention must be paid to the poor soldier in garrison and camp. Perhaps Sidney's openness and honesty had finally registered with her. And, it is certain from ample testimony, she was broken by the news of his death.

All of Europe, Catholic and Protestant alike, was stunned by the death of Sidney, who, at thirty-two, by sixteenth-century statistics had reached middle life, but still with a future ahead. The theme that reverberates through the countless messages of grief received by the Queen, Leicester, and Walsingham and the numerous epitaphs, elegies, and memorials in all languages is that of waste—of great expectations come to naught. The point is soberly captured by his lifelong friend and biographer, Fulke Greville: "What he was to God, his friends and country, fame hath told, though his expectation went beyond her good." But he had lived long enough to establish his worth, to become the true type of chivalry. Camden spoke what all instinctively felt: "whatever we loved in you, whatever we admired in you, still continues, and will continue in the memories of men, the revolutions of ages, and the annals of time." Perhaps the most moving tribute comes from the humble professional soldier, George Whetstone. After enumerating Sidney's condition, education, lingual ability, foreign travel, martial achievement, and intimacy with "men of quality," he concludes with the simple assertion: "he always was a special favorer of soldiers," a moving tribute because it comes from below, from the ranks, and more so because Whetstone was himself in the lines at Zutphen on the 22d of September 1586.

How much Sidney did to plan the defense of England against the sure invasion by Spain is hidden behind the person of Warwick. What he did as Walsingham's agent to keep Scotland free is more easily ascertained, yet how much he was able to help his father-in-law's special protégé Drake is a matter of speculation. More clearly in his death he reminded people that one could live free under God if one had a sense of *virtue*, a sense of what it was to be a man, to be human—to think, to live, to do. One need not cower, beg, lie, and obliterate one's personality or one's sense of self.

This achievement of Sidney's life is also the plea of his criticism and the lesson of his art. But these tend to be lost in the drama of his death. The famous stories told by Greville of the thigh-armor tossed aside before battle and of the canteen passed by the wounded captain to the dying soldier are fitting, and probably true. But they suggest in themselves a man to whom life was a mere gesture and for whom each occasion should be a staged one, whereas the sense of *comraderie* shown by the first act, and the *noblesse* of the second reach deep into the man. In short we lose the whole Sidney if we romanticize him, just as the renaissance tendency to moralize his life also obscured him.

Yet judged fully and objectively, one must conclude that in both his life and his art, Sir Philip Sidney was and is a central figure of the English Renaissance, his life having been the realization of the courtly ideals expressed by Elyot and Hoby, his art having reached lasting success in criticism, poetry, and fiction. But Sidney never separated sharply his endeavors: they were all simply aspects of his way of life as an Elizabethan gentleman.

In preparation for such a life, his education, in school and out, was that of the courtier, so that while Art, Imitation, and Exercise was an academic program, it was for Sidney an ethic and an esthetic consideration as well. Without Exercise such a guide to life and literature would have led to mere grace and formality. But Sidney was constantly engaged with life and was increasingly so by art, with the result that the integrity of the life became more and more apparent in the art. *Because of* Art and Imitation, however, the art never became mere biography or expressionism.

Sidney did not achieve this balance at once, even though he achieved it rapidly, for the duration of his artistic production was relatively short—seven years at the very most. Beginning even in *The Lady of May* there is an engaging quality, a certain energy which becomes even more noticeable in the course of the five books of the *Old Arcadia.* The experiments in poetry led naturally to a kind of fullness and wholeness which possesses, and which I have called "voice." This voice reached poetic maturity in *Astrophel and Stella,* but remains a voice not always fully appreciated because the artistic voice of Sidney has too often been taken as merely his personal voice.

The heroic nature of the *New Arcadia* does not so easily lend itself to this kind of misreading, for Sidney here remained so in control, so kept his Art, Imitation, and Exercise in balance that the work is thoroughly engaging: the impress of the artist is everywhere apparent, but nowhere obtrusive. Paradoxically, the *New Arcadia* became so completely independent, so independently real, however, that Sidney became self-conscious about the implications of his writing: the circumscribed comic world of the *Old Arcadia* could not be accommodated in a world in which death also dwelt.

Even though Sidney did not survive to witness the great outpouring of literature in the 1590s, his works were an integral and stimulating part of the full blossom of the literary Renaissance in England. The three books of his *New Arcadia* were edited by Greville and published by Ponsonby in 1590, then reprinted by the Countess of Pembroke in 1593 along with the last three books of her *Old Arcadia.* In 1591, the publication of *Astrophel and Stella* taught a new generation how to contain the rhythms of speech within the patterns of meter, thereby creating poems of simultaneous song and substance. And, *The Defence of Poesy,* issued three times in 1595, provided writers with the theoretical basis upon which to build more sophisticated artifacts. In fact, such were the breadth of impact of Sidney on his age and the demand for his works, that when the Countess of Pembroke reprinted her 1593 version of the *Arcadia* in the handsome folio of 1598, she included, along with the *Defence* of 1595, versions of *Astrophel and Stella,* the *Certain Sonnets,* and *The Lady of May* from her own manuscript sources. And Sidney's influence continued to be felt: this "collected works," *The Countess of Pembroke's Arcadia,* was reprinted thirteen times by 1739.

CHRONOLOGY

1554 Born, 30 November, at Penshurst, Kent.
1557 Tottel's *Songes and Sonnettes* first published.
1559 *A Mirror for Magistrates* first published.
1564 September, entered Shrewsbury Grammar School (Shropshire).
1566 Visited Oxford, where Leicester entertained the Queen for a week.
1568 February (?), entered Corpus Christi College, Oxford, staying three years.
1572 June to September, at Paris with Sir Francis Walsingham; witnessed St. Bartholomew's Day massacre, 24 August. September to June 1573, at Frankfort with Hubert Languet.
1573 Summer and early fall, en route to Italy via Heidelburg, Strasburg, Hungary, and Vienna.
1573 November to October 1574, lived in Venice and Padua, visited Florence and Genoa.
1574 Winter, at the Imperial Court in Vienna with Languet and Edward Wotton.
1575 Spring, returned home by way of Poland, arriving in England the first of June; July, at Kenilworth when Leicester entertained the Queen; August, saw father off to Ireland; fall and winter, at court.
1576 Made Cupbearer to the Queen; sought out by Drant; Edward's *Paradise of Dainty Devices* first published. Summer, went to Ireland with Essex, and campaigned in

the field with his father. November, returned to England with Essex's body; in December, embassy to Germany.

1577   February to June, with Greville and (later) Dyer, visited: Thomas Wilson in Brussels, Don John of Austria in Louvaine, Prince Casimir of the Palatine in Heidelburg, Emperor Rudolf and Edmund Campion in Prague, and William of Orange in Holland. Spring, sister Mary married the Earl of Pembroke; Phillippe du Plessis Mornay arrived for year and a half stay to plead in behalf of the Protestant cause. Summer and fall, active in behalf of Orange, the Netherlands, and "the cause"; defended in writing his father's conduct of Irish affairs. Christmas, at Wilton with his sister, and uncles Leicester and Warwick.

1578   January, exchanged gifts with the Queen. February, Sir Henry recalled from Ireland (returned to England in September). May, *Lady of May* presented during Queen's visit to Leicester at Wanstead. Spring, denied permission to fight in the Netherlands. Drant died; Proctor's *Gorgeous Gallery of Gallant Inventions* published. Summer (?), began *Old Arcadia*. December, Lyly's *Euphues* published.

1579   January, Prince Casimir of the Palatine and Languet visited England for a month. July, Semier revealed Leicester's secret marriage to Essex's widow. August, the Duke of Anjou arrived as suitor to the Queen; Sidney argued with and challenged Oxford before the French party; Gossen dedicated the *School of Abuse* to Sidney. September, opposed a marriage to Anjou in letter to the Queen. October, Spenser mentioned the "Areopagus" and, in December, published *The Shep-hearde's Calender*, dedicated to Sidney.

1580   January, exchanged New Year's gifts with the Queen; took part in a tournament. Spring and summer, at Wilton, finished *Old Arcadia*. Summer, Harvey-Spenser correspondence published; Spenser went to Ireland with the new Lord Deputy, Lord Grey. September, Languet admonished Sidney concerning his long retirement with friends. Fall, Lyly's *Euphues' England* and Munday's *Zelauto* published; began *The Defence of Poesy.*

1581   January, elected to Parliament; Penelope Devereux presented at court. March, Parliament dissolved, but remained at court; Penelope Devereux engaged to Lord Rich (married him in November). May, the tournament of the "Fortress of Desire." Summer, having finished *The Defence* and most of the *Certain Sonnets* and his share of *The Psalms*, began *Astrophel and Stella.* September, Languet died; Du Mornay published *The Truth of Religion.* Fall, at court; Christmas, at Wilton.

1582   February, part of lavish escort for Anjou to the Netherlands. Late spring and summer in Wales with Father; finished *Astrophel and Stella*, and began the *New Arcadia.*

1583   January, knighted in order to be proxy for Prince Casimir at Garter installation. March, Sir Henry Sidney's long letter to Walsingham concluding almost two years of negotiation for the marriage of Philip and Frances Walsingham (married in September). Spring, finally officially appointed as assistant to Warwick, the Master of Ordinance. Suspended work on the *New Arcadia* and began translating Du Mornay's tract.

1584   February, dinner at Greville's with Giordano Bruno, John Florio, and Matthew Gwinne. Fall, defended in writing Leicester. September, when about to go with Drake to America, finally appointed Governor of Flushing (arriving in November).

1586–87 Summer, father and mother died; 22 September, wounded at Zutphen; 17 October, died at Arnheim; 16 February 1587, buried with great ceremony in St. Pauls.

1590   *New Arcadia* edited by Greville published by William Ponsonby; Frances married Robert, Earl of Essex, son of Walter Devereux and brother of Penelope.

1591   *Astrophel and Stella* published without authority, twice by Thomas Newman and once by Matthew Lownes.

1593   *The Arcadia* (the *New Arcadia* "augmented and ended" by a slightly revised version of the last three books of the *Old Arcadia*) published by Ponsonby for the Countess of Pembroke.

1595   *The Defence of Poesy* published by Ponsonby and, as *An Apology for Poetry*, by Henry Olney.

1598   *The Countess of Pembroke's Arcadia . . . with sundry new additions* published by Ponsonby for the Countess of Pembroke. (Added *Certain Sonnets* and *The Lady of May*, retained the 1593 *Arcadia*, but did not print the *Old Arcadia*.)

1926   *Old Arcadia* first published by Feuillerat. (Since 1905 nine manuscripts of the whole work, prose and poetry, have been discovered, and one of the poems alone.)

SELECTED BIBLIOGRAPHY

WORKS

Duncan-Jones, Katherine, and Van Dorsten, Jan, eds. *Miscellaneous Prose of Sir Philip Sidney.* Oxford: Oxford University Press, 1973. Major critical edition with full introduction, notes, annotation, and bibliographies.

Evans, Maurice, ed. *The Countess of Pembroke's Arcadia.* New York: Penguin, 1977. The 1593 version, amended and modernized.

Feuillerat, Albert. *The Prose Works of Sir Philip Sidney.* 4 vols., Cambridge, England: Cambridge University Press, 1962. (Originally included in *The Complete Works*, 4 vols., Cambridge, 1912–1926.) Complete prose (including the defenses of his father and Leicester and the translation of Du Mornay, as well as selected letters).

Kimbrough, Robert, and Murphy, Philip. "The Helmingham Hall Manuscript of Sidney's *The Lady of May*: A Commentary and Transcription." *Renaissance Drama: New Series I: Essays Principally on Masques and Entertainments.* Evanston, Ill.: Northwestern University Press, 1968.

Pears, Steuart A. *The Correspondence of Sir Philip Sidney and Hubert Languet.* London: W. Pickering, 1845. Translated from Latin, this major collection of correspondence reveals Sidney's good humor and play of mind at firsthand.

Rathmell, J. C. A., ed. *The Psalms of Sir Philip Sidney and The Countess of Pembroke.* New York: Anchor, Doubleday, 1963. Full introduction to, and bibliography of, the "Sydnean Psalmes." Rathmell has higher praise for the countess's work than for Sidney's.

Ringler, William A., Jr. *The Poems of Sir Philip Sidney.* Oxford: Oxford University Press, 1962. Major critical edition with full introduction, notes, annotation, and bibliographies.

Robertson, Jean, ed. *The Countess of Pembroke's Arcadia (The Old Arcadia).* Oxford; Oxford University Press, 1973. Major critical edition with full introduction, notes, annotation, and bibliographies.

SECONDARY SOURCES

Amos, Arthur K. *Time, Space, and Value: the Narrative Structure of the "New Arcadia."* Lewisburg, Pa.: Bucknell University Press, 1977. A close reading of the three books of the 1590 *Arcadia* which emphasizes complexity, yet claims a controlled completeness.

Buxton, John. *Sir Philip Sidney and the English Renaissance.* London: Macmillan, 1954; New York: St. Martin's, 1964. Excellent on the formal nature of Renaissance art and the courtly qualities of the *New Arcadia*. Perhaps overstates the roles of the Sidneys as patrons responsible for the high Renaissance in Elizabethan England.

Danby, John F. *Poets on Fortune's Hill: Studies in Sidney, Shakespeare, Beaumont, & Fletcher.* London: Faber and Faber, 1952. Excellent study of the aristocratic basis, heroic bias, and courtly ethos of the *Arcadia*. Especially perceptive concerning the questions of sexual identity and maturity.

Davis, Walter R. *A Map of Arcadia: Sidney's Romance in Its Tradition.* In *Sidney's Arcadia*, Yale Studies in English, 158. New Haven: Yale, University Press, 1965. A study of the 1593 *Arcadia* as a fulfillment of Sidney's desire to write a pastoral romance. Although the thesis is not persuasive, excellent on the heritage of the *Old* and the *New Arcadia*, and on Sidney's general themes.

Dipple, Elizabeth. "The 'Fore Conceit' of Sidney's Eclogues." *Literary Monographs*, I. Madison, Wis.: University of Wisconsin Press, 1966.

Donow, Herbert S., ed. *A Concordance to the Poems of Sir Philip Sidney.* Ithaca, N.Y.: Cornell University Press, 1975. Based on Ringler's edition.

Doran, Madeleine. *Endeavors of Art: A Study of Form in Elizabethan Drama.* Madison, Wis.: University of Wisconsin Press, 1954. Although primarily devoted to drama, invaluable on Renaissance literary art in general and on the *Defence* in particular.

Godshalk, W. L. "Bibliography of Sidney Studies Since 1935." See Myrick, below, 1965 edition. See also Godshalk, "Recent Sidney Studies," *English Literary Renaissance*, 2 (1972), 148–64, and (with A. J. Colaianne) "Recent Studies in Sidney (1970–1977)," *ELR*, 8 (1978), 212–33. Colaianne and Godshalk have turned their proposed *A Reference Guide to Sir Philip Sidney* over to C. S. Hunter and D. V. Stump, with publication scheduled for 1984 by G. K. Hall, Boston.

Greenfield, Thelma N. *The Eye of Judgment: Reading the "New Arcadia."* Lewisburg, Pa.: Bucknell University Press, 1982. Traces the relationship of language and stylistic variety to meaning and moral vision.

Greville, Sir Fulke (Lord Brooke). *The Life of the Renowned Sir Philip Sidney,* ed. Nowell Smith. Oxford: Clarendon Press, 1907. Written c. 1612 and published in 1652, twenty-four years after Greville's death, this major biography by a life-long friend treats the art as a reflection of Sidney's over-all ideas and ideals.

Hamilton, A. C. *Sir Philip Sidney: A Study of His Life and Works.* Cambridge, England: Cambridge University Press, 1977. Relates the life *to* the works, in an admiring but admirable manner. Learned, loving, and sophisticated.

Hunter, G. K. *John Lyly: The Humanist as Courtier.* Cambridge, Mass.: Harvard University Press, 1962. Introductory chapters on sixteenth-century education and life at court provide excellent pictures of the environment in which Sidney grew.

Kalstone, David. *Sidney's Poetry: Contexts and Interpretations.* Cambridge, Mass.: Harvard University Press, 1965. Excellent on the literary traditions of "Arcadia," and on the Petrarchan heritage of *Astrophel and Stella*.

Kimbrough, Robert. *Sir Philip Sidney.* New York: Twayne, 1971. Short but complete study of the life and works, emphasizing Sidney's artistic theories and development.

Lanham, Richard A. *The Old Arcadia.* In *Sidney's "Arcadia,"* Yale Studies in English, 158. New Haven: Yale University Press, 1965. Good on the pastoral tradition, on the wholeness and humor, and on the "rhetorical" nature of the *Old Arcadia*.

Lawry, Jon S. *Sidney's Two "Arcadias": Pattern and Proceeding.* Ithica, N.Y.: Cornell University Press, 1972. The "pattern" is the ideal; the "proceeding" is the actual: life as it unfolds and is encountered.

Levine, Robert Eril. *A Comparison of Sidney's "Old" and "New Arcadia."* Salzburg, Austria: Salzburg Studies in English Literature, 1974. The *New Arcadia* began as an elaboration of the *Old*, but in Book III shifts in mood and tone.

Lewis, C. S. "Sidney and Spenser," *English Literature in the Sixteenth Century.* Oxford: Clarendon Press, 1954. Pp. 318–93. Most sound and perceptive part of a controversial book.

McCoy, Richard C. *Sir Philip Sidney: Rebellion in Arcadia.* New Brunswick, N.J.: Rutgers University Press, 1979. A study which sees an unresolved personal, political life reflected in the discords of the major works.

Marenco, Franco. *Arcadia Puritana: l'uso della tradizione nella prima "Arcadia" di Sir Philip Sidney.* Bari, Italy: Adriatica, 1968. *Arcadia* is a puritan allegory of one's stay here on earth, where one is a prisoner of the senses.

Moffet, Thomas. *Nobilis, or A View of the Life and Death of a Sidney.* Edited and translated by Virgil B. Heltzel and Hoyt H. Hudson. San Marino, Calif.: Huntington Library, 1940. A fine example of a Renaissance moralized biography, written probably in 1593.

Montgomery, Robert L., Jr. *Symmetry and Sense: The Poetry of Sir Philip Sidney.* Austin: University of Texas, 1961; New York: Greenwood, 1969. An excellent discussion of Sidney's development as a poet within the traditions of sixteenth-century rhetorical-poetical theory and practice.

Muir, Kenneth. *Sir Philip Sidney*, Writers and Their Work, no. 120. London: Longmans, Green, 1960. Short (35 pp.), but perceptive introduction to Sidney (with a selected bibliography).

Myrick, Kenneth O. *Sir Philip Sidney as a Literary Craftsman.* Cambridge, Mass.: Harvard University Press, 1935; Lincoln, Neb.: University of Nebraska Press, 1965. Based on the double thesis that while Sidney's literary ethos reflects the *sprezzatura* of Castiglione's courtier, his actual literary practice is that of the well-trained Renaissance artist. A classic of Sidney scholarship and criticism, with more emphasis on the prose than poetry.

Nichols, John Gordon. *The Poetry of Sir Philip Sidney: An Interpretation in the Context of His Life and Times.* Liverpool, England: Liverpool University Press, 1974. Particularly valuable for the discussion and analysis of *Astrophel and Stella* as a dynamic, objective collection of fine lyric poetry.

Osborn, James Marshall. *Young Philip Sidney, 1572–1577.* New Haven: Yale University Press, 1972. Important study of Sidney's formative years within the context of European politics.

Roberts, Josephine A. *Architectonic Knowledge in the "New Arcadia" (1590): Sidney's Use of the Heroic Journey.* Salzburg, Austria: Salzburg Studies in English Literature, 1978. Detailed exploration of the Renaissance pursuit of the choice of Hercules. Full bibliography.

Robinson, Forrest Glen. *The Shape of Things Known: Sidney's "Apology" in Its Philosophical Tradition.* Cambridge, Mass.: Harvard University Press, 1972. Suggests that the *Defence* must be read within a rather obscure Western philosophical tradition of inner vision and memory: "visual epistemology."

Rose, Mark. *Heroic Love: Studies in Sidney and Spenser.* Cambridge, Mass.: Harvard University Press, 1968. Love as a shaping force in the fashioning of an Elizabethan gentleman.

Rudenstine, Neil L. *Sir Philip Sidney's Poetic Development.* Cambridge, Mass.: Harvard University Press, 1967. Attempts to demonstrate that Sidney was a sophisticated stylist from the very beginning of his career, and that he developed several different manners for very specific purposes.

Sidney Newsletter 1, no. 1 (Spring, 1980). Published twice a year by the Department of English, Wilfrid Laurier University, Waterloo, Ontario.

Spencer, Theodore. "The Poetry of Sir Philip Sidney," *English Literary History* 12 (December, 1945): 251–78. Slightly dated by its new critical orientation, this first full-dress study of all of the poetry *"as* poetry" was important in drawing critical attention to Sidney and is still a valuable, sensitive study.

Stillinger, Jack C. "The Biographical Problem of *Astrophel and Stella,*" *Journal of English and Germanic Philology* 59 (October, 1960): 617–39. A patient and exhaustive examination of all of the "evidence" that Penelope was Stella. Level-headed and skeptical in its conclusions.

Tannenbaum, S. A. *Sir Philip Sidney: A Concise Bibliography.* New York: S. A. Tannenbaum, 1941. See also Washington, below.

Thompson, John. *The Founding of English Metre.* New York: Columbia University Press, 1961. The best book on sixteenth-century prosody ever written. Demonstrates that Sidney discovered how to maintain a maximum tension between the language of the poem and the abstract pattern of the metre.

Tillyard, E. M. W. *The English Epic and its Background.* London: Chatto and Windus, 1954. Contains an excellent criticism of the 1590 *Arcadia* as an epic, as defined by its age. Rejects the *Arcadia* of 1593 as false to Sidney's intentions.

Van Dorsten, J. A. *Poets, Patrons, and Professors: Sir Philip Sidney, Daniel Rogers, and the Leiden Humanists.* Leiden: Published for the Sir Thomas Browne Institute at the University Press, 1962. Especially valuable for reminding us how small and overlapping were the international literary and political worlds in the Renaissance.

Wallace, Malcolm William. *The Life of Sir Philip Sidney.* Cambridge, England: Cambridge University Press, 1915; New York: Octagon, 1969. Full and detailed biography. Most neutral in its point of view. Well documented but all sources not fully indicated.

Washington, Mary A. *Sir Philip Sidney: An Annotated Bibliography of Modern Criticism, 1941–1970.* Columbia, Mo.: University of Missouri Press, 1972. Updates Tannenbaum, above.

Weiner, Andrew D. *Sir Philip Sidney and the Poetics of Protestantism: A Study of Contexts.* Minneapolis, Minn.: University of Minnesota Press, 1978. A landmark study which reads Sidney from the point of view of Calvinist theology.

Wiles, A. G. D. "Parallel Analysis of the Two Versions of Sidney's *Arcadia*," *Studies in Philology* 39 (April, 1942): 167–206. Valuable for its summaries of the two stories in parallel columns.

Wilson, Mona. *Sir Philip Sidney*. London: Duckworth, 1931; R. Hart-Davis, 1950. Biography, romantic in bias, but sound in documentation.

Wolff, S. L. *The Greek Romances in Elizabethan Prose Fiction*. New York: Columbia University Press, 1912. Contains a pioneering source-study.

Young, Richard B. *English Petrarke: A Study of Sidney's Astrophel and Stella*. In *Three Studies in the Renaissance*, Yale Studies in English, 138. New Haven: Yale University Press, 1958. Fine study, emphasizing the sonnet convention.

Zandvoort, R. W. *Sidney's Arcadia: A Comparison Between the Two Versions*. Amsterdam: Swets & Zeitlinger, 1929. Pioneer, detailed work of scholarship, showing Sidney's "growth."

Early Prose, Poetry,
and Criticism

S IDNEY'S EARLY WORK is uneven because he approached it with a true, not a studied, casualness: writing was an appropriate pastime for a courtier. But a developing artistic sincerity or seriousness can be seen in this early work, for Sidney unhesitatingly experimented widely. Although none of them is consistent in tone or level in achievement, each provided Sidney the necessary exercise to prepare him for the good and fine achievement of his later criticism, poetry, and prose.

The Lady of May

Sidney's first work, *The Lady of May*, is preserved in two forms. It was included by Sidney's sister, the Countess of Pembroke, in her edition of his collected works in 1598, and has turned up in a manuscript discovered by Professor Jean Robertson, the Helmingham Hall manuscript (Hm), purchased by Arthur Houghton. Hm is an important manuscript mainly because it contains a conclusion to this entertainment which the Earl of Leicester provided, through his nephew, for a visit of the Queen to Wanstead in May of 1578. This new ending makes it quite clear that the overall purpose of the piece, in addition to providing song, dance, and debate in general entertainment, was to coax a nod of approval from the Queen to her long-time favorite, then somewhat out of favor. The new manuscript, however, does not change the received evaluation of *The Lady of May* as rather slight in and of itself. Although the dialogue which Sidney provided for his actors shows the beginning of his conscious attempt to differentiate among the personalities and

3

voices of his characters, included here is only the first poem, LM 1, Sidney's only poem dedicated to Queen Elizabeth. The text is from Hm, which is now in the British Library.

Old Arcadia

Although the dedicatory letter of *The Countess of Pembroke's Arcadia* first appeared in 1590, introducing the *New Arcadia* as edited by Greville, since the discovery in 1907 of the first of nine manuscripts which have been uncovered in this century of the *Old Arcadia*, no scholar has doubted that this letter belongs with the original version; hence, it is published here along with the entire Book I of the *Old Arcadia*. Book I makes it quite clear that Sidney set out to write a five-act comedy of love in the Terrentian manner, following the rules he had been taught in school. The subject matter, furthermore, shows the lingering influence of Sidney's education, for in many ways, it might be considered a series of extended debates satirizing some of the common topics which schoolboys were so overly exposed to: love v. friendship, the active v. the retired life, the demands of reason v. the demands of passion, the role of the head over the role of the heart, and the duty of rule in the face of the great Elizabethan fear of chaos. (By Book V, however, these topics, especially the last, are treated most seriously.) From the artistic point of view, what is most noteworthy is the voice which Sidney creates for the narrator of the comedy: urbane, detached, and highly ironic, he presents all for the amusement and entertainment of the Countess of Pembroke and her fair lady friends. The source of the present version is the St. John's College (Cambridge) manuscript (St), which is the copy-text used by Robertson in her critical edition.

Other OA Poems

The five *Old Arcadia* poems of Book I have been printed in their appropriate contexts. Furthermore, the *Old Arcadia* poems which have been retained in the selections from the *New Arcadia* at the end of the present anthology have been prefaced by their appropriate designation as *Old Arcadia* poems (following Ringler's notation system). Most of the poems included in these contexts, however, do not reveal very much about Sidney's poetry, but two in particular should be referred to when reading the OA poems. First is the balladlike sonnet describing Mopsa in Book I of the *Old Arcadia*, and the extended catalog lyric sung by Pyrocles describing the beauties of Philoclea in Chapter 11 of Book II of the *New Arcadia*. These two poems, along with the other poems collected in this section, fully show the range of Sidney's experiments in various forms and kinds of English poetry. The question of accentual-syllabic poetry v. quantitative verse, which has been discussed in the General Introduction and which figures in Sidney's digression on English poetry at the end of the *Defence*, was a focal point of Sidney's attention while writing the *Old Arcadia*. In the earliest transcriptions, there is a debate between two shepherds at the end of the First Eclogues based squarely on this topic, but whatever the feelings might have been of Sidney the poet, Sidney the artist gives equal weight, attention, and detail to each side of this particular argument. Then, in St alone (a later transcription), in the margin alongside the first quantitative poem, OA 11, Sidney provides the rules which he feels should govern the writing of quantitative verse in English (and are included in the present text in a footnote to that poem). Sidney suppressed both of these passages in the final transcriptions of the *Old Arcadia*, for it seems clear that after his experimentations he realized that the natural thrust of English poetry could be maintained only within the rhythms and meter of accentual-syllabic verse. All of the poems are from St.

The Twenty-Third Psalm

Sometime during his career, Sidney put the first forty-three Psalms into English meter, and the work was completed by his sister some time after his death. Scholars and critics have never agreed upon the appropriate date for Sidney's part of this joint effort, for the only criterion of judgment seems to be a critical one. For example, Theodore Spencer believes that the Psalms are quite immature when compared to the rest of the poems in Sidney's canon; therefore, he places them early. Ringler, however, feels that they are among the most sophisticated products of Sidney's art and dates them late in Sidney's career. The present editor would date them no later than 1579 because the monotonous regularity of Sidney's accentual-syllabic meter is the result of yet another of his experiments in poetry. Hence, only one, the Twenty-third, is included here to illustrate the absolute woodenness of this particular artistic attempt, a deadness which Sidney must have felt, leading him to drop the project. Copytext is Bodleian MS. 14519 (which Ringler has deduced is closest to Sidney's own) as edited by A. B. Grosart, *The Complete Poems* (2 vols.), London, 1873, Fuller Worthies' Library, vols. 28 and 29. Vol. 29, pp. 250–251.

Certain Sonnets

In 1598 the Countess of Pembroke included at the end of her brother's works a group of poems entitled *Certain Sonnets*. Ringler has proved that these are various early poems (mostly from around 1580), but that Sidney collected them together and gave them a kind of unity by placing framing sonnets on either end of the sequence: at the beginning, two poems looking forward to love, and at the end, two poems rejecting earthly love. The range of experiments and diverse kinds of verse in between clearly indicate, though, that Sidney did not sit down to write any kind of formal sonnet sequence. What is notable is the dominance of an accentual-syllabic poetry which maintains a natural play of voice-rhythms and speech-patterns over the rigidity of meter. Sidney at this stage of his career had clearly rejected quantitative verse and rigid meter, and had settled in the mode appropriate for the eventual writing of *Astrophel and Stella*. Copy-text is 1598 (STC 22541).

Letter to Robert

This hastily penned letter in the fall of 1580 shows almost better than does any single piece of Sidney's art the natural enthusiasm, energy, and openness of the man himself: the words came tumbling out as fast as he could write them, with little regard for syntactical rules. But it shows as well how much Sidney was of his age: the wonderfully mixed idealism and materialism of the Renaissance is captured in his remarks of amazement upon Drake's return from circumnavigating the globe, and the manner of his advice to his brother is a perfect reflection of his conventional, Renaissance, rhetorically-biased education, while the matter of the advice clearly emphasizes practice. Of artistic significance, the letter indicates that Sidney had completed the work on the *Old Arcadia* (or was about to), and that he had not yet settled in his mind the role and nature both of poetry and the poet which he would define in the *Defence*. Nevertheless, in his discussion of historical treatises over historical narrations, one can see him moving toward his eventual definition of poetry, for a treatise contains in it the narration of facts (which instructs), the depiction of lively details (which delights), and the presentation of moral generalizations (which moves). Nascently, then, here is Sidney's definition of poetry as that which instructs, delights, and moves. Copy-text is Albert Feuillerat, ed., *The Prose Works* (4 vols.), Cambridge, Eng., 1962. III, 130–133.

THE LADY OF MAY

Most Gracious Sovereign[1]

To one whose state is raised over all,
Whose face doth oft the bravest sort enchant,
Whose mind is such, as wisest minds appall,[2]
Who in one self these diverse gifts can plant;
   How dare I (wretch) seek there my woes to rest,   5
   Where ears be burnt, eyes dazzled, heart oppres'd?

Your state is great, your greatness is your shield,
Your face hurts oft, but still it doth delight,
Your mind is wise, your wisdom makes you mild;
Such planted gifts enrich ev'n beggars' sight.   10
   So dare I (wretch) my bashful fear subdue,
   And feed mine eyes, mine ears, my heart on you.

[1] Presented to Queen Elizabeth in May 1578 by one of the actors in
The Lady of May, but not read in the presentation. Sidney's only poem to
the Queen.

[2] appall—make pale by comparison.

THE OLD ARCADIA

To My Dear Lady And Sister, The Countess Of Pembroke:

Here now have you (most dear, and most worthy to be most dear, Lady) this idle work of mine, which I fear (like the spider's web) will be thought fitter to be swept away than worn to any other purpose. For my part, in very truth (as the cruel fathers among the Greeks were wont to do to the babes they would not foster) I could well find in my heart to cast out in some desert of forgetfulness this child which I am loth to father. But you desired me to do it, and your desire to my heart is an absolute commandment. Now it is done, only for you, only to you; if you keep it to yourself, or to such friends who will weigh errors in the balance of good will, I hope, for the father's sake, it will be pardoned, perchance made much of, though in itself it have deformities. For indeed for severer eyes it is not, being but a trifle, and that triflingly handled. Your dear self can best witness the manner, being done in loose sheets of paper, most of it in your presence, the rest by sheets sent unto you as fast as they were done. In sum, a young head, not so well stayed as I would it were (and shall be when God will), having many, many fancies begotten in it, if it had not been in some way delivered, would have grown a monster, and more sorry might I be that they came in than that they got out. But his chief safety shall be the not walking abroad; and his chief protection the bearing the livery of your name, which (if much good will do not deceive me) is worthy to be a sanctuary for a greater offender. This say I, because I know the[1] virtue so; and this say I, because it may be ever so; or to say better, because it will be ever so. Read it then at your idle

[1] the—i.e., the strength of your name.

times, and the follies your good judgment will find in it blame not, but laugh at. And so, looking for no better stuff than in an haberdasher's shop, glasses or feathers, you will continue to love the writer, who doth exceedingly love you, and most, most heartily prays you may long live to be a principal ornament to the family of the Sidneys.

Your loving brother,
Philip Sidney

The First Book, or Act

Arcadia among all the provinces of Greece was ever had in singular reputation, partly for the sweetness of the air and other natural benefits, but principally for the moderate and well-tempered minds of the people who (finding how true a contentation is gotten by following the course of nature, and how the shining title of glory, so much affected by other nations, doth indeed help little to the happiness of life) were the only people which (as by their justice and providence) gave neither cause nor hope to their neighbors to annoy them, so were not they stirred with false praise to trouble others' quiet, thinking it a small reward for the wasting of their own lives in ravening, that their posterity should long after say, they had done so. Even the Muses seemed to approve their good determination by choosing that country as their chiefest repairing place, and by bestowing their perfections so largely there, that the very shepherds themselves had their fancies opened to so high conceits (as the most learned of other nations have been long time since content) both to borrow their names and imitate their cunning.

In this place, some time, there dwelt a mighty Duke named Basilius,[2] a prince of sufficient skill to govern so quiet a country, where the good minds of the former princes had set down good laws, and the well bringing up of the people did serve as a most sure bond to keep them. He married Gynecia,[3] daughter of the

---

[2] Basilius—"king."
[3] Gynecia—"womanly."

King of Cyprus,[4] a lady worthy enough to have had her name in
continual remembrance, if her later time had not blotted her well-
governed youth (although the wound fell more to her own conscience than to the knowledge of the world, fortune something
supplying her want of virtue). Of her the Duke had two fair
daughters, the elder Pamela,[5] the younger Philoclea,[6] both so excellent in all those gifts which are allotted to reasonable creatures,
as they seem to be born for a sufficient proof that nature is no
stepmother to that sex, how much so ever the rugged disposition
of some men, sharp witted only in evil-speaking, have sought to
disgrace them. And thus grew they on, in each good increase,
till Pamela, a year older than Philoclea, came to the point of
seventeen years of age; at which time, the Duke Basilius, not so
much stirred with the care of his country and children, as with
the vanity which possesseth many who (making a perpetual
mansion of this poor baiting place of man's life) are desirous to
know the certainty of things to come, wherein there is nothing
so certain as our continual uncertainty. Basilius, I say, would
needs undertake a journey to Delphos,[7] there by the oracle to
inform himself whether the rest of his life should be continued
in like tenor of happiness as thither unto it had been, accompanied with the well-being of his wife and children, whereupon
he had placed greatest part of his own felicity.

Neither did he long stay, but the woman appointed to that
impiety (furiously inspired) gave him in verse this answer:

[OA1]
Thy elder care shall from thy careful face
By princely mean be stolen, and yet not lost;
The younger shall with nature's bliss embrace,
An uncouth love, which nature hateth most;

---

[4] Cyprus—an island in the eastern Mediterranean, sixty miles from the
coast of Syria; the home of Venus.
[5] Pamela—"all sweetness."
[6] Philoclea—"lover of glory."
[7] Delphos—a town in Greece which was famous for its oracle of Pyth-
ian Apollo; the sybil there often uttered obscure prophecies which caused
men to bring down their own ruin.

Thou with thy wife adultery shalt commit,
And in thy throne, a foreign state shall sit;
All this on thee this fatal year shall hit.

Which, as in part it was more obscure than he could understand, so did the whole bear such manifest threatenings, that his
amazement was greater than his fore curiosity (both passions
proceeding out of one weakness: in vain, to desire to know that
of which, in vain, thou shalt be sorry after thou hast known it).
But thus the Duke answered (though not satisfied), he returned
into his country with a countenance well witnessing the dismayedness of his heart, which, notwithstanding upon good considerations, he thought not good to disclose, but only to one chosen
friend of his named Philanax,[8] whom he had ever found a friend,
not only in affection but judgment (and no less of the Duke, than
dukedom): a rare temper, whilst most men either servilely yield
to all appetites, or with an obstinate austerity, looking to that
they fancy good, wholly neglect the prince's person. But such
was this man, and in such a man had Basilius been happy, if his
mind (corrupted with a prince's fortune) had not resolved to
use a friend's secrecy rather for confirmation of fancies, than correcting of errors, which in this mighty matter he well showed;
for, having with many words discovered unto him both the cause
and success of his Delphos journey, in the end he told him that
to prevent all these inconveniences of the loss of his crown and
children (for, as for the point of his wife, he would no way
understand it) he was resolved for this fatal year to retire himself
with his wife and daughters into a solitary place, a place in that
world not so far gone into painted vanities where, being two
lodges built of purpose, he would in the one of them recommend
his daughter Pamela to his principal herdman, of some credit by
name Dametas,[9] in whose blunt truth he had great confidence,
thinking it a contrary salve against the destiny threatening her
mishap by a prince, to place her with a shepherd. In the other

    [8] Philanax—"lover of the lord."
    [9] Dametas—"commoner"; the name is borrowed from a character in
Virgil's *Eclogues*.

lodge he and his wife would keep their younger jewel, Philoclea, and (because the oracle touched some strange love of hers) have the more care of her, in especial keeping away her nearest kinsmen (whom he deemed chiefly understood) and (therewithall) all other likely to move any such humor. And so for himself, being so cruelly menaced by fortune, he would draw himself out of her way by this loneliness, which he thought was the surest mean to avoid her blows, where for his pleasure, he would be recreated with all those sports and eclogues,[10] wherein the shepherds of that country did much excell. As for the government of the country, and in especial manning of his frontiers (for that only way, he thought, a foreign prince might endanger his crown), he would leave the charge to certain selected persons, the superintendence of all which he would commit to Philanax, and so ended he this speech for fashion's sake, asking him his counsel.

But Philanax having forthwith taken into the depth of his consideration both what the Duke said, and with what mind he spoke it, with a true heart and humble countenance, in this sort answered: "Most redoubted and beloved Prince, if as well it had pleased you at your going to Delphos, as now to have used my humble service, both I should in better season and to better purpose have spoken, and you perhaps at this time should have been as no way more in danger, so undoubtedly and much more in quietness. I would have then said unto you that wisdom and virtue be the only destinies appointed for man to follow, wherein one ought to place all his knowledge; since they be such guides as cannot fail, which besides their inward comfort, do make a man see so direct a way of proceeding, as prosperity must necessarily ensue; and, although the wickedness of the world should oppress it, yet could it not be said that evil happened unto him, who should fall accompanied with virtue. So that either standing or falling with virtue, a man is never in evil case.

"I would then have said the heavenly powers to be reverenced and not searched into, and their mercy rather by prayers

---

[10] eclogues—short poems, especially pastoral dialogues.

to be sought, than their hidden counsels by curiosity; these kinds of soothsaying sorcerers (since the heavens have left us in ourselves sufficient guides) to be nothing but fancies wherein there must either be vanity or infallibleness, and so either not to be respected, or not to be prevented. But, since it is weakness too much to remember what should have been done, and that your commandment stretcheth what shall be done, I do (most dear lord) with humble boldness say that the manner of your determination doth in no sort no better please me than the cause of your going. These thirty years past have you so governed this realm that neither your subjects have wanted justice in you, nor you obedience in them, and your neighbors have found you so hurtlessly strong, that they thought it better to rest in your friendship than make new trial of your enmity. If this then have proceeded out of the good constitution of your state, and out of a wise providence generally to prevent all those things which might encumber your happiness, why should you now seek new courses, since your own example comforts you to continue on? And, that it is most certain, no destiny nor influence whatsoever can bring man's wit to a higher point than wisdom and goodness, why should you deprive yourself of governing your dukedom, for fear of losing your dukedom, like one that should kill himself for fear of death? Nay, rather, if this oracle be to be accounted of, arm up your courage the more against it, for who will stick to him that abandons himself? Let your subjects have you in their eyes, let them see the benefits of your justice daily more and more, and so must they needs rather like of present sureties, than uncertain changes. Lastly, whether your time call you to live or die, do both like a prince.

"And even the same mind hold I as touching my ladies your daughters, in whom nature promiseth nothing but goodness; and their education by your fatherly care hath been hitherto such as hath been most fit to restrain all evil, giving their minds virtuous delights, and not grieving them for want of well ruléd liberty: now to fall of a sudden straightening them, what can it do but argue suspicion, the most venomous gall to virtue? Leave women's minds, the most untamed that way of any; see whether any cage can please a bird, or whether a dog grow not fiercer with tying. What doth jealousy else but stir up the mind to think what it is from which they are restrained? For they are treasures, or things of great delight, which men use to hide for the aptness they have to catch men's fancies, and the thoughts once awaked to that, harder sure it is to keep those thoughts from accomplishment, then it had been before to have kept the mind (which being the chief part, by this means is defiled) from thinking. Now, for the recommending so principal a charge of her (whose mind goeth beyond the governing of many hundreds of such) to such a person as Dametas is, besides that the thing in itself is strange, it comes of a very ill ground that ignorance should be the mother of faithfulness. O, no, he cannot be good that knows not why he is good, but stands so far good as his fortune may keep him unassayed; but, coming to that, his rude simplicity is either easily changed, or easily deceived, and so grows that to be the last excuse of his fault, which seemed might have been the first foundation of his faith. Thus far hath your commandment and my zeal drawn me to speak, which I, like a man in a valley may discern hills, or like a poor passenger may spy a rock, so humbly submit to your gracious consideration, beseeching you to stand wholly upon your own virtue, as the surest way to maintain you in that you are, and to avoid any evil which may be imagined."

Whilst Philanax used these words, a man might see in the Duke's face that, as he was wholly wedded to his own opinion, so was he grieved to have any man say that which he had not seen; yet, did the good will he bore to Philanax so far prevail with him, that he passed into no further choler, but, with short manner, asked him: "And would you then," said he, "that in change of fortune I should not change my determination, as we do our apparel according to the air, and as the ship doth her course with the wind?"

"Truly, sir," answered he, "neither do I as yet see any change, and though I did, yet would I think a constant virtue, well settled, little subject unto it. And as in great necessity I would allow a well proportioned change, so in the sight of an enemy, to arm himself the lighter, or at every puff of wind, to strike sail, is such a change as either will breed ill success or no success."

"To give place to blows," said the Duke, "is thought no small wisdom."

"That is true," said Philanax. "But to give place before they come taketh away the occasion, when they come, to give place."

"Yet, the reeds stand with yielding," saith the Duke.

"And so are they but reeds, most worthy prince," said Philanax, "but the rocks stand still and are rocks."

But the Duke having used thus much dukely sophistry to deceive himself and making his will, wisdom, told him resolutely, he stood upon his own determination, and therefore willed him with certain other he named to take the government of the state, and especially to keep narrow watch of the frontiers. Philanax acknowledging himself much honored by so great trust, went with as much care to perform his commandment, as before he had with faith yielded his counsel, which in the later short disputings he had rather proportioned to Basilius' words, than to any soundness of argument. And Basilius, according to his determination, retired himself into the solitary place of the two lodges, where he was daily delighted with the eclogues and pastimes of shepherds; in the one of which lodges he himself remained with his wife and the beauty of the world, Philoclea; in the other, near unto him, he placed his daughter Pamela with Dametas, whose wife was Miso,[11] and daughter Mopsa,[12] unfit company for so excellent a creature, but to exercise her patience and to serve for a foil to her perfections.

Now, newly after that the Duke had begun this solitary life, there came (following the train their virtues led them) into this country, two young princes: the younger, but chiefer, named Pyrocles,[13] only son to Evarchus,[14] King of Macedon;[15] the other,

---

[11] Miso—"hateful."
[12] Mopsa—from Mopsus, a shepherd in Virgil's *Eclogues*.
[13] Pyrocles—"fire and glory."
[14] Evarchus—"good government."
[15] Macedon—a country northwest of the Aegean, north of Thessaly.

his cousin germane,[16] Musidorus,[17] Duke of Thessalia;[18] both like in virtues, near in year, near in blood, but nearest of all in friendship. And because this matter runs principally of them, a few more words, how they came hither, will not be superfluous.

Evarchus, King of Macedon, a prince of such justice that he never thought himself privileged by being a prince, nor did measure greatness by anything but by goodness, as he did thereby root an awful love in his subjects towards him, so yet could he not avoid the assaults of envy (the enemy, and yet the honor, of virtue). For the kings of Thrace,[19] Pannonia,[20] and Epirus,[21] not being able to attain his perfections, thought in their base wickedness best to take away so odious a comparison, lest his virtues joined now to the fame and force of the Macedonians might in time both conquer the bodies and win the minds of their subjects. And thus conspiring together, they did three sundry ways enter into his kingdom at one time, which sudden and dangerous invasions, although they did nothing astonish Evarchus who carried a heart prepared for all extremities (as a man that knew both what ill might happen to a man never so prosperous, and, withal, what the uttermost of that ill was) yet were they cause that Evarchus did send away his young son Pyrocles (at the time but six years old) to his sister, the dowager and regent of Thessalia, there to be brought up with her son Musidorus; which though it proceeded of necessity, yet, was not the counsel in itself unwise, the sweet emulation that grew being an excellent nurse of the good parts in these two princes, two princes indeed born to the exercise of virtue. For they, accounting the increase of their years with the increase of all good inward and outward qualities, and taking very timely into their minds that the divine part of

[16] cousin germane—first cousin.

[17] Musidorus—"gift of the Muses."

[18] Thessalia—a province in northeastern Greece, with the Aegean on the east.

[19] Thrace—a country in northwestern Asia Minor, between the Black Sea and the Aegean.

[20] Pannonia—a Roman province in south central Europe.

[21] Epirus—a region in northwestern Greece, with Macedonia and Thessaly on the east.

man was not enclosed in this body for nothing, gave themselves wholly over to those knowledges which might in the course of their life be ministers to well-being. And so grew they on till Pyrocles came to be seventeen and Musidorus eighteen years of age; at which time Evarchus, having after ten years' war conquered the kingdom of Thrace and brought the other two to be his tributaries, lived in the principal city of Thrace called at that time Byzantium, whither he sent for his son and nephew to delight his aged eyes in them, and to make them enjoy the fruits of his victories. But so pleased it God, who reserved them to greater traverses both of good and evil fortune, that the sea (to which they committed themselves) stirred with terrible tempest, forced them to fall far from their course upon the coast of Lydia.[22] Where, what befell unto them, what valiant acts they did, passing (in one year's space) through the lesser Asia, Syria, and Egypt, how many ladies they defended from wrongs, and disinherited persons restored to their right, it is a work for a higher style than mine. This only shall suffice, that their fame returned so fast before them into Greece, that the King of Macedon received that as the comfort of their absence, although accompanied with so much more longing as he found the manifestation of their worthiness greater. But they desirous more and more to exercise their virtues, and increase their experience, took their journey from Egypt towards Greece, which they did, they two alone because (that being their native country) they might have the most perfect knowledge of it, wherein they that hold the countenances of princes have their eyes most dazzled. And so taking Arcadia in their way for the fame of the country, they came thither newly after that this strange solitariness had possessed Basilius.

Now so fell it unto them, that they lodging in the house of Kerxenus,[23] a principal gentleman in Mantinea[24] (so was the city called, near to the solitary dwelling of the Duke) it was Pyrocles' either evil or good fortune, walking with his host in a fair

[22] Lydia—a country in western Asia Minor, on the Aegean.
[23] Kerxenus—"devoted friend."
[24] Mantinea—a city in central Arcadia.

gallery, that he perceived a picture newly made by an excellent artificer, which contained the Duke and Duchess with their younger daughter Philoclea, with such countenance and fashion as the manner of their life held them in. Both the parents' eyes cast with a loving care upon their beautiful child, she drawn as well as it was possible art should counterfeit so perfect a workmanship of nature; for therein, besides the show of her beauties, a man might judge even the nature of her countenance, full of bashfulness, love, and reverence, and all by the cast of her eye, mixed with a sweet grief to find her virtue suspected. This moved Pyrocles to fall into questions of her, wherein being answered by the gentleman so much as he understood: which was of her strange kind of captivity, neither was it known how long it should last, and there was a general opinion grown, the Duke would grant his daughters in marriage to nobody.

As the most noble heart is subject unto it, from questions grew to pity, and when with pity once his heart was made kinder according to the aptness of the humor, it received straight a cruel impression of that wonderful passion, which to be defined is impossible, by reason no words reach near to the strange nature of it; they only know it which inwardly feel it, it is called love. Yet did not the poor youth at first know his disease, thinking it only such a kind of desire as he was wont to have to see unwonted sights, and his pity to be no other but the fruits of his gentle nature; but even this arguing with himself came oft to a further thought, and the more he argued, the more his thought increased. Desirous he was to see the place where she remained, as though the architecture of the lodges would have been much for his learning, but more desirous to see herself to be judge forsooth of the painter's cunning; for thus at the first did he flatter himself, as though the wound had been no deeper. But when within short time he came to the degree of uncertain wishes and that those wishings grew to unquiet longings; when he could fix his thoughts upon nothing, but that within a little varying, they should end with Philoclea; when each thing he saw seemed to figure out some part of his passions, and that he heard no word spoken, but that he imagined it carried the sound of Philoclea's

name; then did poor Pyrocles yield to the burden, finding himself
prisoner before he had leisure to arm himself, and that he might
well (like the spaniel) gnaw upon the chain that ties him, but
he should sooner mar his teeth than procure liberty. Then was
his chief delight secretly to draw his dear friend, and walking to
the desert[25] of the two lodges, where he saw no grass upon
which he thought Philoclea might hap to tread, but that he
envied the happiness of it, and yet, with a contrary folly, would
sometimes recommend his whole estate unto it.

Till at length, Love, the refiner of invention, put in his head
a way how to come to the sight of his Philoclea for which he
with great speed and secrecy prepared every thing that was
necessary for his purpose. But, yet could not put it in execution,
till he had disclosed it to Musidorus, both to perform the true
laws of friendship and withal to have his counsel and allowance,
and yet out of the sweetness of his disposition was bashfully
afraid to break it with him, to whom (besides other bonds) because he was his elder, he bore a kind of reverence, until some fit
opportunity might, as it were, draw it from him.

Which occasion time shortly presented unto him, for Musidorus having informed himself fully of the strength and riches
of the country, of the nature of the people, and of the manner
of their laws, and seeing the Duke's court could not be visited,
and that they came not without danger to that place (prohibited
to all men, but to certain shepherds) grew no less weary of his
abode there, than marveled of the great delight Pyrocles took
in that place, whereupon, one day at Pyrocles' earnest request
being walked thither again, began in this manner to say unto him:
"A mind well trained and long exercised in virtue, my sweet
and worthy cousin, doth not easily change any course it once
undertakes, but upon well grounded and well weighed causes, for
being witness to itself of his own inward good, it finds nothing
without it of so high a price for which it should be altered. Even
the very countenance and behavior of such a man doth show
forth images of the same constancy by maintaining a right har-

[25] desert—any uncivilized place.

mony betwixt it and the inward good, in yielding itself suitable
to the virtuous resolutions of the mind.

"This speech, I direct to you, noble friend Pyrocles, the
excellency of whose mind and well chosen course in virtue, if I
do not sufficiently know (having seen such rare demonstrations
of it) it is my weakness, and not your unworthiness. But as indeed I do know it, and knowing it, most dearly love both it and
him that hath it, so must I needs say, that since our late coming
into this country I have marked in you (I will not say an alteration) but a relenting truly and slaking of the main career you had
so nobly begun and almost performed. And that in such sort as I
cannot find sufficient reasons in my great love towards you how
to allow it. For, to leave of other secret arguments which my acquaintance with you makes me easily find, this, in effect to any
man, may be manifest, that whereas you were wont in all the
places you came to give yourself vehemently to knowledge of
those things which might better your mind, to seek the familiarity
of excellent men in learning and soldiery, and lastly to put all
these things in practice, both by continual wise proceeds and
worthy enterprises, as occasions fell for them. You now leave all
these things undone; you let your mind fall asleep (besides your
countenance troubled, which surely comes not out of virtue, for
virtue like the clear heaven is without clouds); and lastly, which
seemeth strange unto me, you haunt greatly this place, wherein
besides the disgrace that might fall of it (which that it hath not
already fallen upon you, is more rather luck than providence, the
Duke having sharply forbidden it), now subject yourself to
solitariness, the sly enemy that doth most separate a man from
well doing."

These words spoken vehemently and proceeding from so
dearly an esteemed friend as Musidorus did so pierce poor
Pyrocles, that his blushing cheeks did witness with him, he rather
could not help, than did not know his fault. Yet, desirous by
degrees to bring his friend to a gentler consideration of him,
and beginning with two or three broken sighs, answered him to
this purpose: "Excellent Musidorus, in the praises you gave me
in the beginning of your speech I easily acknowledge the force of

your good will unto me. For, neither could you have thought so well of me if extremity of love had not something dazzled your eyes, nor you could have loved me so entirely, if you had not been apt to make so great (though undeserved) judgment of me. And even so must I say of those imperfections, to which though I have ever through weakness been subject, yet which you by the daily mending of your mind have of late been able to look into, which before you could not discern, so that the change you spake of falls not out by my impairing, but by your bettering. And yet under the leave of your better judgment I must needs say thus much, my dear cousin, that I find not myself wholly to be condemned, because I do not with a continual vehemency follow those knowledges which you call the betterings of my mind. For, both the mind itself must (like other things) sometimes be unbent, or else it will be either weakened or broken, and these knowledges, as they are of good use, so are they not all the mind may stretch itself unto. Who knows whether I feed not my mind with higher thoughts? Truly, as I know not all the particularities, so yet see I the bounds of all those knowledges, but the workings of the mind I find much more infinite than can be led unto by the eye, or imagined by any that distract their thoughts without themselves; and in such contemplations, or as I think more excellent, I enjoy my solitariness, and my solitariness perchance is the nurse of these contemplations. Eagles we see fly alone, and they are but sheep which always herd together. Condemn not therefore my mind sometime to enjoy itself, nor blame not, the taking of such times as serve most fit for it."

And here Pyrocles suddenly stopped, like a man unsatisfied in himself, though his wit might well have served to have satisfied another. And so looking with a countenance as though he desired he should know his mind without hearing him speak, and yet desirous to speak, to breathe out some part of his inward evil, sending again new blood to his face, he continued his speech in this manner.

"And lord, dear cousin," said he, "doth not the pleasantness of this place carry in itself sufficient reward for any time lost in it, or for any such danger that might ensue? Do you not see how everything conspires together to make this place a heavenly dwelling? Do you not see the grass, how in color they excell the emeralds, every one striving to pass his fellow, and yet they are all kept in an equal height? And see you not the rest of all these beautiful flowers, each of which would require a man's wit to know, and his life to express? Do not these stately trees seem to maintain their flourishing old age, with the only happiness of their seat being clothed with a continual spring, because no beauty here should ever fade? Doth not the air breathe health which the birds (both delightful both to the ear and eye) do daily solemnize with the sweet consent of their voices? Is not every echo here a perfect music? And these fresh and delightful brooks, how slowly they slide away, as, loath to leave the company of so many things united in perfection, and with how sweet a murmur they lament their forced departure. Certainly, certainly, cousin, it must needs be, that some goddess this desert belongs unto, who is the soul of this soil, for neither is any less than a goddess worthy to be shrined in such a heap of pleasures, nor any less than a goddess could have made it so perfect a model of the heavenly dwellings."

And so he ended with a deep sigh, ruefully casting his eye upon Musidorus, as more desirous of pity, than pleading. But Musidorus had all this while held his look fixed upon Pyrocles' countenance and with no less loving attention, marked how his words proceeded from him; but in both these he perceived such strange diversities, that they rather increased new doubts, than gave him ground to settle any judgment. For besides his eyes, sometime even great with tears, the oft changing of his color with a kind of shaking unsteadiness over all his body, he might see in his countenance some great determination mixed with fear, and might perceive in him store of thoughts rather stirred than digested, his words interrupted continually with sighs, which served as a burden to each sentence, and the tenor of his speech (though of his wonted phrase) not knit together to one constant end, but rather dissolved in itself, as the vehemency of the inward passion prevailed, which made Musidorus frame his answer nearest to that humor which should soonest put out the secret. For having in the beginning of Pyrocles' speech (which defended his solitariness) framed in his mind a reply against it in the praise of honorable action, in showing that such kind of contemplation is but a glorious title to idleness; that in action a man did not only better himself, but, benefit others; that the God would not have delivered a soul into the body which hath arms and legs only instruments of doing, but that it were intended the mind should employ them; and that the mind should best know his own good or evil by practice, which knowledge was the only way to increase the one and correct the other—besides, many other better arguments, which the plentifulness of the matter yielded to the sharpness of his wit. When he found Pyrocles leave that, and fall to such an affected praising of the place, he left it likewise, and joined therein with him, because he found him in that humor, utter most store of passion.

And even thus kindly embracing him, he said, "Your words are such, noble cousin, so sweetly and strongly handled in the praise of solitariness, as they would make me yield likewise myself up unto it, but that the same words make me know it is more pleasant to enjoy the company of him that can speak such words, than by such words to be persuaded to follow solitariness. And even so do I give you leave, sweet Pyrocles, ever to defend solitariness, so long as to defend it, you ever keep company. But I marvel at the excessive praises you give to this desert; in truth it is not unpleasant, but, yet, if you would return unto Macedon, you should see either many heavens, or find this, no more than earthly. And even Tempe,[26] in my Thessalia, where you and I to my great happiness were brought up together, is nothing inferior unto it. But, I think you will make me see that the vigor of your wit can show itself in any subject, or else you feed sometimes your solitariness, with the conceits of the poets, whose liberal pens can [as] easily travel over mountains as mole hills, and so, like well disposed men, set up everything to the highest note, especially when they put such words in the mouth of one of these

[26] Tempe—a valley in Thessaly, dedicated to Apollo; later, a metaphor for any sequestered vale.

fantastical mind-infected people that children and musicians call lovers."

This word of "lover" did no less pierce poor Pyrocles than the right tune of music touches him that is sick of the tarantula.[27] There was not one part of his body that did not feel a sudden motion, the heart drawing unto itself the life of every part to help it, distressed with the sound of that word. Yet after some pause, lifting up a little his eyes from the ground, and yet not daring to place them in the face of Musidorus, armed with the very countenance of the poor prisoner at the bar whose answer is nothing but "guilty," with much ado he brought forth this question. "And alas," said he, "dear cousin, what if I be not so much the poet, the freedom of whose pen can exercise itself in anything, as even that very miserable subject of his cunning, whereof you speak of."

"Now the eternal gods forbid," mainly[28] cried out Musidorus.

But Pyrocles having broken the ice pursued on in this manner. "And yet such a one am I," said he, "and in such extremity as no man can feel but myself, nor no man believe, since no man ever could taste the hundredth part of that which lies in the innermost part of my soul. For since it was the fatal overthrow of all my liberty to see in the gallery of Mantinea the only Philoclea's picture, that beauty did pierce so through mine eyes to my heart, that the impression of it doth not lie but live there in such sort, as the question is not now, whether I shall love or no, but whether loving I shall live or die."

Musidorus was no less astonished with these words of his friend than if thinking him in health he had suddenly told him that he felt the pangs of death oppress him. So that amazedly looking upon him (even as Apollo is painted when he saw Daphne suddenly turned to a laurel)[29] he was not able to say one word,

---

[27] tarantula—a man sick of the tarantula's bite is subject to frenzy if he hears the music which has exactly the right tones for his particular tarantula.

[28] mainly—strongly.

[29] Apollo and Daphne—Apollo pursued the nymph Daphne, who was changed into a laurel tree in order to escape him; a popular subject for friezes.

but gave Pyrocles occasion, having already made the breach, to pass on in this sort. "And because I have laid open my wound, noble cousin," said he, "I will show you what my melancholy hath brought forth for the preparation at least of a salve, if it be not in itself a medicine. I am resolved (because all direct ways are barred me, of opening my suit to the Duke) to take upon me the estate of an Amazon lady[30] going about the world to practice feats of chivalry, and to seek myself a worthy husband. I have already provided all furniture necessary for it, and my face (you see) will not easily discover me. And hereabout will I haunt, till by the help of these disguisings, I may come to the presence of her whose imprisonment darkens the world; that my own eyes may be witnesses to my heart, it is good reason why he should be thus captive. And then as I shall have attained to the first degree of my happiness, so will fortune, occasion, and mine own industry put forward the rest. For the principal point is to set in a good way the thing we desire, for then will time itself daily discover new secret helps. As for my name it shall be Cleophila,[31] turning Philoclea to myself, as my mind is wholly turned and transformed into her. Now, therefore, do I submit myself to your counsel, dear cousin, and crave your help," and thus he ended (as who should say, "I have told you all, have pity on me").

But Musidorus had by this time gathered his spirits together, dismayed to see him he loved more than himself plunged in such a course of misery. And so, when Pyrocles had ended, casting a ghastful countenance upon him, as if he would conjure some strange spirit he saw possess him, with great vehemency uttered these words: "And is it possible, that this is Pyrocles, the only young prince in the world formed by nature, and framed by education, to the true exercise of virtue? Or is it indeed some Amazon Cleophila, that hath counterfeited the face of my friend in this sort to vex me? For likelier sure I would have thought it that my outward face might have been disguised, than that the face of so excellent a mind could have been thus blemished! O, sweet Pyrocles, separate yourself a little, if it be possible, from

---

[30] Amazon—one of a race of warrior women in Pontus (Asia Minor).
[31] Cleophila—"glory of love," the name of Philoclea reversed.

yourself, and let your own mind look upon your own proceedings, so shall my words be needless and you best instructed. See with yourself, how fit it will be for you in this your tender youth, born so great a prince, of so rare not only expectation, but proof, desired of your old father, and wanted of your native country (now so near your home), to direct your thoughts from the way of goodness; to lose, nay, to abuse your time; lastly, to overthrow all the excellent things you have done, which have filled the world with your fame, as if you should drown your ship in the long desired haven, or like an ill player should mar the last act of his tragedy.

"Remember (for I know you know it) that if we will be men, the reasonable part of your soul is to have absolute commandment, against which if any sensual weakness arise, we are to yield all our sound forces to the overthrowing of so unnatural a rebellion. Wherein, how can we want courage, since we are to deal against so weak an adversary, that in itself is nothing but weakness. Nay, we are to resolve that if reason direct it, we must do it, and if we must do it, we will do it. For, to say I cannot, is childish, and I will not, womanish. And, see how extremely every way you endanger your mind, for to take this womanly habit (without you frame your behavior accordingly) is wholly vain, your behavior can never come kindly[32] from you, but as the mind is proportioned unto it. So that you must resolve, if you will play your part to any purpose (whatsoever peevish imperfections are in that sex) to soften your heart to receive them, the very first downstep to all wickedness. For, do not deceive yourself, my dear cousin, there is no man suddenly either excellently good, or extremely evil, but grows either as he holds himself up in virtue, or lets himself slide to viciousness.

"And let us see, what power is the author of all these troubles? Forsooth, Love. Love, a passion, and the barest and fruitlessest of all passions. Fear breedeth wit, anger is the cradle of courage, joy openeth and enableth the heart, sorrow as it closeth it, so yet draweth it inward to look to the correcting of

[32] kindly—naturally.

itself, and so, all of them generally, have power toward some good by the direction of reason. But this bastard Love (for indeed the name of Love is unworthily applied to so hateful an humor) as it is engendered betwixt lust and idleness,[33] as the matter it works upon is nothing but a certain base weakness which some gentle fools call a gentle heart; as his adjoined companions be unquietness, longings, fond comforts, faint discomforts, hopes, jealousies, ungrounded rages, causeless yieldings; so is the highest end it aspires unto, a little pleasure with much pain before, and great repentance after. But that end (how endless it runs to infinite evils) were fit enough for the matter we speak of, but not for your ears, in whom indeed there is so much true disposition to virtue. Yet thus much of his worthy effects in yourself is to be seen that it utterly subverts the course of nature, in making reason give place to sense, and man, to woman. And truly, (I think) hereupon it first got the name of Love, for indeed the true Love hath that excellent nature in it that it doth transform the very essence of the lover into the thing loved, uniting, and, as it were, incorporating it with a secret and inward working; and herein do these kinds of love imitate the excellent. For, as the love of heaven makes one heavenly, the love of virtue, virtuous, so doth the love of the world make one become worldly, and this effeminate love of a woman doth so womanish a man that if you yield to it, it will not only make you a famous Amazon, but a launder, a distaff spinner,[34] or whatsoever other vile occupation their idle heads can imagine, and their weak hands perform. Therefore, to trouble you no longer with my tedious, but loving words, if either you remember what you are, what you have been, or what you must be, if you consider what it is that moves you, or for what kind of creature you are moved, you shall find the cause so small, the effects so dangerous, yourself so unworthy to run into the one, or to be driven by the other that, I doubt not, I shall quickly have occasion rather to praise you for

[33] lust and idleness—Venus and a Mars rendered effeminate and inert by passion.
[34] launder and distaff spinner—Hercules was reduced to spinning wool by Omphale, Queen of Lydia.

having conquered it, than to give you any further counsel how to do it."

Pyrocles' mind was all this while so fixed upon another devotion that he no more attentively marked his friend's discourse than the child that hath leave to play marks the last part of his lesson, or the diligent pilot in a dangerous tempest doth attend to the unskillful[35] words of the passenger. Yet the very sound having left the general points of his speech in his mind, the respect he bear to his friend brought forth this answer (having first paid up his late accustomed tribute of sighs): "Dear and worthy friend, whatsoever good disposition nature hath bestowed on me, or howsoever that disposition hath been by bringing-up confirmed, this must I confess, that I am not yet come to that degree of wisdom to think lightly of the sex of whom I have my life. Since, if I be anything (which your friendship rather finds, than I acknowledge), I was, to come to it, born of a woman and nursed of a woman; and certainly (for this point of your speech doth nearest touch me) it is strange to see the unmanlike cruelty of mankind, who, not content with their tyrannous ambition, to have brought the others' virtuous patience under them, like childish masters think their masterhood nothing without doing injury unto them who (if we will argue by reason) are framed of nature with the same parts of the mind for the exercise of virtue, as we are. And for example, even this estate of Amazons (which I now for my greatest honor, do seek to counterfeit) doth well witness that if generally the sweetness of their disposition did not make them see the veins of these things (which we account glorious) they neither want valor of mind, nor yet doth their fairness take away their force. And truly, we men, and praisers of men should remember, that if we have such excellencies, it is reason to think them excellent creatures of whom we are, since a kite never brought forth a good flying hawk. But, to tell you true, I do both disdain to use any more words of such a subject, which is so praised in itself as it needs no praises, and withal fear lest my conceit (not able to reach unto them) bring forth words which for their unworthi-

35 unskillful—uninstructed.

ness may be a disgrace to them I so inwardly honor. Let this suffice, that they are capable of virtue, and virtue (you yourself say) is to be loved, and I, too, truly. But this I willingly confess, that it likes me much better when I find virtue in a fair lodging than when I am bound to seek it in an ill-favored creature, like a pearl in a dunghill."

And here, Pyrocles stayed, as to breathe himself having been transported with a little vehemency, because it seemed to him Musidorus had over bitterly glanced against the reputation of womankind. But then quieting his countenance, as well as out of an unquiet mind it might be, he thus proceeded on. "And, poor Love," said he, "dear cousin, is little beholding unto you, since you are not contented to spoil it of the honor of the highest power of the mind, which notable men have attributed unto it; but you deject it below all other passions (in truth) something strangely; since, if Love received any disgrace, it is by the company of those passions you prefer[36] unto it. For those kind of bitter objections, as that lusty idleness and a weak heart should be, as it were, the matter and form of love, rather touch me, dear Musidorus, than Love. But, I am good witness of my own imperfections, and therefore will not defend myself, but herein I must say, you deal contrary to yourself, for if I be so weak, then can you not with reason stir me up, as you did by the remembrance of mine own virtue; or if indeed I be virtuous, then must you confess, that Love hath his working in a virtuous heart, and so no doubt hath it whatsoever I be. For if we love virtue, in whom shall we love it but in virtuous creatures, without your meaning be, I should love this word of virtue when I see it written in a book. Those troublesome effects you say it breeds be not the faults of Love, but of him, that loves, as an unable vessel to bear such a power, like evil eyes not able to look on the sun, or like a weak brain soonest overthrown with the best wine. Even that heavenly Love you speak of is accompanied in some hearts with hopes, griefs, longings, and despairs, and in that heavenly Love since there are two parts, the one the love itself, the other,

[36] prefer—ascribe.

the excellency of the thing loved, I (not able at the first leap, to frame both in myself) do now like a diligent workman, make ready the chief instrument and first part of that great practiced work which is love itself, which, when I have a while practiced in this sort, then, you shall see me turn it to greater matters. And thus gently, you may, if it please you, think of me; neither doubt you because I wear a woman's apparel, I will be the more womanish, since I assure you (for all my apparel) there is nothing I desire more than fully to prove myself a man in this enterprise. Much might be said in my defense, much more for Love, and most of all for that divine creature, which hath joined me and love together. But these disputations are fitter for quiet schools than my troubled brains, which are bent rather in deeds to perform than in words to defend the noble desire that possesseth me."

"O Lord," said Musidorus, "how sharp witted you are to hurt yourself."

"No," answered he, "but it is the hurt you speak of which makes me so sharp-witted."

"Even so," said Musidorus, "as every base occupation makes one sharp in their practice and foolish in all the rest."

"Nay, rather," answered Pyrocles, "as each excellent thing once well learned serves for a measure of all other knowledges."

"And is that become," said Musidorus, "a measure for other things, which never received measure in itself?"

"It is counted without measure," answered Pyrocles, "because the workings of it are without measure, but otherwise in nature it hath measure, since it hath an end alloted unto it. The beginning being so excellent I would gladly know the end enjoying," answered Pyrocles with a deep sigh.

"Oh," said Musidorus, "now set you forth the baseness of it, since, if it end in enjoying, it shows all the rest was nothing."

"You mistake me," answered Pyrocles. "I spake of the end, to which it is directed, which end ends not, no sooner than the life."

"Alas, let your own brain disenchant you," said Musidorus.

"My heart is too far possessed," said Pyrocles. "But the head gives you direction and the heart gives me life," answered Pyrocles.

But Musidorus was so grieved to see his beloved friend obstinate (as he thought) to his own destruction, that it forced him with more than accustomed vehemency to speak these words. "Well, well," said he, "you list[37] to abuse yourself; it was a very white and red[38] virtue which you could pick out by the sight of a picture. Confess the truth, and you shall find the uttermost was but beauty: a thing which though it be in as great excellency in yourself as may be in any, yet I am sure you make no further reckoning of it than of an outward fading benefit nature bestowed upon you. And yet, such is your want of a true grounded virtue, which must be like itself in all points that what you wisely count a trifle in yourself, you fondly become a slave unto in another. For my part, I now protest, I have left nothing unsaid which my wit could make me know, or my most entire friendship to you requires of me. I do now beseech you, even for the love betwixt us (if this other love have left any in you towards me), and for the remembrance of your old careful father (if you can remember him, that forgets yourself), lastly for Pyrocles' own sake who is now upon the point of falling or rising, to purge your head of this vile infection. Otherwise, give me leave rather in absence to bewail your mishap, than to bide the continual pang of seeing your danger with mine eyes."

The length of these speeches before had not so much cloyed Pyrocles, though he were very impatient of long deliberations, as this last farewell of him he loved as his own life did wound his soul. As, indeed, they that think themselves afflicted are apt to conceive unkindness deeply, in so much that shaking his head, and delivering some show of tears, he thus uttered his griefs. "Alas," said he, "Prince Musidorus, how cruelly you deal with me; if you seek the victory, take it; and if you list, triumph. Have you all the reason of the world, and with me remain all the imperfections? Yet such as I can no more lay from me than the

[37] list—desire.
[38] white and red—the colors of passion.

crow can be persuaded by the swan to cast off his blackness. But, truly you deal with me like a physician that, seeing his patient in a pestilent fever, should chide him instead of ministering help, and bid him be sick no more; or, rather, like such a friend, that visiting his friend condemned to perpetual prison and loaded with grievous fetters, should will him to shake off his fetters, or he would leave him. I am sick, and sick to the death; I am prisoner; neither is there any redress, but by her, to whom I am slave. Now, if you list, leave him that loves you in the highest degree, but remember ever to carry this with you, that you abandon your friend in his greatest need."

And herewith the deep wound of his love, being rubbed afresh with this new unkindness, began as it were to bleed again in such sort that he was unable to bear it any longer. But gushing out abundance of tears, and crossing his arms over his woeful heart, he sank down to the ground. Which sudden trance went so to the heart of Musidorus, that falling down by him, and kissing the weeping eyes of his friend, he besought him not to make account of his speech, which if it had been over-vehement, yet was it to be borne withal because it came out of a love much more vehement, that he had never thought fancy could have received so deep a wound. But, now finding in him the force of it, he would no further contrary it, but employ all his service to medicine it in such sort as the nature of it required. But even this kindness made Pyrocles the more melt in the former unkindness, which his manlike tears well showed with a silent look upon Musidorus (as who should say, "And is it possible, that Musidorus, should threaten to leave me?"). And this struck Musidorus' mind and senses so dumb, too, that for grief, not being able to say anything, they rested with their eyes placed one upon another in such sort as might well paint out the true passion of unkindness, which is never aright,[39] but betwixt them that most dearly love. And thus remained they a time, till at length Musidorus, embracing him, said, "And will you thus shake off your friend?"

[39] aright—real, true.

"It is you that shake off me," said Pyrocles, "being for mine unperfectness unworthy of your friendship."

"But this," said Musidorus, "shows you much more unperfect, to be cruel to him that submitteth himself unto you." "But since you are unperfect," said he smiling, "it is reason you be governed by us wise and perfect men. And that authority will I begin to take upon me with three absolute commandments: the first, that you increase not your evil with further griefs; the second, that you love Philoclea with all the powers of your mind; and the last commandment shall be that you command me to do you what service I can toward the obtaining of your desires."

Pyrocles' heart was not so oppressed with the two mighty passions of love and unkindness but that it yielded to some mirth at this commandment of Musidorus, that he should love Philoclea; so that something clearing his face from his former shows of grief, "Well," said he, "dear cousin, I see by the well choosing of your commandments that you are far fitter to be a prince than a counselor. And therefore, I am resolved to employ all my endeavor to obey you with this condition, that the commandments you command me to lay upon you shall only be that you continue to love me, and look upon my imperfections with more affection than judgment."

"Love you?" said he, "Alas how can my heart be separated from the true embracing of it without it burst by being too full of it." "But," said he, "let us leave of these flowers[40] of new begun friendship, and since you have found out that way as your readiest remedy, let us go put on your transforming apparel. For my part, I will ever remain hereabouts, either to help you in any necessity, or at least to be partaker of any evil may fall unto you."

Pyrocles, accepting this as a most notable testimony of his long approved friendship, and returning to Mantinea, where having taken leave of their host, who though he knew them not was in love with their virtue, and leaving with him some apparel and jewels, with opinion they would return after some time unto him,

---

[40] flowers—rhetorical expressions.

they departed thence to the place where he had left his womanish apparel, which with the help of his friend, he had quickly put on in such sort as it might seem love had not only sharpened his wits, but nimbled his hands in anything which might serve to his service.

And to begin with his head, thus was he dressed. His hair (which the young men of Greece wear very long, accounting them most beautiful that had that in fairest quantity) lay upon the upper part of his forehead in locks, some curled, and some, as it were, forgotten—with such a careless care and with an art so hiding art, that he seemed he would lay them for a trial whether nature simply, or nature helped by cunning, be the more excellent—the rest whereof was drawn into a coronet of gold, richly set with pearls, and so joined all over with gold wires, and covered with feathers of diverse colors, that it was not unlike to a helmet, such a glittering show it bear, and so bravely it was held up from the head. Upon his body he wore a kind of doublet[41] of skycolor satin, so plaited over with plaits[42] of massy gold, that he seemed armed in it. His sleeves of the same, instead of plaits, was covered with purled lace,[43] and such was the nether part of his garment (but that made so full of stuff,[44] and cut after such a fashion) that though the length fell under his ankles, yet in his going one might well perceive the small of the leg, which, with the foot, was covered with a little short pair of crimson velvet buskins,[45] in some places open, as the ancient manner was, to show the fairness of the skin. Over all this, he wore a certain mantle of like stuff, made in such manner that, coming under his right arm and covering most part of that side, it touched not the left side but upon the top of the shoulder where the two ends met and were fastened together with a very rich jewel, the device[46] whereof was this: an eagle covered with the feathers of a

41 doublet—a kind of close-fitting body garment, with or without sleeves.
42 plaits—folds.
43 purled lace—lace ornamented with embroidered loops.
44 stuff—a woolen fabric.
45 buskins—high boots.
46 device—a figure or design.

dove, and yet lying under another dove, in such sort as it seemed the dove preyed upon the eagle, the eagle casting up such a look as though the state he was in, liked him, though the pain grieved him. Upon the same side upon his thigh, he wore a sword, such as we now call scimitars,[47] the pommel[48] whereof was so richly set with precious stones, as they were sufficient testimony it could be no mean personage that bore it.

Such was this Amazon's attire, and thus did Pyrocles become Cleophila, which name for a time hereafter I will use, for I myself feel such compassion of his passion that I find even part of his fear lest his name should be uttered before fit time were for it. Which, you fair ladies, that vouchsafe to read this, I doubt not will account excusable. But Musidorus that had helped to dress his friend could not satisfy himself with looking upon him, so did he find his excellent beauty set out with this new change like a diamond set in a more advantageous sort, insomuch that he could not choose, but (smiling) said unto him: "Well," said he, "sweet cousin, since you are framed of such a loving mettle, I pray you take heed of looking yourself in a glass, lest Narcissus'[49] fortune fall unto you. For my part, I promise you, if I were not fully resolved never to submit my heart to those fancies, I were like enough, while I dressed you, to become a young Pygmalion."[50]

"Alas," answered Cleophila, "if my beauty be anything, then will it help me to some part of my desires; otherwise, I am no more to set by it than the orator by his eloquence that persuades nobody."

"She is a very invincible creature then," said he, "for I doubt me much (under your patience) whether my mistress, your mistress, have a greater portion of beauty."

"Speak not that blasphemy, dear friend," said Cleophila, "for if I have any beauty, it is the beauty which the imagination

---

[47] scimitars—short, curved, single-edged swords.
[48] pommel—knob on the hilt of a sword.
[49] Narcissus—Pined away through love of his own reflection in a pool.
[50] Pygmalion—Cyprian king who made a woman out of ivory, fell in love with it, and begged Venus to give it life, which she did.

of her strikes into my fancies, which in part shines through my face into your eyes."

"Truly," said Musidorus, "you are grown a notable philosopher of fancies."

"Astronomer," answered Cleophila, "for they are heavenly fancies."

In such friendly speeches they returned again to the desert of the two lodges, where Cleophila desired Musidorus he would hide himself in a little grove, where he might see how she could play her part. For there (she said) she was resolved to remain till by some good favor of fortune she might obtain the sight of her whom she bore continually in the eyes of her mind. Musidorus obeyed her request, full of extreme grief to see so worthy a mind thus infected, besides he could see no hope of success, but great appearance of danger. Yet finding it so deeply grounded that striving against it did rather anger than heal the wound, and rather call his friendship in question than give place to any friendly counsel, he was contented to yield to the force of the present stream, with hope afterwards as occasion fell out to prevail better with him, or at least, to adventure his life in preserving him from any injury might be offered him. And with the beating of those thoughts, remained he in the grove, till with a new fullness he was emptied of them, as you shall after hear. In the meantime Cleophila walking up and down in that solitary place, with many intricate determinations, at last wearied both in mind and body sat her down, and beginning to tune her voice with many sobs and tears, sang this song, which she had made since her first determination thus to change her estate:

[OA2]

Transformed in show, but more transformed in mind,
I cease to strive, with double conquest foiled;
For, woe is me, my powers all, I find,
With outward force and inward treason spoiled.

For, from without, came to mine eyes the blow
Whereto mine inward thoughts did faintly yield;

Both these conspired poor reason's overthrow,
False in myself, thus have I lost the field.

And thus mine eyes are placed still in one sight,
And thus my thoughts can think but one thing still;
Thus reason to his servant gives his right;
Thus is my power transformed to your will.

What marvel then I take a woman's hue?
Since what I see, think, know, is all but you?

I might entertain you, fair ladies, a great while, if I should
make as many interruptions in the repeating as she did in the
singing. For no verse did pass out of her mouth, but that it was
waited on with such abundance of sighs, and, as it were, witnessed with her flowing tears that though the words were few,
yet the time was long she employed in uttering them, although
her pauses chose so fit times that they rather strengthened a
sweeter passion than hindered the harmony. Musidorus himself
that lay so as he might see and hear these things was yet more
moved to pity by the manner of Cleophila's singing, than with
anything he had ever seen, so lively an action doth the mind,
truly touched, bring forth.

But so fell it out that, as with her sweet voice, she recorded
once or twice the last verse of her song, it awakened the shepherd Dametas, who at that time had laid his sleepy back upon
a sunny bank, not far thence, gaping as far as his jaws would
suffer him. But being troubled out of his sleep (the best thing his
life could bring forth) his dull senses could not convey the
pleasure of the excellent music to his rude mind, but that he fell
into a notable rage, insomuch that, taking a hedging bill[51] lay by
him, he guided himself by the voice till he came to the place
where he saw Cleophila sitting, wringing her hands and, with
some few words to herself, breathing out part of the vehemency
of that passion which she had not fully declared in her song. But
no more were his eyes taken with her beauty than his ears with

[51] hedging bill—a long staff with a hooked blade used for cutting
hedges.

her music, but beginning to swear by the pantaple[52] of Pallas, Venus' waistcoat, and such other oaths as his rustical bravery could imagine, leaning his hands upon his bill and his chin upon his hands, he fell to mutter such railings and cursings against her, as a man might well see he had passed through the discipline of an alehouse; and because you may take the better into your fancies his mannerliness, the manner of the man shall in few words be described.

He was a short, lean fellow, of black hair, and notably backed for a burden, one of his eyes out, his nose turned up to take more air, seven or eight long black hairs upon his chin, which he called his beard, his breast he wore always unbuttoned, for heat, and yet, a stomacher[53] before it for cold, even untrussed, yet points hanging down, because he might be trussed, if he list, ill-gartered for a courtlike carelessness, only well shod for his father's sake, who had upon his death bed charged him to take heed of going wet. He had, for love, chosen his wife, Miso, yet so handsome a beldame that she was counted a witch only for her face and her splayfoot; neither inwardly nor outwardly was there any thing good in her, but that she observed decorum, having in a wretched body a froward mind; neither was there any humor in which her husband and she could ever agree, but in disagreeing. Betwixt these two issued forth Mistress Mopsa, a fit woman to participate of both their perfections. But because Alethes[54] an honest man of that time did her praises in verse, I will only repeat them and spare mine own pen because she bore the sex of a woman, and these they were:

[OA3][55]

What length of verse can serve brave Mopsa's good to show,
Whose virtues strange, and beauties such, as no man them may
    know?

[52] pantaple—slipper.
[53] stomacher—waistcoat.
[54] Alethes—"truthful."
[55] This delightful poem, written at the same time that Sidney was discussing the nature and fate of English poetry with friends, reveals a great

Thus shrewdly burdened, then, how can my Muse escape?
The gods must help, and precious things must serve to show her
    shape.

Like great god Saturn, fair, and like fair Venus, chaste;
As smooth as Pan, a Juno mild, like goddess Iris faced.
With Cupid she foresees, and goes god Vulcan's pace;
And for a taste of all these gifts, she borrows Momus' grace.

Her forehead jacinth-like,[56] her cheeks of opal hue,
Her twinkling eyes bedecked with pearl, her lips of sapphire blue,
Her hair pure crapall stone[57] her mouth, O heavenly wide,
Her skin like burnished gold, her hands like silver ore untried.

As for those parts unknown, which hidden sure are best,
Happy be they which will believe, and never seek the rest.

The beginning of this Dametas' credit with Basilius was by
the Duke's straying out of his way one time, ahunting, where
meeting this fellow and asking him the way, and so falling into
other questions, he found some of his answers touching husbandry matters (as a dog, sure if he could speak had wit enough
to describe his kennel) not unsensible; and all uttered with such
a rudeness which the Duke interpreted plainness (although there
be great difference betwixt them) that the Duke conceiving a
sudden delight in his entertainment, took him to his court, with
apparent show of his good opinion. Where the flattering courtier
had no sooner taken the Prince's mind, but that there were
straight reasons to confirm the Duke's doing, and shadows of
virtues found for Dametas: his silence grew wit, his bluntness

---

deal about his thought. That it is a sonnet shows that he knew what form to
use in praise of a lady, but that it is in the merely popular poulter's measure
reveals his contempt for that balladlike meter. The invocations and the
comparisons are satiric of poetry that is only conventional and is written (or
miswritten) from an open commonplace book, criticisms which he then later
elaborated in the *Defence*, especially in the discussion of English poetry.
    [56] jacinth—reddish-orange.
    [57] crapall stone—crapaud stone, believed to be produced in a toad's head.

integrity, his beastly ignorance, virtuous simplicity. And the Duke (according to the nature of great persons, in love with that he had done himself) fancied that the weakness was in him, with his presence would grow wisdom, and so like a creature of his own making he liked him more and more. And thus gave he himself the office of principal herdman, and thus lastly did he put his life into his hands, although he grounded upon a great error. For his quality was not to make men, but to use men according as men were, no more than an ass will be taught to manage a horse to hunt, or a hound to bear a saddle, but each to be used according to the force of his own nature.

But, Dametas (as I said) suddenly awaked, remembering the Duke's commandment, and glad he might use his authority in chiding, came swearing to the place where Cleophila was, with a voice like him that plays Hercules in [a] play and God knows never had Hercules' fancy in his head. The first word he spake after his railing oaths was: "Am not I Dametas? Why, am not I Dametas?"

These words made Cleophila lift up her eyes upon him, and seeing what manner of man he was, the height of her thoughts would not suffer her to yield any answer to so base a creature, but casting again down her eyes, leaning upon the ground, and putting her cheek in the palm of her hand, fetched a great sigh (as if she had answered him, "My head is troubled with greater matters"). Which Dametas (as all persons, witnesses of their own unworthiness, are apt to think they are contemned) took in so heinous a chafe that, standing upon his tiptoes and staring as if he would have had a mote pulled out of his eye, "Why," said he, "thou woman, or boy, or both, or whatsoever thou be, I tell thee there is no place for thee; get thee gone; I tell thee it is the Duke's pleasure; I tell thee it is Master Dametas' pleasure."

Cleophila could not choose but smile at him, and, yet taking herself with the manner, spoke these words to herself. "O spirit," said she, "of mine, how canst thou receive my mirth in the midst of thine agonies and thou, mirth, how darest thou enter into a mind so grown of late thy professed enemy?"

"Thy spirit," said Dametas. "Dost thou think me a spirit?

I tell thee I am the Duke's officer, and have the charge of him and his daughters."

"O pearl," said sobbing Cleophila, "that so vile an oyster should keep thee?"

"By the comb-case of Diana," swore Dametas, "this woman is mad. Oysters and pearls? Dost thou think I will buy oysters? I tell thee get thee packing, or else I must needs be offended."

"O sun," said Cleophila, "how long shall this cloud live to darken thee? and the poor creatures that live only by thee be deprived of thee?"

These speeches to herself put Dametas out of all patience; so that hitting her upon the breast with the blunt end of his bill, "Maid Marion,"[58] said he, "am not I a personage to be answered?"

But Cleophila no sooner felt the blow but that the fire sparkling out of her eyes, and rising up with a right Pyrocles countenance in a Cleophila face, "Vile creature," said she, laying her hand upon her sword, "force me not to defile this sword in thy base blood!"

Dametas that from his childhood had ever feared the blade of a sword, ran back backward with his hands above his head at least twenty paces, gaping and staring with the very countenance of those clownish churls that by Latona's prayer were turned into frogs.[59] At length staying, he came a little nearer her again, but still without the compass of blows, holding one leg, as it were, ready to run away, and then fell to scolding and railing, swearing it was but a little bashfulness in him, that had made him go back, and that if she stayed any longer, he would make her see his blood come out of the eldest shepherd's house in that country. But, seeing her walk up and down without marking what he said, he went for more help to his own lodge, where knocking a good while, at length he cried to his wife Miso that in a whore's name she should come out to him; but instead of that he might hear a hollow rotten voice that bid him let her alone, like a knave as he was, for she was busy about my Lady

---

[58] Maid Marion—strumpet.
[59] Latona—Latona, a goddess, metamorphosed some peasants who ignored her plea for water.

Pamela. This dashed poor Dametas more than anything, for old acquaintance had taught him to fear that place,[60] and, therefore, calling with a more pitiful voice to his daughter, he might see a face look out of a window enough to have made any blind man in love; it was Mistress Mopsa, that instead of answer asked him whether he was mad to forget his duty to her mother? Dametas shrunk down his shoulders, like the poor ass that lays down his ears when he must needs yield to the burden. And yet his tongue, the valiantest part of him, could not forbear to say these words: "Here is foreign wars abroad and uncivil wars at home, and all with women. Now," said he, "the black jaunders[61] and the red fly[62] take all the warlled[63] kind of you."

And with this prayer he went to the other lodge, where the Duke lay at that time sleeping, as it was in the heat of the day, and there he whistled, and stamped, and knocked, crying, "O, my liege!," with such faces as might well show what a deformity a passion can bring a man into, when it is not governed with reason. Till at length the fair Philoclea came down, in such loose apparel as was enough to have bound any man's fancies, and, with a sweet look, asking him what he would have. Dametas without any reverence commanded her in the Duke's name, she should tell the Duke, he was to speak with the Duke, for he, forsooth, had things to tell the Duke, that pertained to the Duke's service. She answered him he should be obeyed, since such was the fortune of her and her sister. And so went she to tell her father of Dametas' being there, leaving him chafing at the door, and whetting his bill, swearing if he met her again, neither she nor the tallest[64] woman in the parish should make him run away any more. But, the Duke understanding by his jewel Philoclea that something there was which greatly troubled Dametas' conscience, came presently down unto him to know the matter. Where he found Dametas talking to himself and making faces like an ape that had newly taken a purgation, pale, shaking, and

---

[60] place—subject.
[61] black jaunders—a kind of jaundice.
[62] red fly—red flux, dysentery.
[63] warlled—from "warly," therefore, warlike.
[64] tallest—bravest.

foaming at the mouth, and a great while it was before the Duke could get any word of him. At length, putting his leg before him (which was the manner of his courtesy), he told the Duke that, saving the reverence of his duty, he should keep himself from henceforward, he would take no more charge of him. The Duke, accustomed to take all well at his hands, did but laugh to see his rage, and stroking his head, desired him of fellowship to let him know the matter. "I tell you," saith Dametas, "it is not for me to be an officer, without I may be obeyed."

"But what troubles thee, my good Dametas?" said the Duke.

"I tell you," said Dametas, "I have been a man in my days, whatsoever I be now."

"And reason," answered the Duke, "but let me know, that I may redress thy wrongs."

"Nay," said Dametas, "no wrongs neither, but thus falls out the case, my liege. I met with such a mankind creature yonder with her sword by her hip, and with such a visage, as if it had not been for me and this bill, God save it, she had come hither, and killed you and all your house."

"What? Strike a woman?" said the Duke.

"Indeed," said Dametas, "I made her but a little weep, and after I had pity of her."

"It was well and wisely done," said the Duke, "but I pray thee show me her."

"I pray you," said Dametas, "first call for more company, to hold me from hurting her, for my stomach riseth against her."

"Let me but see the place," said the Duke, "and then you shall know whether my words or your bill be the better weapon."

Dametas went stalking on before the Duke, as if he had been afraid to wake his child, and then, pointing with his bill towards her, was not hasty to make any near approaches. But the Duke no sooner saw Cleophila but that he remained amazed at the goodliness of her stature, and the stateliness of her march (for at that time she was walking with a countenance well setting forth an extreme distraction of her mind), and, as he came nearer her, at the excellent perfection of her beauty; insomuch, that forgetting any anger he conceived in Dametas' behalf and doing

reverence to her as to a lady in whom he saw much worthy of
great respect, "Fair lady," said he, "it is nothing strange that
such a solitary place as this should receive solitary persons, but
much do I marvel how such a beauty as yours is, could be
suffered to be thus alone."

She looking with a grave majesty upon him, as if she found
in herself cause why she should be reverenced, "They are never
alone," said she, "that are accompanied with noble thoughts."

"But, those thoughts," said the Duke, replying for the delight he had to speak further with her, "cannot in this your loneliness neither warrant you from suspicion in others, nor defend
you from melancholy in yourself."

Cleophila looking upon him as though he pressed further
than he needed, "I seek no better warrant," said she, "than mine
own conscience, nor no greater pleasure than mine own contentation."[65]

"Yet virtue seeks to satisfy others," said Basilius.

"Those that be good," answered Cleophila, "and they will
be satisfied so long as they see no evil."

"Yet will the best in this country," said the Duke, "suspect
so excellent a beauty, being so weakly guarded."

"Then are the best but stark naughty," answered Cleophila,
"for open suspecting others comes of secret condemning themselves." "But in my country," said she, continuing her speech
with a brave vehemency, "whose manners I am in all places to
maintain and reverence, the general goodness which is nourished
in our hearts makes everyone think that strength of virtue in
another, whereof they find the assured foundation in themselves."

But, Basilius, who began to feel the sparkles of those flames
which shortly after burned all other thoughts out of his heart,
felt such a music, as he thought, in her voice, and such an eye-
pleasing in her face, that he thought his retiring into this solitary
place was well employed, if it had been only to have met with
such a guest. And therefore, desirous to enter into nearer points
with her, "Excellent lady," said he, "you praise so greatly and

65 contentation—contentment.

yet so wisely your country that I must needs desire to know what the nest is out of which such birds do fly."

"You must first deserve that knowledge," said she, "before you obtain it."

"And by what means," said Basilius, "shall I deserve to know your estate?"

"By letting me first know yours," said she.

"To obey you," said he, "I will do it, although it were so much more reason yours should be known first, as you do deserve in all points to be preferred." "Know you, fair lady," said he, "that my name is Basilius, unworthy Duke of this country; the rest either fame hath all ready brought to your ears, or if it please you to make this place happy by your presence, at more leisure you shall understand of me."

Cleophila, who had from the beginning suspected it should be he, but would not seem she did so (to keep her majesty the better) making some reverence unto him, "Mighty Prince," said she, "let my not knowing of you serve for the excuse of my boldness, and the little reverence I do you, impute it to the manner of my country, which is the invincible land of the Amazons, myself niece to Senicia,[66] queen thereof, lineally descended of the famous Penthesilea,[67] slain before Troy by the bloody hand of Pyrrhus.[68] I, having in this my youth determined to make the world see the Amazons' excellencies, as well in private as in public virtues, have passed many dangerous adventures in diverse countries, till the unmerciful sea deprived me of all my company, so that shipwreck brought me to this realm, and uncertain wandering guided me to this place."

Whoever saw a man to whom a beloved child long lost did (unlooked for) return, might easily figure unto his fancy the very fashion of Basilius' countenance, so far had love become his master, and so had this young siren charmed his old ears; insomuch, that with more vehement importunacy than any greedy host would use to well acquainted passengers, he fell to

[66] Senicia—"sign of the goddess."
[67] Penthesilea—Amazon queen who fought on Trojan side.
[68] Pyrrhus—Achilles actually slew Penthesilea, not his son Pyrrhus.

entreat her abode there for some time. She, although nothing could come fitter to the very point of her desire, yet had she already learned that womanish quality to counterfeit backwardness in that she most wished; so that he, desirous to prove whether intercession coming out of fitter mouths might better prevail, called to Dametas and commanded him to bring forth his wife and two daughters, three ladies, although of diverse, yet all of excellent beauty:

The Duchess Gynecia in grave matronlike attire with a countenance and behavior far unlike to fall into those inconveniences[69] she afterwards tasted of. The fair Pamela, whose noble heart had long disdained to find the trust of her virtue reposed in the hands of a shepherd, had yet (to show an obedience) taken on a shepherdish apparel, which was of russet velvet, cut after their fashion with a straight body open-breasted, the nether part full of plaits with wide open sleeves hanging down very low, her hair at the full length only wound about with gold lace; by the comparison, to show how far her hair did excell in color, betwixt her breasts, which sweetly rose up like two fair mountainettes in the pleasant vale of Tempe, there hanged down a jewel which she had devised as a picture of her own estate; it was a perfect white lamb tied at a stake with a great number of chains, as it had been feared lest the silly creature should do some great harm; neither had she added any word unto it, but even took silence as the word of the poor lamb, showing such humbleness, as not to use her own voice for complaint of her misery. But when the ornament of the earth, young Philoclea appeared in her nymphlike apparel so near nakedness, as one might well discern part of her perfections—and yet so appareled as did show she kept the best store of her beauties to herself; her excellent fair hair drawn up into a net, made only of itself, a net indeed to have caught the wildest disposition; her body covered with a light taffeta garment, so cut as the wrought smock[70] came through it in many places, enough to have made a very restrained imagination have thought what was under it—with the sweet

---

[69] inconveniences—moral improprieties.
[70] wrought smock—undergarment decorated with needlework.

cast of her black eye, which seemed to make a contention whether that in perfect blackness, or her skin in perfect whiteness were the most excellent, then, I say, the very clouds seemed to give place to make the heaven more fair.

At least the clouds of Cleophila's thoughts quite vanished, and so was her brain fixed withal that her sight seemed more forcible and clear than ever before, or since, she found it. With such strange delight unto her (for still, fair ladies, you remember that I use the "she" title to Pyrocles since so he would have it) that she stood like a well wrought image, with show of life, but without all exercise of life, so forcible had love transferred all her spirits into the present contemplation of the lovely Philoclea, and so had it been like enough she would have stayed long time, but that by chance Gynecia stepped betwixt her sight, and the Lady Philoclea. And the change of the object made her recover her senses, so that she could with good manner receive the salutation of the Duchess and the Princess Pamela, doing them yet no further reverence than one princess useth to another. But when she came to the Lady Philoclea, she fell down on her knees, taking by force her fair hands, and kissing them with great show of extreme affection, and with a bowed down countenance began this speech unto her. "Divine lady," said she, "let not the world nor this great princess marvel to see me, contrary to my manner, do this especial honor unto you, since all, both men and women, owe this homage to the perfection of your beauty."

Philoclea's blushing cheeks quickly witnessed how much she was abashed to see the singularity used to herself, and, therefore, causing Cleophila to rise, "Noble lady," said she, "it is no marvel to see your judgment much mistaken in my beauty, since you begin with so great an error, as to do more honor unto me than to them, to whom I myself owe all service."

"Rather," answered Cleophila, "that shows the power of your beauty which hath forced me to fall into such an error, if it were an error."

"You are so acquainted," said Philoclea, sweetly smiling, "with your own beauty, that it makes you easily fall into the discourse of beauty."

"Beauty in me?" said Cleophila, deeply sighing, "alas, if there be any, it is in my eyes, which your happy presence hath imparted unto them."

Basilius was even transported with delight to hear these speeches betwixt his well-beloved daughter and his better-loved lady, and so made a sign to Philoclea that she should entreat her to remain with them; which she willingly obeyed, for already she conceived delight in Cleophila's presence, and therefore said unto her: "It is a great happiness (I must confess) to be praised of them that are themselves most praiseworthy; and well I find you an invincible Amazon, since you will overcome in a wrong matter." "But if my beauty be anything," said she, "then let it obtain thus much of you, that you will remain in this company sometime to ease your own travel, and our solitariness."

"First, let me die," said Cleophila, "before any word spoken by such a mouth should come in vain. I yield wholly to your commandment, fearing nothing. But that you command that which may be troublesome to yourself."

Thus, with some other words of entertaining, her staying was concluded to the inspeakable joy of the Duke, although perchance with some little envy in the other ladies to see young Philoclea's beauty so advanced. You ladies know best whether sometimes you feel impression of that passion; for my part, I would hardly think that the affection of a mother and the noble mind of Pamela could be overthrown with so base a thing as envy is; especially Pamela, to whom fortune had already framed another who no less was dedicated to her excellencies than Cleophila was to Philoclea's perfection, as you shall shortly hear.

For the Duke going into the lodge with his wife and daughters, Cleophila desired them to excuse her for a while, for that she had thoughts to pass over with herself, and that shortly after she would come into them, indeed meaning to find her friend Musidorus, and to glory with him of the happiness of her choice; but when she looked in the grove, and could nowhere find him, marveling something at it, she gave herself to feed these sweet thoughts, which now had the full possession of her heart, sometimes thinking how far Philoclea herself passed her picture, sometimes foreimagining with herself how happy she should be if she could obtain her desires. Till having spent thus an hour or two, she might perceive afar off one coming towards her in the apparel of a shepherd, with his arms hanging down, going a kind of languishing pace, with his eyes sometimes cast up to heaven, as though his fancies strove to mount up higher, sometimes thrown down to the ground, as if the earth could not bear the burden of his pains; at length she heard him with a lamentable tune sing these few verses:

[*OA4*]

Come shepherd weeds,[71] become your master's mind,
Yield outward show, what inward change he tries;
Nor be abashed, since such a guest you find,
Whose strongest hope in your weak comfort lies.

Come shepherd weeds, attend my woeful cries,
Disuse yourselves from sweet Menalcas'[72] voice;
For other be those tunes which sorrow ties,
From those clear notes which freely may rejoice.

Then pour out plaint, and in one word say this:
Helpless is plaint, who spoils himself of bliss.

And having ended, she might see him strike himself upon the breast, uttering these words: "O miserable wretch, whither do thy destinies guide thee?" It seemed to Cleophila she knew the voice, and, therefore, drawing nearer that her sight might receive a perfect discerning, she saw plainly, to her great amazement, it was her dear friend Musidorus.
    And now, having named him, methinks it reason, I should tell you what chance brought him to this change. I left him lately (if you remember, fair ladies) in the grove, by the two lodges, there to see what should befall to his dear new-transformed friend. There heard he all the complaints (not without great com-

---

[71] weeds—garments.
[72] Menalcas—"truly valiant"; borrowed from Virgil's *Eclogues*.

passion) that his friend made to himself, and there (not without some laughter) did he see what passed betwixt him and Dametas, and how stately he played the part of Cleophila, at the Duke's first coming. And falling into many kind fancies towards him, sometimes pitying his case, sometimes praising his behavior, he would often say to himself: "O sweet Pyrocles, how art thou bewitched? Where is thy virtue? Where is the use of thy reason? Much am I inferior to thee in all the powers of the mind, and yet know I that all the heavens cannot bring me to such a thralldom."

Scarcely (think I) he had spoken these words, but that the Duchess (being sent for to entertain Cleophila) came out with her two daughters, where the beams of the Princess Pamela's beauty had no sooner stricken into his eyes but that he was wounded with more sudden violence of love than ever Pyrocles was. Whether indeed it were that this strange power would be bravely revenged of him for the bitter words he had used, or that his very resisting made the wound the crueler (as we see the harquebus[73] doth most endamage the stiffest metal), or rather that the continual healthfulness of his mind made this sudden evil the more incurable (as the soundest bodies once infected are most mortally endangered). But, howsoever the cause was, such was the effect, that not being able to bear the vehement pain, he ran away through the grove like a mad man, hoping perchance (as the fever-sick folks do) that the change of places might ease his grief, but therein was his luck indeed better than his providence.[74] For he had not gone a little, but that he met with a shepherd (according to his estate) handsomely appareled, who was then going to meet with other shepherds (as upon certain days they had accustomed) to do exercises of activity, and to play new-invented eclogues before the Duke, which, when Musidorus had learned of him (for love is full of desire, and desire is always inquisitive) it came straight into his head that there were no better way for him to come by the often enjoying of the Princess Pamela's sight than to take the apparel of this shepherd upon

[73] harquebus—a portable gun.
[74] providence—foresight.

him. Which he quickly did giving him his own, much richer worth, and withal lest the matter by him might be discovered, hired him to go without stay into Thessalia, writing two or three words by him (in a pair of tables[75] well closed up) to a servant of his, that he should upon the receipt arrest and keep him in good order, till he heard his further pleasure. Yet before Menalcas departed (for so was his name) he learned of him both his own estate, and the manner of their pastimes and eclogues.

And thus furnished he returned again to the place where his heart was pledged, so oppressed in mind that, it seemed to him, his legs were unneth[76] able to bear him, which grief he uttered in the doleful song I told you of before, and was cause that his dear he-she-friend Cleophila came unto him. Who, when she was assured it was he (with wonted entireness embracing him) demanded of him what sudden change had thus suddenly changed him? Whether the goddess of these woods had such a power to transform everybody, or whether indeed, as he had always in all enterprises most faithfully accompanied her, so he would continue to match her in this new metamorphosis? But Musidorus looking dolefully upon her, wringing his hands, and pouring out abundance of tears, began to recount unto her all this I have already told you; but with such passionate debating of it, that for my part I have not a feeling insight enough into the matter to be able lively to express it; suffiseth it, that whatsoever a possessed heart, with a good tongue to a dear friend could utter, was at that time largely set forth.

The perfect friendship Cleophila bare him, and the great pity she by good experience had of his case, could not keep her from smiling at him, remembering how vehemently he had cried out against the folly of lovers, so that she thought good a little to punish him, playing with him in this manner.

"Why, how now, dear cousin," said she. "You that were even now so high in the pulpit against love, are you now become so mean an auditor? Remember that love is a passion, and that a worthy man's reason must ever have the masterhood."

[75] tables—small, smooth stiff sheets for writing, hinged together.
[76] unneth—with difficulty.

"I recant, I recant," cried Musidorus, and withal falling down prostrate, "O thou celestial, or infernal spirit of Love," said he, "or what other heavenly or hellish title thou list to have (for both those effects I find in myself) have compassion of me, and let thy glory be as great in pardoning them that be submitted to thee, as in conquering those that were rebellious."

"No, no," said Cleophila (yet further to urge him), "I see you well enough, you make but an interlude[77] of my mishaps, and do but counterfeit thus to make me see the deformity of my passions." "But take heed," said she, "cousin, that this jest do not one day turn into earnest."

"Now, I beseech thee," said Musidorus, taking her fast by the hand, "even by the truth of our friendship, of which (if I be not altogether an unhappy man) thou hast some remembrance, and by those secret flames which (I know) have likewise nearly touched thee, make no jest of that which hath so earnestly pierced me through, nor let that be light to thee which is to me so burdenous that I am not able to bear it."

Musidorus did so lively deliver out his inward griefs that Cleophila's friendly heart felt a great impression of pity withal, as certainly all persons that find themselves afflicted easily fall to compassion of them who taste of like misery, partly led by the common course of humanity, but principally because under the image of them, they lament their own mishaps, and so the complaints the others make, seem to touch the right tune of their own woes, which did mutually work so in these two young princes that, looking ruefully one upon the other, they made their speech a great while nothing but doleful sighs, yet sometimes they would yield out suchlike lamentations: "Alas, what farther evil hath fortune reserved for us? What shall be the end of this our tragical pilgrimage? Shipwrecks, daily dangers, absence from our country, have at length brought forth this captiving of us within ourselves, which hath transformed the one in sex, and the other in state as much as the uttermost work of changeable fortune can be extended unto."

And then would they kiss one another, vowing to continue

[77] interlude—comedy.

partakers of all either good or evil fortune, and thus perchance would they have forgotten themselves some longer time, but that Basilius, whose heart was now set on fire with his new mistress, finding her absence long, sent out Dametas to her, to know if she would command anything, and to invite her to go with his wife and daughters to a fair meadow thereby, to see the sports and hear the eclogues of his country shepherds. Dametas came out with two or three swords about him, his hedging bill on his neck, and a chopping knife under his girdle, armed only behind, as fearing most the blows that might fall upon the reins[78] of his back, for, indeed, Cleophila had put such a sudden fear into his head, that from thenceforth he was resolved never to come out any more ill-provided. Yet had his blunt brains perceived some favor the Duke bare to his new-come lady, and so framing himself thereunto (as without doubt the most servile flattery is most easy to be lodged in the most gross capacity, for their ordinary conceit draws a yielding to their greaters, and then have they not wit to discern right degrees of goodness), he no sooner saw her, but with head and arms he laid his reverence before her, enough to have made any man forsworn all courtesy.

And, then, in the Duke's name did he require her, she would take pains to see their pastorals, for so their sports were termed, but when he espied Musidorus standing by her (for his eye had been placed all this while upon her) not knowing him, he would fain have persuaded himself to have been angry, but that he durst not. Yet muttering and champing as though his cud troubled him, he gave occasion to Musidorus to come nearer him, and to frame a tale of his own life, that he was a younger brother of the shepherd Menalcas, by name Dorus,[79] sent by his father in his tender age to Athens, there to learn some cunning more than ordinary, for to excell his fellow shepherds in their eclogues; and that his brother Menalcas, lately gone thither to fetch him home, was deceased, where upon his deathbed he had charged him to seek the service of Dametas, and to be wholly and only guided by his counsel, as one in whose judgment and integrity the Duke had

---

[78] reins—loins or kidney region.
[79] Dorus—"gift."

singular confidence. For token whereof he gave him a sum of gold in ready coin, which Menalcas had bequeathed him, upon condition he should receive this poor Dorus into his service, that his mind and manners might grow the better by his daily ensample. Dametas no sooner saw the gold but that his heart was presently infected with the self-conceit he took of it, which being helped with the tickling of Musidorus' praises, so turned the brain of good Dametas that he became slave to that which he that would be his servant bestowed of him, and gave in himself an ensample forever that the fool can never be honest, since (not being able to balance what points virtue stands upon) every present occasion catches his senses, and his senses are masters of his silly mind. Yet for countenance sake, he seemed very squeamish (in respect he had the charge of the Princess Pamela) to accept any new servant into his house. But, such was the secret operation of the gold, helped with the persuasion of the Amazon Cleophila (who said it was pity so proper a young man should be anywhere else than with so good a master) that, in the end, he agreed to receive him for his servant, so as that day in their pastorals he proved himself active in mind and body.

And thus went they to the lodge, with greater joy to Musidorus (now only poor shepherd Dorus) than all his life before had ever brought forth unto him; so manifest it is, that the greatest point outward things can bring a man unto is the contentment of the mind (which once obtained) no estate is miserable, and without that no prince's state restful. There found they Gynecia with her two daughters, ready to go to the meadow, whither also they went. For, as for Basilius, he desired to stay behind them to debate a little with himself of this new guest that had entered and possessed his brains.

There it is said the poor Basilius now alone (for as I said, the rest were gone to see the pastorals) had a sufficient eclogue in his own head betwixt honor, with the long experience he had had of the world, on the one side, and this new assault of Cleophila's beauty on the other side. There hard by the lodge walked he, carrying this unquiet contention about him, but passion ere long had gotten the absolute masterhood, bringing with it the show of present pleasure, fortified with the authority of a prince, whose power might easily satisfy his will against the farfetched (though true) reasons of the spirit, which in a man not trained in the way of virtue, have but slender working; so that ere long he utterly gave himself over to the longing desire to enjoy Cleophila, which finding an old broken vessel of him, had the more power in him than perchance it would have had in a younger man; and so, as all vice is foolish, it wrought in him the more absurd follies.

But, thus as I say, in a number of intermixed imaginations he stayed solitary by the lodge, waiting for the return of his company from the pastorals some good space of time, till he was suddenly stirred out of his deep muses by the hasty and fearful running unto him of most part of the shepherds, who came flying from the pastoral sports, crying one to another, to stay and save the Duchess and young ladies. But, even whilst they cried so, they ran away as fast as they could so that the one tumbled over the other, each one showing he would be glad his fellow should do valiantly, but his own heart served him not. The Duke amazed to see such extreme shows of fear asked the matter of them, but fear had so possessed their inward parts that their breath could not serve to tell him, but after such a broken manner that I think it best not to trouble you, fair ladies, with their panting speeches, but to make a full declaration of it myself, and thus it was.

Gynecia with her two daughters, Cleophila, the shepherds Dorus and Dametas, being parted from the Duke whom they left solitary at the lodge, came into the fair meadow appointed for their shepherdish pastimes. It was indeed a place of great delight, for through the midst of it there ran a sweet brook, which did both hold the eye open with her beautiful streams, and close the eye with the sweet purling noise it made upon the pebble stones it ran over. The meadow itself yielding so liberally all sorts of flowers that it seemed to nourish a contention betwixt the color and the smell, whether[80] in his kind were the more delightful. Round about the meadow (as if it had been to enclose a theater) grew all such sort of trees, as either excellency of fruit, stateliness

[80] whether—which of the two.

of growth, continual greens, or poetical fancies have made at any
time famous. In most part of which trees there had been framed
by art such pleasant arbors, that it became a gallery aloft from
one tree to the other, almost round about, which below yielded
a perfect shadow, in those hot countries counted a great pleasure.
In this place, under one of the trees the ladies sat down, inquiring many questions of young Dorus, now newly perceived of
them. Whilst the other shepherds made them ready to the
pastimes, Dorus, keeping his eye still upon the Princess Pamela,
answered with such a trembling voice, and abashed countenance,
and often times so far from the matter, that it was some sport to
the ladies, thinking it had been want of education which made
him so discountenanced with unwonted presence.[81]

But Cleophila that saw in him the glass of her own misery,
taking the fair hand of Philoclea, and with more than womanish
ardency, kissing it began to say these words: "O Love, since thou
art so changeable in men's estates, how art thou so constant in
their torments?" When, suddenly, there came out of the wood a
monstrous lion, with a she bear of little less fierceness, which
having been hunted in forests far off had by chance come to this
place, where such beasts had never before been seen. Which
when the shepherds saw, like silly wretches that think all evil is
ever next themselves, ran away in such sort, as I told you, till
they came to the Duke's presence.

There might one have seen at one instant all sorts of passions
lively painted out in the young lovers' faces, an extremity of love
shining in their eyes, fear for their mistresses, assured hope in
their own virtue, anger against the beasts, joy that occasion employed their services, sorrow to see their ladies in agony. For,
indeed, the sweet Philoclea no sooner espied the ravenous lion,
but that opening her arms she fell so right upon the breast of
Cleophila, sitting by her, that their faces at unawares closed
together, which so transported all whatsoever Cleophila was, that
she gave leisure to the lion to come very near them, before she
rid herself from the dear arms of Philoclea. But, necessity, the
only over-ruler of affections, did force her then gently to unfold

[81] presence—majesty.

herself from those sweet embracements, and so drawing her sword, waited the present assault of the lion, who, seeing Philoclea flee away, suddenly turned after her, for as soon as she had risen up with Cleophila, she ran as fast as her delicate legs would carry her towards the lodge, after the fugitive shepherds.

But Cleophila, seeing how greedily the lion went after the prey she herself so much desired, it seemed all her spirits were kindled with an unwonted fear, so that equalling the lion in swiftness, she overtook him, as he was ready to have seized himself of his beautiful chase, and (disdainfully saying, "Are you become my competitor?") struck him so great a blow upon the shoulder that she almost cleaved him assunder, yet, the valiant beast turned withal so far upon the weapon that with his paw he did hurt a little the left shoulder of Cleophila. And mortal it would have been, had not the death wound Cleophila, with a new thrust gave unto him, taken away the effect of his force, but, therewithal, he fell down, and gave Cleophila leisure to take off his head, to carry it for a present to her Lady Philoclea. Who, all this while, not knowing what was done behind her, kept on her course, as Arethusa when she ran from Alpheus,[82] her light nymphlike apparel being carried up with the wind, that much of those beauties she would at another time have willingly hidden, were presented to the eye of the twice wounded Cleophila.

Which made Cleophila not follow her over hastily, lest she should too soon deprive herself of that pleasure, but, carrying the lion's head in her hand, did not fully overtake her, till they came both in the presence of Basilius, at that time examining the shepherds of what was past, and preparing himself to come to their succor. Neither were they long there, but that Gynecia came to them, whose look had all this while been upon the combat, eyeing so fixedly Cleophila's manner of fighting, that no fear did prevail over her. But as soon as Cleophila had cut off his head, and ran after Philoclea, she could not find in her heart but to run likewise after Cleophila, so that it was a new sight fortune

---

[82] Arethusa when she ran from Alpheus—the river nymph Arethusa was changed into a spring by Diana in order to save her from the river god Alpheus, but the god then mingled his waters with hers.

had prepared to those woods, to see these three great personages thus run one after the other, each carried away in the violence of inward evil: the sweet Philoclea, with such fear, that she thought she was still in the lion's mouth; Cleophila with a painful delight she had to see, without hope of enjoying; Gynecia, not so much with the love she bare to her best loved daughter, as with a new wonderful passionate love had possessed her heart of the goodly Cleophila.

For so the truth is that, at the first sight she had of Cleophila, her heart gave her she was a man, thus for some strange cause disguised, which now this combat did in effect assure her of, because she measured the possibility of all women's hearts out of her own. And this doubt framed in her a desire to know, and desire to know brought forth shortly such longing to enjoy, that it reduced her whole mind to an extreme and unfortunate slavery, pitifully, truly considering her beauty and estate. But for a perfect mark of the triumph of love, who could in one moment overthrow the heart of a wise lady, so that neither honor long maintained, nor love of husband and children could withstand it, but of that you shall after hear. For, now, they being come before the Duke, and the fair Philoclea scarcely then stayed from her fear, Cleophila kneeling down presented the head of the lion unto her with these words. "Only lady," said she, "here see you the punishment of that unnatural beast, which contrary to his own kind[83] would have wronged princess' blood; neither were his eyes vanquished with the duty all eyes bear to your beauty."

"Happy am I and my beauty both," answered the fair Philoclea (the blood coming again to her cheeks, pale before for fear), "that you, excellent Amazon, were there to teach him good manners."

"And even thank that beauty," said Cleophila, "which forceth all noble swords to be ready to serve it."

Having finished these words the Lady Philoclea perceived

[83] contrary to his own kind—the lion supposedly symbolized natural honor and would instinctively recognize and respect the virtue of maidens and the nobility of royal persons.

the blood that ran abundantly down upon Cleophila's shoulder, so that starting aside with a countenance full of sweet pity, "Alas," said she, "now perceive I my good hap is waited on with great misfortune, since my safety is wrought with the danger of a much more worthy person."

"Noble lady," answered she, "if your inward eyes could discern the wounds of my soul, you should have a plentifuller cause to exercise your compassion."

But it was sport to see how in one instant both Basilius and Gynecia (like a father and mother to a beloved child) came running to see the wound on Cleophila, into what rages Basilius grew, and what tears Gynecia spent. For so it seemed that Love had purposed to make in those solitary woods a perfect demonstration of his unresistible force, to show that no desert place can avoid his dart; he must fly from himself that will shun his evil. But so wonderful, and in effect incredible, was the passion which reigned as well in Gynecia as Basilius, and all for the poor Cleophila, dedicated another way, that it seems to myself I use not words enough to make you see how they could in one moment be so overtaken. But, you worthy ladies that have at any time feelingly known what it means, will easily believe the possibility of it; let the ignorant sort of people give credit to them that have passed the doleful passage, and duly find that quickly is the infection gotten, which in long time is hardly cured.

Basilius sometime would kiss her forehead, blessing the destinies that had joined such beauty and valor together, Gynecia would kiss her more boldly by the liberty of her womanish show, although her heart were set on nothing less. For already was she fallen into a jealous envy against her daughter Philoclea, because she found Cleophila showed such extraordinary dutiful favor unto her, and even that settled her opinion the more of her manhood. And this doubtful jealousy served as a bellows to kindle the violent coals of her passion, but as the overkind nurse may sometime with kissing forget to give the child suck, so had they with too much kindness unkindly forgotten the wound of Cleophila, had not Philoclea (whose heart had not yet gone be-

yond the limits of a right good will) advised herself, and desired
her mother to help her to dress the wound of Cleophila. For both
those great ladies were excellently seen in that part of surgery,
an art in that age greatly esteemed because it served as a minister
to virtuous courage, which in those worthy days was even by
ladies more beloved than any outward beauty. So to the great
comfort of Cleophila, more to feel the delicate hands of Philoclea
than for the care she had of her wound, these two ladies had
quickly dressed it, applying so precious a balm as all the heat
and pain was presently assuaged with apparent hope of some
amendment, in which doing I know not whether Gynecia took
some greater conjectures of Cleophila's sex.

But even then and not before, did Cleophila remember herself of her dear friend Musidorus, for having only had care of
the execllent Philoclea, she neither missed her friend, nor the
Princess Pamela; not so much to be marveled at in her, since both
the Duke and Duchess had forgotten their daughter, so were all
their thoughts plunged in one place. Besides Cleophila had not
seen any danger was like to fall unto him, for her eye had been
still fixed upon Philoclea, and that made her the more careless.
But now with a kind of rising in her heart, lest some evil should
be fallen to her chosen friend, she hastily asked what was become
of the Princess Pamela with the two shepherds Dametas and
Dorus. And then the Duke and Gynecia remembered their forgetfulness, and with great astonishment made like inquiry for her.
But of all the company of the shepherds (so had the lion's sight
put them from themselves) there was but one could say anything of her, and all he said was this, that as he ran away, he
might perceive a great bear run directly towards her. Cleophila
(whose courage was always ready without deliberation) took up
the sword lying by her [with mind to bestow her life for the
succor or revenge of her Musidorus and the gracious Pamela.][84]
But as she had run two or three steps, they might all see Pamela
coming betwixt Dametas and Dorus, Pamela having in her hand
the paw of the bear, which the shepherd Dorus had newly presented unto her, desiring her to keep it as of such a beast, which

[84] from the Clifford and earlier manuscripts.

though she was to be punished for her over great cruelty, yet was her wit to be esteemed, since she could make so sweet a choice. Dametas, for his part, came piping and dancing, the merriest man of a parish, but when he came so near as he might be heard of the Duke, he sang this song, for joy of their success:

[OA5]

Now thanked be the great god Pan,
That thus preserves my loved life;
Thanked be I that keep a man,
Who ended hath this fearful strife.
So, if my man must praises have,
What then must I that keep the knave?

For as the moon the eye doth please,
With gently beams not hurting sight,
Yet hath Sir Sun the greatest praise,
Because from him doth come her light.
So, if my man must praises have;
What then must I that keep the knave?

It were a very superfluous thing to tell you how glad each party was of the happy returning from these dangers. And doubt you not, fair ladies, there wanted no questioning how things had passed, but because I will have the thanks myself, it shall be I you shall hear of it. And thus the ancient records of Arcadia say it fell out.

The lion's presence had no sooner driven away the heartless shepherds, and followed, as I told you, the excellent Philoclea, but there came out of the same woods a monstrous she bear, which fearing to deal with the lion's prey, came furiously towards the Princess Pamela, who, whether it were she had heard that such was the best refuge against that beast, or that fear (as it fell out most likely) brought forth the effects of wisdom, she no sooner saw the bear coming towards her but she fell down flat upon her face. Which, when the Prince Musidorus saw (whom because such was his pleasure, I am bold to call the shepherd

Dorus), with a true resolved magnanimity, although he had no other weapon but a great shepherd's knife, he leapt before the head of his dear lady, and (saying these words unto her, "Receive here the sacrifice of that heart, which is only vowed to your service") attended with a quiet courage the coming of the bear, which according to the manner of that beast's fight (especially against a man that resists them) rose up upon her hinder feet, so to take him in her ugly paws. But as she was ready to give him a mortal embracement, the shepherd Dorus, with a lusty strength and good fortune, thrust his knife so right into the heart of the beast that she fell down dead, without ever being able to touch him. Which, being done, he turned to his lady Pamela, that time in a swound with extremity of fear, and softly taking her in his arms, he took the advantage to kiss and rekiss her a hundred times, with such exceeding delight that he would often after say, he thought the joy would have carried his life from him, had not the grief he conceived to see her in such case something diminished it.

But, long in that delightful agony he was not, for the Lady Pamela, being come out of her swound, opened her fair eyes, and seeing herself in the hands of this new come shepherd, with great disdain put him from her. But when she saw the ugly bear lying hard by her, starting aside (for fear gave not reason leave to determine whether it were dead or no) she forgat her anger, and cried to Dorus to help her; wherefore, he cutting off the forepaw of the bear, and showing unto her the bloody knife, told her she might well by this perceive that there was no heart so base, nor weapon so feeble but that the force of her beauty was well able to enable them for the performance of great matters. She inquiring the manner, whether himself were hurt, gave him great thanks for his pains, with promise of reward; but, being ashamed to find herself so alone with this young shepherd, looked round about if she could see anybody, and at length they both perceived the gentle Dametas, lying with his head and breast, as far as he could thrust himself, into a bush, drawing up his legs as close unto him as he could.

For, indeed, as soon as he saw the bear coming towards

them (like a man that was very apt to take pity of himself) he ran headlong into the bush, with full resolution that at the worst hand he would not see his own death. And when Dorus pushed him, bidding him be of good courage, it was a great while before that he could persuade him that Dorus was not the bear, so that he was fain to pull him out by the heels, and show him her as dead as he could wish her, which, you may believe me, was a very joyful sight unto him. And yet like a man of revengeful spirit, he gave the dead body many a wound, swearing by much it was pity such beasts should be suffered in a commonwealth. And then with as immoderate joy as before with fear (for his heart was framed never to be without a passion) he went by his fair charge, dancing, piping, and singing, till they all came to the presence of the careful company, as before I told you.

Thus now this little (but noble) company united again together, the first thing was done, was the yielding of great thanks and praises of all sides to the virtuous Cleophila. The Duke told with what a gallant grace she ran after Philoclea with the lion's head in her hand, like another Pallas with the spoils of Gorgon.[85] Gynecia swore she saw the very face of young Hercules killing the Nemean lion,[86] and all with a grateful assent confirmed the same praises; only poor Dorus (though of equal desert) yet not proceeding from equal estate, should have been left forgotten had not Cleophila (partly to put by the occasion of her own excessive praises, but principally for the true remembrance she had of her professed friend) with great admiration spoken of his hazardous act, asking afresh (as if she had never known him) what he was, and whether he had haunted that place before, protesting that, upon her conscience, she could not think but that he came of some very noble blood, so noble a countenance he bore, and so worthy an act he had performed.

This Basilius took (as the lover's heart is apt to receive all

[85] Pallas with the spoils of Gorgon—Perseus gave the head of the Medusa, which he killed, to Pallas Athena, who always carried it upon the aegis, Jupiter's shield, which she bore before her.

[86] Hercules killing the Nemean lion—the first of the twelve labors laid upon Hercules as punishment for killing his own family in a fit of madness; after he strangled the lion, he always wore its skin.

sudden sorts of impression) as though his mistress had given him a secret reprehension that he had not showed more gratefulness to the valiant Dorus; and, therefore, as nimbly as he could, began forthwith to inquire of his estate, adding promise of great rewards, among the rest offering to him that, if he would exercise his valor in soldiery, he would commit some charge unto him under Philanax, governor of his frontiers. But, Dorus, whose ambition stretched a quite other way, having first answered (touching his estate) that he was brother to the shepherd Menalcas, whom the Duke had well known, and excused his going to soldiery by the unaptness he found in himself that way, told the Duke that his brother in last testament had commanded him to dedicate his service to Dametas; and therefore, as well for the due obedience thereto as for the satisfaction of his own mind (which was wholly set upon pastoral affairs) he would think his service greatly rewarded if he might obtain (by that means) to live in the sight of the Duke, more than the rest of his fellows, and yet practice that his chosen vocation. The Duke liking well of his modest manner charged Dametas to receive him like a son in his house telling him because of his tried valor, he would have him be as a guard to his daughter Pamela, to whom likewise he recommended him, sticking not to say, such men were to be cherished, since she was in danger of some secret misadventure.

All this while Pamela said little of him and even as little did Philoclea of Cleophila, although everybody else filled their mouths with their praises. Whereof seeking the cause that they which most were bound said least, I note this to myself (fair ladies) that, even at this time they did begin to find, they themselves could not tell, what kind of inclination towards them. Whereof feeling a secret accusation in themselves, and in their simplicity not able to warrant it, closed up all such motion in secret, without daring scarcely to breathe out the names of them, who already began to breed unwonted war in their spirits. For, indeed, fortune had framed a very stage play of love among these few folks, making the old age of Basilius, the virtue of Gynecia, and the simplicity of Philoclea, all affected to one. But, by a three-headed kind of passion, Basilius assuring himself she was (as she pretended) a young lady, but greatly despairing for his own unworthiness' sake; Gynecia hoping her judgment to be right of his disguising, but therein fearing a greater sore if his heart already were pledged to her daughter. But, sweet Philoclea grew shortly after of all other into worst terms, for taking her to be such as she professed, desire she did, but she knew not what. And she longed to obtain that whereof she herself could not imagine the name, but full of unquiet imaginations, rested only unhappy, because she knew not her good hap. Cleophila hath (I think) said enough for herself to make you know (fair ladies) that she was not a little enchanted. And as for Dorus, a shepherd's apparel upon a duke of Thessalia will answer for him. Pamela was the only lady that would needs make open war upon herself, and obtain the victory, for, indeed, even now find she did a certain working of a new come inclination to Dorus. But when she found perfectly in herself whither it must draw her, she did over-master it with the consideration of his meanness.

But how therein Dorus thought to satisfy her, you shall after hear, for now the day being closed up in darkness, the Duke would fain have had Cleophila gone to rest because of the late received wound. But she that found no better salve than Philoclea's presence, desired first, that by torch light, they might see some of the pastorals the lion's coming had disordered, which accordingly was done, whereof I will repeat you a few, to ease you, fair ladies, of the tediousness of this long discourse.[87]

[87] The First Eclogues follow here and, appropriately, deal with unrequited love (see OA 11 and OA 12, in next section). Nothing of narrative is accomplished, but Histor ("story") tells of the plight of Plangus in search of the famous princes Pyrocles and Musidorus.

The Second Book, or Act, opens with each of the principals lamenting his or her situation (e.g., OA 22 reprinted in NA, Bk II, Chapter 25, below), but only Musidorus has the wit to act, wooing Pamela by "wooing" Mopsa (see OA 17, below). Pamela, knowing now he is a prince, agrees to an elopement. Pyrocles, then, woos Philoclea openly and they, too, become engaged. The book ends with another outbreak, now by rebels who fear Basilius has been murdered, but who are put down and dispersed by Pyrocles' sword and oratory, delivered from Basilius's throne. Basilius thus believes the oracle is fulfilled and there is rejoicing all around (see OA 25, reprinted in NA, Book II, Chapter 28, below).

The Second Eclogues focus on the conflicts of reason and passion in love (see OA 31 and OA 34, below), and Histor continues telling about Musidorus and Pyrocles, whom the sisters can now identify.

The Third Book, or Act, deals with the plots of the two princes to consummate their loves. First, Pyrocles, after repulsing Basilius in love (see OA 38, below), discovers Gynecia in a cave and agrees to return there at night for an assignation, but plans to send Basilius in his stead. Meanwhile Musidorus gets rid of Dametas and his family by sending Dametas out to find hidden treasure, by telling Miso that her husband is on his way to his lover (whom Musidorus has heard sing OA 45, below, to Dametas) and sending her after him, and by placing Mopsa all night in a "wishing tree." He and Pamela then escape, but are captured by the dispersed rebels just as Musidorus was seeking a kiss. After Basilius and Gynecia sneak out for their "adulterous" affairs, Pyrocles, going to Philoclea's room, overhears her singing to her lute (OA 60, below), waits, then steals in to see her, half naked, asleep. Immediately, a long, sensuous lyric passes through his mind (OA 62, reprinted in NA, Book II, Chapter 11, below), and he gets in bed with her.

The Third Eclogues celebrate, somewhat ironically, the rituals and joys of marriage (OA 63, below), and no significant mention is made of the princes.

The Fourth Book, or Act, opens with Dametas returning empty-handed only to discover Pamela missing. Rushing to Philoclea's room in search of her, he discovers Pyrocles and rushes to tell the King, but he meets the shepherds who tell him the King is dead. We then are given a flashback to the night before and discover that Gynecia has given Basilius a sleep-potion which she thinks is a love-potion, so believes she has killed him. Philanax arrives and arrests her. In a second flashback we discover that Pyrocles and Philoclea merely spent the night in the same bed, but realize after discovery by Dametas that they will be judged guilty by the world, and, indeed, Philanax does arrest Pyrocles for "raping" Philoclea and aiding Gynecia in "murder." Then, in a third flashback, the rebels decide to return Musidorus and Pamela to her father as a means of seeking their pardon, and, on return, Musidorus is arrested for abducting the princess and probable complicity in murder of Basilius. The book then ends in general political discord and strife.

The Fourth Eclogues contain only the pastoral laments of the shepherds for their "dead" king.

The Fifth Book, or Act, opens with the fortuitous arrival in Arcadia of King Evarchus of Macedonia (Pyrocles' father) who assumes Basilius's throne in order to try the three prisoners, all of whom are sentenced to death, in spite of the fact that the princes' identities are revealed; but Basilius awakes; all are forgiven; and the story-play ends happily.

OTHER POEMS FROM
THE OLD ARCADIA

OA11

```
-------⌣⌣---⌣⌣--
---⌣⌣--⌣⌣--⌣⌣-¹
```

Fortune, Nature, Love, long have contended about me,
   Which should most miseries, cast on a worm that I am.
Fortune thus gan say: "Misery and misfortune is all one,
   And of misfortune, fortune hath only the gift.²
With strong foes on land, on seas with contrary tempests   5
   Still do I cross this wretch, what so he taketh in hand."
"Tush, tush," said Nature, "this is all but a trifle, a man's self
   Gives haps or mishaps, ev'n as he ord'reth his heart.
But so his humor I frame, in a mould of choler adusted,³
   . That the delights of life shall be to him dolorous."   10

Love smiled, and thus said: "Want join'd to desire is
   unhappy.
   But if he nought do desire, what can Heraclitus⁴ ail?
None but I, works by desire; by desire have I kindled in his
   soul
   Infernal agonies unto a beauty divine,
Where thou poor Nature left all thy due glory, to Fortune   15
   Her virtue is sovereign, Fortune a vassal of hers."
Nature abash'd went back; Fortune blush'd; yet she replied
   thus:
   "And ev'n in that love, shall I reserve him a spite."⁵
Thus, thus, alas! woeful in Nature, unhappy by Fortune,
   But most wretched I am, now Love awakes my desire.   20

68

---

¹ This elegiac, quantitative poem is sung by Musidorus to Pamela in the First Eclogues. As a prince of blood it is appropriate that he would imitate a classical meter. The following "Nota" appear only in St, in the margin next to OA 11, on folios 40 and 41: The rules observed in these English measured [i.e., quantitative] verses be these:

Consonant before consonant, always long—except a mute and a liquid, as *refrain* (such indifferent single consonants, commonly short). But such as have a double sound, as *lack, will, till*, or such as the vowel before, doth produce long, as *hāte, debāte*.

Vowel before vowel, or diphthong before vowel, always short—except such an exclamation as *oh*. Else the diphthongs always long, and the single vowels short.

Because our tongue being full of consonants and monosyllables, the vowel slides away quicklier than in Greek or Latin, which be full of vowels and long words. Yet are such vowels long as the pronunciation makes long, as *glōry, lādy*, and such like as seem to have a diphthong sound, as *shōw, blōw, dīe, hīgh*.

Elisions, when one vowel meets with another, used indifferently as the advantage of the verse best serves—for so in our ordinary speech we do (for as well we say *thou art* as *th'art*), and like scope doth Petrarch take to himself sometimes to use apostrophe, sometimes not.

For the words derived out of Latin and other languages, they are measured as they are denizened [i.e., naturalized] in English, and not as before they came over sea (for we say not *fortúnate*, though the Latin says *fortuna*; nor *usúry*, but *úsury* in the first [syllable]); so our language hath a special gift in altering them and making them our own, some words especially short.

Particles, used now long, now short, as *but, or, nor, on, to*.

Some words, as they have diverse pronunciations, to be written diversely, as some say *though*, some pronounce it *tho*.

As for *wee, thee, shee*, though they may seem to be a double vowel by the wrong orthography, be here short (being indeed no other than the Greek iota), and the like of our "o" which some write double in this word *doo*.

² hath only the gift—is the sole dispenser.

³ mould of choler adusted — body scorched by choler (the hot, dry humor).

⁴ Heraclitus—a misanthropic Ephesian philosopher who believed that all things, including the gods, would eventually be consumed by change and urged that men cultivate a detached indifference to fortune.

⁵ reserve him a spite—grant him only hatred.

OA *12*[1]

‒∪‒‒‒∪∪‒∪‒∪
‒∪‒‒‒∪∪‒∪‒∪
‒∪‒‒‒∪∪‒∪‒∪
‒∪∪‒‒

If mine eyes can speak to do hearty errand,
Or mine eyes' language she do hap to judge of,
So that eyes' message be of her received,
 Hope, we do live yet.

But if eyes fail then when I most do need them,   5
Or if eyes' language be not unto her known,
So that eyes' message do return rejected,
 Hope, we do both die.

Yet, dying and dead, do we sing her honor;
So become our tombs monuments of her praise;   10
So becomes our loss the triumph of her gain;
 Hers be the glory.

If the senseless spheres do yet hold a music
If the swan's sweet voice be not heard but at death,
If muett[2] timber when it hath the life lost   15
 Yieldeth a lute's tune,

Are then human minds privileged so meanly
As that hateful Death can abridge them of power
With the vow of truth to record to all worlds
 That we be her spoils?   20

Thus, not ending, ends the due praise of her praise:
Fleshly veil consumes, but a soul hath his life
Which is held in love; love it is that hath join'd
 Life to this our soul.

But if eyes can speak to do hearty errand,   25
Or mine eyes' language she do hap to judge of,
So that eyes' message be of her received,
 Hope, we do live yet.

---

[1] This sapphic is sung by Pyrocles to Philoclea in the First Eclogues.
[2] muett—mute, but spelled to get two "long" syllables.

OA 17[1]

My sheep are thoughts, which I both guide and serve;
Their pasture is fair hills of fruitless love.
In barren sweets they feed, and feeding sterve.[2]
I wail their lot but will not other prove;[3]
My sheephook is wanhope,[4] which all upholds;   5
My weeds, desire, cut out in endless folds;
What wool my sheep shall bear, while thus they live,
In you it is, you must the judgment give.

OA 31[1]

----⏑⏑----⏑⏑-⏑⏑--

Fair rocks, goodly rivers, sweet woods, when shall I see peace?	Peace.
Peace! what bars me my tongue? who is it that comes me so nigh?	I.
Oh, I do know what guest I have met, it is Echo.	'Tis Echo.
Well met, Echo, approach; then tell me thy will too.	I will too.
Echo, what do I get yielding my sprite to my griefs?	Griefs. 5
What medicine may I find for a pain that draws me to death?	Death.
O poisonous medicine! what worse to me can be than it?	It.
In what state was I then, when I took this deadly disease?	Ease.

[1] This absolutely regular iambic pentameter poem is sung by Musidorus to Pamela in Book Two.
[2] sterve—starve.
[3] prove—try.
[4] wanhope—despair.
[1] This hexameter echo poem is sung by the stranger shepherd Philisides (Sidney) in the Second Eclogues. Philisides sings the first column of verses and "Echo" punctuates each with the word or phrase in the second column.

And what manner a mind which had to that
 humor a vein?   Vain.
Hath not Reason enough vehemence the
 desire to reprove?   Prove.   10
Oft prove I: but what salve, when Reason
 seeks to be gone?   One.
Oh, what is it? what is it that may be a salve
 to my love?   Love.
What do lovers seek for, long seeking for to
 enjoy?   Joy.
What be the joys for which to enjoy they
 went to the pains?   Pains.
Then to an earnest love what doth best vic-
 tory lend?   End.   15
End! but I can never end, Love will not give
 me leave?   Leave.
How be the minds dispos'd that cannot taste
 thy physic?   Sick.
Yet say again thy advice for the evils that I
 told thee?   I told thee.
Doth the infected wretch of his harm the ex-
 tremity know?   No.
But if he know not his harms, what guides
 hath he whilst he be blind?   Blind.   20
What blind guides can he have that leans to a
 fancy?   A fancy.
Can fancies want eyes, or he fall that steppeth
 aloft?   Oft.
What causes first made these torments on me
 to light?   Light.
Can then a cause be so light that forceth a
 man to go die?   I.
Yet tell what light thing I had in me to draw
 me to die?   Eye.   25
Eyesight made me to yield; but what first
 pierc'd to my eyes?   Eyes.

Eyes hurters, eyes hurt; but what from them
   to me falls?   Falls.

But when I first did fall, what brought most
   fall to my heart?   Art.

Art! what can be that art which thou dost
   mean by thy speech?   Speech.

What be the fruits of speaking art? what
   grows by the words?   Words.   30

O, much more than words: those words
   serv'd more to me bless.   Less.

Oh, when shall I be known where most to be
   known I do long?   Long.

Long be thy woes for such news; but how
   rocks she my thoughts?   Oughts.

Then, then, what do I gain, since unto her
   will I do wind?   Wind.

Wind, tempests, and storms, yet in end what
   gives she desire?   Ire.   35

Silly reward! yet among women hath she of
   virtue the most.   Most.

What great name may I give to so heavenly a
   woman?   A wo-man.

Woe but seems to me joy, that agrees to my
   thought so.   I thought so.

Think so, for of my desired bliss it is only the
   course.   Curse.

Curs'd be thyself for cursing that which leads
   me to joys.   Toys.   40

What be the sweet creatures where lowly demands be not heard?   Hard.

Hard to be got, but got constant, to be held
   like steels.   Eels.

How can they be unkind? speak, for thou
   hast nearly pried?   Pride.

Whence can pride come there, since springs
   of beauty be thence?   Thence.

Horrible is this blasphemy unto the most holy.	O lie.	45
Thou liest, false Echo; their minds as virtue be just.	Just.	
Mock'st thou those diamonds which only be match'd by the gods?	Odds.	
Odds! what an odds is there! since them to the heavens I prefer.	Err.	
Tell yet again me the names of these fair form'd to do evils?	Devils.	
Devils! if in hell such devils do abide, to the hell I do go.	Go.	50

from OA 34[1]

‒‒‒∪∪‒‒∪∪‒∪∪

O sweet woods, the delight of solitariness!
Oh, how much I do like your solitariness!
Where man's mind hath a freed consideration,
Of goodness to receive lovely direction.
Where senses do behold th'order of heav'nly host,   5
And wise thoughts do behold what the creator is;
Contemplation here holdeth his only seat,
Bounded with no limits, born with a wing of hope,
Climbs even unto the stars, nature is under it.
Nought disturbs thy quiet, all to thy service yields,   10
Each sight draws on a thought (thought, mother of
     science)[2]
Sweet birds kindly do grant harmony unto thee,
     Fair trees' shade is enough fortification,
     Nor danger to thyself if it be not in thyself.

[1] This complex, complicated asclepiadic is sung by Musidorus in the Second Eclogues. Only the first of three stanzas is included to illustrate how flat in English poetry the patterns of Latin poetry are.
[2] science—knowledge.

OA 38[1]

Phoebus, farewell! A sweeter saint I serve.
The high conceits thy heavenly wisdoms breed
My thoughts forget, my thoughts which never swerve
From her in whom is sown their freedom's seed,
And in whose eyes my daily doom I read.   5

Phoebus, farewell! A sweeter saint I serve.
Thou art far off, thy kingdom is above:
She heaven on earth with beauties doth preserve.
Thy beams I like, but her clear rays I love:
Thy force I fear, her force I still do prove.   10

Phoebus, yield up thy title in my mind,
She does possess; thy image is defac'd;
But if thy rage some brave revenge will find
On her who hath in me thy temple raz'd,
Employ thy might that she my fires may taste: 15
    And, how much more her worth surmounteth thee
    Make her as much more base by loving me.

OA 45[1]

My true love hath my heart, and I have his
By just exchange, one for the other given;
I hold his dear, and mine he cannot miss;[2]
There never was a better bargain driven.

His heart in me, keeps me and him in one;   5
My heart in him his thoughts and senses guides;

[1] In Book Three, after having thanked Apollo for saving him and his group at the end of Book Two, Basilius now resumes his courtship of Pyrocles with this delightful iambic, pentametric lyric.

[1] Musidorus, in order to force Miso to pursue Dametas on a fictional assignation, repeats this song which he says he heard some shepherdess sing to Dametas while she cradled his head on her lap. Sidney captures the charm of the native English lyric in this completely regular iambic, accentual-syllabic, pentametric poem.

[2] miss—live without.

He loves my heart, for once it was his own;
I cherish his, because in me it bides.

His heart his wound received from my sight;
My heart was wounded with his wounded heart,   10
For as from me on him his hurt did light,
So still methought in me his hurt did smart;
    Both equal hurt, in this change³ sought our bliss:
    My true love hath my heart, and I have his.

OA60¹

  1   2   3   1   2   3
Virtue, beauty, and speech, did strike, wound, charm,
     1   2 3   1   2   3
My heart, eyes, ears, with wonder, love, delight:
  1   2   3   1   2   3
First, second, last, did bind, enforce, and arm,
     1   2   3   1   2   3
His works, shows, suits, with wit, grace, and vow's might.

      1   2   3   1   2   3
Thus honor, liking, trust, much, far, and deep,   5
  1   2   3   1   2   3
Held, pierc'd, possess'd, my judgment, sense, and will,
  1   2   3   1   2   3
Till wrong, contempt, deceit, did grow, steal, creep,
  1   2   3   1   2   3
Bands, favor, faith, to break, defile, and kill.

     1   2   3 1   2   3
Then grief, unkindness, proof, took, kindled, taught,
  1   2   3   1   2   3
Well grounded, noble, due, spite, rage, disdain,   10

---

³ change—exchange.

¹ Philoclea sings this sonnet to her lute before Pyrocles enters her room at the end of Book Three. Although the poem is in iambic pentameter, Sidney's adherence to the correlative design where all similarly numbered items must bear a relation to one another actually prevents the generation of real poetry.

```
1   2     3              1     2      3
```
But ah, alas! (In vain) my mind, sight, thought,
```
   1        2        3     1      2      3
```
Doth him, his face, his words, leave, shun, refrain,
```
      1        2        3          1      2     3
```
For no thing, time, nor place, can loose, quench, ease,
```
      1       2        3      1     2      3
```
Mine own, embraced, sought, knot, fire, disease.

OA63[1]

Let mother Earth now deck herself in flowers,
To see her offspring seek a good increase,
Where justest love doth vanquish Cupid's powers,
And war of thoughts is swallow'd up in peace,
    Which never may decrease,   5
    But, like the turtles[2] fair,
Live one in two, a well-united pair,
    Which that no chance may stain,
O Hymen, long their coupled joys maintain!

O Heaven, awake, show forth thy stately face;   10
Let not these slumb'ring clouds thy beauties hide,
But with thy cheerful presence help to grace
The honest Bridegroom and the bashful Bride;
    Whose loves may ever bide,
    Like to the elm and vine,   15
With mutual embracements them to twine:
    In which delightful pain,
O Hymen, long their coupled joys maintain!

Ye Muses all, which chaste affects[3] allow,

---

[1] Because the relationships among the items are more fully and naturally developed, this correlative poem is able to develop in natural iambic, accentual-syllabic verses. This epithalamion is sung by a shepherd in the Third Eclogues to celebrate a country marriage. Ringler points out that it is the first formal marriage-hymn in English.

[2] turtles—turtle doves.

[3] affects—affections.

And have to Lalus show'd your secret skill,   20
To this chaste love your sacred favors bow,[4]
And so to him and her your gifts distil,
   That they all vice may kill,
   And, like to lilies pure,
Do please all eyes, and spotless do endure,   25
   Where that all bliss may reign,
O Hymen, long their coupled joys maintain!

Ye Nymphs which in the waters empire have,
Since Lalus' music oft doth yield you praise,
Grant to the thing which we for Lalus crave;   30
Let one time—but long first—close up their days,
   One grave their bodies seize;
   And like two rivers sweet,
When they though divers do together meet,
   One stream both streams contain,   35
O Hymen, long their coupled joys maintain!

Pan, father Pan, the god of silly sheep,
Whose care is cause that they in number grow,
Have much more care of them that them do keep—
Since from these good the others' good doth flow—   40
   And make their issue show
   In number like the herd
O younglings which thyself with love hast rear'd,
   Or like the drops of rain.
O Hymen, long their coupled joys maintain!   45

Virtue, if not a god, yet God's chief part,
Be thou the knot of this their open vow,
That still he be her head, she be his heart,
He lean to her, she unto him do bow,
   Each other still allow:[5]   50
   Like oak and mistletoe,

[4] bow—grant.
[5] allow—tolerate.

Her strength from him, his praise from her do grow:
  In which most lovely train,[6]
O Hymen, long their coupled joys maintain!

But thou, foul Cupid, sire to lawless lust,   55
Be thou far hence with thy empoison'd dart,
Which, though of glitt'ring gold, shall here take rust
Where simple love, which chasteness doth impart,
  Avoids thy hurtful art,
  Not needing charming skill   60
Such minds with sweet affections for to fill:
  Which begin pure and plain,
O Hymen, long their coupled joys maintain!

All churlish words, shrewd answers, crabbed looks,
All privateness, self-seeking, inward spite,   65
All waywardness which nothing kindly brooks,
All strife for toys and claiming master's right,
  Be hence aye put to flight!
  All stirring husband's hate
Gainst neighbours good, for womanish debate,   70
  Be fled, as things most vain!
O Hymen, long their coupled joys maintain!

All peacock pride, and fruits of peacock's pride,
Longing to be with loss of substance gay;
With recklessness what may thy house betide,   75
So that you may on higher slippers stay,[7]
  For ever hence away:
  Yet let not sluttery,
The sink of filth, be counted huswifery,
  But keeping whole your mean,   80
O Hymen, long their coupled joys maintain!

But above all, away vile Jealousy,
The evil of evils, just cause to be unjust;

[6] train—course.

[7] on higher slippers stay—walk on shoes with heels high enough to make you taller than everyone else.

How can he love suspecting treachery?
How can she love where love cannot win trust?   85
   Go, snake, hide thee in dust,
   Nor dare once show thy face
Where open hearts do hold so constant place
   That they thy sting restrain:
O Hymen, long their coupled joys maintain!   90

The Earth is decked with flowers; the Heavens display'd
Muses, grant gifts; Nymphs, long and joined life;
Pan, store of babes; Virtue their thoughts well staid;
Cupid's lust gone, and gone is bitter Strife.
   Happy man, happy wife!   95
   No Pride shall them oppress
Not yet shall yield to loathsome sluttishness,
   And Jealousy is slain;
For Hymen will their coupled joys maintain.

    OA71[1]

STREPHON   Ye goatherd gods, that love the grassy
          mountains,
      Ye nymphs that haunt the springs in pleasant
          valleys,
      Ye satyrs joy'd with free and quiet forests,
      Vouchsafe your silent ears to plaining music,
      Which to my woes gives still an early
          morning,   5
      And draws the dolor on till weary evening.

[1] Although the burden of the Fourth Eclogues is the grief of the Arcadian shepherds over the "death" of Basilius, here two foreign (like Philisides, strangers) shepherds sing of their private loss, their mutual love, Urania, who has forsaken them. One should note that Sidney opens the *New Arcadia* with these same two in the same lament, but he does not there give them this or any song.

    This much praised poem is a sestina which has six-line stanzas and a final triplet of three lines; the terminal words of each stanza are the same, but rearranged according to a definite pattern in the final triplet. Sestinas usually have six stanzas, but Sidney has here created a double sestina, of twelve stanzas.

KLAIUS   O Mercury, foregoer to the evening,
      O heavenly huntress of the savage
          mountains,[2]
      O lovely star, entitled of the morning,[3]
      While that my voice doth fill these woeful
          valleys,   10
      Vouchsafe your silent ears to plaining music,
      Which oft hath Echo tir'd in secret forests.

STREPHON   I, that was once free burgess of the forests,
      Where shade from sun, and sport I sought at
          evening,
      I, that was once esteem'd for pleasant music,   15
      Am banish'd now among the monstrous
          mountains
      Of huge despair, and foul affliction's valleys,
      Am grown a screech owl to myself each
          morning.

KLAIUS   I, that was once delighted every morning,
      Hunting the wild inhabiters of forests,   20
      I, that was once the music of these valleys,
      So darkened am that all my day is evening,
      Heartbroken so that molehills seem high
          mountains
      And fill the vales with cries instead of music.

STREPHON   Long since, alas, my deadly swannish music[4]   25
      Hath made itself a crier of the morning,
      And hath with wailing strength climb'd
          highest mountains;
      Long since my thoughts more desert be than
          forests,
      Long since I see my joys come to their
          evening,

[2] huntress . . . mountains—Diana.
[3] star . . . morning—Lucifer.
[4] deadly swannish music—music like that of the swan, a bird which supposedly sings as it dies.

And state thrown down to overtrodden
    valleys.   30

KLAIUS   Long since the happy dwellers of these
                valleys
Have prayed me leave my strange exclaiming
    music
Which troubles their day's work and joys of
    evening;
Long since I hate the night, more hate the
    morning,
Long since my thoughts chase me like beasts
    in forests   35
And make me wish myself laid under
    mountains.

STREPHON   Meseems I see the high and stately mountains
Transform themselves to low dejected
    valleys;
Meseems I hear in these ill-changed forests
The nightingales do learn of owls their
    music;   40
Meseems I feel the comfort of the morning
Turned to the mortal serene[5] of an evening.

KLAIUS   Meseems I see a filthy cloudy evening
As soon as sun begins to climb the mountains;
Meseems I feel a noisome scent, the morning   45
When I do smell the flowers of these valleys;
Meseems I hear, when I do hear sweet music,
The dreadful cries of murder'd men in forests.

STREPHON   I wish to fire the trees of all these forests;
I give the sun a last farewell each evening;   50
I curse the fiddling finders-out of music;
With envy I do hate the lofty mountains

[5] serene—mist.

And with despite despise the humble valleys;
I do detest night, evening, day, and morning.

KLAIUS   Curse to myself my prayer is, the morning;   55
My fire is more than can be made with
            forests,
My state more base than are the basest
            valleys.
I wish no evenings more to see, each evening;
Shamed, I hate myself in sight of mountains
And stop mine ears, lest I grow mad with
            music.   60

STREPHON   For she whose parts maintain'd a perfect
            music,
Whose beauty shin'd more than the blushing
            morning,
Who much did pass in state the stately
            mountains,
In straightness pass'd the cedars of the
            forests,
Hath cast me, wretched, into eternal evening   65
By taking her two suns from these dark
            valleys.

KLAIUS   For she, to whom compar'd, the Alps are
            valleys,
She, whose least word brings from the
            spheres their music,
At whose approach the sun rose in the
            evening,
Who where she went bare in her forehead
            morning,   70
Is gone, is gone, from these our spoiled
            forests,
Turning to deserts our best pastur'd
            mountains.

STREPHON   These mountains witness shall, so shall these valleys,

KLAIUS   These forests eke, made wretched by our music,
Our morning hymn this is, and song at evening.   75

THE TWENTY-THIRD PSALM

Dominus regit me[1]

The Lord the Lord my shepherd is,
  And so can never I
    Taste misery.
He rests me in green pasture His.
  By waters still and sweet   5
    He guides my feet.

He me revives, leads me the way
  Which righteousness doth take,
    For His name's sake.
Yea though I should through valleys stray   10
  Of death's dark shade I will
    No whit fear ill.

For Thou dear Lord Thou me beset'st,
  Thy rod and Thy staff be
    To comfort me.   15
Before me Thou a table set'st,
  Ev'n when foe's envious eye
    Doth it espy.

With oil Thou dost anoint my head,
  And so my cup dost fill   20
    That it doth spill.
Thus thus shall all my days be fed,

[1] The Lord guides me.

This mercy is so sure
It shall endure,
And long yea long abide I shall,   25
There where the Lord of all
Doth hold His hall.

FROM THE CERTAIN SONNETS

CS 4

The nightingale, as soon as April bringeth
  Unto her rested sense a perfect waking,
While late bare earth, proud of new clothing, springeth,
  Sings out her woes, a thorn her song-book making,[1]
  And mournfully bewailing,   5
Her throat in tunes expresseth
What grief her breast oppresseth
  For Tereus' force on her chaste will prevailing.
O Philomela fair, O take some gladness,
That here is juster cause of plaintful sadness: 10
Thine earth now springs, mine fadeth;
Thy thorn without, my thorn my heart invadeth.

Alas, she hath no other cause of anguish
  But Tereus' love, on her by strong hand wroken,[2]
Wherein she suff'ring, all her spirits languish;   15
  Full womanlike complains her will was broken.
  But I, who daily craving,
Cannot have to[3] content me,
Have more cause to lament me,
  Since wanting is more woe than too much having.   20

[1] a thorn her song-book making—the nightingale is said to sing with
her breast pressed against a thorn; her music, in other words, is the result
of pain, an idea related to the myth of Philomela, who, after being raped
and muted by her brother-in-law Tereus, was changed into a nightingale.
[2] wroken—wreaked.
[3] to—what would.

87

O Philomela fair, O take some gladness,
That here is juster cause of plaintful sadness:
Thine earth now springs, mine fadeth;
Thy thorn without, my thorn my heart invadeth.

CS *13*

Out of Catullus[1]

Nulli se dicit mulier mea nubere malle,
  Quam mihi non si se Iupiter ipse petat,
Dicit sed mulier Cupido quædicit amanti,
  In vento aut rapida scribere oportet aqua.

Unto no body my woman saith she had rather a wife be,
  Than to myself, not though Jove grew a suitor of hers.
These be her words, but a woman's words to a love that is eager,
  In wind or water stream do require to be writ.

CS *18*

In wonted walks, since wonted fancies change,
Some cause there is, which of strange cause doth rise;
For in each thing whereto mine eye doth range,
Part of my pain meseems engraved lies.

The rocks which were of constant mind the mark   5
In climbing steep, now hard refusal show;
The shading woods seem now my sun to dark,
And stately hills disdain to look so low.

The restful caves now restless visions give,
In dales I see each way a hard assent;[1]   10
Like late mown meads, late cut from joy I live.
Alas sweet brooks do in my tears augment.

[1] For scansion, see footnote #1 to OA 11
[1] The pun assent—ascent is lost in modern spelling.

Rocks, woods, hills, caves, dales, meads, brooks, answer me:[1]
Infected minds infect each thing they see.

CS *30*

Ring our your bells, let mourning shows be spread;
    For Love is dead.
His Love is dead, infected
With plague of deep disdain:
Worth, as nought worth, rejected,   5
And Faith fair scorn doth gain.
From so ungrateful fancy,
From such a female franzy,[1]
From them that use men thus,
Good Lord, deliver us!   10

Weep, neighbors, weep! do you not hear it said
    That Love is dead?
His death-bed, peacock's folly;[2]
His winding-sheet is shame;
His will, false-seeming holy;   15
His sole exec'tor, blame.
From so ungrateful fancy,
From such a female franzy,
From them that use men thus,
Good Lord, deliver us!   20

Let dirge be sung and trentals[3] rightly read,
    For Love is dead.
Sir Wrong his tomb ordaineth
My mistress' marble heart,
Which epitaph containeth: 25
'Her eyes were once his dart.'
From so ungrateful fancy,
From such a female franzy,

---

[1] Compare Milton, *Paradise Lost*, Book II, line 621: "Rocks, Caves, Lakes, Fens, Bogs, Dens, and shades of death."

[1] franzy—frenzy.

[2] peacock's folly—pride.

[3] trentals—thirty masses for the soul of the deceased.

From them that use men thus,
Good Lord, deliver us!   30

Alas, I lie! rage hath this error bred.
        Love is not dead.
    Love is not dead, but sleepeth
    In her unmatched mind,
    Where she his counsel keepeth   35
    Till due desert she find.
    Therefore from so vile fancy,
    To call such wit a franzy,
    Who Love can temper thus,
    Good Lord, deliver us!   40

CS 31

Thou blind man's mark,[1] thou fool's self-chosen snare,
Fond fancy's scum, and dregs of scatter'd thought,
Band of all evils, cradle of causeless care,
Thou web of will, whose end is never wrought,

Desire, desire! I have too dearly bought   5
With price of mangled mind thy worthless ware;
Too long, too long, asleep thou hast me brought
Who should my mind to higher things prepare.

But yet in vain thou hast my ruin sought;
In vain thou madest me to vain things aspire;   10
In vain thou kindlest all thy smoky fire;
For virtue hath this better lesson taught:
    Within myself to seek my only hire,[2]
    Desiring naught but how to kill desire.

CS 32

Leave me, O love, which reachest but to dust;
And thou, my mind, aspire to higher things;

---

[1] mark—target; hence, slang for "dupe."
[2] hire—reward.

Grow rich in that which never taketh rust;
Whatever fades but fading pleasure brings.

Draw in thy beams, and humble all thy might   5
To that sweet yoke, where lasting freedoms be,
Which breaks the clouds, and opens forth the light
That doth both shine and give us sight to see.

O take fast hold; let that light be thy guide
In this small course which birth draws out to death,   10
And think how evil becometh him to slide,
Who seeketh heav'n, and comes of heav'nly breath.
    Then farewell, world; thy uttermost I see;
    Eternal Love, maintain thy life in me.

    Splendidis longum valedico nugis.[1]

---

[1] *Splendidis . . . nugis*—I bid a long farewell to these fine trifles.

LETTER TO ROBERT SIDNEY

My dear brother,

For the money you have received, assure yourself (for it is true), there is nothing I spend so pleaseth me as that which is for you. If ever I have ability you will find it; if not, yet shall not any brother living be better beloved than you of me. . . . For your countenance, I would for no cause have it diminished in Germany; in Italy your greatest expense must be upon worthy men, and not upon householding. Look to your diet, sweet Robin, and hold up your heart in courage and virtue. Truly, great part of my comfort is in you. I know not myself what I meant by bravery in you, so greatly you may see I condemn you. Be careful of yourself and I shall never have cares. . . .

For the method of writing history, Boden[1] hath written at large; you may read him and gather out of many words some matter. This I think in haste: a story is either to be considered as a story, or as a treatise, which besides that addeth many things for profit and ornament.

As a story, he is nothing but a narration of things done with beginnings, causes, and appendices thereof. In that kind your method must be to have *seriem temporum* very exactly, which the Chronologies of Melanchton, Tarchagnota, Languet,[2] and

---

[1] Jean Bodin (1530–1596), French political philosopher, most noted for his *Six Livres de la Republique*, 1576, considered the beginning of the science of political economy. Ironically, he was a secretary to Anjou when he came to England in 1581 to seek the hand of Elizabeth.

[2] *seriem temporum* . . . Melanchton, Tarchagnota, Languet—"chain of events"; Philip Melanchthon (1497–1560), influential theologian, educator, and voluminous writer during the German Reformation; Giovanni Tarcagnota (c. 1513–1566), author of *Delle Histoire del Mondo*, 1562; Hubert Languet (1518–1581) had been with Sidney on his grand tour and was currently with Robert (see General Introduction).

such other will help you to. . . . In that kind you have principally to note the examples of virtue or vice, with their good or evil successes, the establishments or ruins of great estates, with the causes, the time and circumstances of the laws they write of, the enterings and endings of wars, and therein the stratagems against the enemy, and the discipline upon the soldier, and thus much as a very historiographer.

Besides this, the historian makes himself a discourser[3] for profit, and an orator, yea, a poet sometimes for ornament: an orator in making excellent oration *e re nata*[4] which are to be marked, but marked with the note of rhetorical remembrances; a poet in painting forth the effects, the motions, the whisperings of the people, which though in disputation one might say were true, yet, who will mark them well shall find them to taste of a poetical vein, and in that kind are gallantly to be marked, for though perchance they were not so, yet it is enough they might be so.

The last point which tends to reach profit is of a discourser, which name I give to whosoever speaks *non simpliciter de facto, sed de qualitatibus et circumstantiis facti*[5] (and that is it which makes me and many others rather note much with our pen than with our mind, because we leave all these discourses to the confused trust of our memory because they being not tied to the tenor of a question)[6] as philosophers use sometimes plays, the divine in telling his opinion and reasons in religion, sometimes the lawyer in showing the causes and benefits of laws, sometimes a natural philosopher in setting down the causes of any strange thing which the story binds him to speak of, but most commonly

[3] discourser—philosopher.
[4] *e re nata*—from things as they are.
[5] *non simpliciter . . . facti*—not simply of the fact, but of the qualities and circumstances of the fact.
[6] (and that . . . a question)—Sidney's parenthetical advice is rather garbled, but the general tenor of his remark pertains to the use of a commonplace book to jot down observations and ideas under categories and topics which permit them later to be matched against appropriate illustrations and examples topically arranged in history, and other, books, to be used in elaboration of one's own thoughts.

a moral philosopher, either in the ethic part when he sets forth virtues or vices and the natures of passions, or in the politic when he doth, as he often doth, meddle sententiously with matters of estate. Again, sometimes he gives precept of war, both offensive and defensive, and so lastly not professing any art, as his matter leads him, he deals with all arts which, because it carrieth the life of a lively example, it is wonderful what light it gives to the arts themselves.

So as the great civilians help themselves with the discourses of the historians, so do soldiers, and even philosophers, and astronomers. But that I wish herein, is this, that when you read any such thing, you straight bring it to his head, not only of what art, but by your logical subdivisions, to the next member and parcel of the art. And so as in a table—be it witty word of which Tacitus is full, sentences of which Livy, or similitudes whereof Plutarch—straight to lay it up in the right place of his storehouse as either military, or more specially, defensive military, or more particularly, defensive by fortification, and so lay it up. And such a little table you may easily make, wherewith I would have you ever join the historical part, which is only the example of some stratagem, or good counsel, or such like. This write I to you in great haste, of method, without method, but with more leisure and study (if I do not find some book that satisfies) I will venture to write more largely of it unto you. . . .

I write this to you as one that for myself have given over the delight in the world, but wish to you as much if not more than to myself. So you can speak and write Latin not barbarously, I never require great study in Ciceronianism, the chief abuse of Oxford, *Qui dum verba sectantur, res ipsas negligunt.*[7] My toyful book I will send with God's help by February.[8] . . .

Now, sweet brother, take a delight to keep and increase your music; you will not believe what a want I find of it in my melancholy times. At horsemanship, when you exercise it, read

[7] *Qui dum verba . . . negligunt*—where, while they eagerly pursue words, they neglect things themselves. Here Sidney fires a shot in the growing "matter v. manner" debate which broke out among the humanists.

[8] Sidney had just finished, or was finishing, the *Old Arcadia.*

Grison Claudio, and a book that is called *La Gloria de Cavallo*,[9] withal that you may join the thorough contemplation of it with the exercise, and so shall you profit more in a month than others in a year, and mark the bitting, saddling, and curing[10] of horses.

Sir, for news I refer myself to this bearer. He can tell you how idly we look on our neighbor's fires; and nothing is happened notable at home, save only Drake's return, of which yet I know not the secret points, but about the world he hath been, and rich he is returned. . . .

When you play at weapons I would have you get thick caps and brasers,[11] and play out your play lustily, for indeed ticks and daliances[12] are nothing in earnest for the time of the one and the other greatly differs, and use as well the blow as the thrust; it is good in itself, and besides exerciseth your breath and strength, and will make you a strong man at the tourney and barriers.[13] First, in any case, practice the single sword, and then with the dagger. Let no day pass without an hour or two such exercise; the rest study or confer diligently, and so shall you come home to my comfort and credit. Lord, how I have babbled; once again, farewell dearest brother.

Your most loving and careful brother,
Philip Sidney

At Leicesterhouse, this 18th of October, 1580

---

[9] Claudio . . . *La Gloria de Cavallo*—The title Sidney uses is to a work by Pasqual Caracciolo, published in Venice, 1567; however, *Federico* Grisson was a contemporary, voluminous Spanish writer on horsemanship.

[10] curing—currying.

[11] caps and brasers—chest armor and fore-arm guards.

[12] ticks and daliances—light touches and toying.

[13] barriers—a tournament (from the palisades enclosing the lists).

The Defence of Poesy

THE TWO TITLES given Sidney's major critical treatise in 1595, *The Defence of Poesy* and *An Apology for Poetry*, are apt to be misleading to the modern eye, but when the word "case" is substituted for either "defence" or "apology" and some such phrase as "creative writing," "fine arts," or "imaginative fiction" is substituted for "poesy" or "poetry," one can readily prepare the mind for the large and positive discussion of the role and function of both the artist and art which Sidney presents. Sidney's conception of art concurs completely with that of his age: the finest art hides its art, and as such, appears to have an independent existence. Sidney was one of the first to discover, however, the paradox that fine art is the result only of an artist's complete dedication to, and immersion in, his artifact.

Some have called this artistic integrity, some have called it negative capability, and some have called it an escape from personality, but Sidney's word was *"energia,"* or a kind of "forcibleness" as he translated the term. But this release of energy is not untamed or unshaped. Indeed, the program which was discussed under the General Introduction—Art, Imitation, and Exercise—serves as the basis for creative effort. While all art shares this common base, what separates great art from ordinary, even as a great life is separated from an ordinary life, is the quality of Exercise—better understood possibly by the concept of engagement, total engagement with all possible worlds, imaginary and real. Through this kind of engagement the artist makes discoveries and connections about the data of the world which we ordinary mortals tend to miss. The Renaissance term was simply invention, meaning not, something made-up, rather, something discovered, something found out about that which already exists. In order to make an invention, then, artists had to utilize their God-given reason, or powers of observation and reflection, and here it must be recalled that to the Renaissance, reason so exercised was analogous to the romantic imagination, which, after all, Wordsworth defined as reason in her most exalted mood.

Although all of this is commonplace to the Renaissance, Sidney in the *Defence* gives it shape and meaning, showing the connection between the function of the artist and the efficacy of art: because reason resides in the rational soul—that touch of the divine within each person—when the artist, or poet, or maker, allows reason to entertain, weigh, and measure the sensory data of second nature, the artist can be creative. Because God is the exalted and first creator, man is able to create: God is the "Maker of that maker." Thus, Sidney is the first in the history of esthetics to give a logical and comprehensible definition of that vexing problem, "inspiration."

To the Renaissance, Sidney's *Defence of Poesy* would itself be an example of art, for it is an oration after the manner of Cicero, the grand master in Renaissance education. Particularly, as any Renaissance schoolboy would readily recognize, what we have here is "the case for poetry," or a legal defense, a plea before the bar. Such a schoolboy would also immediately call to mind the conventional parts of such an oration, but this skill or art is no longer a part of our literary training. As a result, I have divided the various parts of Sidney's defense from one another, labeled each with its appropriate title, and explained its function in the footnotes. Even with the division, however, the art of the whole is so graceful and complete that it tends to hide the very art of its creation. The *Defence* is not art simply because it is an oration; it is art because it is so well done.

Sidney began the *Defence* sometime after the fall of 1580, and most likely completed it by 1582. Although there is evidence that it circulated during his lifetime, it was not published until 1595, when it appeared three times. The first publication was by William Ponsonby under the title *The Defence of Poesy*, which was followed by *An Apology for Poetry*, published by Henry

Olney. Ponsonby contested within the Stationers' Company that he had the rights to the text, and, indeed, won his case, for the third appearance of the *Defence* has Ponsonby's original title page, but carries the text made up of sheets from Olney's press. Although this third issue is an indication of the obliviousness of Elizabethan printers to textual problems, the fact that the Countess of Pembroke and Ponsonby in 1598 included the first text of the *Defence* of 1595 (STC 22535) as part of the collected works, that is the text which has been selected for the present edition, silently corrected, however, from the text of 1598 (STC 22541) and including in brackets significant readings from the *Apology* (STC 22534).

THE DEFENCE OF POESY

1

Exordium[1]

When the right virtuous E[dward] W[otton] and I were at the Emperor's court together, we gave ourselves to learn horsemanship of John Pietro Pugliano, one that with great commendation had the place of an esquire in his stable.[2] And he, according to the fertileness of the Italian wit, did not only afford us the demonstration of his practice, but sought to enrich our minds with the contemplations therein which he thought most precious. But with none I remember mine ears were at any time more loaden, than when (either angered with slow payment, or moved with our learned-like admiration) he exercised his speech in the praise of his faculty. He said, soldiers were the noblest estate of mankind, and horsemen the noblest of soldiers. He said they were the masters of war and ornaments of peace; speedy goers and strong abiders; triumphers both in camps and courts. Nay, to so unbelieved a point he proceeded, as that no earthly thing bred such wonder to a prince as to be a good horseman. Skill of government was but a *pedanteria*[3] in comparison. Then would he add certain praises, by telling what a peerless beast the horse was, the only serviceable courtier without flattery, the beast of most beauty, faithfulness, courage, and such more that if I had not been a piece of a logician before I came to him, I think he would have per-

[1] exordium—in rhetoric, the introduction to a speech.
[2] an esquire in his stable—John Pietro Pugliano was an equerry at the court of Emperor Maximilian II.
[3] *pedanteria*—in Italian, "school learning."

suaded me to have wished myself a horse. But this much at least with his no few words he drove into me, that self-love is better than any gilding to make that seem gorgeous wherein ourselves be parties.

Wherein, if Pugliano's strong affection and weak arguments will not satisfy you, I will give you a nearer example of myself, who (I know not by what mischance) in these my not old years and idlest times having slipped into the title of a poet, am provoked to say something unto you in the defense of that my unelected vocation, which if I handle with more good will than good reasons, bear with me, since the scholar is to be pardoned that followeth the steps of his master. And yet I must say that, as I have more just cause to make a pitiful defence of poor poetry, which from almost the highest estimation of learning is fallen to be the laughingstock of children, so have I need to bring some more available proofs, since the former is by no man barred of his deserved credit, the silly latter hath had even the names of philosophers used to the defacing of it, with great danger of civil war among the Muses.

II
Narratio[4]

And first, truly, to all them that professing learning inveigh against poetry may justly be objected, that they go very near to ungratefulness, to seek to deface that which, in the noblest nations and languages that are known, hath been the first light-giver to ignorance, and first nurse, whose milk little and little enabled them to feed afterwards of tougher knowledges. And will you play the hedgehog that, being received into the den, drove out his host, or rather the vipers, that with their birth kill their parents? Let learned Greece in any of |her| manifold sciences be able to show me one book before Musaeus, Homer, and Hesiod, all three nothing else but poets. Nay, let any history be brought that can say any writers were there before them, if they

[4] narratio—the part of an oration which outlines the subject matter and indicates the points to be covered.

were not men of the same skill, as Orpheus, Linus, and some other are named, who, having been the first of that country that made pens deliverers of their knowledge to the[ir] posterity, may justly challenge to be called their fathers in learning, for not only in time they had their priority (although in itself antiquity be venerable) but went before them, as causes to draw with their charming sweetness the wild untamed wits to an admiration of knowledge, so, as Amphion was said to move stones with his poetry to build Thebes, and Orpheus to be listened to by beasts —indeed stony and beastly people. So among the Romans were Livius Andronicus and Ennius. So in the Italian language the first that made it aspire to be a treasure-house of science were the poets Dante, Boccaccio, and Petrarch. So in our English were Gower and Chaucer, after whom, encouraged and delighted with their excellent foregoing, others have followed, to beautify our mother tongue, as well in the same kind as [in] other arts.

This did so notably show itself, that the philosophers of Greece durst not a long time appear to the world but under the mask of poets. So Thales, Empedocles, and Parmenides sang their natural philosophy in verses; so did Pythagoras and Phocylides their moral counsels; so did Tyrtaeus in war matters, and Solon in matters of policy; or rather, they, being poets, did exercise their delightful vein in those points of highest knowledge, which before them lay hidden to the world. For that wise Solon was directly a poet it is manifest, having written in verse the notable fable of the Atlantic Island, which was continued by Plato. And truly, even Plato, whosoever well considereth shall find that in the body of his work, though the inside and strength were philosophy, the skin as it were and beauty depended most of poetry; for all stands upon dialogues, wherein he feigns many honest burgesses of Athens speak of such matters, that, if they had been set on the rack, they would never have confessed them, besides his poetical describing the circumstances of their meetings, as the well ordering of a banquet, the delicacy of a walk, with interlacing mere tales, as Gyges' Ring,[5] and others, which

[5] Gyges' Ring—Plato's mythological Lydian shepherd, Gyges, owned a ring which could render him invisible.

who knows not to be flowers of poetry did never walk into Apollo's garden.

And even historiographers (although their lips sound of things done, and verity be written in their foreheads) have been glad to borrow both fashion and perchance weight of the poets. So Herodotus entitled his history by the name of the nine Muses; and both he and all the rest that followed him either stole or usurped of poetry their passionate describing of passions, the many particularities of battles, which no man could affirm, or, if that be denied me, long orations put in the mouths of great kings and captains, which it is certain they never pronounced. So that, truly, neither philosopher nor historiographer could at the first have entered into the gates of popular judgments, if they had not taken a great passport of poetry, which in all nations at this day, where learning flourisheth not, is plain to be seen, in all which they have some feeling of poetry.

In Turkey, besides their law-giving divines, they have no other writers but poets. In our neighbor country Ireland, where truly learning goes very bare, yet are their poets held in a devout reverence. Even among the most barbarous and simple Indians where no writing is, yet have they their poets, who make and sing songs, which they call *Areytos*,[6] both of their ancestors' deeds and praises of their gods—a sufficient probability that, if ever learning come among them, it must be by having their hard dull wits softened and sharpened with the sweet delights of poetry. For until they find a pleasure in the exercise of the mind, great promises of much knowledge will little persuade them that know not the fruits of knowledge. In Wales, the true remnant of the ancient Britons, as there are good authorities to show, the long time they had poets, which they called bards, so through all the conquests of Romans, Saxons, Danes, and Normans, some of whom did seek to ruin all memory of learning from among them, yet do their poets, even to this day, last; so as it is not more notable in the soon beginning than in long continuing. But since the authors of most of our sciences were the Romans, and before

---

[6] *Areytos*—Spanish *aréito*, a word used by the West Indians to describe songs which accompany dances.

them the Greeks, let us a little stand upon their authorities, but even so far as to see what names they have given unto this now scorned skill.

Among the Romans a poet was called *Vates*, which is as much as a diviner, foreseer, or prophet, as by his conjoined words *vaticinium* and *vaticinari* is manifest: so heavenly a title did that excellent people bestow upon this heart-ravishing knowledge. And so far were they carried into the admiration thereof, that they thought in the chanceable hitting upon any of such verses great foretokens of their following fortunes were placed. Whereupon grew the word of *Sortes Virgilianae*, when, by sudden opening Virgil's book, they lighted upon some verse of his, as it is reported by many, whereof the histories of the emperors' lives are full, as of Albinus, the governor of our island, who in his childhood met with this verse,

Arma amens capio, nec sat rationis in armis;[7]

and in his age performed it. Although it were a very vain and godless superstition, as also it was to think spirits were commanded by such verses (whereupon this word charms, derived of *carmina*,[8] cometh), so yet serveth it to show the great reverence those wits were held in. And altogether not without ground, since both the Oracles of Delphos and Sibylla's prophecies were wholly delivered in verses. For that same exquisite observing of number and measure in the words, and that high-flying liberty of conceit proper to the poet, did seem to have some divine force in it.

And may not I presume a little farther, to show the reasonableness of this word *Vates*, and say that the holy David's Psalms are a divine poem? If I do, I shall not do it without the testimony of great learned men, both ancient and modern. But even the name of Psalms will speak for me, which, being interpreted, is nothing but Songs; then, that it is fully written in meter, as all

---

[7]Albinus, Roman commander in Britain, 192–197 A.D.; *Arma* . . . "Madly I take up arms, though arms are useless now" (*Aeneid* 2.314).

[8] *carmina*—songs.

learned Hebricians agree, although the rules be not yet fully found; lastly and principally, his handling his prophecy, which is merely poetical. For what else is the awaking his musical instruments, the often and free changing of persons, his notable *prosopopeias*,[9] when he maketh you, as it were, see God coming in his majesty, his telling of the beasts' joyfulness, and hills' leaping, but a heavenly poesy, wherein almost he showeth himself a passionate lover of that unspeakable and everlasting beauty to be seen by the eyes of the mind, only cleared by faith? But truly now having named him, I fear I seem to profane that holy name, applying it to Poetry, which is among us thrown down to so ridiculous an estimation: but they that with quiet judgments will look a little deeper into it, shall find the end and working of it such, as, being rightly applied, deserveth not to be scourged out of the Church of God.

But now, let us see how the Greeks have named it, and how they deemed of it. The Greeks named him ποιητήν,[10] which name hath, as the most excellent, gone through other languages. It cometh of this word ποιεῖν, which is to make; wherein, I know not whether by luck or wisdom, we Englishmen have met with the Greeks in calling him a maker; which name, how high and incomparable a title it is, I had rather were known by marking the scope of other sciences than by any partial allegation.

There is no art delivered unto mankind that hath not the works of Nature for his principal object, without which they could not consist, and on which they so depend, as they become actors and players, as it were, of what Nature will have set forth. So doth the astronomer look upon the stars, and, by that he seeth set down what order Nature hath taken therein. So doth the geometrician and arithmetician in their diverse sorts of quantities. So doth the musician in times tell you which by nature agree, which not. The natural philosopher thereon hath his name, and the moral philosopher standeth upon the natural virtues, vices, or passions of man; and "follow Nature" (saith he) "therein, and

9 *prosopopeias*—personifications.
10 *poieten*—Greek term meaning "maker."

thou shalt not err." The lawyer saith what men have determined; the historian what men have done. The grammarian speaketh only of the rules of speech; and the rhetorician and logician, considering what in Nature will soonest prove and persuade, thereon give artificial rules, which still are compassed within the circle of a question according to the proposed matter. The physician weigheth the nature of man's body, and the nature of things helpful or hurtful unto it. And the metaphysic, though it be in the second and abstract notions, and therefore be counted supernatural, yet doth he indeed build upon the depth of Nature.

Only the poet, disdaining to be tied to any such subjection, lifted up with the vigor of his own invention, doth grow in effect into another Nature, in making things either better than Nature bringeth forth, or, quite anew, forms such as never were in Nature, as the Heroes, Demigods, Cyclops, Chimeras, Furies, and such like: so as he goeth hand in hand with Nature, not enclosed within the narrow warrant of her gifts, but freely ranging within the zodiac of his own wit.

Nature never set forth the earth in so rich tapestry as divers poets have done, neither with so pleasant rivers, fruitful trees, sweet-smelling flowers, nor whatsoever else may make the too much loved earth more lovely. Her world is brazen, the poets only deliver a golden. But let those things alone, and go to man (for whom as the other things are, so it seemeth in him her uttermost cunning is employed), and know whether she have brought forth so true a lover as Theagenes, so constant a friend as Pylades, so valiant a man as Orlando, so right a prince as Xenophon's Cyrus, and so excellent a man every way as Virgil's Aeneas.[11] Neither let this be jestingly conceived because the works of the one be essential, the other in imitation or fiction, for every understanding knoweth the skill of each artificer standeth in that Idea or foreconceit of the work, and not in the work itself.

[11] Theagenes . . . Pylades . . . Orlando . . . Cyrus—Theagenes is the hero of the Greek prose romance *Aethiopica*, which was written by Heliodorus about 400 A.D.; Pylades is the faithful friend of Orestes in the *Oresteia* by Aeschylus; Orlando is the hero of Ariosto's Italian epic, *Orlando Furioso*, which is based on the story of Roland, Charlemagne's courageous lieutenant; Cyrus is the subject of Xenophon's *Cyropaedia*.

And that the poet hath that Idea is manifest, by delivering them forth in such excellency as he had imagined them. Which delivering forth also is not wholly imaginative, as we are wont to say by them that build castles in the air, but so far substantially it worketh, not only to make a Cyrus, which had been but a particular excellency, as Nature might have done, but to bestow a Cyrus upon the world to make many Cyruses, if they will learn aright why and how that maker made him.[12]

Neither let it be deemed too saucy a comparison to balance the highest point of man's wit with the efficacy of Nature; but rather give right honor to the heavenly Maker of that maker, who, having made man to his own likeness, set him beyond and over all the works of that second nature, which in nothing he showeth so much as in Poetry, when with the force of a divine breath he bringeth things forth surpassing her doings, with no small [argument] to the incredulous of that first accursed fall of Adam, since our erected wit maketh us know what perfection is, and yet our infected will keepeth us from reaching unto it. But these arguments will by few be understood, and by fewer granted. Thus much (I hope) will be given me, that the Greeks with some probability of reason gave him the name above all names of learning.

Now let us go to a more ordinary opening of him, that the truth may be the more palpable: and so I hope, though we get not so unmatched a praise as the etymology of his names will grant, yet his very description, which no man will deny, shall not justly be barred from a principal commendation.

III
Propositio[13]

Poesy, therefore, is an art of imitation, for so Aristotle termeth it in the word μίμησις;[14] that is to say, a representing,

---

[12] that maker—Sidney here prepares to introduce his most important contribution to Renaissance critical theory.

[13] propositio—that part of an oration which presents the thesis sentence.

[14] *mimesis*—"imitation."

counterfeiting, or figuring forth—to speak metaphorically, a speaking picture—with this end, to teach and delight. (Of this have been three general kinds.)

IV
Divisio[15]

The chief, both in antiquity and excellency, were they that did imitate the unconceivable excellencies of God. Such were David in his Psalms; Solomon in his Song of Songs, in his Ecclesiastes, and Proverbs; Moses and Deborah in their Hymns; and the writer of Job; which, beside other, the learned Emanuel Tremellius and F[ranciscus] Junius do entitle the poetical part of the Scripture.[16] Against these none will speak that hath the Holy Ghost in due holy reverence. In this kind, though in a full wrong divinity, were Orpheus, Amphion, Homer in his Hymns, and many other, both Greek[s] and Romans. And this poesy must be used by whosoever will follow [St. James's][17] counsel in singing psalms when they are merry, and I know is used with the fruit of comfort by some, when in sorrowful pangs of their death-bringing sins, they find the consolation of the never-leaving goodness.

The second kind is of them that deal with matters philosophical: either moral, as Tyrtaeus, Phocylides, [and] Cato; or natural, as Lucretius, and Virgil's Georgics; or astronomical, as Manilius and Pontanus; or historical, as Lucan; which who mislike, the fault is in their judgment quite out of taste, and not in the sweet food of sweetly uttered knowledge.

But because this second sort is wrapped within the fold of the proposed subject, and takes not the free course of his own invention, whether they properly be poets or no let gram-

15 divisio—the part of the oration in which the argument is divided up into parts or topics for discussion.

16 Emanuel Tremellius and Franciscus Junius—two sixteenth-century Protestant scholars who published a widely used Latin translation of the Bible between 1575 and 1580.

17 St. James's counsel—"Is any merry? Let him sing psalms" (5.13).

marians dispute; and go to the third, indeed right poets, of whom chiefly this question ariseth; betwixt whom and these second is such a kind of difference as betwixt the meaner sort of painters, who counterfeit only such faces as are set before them, and the more excellent, who, having no law but wit, bestow that in colors upon you which is fittest for the eye to see: as the constant though lamenting look of Lucretia, when she punished in herself another's fault; wherein he painteth not Lucretia whom he never saw, but painteth the outward beauty of such a virtue.[18] For these third be they which most properly do imitate to teach and delight, and to imitate borrow nothing of what is, hath been, or shall be; but range, only reined with learned discretion, into the divine consideration of what may be, and should be.

These be they that, as the first and most noble sort may justly be termed *Vates*, so these are waited on in the excellentest languages and best understandings, with the foredescribed names of poets; for these indeed do merely make to imitate, and imitate both to delight and teach, and delight to move men to take that goodness in hand, which without delight they would fly as from a stranger, and teach, to make them know that goodness whereunto they are moved—which being the noblest scope to which ever any learning was directed, yet want there not idle tongues to bark at them.

These be subdivided into sundry more special denominations. The most notable be the heroic, lyric, tragic, comic, satiric, iambic, elegiac, pastoral, and certain others, some of these being termed according to the matter they deal with, some by the sort of verse they liked best to write in; for indeed the greatest part of poets have appareled their poetical inventions in that numbrous kind of writing which is called verse—indeed, but appareled, verse being but an ornament and no cause to poetry, since there have been many most excellent poets that never versified, and now swarm many versifiers that need never answer to the name of poets. For Xenophon, who did imitate so excellently as to

[18] Lucretia . . . such a virtue—Lucretia was the wife of L. Tarquinius Colatinus; raped by Sextus, son of Tarquinius Superbus, she committed suicide rather than live in shame. See Shakespeare's *Lucrece*.

give us *effigiem iusti imperii*, "the portraiture of a just Empire," under the name of Cyrus (as Cicero saith of him), made therein an absolute heroical poem. So did Heliodorus in his sugared invention of that picture of love in Theagenes and Chariclea; and yet both these wrote in prose, which I speak to show that it is not rhyming and versing that maketh a poet, no more than a long gown maketh an advocate, who though he pleaded in armor should be an advocate and no soldier. But it is that feigning notable images of virtues, vices, or what else, with that delightful teaching, which must be the right describing note to know a poet by, although indeed the Senate of Poets have chosen verse as their fittest raiment, meaning, as in matter they passed all in all, so in manner to go beyond them, not speaking (table-talk fashion or like men in a dream) words as they chanceably fall from the mouth, but peizing[19] each syllable of each word by just proportion according to the dignity of the subject.

V
Confirmatio[20]

Now, therefore, it shall not be amiss first to weigh this latter sort of poetry by his works, and then by his parts, and, if in neither of these anatomies he be condemnable, I hope we shall obtain a more favorable sentence.

This purifying of wit, this enriching of memory, enabling of judgment, and enlarging of conceit, which commonly we call learning, under what name soever it come forth, or to what immediate end soever it be directed, the final end is to lead and draw us to as high a perfection as our degenerate souls, made worse by their clay lodgings, can be capable of. This, according to the inclination of the man, bred many formed impressions. For some that thought this felicity principally to be gotten by knowledge and no knowledge to be so high of heavenly as acquaintance with the stars, gave themselves to astronomy;

[19] peizing—pressing down, weighing.
[20] confirmatio—the part of the oration which outlines the argument and gives proofs.

others, persuading themselves to be demigods if they knew the causes of things, became natural and supernatural philosophers; some an admirable delight drew to music; and some the certainty of demonstration to the mathematics. But all, one and other, having this scope—to know, and by knowledge to lift up the mind from the dungeon of the body to the enjoying his own divine essence.

But when by the balance of experience it was found that the astronomer looking to the stars might fall in a ditch, that the inquiring philosopher might be blind in himself, and the mathematician might draw forth a straight line with a crooked heart, then, lo, did proof, the overruler of opinions, make manifest that all these are but serving sciences, which, as they have a private end in themselves, so yet are they all directed to the highest end of the mistress knowledge, by the Greeks [called] ἀρχιτεκτονική,[21] which stands (as I think) in the knowledge of a man's self, in the ethic and politic consideration, with the end of well doing and not of well knowing only; even as the saddler's next end is to make a good saddle, but his further end to serve a nobler faculty, which is horsemanship; so the horseman's to soldiery, and the soldier not only to have the skill, but to perform the practice of a soldier. So that, the ending end of all earthly learning being virtuous action, those skills that most serve to bring forth that, have a most just title to be princes over all the rest. Wherein we can show the poet is worthy to have it before any other competitors, among whom principally to challenge it step forth the moral philosophers, whom methinks I see coming towards me with a sullen gravity, as though they could not abide vice by daylight, rudely clothed for to witness outwardly their contempt of outward things, with books in their hands against glory, whereto they set their names, sophistically speaking against subtlety, and angry with any man in whom they see the foul fault of anger.

These men casting largesse as they go of definitions, divi-

[21] *architektonike*—construction—the Platonic concept of a "master builder"—one who knows and does; the Aristotelian concept of active, purposive striving.

sions, and distinctions, with a scornful interrogative do soberly
ask whether it be possible to find any path so ready to lead a
man to virtue as that which teacheth what virtue is, and teacheth
it not only by delivering forth his very being, his causes, and
effects, but also by making known his enemy Vice, which must
be destroyed, and his cumbersome servant Passion, which must
be mastered; by showing the generalities that contains it, and by
the specialties that are derived from it; lastly, by plain setting
down, how it extends itself out of the limits of a man's own little
world to the government of families, and maintaining of public
societies.

The historian scarcely gives leisure to the moralist to say so
much, but that he, loaden with old mouse-eaten records, author-
izing himself (for the most part) upon other histories, whose
greatest authorities are built upon the notable foundation of hear-
say; having much ado to accord differing writers and to pick truth
out of partiality; better acquainted with a thousand years ago
than with the present age, and yet better knowing how this world
goes than how his own wit runs; curious for antiquities and inquisitive of novelties; a wonder to young folks and a tyrant in
table talk; denieth, in a great chafe, that any man for teaching of
virtue, and virtuous actions, is comparable to him. "I am *testis
temporum, lux veritatis, vita memoriae, magistra vitae, nuntia
vetustatis.*[22] The philosopher," saith he, "teacheth a disputative
virtue, but I do an active. His virtue is excellent in the dangerless
Academy of Plato, but mine showeth forth her honorable face
in the battles of Marathon, Pharsalia, Poitiers, and Agincourt.[23]
He teacheth virtue by certain abstract considerations, but I only
bid you follow the footing of them that have gone before you.
Old-aged experience goeth beyond the fine-witted philosopher,
but I give the experience of many ages. Lastly, if he make the

[22] I am *testis temporum, lux veritatis, vita memoriae, magistra vitae, nuntia
vetustatis.*—"I am the witness of the times, the light of truth, the life of
memory, the teacher of life, and the messenger of antiquity" (Cicero, *De
oratore* 2.9.36).
[23] battles of Marathon, Pharsalia, Poitiers, and Agincourt—Marathon,
490 B.C.; Pharsalia, 48 B.C.; Poitiers, 1356; Agincourt, 1415.

songbook, I put the learner's hand to the lute; and if he be the guide, I am the light."

Then would he allege you innumerable examples, confirming story by stories how much the wisest senators and princes have been directed by the credit of history, as Brutus, Alphonsus of Aragon, and who not, if need be?[24] At length the long line of their disputation makes a point in this, that the one giveth the precept, and the other the example.

Now, whom shall we find (since the question standeth for the highest form in the school of learning) to be moderator? Truly, as me seemeth, the poet; and if not a moderator, even the man that ought to carry the title from them both, and much more from all other serving sciences; therefore, compare we the poet with the historian, and with the moral philosopher; and, if he go beyond them both, no other human skill can match him. For, as for the divine, with all reverence he is ever to be excepted, not only for having his scope as far beyond any of these as eternity exceedeth a moment, but even for passing each of these in themselves. And for the lawyer, though *Jus* be the daughter of Justice, the chief of virtues, yet because he seeks to make men good rather *formidine poenae* than *virtutis amore*,[25] or, to say righter, doth not endeavor to make men good, but that their evil hurt not others, having no care, so he be a good citizen, how bad a man he be; therefore, as our wickedness maketh him necessary, and necessity maketh him honorable, so is he not in the deepest truth to stand in rank with these who all endeavor to take naughtiness away, and plant goodness even in the secretest cabinet of our souls. And these four are all that any way deal in the consideration of men's manners, which being the supreme knowledge, they that best breed it deserve the best commendation.

The philosopher, therefore, and the historian are they which

[24] Brutus, Alphonsus of Aragon—Brutus was a noted humanist, and Alphonso V of Aragon (1416–58) carried Livy, Caesar, and Quintus Curtius into battle with him.

[25] rather *formidine poenae* than *virtutis amore*—rather from fear of punishment than from love of virtue.

would win the goal, the one by precept, the other by example. But both, not having both, do both halt. For the philosopher, setting down with thorny arguments the bare rule, is so hard of utterance, and so misty to be conceived, that one that hath no other guide but him shall wade in him till he be old before he shall find sufficient cause to be honest: for his knowledge standeth so upon the abstract and general, that happy is that man who may understand him, and more happy that can apply what he doth understand. On the other side, the historian, wanting the precept, is so tied, not to what should be but to what is, to the particular truth of things and not to the general reason of things, that his example draweth no necessary consequence, and therefore a less fruitful doctrine.

Now doth the peerless poet perform both: for whatsoever the philosopher saith should be done, he giveth a perfect picture of it by some one by whom he presupposeth it was done; so as he coupleth the general notion with the particular example. A perfect picture, I say, for he yieldeth to the powers of the mind an image of that whereof the philosopher bestoweth but a wordish description, which doth neither strike, pierce, nor possess the sight of the soul so much as that other doth. For, as in outward things, to a man that had never seen an elephant or a rhinoceros, who should tell him most exquisitely all their shape[s], color, bigness, and particular marks, or of a gorgeous palace [the] architecture, who declaring the full beauties might well make the hearer able to repeat, as it were by rote, all he had heard, yet should never satisfy his inward conceit with being witness to itself of a true lively knowledge; but the same man, as soon as he might see those beasts well painted, or that house well in model, should straightways grow, without need of any description, to a judicial comprehending of them: so no doubt the philosopher with his learned definitions, be it of virtues or vices, matters of public policy or private government, replenisheth the memory with many infallible grounds of wisdom, which, notwithstanding, lie dark before the imaginative and judging power, if they be not illuminated, or figured forth, by the speaking picture of poesy.

Tully taketh much pains, and many times not without poetical helps, to make us know the force love of our country hath in us. Let us but hear old Anchises speaking in the middest of Troy's flames, or see Ulysses in the fullness of all Calypso's delights bewail his absence from barren and beggarly Ithaca.[26] Anger, the Stoics said, was a short madness: let but Sophocles bring you Ajax on a stage, killing and whipping sheep and oxen, thinking them the army of Greeks, with their chieftains Agamemnon and Menelaus, and tell me if you have not a more familiar insight into anger than finding in the Schoolmen his genus and difference.[27] See whether wisdom and temperance in Ulysses and Diomedes, valor in Achilles, friendship in Nisus and Euryalus,[28] contrarily, the remorse of conscience in Oedipus, the soon repenting pride in Agamemnon, the self-devouring cruelty in his father Atreus, the violence of ambition in the two Theban brothers,[29] the sour-sweetness of revenge of Medea, and, to fall even to an ignorant man carry not an apparent shining, and, lower, the Terentian Gnatho and our Chaucer's Pandar so expressed that we now use their names to signify their trades; and finally, all virtues, vices, and passions so in their own natural states laid to the view, that we seem not to hear of them, but clearly to see through them. But even in the most excellent determination of goodness, what philosopher's counsel can so readily direct a prince, as the feigned Cyrus in Xenophon; or a virtuous man in all fortunes, as Aeneas in Virgil; or a whole Commonwealth, as the way of Sir Thomas More's *Utopia?* I say the way, because where Sir Thomas More erred, it was the fault of the man and not of the poet, for that way of patterning a Commonwealth was most absolute, though he perchance hath not so absolutely performed it. For the question is, whether the feigned image of poetry or the regular instruction of philosophy

[26] Ithaca—Ionian island west of Greece, Ulysses' home.
[27] genus and difference—definition; type and distinguishing characteristics.
[28] Nisus and Euryalus—*Aeneid*, 9, Nisus died revenging his friend.
[29] two Theban brothers—Polynices and Eteocles, who exiled his brother (see Aeschylus, *Seven Against Thebes*).

hath the more force in teaching: wherein if the philosophers have more rightly showed themselves philosophers than the poets have attained to the high top of their profession, as in truth,

> *Mediocribus esse poetis,*
> *Non dii, non homines, non concessere columnae;* [30]

it is, I say again, not the fault of the art, but that by few men that art can be accomplished. Certainly, even our Savior Christ could as well have given the moral commonplaces of uncharitableness and humbleness as the divine narration of Dives and Lazarus; or of disobedience and mercy, as that heavenly discourse of the lost child and the gracious father; but that his thorough-searching wisdom knew the estate of Dives burning in hell, and of Lazarus in Abraham's bosom, would more constantly (as it were) inhabit both the memory and judgment. Truly, for myself, meseems I see before mine eyes the lost child's disdainful prodigality, turned to envy a swine's dinner: which by the learned divines are thought not historical acts, but instructing parables.

For conclusion, I say the Philosopher teacheth, but he teacheth obscurely, so as the learned only can understand him; that is to say, he teacheth them that are already taught. But the poet is the food for the tenderest stomachs, the poet is indeed the right popular philosopher, whereof Aesop's tales give good proof: whose pretty allegories, stealing under the formal tales of beasts, make many, more beastly than beasts, begin to hear the sound of virtue from these dumb speakers.

But now may it be alleged that, if this imagining of matters be so fit for the imagination, then must the historian needs surpass, who brings you images of true matters, such as indeed were done, and not such as fantastically or falsely may be suggested to have been done. Truly, Aristotle himself, in his discourse of poesy, plainly determineth this question, saying that poetry is φιλοσοφώτερον and σπουδαιότερον, that is to say, it is more philo-

---

[30] *Mediocribus esse poetis,/ Non dii, non homines, non concessere columnae*— "neither gods nor men nor bookstalls have allowed mediocrity in poets," *Ars Poetica*, Horace (*Epist.* 3.2.373–74).

sophical and more [studiously serious] than history. His reason is, because poesy dealeth with καθόλου, that is to say, with the universal consideration, and the history with καθ᾽ ἕκαστον the particular:[31] "now," saith he, "the universal weighs what is fit to be said or done, either in likelihood or necessity (which the poesy considereth in his imposed names), and the particular only marketh whether Alcibiades did, or suffered, this or that."[32] Thus far Aristotle: which reason of his (as all his) is most full of reason. For indeed, if the question were whether it were better to have a particular act truly or falsely set down, there is no doubt which is to be chosen, no more than whether you had rather have Vespasian's picture right as he was, or at the painter's pleasure nothing resembling. But if the question be for your own use and learning, whether it be better to have it set down as it should be, or as it was, then certainly is more doctrinable the feigned Cyrus in Xenophon than the true Cyrus in Justin, and the feigned Aeneas in Virgil than the right Aeneas in Dares Phrygius: as to a lady that desired to fashion her countenance to the best grace, a painter should more benefit her to portrait a most sweet face, writing Canidia upon it, than to paint Canidia as she was, who, Horace sweareth, was full ill favored.[33]

If the poet do his part aright, he will show you in Tantalus, Atreus, and such like, nothing that is not to be shunned; in Cyrus, Aeneas, Ulysses, each thing to be followed; where the historian, bound to tell things as things were, cannot be liberal (without he will be poetical) of a perfect pattern, but as in Alexander or Scipio himself, show doings, some to be liked, some to be misliked. And then how will you discern what to follow but by

[31] philosophoteron, spoudaioteron, katholou, and kathekaston, all of which Sidney translates.
[32] Aristotle's *Poetics* 9.3.
[33] the feigned Cyrus in Xenophon . . . the true Cyrus in Justin . . . Dares Phrygius . . . Canidia—Xenophon's *Cyropaedia* was a manual for the education of princes; Justin's *Historiae Philipicae* is a collection of extracts from Trogus Pompeius, very famous in Middle Ages; Dares Phrygius wrote a supposed eyewitness account of the fall of Troy called *De excidio Troiae historia*; Canidia was a Neapolitan courtesan who jilted Horace and then became the maligned old sorceress of *Satires* 1.8 and *Epod.* 5.

your own discretion, which you had without reading Q[uintus] Curtius?[34] And whereas a man may say, "though in universal consideration of doctrine the poet prevaileth, yet that the history, in his saying such a thing was done, doth warrant a man more in that he shall follow"; the answer is manifest: that if he stand upon that *was*—as if he should argue, because it rained yesterday, therefore it should rain today—then, indeed, hath it some advantage to a gross conceit; but if he know an example only informs a conjectured likelihood, and so go by reason, the poet doth so far exceed him, as he is to frame his example to that which is most reasonable, be it in warlike, politic, or private matters—where the historian in his bare *was* hath many times that which we call fortune to overrule the best wisdom. Many times he must tell events whereof he can yield no cause: or, if he do, it must be poetically.

For that a feigned example hath as much force to teach as a true example (for, as for to move, it is clear, since the feigned may be tuned to the highest key of passion), let us take one example wherein an historian and a poet did concur. Herodotus and Justin do both testify that Zopyrus, King Darius's faithful servant, seeing his master long resisted by the rebellious Babylonians, feigned himself in extreme disgrace of his king; for verifying of which, he caused his own nose and ears to be cut off, and so flying to the Babylonians, was received, and for his known valor so far credited, that he did find means to deliver them over to Darius.[35] Much like matter doth Livy record of Tarquinius and his son.[36] Xenophon excellently feigned such another stratagem performed by Abradates in Cyrus's behalf.[37] Now would I fain know, if occasion be presented unto you to serve your

[34] Quintus Curtius—the Roman author of a life of Alexander called *Historiarum Alexandri Magni Libri Decem.*

[35] Zopyrus—Herodotus, in *Persian Wars* 3.153–60, tells the story of Zopyrus, a servant of Darius who cut off his own ears and nose and fled to the Babylonians, pretending to be a victim of his master's cruelty; he then found an opportunity to betray the city to Darius.

[36] Livy record of Tarquinius and his son—Livy 1. 53–54.

[37] Abradates—actually Araspes in *Cyropaedia* 6.1.31.

prince by such an honest dissimulation, why you do not as well learn it of Xenophon's fiction as of the other's verity—and truly so much the better, as you shall save your nose by the bargain; for Abradates did not counterfeit so far. So, then, the best of the historian is subject to the poet; for whatsoever action, or faction, whatsoever counsel, policy, or war stratagem the historian is bound to recite, that may the poet (if he list) with his imitation make his own, beautifying it both for further teaching, and more delighting, as it please him, having all, from Dante's heaven to his hell, under the authority of his pen. Which if I be asked what poets have done so, as I might well name some, yet say I, and say again, I speak of the art, and not of the artificer.

Now, to that which commonly is attributed to the praise of history, in respect of the notable learning got by marking the success (as though therein a man should see virtue exalted and vice punished), truly that commendation is peculiar to poetry, and far off from history. For indeed, poetry ever sets virtue so out in her best colors, making fortune her well-waiting hand-maid, that one must needs be enamored of her. Well may you see Ulysses in a storm, and in other hard plights; but they are but exercises of patience and magnanimity, to make them shine the more in the near-following prosperity. And of the contrary part, if evil men come to the stage, they ever go out (as the tragedy-writer answered to one that misliked the show of such persons) so manacled as they little animate folks to follow them. But the history, being captived to the truth of a foolish world, is many times a terror from well-doing, and an encouragement to un-bridled wickedness.

For see we not valiant Miltiades rot in his fetters; the just Phocion and the accomplished Socrates put to death like traitors; the cruel Severus live prosperously; the excellent Severus miserably murdered; Sylla and Marius dying in their beds; Pompey and Cicero slain then when they would have thought exile a happiness? See we not virtuous Cato driven to kill himself, and rebel Caesar so advanced that his name yet, after 1,600 years, lasteth in the highest honor?[38] And mark but even Caesar's own words of the forenamed Sylla (who in that only did honestly, to put down his dishonest tyranny), *Literas nescivit,*[39] as if want of learning caused him to do well. He meant it not by poetry, which, not content with earthly plagues, deviseth new punishments in hell for tyrants, nor yet by philosophy, which teacheth *Occidendos esse;*[40] but no doubt by skill in history, for that indeed can afford you Cypselus, Periander, Phalaris, Dionysius, and I know not how many more [of] the same kennel, that speed well enough in their abominable injustice or usurpation.[41]

I conclude, therefore, that he excelleth History, not only in furnishing the mind with knowledge, but in setting it forward to that which deserves to be called and accounted good: which setting forward, and moving to well-doing, indeed setteth the laurel crown upon the poets as victorious, not only of the historian, but over the philosopher, howsoever in teaching it may be questionable. For suppose it be granted (that which I suppose with great reason may be denied) that the philosopher, in respect of his methodical proceeding, teach more perfectly than the poet,

---

[38] Miltiades . . . Phocion . . . cruel Severus . . . excellent Severus . . . Sylla and Marius . . . Pompey and Cicero—Miltiades was an Athenian general (540?–?489 B.C.) who conquered the Persians at Marathon in 490 B.C. but was later imprisoned by the Athenians for leading government troops in an unauthorized campaign; Phocion was an Athenian general and statesman (402?–317 B.C.) executed for treason because he opposed an unjust war; cruel Severus—Lucius Septimus Severus, emperor from 193–211, a great plunderer of cities; excellent Severus—Alexander Severus, emperor from 222–235, a great reformer slain by mutinous troops; Sylla and Marius were rival dictators in the Rome of Julius Caesar's boyhood; Pompey and Cicero: Pompey the Great (106–48 B.C.) was a triumvir with Caesar and Crassus, conqueror of Mithridates, defeated by Caesar at Pharsalia, and slain off Egypt; Cicero was a great statesman, orator, and writer (106–43B.C.) killed at Antony's behest.

[39] *Literas nescivit*—he did not know literature.

[40] *Occidendos esse*—that they must be killed.

[41] Cypselus, Periander, Phalaris, Dionysius—four famous tyrants, the first two of seventh century B.C. Corinth; Phalaris was a tyrant of Agrigentum (570–549) noted for his excessive cruelty; Dionysius the Elder was tyrant of Syracuse from 406–367.

yet do I think that no man is so much φιλοφιλόσοφος[42] as to compare the philosopher, in moving, with the poet.

And that moving is of a higher degree than teaching, it may by this appear, that it is well-nigh both the cause and effect of teaching. For who will be taught, if he be not moved with desire to be taught? and what so much good doth that teaching bring forth (I speak still of moral doctrine) as that it moveth one to do that which it doth teach? For, as Aristotle saith, it is not γνῶσις but πρᾶξις must be the fruit.[43] And how πρᾶξις cannot be, without being moved to practise, it is no hard matter to consider.

The philosopher showeth you the way, he informeth you of the particularities, as well of the tediousness of the way, as of the pleasant lodging you shall have when your journey is ended, as of the many by-turnings that may divert you from your way. But this is to no man but to him that will read him, and read him with attentive studious painfulness; which constant desire whosoever hath in him, hath already passed half the hardness of the way, and therefore is beholding to the philosopher but for the other half. Nay truly, learned men have learnedly thought that where once reason hath so much overmastered passion as that the mind hath a free desire to do well, the inward light each mind hath in itself is as good as a philosopher's book, since in nature we know it is well to do well, and what is well and what is evil, although not in the words of art[44] which philosophers bestow upon us. For out of natural conceit the philosophers drew it; but to be moved to do that which we know, or to be moved with desire to know, *Hoc opus, hic labor est.*[45]

Now therein of all sciences (I speak still of human, and according to the human conceit) is our poet the monarch; for he doth not only show the way, but giveth so sweet a prospect into the way, as will entice any man to enter into it. Nay, he doth, as

[42] *philophilosophos*—a lover of philosophers.
[43] *gnosis . . . praxis*—knowing . . . acting; *Ethics* 1.1.
[44] words of art—skill; i.e., the special language and terms of philosophy.
[45] *Hoc opus, hic labor est*—"This is the job, here is the work to be done" (*Aeneid* 6.129).

if your journey should lie through a fair vineyard, at the very first give you a cluster of grapes, that, full of that taste, you may long to pass further. He beginneth not with obscure definitions, which must blur the margent with interpretations, and load the memory with doubtfulness; but he cometh to you with words set in delightful proportion, either accompanied with, or prepared for, the well-enchanting skill of music; and with a tale, forsooth, he cometh unto you, with a tale which holdeth children from play, and old men from the chimney corner. And, pretending no more, doth intend the winning of the mind from wickedness to virtue: even as the child is often brought to take most wholesome things by hiding them in such other as have a pleasant taste: which, if one should begin to tell them the nature of the aloes[46] or rhubarb they should receive, would sooner take their physic at their ears than at their mouth. So it is in men (most of which be childish in the best things, till they be cradled in their graves): glad they will be to hear the tales of Hercules, Achilles, Cyrus, and Aeneas; and, hearing them, must needs hear the right description of wisdom, valor, and justice; which, if they had been barely, that is to say philosophically, set out, they would swear they be brought to school again.

That imitation whereof poetry is, hath the most conveniency to nature of all other, insomuch that, as Aristotle saith, those things which in themselves are horrible, as cruel battles, unnatural monsters, are made in poetical imitation delightful.[47] Truly, I have known men, that even with reading *Amadis de Gaule*[48] (which God knoweth wanteth much of a perfect poesy) have found their hearts moved to the exercise of courtesy, liberality, and especially courage. Who readeth Aeneas carrying old Anchises on his back, that wisheth not it were his fortune to perform so excellent an act? Whom do not those words of Turnus move, the tale of Turnus having planted his image in the imagination?—

[46] aloes—a bitter purgative drink from the juice of the herb, aloe.
[47] as Aristotle saith—*Poetics* 1.5.
[48] *Amadis de Gaule*—popular Spanish romance of chivalry, completed by Garcia del Montalvo in the second half of the fifteenth century.

Fugientem haec terra videbit?
Usque adeone mori miserum est?[49]

Where the philosophers, as they think scorn to delight, so must they be content little to move, saving wrangling whether virtue be the chief or the only good, whether the contemplative or the active life do excel: which Plato and Boethius[50] well knew, and therefore made mistress philosophy very often borrow the masking raiment of poesy. For even those hard-hearted evil men who think virtue a school name, and know no other good but *indulgere genio*,[51] and therefore despise the austere admonitions of the philosopher, and feel not the inward reason they stand upon, yet will be content to be delighted—which is all the good fellow poet seems to promise—and so steal to see the form of goodness, which seen they cannot but love ere themselves be aware, as if they took a medicine of cherries. Infinite proofs of the strange effects of this poetical invention might be alleged; only two shall serve, which are so often remembered as I think all men know them.

The one, of Menenius Agrippa,[52] who, when the whole people of Rome had resolutely divided themselves from the Senate, with apparent show of utter ruin, though he were (for that time) an excellent orator, came not among them upon trust either of figurative speeches or cunning insinuations, and much less with far-fetched maxims of philosophy, which (especially if they were Platonic) they must have learned geometry before they could well have conceived; but forsooth he behaves himself like

[49] *Fugientem haec terra videbit? / Usque adeone mori miserum est?* "Shall this ground see [Turnus] fleeing? Is it so hard to die?" (*Aeneid* 12.645–46).

[50] Boethius—d. 524 A.D., author of *De Consolatione Philosophiae*, a work on the desirability of contemplative retreat from Fortune; the form mixes prose dialogue with poetic passages.

[51] *indulgere genio*—"to indulge one's own inclinations" (*Satires* 5.151, Persius).

[52] Menenius Agrippa—a Roman general said to have reconciled patricians and plebeians at the secession of 494 B.C.

a homely and familiar poet. He telleth them a tale, that there was a time when all the parts of the body made a mutinous conspiracy against the belly, which they thought devoured the fruits of each other's labor; they concluded they would let so unprofitable a spender starve. In the end, to be short (for the tale is notorious, and as notorious that it was a tale), with punishing the belly they plagued themselves. This applied by him wrought such effect in the people, as I never read that only words brought forth but then so sudden and so good an alteration; for upon reasonable conditions a perfect reconcilement ensued.

The other is of Nathan the Prophet,[53] who, when the holy David had so far forsaken God as to confirm adultery with murder, when he was to do the tenderest office of a friend, in laying his own shame before his eyes, sent by God to call again so chosen a servant, how doth he it but by telling of a man whose beloved lamb was ungratefully taken from his bosom—the application most divinely true, but the discourse itself feigned. Which made David (I speak of the second and instrumental cause) as in a glass see his own filthiness, as that heavenly Psalm of mercy well testifieth.

By these, therefore, examples and reasons, I think it may be manifest that the poet, with that same hand of delight, doth draw the mind more effectually than any other art doth: and so a conclusion not unfitly ensue, that, as virtue is the most excellent resting place for all worldly learning to make his end of, so poetry, being the most familiar to teach it, and most princely to move towards it, in the most excellent work is the most excellent workman.

But I am content not only to decipher him by his works (although works in commendation and dispraise must ever hold a high authority), but more narrowly will examine his parts:[54] so that, as in a man, though all together may carry a presence full of majesty and beauty, perchance in some one defectious piece we

[53] Nathan the Prophet—2 *Samuel* 12:1–7.
[54] parts—Sidney here moves from the first half of the confirmation to the second.

may find a blemish. Now in his parts, kinds, or species (as you list to term them), it is to be noted that some poesies have coupled together two or three kinds, as the tragical and comical, whereupon is risen the tragicomical. Some in the [like] manner, have mingled prose and verse, as Sannazaro[55] and Boethius. Some have mingled matters heroical and pastoral. But that cometh all to one in this question, for if severed they be good, the conjunction cannot be hurtful. Therefore, perchance forgetting some, and leaving some as needless to be remembered, it shall not be amiss in a word to cite the special kinds, to see what faults may be found in the right use of them.

Is it then the pastoral poem which is misliked? For perchance where the hedge is lowest they will soonest leap over. Is the poor pipe disdained, which sometimes out of Melibaeus' mouth can show the misery of people under hard lords and ravening soldiers? and again, by Tityrus, what blessedness is derived to them that lie lowest from the goodness of them that sit highest? sometimes, under the pretty tales of wolves and sheep, can include the whole considerations of wrongdoing and patience? sometimes show that contentions for trifles can get but a trifling victory, where perchance a man may see that even Alexander and Darius, when they strave who should be cock of this world's dunghill, the benefit they got was that the after-livers may say,

> *Haec memini et victum frustra contendere Thyrsin:*
> *Ex illo Coridon, Coridon est tempore nobis?*[56]

Or is it the lamenting elegiac, which in a kind heart would move rather pity than blame, who bewaileth with the great phi-

---

[55] Sannazaro—Italian poet (1458-1530), author of the *Arcadia*, a pastoral romance of mixed prose and verse which influenced Sidney.

[56] *Haec memini . . . tempore nobis*—"These things I remember, how the vanquished Thyrsis struggled in vain. From that day on it has been Coridon, only Coridon with us" (Virgil's *Eclogues* 7.69-70).

losopher Heraclitus[57] the weakness of mankind and the wretchedness of the world; who surely is to be praised, either for compassionate accompanying just causes of lamentations, or for
rightly painting out how weak be the passions of woefulness?

Is it the bitter but wholesome iambic, who rubs the galled
mind, in making shame the trumpet of villainy with bold and
open crying out against naughtiness?

Or the satiric, who

Omne vafer vitium ridenti tangit amico;[58]

who sportingly never leaveth till he make a man laugh at folly,
and (at length ashamed) to laugh at himself, which he cannot
avoid without avoiding the folly; who, while

circum praecordia ludit,[59]

giveth us to feel how many headaches a passionate life bringeth
us to—how, when all is done,

Est Ulubris, animus si nos non deficit aequus?[60]

No, perchance it is the comic, whom naughty play-makers
and stage-keepers have justly made odious. To the arguments of
abuse I will after answer. Only thus much now is to be said, that
the comedy is an imitation of the common errors of our life,
which he representeth in the most ridiculous and scornful sort
that may be, so as it is impossible that any beholder can be con-

[57] Heraclitus—an Ephesian philosopher of 6–5th century B.C. who was
highly pessimistic and believed that the whole world would be consumed
by mutability; he counseled indifference to the workings of Fortune.

[58] *Omne vafer vitium ridenti tangit amico*—"manages to probe every
fault while making his friend laugh" (Persius, *Satires* 1.116).

[59] *circum praecordia ludit*—"he plays about the innermost feelings"
(Persius, *Satires* 1.117).

[60] *Est Ulubris . . . aequus?*—The whole phrase is: "What you seek is
here; it is at Ulubrae, if a well-balanced mind does not fail you there"
(Horace, *Epistles* 1.11.30).

tent to be such a one. Now, as in geometry the oblique must be known as well as the right, and in arithmetic the odd as well as the even, so in the actions of our life who seeth not the filthiness of evil wanteth a great foil[61] to perceive the beauty of virtue. This doth the comedy handle so in our private and domestical matters as with hearing it we get, as it were, an experience, what is to be looked for of a niggardly Demea, of a crafty Davus, of a flattering Gnatho, of a vainglorious Thraso,[62] and not only to know what effects are to be expected, but to know who be such, by the signifying badge given them by the comedian. And little reason hath any man to say that men learn the evil by seeing it so set out; since, as I said before, there is no man living but, by the force truth hath in nature, no sooner seeth these men play their parts, but wisheth them in *pistrinum*:[63] although perchance the sack of his own faults lie so behind his back that he seeth not himself to dance the same measure; whereto yet nothing can more open his eyes than to see his own actions contemptibly set forth.

So that the right use of comedy will (I think) by nobody be blamed, and much less of the high and excellent tragedy, that openeth the greatest wounds, and showeth forth the ulcers that are covered with tissue; that maketh kings fear to be tyrants, and tyrants manifest their tyrannical humors; that, with stirring the affects of admiration and commiseration, teacheth the uncertainty of this world, and upon how weak foundations gilden roofs are builded; that maketh us know,

> *Qui sceptra saevus duro imperio regit,*
> *Timet timentes, metus in auctorem redit.*[64]

[61] foil—reflecting setting used behind jewels to show their facets.

[62] niggardly Demea . . . crafty Davus . . . flattering Gnatho . . . vainglorious Thraso—the Terentian heavy father, clever servant, parasite, and braggart, respectively.

[63] *pistrinum*—a pounding mill, used as a punishment for slaves.

[64] *Qui sceptra . . . redit*—"He who rules his people with a harsh government fears those who fear him; the fear returns upon its author" (Seneca, *Oedipus* 705).

But how much it can move, Plutarch yieldeth a notable testimony of the abominable tyrant Alexander Pheraeus,[65] from whose eyes a tragedy, well made and represented, drew abundance of tears, who, without all pity, had murdered infinite numbers, and some of his own blood, so as he that was not ashamed to make matters for tragedies, yet could not resist the sweet violence of a tragedy. And if it wrought no further good in him, it was that he, in despite of himself, withdrew himself from hearkening to that which might mollify his hardened heart. But it is not the tragedy they do mislike; for it were too absurd to cast out so excellent a representation of whatsoever is most worthy to be learned.

Is it the lyric[66] that most displeaseth, who with his tuned lyre, and well-accorded voice, giveth praise (the reward of virtue) to virtuous acts? who giveth moral precepts, and natural problems? who sometime raiseth up his voice to the height of the heavens in singing the lauds of the immortal God? Certainly, I must confess my own barbarousness, I never heard the old song of Percy and Douglas that I found not my heart moved more than with a trumpet; and yet is it sung but by some blind crowder,[67] with no rougher voice than rude style, which being so evil appareled in the dust and cobwebs of that uncivil age,[68] what would it work, trimmed in the gorgeous eloquence of Pindar? In Hungary I have seen it the manner at all feasts, and other such like meetings, to have songs of their ancestors' valor, which that right soldierlike nation think one of the chiefest kindlers of brave courage. The incomparable Lacedemonians did not only carry that kind of music ever with them to the field, but even at home, as such songs were made, so were they all content to be singers of them, when the lusty men were to tell what they did, the old men what they had done, and the young what they would do. And where a man may say that Pindar many times praiseth highly victories of small moment (rather

[65] Plutarch . . . Alexander Pheraeus—Plutarch describes this tyrant of Pherae in his *Life of Pelopidas*, 20.
[66] lyric—Pindaric ode.
[67] crowder—fiddler.
[68] uncivil age—Middle Ages.

matters of sport than virtue), as it may be answered it was the
fault of the poet and not of the poetry, so indeed the chief fault
was in the time and custom of the Greeks, who set those toys at
so high a price that Philip of Macedon reckoned a horse race
won at Olympus among his three fearful felicities. But as the
inimitable Pindar often did, so is that kind most capable and most
fit to awake the thoughts from the sleep of idleness to embrace
honorable enterprises.

There rests the heroical, whose very name (I think) should
daunt all backbiters (for by what conceit can a tongue be
directed to speak evil of that which draweth with him no less
champions than Achilles, Cyrus, Aeneas, Turnus, Tydeus, [and]
Rinaldo?): who doth not only teach and move to a truth, but
teacheth and moveth to the most high and excellent truth; who
maketh magnanimity and justice shine through all misty fearful-
ness and foggy desires; who, if the saying of Plato and Tully be
true—that who could see virtue would be wonderfully ravished
with the love of her beauty—this man setteth her out to make her
more lovely in her holiday apparel, to the eye of any that will
deign not to disdain until they understand. But if anything be
already said in the defense of sweet poetry, all concurreth to the
maintaining the heroical, which is not only a kind, but the best
and most accomplished kind of poetry. For as the image of each
action stirreth and instructeth the mind, so the lofty image of
such worthies most inflameth the mind with desire to be worthy,
and informs with counsel how to be worthy. Only let Aeneas be
worn in the tablet of your memory, how he governeth himself in
the ruin of his country, in the preserving his old father, and
carrying away his religious ceremonies, in obeying gods' commandment to leave Dido, though not only all passionate kindness
but even the human consideration of virtuous gratefulness would
have craved other of him; how in storms, how in sports, how in
war, how in peace, how a fugitive, how victorious, how besieged,
how besieging, how to strangers, how to allies, how to enemies,
how to his own, (lastly) how in his inward self and how in his
outward government, and (I think, in a mind most prejudiced

with a prejudicating humor) he will be found in excellency fruitful, yea, as Horace saith,

Melius Chrysippo et Crantore.[69]

But truly I imagine it falleth out with these poet-whippers, as with some good women who often are sick but in faith they cannot tell where, so the name of poetry is odious to them, but neither his cause nor effects, neither the sum that contains him nor the particularities descending from him, give any fast handle to their carping dispraise.

Since then poetry[70] is of all human learnings the most ancient and of most fatherly antiquity, as from whence other learnings have taken their beginnings; since it is so universal that no learned nation doth despise it, nor barbarous nation is without it; since both Roman and Greek gave such divine names unto it, the one of "prophesying," the other of "making," and that indeed that name of "making" is fit for him, considering that where all other arts retain themselves within their subject, and receive, as it were, their being from it, the poet only bringeth his own stuff, and doth not learn a conceit out of a matter, but maketh matter for a conceit; since neither his description nor end containing any evil, the thing described cannot be evil; since his effects be so good as to teach goodness and delight the learners of it; since therein (namely in moral doctrine, the chief of all knowledges) he doth not only far pass the historian, but, for instructing, is well-nigh comparable to the philosopher, for moving, leaveth him behind him; since the Holy Scripture (wherein there is no uncleanness) hath whole parts in it poetical, and that even our Savior Christ vouchsafed to use the flowers of it; since all his kinds are not only in their united forms but in their severed dissections fully commendable; I think (and think I think rightly)

---

[69] *Melius Chrysippo et Crantore*—"Better than [the philosophers] Chrysippus and Crantor" (Horace, *Epist.* 1.2.4).

[70] Since then poetry—Sidney here summarizes the entire argument so far presented.

the laurel crown appointed for triumphant captains does worthily (of all other learnings) honor the poet's triumph.

VI
Refutatio[71]

But because we have ears as well as tongues, and that the lightest reasons that may be will seem to weigh greatly if nothing be put in the counterbalance, let us hear, and, as well as we can, ponder, what objections be made against this art, which may be worthy either of yielding or answering.

First, truly I note not only in these μισομούσοι,[72] poet-haters, but in all that kind of people who seek a praise by dispraising others, that they do prodigally spend a great many wandering words in quips and scoffs, carping and taunting at each thing, which, by stirring the spleen, may stay the brain from a thorough beholding the worthiness of the subject. Those kind of objections, as they are full of a very idle easiness, since there is nothing of so sacred a majesty but that an itching tongue may rub itself upon it, so deserve they no other answer, but, instead of laughing at the jest, to laugh at the jester. We know a playing wit can praise the discretion of an ass, the comfortableness of being in debt, and the jolly commodities of being sick of the plague. So of the contrary side, if we will turn Ovid's verse,

Ut lateat virtus proximitate mali,[73]

that "good lie hid in nearness of the evil," Agrippa will be as merry in showing the vanity of science as Erasmus was in the commending of folly.[74] Neither shall any man or matter escape

---

[71] *refutatio*—the consideration and rejection of opposing arguments.
[72] *misomousoi*—poet-haters.
[73] *Ut lateat virtus proximitate mali*—"That virtue lies hidden by the proximity of evil" (*Ars Amatoria* 2.662).
[74] Agrippa . . . Erasmus—Henricus Cornelius Agrippa (1486–1535), German humanist, wrote *De incertitudine et vanitate scientiarum*, an attack on the educational methods of his day (1531); Desiderius Erasmus (1466–1536) published the *Praise of Folly* in 1510.

some touch of these smiling railers. But for Erasmus and Agrippa, they had another foundation than the superficial part would promise. Marry, these other pleasant fault-finders, who will correct the verb before they understand the noun, and confute others' knowledge before they confirm their own, I would have them only remember that scoffing cometh not of wisdom; so as the best title in true English they get with their merriments is to be called good fools, for so have our brave forefathers ever termed that humorous kind of jesters.

But that which giveth greatest scope to their scorning humor is "riming" and "versing."[75] It is already said (and, as I think, truly said) it is not rhyming and versing that maketh poesy. One may be a poet without versing, and a versifier without poetry. But yet presuppose it were inseparable (as indeed it seemeth Scaliger judgeth)[76] truly it were an inseparable commendation. For if *Oratio* next to *Ratio*, speech next to reason, be the greatest gift bestowed upon mortality, that cannot be praiseless which doth most polish that blessing of speech; which considereth each word, not only (as a man may say) by his forcible quality, but by his best measured quantity, carrying even in themselves a harmony (without, perchance, number, measure, order, proportion be in our time grown odious). But lay aside the just praise it hath, by being the only fit speech for music (music, I say, the most divine striker of the senses), thus much is undoubtedly true, that if reading be foolish without remembering, memory being the only treasure of knowledge, those words which are fittest for memory are likewise most convenient for knowledge.

Now, that verse far exceedeth prose in the knitting up of the memory, the reason is manifest—the words (besides their delight, which hath a great affinity to memory) being so set as one [word] cannot be lost but the whole work fails; which accusing itself, calleth the remembrance back to itself, and so most strongly confirmeth it. Besides, one word so, as it were, begetting another, as, be it in rhyme or measured verse, by the former

---

[75] "riming" and "versing"—16th century terms, respectively, for accentual-syllabic and quantitative verse.

[76] Scaliger—Julius Caesar Scaliger (1484-1558) wrote *Poetice*.

a man shall have a near guess to the follower: lastly, even they that have taught the art of memory have showed nothing so apt for it as a certain room divided into many places well and thoroughly known. Now, that hath the verse in effect perfectly, every word having his natural seat, which seat must needs make the word remembered. But what needs more in a thing so known to all men? Who is it that ever was scholar that doth not carry away some verses of Virgil, Horace, or Cato, which in his youth he learned, and even to his old age serve him for hourly lessons? As,

> *Percontatorem fugito nam garrulus idem est;*[77]
> *Dum sibi quisque placet credula turba sumus.*[78]

But the fitness it hath for memory is notably proved by all delivery of arts: wherein for the most part, from grammar to logic, mathematics, physic, and the rest, the rules chiefly necessary to be borne away are compiled in verses. So that, verse being in itself sweet and orderly, and being best for memory, the only handle of knowledge, it must be in jest that any man can speak against it.

Now then go we to the most important imputations laid to the poor poets. For aught I can yet learn, they are these. First, that there being many other more fruitful knowledges, a man might better spend his time in them than in this. Secondly, that it is the mother of lies. Thirdly, that it is the nurse of abuse, infecting us with many pestilent desires, with a siren['s] sweetness drawing the mind to the serpent's tale of sinful fancies—and herein, especially, comedies give the largest field to ear (as Chaucer saith)[79]—how both in other nations and in ours, before poets did soften us, we were full of courage, given to martial exercises, the pillars of manlike liberty, and not lulled asleep in shady idleness with poets' pastimes. And lastly, and chiefly, they

[77] *Percontatorem . . . est*—"Flee the inquisitive man, for he will repeat what you tell him" (Horace, *Epist.* 1.18.69).
[78] *Dum . . . sumus*—"While each of us flatters himself, we are all a credulous mob" (Ovid, *Remedia Amores*, 686).
[79] as Chaucer saith—*Knight's Tale*, 28.

cry out with an open mouth, as if they had overshot Robin Hood, that Plato banished them out of his Commonwealth. Truly, this is much, if there be much truth in it.

First, to the first, that a man might better spend his time is a reason indeed: but it doth (as they say) but *petere principium:*[80] for if it be, as I affirm, that no learning is so good as that which teacheth and moveth to virtue, and that none can both teach and move thereto so much as poesy, then is the conclusion manifest that ink and paper cannot be to a more profitable purpose employed. And certainly, though a man should grant their first assumption, it should follow (methinks) very unwillingly, that good is not good because better is better. But I still and utterly deny that there is sprung out of earth a more fruitful knowledge.

To the second therefore, that they should be the principal liars, I answer paradoxically (but truly, I think truly) that of all writers under the sun the poet is the least liar, and, though he would, as a poet can scarcely be a liar. The astronomer, with his cousin the geometrician, can hardly escape, when they take upon them to measure the height of the stars. How often, think you, do the physicians lie, when they aver things good for sicknesses, which afterwards send Charon a great number of souls drowned in a potion before they come to his ferry? And no less of the rest, which take upon them to affirm. Now, for the poet, he nothing affirmeth, and therefore never lieth. For, as I take it, to lie is to affirm that to be true which is false; so as the other artists, and especially the historian, affirming many things, can, in the cloudy knowledge of mankind, hardly escape from many lies. But the poet (as I said before) never affirmeth. The poet never maketh any circles about your imagination, to conjure you to believe for true what he writeth. He citeth not authorities of other histories, but even for his entry calleth the sweet Muses to inspire unto him a good invention; in truth, not laboring to tell you what is, or is not, but what should or should not be. And

[80] *petere principium*—beg the question.

therefore, though he recount things not true, yet because he telleth them not for true, he lieth not—without we will say that Nathan lied in his speech, before alleged, to David; which as a wicked man durst scarce say, so think I none so simple would say that Aesop lied in the tales of his beasts: for who thinketh that Aesop wrote it for actually true were well worthy to have his name chronicled among the beasts he writeth of. What child is there that, coming to a play, and seeing *Thebes* written in great letters upon an old door, doth believe that it is Thebes? If then a man can arrive to the child's age, to know that the poets' persons and doings are but pictures what should be, and not stories what have been, they will never give the lie to things not affirmatively but allegorically and figuratively written. And therefore, as in history, looking for truth, they may go away full fraught with falsehood, so in poesy, looking but for fiction, they shall use the narration but as an imaginative groundplot of a profitable invention. But hereto is replied, that the poets give names to men they write of, which argueth a conceit of an actual truth, and so, not being true, proveth a falsehood. And doth the lawyer lie then, when under the names of "John of the Stile" and "John of the Noakes" he puteth his case?[81] But that is easily answered. Their naming of men is but to make their picture the more lively, and not to build any history; painting men, they cannot leave men nameless. We see we cannot play at chess but that we must give names to our chessmen; and yet, methinks, he were a very partial champion of truth that would say we lied for giving a piece of wood the reverend title of a bishop. The poet nameth Cyrus and Aeneas no other way than to show what men of their fames, fortunes, and estates should do.

Their third is, how much it abuseth men's wit, training it to wanton sinfulness and lustful love, for, indeed, that is the principal, if not only, abuse I can hear alleged. They say the comedies rather teach than reprehend amorous conceits. They say the lyric

---

[81] "John of the Stile" and "John of the Noakes"—the British law court's equivalent of "John Doe" and "Richard Roe."

is larded with passionate sonnets, the elegiac weeps the want of his mistress, and that even to the heroical Cupid hath ambitiously climbed. Alas, Love, I would thou couldst as well defend thyself as thou canst offend others. I would those on whom thou dost attend could either put thee away, or yield good reason why they keep thee. But grant love of beauty to be a beastly fault (although it be very hard, since only man, and no beast, hath that gift to discern beauty); grant that lovely name of love to deserve all hateful reproaches (although even some of my masters the philosophers spent a good deal of their lamp-oil in setting forth the excellency of it); grant, I say, what they will have granted; that not only love, but lust, but vanity, but (if they list) scurrility, possess many leaves of the poets' books: yet think I, when this is granted, they will find their sentence may with good manners put the last words foremost, and not say that poetry abuseth man's wit, but that man's wit abuseth poetry.

For I will not deny but that man's wit may make poesy, which should be εἰκαστική, which some learned have defined, "figuring forth good things," to be φανταστική,[82] which doth, contrariwise, infect the fancy with unworthy objects, as the painter should give to the eye either some excellent perspective, or some fine picture, fit for building or fortification, or containing in it some notable example, as Abraham sacrificing his son Isaac, Judith killing Holofernes, David fighting with Goliath, may leave those, and please an ill-pleased eye with wanton shows of better hidden matters. But what, shall the abuse of a thing make the right use odious? Nay truly, though I yield that poesy may not only be abused, but that being abused, by the reason of his sweet charming force, it can do more hurt than any other army of words, yet shall it be so far from concluding that the abuse should give reproach to the abused, that contrariwise it is a good reason, that whatsoever, being abused, doth most harm, being rightly used (and upon the right use each thing receives his title), doth most good.

[82] *eikastike . . . phantastike*—representing, imitating . . . producing images.

Do we not see the skill of physic (the best rampire[83] to our often-assaulted bodies), being abused, teach poison, the most violent destroyer? Doth not knowledge of law, whose end is to even and right all things, being abused, grow the crooked fosterer of horrible injuries? Doth not (to go to the highest) God's word abused breed heresy, and his Name abused become blasphemy? Truly, a needle cannot do much hurt, and as truly (with leave of ladies be it spoken) it cannot do much good. With a sword thou mayest kill thy father, and with a sword thou mayest defend thy prince and country. So that, as in their calling poets fathers of lies they said nothing, so in this their argument of abuse they prove the commendation.

They allege herewith, that before poets began to be in price our nation had set their hearts' delight upon action, and not imagination, rather doing things worthy to be written, than writing things fit to be done. What that before-time was, I think scarcely Sphinx can tell, since no memory is so ancient that hath the precedence of poetry. And certain it is that, in our plainest homeliness, yet never was the Albion nation without poetry. Marry, this argument, though it be leveled against poetry, yet is it indeed a chain shot against all learning, or bookishness, as they commonly term it. Of such mind were certain Goths, of whom it is written that, having in the spoil of a famous city taken a fair library, one hangman, belike, fit to execute the fruits of their wits, who had murdered a great number of bodies, would have set fire in it. "No," said another very gravely, "take heed what you do, for while they are busy about those toys, we shall with more leisure conquer their countries."

This indeed is the ordinary doctrine of ignorance, and many words sometimes I have heard spent in it: but because this reason is generally against all learning, as well as poetry, or rather, all learning but poetry; because it were too large a digression to handle it, or at least too superfluous (since it is manifest that all government of action is to be gotten by knowledge, and knowledge best by gathering many knowledges, which is reading), I only, with Horace, to him that is of that opinion,

[83] rampire—rampart.

Iubeo stultum esse libenter;[84]

for as for poetry itself, it is the freest from this objection. For poetry is the companion of camps.

I dare undertake, Orlando Furioso, or honest King Arthur, will never displease a soldier: but the quiddity of *ens* and *prima materia*[85] will hardly agree with a corslet. And therefore, as I said in the beginning, even Turks and Tartars are delighted with poets. Homer, a Greek, flourished before Greece flourished. And if to a slight conjecture a conjecture may be opposed, truly it may seem, that, as by him their learned men took almost their first light of knowledge, so their active men received their first motions of courage. Only Alexander's example may serve, who by Plutarch is accounted of such virtue, that fortune was not his guide but his footstool; whose acts speak for him—though Plutarch did not—indeed the Phoenix of warlike princes. This Alexander left his schoolmaster, living Aristotle, behind him, but took dead Homer with him. He put the philosopher Callisthenes to death for his seeming philosophical, indeed mutinous, stubbornness, but the chief thing he was ever heard to wish for was that Homer had been alive. He well found he received more bravery of mind by the pattern of Achilles than by hearing the definition of fortitude, and therefore, if Cato misliked Fulvius for carrying Ennius with him to the field, it may be answered that, if Cato misliked it, the noble Fulvius liked it, or else he had not done it: for it was not the excellent Cato Uticensis (whose authority I would much more have reverenced), but it was the former, in truth a bitter punisher of faults, but else a man that had never sacrificed to the Graces.[86] He misliked and cried out against all Greek learning, and yet, being four score years old, began to

---

[84] *Iubeo stultum esse libenter*—"I bid him be a fool to his heart's content" (*Satires* 1.1.63).

[85] quiddity of *ens* and *prima materia*—philosophical terms, meaning the thisness of essence and the prime matter of the universe.

[86] Cato . . . a bitter punisher of faults, but else a man that had never sacrificed to the Graces—Cato the Censor, public censor in third century Rome, a very rigid adherent to old Roman mores, an opponent of all Grecian learning, grace, and beauty.

learn it, belike fearing that Pluto understood not Latin. Indeed, the Roman laws allowed no person to be carried to the wars but he that was in the soldier's roll, and therefore, though Cato misliked his unmustered person, he misliked not his work. And if he had, Scipio Nasica, judged by common consent the best Roman, loved him.[87] Both the other Scipio brothers, who had by their virtues no less surnames than of Asia and Afric, so loved him that they caused his body to be buried in their sepulcher. So as Cato's authority being but against his person, and that answered with so far greater than himself, is herein of no validity.

But now indeed my burden is great, that Plato's name is laid upon me, whom, I must confess, of all philosophers I have ever esteemed most worthy of reverence, and with good reason, since of all philosophers he is the most poetical. Yet if he will defile the fountain out of which his flowing streams have proceeded, let us boldly examine with what reasons he did it. First truly, a man might maliciously object that Plato, being a philosopher, was a natural enemy of poets. For indeed, after the philosophers had picked out of the sweet mysteries of poetry the right discerning true points of knowledge, they forthwith, putting it in method, and making a school art of that which the poets did only teach by a divine delightfulness, beginning to spurn at their guides, like ungrateful prentices, were not content to set up shops for themselves, but sought by all means to discredit their masters; which by the force of delight being barred them, the less they could overthrow them, the more they hated them. For indeed, they found for Homer seven cities strove who should have him for their citizen; where many cities banished philosophers as not fit members to live among them. For only repeating certain of Euripides' verses, many Athenians had their lives saved of the Syracusians, where the Athenians thought many philosophers unworthy to live. Certain poets, as Simonides and Pindarus, had so prevailed with Hiero the First, that of a tyrant they made him a just king; where Plato could do so little with

[87] Scipio Nasica—P. Cornelius Scipio Nasica Corculum, a famous jurist and consul, a renowned and respected man, a follower of republican morals.

Dionysius, that he himself of a philosopher was made a slave.[88] But who should do thus, I confess, should requite the objections made against poets with like cavilations against philosophers; as likewise one should do that should bid one read *Phaedrus* or *Symposium* in Plato, or the discourse of love in Plutarch, and see whether any poet do authorize abominable filthiness, as they do. Again, a man might ask out of what commonwealth Plato doth banish them. In sooth, thence where he himself alloweth community of women. So as belike this banishment grew not for effeminate wantonness, since little should poetical sonnets be hurtful when a man might have what woman he listed. But I honor philosophical instructions, and bless the wits which bred them: so as they be not abused, which is likewise stretched to poetry.

St. Paul himself [who yet, for the credit of poets, allegeth twice two poets, and one of them by the name of a prophet] sets a watchword upon philosophy—indeed upon the abuse.[89] So doth Plato upon the abuse, not upon poetry. Plato found fault that the poets of his time filled the world with wrong opinions of the gods, making light tales of that unspotted essence, and therefore would not have the youth depraved with such opinions. Herein may much be said; let this suffice: the poets did not induce such opinions, but did imitate those opinions already induced. For all the Greek stories can well testify that the very religion of that time stood upon many and many-fashioned gods, not taught so by poets, but followed according to their nature of imitation. Who list may read in Plutarch the discourses of Isis and Osiris, of the cause why oracles ceased, of the divine providence, and see whether the theology of that nation stood not upon such dreams which the poets indeed superstitiously observed, and truly (since they had not the light of Christ) did much better in it than the philosophers, who, shaking off superstition, brought in

[88] Dionysius—Dionysius the Younger, tyrant of Syracuse, was infamous for his immorality; when Plato visited his city in 364 B.C., he reformed for a while, but Plato was forced to leave after his friend and host, Dion, was exiled.
[89] St. Paul . . . *Colossians* 2.8.

atheism. Plato therefore (whose authority I had much rather
justly construe than unjustly resist) meant not in general of
poets, in those words of which Julius Scaliger saith, *Qua authoritate barbari quidam atque hispidi abuti velint ad poetas e republica
exigendos;*[90] but only meant to drive out those wrong opinions
of the Deity (whereof now, without further law, Christianity
hath taken away all the hurtful belief), perchance (as he thought)
nourished by then esteemed poets. And a man need go no further
than to Plato himself to know his meaning: who, in his dialogue
called *Ion*, giveth high and rightly divine commendation unto
poetry. So as Plato, banishing the abuse, not the thing, not
banishing it, but giving due honor to it, shall be our patron and
not our adversary. For indeed, I had much rather (since truly
I may do it) show their mistaking of Plato (under whose lion's
skin they would make an ass-like braying against poesy) than go
about to overthrow his authority; whom, the wiser a man is, the
more just cause he shall find to have in admiration; especially
since he attributeth unto poesy more than myself do, namely, to
be a very inspiring of a divine force, far above man's wit, as in
the afore-named dialogue is apparent.

Of the other side, who would show the honors have been by
the best sort of judgments granted them, a whole sea of examples
would present themselves: Alexanders, Caesars, Scipios, all favor-
ers of poets; Laelius, called the Roman Socrates, himself a poet
(so as part of *Heautontimorumenos*[91] in Terence was supposed
to be made by him) and even the Greek Socrates, whom Apollo
confirmed to be the only wise man, is said to have spent part of
his old time in putting Aesop's fables into verses. And therefore,
full evil should it become his scholar Plato to put such words in
his master's mouth against poets. But what needs more? Aristotle
writes the Art of Poesy: and why, if it should not be written?
Plutarch teacheth the use to be gathered of them, and how, if
they should not be read? And who reads Plutarch's either history

[90] *Qua authoritate . . . exigendos*—"which authority certain barbarous
and uncultivated persons would use for expelling poets from the state"
(*Poetice*, 1.2).

[91] *Heautontimorumenos*—"The self-tormentor."

or philosophy, shall find he trimmeth both their garments with guards of poesy. But I list not to defend poesy with the help of his underling historiography. Let it suffice to have showed it is a fit soil for praise to dwell upon; and what dispraise may set upon it, is either easily overcome, or transformed into just commendation. So that, since the excellencies of it may be so easily and so justly confirmed, and the low-creeping objections so soon trodden down; it not being an art of lies, but of true doctrine; not of effeminateness, but of notable stirring of courage; not of abusing man's wit, but of strengthening man's wit; not banished, but honored by Plato; let us rather plant more laurels for to engarland the poets' heads (which honor of being laureate, as besides them only triumphant captains wear, is a sufficient authority to show the price they ought to be held in) than suffer the ill-savoured breath of such wrong-speakers once to blow upon the clear springs of poesy.

VII
Digressio[92]

But since I have run so long a career in this matter, methinks, before I give my pen a full stop, it shall be but a little more lost time to inquire why England (the mother of excellent minds) should be grown so hard a stepmother to poets, who certainly in wit ought to pass all others, since all only proceeds from their wit, being indeed makers of themselves, not takers of others. How can I but exclaim,

> *Musa, mihi causas memora, quo numine laeso!*[93]

Sweet poesy, that hath anciently had kings, emperors, senators, great captains, such as, besides a thousand others, David, Adrian, Sophocles, Germanicus, not only to favor poets, but to be poets;

---

[92] *digressio*—not technically one of the seven parts of an oration, the digression nevertheless is an oblique recapitulation and summary of the whole argument, or defense.

[93] *Musa, mihi causas memora, quo numine laeso!*—"Oh, Muse, call to mind the causes: what divinity was injured" (*Aeneid* 1.8).

and of our nearer times can present for her patrons a Robert, King
of Sicily, the great King Francis of France, King James of Scotland; such cardinals as Bembus and Bibbiena; such famous preachers and teachers as Beza and Melancthon; so learned philosophers as
Fracastorius and Scaliger; so great orators as Pontanus and
Muretus; so piercing wits as George Buchanan; so grave coun-
selors as, besides many, but before all, that Hospital of France,
than whom (I think) that realm never brought forth a more accomplished judgment, more firmly builded upon virtue—[94] I
say these, with numbers of others, not only to read others'
poesies, but to poetize for others' reading—that poesy, thus
embraced in all other places, should only find in our time a
hard welcome in England, I think the very earth laments it, and
therefore decks our soil with fewer laurels than it was accustomed. For heretofore poets have in England also flourished,
and, which is to be noted, even in those times when the trumpet
of Mars did sound loudest. And now that an overfaint quietness
should seem to strew the house for poets, they are almost in as
good reputation as the mountebanks at Venice.[95] Truly even
that, as of the one side it giveth great praise to poesy, which
like Venus (but to better purpose) had rather be troubled in
the net with Mars than enjoy the homely quiet of Vulcan; so
serveth it for a piece of a reason why they are less grateful to
idle England, which now can scarce endure the pain of a pen.
Upon this necessarily followeth, that base men with servile

[94] Robert . . . Hospital of France—Robert d'Anjou, King of Naples
(1309–43), was a friend of Boccaccio and Petrarch; Francis I (1515–47)
was a great patron of arts and letters; James I of Scotland (1406–37); Pietro
Bembo (1470–1547) was a scholar and man of letters who figures in
Castiglione's *Courtier;* Bernardo de Bibbiena (1470–1520) wrote comedies
and was secretary to Lorenzo de Medici; Theodore Beza (1519–1605) was
one of the most eminent Protestant clerics in Europe and succeeded Calvin
at Geneva; Philip Melanchthon (1497–1560) was an intimate friend of Martin
Luther; Fracastorius (1483–1553) was a Veronese poet, philosopher, astronomer, and physician; John Jovius Pontanus (1420–1503) was an Italian poet;
Marc Antoine Muret (1526–85) was a French scholar and writer; George
Buchanan (1506–82) was one of the most influential of sixteenth-century
Scotch writers; Michel de l'Hospital (1504–73) was a chancellor of France
who later promoted toleration for Huguenots.
[95] mountebanks—quacks, pitch-men.

wits undertake it, who think it enough if they can be rewarded of the printer. And so as Epaminondas is said,[96] with the honor of his virtue, to have made an office, by his exercising it, which before was contemptible, to become highly respected, so these men, no more but setting their names to it, by their own disgracefulness disgrace the most graceful poesy. For now, as if all the Muses were got with child, to bring forth bastard poets, without any commission they do post over the banks of Helicon, till they make the readers more weary than posthorses, while, in the meantime, they,

Queis meliore luto finxit praecordia Titan,[97]

are better content to suppress the outflowing of their wit, than, by publishing them, to be accounted knights of the same order. But I that, before ever I durst aspire unto the dignity, am admitted into the company of the paper-blurrers, do find the very true cause of our wanting estimation is want of desert, taking upon us to be poets in despite of Pallas. Now, wherein we want desert were a thankworthy labor to express; but if I knew, I should have mended myself. But, as I never desired the title, so have I neglected the means to come by it. Only, overmastered by some thoughts, I yielded an inky tribute unto them.

Marry, that they delight in poesy itself should seek to know what they do, and how they do, and especially, look themselves in an unflattering glass of reason, if they be inclinable unto it. For poesy must not be drawn by the ears; it must be gently led, or rather it must lead; which was partly the cause that made the ancient-learned affirm it was a divine gift, and no human skill, since all other knowledges lie ready for any that have strength of it; a poet no industry can make, if his own genius be not carried into it; and therefore is an old proverb, *Orator fit, poeta nascitur.*[98] Yet confess I always that as the fertilest ground must

---

[96] Epaminondas—a Theban statesman and soldier of great rectitude who made Thebes a major fourth-century power.

[97] *Queis meliore luto finxit praecordia Titan*—"whose hearts Titan had formed of better clay" (Juvenal, *Satires* 14.34-35).

[98] *Orator fit, poeta nascitur*—The orator is made, the poet born.

be manured, so must the highest-flying wit have a Daedalus to guide him. That Daedalus, they say, both in this and in other, hath three wings to bear itself up into the air of due commendation: that is, Art, Imitation, and Exercise. But these, neither artificial rules nor imitative patterns, we much cumber ourselves withal. Exercise indeed we do, but that very fore-backwardly: for where we should exercise to know, we exercise as having known: and so is our brain delivered of much matter which never was begotten by knowledge. For, these being two principal parts—matter to be expressed by words and words to express the matter—in neither we use Art or Imitation rightly. Our matter is *Quodlibet*[99] indeed, though wrongly performing Ovid's verse,

Quicquid conabar dicere, versus erit:[100]

never marshaling it into any assured rank, that almost the readers cannot tell where to find themselves.

Chaucer, undoubtedly, did excellently in his *Troilus and Creseid;* of whom, truly, I know not whether to marvel more, either that he in that misty time could see so clearly, or that we in this clear age go so stumblingly after him. Yet had he great wants, fit to be forgiven in so reverent an antiquity. I account the *Mirror of Magistrates* meetly furnished of beautiful parts, and in the Earl of Surrey's *Lyrics*[101] many things tasting of a noble birth, and worthy of a noble mind. *The Shepherd's Calendar* hath much poetry in his Eclogues, indeed worthy the reading, if I be not deceived. That same framing of his style to an old rustic language I dare not allow, since neither Theocritus in Greek, Virgil in Latin, nor Sannazaro in Italian did affect it.[102] Besides these, do I not remember to have seen but few (to speak

99 *Quodlibet*—what you will.
100 *Quicquid conabar dicere, versus erit*—"Whatever I shall try to say shall become verse" (*Tristia* 4.10.26).
101 Earl of Surrey's *Lyrics*—first published in 1557 as *Songs and Sonnets* along with Sir Thomas Wyatt's.
102 Theocritus . . . Virgil . . . Sannazaro—the chief writers of pastoral in the respective languages.

boldly) printed, that have poetical sinews in them: for proof
whereof, let but most of the verses be put in prose, and then
ask the meaning; and it will be found that one verse did but
beget another, without ordering at the first what should be at
the last; which becomes a confused mass of words, with a tingling
sound of rhyme, barely accompanied with reason.

Our tragedies and comedies (not without cause cried out
against), observing rules neither of honest civility nor skillful
poetry, excepting *Gorboduc*[103] (again, I say, of those that I have
seen), which notwithstanding, as it is full of stately speeches
and well-sounding phrases, climbing to the height of Seneca's
style, and as full of notable morality, which it doth most delightfully teach, and so obtain the very end of poesy, yet in truth
it is very defectious in the circumstances (which grieves me, because it might not remain as an exact model of all tragedies),
for it is faulty both in place and time, the two necessary companions of all corporal actions. For where the stage should always
represent but one place, and the uttermost time presupposed
in it should be, both by Aristotle's precept and common reason,
but one day, there is both many days and many places, inarti-
ficially imagined. But if it be so in *Gorboduc*, how much more in
all the rest, where you shall have Asia of the one side, and
Afric of the other, and so many other under-kingdoms, that the
player, when he comes in, must ever begin with telling where
he is, or else the tale will not be conceived? Now you shall have
three ladies walk to gather flowers, and then we must believe
the stage to be a garden. By and by we hear news of shipwreck
in the same place, then we are to blame if we accept it not for
a rock. Upon the back of that comes out a hideous monster, with
fire and smoke, and then the miserable beholders are bound to
take it for a cave. While in the meantime two armies fly in,
represented with four swords and bucklers, and then what hard
heart will not receive it for a pitched field? Now, of time they
are much more liberal, for ordinary it is that two young princes

[103] *Gorboduc*—Senecan blank verse tragedy by Thomas Sackville and
Thomas Norton, published in 1565.

fall in love. After many traverses, she is got with child, delivered of a fair boy; he is lost, groweth a man, falleth in love, and is ready to get another child; and all this in two hours' space: which, how absurd it is in sense, even sense may imagine, and art hath taught, and all ancient examples justified, and at this day, the ordinary players in Italy will nor err in. Yet will some bring in an example of *Eunuchus* in Terence, that containeth matter of two days, yet far short of twenty years. True it is, and so was it to be played in two days, and so fitted to the time it set forth. And though Plautus have in one place done amiss, let us hit it with him, and not miss with him. But they will say, "How then shall we set forth a story, which contains both many places and many times?" And do they not know that a tragedy is tied to the laws of poesy, and not of history; not bound to follow the story, but, having liberty, either to feign a quite new matter, or to frame the history to the most tragical conveniency? Again, many things may be told which cannot be showed, if they know the difference betwixt reporting and representing. As, for example, I may speak (though I am here) of Peru, and in speech digress from that to the description of Calicut; but in action I cannot represent it without Pacolet's horse.[104] And so was the manner the ancients took, by some Nuntius[105] to recount things done in former time or other place. Lastly, if they will represent an history, they must not (as Horace saith) begin *ab ovo*,[106] but they must come to the principal point of that one action which they will represent. By example this will be best expressed. I have a story of young Polydorus, delivered for safety's sake, with great riches, by his father Priam to Polymnestor, king of Thrace, in the Trojan war time.[107] He, after some years, hearing the overthrow of Priam, for to make the treasure his own, murdereth the child. The body of the child is taken

---

[104] Pacolet's horse—a magic horse made by the dwarf Pacolet in the old French romance, *Valentine and Orson.*

[105] Nuntius— the messenger, useful in classical tragedies because most of the action took place offstage and had to be described.

[106] *ab ovo*—"from the egg" (*Ars Poetica* 147).

[107] I have a story—the plot of Euripides' *Hecuba.*

up by Hecuba. She, the same day, findeth a slight to be revenged most cruelly of the tyrant. Where now would one of
our tragedy writers begin, but with the delivery of the child?
Then should he sail over into Thrace, and so spend I know not
how many years, and travel numbers of places. But where doth
Euripides? Even with the finding of the body, the rest leaving
to be told by the spirit of Polydorus. This need no further to be
enlarged; the dullest wit may conceive it.

But besides these gross absurdities, how all their plays be
neither right tragedies, nor right comedies, mingling kings and
clowns, not because the matter so carrieth it, but thrust in the
clown by head and shoulders, to play a part in majestical matters,
with neither decency nor discretion, so as neither the admiration
and commiseration, nor the right sportfulness, is by their mongrel
tragicomedy obtained. I know Apuleius[108] did somewhat so, but
that is a thing recounted with space of time, not represented in one
moment: and I know the ancients have one or two examples of
tragicomedies, as Plautus hath *Amphitryo*. But, if we mark them
well, we shall find that they never, or very daintily, match horn-
pipes and funerals. So falleth it out that, having indeed no right
comedy, in that comical part of our tragedy we have nothing but
scurrility, unworthy of any chaste ears, or some extreme show of
doltishness, indeed fit to lift up a loud laughter, and nothing else:
where the whole tract of a comedy should be full of delight, as the
tragedy should be still maintained in a well-raised admiration.
But our comedians think there is no delight without laughter;
which is very wrong, for though laughter may come with delight, yet cometh it not of delight, as though delight should be
the cause of laughter; but well may one thing breed both
together. Nay, rather in themselves they have, as it were, a kind
of contrariety: for delight we scarcely do but in things that
have a conveniency to ourselves or to the general nature:
laughter almost ever cometh of things most disproportioned
to ourselves and nature. Delight hath a joy in it, either permanent or present. Laughter hath only a scornful tickling. For

---

[108] Apuleius—writer of the 2nd century, not a dramatist, known for his
satirical romance popularly called *The Golden Ass*.

example, we are ravished with delight to see a fair woman, and yet are far from being moved to laughter. We laugh at deformed creatures, wherein certainly we cannot delight. We delight in good chances, we laugh at mischances; we delight to hear the happiness of our friends and country, at which he were worthy to be laughed at that would laugh. We shall, contrarily, laugh sometimes to find a matter quite mistaken and go down the hill against the bias, in the mouth of some such men, as for the respect of them one shall be heartily sorry, [yet] he cannot choose but laugh; and so is rather pained than delighted with laughter. Yet deny I not but that they may go well together. For as in Alexander's picture well set out we delight without laughter, and in twenty mad antics we laugh without delight, so in Hercules, painted with his great beard and furious countenance, in a woman's attire, spinning at Omphale's commandment, it breeds both delight and laughter. For the representing of so strange a power in love procures delight, and the scornfulness of the action stirreth laughter. But I speak to this purpose, that all the end of the comical part be not upon such scornful matters as stirreth laughter only, but, mix with it that delightful teaching which is the end of poesy. And the great fault even in that point of laughter, and forbidden plainly by Aristotle, is that they stir laughter in sinful things, which are rather execrable than ridiculous; or in miserable, which are rather to be pitied than scorned. For what is it to make folks gape at a wretched beggar, and a beggarly clown; or, against law of hospitality, to jest at strangers, because they speak not English so well as we do? What do we learn? Since it is certain

> *Nil habet infelix paupertas durius in se,*
> *Quam quod ridiculos homines facit.*[109]

But rather a busy loving courtier, and a heartless threatening Thraso, a self-wise-seeming schoolmaster, a wry-transformed traveler—these if we saw walk in stage names, which we play

[109] *Nil habet . . . facit*—"Unfortunate poverty has nothing in itself harder to bear than that it makes men ridiculous" (Juvenal, *Satires* 3.152–53).

naturally, therein were delightful laughter, and teaching delightfulness: as in the other, the tragedies of Buchanan do justly bring forth a divine admiration. But I have lavished out too many words of this play matter. I do it because, as they are excelling parts of poesy, so is there none so much used in England, and none can be more pitifully abused; which, like an unmannerly daughter showing a bad education, causeth her mother poesy's honesty to be called in question.

Other sort of poetry almost have we none, but that lyrical kind of songs and sonnets which, Lord, if he gave us so good minds, how well it might be employed, and with how heavenly fruit, both private and public, in singing the praises of the immortal beauty, the immortal goodness of that God who giveth us hands to write and wits to conceive; of which we might well want words, but never matter; of which we could turn our eyes to nothing, but we should ever have new budding occasions. But truly many of such writings as come under the banner of unresistible love, if I were a mistress, would never persuade me they were in love; so coldly they apply fiery speeches, as men that had rather read lovers' writings, and so caught up certain swelling phrases (which hang together like a man that once told me the wind was at northwest, and by south, because he would be sure to name winds enough), than that in truth they feel those passions, which easily (as I think) may be bewrayed by that same forcibleness, or *energia* (as the Greeks call it) of the writer. But let this be a sufficient though short note, that we miss the right use of the material point of poesy.

Now, for the outside of it, which is words, or (as I may term it) diction, it is even well worse. So is that honey-flowing matron Eloquence appareled, or rather disguised, in a courtesan-like painted affectation: one time with so farfetched words, that many seem monsters, but must seem strangers, to any poor Englishman; another time, with coursing of a letter,[110] as if they were bound to follow the method of a dictionary; another time, with figures and flowers, extremely winter-starved. But I would

---

[110] with coursing of a letter—alliteration.

this fault were only peculiar to versifiers, and had not as large possession among prose-printers, and (which is to be marveled) among many scholars, and (which is to be pitied) among some preachers. Truly I could wish, if at least I might be so bold to wish in a thing beyond the reach of my capacity, the diligent imitators of Tully and Demosthenes (most worthy to be imitated) did not so much keep Nizolian paper-books of their figures and phrases,[111] as by attentive translation (as it were) devour them whole, and make them wholly theirs. For now they cast sugar and spice upon every dish that is served at the table, like those Indians, not content to wear earrings at the fit and natural place of the ears, but they will thrust jewels through their nose and lips, because they will be sure to be fine. Tully, when he was to drive out Catiline, as it were with a thunderbolt of eloquence, often used that figure of repetition, as: *Vivit et vincit, immo in senatum, Venit immo, in senatum venit, etc.*[112] Indeed, inflamed with a well-grounded rage, he would have his words (as it were) double out of his mouth, and so do that artificially which we see men in choler do naturally. And we, having noted the grace of those words, hale them in sometimes to a familiar epistole, when it were too much choler to be choleric. How well store of *similiter cadenses* doth sound with the gravity of the pulpit, I would but invoke Demosthenes' soul to tell, who with a rare daintiness useth them. Truly they have made me think of the sophister that with too much subtlety would prove two eggs three and, though he might be counted a sophister, had none for his labor. So these men, bringing in such a kind of eloquence, well may they obtain an opinion of a seeming fineness but persuade few, which should be the end of their fineness.

Now for similitudes in certain printed discourses, I think all herbarists,[113] all stories of beasts, fowls, and fishes are rifled up,

---

[111] Nizolian paper-books of their figures and phrases—Marius Nizolius (1498?–1576), an Italian rhetorician and lexicographer, published a collection of Ciceronian phrases in 1535.

[112] *Vivit . . . venit*—freely quoted from Cicero's *Catiline* 1.2: *Hic tamen vivit. Vivit? Immo vero etiam in senatum venit;* "This man still lives. Lives? Nay more, he comes into the senate."

[113] herbarists—men skilled in herbs (the jab is against Lyly).

that they come in multitudes to wait upon any of our conceits; which certainly is as absurd a surfeit to the ears as is possible: for the force of a similitude not being to prove anything to a contrary disputer, but only to explain to a willing hearer; when that is done, the rest is a most tedious prattling, rather over-swaying the memory from the purpose whereto they were applied, than any whit informing the judgment, already either satisfied, or by similitudes not to be satisfied. For my part, I do not doubt, when Antonius and Crassus, the great forefathers of Cicero in eloquence, the one (as Cicero testifieth of them) pretended not to know art, the other not to set by it, because with a plain sensibleness they might win credit of popular ears; which credit is the nearest step to persuasion; which persuasion is the chief mark of oratory—I do not doubt (I say) but that they used these knacks very sparingly; which, who doth generally use, any man may see doth dance to his own music; and so to be noted by the audience more careful to speak curiously than truly.

Undoubtedly (at least to my opinion undoubtedly) I have found in divers small-learned courtiers a more sound style than in some professors of learning: of which I can guess no other cause, but that the courtier, following that which by practice he findeth fittest to nature, therein (though he know it not) doth according to art, though not by art; where the other, using art to show art, and not hide art (as in these cases he should do), flieth from nature, and indeed abuseth art.

But what? Methinks I deserve to be pounded for straying from poetry to oratory; but both have such an affinity in the wordish consideration, that I think this digression will make my meaning receive the fuller understanding—which is not to take up me to teach poets how they should do, but only, finding myself sick among the rest, to show some one or two spots of the common infection grown among the most part of writers: that, acknowledging ourselves somewhat awry, we may bend to the right use both of matter and manner; whereto our language giveth us great occasion, being indeed capable of any excellent exercising of it. I know some will say it is a mingled language. And why not so much the better, taking the best of both the other? Another will say it wanteth grammar. Nay truly, it hath that praise, that it wants not grammar: for grammar it might have, but it needs it not; being so easy in itself, and so void of those cumbersome differences of cases, genders, moods, and tenses, which I think was a piece of the Tower of Babylon's curse, that a man should be put to school to learn his mother tongue. But for the uttering sweetly and properly the conceit of the mind, which is the end of speech, that hath it equally with any other tongue in the world: and is particularly happy in compositions of two or three words together, near the Greek, far beyond the Latin: which is one of the greatest beauties can be in a language.

Now, of versifying there are two sorts, the one ancient, the other modern: the ancient marked the quantity of each syllable, and according to that framed his verse; the modern observing only number (with some regard of the accent), the chief life of it standeth in that like sounding of the words, which we call "rime." Whether of these be the more excellent, would bear many speeches. The ancient, no doubt, more fit for music, both words and time observing quantity, and more fit lively to express divers passions, by the low or lofty sound of the well-weighted syllable. The latter likewise, with his rhyme, striketh a certain music to the ear: and, in fine, since it doth delight, though by another way, it obtaineth the same purpose: there being in either sweetness, and wanting in neither, majesty. Truly the English, before any vulgar language I know, is fit for both sorts: for, for the ancient, the Italian is so full of vowels that it must ever be cumbered with elisions; the Dutch[114] so, of the other side, with consonants, that they cannot yield the sweet sliding fit for a verse; the French, in his whole language, hath not one word that hath his accent in the last syllable saving two, called *Antepenultima;* and little more hath the Spanish: and, therefore, very gracelessly may they use dactyls. The English is subject to none of these defects.

[114] Dutch—German.

Now, for rhyme, though we do not observe quantity, yet we observe the accent very precisely: which other languages either cannot do, or will not do so absolutely. That *caesura*, or breathing place in the midst of the verse, neither Italian nor Spanish have, the French, and we, never almost fail of. Lastly, even the very rhyme itself the Italian cannot put it in the last syllable, by the French named the "masculine rhyme," but still in the next to the last, which the French call the "female," or the next before that, which the Italian [term] *sdrucciola*.[115] The example of the former is *buono: suono*, of the *sdrucciola* is *femina: semina*. The French, of the other side, hath both the male, as *bon: son*, and the female, as *plaise: taise*, but the *sdrucciola* he hath not; where the English hath all three, as *due: true, father: rather, motion: potion*, with much more which might be said, but that already I find that trifling of this discourse is much too much enlarged.

VIII
Peroratio[116]

So that since the ever-praiseworthy poesy is full of virtue-breeding delightfulness, and void of no gift that ought to be in the noble name of learning; since the blames laid against it are either false or feeble; since the cause why it is not esteemed in England is the fault of poet-apes, not poets; since, lastly, our tongue is most fit to honor poesy, and to be honored by poesy; I conjure you all that have had the evil luck to read this ink-wasting toy of mine, even in the name of the Nine Muses, no more to scorn the sacred mysteries of poesy, no more to laugh at the name of "poets," as though they were next inheritors to fools, nor more to jest at the reverent title of a "rimer"; but to believe, with Aristotle, that they were the ancient treasurers of the Grecians' divinity; to believe, with Bembus, that they were first bringers-in of all civility; to believe, with Scaliger,

---

[115] *sdrucciola*—in grammar, proparoxytonal, that is, having the accent on the antepenultimate syllable.

[116] *peroratio*—the conclusion to a speech.

that no philosopher's precepts can sooner make you an honest man than the reading of Virgil; to believe, with Clauserus,[117] the translator of Cornutus, that it pleased the heavenly Deity, by Hesiod and Homer, under the veil of fables, to give us all knowledge, logic, rhetoric, philosophy, natural and moral, and *quid non?*; to believe, with me, that there are many mysteries contained in poetry, which of purpose were written darkly, lest by profane wits it should be abused; to believe, with Landin,[118] that they are so beloved of the gods that whatsoever they write proceeds of a divine fury; lastly, to believe themselves, when they tell you they will make you immortal by their verses.

Thus doing, your name shall flourish in the printers' shops; thus doing, you shall be of kin to many a poetical preface; thus doing, you shall be most fair, most rich, most wise, most all; you shall dwell upon superlatives. Thus doing, though you be *libertino patre natus*, you shall suddenly grow *Herculae proles*,

Si quid mea carmina possunt.[119]

Thus doing, your soul shall be placed with Dante's Beatrix, or Virgil's Anchises. But if (fie of such a but) you be born so near the dull-making cataract of Nilus[120] that you cannot hear the planet-like music of poetry, if you have so earth-creeping a mind that it cannot lift itself up to look to the sky of poetry, or rather, by a certain rustical disdain, will become such a mome as to be a Momus of poetry;[121] then, though I will not wish unto you the

[117] Clauserus—Latin name of Conrad Clauser (1520?–1611), German scholar. Sidney alludes to Clauser's preface to his Latin translation of a Greek treatise by Cornutus, who flourished in the reign of Nero.
[118] Landin—Cristofero Landino (1424?–1504), an Italian scholar and one-time tutor to Lorenzo de Medici.
[119] *libertino patre natus . . . Herculea proles . . . Si quid mea carmina possunt*—"born of a freed slave father" . . . "a descendant of Hercules" . . . "If my songs are of any avail" (the first two are from Horace, *Epistles* 1.20.20 and *Satires* 1.6.45; the last from *Aeneid* 9.446).
[120] Nilus—Nile River, which, according to Cicero in *Somnium Scipionis*, makes people deaf.
[121] Momus of poetry—Momus was god of ridicule.

ass's ears of Midas,[122] nor to be driven by a poet's verses (as Bubonax was)[123] to hang himself, nor to be rhymed to death, as is said to be done in Ireland;[124] yet thus much curse I must send you, in the behalf of all poets, that while you live, you live in love, and never get favor for lacking skill of a sonnet, and, when you die, your memory die from the earth for want of an epitaph.

[122] ass's ears of Midas—Midas, wealthy king of Phrygia, whose ears were changed into an ass's because he preferred Pan's playing to Apollo's (Ovid, *Metamorphoses* 11.146-79).

[123] Bubonax—combination of Hipponax and Bupalus, Hipponax being an Ephesian poet who satirized the statuary of Bupalus so bitterly that the latter hanged himself (c. 500 B.C.).

[124] as is said to be done in Ireland—Irish bards are said to have the power to cause death with their incantations.

Astrophel and Stella

T HE ARTISTIC ACHIEVEMENT of *Astrophel and Stella* has not always been fully appreciated because Sidney here so employed
his artistic skill, and so utilized his exercise in the world of love,
in so perfect an imitation of Petrarch that the world has too
readily accepted as merely literal what is deeply real. *Astrophel
and Stella* is real because it is fine art. That is to say, Sidney fully
immersed himself within his artifact and released his artistic
energy totally. As a result, *Astrophel and Stella* comes alive.

Such an achievement was possible because Sidney had at last
mastered the secret of English prosody. Through the bias of his
education, and through the evidence of his friends, we know that
Sidney realized that English poetry could not come into maturity
unless it was based in some sort of metrical regularity—all
the great poetry of history so testified. But Sidney, the man,
realized at the same time that poetry had to be natural, had to
reflect the speaking, living, feeling human being. On the one
hand, English poetry demanded the discipline and regularity of
meter; on the other hand, it cried for the freedom of the rhythms
and range of the speaking voice. What Sidney discovered was
that these two demands were not essentially in conflict, but could
be pulled together in a harmonious tension. When Sidney allowed
the rhythms of natural speech to play across the regularity and
rigidity of meter, with occasional, rhetorically-demanded substitutions, what he created was "voice." While this voice is his in
the sense that it stems from him, it is not really his. It is the voice
of poetry, the voice of each individual poem.

Because of the artistic integrity of *Astrophel and Stella*, and
because it is a perfect imitation of Petrarch, readers tend to

interpret *Astrophel and Stella* autobiographically, believing that it is Sidney himself who is suffering all the typical tortures, pain, anguish, and frustration of the Petrarchan lover. Further, scholars have fastened on partial and inconclusive evidence to identify Stella as Penelope Devereux Rich. There is no need here to go into the background and characteristics of Petrarchism, nor is there reason to rehearse an essentially extraliterary controversy. Suffice it to say that Sidney fully embraced a particular literary convention and completely mastered it. So also did Shakespeare and Spenser, and so also is the breadth and variety of their lyric achievement too often missed because they are couched in the conventions of the sonnet sequence. But when sonnets are understood to be lyrics, and sequences are understood to be merely miscellaneous collections of poetry, loosely organized around some unobtainable beloved, then we can open our ears to the ranges of some of the finest music achieved within English poetry.

Sidney probably began *Astrophel and Stella* sometime in 1581, but may not have completed the sequence until late in 1582. We know that it circulated rather widely in manuscript; however, it did not appear in print until 1591, when three unauthorized versions were printed, two by Thomas Newman, and one by Matthew Lownes. The first and only authoritative version of *Astrophel and Stella* appeared in the collected works of 1598 (STC 22541), which has been used as the copy text for the present edition.

no narrative - rather a sequence of writing sequences -
huge #s of ghost poems to Stella that we never see -

Poetry is figuring
forth, counterfeiting

(defense of poetry)

is this an anthology of different
styles that Astrophil tries &
which don't work.
— Neoplatonic
— petrarchan ⟩ elems of
petrarchan in English
form: Ready, willing + happy
required,

108 sonnets
suitors for
penelope

ASTROPHEL AND STELLA

confusion of invention & eloquence?
on faulty rhetoric: if he succeeds as a
praise of her virtue   lover or rhetor he fails in

inner   vs. outer   don't equate Astrophil
truth   show   w/ Sidney —
                   "many the lies the poets tell"
1   to feign (as in madness)
                                    indirect or direct object?
                                                             spectacle

A Loving in truth, and fain in verse my love to show,   truth/fain
B That she, dear she, might take some pleasure of my pain,   grace/sex
A Pleasure might cause her read, reading might make her
       know,   rhetoric leads to
                                                                          vice not virtue
                                         sex
B Knowledge might pity win, and pity grace obtain,
A I sought fit words to paint the blackest face of woe: artificiality 5
B Studying inventions fine,[1] her wits to entertain,   influence
A Oft turning others' leaves, to see if thence would flow   + birth —
B Some fresh and fruitful showers upon my sunburn'd brain.
B But words came halting forth, wanting invention's stay;   support   poem
A Invention, Nature's child, fled stepdame study's blows;   10 reverses
A And others' feet still seem'd but stranger in my way.   the
A Thus, great with child to speak, and helpless in my throes,   standard
C   Biting my truant pen, beating myself for spite: procedure of
C   "Fool," said my Muse to me, "look in thy heart and   rhetoric
     write!"[2]
look for Stella not   Zeus a model for male pregnancy —
romantic   Dionysus from thigh, Athena from head
2   subjectivity
         see #32   also trojan horse pregnant

Not at the first sight, nor with a dribbed[1] shot,
Love gave the wound which, while I breathe, will bleed;

  [1] inventions fine—subjects treated artistically by others (see Gen.
Intro.).
  [2] look in thy heart—the injunction of the low, or plain, style.
  [1] dribbed—random.

163

Auden's poem "The truest poetry is most
                              Feigning"

But known worth did in mine of time proceed,[2]
Till, by degrees, it had full conquest got.
I saw, and liked; I liked, but loved not;   5
I loved, but straight did not what love decreed;
At length to love's decrees I, forc'd, agreed,
Yet with repining at so partial lot.[3]
Now even that footstep[4] of lost liberty
Is gone; and now, like slave-born Muscovite,   10
I call it praise to suffer tyranny;
And now employ the remnant of my wit
    To make myself believe that all is well,
    While, with a feeling skill,[5] I paint my hell.

3

Let dainty wits cry on the sisters nine,
That bravely mask'd, their fancies may be told;
Or, Pindar's apes,[1] flaunt they in phrases fine,   *Ronsard*
Enam'ling with pied flowers their thoughts of gold;
Or else let them in statelier glory shine,   5
Ennobling new-found tropes[2] with problems[3] old;
Or with strange similes enrich each line,
Of herbs or beasts which Ind or Afric hold.
For me, in sooth, no Muse but one I know;
Phrases and problems from my reach do grow,   10
And strange[4] things cost too dear for my poor sprites.[5]
How then? Even thus—in Stella's face I read

[2] in mine of time proceed—the passage of time as a tunnel mined under the walls of a fort, dug by the enemy for the laying of explosives.
[3] partial lot—unjust fate.
[4] footstep—footprint.
[5] feeling skill—dexterity born of deeply felt emotion.
[1] Pindar's apes—imitators of the ornate Greek poet, Pindar.
[2] tropes—turns, figures.
[3] problems—subjects, especially for debates.
[4] strange—exotic.
[5] sprites—spirits.

What love and beauty be; then all my deed
But copying is, what, in her, Nature writes.[6]

[handwritten marginalia: inspiration ... just copying is good poetry? In Defense poetry = mimesis not poesis - p. 138 ekphastic fantastic]

4

Virtue, alas, now let me take some rest;
Thou set'st a bate[1] between my will and wit;
If vain love have my simple soul oppress'd,
Leave what thou lik'st not; deal not thou with it.
Thy scepter use in some old Cato's breast;[2]   5
Churches or schools are for thy seat more fit.
I do confess—pardon a fault confess'd—
My mouth too tender is for thy hard bit.
But if that needs thou wilt usurping be
The little reason that is left in me,   10
And still the effect of thy persuasions prove,
I swear, my heart such one shall show to thee
    That shrines in flesh so true a deity
    That, virtue, thou thyself shalt be in love.

5

It is most true that eyes are form'd to serve
The inward light, and that the heavenly part
Ought to be king, from whose rules who do swerve,
Rebels to nature, strive for their own smart.
It is most true, what we call Cupid's dart,   5
An image is, which for ourselves we carve,
And, fools, adore in temple of our heart,
Till that good god make church and churchmen starve.
True, that true beauty virtue is indeed,
Whereof this beauty can be but a shade,   10
Which elements with mortal mixture breed.

---

[6] Nature writes—first reference to Stella as a "book of Nature."
[1] bate—debate.
[2] Cato's breast—Cato the Censor, a Stoic philosopher.

True, that on earth we are but pilgrims made,
    And should in soul up to our country move.
    True, and yet true that I must Stella love.

6

Some lovers speak, when they their Muses entertain,
Of hopes begot by fear, of wot not what desires,[1]
Of force of heavenly beams infusing hellish pain,
Of living deaths, dear wounds, fair storms, and freezing fires;
Someone his song in Jove and Jove's strange tales attires,   5
Border'd with bulls and swans, powder'd with golden rain;[2]
Another humbler wit to shepherd's pipe retires,
Yet hiding royal blood full oft in rural vein.
To some a sweetest plaint a sweetest style affords,
While tears pour out his ink, and sighs breathe out his
        words,   10
His paper pale despair, and pain his pen doth move.
I can speak what I feel, and feel as much as they,
    But think that all the map of my state I display
    When trembling voice brings forth, that I do Stella love.

7

When Nature made her chief work, Stella's eyes,
In color black why wrapt she beams so bright?
Would she, in beamy black, like painter wise,
Frame daintiest luster, mix'd of shades and light?
Or did she else that sober hue devise   5
In object best to knit and strength our sight;
Lest, if no veil these brave gleams did disguise,
They, sun-like, should more dazzle than delight?

[1] wot not what—incomprehensible.
[2] bulls and swans . . . golden rain—Jupiter abducted Europa by changing into a white bull and carrying her off; in the form of a swan, he mated
with Leda; and he united with Danae in the guise of a shower of gold.

Or would she her miraculous power show,
That, whereas black seems beauty's contrary,   10
She, even in black, doth make all beauties flow?
Both so, and thus—she, minding[1] Love should be
  Placed ever there, gave him this mourning weed
  To honor all their deaths who for her bleed.

8   *cf. # 3*

Love, born in Greece, of late fled from his native place,
Forc'd, by a tedious proof, that Turkish harden'd heart
Is not fit mark to pierce with his fine-pointed dart,
And, pleas'd with our soft peace, stay'd here his flying race;
But, finding these north climes do coldly him embrace,   5
Not used to frozen clips,[1] he strave to find some part
Where with most ease and warmth he might employ his art.
At length he perch'd himself in Stella's joyful face,
Whose fair skin, beamy eyes, like morning sun on snow,
Deceiv'd the quaking boy, who thought from so pure light   10
Effects of lively heat must needs in nature grow;
But she, most fair, most cold, made him thence take his
  flight
  To my close heart, where, while some firebrands he did
  lay,
  He burnt unawares his wings, and cannot fly away.

9

Queen virtue's court, which some call Stella's face,
Prepar'd by Nature's choicest furniture,[1]
Hath his front[2] built of alabaster pure;

   [1] minding—remembering.
   [1] clips—embraces.
   [1] furniture—bedecked with the most beautiful materials at Nature's disposal.
   [2] front—forehead.

Gold is the covering of that stately place.
The door by which sometimes comes forth her grace   5
Red porphir[3] is, which lock of pearl makes sure,
Whose porches rich—which name of cheeks endure—
Marble, mix'd red and white, do interlace.
The windows now, through which this heavenly guest
Looks over the world and can find nothing such   10
Which dare claim from those lights the name of best,
Of touch[4] they are, that without touch doth touch,
    Which Cupid's self, from beauty's mine did draw:
    Of touch they are, and poor I am their straw.[5]

        10

Reason, in faith thou art well serv'd, that still
Wouldst brabbling[1] be with sense and love in me;
I rather wish'd thee climb the Muses' hill;[2]
Or reach the fruit of Nature's choicest tree;[3]
Or seek heaven's course or heaven's inside to see.   5
Why shouldst thou toil our thorny soil to till?
Leave sense and those which sense's objects be;
Deal thou with powers of thoughts; leave love to will.
But thou wouldst needs fight both with love and sense,
With sword of wit giving wounds of dispraise,   10
Till downright blows did foil thy cunning fence;[4]
For, soon as they strake thee with Stella's rays,
    Reason, thou kneel'dst, and offer'dst straight to prove,
    By reason good, good reason her to love.

[3] porphir—porphyry, an ornamental red or purple stone.
[4] touch—a lignite stone capable of magnetic attraction when rubbed, and can touch (affect) without touch (contact).
[5] straw—the material drawn by magnetism.
[1] brabbling—brawling.
[2] Muses' hill—Mt. Helicon.
[3] Nature's choicest tree—the tree of knowledge.
[4] fence—swordsmanship.

11

In truth O Love, with what a boyish kind
Thou dost proceed in thy most serious ways,
That when the heaven to thee his best displays,
Yet of that best thou leav'st the best behind!
For, like a child that some fair book doth find,   5
With gilded leaves or color'd vellum plays,
Or, at the most, on some fine picture stays,
But never heeds the fruit of writer's mind;
So when thou saw'st, in Nature's cabinet,
Stella, thou straight look'st babies in her eyes,[1]   10
In her cheeks' pit thou didst thy pitfold[2] set,
In her breast bo-peep or couching[3] lies,
     Playing and shining in each outward part;
     But, fool, seek'st not to get into her heart.

12

Cupid, because thou shin'st in Stella's eyes,
That from her locks, thy day-nets,[1] none 'scapes free,
That those lips swell, so full of thee they be,
That her sweet breath makes oft thy flames to rise,
That in her breast thy pap well sugar'd lies,   5
That her grace gracious makes thy wrongs, that she,
What words soe'er she speak, persuades for thee,
That her clear voice lifts thy fame to the skies—
Thou countest Stella thine, like those whose powers[2]
Having got up a breach by fighting well,   10
Cry, "Victory, this fair day all is ours!"

[1] look'st babies—see a tiny image of yourself in her pupils.
[2] pitfold—net.
[3] bo-peep or couching lies—plays hide-and-seek.
[1] day-nets—bird lures made with bits of shining metal, used to dazzle
larks and entrap them in nets.
[2] powers—soldiers.

Oh no! Her heart is such a citadel,
  So fortified with wit, stor'd with disdain,
  That to win it, is all the skill and pain.

13

Phoebus was judge between Jove, Mars, and Love,
Of these three gods, whose arms the fairest were.
Jove's golden shield did eagle sables[1] bear,
Whose talons held young Ganymede[2] above;
But in vert[3] field Mars bare a golden spear   5
Which through a bleeding heart his point did shove.
Each had his crest:[4] Mars carried Venus' glove,
Jove on his helm the thunderbolt did rear.
Cupid then smiles, for on his crest there lies
Stella's fair hair; her face he makes his shield,   10
Where roses gules[5] are borne in silver field.[6]
Phoebus drew wide the curtains of the skies
  To blaze[7] these last, and sware devoutly then
  The first, thus match'd, were scantly[8] gentlemen.

14

Alas, have I not pain enough, my friend,
Upon whose breast a fiercer gripe doth tire[1]
Than did on him who first stole down the fire,[2]

1 eagle sables—heraldic term for black eagles.
2 Ganymede—a Trojan boy whom Jupiter, in the form of an eagle, carried off to be his cup-bearer and minion.
3 vert—heraldic term for green.
4 crest—topmost figure on a shield.
5 roses gules—red roses, in heraldic terminology.
6 field—background.
7 blaze—emblazon.
8 scantly—scarcely.
1 gripe doth tire—grasp does tear.
2 him who first stole down the fire—Prometheus, the Titan who gave fire to man, was punished by being chained to a rock and subjected to a vulture, which gnawed at his liver.

While Love on me doth all his quiver spend—
But with your rhubarb[3] words ye must contend,   5
To grieve me worse, in saying that desire
Doth plunge my well-form'd soul even in the mire
Of sinful thoughts, which do in ruin end?
If that be sin which doth the manners[4] frame,
Well stayed with truth in word and faith of deed,   10
Ready of wit, and fearing naught but shame;
If that be sin, which in fix'd hearts doth breed
   A loathing of all loose unchastity,
     Then love is sin, and let me sinful be.

15

You that do search for every purling spring
Which from the ribs of old Parnassus[1] flows,
And every flower, not sweet perhaps, which grows
Near thereabouts, into your poesy wring;
You that do dictionary's method[2] bring   5
Into your rhymes, running in rattling rows;
You that poor Petrarch's long deceased woes
With newborn sighs and denizen'd[3] wit do sing:
You take wrong ways; those far-fet[4] helps be such
As do bewray a want of inward touch,[5]   10
And sure at length stolen goods do come to light;
But if, both for your love and skill, your name
   You seek to nurse at fullest breasts of fame,
     Stella behold, and then begin to indite.

[3] rhubarb—bitter when used as a purgative.
[4] manners—full courtly, virtuous behavior.
[1] Parnassus—the symbolic home of ancient poetry.
[2] dictionary's method—alliterations.
[3] denizen'd—native English.
[4] far-fet—far-fetched.
[5] inward touch—genuine creative sensibility, or "*energia*" (see *Def.*).

16

In nature apt to like, when I did see
Beauties which were of many carats fine,
My boiling sprites did thither soon incline,
And, Love, I thought that I was full of thee.
But finding not those restless flames in me   5
Which others said did make their souls to pine,
I thought those babes of some pin's hurt did whine,
By my soul judging what love's pain might be.
But while I thus with this young lion play'd,
Mine eyes—shall I say curs'd or bless'd?—beheld   10
Stella; now she is nam'd, need more be said?
In her sight I a lesson new have spell'd.
    I now have learn'd love right, and learn'd ev'n so
    As who by being poison'd, doth poison know.

17

His mother dear, Cupid offended late
Because that Mars, grown slacker in her love,
With pricking shot he did not th'roughly move
To keep the pace of their first loving state.
The boy refus'd, for fear of Mars's hate   5
Who threatened stripes if he his wrath did prove;
But she, in chafe, him from her lap did shove,
Brake bow, brake shafts, while Cupid weeping sate;
Till that his grandam Nature,[1] pitying it,
Of Stella's brows made him two better bows,   10
And in her eyes of arrows infinite.
O how for joy he leaps! O how he crows!
    And straight therewith, like wags new got to play,[2]
    Falls to shrewd[3] turns! And I was in his way.

[1] grandam Nature—Nature is the mother of Beauty (Venus) and Beauty is the mother of Desire (Cupid).
[2] wags new got to play—boys newly begun to play.
[3] shrewd—mischievous.

18

With what sharp checks I in myself am shent[1]
When into reason's audit I do go,
And by just counts myself a bankrupt know
Of all those goods which heaven to me hath lent;
Unable quite[2] to pay even Nature's rent,   5
Which unto it by birthright I do owe;[3]
And, which is worse, no good excuse can show,
But that my wealth I have most idly spent.
My youth doth waste,[4] my knowledge brings forth toys;[5]
My wit doth strive those passions to defend,   10
Which, for reward, spoil it with vain annoys.[6]
I see my course to lose[7] myself doth bend;
   I see—and yet no greater sorrow take
    Than that I lose no more for Stella's sake.

19

On Cupid's bow how are my heart-strings bent,
That see my wrack[1] and yet embrace the same?
When most I glory, then I feel most shame;
I willing run, yet while I run repent;
My best wits still their own disgrace invent,   5
My very ink turns straight to Stella's name,
And yet my words, as them my pen doth frame,
Advise themselves that they are vainly spent.
For though she pass all things, yet what is all
That unto me, who fare like him[2] that both   10

[1] shent—blamed.
[2] quite—completely.
[3] to pay even . . . do owe—to return the basic obligations received at birth: to stay alive.
[4] waste—inactivity.
[5] toys—trivial writing.
[6] vain annoys—empty griefs.
[7] lose—ruin.
[1] wrack—ruin.
[2] him—the proverbial astronomer.

Looks to the skies and in a ditch doth fall?
O let me prop[3] my mind, yet in his growth
   And not in Nature, for best fruits unfit.[4]
   "Scholar," saith Love, "bend hitherward your wit."

20

Fly, fly, my friends, I have my death wound, fly!
See there that boy, that murth'ring boy, I say,
Who, like a thief, hid in dark bush doth lie
Till bloody bullet get him wrongful prey.
So tyrant he no fitter place could spy,   5
Nor so fair level in so secret stay,[1]
As that sweet black which veils the heavenly eye;
There himself with his shot he close doth lay.
Poor passenger,[2] pass now thereby I did,
And stay'd, pleas'd with the prospect of the place,   10
While that black hue from me the bad guest hid;
But straight I saw motions of lightning grace,
   And then descried the glist'ring of his dart;
   But ere I could fly thence, it pierc'd my heart.

21

Your words, my friend, right healthful caustics,[1] blame
My young mind marr'd, whom love doth windlass[2] so
That mine own writings, like bad servants, show
My wits quick in vain thoughts, in virtue lame;
That Plato I read for naught but if he tame   5
Such coltish years; that to my birth I owe

---

   [3] prop—give support to, as in gardening with growing things.
   [4] yet in his growth . . . unfit—still in its growing stage and not yet fully mature, not able to entertain the best things in life.
   [1] so fair level . . . stay—such a hidden but strategically good aiming place.
   [2] passenger—passer-by.
   [1] caustics—medical application used for burning away diseased tissue.
   [2] windlass—ensnare.

Nobler desires, lest else that friendly foe,
Great expectation, wear a train of shame;
For since mad March great promise made of me,
If now the May of my years much decline, 10
What can be hoped my harvest-time will be?
Sure, you say well. Your wisdom's golden mine
    Dig deep with learning's spade. Now tell me this—
    Hath this world aught so fair as Stella is?

22

In highest way of heaven the sun did ride,
Progressing then from fair Twins'[1] golden place,
Having no scarf of clouds before his face,
But shining forth of heat in his chief pride;
When some fair ladies, by hard promise tied, 5
On horseback met him in his furious race;
Yet each prepar'd with fans' well-shading grace
From that foe's wounds their tender skins to hide.
Stella alone with face unarmed march'd,
Either to do like him which open shone, 10
Or careless of the wealth, because her own.
Yet were the hid and meaner beauties parch'd;
    Her daintiest bare went free. The cause was this—
    The sun, which others burn'd, did her but kiss.

23

The curious wits, seeing dull pensiveness
Bewray itself in my long-settled[1] eyes,
Whence those same fumes of melancholy rise,
With idle pains and missing aim do guess.
Some, that know how my spring[2] I did address, 5

[1] fair Twins—the Zodiacal sign Gemini, which houses the sun from the last week in May through the first three weeks in June, i.e., midsummer.
[1] long-settled—usually calm.
[2] spring—youth.

Deem that my Muse some fruit of knowledge plies;
Others, because the prince my service tries,
Think that I think state errors to redress.
But harder judges judge ambition's rage,
Scourge of itself, still climbing slipp'ry place,   10
Holds my young brain captiv'd in golden cage.
O fools, or over-wise: alas, the race
    Of all my thoughts hath neither stop nor start
    But only Stella's eyes and Stella's heart.

24

Rich fools there be whose base and filthy heart
Lies hatching still the goods wherein they flow,
And damning their own selves to Tantal's smart,[1]
Wealth breeding want, more bliss'd, more wretched grow.
Yet to those fools heav'n such wit doth impart   5
As what their hands do hold, their heads do know,
And knowing, love, and loving, lay apart
As sacred things, far from all danger's show.
But that rich fool who by blind Fortune's lot
The richest gem of love and life enjoys,   10
And can with foul abuse such beauties blot,
Let him, deprived of sweet but unfelt joys,
    Exil'd for aye from those high treasures which
    He knows not, grow in only folly rich!

25

The wisest scholar of the wight most wise
By Phoebus' doom,[1] with sugar'd sentence says
That virtue, if it once met with our eyes,

_____

[1] Tantal's smart—Tantalus' punishment in Hades, to have food and drink always just beyond his reach, receding when he tries to grasp them.
[1] The wisest scholar . . . doom—Plato, the wisest pupil of Socrates, who was judged the wisest of mortals by Apollo's oracle.

Strange flames of love it in our souls would raise;
But, for that man with pain this truth descries,   5
Whiles he each thing in sense's balance weighs,
And so nor will nor can behold those skies
Which inward sun to heroic mind displays,
Virtue of late, with virtuous care to stir
Love of herself, took Stella's shape, that she   10
To mortal eyes might sweetly shine in her.
It is most true; for since I her did see,
 Virtue's great beauty in that face I prove,
 And find the effects, for I do burn in love.

26

Though dusty[1] wits dare scorn astrology,
And fools can think those lamps of purest light
(Whose numbers, ways,[2] greatness, eternity,
Promising wonders, wonder do invite)
To have for no cause birthright in the sky   5
But for to spangle the black weeds of night;
Or for some brawl[3] which in that chamber high
They should still dance to please a gazer's sight.
For me, I do Nature unidle know,[4]
And know great causes great effects procure;   10
And know those bodies high, reign on the low
And if these rules did fail, proof makes me sure,
 Who oft forejudge my after-following race[5]
 By only those two stars in Stella's face.

27

Because I oft in dark abstracted guise
Seem most alone in greatest company,

---

[1] dusty—mere earth-bound.
[2] ways—orbits.
[3] brawl—a circular dance.
[4] I do Nature unidle know—I know Nature is active.
[5] race—experience in life.

With dearth of words, or answers quite awry,
To them that would make speech of speech arise,
They deem, and of their doom the rumor flies,   5
That poison foul of bubbling pride doth lie
So in my swelling breast that only I
Fawn on myself, and others do despise.
Yet pride, I think, doth not my soul possess,
Which looks too oft in his unflatt'ring glass;   10
But one worse fault, ambition, I confess,
That makes me oft my best friends overpass,
    Unseen, unheard, while thought to highest place
    Bends all his powers, even unto Stella's grace.

28

You that with allegory's curious frame[1]
Of others' children changelings use to make,
With me those pains, for God's sake, do not take;   *or gold, silver*
I list[2] not dig so deep for brazen fame.
When I say Stella, I do mean the same   5
Princess of beauty, for whose only sake
The reins of Love I love, though never slake,
And joy therein, though nations count it shame.
I beg no subject to use eloquence,[3]
Nor in hid ways do guide philosophy;[4]   10
Look at my hands for no such quintessence;[5]
But know that I in pure simplicity
    Breathe out the flames which burn within my heart,
    Love only reading unto me this art.

[1] allegory's curious frame—literary deduction of hidden meanings.
[2] list—desire.
[3] I beg no subject to use eloquence—I am not at a loss for matter (invention) to display (disposition) my ability to exploit the flowers and figures of language (elocution) (see Gen. Intro.).
[4] in hid ways . . . philosophy—the old idea that knowledge must not be profaned, therefore must be hidden.
[5] quintessence—the complex fifth essence which was the object of alchemical science.

29

Like some weak lords, neighbor'd by mighty kings,
To keep themselves and their chief cities free
Do easily yield that all their coasts may be
Ready to store their camps of needful things,
So Stella's heart, finding what power Love brings
To keep itself in life and liberty,
Doth willing grant that in the frontiers he
Use all to help his other conquerings.
And thus her heart escapes, but thus her eyes
Serve him with shot, her lips his heralds are,   10
Her breasts his tents, legs his triumphal car,
Her flesh his food, her skin his armor brave.
   And I, but for because my prospect lies
   Upon that coast, am giv'n up for a slave.

30

Whether the Turkish new moon minded be
To fill his horns this year on Christian coast[1]—
How Poles' right king means, without leave of host,
To warm with ill-made fire cold Muscovy[2]—
If French can yet three parts in one agree[3]—   5
What now the Dutch in their full diets boast[4]—
How Holland hearts, now so good towns be lost,
Trust in the shade of pleasing Orange-tree[5]—

[1] Turkish new moon . . . coast—the crescent moon, symbol of the
Turkish Empire, traditional foe of the Christian world (cf. *Othello*).

[2] Poles' right king . . . Muscovy—King Stephen, the legitimate ruler
of Poland, conducted an invasion of Muscovy in 1580 which lasted until
December 1581. ("ill-made fire" is obscure but has been annotated as "red-
hot cannon shot.")

[3] If French can yet three parts in one agree—the three warring factions
in France from 1575 to 1589 were the Catholics, Huguenots, and moderates.

[4] The Dutch in their full diets boast—according to E. G. Fogel this
refers to the Diet of the Holy Roman Empire held at Augsburg (Germany)
1576–1582.

[5] How Holland hearts . . . Orange-tree—How the subjects of William
of Orange, king of Holland, feel about his rule now that he has lost so many
towns to the Spaniards.

How Ulster likes of that same golden bit
Wherewith my father once made it half tame[6]—   10
If in the Scotch court be no welt'ring yet[7]—
These questions busy wits to me do frame.
  I, cumber'd with good manners, answer do,
  But know not how; for still I think of you.

31

With how sad steps, O moon, thou climb'st the skies!
How silently, and with how wan a face!
What, may it be that even in heavenly place
That busy archer his sharp arrows tries?
Sure, if that long-with-love-acquainted eyes   5
Can judge of love, thou feel'st a lover's case;
I read it in thy looks; thy languish'd grace,
To me, that feel the like, thy state descries.
Then, even of fellowship, O moon, tell me,
Is constant love deem'd there but want of wit?   10
Are beauties there as proud as here they be?
Do they above love to be lov'd, and yet
  Those lovers scorn whom that love doth possess?
  Do they call "virtue" there, ungratefulness?[1]

32

Morpheus,[1] the lively son of deadly sleep,
Witness of life to them that living die,
A prophet oft, and oft an history,
A poet eke, as humors fly or creep:[2]

   [6] How Ulster . . . half tame—Sir Henry Sidney, three times Lord
Deputy of Ireland, had imposed internal taxation.
   [7] welt'ring yet—from the accession of Queen Elizabeth (1558), until the
death of Mary, Queen of Scots (1587), there was constant "unrest" in Scotland.
   [1] "virtue" . . . ungratefulness?—there in heaven, do proud beauties
call their ungratefulness, "virtue"?
   [1] Morpheus—god of dreams, son of Somnus.
   [2] as humors fly or creep—the humors in the dreamer's body dictate the
nature of his dreams.

Since thou in me so sure a power dost keep   5
That never I with clos'd-up sense do lie
But, by thy work, my Stella I descry,
Teaching blind eyes both how to smile and weep,
Vouchsafe, of all acquaintance,[3] this to tell:
Whence hast thou ivory, rubies, pearl, and gold,   10
To show her skin, lips, teeth, and head so well?
"Fool!" answers he, "no Indies such treasures hold;
  But from thy heart, while my sire charmeth thee,
  Sweet Stella's image I do steal to me."

33

I might—unhappy word—oh me, I might,
And then would not, or could not, see my bliss;
Till now wrapp'd in a most infernal night,
I find how heav'nly day (wretch) I did miss.
Heart, rend thyself, thou dost thyself but right;   5
No lovely Paris made thy Helen his;
No force, no fraud robb'd thee of thy delight,
Nor Fortune of thy fortune author is;
But to myself myself did give the blow,
While too much wit,[1] forsooth, so troubled me   10
That I respects[2] for both our sakes must show;
And yet could not, by rising morn, foresee
  How fair a day was near. O punish'd eyes,
  That I had been more foolish, or more wise!

34

Come, let me write. "And to what end?" To ease
A burthen'd heart. "How can words ease, which are
The glasses[1] of thy daily vexing care?"

---

[3] of all acquaintance—out of all that you know.
[1] wit—reason.
[2] respects—caution.
[1] glasses—reflection.

Oft cruel fights well pictured forth do please.
"Art not asham'd to publish thy disease?"   5
Nay, that may breed my fame, it is so rare.
"But will not wise men think thy words fond ware?"[2]
Then be they close,[3] and so none shall displease.
"What idler thing than speak and not be heard?"
What harder thing than smart and not to speak?   10
Peace, foolish wit! with wit my wit is marr'd.
Thus write I, while I doubt to write, and wreak
    My harms on ink's poor loss. Perhaps some find
    Stella's great powers, that so confuse my mind.

35

What may words say, or what may words not say,
Where·truth itself must speak like flattery?
Within what bounds can one his liking stay,[1]
Where Nature doth with infinite agree?
What Nestor's counsel[2] can my flames allay,   5
Since reason's self doth blow the coal in me?
And ah, what hope that hope should once see day,
Where Cupid is sworn page to chastity?
Honor is honor'd, that thou dost possess
Him as thy slave, and now long-needy fame   10
Doth even grow rich, naming my Stella's name.
Wit learns in thee perfection to express,
    Not thou by praise, but praise in thee is rais'd;
    It is a praise to praise, when thou art prais'd.

36

Stella, whence doth this new assault arise,
A conquer'd, yielded, ransack'd heart to win,

---

[2] fond ware—foolish stuff.
[3] close—secret.
[1] his liking stay—confine his love.
[2] Nestor's counsel—Nestor, venerable Greek, famous for his wisdom.

Whereto long since, through my long-batter'd eyes,
Whole armies of thy beauties enter'd in?
And there, long since, Love, thy lieutenant, lies;   5
My forces raz'd, thy banners rais'd within,
Of conquest do not these effects suffice,
But wilt new war upon thine own begin?
With so sweet voice, and by sweet Nature so
In sweetest strength, so sweetly skill'd withal   10
In all sweet stratagems sweet art can show,
That not my soul, which at thy foot did fall
  Long since, forc'd by thy beams, but stone or tree,
  By sense's privilege, can 'scape from thee.

37

My mouth doth water, and my breast doth swell,
My tongue doth itch, my thoughts in labor be.
Listen then, lordings, with good ear to me,
For, of my life,[1] I must a riddle tell.
Toward Aurora's court[2] a nymph doth dwell,   5
Rich in all beauties which man's eye can see
(Beauties so far from reach of words, that we
Abase her praise saying she doth excel),
Rich in the treasure of deserv'd renown,
Rich in the riches of a royal heart,   10
Rich in those gifts which give the eternal crown,
Who (though most rich in these and every part
  Which make the patents[3] of true worldly bliss)
  Hath no misfortune but that Rich she is.[4]

---

[1] of my life—"by my life."
[2] Aurora's court—Elizabeth's court, in the east of England.
[3] patents—royal grants.
[4] Rich she is—a satiric jab at Penelope Devereux, who had married
Lord Rich, inheritor of his grandfather's ill-gotten wealth.

38

This night, while sleep begins with heavy wings
To hatch[1] mine eyes, and that unbitted[2] thought
Doth fall[3] to stray, and my chief powers are brought
To leave the scepter of all subject things,
The first that straight my fancy's error[4] brings   5
Unto my mind is Stella's image, wrought
By Love's own self, but with so curious draught[5]
That she, methinks, not only shines but sings.
I start, look, hark: but what in clos'd-up sense
Was held, in open'd sense it flies away,   10
Leaving me nought but wailing eloquence.
I, seeing better sights in sight's decay,
    Call'd it[6] anew, and woo'd sleep again:
    But him, her host, that unkind guest had slain.

39

Come sleep! O sleep, the certain knot of peace,
The baiting place[1] of wit, the balm of woe,
The poor man's wealth, the prisoner's release,
The indifferent judge between the high and low;
With shield of proof shield me from out the prease[2]   5
Of those fierce darts despair at me doth throw;
O make in me those civil wars to cease;
I will good tribute pay, if thou do so.
Take thou of me smooth pillows, sweetest bed,
A chamber deaf to noise and blind to light,   10
A rosy garland and a weary head;

[1] hatch—seal.
[2] unbitted—unrestrained, unbridled.
[3] fall—begin.
[4] error—wandering.
[5] curious draught—skillful draughtsmanship.
[6] it—Stella's image.
[1] baiting place—resting place.
[2] prease—press or crowd.

And if these things, as being thine by right,
  Move not thy heavy grace,[3] thou shalt in me,
  Livelier than elsewhere, Stella's image see.

40

As good to write, as for to lie and groan:
O Stella dear, how much thy power hath wrought,
That hast my mind—now of the basest—brought
My still-kept course, while others sleep, to moan!
Alas, if from the height of virtue's throne   5
Thou canst vouchsafe the influence of a thought
Upon a wretch that long thy grace hath sought,
Weigh then how I by thee am overthrown,
And then think thus—although thy beauty be
Made manifest by such a victory,   10
Yet noblest conquerors do wrecks[1] avoid.
Since then thou hast so far subdued me
  That in my heart I offer still to thee,
  O do not let thy temple be destroy'd!

41

Having this day my horse, my hand, my lance
Guided so well that I obtain'd the prize,
Both by the judgment of the English eyes,
And of some sent from that sweet enemy, France,[1]
Horsemen my skill in horsemanship advance,[2]   5
Town-folks, my strength; a daintier[3] judge applies
His praise to sleight[4] which from good use[5] doth rise;

[3] heavy grace—weighty favor.
[1] wrecks—total annihilation of the defeated army.
[1] France—attempts to identify this tournament, if in fact it refers to an actual tournament, have proved fruitless.
[2] advance—praise.
[3] daintier—finer.
[4] sleight—dexterity.
[5] good use—practice, exercise.

Some lucky wits impute it but to chance;
Others, because of both sides I do take
My blood from them who did excell in this,[6]   10
Think Nature me a man of arms did make.
How far they shoot awry! The true cause is,
   Stella look'd on, and from her heav'nly face
   Sent forth the beams which made so fair my race.

42

O eyes, which do the spheres of beauty move,
Whose beams be joys, whose joys all virtues be,
Who, while they make love conquer, conquer love,
The schools where Venus hath learn'd chastity,
O eyes, where humble looks most glorious prove,   5
Only-lov'd tyrants, just in cruelty,
Do not, O do not, from poor me remove;
Keep still my zenith, ever shine on me.
For though I never see them but straightways
My life forgets to nourish languish'd sprites,   10
Yet still on me, O eyes, dart down your rays!
And if from majesty of sacred lights
   Oppressing mortal sense my death proceed,
   Wracks triumphs be[1] which love high-set doth breed.

43

Fair eyes, sweet lips, dear heart, that foolish I
Could hope, by Cupid's help, on you to prey,
Since to himself he doth your gifts apply,
As his main force, choice sport, and easeful stay.
For when he will see who dare him gainsay,   5
Then with those eyes he looks; lo, by-and-by,

[6] them who did excell in this—Sidney's father told Philip always to be proud to be descended from both the Dudleys and the Sidneys.

[1] Wracks triumphs be— things totally destroyed become signs of complete victory.

Each soul doth at Love's feet his weapons lay,
Glad if for her he give them leave to die.
When he will play, then in her lips he is,
Where, blushing red that Love's self them doth love,   10
With either lip he doth the other kiss;
But when he will, for quiet's sake, remove
　　From all the world, her heart is then his room,
　　Where well he knows no man to him can come.

44

My words I know do well set forth my mind;
My mind bemoans his sense of inward smart;
Such smart may pity claim of any heart;
Her heart, sweet heart, is of no tiger's kind,
And yet she hears and yet no pity I find,   5
But more I cry, less grace she doth impart.
Alas, what cause is there so overthwart
That nobleness itself makes thus unkind?[1]
I much do guess, yet find no truth save this,
That when the breath of my complaints doth touch   10
Those dainty doors unto the court of bliss,
The heavenly nature of that place is such
　　That, once come there, the sobs of mine annoys
　　Are metamorphos'd straight to tunes of joys.

45

Stella oft sees the very face of woe
Painted in my beclouded stormy face,
But cannot skill[1] to pity my disgrace,[2]
Not though thereof the cause herself she know.[3]

---

[1] what cause . . . thus unkind?—what evil effects does it have, that even nobility is driven by it to cruel behavior?
　[1] cannot skill—does not have the "know how."
　[2] disgrace—lack of blessing; therefore, unhappiness.
　[3] the cause herself she know—she knows herself to be the cause.

Yet hearing late a fable which did show   5
Of lovers-never-known a grievous case;
Pity thereof got in her breast such place
That, from that sea deriv'd, tears' spring did flow.
Alas, if fancy, drawn by imag'd things,
Though false, yet with free scope more grace doth breed   10
Than servant's wreck (where new doubts honor brings),[4]
Then think, my dear, that you in me do read
    Of lovers' ruin, some sad tragedy.
    I am not I; pity the tale of me.

46

I curst thee oft, I pity now thy case,
Blind-hitting boy, since she, that thee and me
Rules with a beck, so tyrannizeth thee
That thou must want or food or dwelling-place,
For she protests[1] to banish thee her face.   5
Her face! O Love, a rogue[2] thou then shouldst be
If Love learn not alone to love and see
Without desire to feed of further grace.
Alas, poor wag, that now a scholar art
To such a schoolmistress, whose lessons new   10
Thou needs must miss, and so thou needs must smart.
Yet, dear, let me his pardon get of you,
    So long, though he from book much to desire,
    Till without fuel you can make hot fire.

47

What, have I thus betrayed my liberty?
Can those black beams such burning marks[1] engrave

---

[4] where new doubts honor brings—obscure, possibly: as is not the case
in imagined ruin, out of the real ruin of a true lover there is the chance for
reassessment ("new doubt") and recognition ("honor").
[1] protests—formally intends.
[2] rogue—vagabond.
[1] burning marks—brands, sign of slavery.

In my free side; or am I born a slave,
Whose neck becomes² such yoke of tyranny?
Or want I sense to feel my misery,   5
Or sprite, disdain of such disdain to have,
Who for long faith, though daily help I crave,
May get no alms, but scorn of beggary?
Virtue, awake! Beauty but beauty is;
I may, I must, I can, I will, I do   10
Leave following that which it is gain to miss.
Let her go! Soft, but here she comes! Go to;
    Unkind, I love you not. Oh me, that eye
    Doth make my heart give to my tongue the lie!

48

Soul's joy, bend not those morning stars from me
Where virtue is made strong by beauty's might,
Where love is chasteness, pain does learn delight,
And humbleness grows one with majesty.
Whatever may ensue, O let me be   5
Co-partner of the riches of that sight.
Let not mine eyes be hell-driven from that light:
O look, O shine, O let me die, and see.
For though I oft myself of them bemoan
That through my heart their beamy darts be gone   10
Whose cureless wounds even now most freshly bleed,
Yet since my death-wound is already got,
    Dear killer, spare not thy sweet-cruel shot:
    A kind of grace it is to slay with speed.

49

I on my horse, and Love on me, doth try
Our horsemanships, while by strange work I prove
A horseman to my horse, a horse to Love,

² becomes—is naturally suited to.

And now man's wrongs[1] in me, poor beast, descry.
The reins wherewith my rider doth me tie   5
Are humbled thoughts, which bit of reverence move,
Curb'd in with fear, but with gilt boss[2] above
Of hope, which makes it seem fair to the eye;
The wand[3] is will; thou, fancy, saddle art,
Girt fast by memory; and while I spur   10
My horse, he spurs with sharp desire my heart;
He sits me fast, however I do stir;
    And now hath made me to his hand so right
    That in the manage[4] myself takes delight.

50

Stella, the fullness of my thoughts of thee
Cannot be stay'd within my panting breast,
But they do swell and struggle forth of me
Till that in words thy figure be express'd;
And yet, as soon as they so formed be,   5
According to my Lord Love's own behest,
With sad eyes I their weak proportion see
To portrait that which in this world is best.
So that I cannot choose but write my mind,
And cannot choose but put out[1] what I write,   10
While[2] these poor babes their death in birth do find;
And now my pen these lines had dashed quite[3]
    But that they stopp'd his fury from the same
    Because their forefront[4] bare sweet Stella's name.

[1] wrongs—cruelties.
[2] gilt boss—ornamental gold studs adorning the reins.
[3] wand—whip.
[4] manage—art of horsemanship.
[1] put out—put to death.
[2] while—as long as.
[3] dashed quite—blotted out.
[4] forefront—the first word.

51

Pardon mine ears, both I and they do pray,
So may your tongue still fluently proceed
To them that do such entertainment need,
So may you still have somewhat new to say.
On silly me do not the burthen lay   5
Of all the grave conceits your brain doth breed,
But find some Hercules to bear, instead
Of Atlas tired,[1] your wisdom's heavenly sway.
For me, while you discourse of courtly tides,
Of cunning fishers in most troubled streams,   10
Of straying ways, when valiant error[2] guides,
Meanwhile my heart confers with Stella's beams,
    And is even irk'd that so sweet comedy
    By such unsuited speech should hinder'd be.

52

A strife is grown between Virtue and Love,
While each pretends[1] that Stella must be his.
Her eyes, her lips, her all, saith Love, do this,
Since they do wear his badge,[2] most firmly prove.
But Virtue thus that title does disprove   5
That Stella (oh dear name!), that Stella is
That virtuous soul, sure heir of heavenly bliss,
Not this fair outside which our hearts doth move;
And therefore, though her beauty and her grace
Be Love's indeed, in Stella's self he may   10
By no pretense claim any manner place.
Well, Love, since this demur[3] our suit doth stay,

1 Atlas—Atlas once tricked Hercules into relieving him from bearing
the world on his shoulders.
2 error—to wander; therefore, to be wrong.
1 pretends—claims.
2 badge—livery.
3 demur—objection.

Let Virtue have that Stella's self; yet thus,
That Virtue but that body grant to us.

53

In martial sports I had my cunning tried,
And yet to break more staves[1] did me address,
While, with the people's shouts, I must confess,
Youth, luck, and praise even fill'd my veins with pride;
When Cupid, having me his slave descried   5
In Mars's livery prancing in the press,[2]
"What now, sir fool!" said he. I would no less.
"Look here, I say!" I look'd, and Stella spied,
Who, hard by, made a window send forth light.
My heart then quak'd, then dazzled were mine eyes;   10
One hand forgot to rule,[3] the other to fight;
Nor trumpets' sound I heard, nor friendly cries.
    My foe came on, and beat the air for me,[4]
    Till that her blush taught me my shame to see.

54

Because I breathe not love to every one,
Nor do not use set colors[1] for to wear,
Nor nourish special locks of vowed hair,[2]
Nor give each speech a full point of a groan,[3]
The courtly nymphs, acquainted with the moan   5
Of them who in their lips Love's standard bear,
"What, he!" say they of me, "now I dare swear

[1] staves—lances.
[2] press—crowd.
[3] rule—control the horse.
[4] beat the air for me—struck the empty air instead of me.
[1] set colors—either established, conventional colors of the lover, or his lady's colors.
[2] vowed—symbolizing devotion.
[3] full point of a groan—sigh after each sentence.

He cannot love; no, no, let him alone."
And think so still, so Stella know my mind;
Profess indeed I do not Cupid's art.   10
But you, fair maids, at length this true shall find,
That his right badge is but worn in the heart:
   Dumb swans, not chatt'ring pies,[4] do lovers prove;
   They love indeed who quake to say they love.

55

Muses, I oft invoked your holy aid,
With choicest flowers my speech t' engarland so
That it, despis'd in true but naked show,
Might win some grace in your sweet grace array'd;
And oft whole troops of saddest words I stay'd,   5
Striving abroad a-foraging to go,
Until by your inspiring I might know
How their black banner might be best display'd.
But now I mean no more your help to try,
Nor other sug'ring of my speech to prove,   10
But on her name incessantly to cry;
For let me but name her whom I do love,
   So sweet sounds straight mine ear and heart do hit,
   That I well find no eloquence like it.

56

Fie, school of patience, fie! Your lesson is
Far, far too long to learn it without book.[1]
What, a whole week without one piece of look,
And think I should not your large precepts miss?[2]
When I might read those letters fair of bliss   5

[4] pies—magpies.
[1] without book—by heart.
[2] what, . . . large precepts miss?—"Do you think I should be able to recite perfectly your heavy, abstract principles without having looked in my 'lesson book' for a week?"

Which in her face teach virtue, I could brook
Somewhat thy leaden counsels, which I took
As of a friend that meant not much amiss.
But now that I, alas, do want her sight,
What, dost thou think that I can ever take   10
In thy cold stuff a phlegmatic delight?
No, patience; if thou wilt my good, then make
   Her come and hear with patience my desire,
   And then with patience bid me bear my fire.

57

Woe having made, with many fights, his own
Each sense of mine, each gift, each power of mind;
Grown now his slaves, he forc'd them out to find
The thoroughest[1] words fit for woe's self to groan,
Hoping that when they might find Stella alone,   5
Before she could prepare to be unkind,
Her soul, arm'd but with such a dainty rind,
Should soon be pierc'd with sharpness of the moan.
She heard my plaints, and did not only hear,
But them (so sweet is she) most sweetly sing,   10
With that fair breast making woe's darkness clear.
A pretty case! I hoped her to bring
   To feel my griefs, and she, with face and voice
   So sweets my pains that my pains me rejoice.

58

Doubt there hath been,[1] when with his golden chain
The orator so far men's hearts doth bind
That no pace else their guided steps can find
But as he them more short or slack doth rein,[2]

[1] thoroughest—most penetrating.
[1] Doubt there hath been—there has been some question.
[2] orator . . . rein—Alciati's emblem portrays Hercules as leading a crowd by a golden chain attached to his tongue, thereby depicting the power of oratory.

Whether with words this sovereignty he gain,   5
Cloth'd with fine tropes, with strongest reasons lin'd,
Or else pronouncing grace,[3] wherewith his mind
Prints his own lively form in rudest brain.
Now judge by this: in piercing phrases late
The anatomy of all my woes I wrate;   10
Stella's sweet breath the same to me did read.
Oh voice, oh face! Mauger[4] my speech's might
    Which wooed woe, most ravishing delight
    Even those sad words even in sad me did breed.

59

Dear, why make you more of a dog than me?
If he do love, I burn, I burn in love;
If he wait well, I never thence would move;
If he be fair, yet but a dog can be.
Little he is, so little worth is he;   5
He barks, my songs thine own voice oft doth prove;
Bidd'n, perhaps he fetcheth thee a glove,
But I, unbid, fetch even my soul to thee.
Yet, while I languish, him that bosom clips,[1]
That lap doth lap, nay lets, in spite of spite,   10
This sour-breath'd mate taste of those sugar'd lips.
Alas, if you grant only such delight
    To witless things, then Love, I hope, since wit
    Becomes a clog,[2] will soon ease me of it.

60

When my good angel guides me to the place
Where all my good I do in Stella see,

---

[3] pronouncing grace—graceful delivery (cf. the matter vs. manner debate, in Letter to Robert Sidney).
    [4] Mauger—in spite of.
    [1] clips—embraces.
    [2] clog—wooden block attached to a horse's leg to prevent its straying.

That heav'n of joys throws only down on me
Thund'red disdains and lightnings of disgrace;
But when the ruggedest step of Fortune's race   5
Makes me fall from her sight, then sweetly she,
With words wherein the Muses' treasures be,
Shows love and pity to my absent case.
Now I, wit-beaten long by hardest fate,
So dull am that I cannot look into   10
The ground of this fierce love and lovely hate.
Then, some good body, tell me how I do,
    Whose presence absence, absence presence is:
    Bliss'd in my curse, and cursed in my bliss.

61

Oft with true sighs, oft with uncalled tears,
Now with slow words, now with dumb eloquence,
I Stella's eyes assay'd, invade her ears;
But this, at last, is her sweet-breath'd defense:
That who indeed in-felt affection bears[1]   5
So captives to his saint both soul and sense
That, wholly hers, all selfness he forebears;
Then, his desires he learns, his life's course thence.
Now, since her chaste mind hates this love in me,
With chasten'd mind I straight must show that she   10
Shall quickly me from what she hates remove.
O Doctor Cupid, thou for me reply;
    Driven else to grant, by angel's sophistry,
    That I love not without I leave to love.

62

Late tir'd with woe, even ready for to pine
With rage of love, I call'd my love unkind;
She in whose eyes love, though unfelt, doth shine,

---

[1] in-felt affection—love rooted in the soul rather than in the body.

Sweet said, that I true love in her should find.
I joyed; but straight thus water'd was my wine—   5
That love she did, but loved a love not blind,
Which would not let me, whom she loved, decline
From nobler course, fit for my birth and mind;
And therefore, by her love's authority,
Will'd me these tempests of vain love to fly,   10
And anchor fast myself on virtue's shore.
Alas, if this the only metal be
   Of love new coin'd to help my beggary,
   Dear, love me not, that ye may love me more.

63

O grammar-rules, O now your virtues show,
So children still read you with awful[1] eyes,
As my young dove may, in your precepts wise,
Her grant to me by her own virtue know;
For late, with heart most high, with eyes most low,   5
I crav'd the thing which ever she denies;
She, lightning love, displaying Venus' skies,
Lest once should not be heard, twice said, "No, no!"
Sing then, my muse, now Io Pæan sing;[2]
Heavens envy not at my high triumphing,   10
But grammar's force with sweet success confirm,
For grammar says,—oh this, dear Stella, weigh,—
   For grammar says,—to grammar who says nay?—
   That in one speech two negatives affirm!

First song

Doubt you to whom my Muse these notes intendeth
Which now my breast, o'ercharg'd, to music lendeth?

---

[1] awful—awed.
[2] Io Pæan—hymn of thanksgiving for deliverance.

To you, to you, all song of praise is due;
Only in you my song begins and endeth.

Who hath the eyes which marry state[1] with pleasure?   5
Who keeps the key of Nature's chiefest treasure?
To you, to you, all song of praise is due;
Only for you the heaven forgot all measure.

Who hath the lips where wit in fairness reigneth?
Who womankind at once both decks and staineth?   10
To you, to you, all song of praise is due;
Only by you Cupid his crown maintaineth.

Who hath the feet whose step of sweetness planteth?
Who else, for whom fame worthy trumpets wanteth?
To you, to you, all song of praise is due;   15
Only to you her scepter Venus granteth.

Who hath the breast whose milk doth passions nourish?
Whose grace is such that when it chides doth cherish?
To you, to you, all song of praise is due;
Only through you the tree of life doth flourish.   20

Who hath the hand which without stroke subdueth?
Who long dead beauty with increase reneweth?
To you, to you, all song of praise is due;
Only at you all envy hopeless rueth.

Who hath the hair which, loosest, fastest tieth?   25
Who makes a man live then glad, when he dieth?
To you, to you, all song of praise is due;
Only of you the flatterer never lieth.

Who hath the voice which soul from senses sunders?
Whose force but yours the bolts of beauty thunders?   30
To you, to you, all song of praise is due;
Only with you, not miracles, are wonders.

[1] state—dignity.

Doubt you to whom my Muse these notes intendeth,
Which now my breast, o'ercharg'd, to music lendeth?
To you, to you, all song of praise is due;   35
Only in you my song begins and endeth.

64

No more, my dear, no more these counsels try;
O give my passions leave to run their race;
Let Fortune lay on me her worst disgrace;
Let folk o'ercharg'd with brain against me cry;
Let clouds bedim my face, break in mine eye;   5
Let me no steps but of lost labor trace;
Let all the earth with scorn recount my case;
But do not will me from my love to fly.
I do not envy Aristotle's wit,
Nor do aspire to Caesar's bleeding fame,   10
Nor aught do care though some above me sit,
Nor hope nor wish another course to frame
   But that which once may win thy cruel heart.
   Thou art my wit, and thou my virtue art.

65

Love, by sure proof I may call thee unkind
That giv'st no better ear to my just cries,
Thou whom to me such my good turns should bind
As I may well recount but none can prize;[1]
For when, nak'd boy, thou couldst no harbor find   5
In this old world grown now so too, too wise,
I lodg'd thee in my heart, and being blind
By nature born, I gave to thee mine eyes.
Mine eyes, my light, my heart, my life, alas!
If so great services may scorned be,   10
Yet let this thought thy tig'rish courage pass,[2]

[1] prize—appraise.
[2] pass—surpass.

That I perhaps am somewhat kin to thee,
　　Since in thine arms, if learn'd fame truth hath spread,
　　Thou bear'st the arrow, I the arrow-head.

66

And do I see some cause a hope to feed,
Or doth the tedious burden of long woe
In weakened minds quick apprehending breed
Of every image which may comfort show?
I cannot brag of word, much less of deed,　　　　　5
Fortune wheels still with me, in one sort, slow;
My wealth no more, and no whit less my need;
Desire still on the stilts of fear doth go.
And yet amid all fears a hope there is,
Stolen to my heart since, last fair night, nay day,　　10
Stella's eyes sent to me the beams of bliss,
Looking on me while I look'd other way.
　　But when mine eyes back to their heaven did move,
　　They fled with blush which guilty seem'd of love.

67

Hope, art thou true, or dost thou flatter me?
Doth Stella now begin with piteous eye
The ruins of her conquest to espy?
Will she take time[1] before all wracked be?
Her eyes' speech is translated thus by thee,　　　　5
But fail'st thou not in phrase so heavenly high?
Look on again, the fair text better try;
What blushing notes dost thou in margin see?
What sighs stolen out, or kill'd before full-born?
Hast thou found such and such-like arguments,　　10
Or art thou else to comfort me forsworn?
Well, how so thou interpret the contents,

　　[1] take time—stop her conquest, call "time out."

I am resolved thy error to maintain,
Rather than by more truth to get more pain.

68

Stella, the only planet of my light,
Light of my life, and life of my desire,
Chief good whereto my hope doth only aspire,
World of my wealth, and heaven of my delight,
Why dost thou spend the treasures of thy sprite   5
With voice more fit to wed Amphion's lyre,[1]
Seeking to quench in me the noble fire
Fed by thy worth and blinded by thy sight?
And all in vain; for while thy breath most sweet
With choicest words, thy words with reasons rare,   10
Thy reasons firmly set on virtue's feet,
Labor to kill in me this killing care;
   O think I then, what paradise of joy
   It is, so fair a virtue to enjoy!

69

O joy too high for my low style to show!
O bliss fit for a nobler state than me!
Envy, put out thine eyes, lest thou do see
What oceans of delight in me do flow.
My friend, that oft saw through all masks my woe,   5
Come, come, and let me pour myself on thee.
Gone is the winter of my misery!
My spring appears; oh see what here doth grow.
For Stella hath, with words where faith doth shine,
Of her high heart given me the monarchy.   10
I, I—O—I may say that she is mine!
And though she give but thus condition'ly

[1] Amphion's lyre—Amphion's lyre had the power to make even stones obey; he used it to build the walls of Thebes. The whole line says: your spirit is better suited to creating affection than to tearing it down.

This realm of bliss, while virtuous course I take,
No kings be crown'd but they some covenants make.

70

My Muse may well grudge at my heavenly joy
If still I force her in sad rhymes to creep.
She oft hath drunk my tears, now hopes to enjoy
Nectar of mirth, since I Jove's cup do keep.
Sonnets be not bound prentice to annoy;   5
Trebles sing high, as well as basses deep;
Grief but Love's winter livery is; the boy
Hath cheeks to smile as well as eyes to weep.
Come then, my Muse, show thou height of delight
In well-rais'd notes; my pen, the best it may,   10
Shall paint out joy, though but in black and white.
Cease, eager Muse; peace, pen, for my sake stay.
  I give you here my hand for truth of this:
  Wise silence is best music unto bliss.

71   Petrarchan + Neoplatonic

Who will in fairest book of Nature know
How virtue may best lodg'd in beauty be,
Let him but learn of love to read in thee,
Stella, those fair lines which true goodness show.
There shall he find all vices' overthrow,   5
Not by rude force, but sweetest sovereignty
Of reason, from whose light those night birds[1] fly,
That inward sun in thine eyes shineth so.
And, not content to be perfection's heir
Thyself, dost strive all minds that way to move,   10
Who mark in thee what is in thee most fair.
So while thy beauty draws the heart to love,

  [1] night birds—emblems of vice and error.

As fast thy virtue bends that love to good.
But, ah, desire still cries, "Give me some food."

72

Desire, though thou my old companion art,
And oft so clings to my pure love that I
One from the other scarcely can descry,
While each doth blow the fire of my heart,
Now from thy fellowship I needs must part;   5
Venus is taught with Dian's wings to fly;
I must no more in thy sweet passions lie;
Virtue's gold now must head my Cupid's dart.
Service and honor, wonder with delight,
Fear to offend, will worthy to appear,   10
Care shining in mine eyes, faith in my sprite—
These things are left me by my only dear.
   But thou, desire, because thou wouldst have all,
   Now banish'd art; but yet, alas, how shall?

Second song

Have I caught my heavenly jewel
Teaching sleep most fair to be?
Now will I teach her that she,
When she wakes, is too too cruel.

Since sweet sleep her eyes hath charm'd   5
The two only darts of Love,
Now will I with that boy prove
Some play[1] while he is disarmed.

Her tongue, waking, still refuseth,
Giving frankly niggard no;   10
Now will I attempt to know
What no her tongue, sleeping, useth.

   [1] prove / Some play—have a contest.

See the hand which, waking, guardeth,
Sleeping, grants a free resort.
Now will I invade the fort.   15
Cowards love with loss rewardeth.

But, O fool, think of the danger
Of her just and high disdain!
Now will I, alas, refrain.
Love fears nothing else but anger.   20

Yet those lips, so sweetly swelling,
Do invite a stealing kiss.
Now will I but venture this.
Who will read must first learn spelling.

O, sweet kiss! but ah, she's waking!   25
Louring beauty chastens me.
Now will I away hence flee:
Fool, more fool, for no more taking!

73

Love still a boy, and oft a wanton, is,
School'd only by his mother's tender eye.
What wonder then if he his lesson miss,
When for so soft a rod, dear play he try?
And, yet, my star, because a sugar'd kiss   5
In sport I suck'd while she asleep did lie,
Doth lour, nay chide, nay threat for only this.
Sweet, it was saucy love, not humble I.
But no 'scuse serves; she makes her wrath appear
In beauty's throne. See now, who dares come near   10
Those scarlet judges, threat'ning bloody pain?
O heavenly fool,[1] thy most kiss-worthy face
    Anger invests with such a lovely grace
    That anger self I needs must kiss again.

[1] fool—often a term of endearment.

74

I never drank of Aganippe well,[1]
Nor ever did in shade of Tempe[2] sit,
And Muses scorn with vulgar brains to dwell,
Poor layman I, for sacred rites unfit.
Some do I hear of poets' fury[3] tell,   5
But, God wot, wot not what they mean by it;
And this I swear by blackest brook of hell,[4]
I am no pick-purse of another's wit.
How falls it then that with so smooth an ease
My thoughts I speak; and what I speak doth flow   10
In verse, and that my verse best wits doth please?
Guess we the cause. "What, is it thus?" Fie, no.
    "Or so?" Much less. "How then?" Sure thus it is:
    My lips are sweet, inspired with Stella's kiss.

75

Of all the kings that ever here did reign,
Edward, named fourth, as first in praise I name:[1]
Not for his fair outside nor well-lined brain,
Although less gifts imp[2] feathers oft on Fame;
Nor that he could, young-wise, wise-valiant, frame   5
His sire's revenge join'd with a kingdom's gain,[3]

    [1] Aganippe well—a fountain at the base of Mt. Helicon, the Muses'
dwelling place.
    [2] Tempe—a valley in Thessaly.
    [3] poets' fury—Plato called poetic inspiration a divine frenzy (cf. *Defence*).
    [4] I swear . . . of hell— the most binding of all oaths, honored even by
the gods, was that sworn on the river Styx.
    [1] first in praise I name—the irony of this poem would be immediately
apparent to Sidney's audience, familiar with the Tudor myth (see Shakespeare's *Henry VI* plays).
    [2] imp—graft new feathers onto a bird's wing to replace lost or broken
ones which being natural were better; therefore: "lesser gifts than beauty
and intelligence often bring fame."
    [3] Nor that . . . gain—Richard, Duke of York, leader of the Yorkist
faction, killed by the Lancastrians in the Wars of the Roses, was revenged
by his sons, Edward becoming king.

And, gain'd by Mars, could yet mad Mars so tame
That balance weigh'd what sword did late obtain:[4]
Nor that he made the fleur-de-luce so 'fraid
—Though strongly hedg'd—of bloody lions' paws,   10
That witty Lewis to him a tribute paid:[5]
Nor this, nor that, nor any such small cause,
    But only for this worthy knight durst prove
    To lose his crown rather than fail his love.[6]

76

She comes, and straight therewith her shining twins do
        move
Their rays to me, who in her tedious absence lay
Benighted in cold woe; but now appears my day,
The only light of joy, the only warmth of love.
She comes with light and warmth which, like Aurora,[1]
        prove   5
Of gentle force, so that mine eyes dare gladly play
With such a rosy morn whose beams, most freshly gay,
Scorch not, but only do dark chilling sprites remove.
But, lo, while I do speak, it groweth noon with me,
Her flamy-glist'ring lights increase with time and place;   10
My heart cries, "ah, it burns," mine eyes now dazzled be;
No wind, no shade can cool: what help then in my case?
    But with short breath, long looks, staid feet, and
        walking head,
    Pray that my sun go down with meeker beams to bed.

    [4] And . . . obtain—Edward, of course, did not bring a "just and lasting peace" to England.
    [5] Nor that . . . paid—Edward invaded France in 1474 and demanded tribute, which Louis XI granted if Edward withdrew across the channel, which he did and Louis continued to pay even "though strongly hedged."
    [6] To lose . . . fail his love—Edward rejected his French fiancée in order to marry Lady Elizabeth Grey, whom he rejected in favor of his mistress, Jane Shore.
    [1] Aurora—goddess of dawn.

77

Those looks, whose beams be joy, whose motion is delight,
That face whose lecture[1] shows what perfect beauty is,
That presence which doth give dark hearts a living light,
That grace which Venus weeps that she herself doth miss,
That hand which without touch holds more than Atlas
    might,   5
Those lips which make death's pay a mean price for a kiss,
That skin whose past-praise hue scorns this poor term of
    white,
Those words which do sublime the quintessence[2] of bliss,
That voice which makes the soul plant himself in the ears,
That conversation sweet where such high comforts be   10
As, conster'd[3] in true speech, the name of heaven it bears,
Make me in my best thoughts and quietest judgment see
    That in no more but these I might be fully blest;
    Yet, ah, my maiden Muse does blush to tell the best.

78

O how the pleasant airs of true love be
Infected by those vapors which arise
From out that noisome gulf which gaping lies
Between the jaws of hellish jealousy,
A monster (others' harm, self-misery,   5
Beauty's plague, virtue's scourge, succor of lies),
Who (his own joy to his own hurt applies,
And only cherish doth with injury),
Who (since he hath by Nature's special grace
So piercing paws as spoil when they embrace,   10
So nimble feet as stir still, though on thorns,
So many eyes aye seeking their own woe,

---

[1] lecture—lesson.
[2] sublime the quintessence—in alchemical terms, abstract the fifth essence.
[3] conster'd—construed.

So ample ears as never good news know)
Is it not evil that such a devil wants horns?

79

Sweet kiss, thy sweets I fain would sweetly indite:
Which, even of sweetness sweetest sweet'ner art;
Pleasing'st consort,[1] where each sense holds a part;
Which, coupling doves, guides Venus' chariot right;
Best charge and bravest retreat in Cupid's fight;   5
A double key, which opens to the heart,
Most rich when most his riches it impart;
Nest of young joys, schoolmaster of delight,
Teaching the mean[2] at once to take and give;
The friendly fray, where blows both wound and heal, 10
The pretty death,[3] while each in other live;
Poor hope's first wealth, hostage of promis'd weal;
 Breakfast of love. But lo, lo, where she is!
 Cease we to praise; now pray we for a kiss.

80

Sweet-swelling lip, well mayst thou swell in pride,
Since best wits think it wit thee to admire;
Nature's praise, virtue's stall,[1] Cupid's cold fire,
Whence words, not words but heavenly graces slide;
The new Parnassus, where the Muses bide;   5
Sweet'ner of music, wisdom's beautifier,
Breather of life, and fast'ner of desire,
Where beauty's blush in honor's grain[2] is dyed.
Thus much my heart compell'd my mouth to say;
But now, spite of my heart, my mouth will stay, 10

[1] consort—harmony.
[2] mean—means.
[3] pretty death—consummation.
[1] stall—throne.
[2] grain—scarlet.

Loathing all lies, doubting this flattery is,
And no spur can his resty race³ renew
  Without, how far this praise is short of you,
  Sweet lip, you teach my mouth with one sweet kiss.

   8 1

O kiss, which dost those ruddy gems impart,
Or gems or fruits of new-found Paradise,
Breathing all bliss and sweet'ning to the heart,
Teaching dumb lips a nobler exercise;
O kiss, which souls, even souls, together ties   5
By links of love and only Nature's art,
How fain would I paint thee to all men's eyes,
Or of thy gifts at least shade out some part!
But she forbids; with blushing words she says
She builds her fame on higher-seated praise.   10
But my heart burns; I cannot silent be.
Then, since, dear life, you fain would have me peace,¹
  And I, mad with delight, want wit to cease,
  Stop you my mouth with still, still kissing me.

   82

Nymph of the garden where all beauties be,
Beauties which do in excellency pass
His¹ who till death look'd in a wat'ry glass,
Or hers² whom naked the Trojan boy did see;
Sweet garden-nymph, which keeps the cherry-tree³   5
Whose fruit doth far the Hesperian taste⁴ surpass,

    ³ resty race—restless running.
    ¹ peace—be quiet.
    ¹ His—Narcissus, who fell in a stream while admiring his own reflection.
    ² hers—Venus, judged most beautiful by Paris, who thereby won Helen.
    ³ cherry-tree—symbol of virginity.
    ⁴ Hesperian taste—the golden apples of the Hesperides, symbols of immortality.

Most sweet-fair, most fair-sweet, do not, alas,
From coming near those cherries banish me.
For though, full of desire, empty of wit,
Admitted late by your best-graced grace,   10
I caught at one of them, and hungry bit,
Pardon that fault; once more grant me the place,
　And I do swear, even by the same delight,
　I will but kiss; I never more will bite.

83

Good brother Philip,[1] I have borne you long.
I was content you should in favor creep,
While craftily you seem'd your cut to keep,[2]
As though that fair soft hand did you great wrong;
I bare, with envy, yet I bare your song,   5
When in her neck you did love-ditties peep;
Nay—more fool I—oft suffer'd you to sleep
In lilies' nest where Love's self lies along.
What, doth high place ambitious thoughts augment?
Is sauciness reward of courtesy?   10
Cannot such grace your silly self content
But you must needs with those lips billing be,
　And through those lips drink nectar from that tongue?
　Leave that, Sir Philip, lest off your neck be wrung!

Third Song

If Orpheus' voice[1] had force to breathe such music's love
Through pores of senseless trees as it could make them
　　move,

　[1] brother Philip—Stella's pet sparrow who gets his name from Jane
Scrope's pet in Skelton's *Philip Sparrow.*
　[2] craftily . . . cut to keep—pretended to nurse some hurt.
　[1] Orpheus' voice—Orpheus, the Thracian bard, had the power to
harmonize all nature with his music.

If stones good measure danc'd the Theban walls to build
To cadence of the tunes which Amphion's lyre did yield,[2]
More cause a like effect at leastwise bringeth: 5
O stones, O trees, learn hearing—Stella singeth.

If love might sweeten so a boy of shepherd brood
To make a lizard dull to taste love's dainty food,[3]
If eagle fierce could so in Grecian maid delight
As his light was her eyes, her death his endless night,[4]   10
Earth gave that love, heaven, I trow, love refineth:
O beasts, O birds, look love—lo, Stella shineth.

The birds, beasts, stones, and trees feel this, and feeling love;
And if the trees nor stones stir not the same to prove,
Nor beasts nor birds do come unto this blessed gaze,   5   15
Know that small love is quick, and great love doth amaze.
They are amaz'd, but you, with reason arm'd,
O eyes, O ears of men, how are you charm'd!

84

Highway, since you my chief Parnassus[1] be,
And that my Muse, to some ears not unsweet,
Tempers her words to trampling horses' feet
More oft than to a chamber melody,
Now blessed you bear onward blessed me   5
To her, where I my heart, safest shall meet;
My Muse and I must you of duty greet
With thanks and wishes, wishing thankfully:

[2] yield—see AS68, note 1.
[3] If love . . . dainty food—Thoas, an Arcadian shepherd lad, was so beautiful that a dragon was moved to rescue him from bandits.
[4] If eagle . . . night—a Sestain maid tamed an eagle; when she died, it flew into her funeral pyre and was consumed.
[5] small love is quick, and great love doth amaze—Cupid's love (earthly, human love) inspires activity; Venus' love (great creating Nature's love) stuns the mind.
[1] my chief Parnassus—my inspiration.

Be you still fair, honor'd by public heed,[2]
By no encroachment wrong'd, nor time forgot,   10
Nor blam'd for blood, nor sham'd for sinful deed;
And that you know I envy you no lot
   Of highest wish, I wish you so much bliss,
   Hundreds of years you Stella's feet may kiss.

85

I see the house. My heart thyself contain!
Beware full sails drown not thy tottering barge,
Lest joy, by nature, apt sprites to enlarge,
Thee to thy wrack beyond thy limits strain;
Nor do like lords whose weak confus'd brain,   5
Not 'pointing to fit folks[1] each undercharge,
While every office themselves will discharge,
With doing all leave nothing done but pain.[2]
But give apt servants their due place: let eyes
See beauty's total sum summ'd in her face,   10
Let ears hear speech which wit to wonder ties,
Let breath suck up those sweets, let arms embrace
   The globe of weal,[3] lips love's indentures make.[4]
   Thou but of all the kingly tribute take.

Fourth Song

Only joy, now here you are,
Fit to hear and ease my care;
Let my whispering voice obtain
Sweet reward for sharpest pain;
Take me to thee, and thee to me—   5
"No, no, no, no, my dear, let be."

[2] heed—care.
[1] 'pointing to fit folks—appointing to reliable servants.
[2] pain—trouble.
[3] globe of weal—world of good.
[4] lips love's indentures make—lips draw up love's contracts.

Night hath clos'd all in her cloak,
Twinkling stars love-thoughts provoke,
Danger hence, good care doth keep,
Jealousy itself doth sleep;   10
Take me to thee, and thee to me—
"No, no, no, no, my dear, let be."

Better place no wit can find,
Cupid's yoke to loose or bind;
These sweet flowers on fine bed too,   15
Us in their best language woo;
Take me to thee, and thee to me—
"No, no, no, no, my dear, let be."

This small light the moon bestows
Serves thy beams but to disclose;   20
So to raise my hap more high,
Fear not else, none can us spy;
Take me to thee, and thee to me—
"No, no, no, no, my dear, let be."

That you heard was but a mouse,   25
Dumb sleep holdeth all the house;
Yet asleep, methinks they say,
Young folks, take time while you may;
Take me to thee, and thee to me—
"No, no, no, no, my dear, let be."   30

Niggard time threats, if we miss
This large offer of our bliss,
Long stay ere he grant the same;
Sweet, then, while each thing doth frame,[1]
Take me to thee, and thee to me—   35
"No, no, no, no, my dear, let be."

Your fair mother is abed,
Candles out and curtains spread;

[1] frame—is of service.

She thinks you do letters write;
Write, but let me first endite: 40
Take me to thee, and thee to me—
"No, no, no, no, my dear, let be."

Sweet, alas, why strive you thus?
Concords better fitteth us;
Leave to Mars the force of hands,   45
Your power in your beauty stands;
Take thee to me, and me to thee—
"No, no, no, no, my dear, let be."

Woe to me, and do you swear
Me to hate? but I forbear;   50
Cursed be my destines all,
That brought me so high to fall;
Soon with my death I will please thee—
"No, no, no, no, my dear, let be."

86

Alas, whence came this change of looks? If I
Have chang'd desert let mine own conscience be
A still-felt plague to self-condemning me,
Let woe gripe on my heart, shame load mine eye;
But if all faith like spotless ermine[1] lie   5
Safe in my soul, which only doth to thee
As his sole object of felicity
With wings of Love in air of wonder fly,
O ease your hand, treat not so hard your slave:
In justice pains come not till faults do call.   10
Or if I needs, sweet judge, must torments have,
Use something else to chasten me withal
    Than those bless'd eyes where all my hopes do dwell:
No doom[2] should make one's heaven become his hell.

[1] spotless ermine—emblem of purity.
[2] doom—judgment.

Fifth Song

While favor fed my hope, delight with hope was brought,
Thought waited on delight, and speech did follow thought;
Then grew my tongue and pen records unto thy glory;
I thought all words were lost, that were not spent of thee;
I thought each place was dark but where thy lights would
    be,   5
And all ears worse than deaf, that heard not out thy story.

I said, thou wert most fair, and so indeed thou art;
I said, thou were most sweet, sweet poison to my heart;
I said, my soul was thine (O that I then had lied);
I said, thine eyes were stars, thy breasts the milken way,   10
Thy fingers Cupid's shafts, thy voice the angels' lay:[1]
And all I said so well, as no man it denied.

But now that hope is lost, unkindness kills delight,
Yet thought and speech do live, though metamorphos'd
    quite;
For rage now rules the reins, which guided were by
    pleasure.   15
I think now of thy faults, who late thought of thy praise,
That speech falls now to blame, which did thy honor raise,
The same key open can, which can lock up a treasure.

Thou then whom partial heavens conspir'd in one to frame,
The proof of beauty's worth, th' inheritrix of fame,   20
The mansion seat of bliss, and just excuse of lovers;
See now those feathers pluck'd, wherewith thou flew most
    high;
See what clouds of reproach shall dark thy honor's sky,
Whose own fault casts him down, hardly high seat
    recovers.

And O my Muse, though oft you lull'd her in your lap,   25
And then, a heavenly child, gave her Ambrosia pap,
And to that brain of hers your hidd'nest gifts infused,

[1] lay—song

Since she disdaining me, doth you in me disdain,
Suffer not her to laugh, while both we suffer pain:
Princes in subjects wrong'd, must deem themselves abused.   30

Your client, poor myself, shall Stella handle so?
Revenge, revenge, my Muse, defiance' trumpet blow;
Threaten what may be done, yet do more than you threat'n.
Ah, my suit granted is, I feel my breast doth swell;
Now child, a lesson new you shall begin to spell: 35
Sweet babes must babies[2] have, but shrewd[3] girls must be
    beat'n
Think now no more to hear of warm fine odor'd snow,
Nor blushing lilies, nor pearls' ruby-hidden row,
Nor of that golden sea, whose waves in curls are broken;
But of thy soul, so fraught with such ungratefulness,   40
As where thou soon might'st help, most faith doth most
    oppress:
Ungrateful who is call'd, the worst of evils is spoken.

Yet worse than worst, I say thou art a thief. A thief?
Now God forbid. A thief, and of worst thieves the chief:
Thieves steal for need, and steal but goods, which pain
    recovers,   45
But thou rich in all joys, dost rob my joys from me,
Which cannot be restor'd by time nor industry:
Of foes the spoil is evil, far worse of constant lovers.

Yet gentle English thieves do rob, but will not slay;
Thou English murd'ring thief, wilt have hearts for thy prey;   50
The name of murd'rer now on thy fair forehead sitteth,
And even while I do speak, my death wounds bleeding be,
Which (I protest) proceeds from only cruel thee,
Who may and will not save, murder in truth committeth.

But murder, private fault, seems but a toy to thee,   55
I lay then to thy charge unjustest tyranny,
If rule by force without all claim a tyrant showeth,

2 babies—dolls.
3 shrewd—shrewish.

For thou dost lord my heart, who am not born thy slave,
And which is worse, makes me most guiltless torments
    have,
A rightful prince by unright deeds a tyrant groweth.   60

Lo you grow proud with this, for tyrants make folk bow;
Of foul rebellion, then, I do appeach[4] thee now;
Rebel by Nature's law, rebel by law of reason,
Thou, sweetest subject, were born in the realm of Love,
And yet against thy prince thy force dost daily prove: 65
No virtue merits praise, once touch'd with blot of treason.

But valiant rebels oft in fools' mouth purchase fame;
I now then stain thy white with vagabonding shame,
Both rebel to the son, and vagrant from the mother;
For wearing Venus' badge, in every part of thee,   70
Unto Diana's train thou runaway didst flee:
Who faileth one is false, though trusty to another.

What, is not this enough? nay far worse cometh here;
A witch I say thou art, though thou so fair appear;
For I protest, my sight never thy face enjoyeth,   75
But I in me am chang'd; I am alive and dead:
My feet are turn'd to roots, my heart becometh lead,
No witchcraft is so evil, as which man's mind destroyeth.

Yet witches may repent, thou art far worse than they;
Alas, that I am forc'd such evil of thee to say,   80
I say thou art a devil, though cloth'd in angel's shining;
For thy face tempts my soul to leave the heav'n for thee,
And thy words of refuse, do pour even hell on me:
Who tempt, and tempted plague, are devils in true defining.

You then ungrateful thief, you murd'ring tyrant you,   85
You rebel run away, to lord and lady untrue,
You witch, you devil, (alas) you still of me beloved,
You see what I can say, mend yet your froward mind,

---

[4] appeach—impeach.

And such skill in my Muse you reconcil'd shall find,
That all these cruel words your praises shall be proved.   90

Sixth Song

O you that hear this voice,
O you that see this face,
Say whether[1] of the choice
Deserves the former place;[2]
Fear not to judge this bate,[3]   5
For it is void of hate.

This side doth Beauty take,
For that doth Music speak,
Fit orators to make
The strongest judgments weak;   10
The bar[4] to plead their right
Is only true Delight.

Thus doth the voice and face,
These gentle lawyers wage,
Like loving brothers' case,   15
For father's heritage;
That each, while each contends,
Itself to other lends.[5]

For Beauty beautifies
With heavenly hue and grace   20
The heavenly harmonies,
And in this faultless face
The perfect beauties be
A perfect harmony.

Music more loftly swells   25
In speeches nobly placed;

1 whether—which one.
2 former place—precedence.
3 bate—contest.
4 bar—barrister.
5 Itself to other lends—aids his opponent.

Beauty as far excels
In action aptly graced.
A friend each party draws
To countenance his cause.   30

Love more affected seems
To Beauty's lovely light,
And Wonder more esteems
Of Music's wondrous might:
But both to both so bent,   35
As both in both are spent.

Music doth witness call
The Ear his truth to try,
Beauty brings to the hall
The judgment of the Eye;   40
Both in their objects such
As no exceptions[6] touch.

The Common Sense which might
Be arbiter of this,
To be forsooth upright,   45
To both sides partial is;
He lays on this chief praise,
Chief praise on that he lays.

Then Reason, princess high,
Whose throne is in the mind,   50
Which Music can in sky
And hidden beauties find,
Say, whether thou wilt crown
With limitless renown.

Seventh Song

Whose senses in so evil consort, their stepdame Nature lays,
That ravishing delight in them most sweet tunes do not
    raise;

---

[6] exceptions—legal objections.

Or if they do delight therein, yet are so cloyed with wit,
As with sententious lips to set a title vain on it:
O let them hear these sacred tunes, and learn in wonder's
    schools,   5
To be (in things past bounds of wit) fools, if they be not
    fools.

Who have so leaden eyes, as not to see sweet beauty's show,
Or seeing, have so wodden wits,[1] as not that worth to
    know;
Or knowing, have so muddy minds, as not to be in love;
Or loving, have so frothy thoughts, as easily thence to
    move?   10
O let them see these heavenly beams, and in fair letters read
A lesson fit, both sight and skill, love and firm love to breed.

Hear then, but then with wonder hear; see, but adoring see:
No mortal gifts, no earthly fruits, now here descended be:
See, do you see this face? a face? nay image of the skies,   15
Of which the two life-giving lights are figured in her eyes.
Hear you this soul-invading voice, and count it but a voice?
The very essence of their tunes, when angels do rejoice.

   Eighth Song

In a grove most rich of shade,
Where birds wanton music made,
May, then young, his pied weeds[1] showing,
New-perfumed with flowers fresh growing,

Astrophel with Stella sweet   5
Did for mutual comfort meet,
Both within themselves oppressed,
But each in the other blessed.

Him great harms had taught much care,
Her fair neck a foul yoke bare;   10

    1 wodden wits—mad minds.
    1 pied weeds—multi-colored clothes.

But her sight his cares did banish,
In his sight her yoke did vanish.

Wept they had, alas the while,
But now tears themselves did smile,
While their eyes, by love directed,   15
Interchangeable reflected.

Sigh they did, but now betwixt
Sighs of woe were glad sighs mix'd,
With arms cross'd, yet testifying
Restless rest and living dying.   20

Their ears hungry of each word
Which the dear tongue would afford,
But their tongues restrain'd from walking
Till their hearts had ended talking.

But, when their tongues could not speak,   25
Love itself did silence break;
Love did set his lips asunder,
Thus to speak in love and wonder:

"Stella, sovereign of my joy,
Fair triumpher of annoy,²   30
Stella, star of heavenly fire,
Stella, lodestar of desire,

"Stella, in whose shining eyes
Are the lights of Cupid's skies,
Whose beams, where they once are darted,   35
Love therewith is straight imparted,

"Stella whose voice, when it speaks,
Senses all asunder breaks,
Stella whose voice, when it singeth,
Angels to acquaintance bringeth,   40

"Stella, in whose body is
Writ each character of bliss,

² annoy—grief

Whose face all, all beauty passeth,
Save thy mind, which yet surpasseth,

"Grant, O grant—but speech, alas,   45
Fails me, fearing on to pass!—
Grant, O me! what am I saying?
But no fault there is in praying.

"Grant, O dear, on knees I pray,"
(Knees on ground he then did stay)   50
"That, not I, but, since I love you,
Time and place for me may move you.

"Never season was more fit,
Never room more apt for it;
Smiling air allows my reason;   55
These birds sing, 'Now use the season.'

"This small wind, which so sweet is,
See how it the leaves doth kiss;
Each tree in his best attiring
Sense of love to love inspiring.   60

"Love makes earth the water drink,
Love to earth makes water sink;
And, if dumb things be so witty,
Shall a heavenly grace want pity?"

There his hands, in their speech, fain   65
Would have made tongue's language plain;
But her hands, his hands repelling,
Gave repulse all grace excelling.

Then she spake; her speech was such,
As not ears but heart did touch,   70
While suchwise she love denied,
As yet love she signified.

"Astrophel," said she, "my love,
Cease in these effects to prove;

Now be still, yet still believe me,   75
Thy grief more than death would grieve me.

"If that any thought in me
Can taste comfort but of thee,
Let me, fed with hellish anguish,
Joyless, hopeless, endless languish.   80

"If those eyes you praised be
Half so dear as you to me,
Let me home return, stark blinded
Of those eyes, and blinder minded.[3]

"If to secret of my heart   85
I do any wish impart
Where thou art not foremost placed,
Be both wish and I defaced.[4]

"If more may be said, I say
All my bliss in thee I lay;   90
If thou love, my love, content thee,
For all love, all faith, is meant thee.

"Trust me, while I thee deny,
In myself the smart I try;
Tyrant honor doth thus use thee: 95
Stella's self might not refuse thee.

"Therefore, dear, this no more move,
Lest, though I leave not thy love,
Which too deep in me is framed,
I should blush when thou art named."   100

Therewithal away she went,
Leaving him to passion, rent
With what she had done and spoken,
That therewith my song is broken.

[3] blinder minded—my mind even more blinded.
[4] defaced—utterly destroyed.

Ninth Song

Go, my flock, go get you hence,
Seek a better place of feeding,
Where you may have some defence
From the storms in my breast breeding,
And showers from mine eyes proceeding.   5

Leave a wretch in whom all woe
Can abide to keep no measure;
Merry flock, such one forgo,
Unto whom mirth is displeasure,
Only rich in mischief's treasure.   10

Yet, alas, before you go,
Hear your woeful master's story,
Which to stones I else would show:
Sorrow only then hath glory
When 'tis excellently[1] sorry.   15

Stella, fiercest shepherdess,
Fiercest but yet fairest ever,
Stella whom, O heavens, do bless,
Though against me she persever,
Though I bliss inherit never,   20

Stella hath refused me;
Stella who more love hath proved
In this caitiff[2] heart to be
Than can in good ewes be moved
Toward lambkins best beloved.   25

Stella hath refused me,
Astrophel, that so well served
In this pleasant spring must see,
While in pride flowers be preserved,
Himself only winter-starved.   30

[1] excellently—exceedingly.
[2] caitiff—lowest of the low, most wretched.

Why, alas, doth she then swear
That she loveth me so dearly,
Seeing me so long to bear
Coals of love that burn so clearly,
And yet leave me helpless merely?   35

Is that love? forsooth I trow,
If I saw my good dog grieved,
And a help for him did know,
My love should not be believed
But he were by me relieved.   40

No, she hates me (wellaway!)
Feigning love somewhat to please me,
For she knows if she display
All her hate, death soon would seize me
And of hideous torments ease me.   45

Then adieu, dear flock, adieu!
But, alas, if in your straying
Heavenly Stella meet with you,
Tell her, in your piteous blaying,
Her poor slave's unjust decaying.   50

87

When I was forc'd from Stella ever dear
(Stella, food of my thoughts, heart of my heart;
Stella, whose eyes make all my tempest clear)
By iron laws of duty to depart,
Alas, I found that she with me did smart;   5
I saw that tears did in her eyes appear,
I saw that sighs her sweetest lips did part,
And her sad words my sadded sense did hear.
For me, I wept to see pearls scattered so,
I sigh'd her sighs and wailed for her woe,   10
Yet swam in joy, such love in her was seen.
Thus, while the effect most bitter was to me,

And nothing than the cause more sweet could be.
I had been vex'd, if vex'd I had not been.

88

Out, traitor absence, darest thou counsel me
From my dear captainess to run away
Because in brave array here marcheth she
That to win me oft shows a present pay?[1]
Is faith so weak? Or is such force in thee?   5
When sun is hid, can stars such beams display?
Cannot heaven's food, once felt, keep stomach free
From base desire on earthly cates[2] to prey?
Tush, absence! While thy mists eclipse that light,
My orphan sense flies to the inward sight,   10
Where memory sets forth the beams of love,
That, where before heart loved and eyes did see,
    In heart both sight and love now coupled be:
    United powers make each the stronger prove.

89

Now that, of absence, the most irksome night
With darkest shade doth overcome my day,
(Since Stella's eyes, wont to give me my day,
Leaving my hemisphere, leave me in night)
Each day seems long and longs for long-stay'd night;   5
The night, as tedious, woos the approach of day;
Tired with the dusty toils of busy day,
Languish'd with horrors of the silent night,
Suff'ring the evils both of the day and night,
(While no night is more dark than is my day,   10
Nor no day hath less quiet than my night)

[1] shows a present pay—offers immediate return on my love.
[2] cates—delicacies.

With such bad-mixture of my night and day
  That living thus in blackest winter night,
  I feel the flames of hottest summer day.

90

Stella, think not that I by verse seek fame—
Who seek, who hope, who love, who live—but thee,
Thine eyes my pride, thy lips mine history.
If thou praise not, all other praise is shame.
Nor so ambitious am I as to frame   5
A nest for my young praise in laurel tree.
In truth, I swear I wish not there should be
Graved in mine epitaph a poet's name.
Nay, if I would, I could just title make
That any laud to me thereof should grow   10
Without my plumes from others' wings I take,
For nothing from my wit or will doth flow
  Since all my words thy beauty doth indite,
  And love doth hold my hand, and makes me write.

91

Stella, while now by honor's cruel might
I am from you (light of my life) misled,
And that fair you, my sun, thus overspread
With absence' veil, I live in sorrow's night,
If this dark place yet show like candle-light,   5
Some beauty's piece (as amber-color'd head,
Milk hands, rose cheeks, or lips more sweet, more red
Or seeing jets, black,[1] but in blackness bright)
They please, I do confess, they please mine eyes.
But why? Because of you they models be,   10
Models such be wood-globes of glist'ring skies.

[1] seeing jets, black—black eyes.

Dear, therefore be not jealous over me,
  If you hear that they seem my heart to move;
  Not them, O no, but you in them I love.

92

Be your words made, good sir, of Indian ware,[1]
That you allow me them by so small rate?[2]
Or do you cutted Spartans imitate?
Or do you mean my tender ears to spare,
That to my questions you so total are?   5
When I demand of Phoenix-Stella's state
You say, forsooth, you left her well of late.
Oh God, think you that satisfies my care?
I would know whether she did sit or walk;
How cloth'd; how waited on; sigh'd she, or smil'd;   10
Whereof, with whom, how often did she talk;
With what pastime time's journey she beguil'd;
  If her lips deign'd to sweeten my poor name.
  Say all; and all well said, still say the same.

Tenth Song

O dear life, when shall it be
That mine eyes thine eyes may see,
And in them thy mind discover
Whether absence have had force
Thy remembrance to divorce   5
From the image of thy lover?

Or if myself find not
After parting aught forgot,
Nor debarr'd from beauty's treasure,
Let no tongue aspire to tell   10

----

[1] Indian ware—precious materials from the Indies.
[2] small—as is "cutted" (ln 3) and as is "total" (ln 5), this is, of course, ironic.

In what high joys I shall dwell:
Only thought aims at the pleasure.

Thought, therefore, I will send thee
To take up the place for me;
Long I will not after tarry.   15
There, unseen, thou mayst be bold
Those fair wonders to behold
Which in them my hopes do carry.

Thought, see thou no place forbear,
Enter bravely everywhere;   20
Seize on all to her belonging.
But if thou wouldst guarded be,
Fearing her beams, take with thee
Strength of liking, rage of longing.

Think of that most grateful time   25
When my leaping heart will climb
In my lips to have his biding,
There those roses for to kiss
Which do breathe a sugar'd bliss,
Opening rubies, pearls dividing.   30

Think of my most princely power
When I blessed shall devour
With my greedy licorous senses
Beauty, music, sweetness, love,
While she doth against me prove   35
Her strong darts but weak defenses.

Think, think of those dallyings
When with dovelike murmurings,
With glad moaning, passed anguish,
We change eyes, and heart for heart   40
Each to other do impart,
Joying till joy makes us languish.

O my thought, my thoughts surcease!
Thy delights my woes increase:

My life melts with too much thinking.   45
Think no more, but die in me,
Till thou shalt revived be
At her lips, my nectar drinking.

93

O fate, O fault, O curse, child of my bliss!
What sobs can give words grace my grief to show?
What ink is black enough to paint my woe?
Through me—wretch me—even Stella vexed is.
Yet, truth—if caitiff's breath may call thee—this   5
Witness with me, that my foul stumbling so
From carelessness did in no manner grow,
But wit confus'd with too much care did miss.
And do I, then, myself this vain 'scuse give?
I have—live I, and know this—harmed thee;   10
Tho' worlds 'quit me, shall I myself forgive?
Only with pains my pains thus eased be,
    That all thy hurts in my heart's wrack I read:
    I cry thy sighs, my dear, thy tears I bleed.

94

Grief, find the words; for thou hast made my brain
So dark with misty vapors which arise
From out thy heavy mold, that inbent eyes
Can scarcely discern the shape of mine own pain.
Do thou, then—for thou canst—do thou complain   5
For my poor soul, which now that sickness tries
Which even to sense, sense of itself denies,
Though harbingers of death lodge there his train.
Or if thy love of plaint yet mine forbears,
As of a caitiff worthy so to die,   10
Yet wail thyself, and wail with causeful tears,
That though in wretchedness thy life doth lie,

Yet growest more wretched than thy nature bears
By being placed in such a wretch as I.

95

Yet sighs, dear sighs, indeed true friends you are,
That do not leave your left[1] friend at the worst,
But as you with my breast I oft have nurs'd,
So, grateful now, you wait upon my care
Faint coward joy no longer tarry dare,   5
Seeing hope yield when this woe strake him first;
Delight protests he is for the accurs'd,
Though oft himself my mate in arms he sware;
Nay, sorrow comes with such main rage, that he
Kills his own children, tears, finding that they   10
By Love were made apt to consort with me.
Only, true sighs, you do not go away.
    Thank may you have for such a thankful part,
    Thank-worthiest yet when you shall break my heart.

96

Thought, with good cause thou likest so well the night,
Since kind or chance gives both one livery,
Both sadly black, both blackly darken'd be;
Night barr'd from sun, thou from thy own sunlight;
Silence in both displays his sullen might;   5
Slow heaviness in both holds one degree,
That full of doubts, thou of perplexity;
Thy tears express night's native moisture right;
In both a mazeful solitariness;
In night, of sprites the ghastly pow'rs do stir,   10
In thee, or sprites or sprited ghastliness,
But, but, alas, night's side the odds hath fur,[1]

---

1 left—i.e., left by all others.
1 fur—far.

For that, at length, yet doth invite some rest;
Thou, though still tired, yet still doth it detest.

97

Dian, that fain would cheer her friend the night,
Shows her oft, at the full, her fairest face,
Bringing with her those starry nymphs, whose chase
From heavenly standing[1] hits each mortal wight.
But ah, poor night, in love with Phoebus' light   5
And endlessly despairing of his grace,
Herself, to show no other joy hath place,
Silent and sad, in mourning weeds doth dight.
Even so, alas, a lady, Dian's peer,
With choice delights and rarest company   10
Would fain drive clouds from out my heavy cheer.
But, woe is me, though joy itself were she,
　　She could not show my blind brain ways of joy,
　　While I despair my sun's sight to enjoy.

98

Ah, bed! the field where joy's peace some do see,
The field where all my thoughts to war be trained,
How is thy grace by my strange fortune stain'd!
How thy lee[1] shores by my sighs stormed be!
With sweet soft shades thou oft invitest me   5
To steal some rest; but, wretch, I am constrain'd
Spurr'd with love's spur, though gold, and shortly rein'd
With care's hard hand—to turn and toss in thee,
While the black horrors of the silent night
Paint woe's black face so lively to my sight   10
That tedious leisure makes each wrinkled line.
But when Aurora leads out Phoebus' dance

[1] standing—station for an ambush.
[1] lee—protected.

Mine eyes then only wink; for spite, perchance,
That worms should have their sun, and I want mine.

99

When far-spent night persuades each mortal eye
(To whom nor Art nor Nature granteth light)
To lay his then mark-wanting shafts[1] of sight,
Clos'd with their quivers, in sleep's armory,
With windows ope then most my mind doth lie,   5
Viewing the shape of darkness, and delight
Takes in that sad hue which with the inward night
Of his maz'd[2] powers keeps perfect harmony.
But when birds charm and that sweet air which is
Morn's messenger, with rose-enamel'd skies   10
Calls each wight to salute the flower of bliss,
In tomb of lids then buried are mine eyes,
    Forc'd by their lord, who is asham'd to find
    Such light in sense, with such a darken'd mind.

100

O tears! no tears, but rain from beauty's skies,
Making those lilies and those roses grow
Which, aye most fair, now more than most fair show,
While graceful pity beauty beautifies.
O honied sighs, which from that breast do rise,   5
Whose pants do make unspilling cream to flow,
Wing'd with whose breath so pleasing zephyrs blow
As can refresh the hell where my soul fries.
O plaints! conserv'd in such a sugar'd phrase
That eloquence itself envies your praise,   10
While sobb'd-out words a perfect music give.
Such tears, sighs, plaints, no sorrow is, but joy.

[1] mark-wanting shafts—arrows without a target.
[2] maz'd—confused.

Or, if such heavenly signs must prove annoy,[1]
All mirth farewell, let me in sorrow live.

101

Stella is sick, and in that sick-bed lies
Sweetness which breathes and pants as oft as she;
And grace, sick too, such fine conclusions tries[1]
That sickness brags itself best graced to be.
Beauty is sick, but sick in so fair guise   5
That in that paleness beauty's white we see,
And joy, which is inseparate from those eyes,
Stella, now learns, strange case, to weep in thee.
Love moans thy pain, and like a faithful page,
As thy looks stir, comes up and down to make   10
All folks, press'd at thy will,[2] thy pain to 'swage.
Nature with care sweats for her darling's sake,
    Knowing worlds pass ere she enough can find
    Of such heaven-stuff[3] to clothe so heavenly a mind.

102

Where be those roses gone which sweeten'd so our eyes?
Where those red cheeks which oft with fair increase[1] did
    frame
To height of honor in the kindly badge of shame?
Who hath the crimson weeds stolen from my morning skies?
How doth the color fade of those vermilion dyes,   5
Which Nature's self did make and self-ingrain'd[2] the same?
I would know by what right this paleness overcame
That hue whose force my heart still unto thraldom ties?

[1] prove annoy—indicate sorrow.
[1] tries—proves.
[2] press'd at thy will—drafted by you into your service.
[3] heaven-stuff—heavenly material, Stella's beautiful body.
[1] increase—heightening (blush).
[2] self-ingrain'd—dyed.

Galen's adoptive sons, who by a beaten way
Their judgments hackney on, the fault on sickness lay;[3]   10
But feeling proof makes me say they mistake it fur:[4]
It is but Love which makes his paper perfect white,
   To write therein more fresh the story of delight,
   Whiles beauty's reddest ink, Venus for him doth stir.

103

O happy Thames, that didst my Stella bear!
I saw thyself with many a smiling line
Upon thy cheerful face, joy's livery wear,
While those fair planets on thy streams did shine.
The boat for joy could not to dance forbear,   5
While wanton winds, with beauties so divine
Ravish'd, stay'd not, till in her golden hair
They did themselves—O sweetest prison!—twine.
And fain those Aeol's youth[1] there would their stay
Have made, but forc'd by Nature still to fly,   10
First did, with puffing kiss, those locks display.
She, so dishevel'd, blush'd. From window I
   With sight thereof cried out, "O fair disgrace![2]
   Let honor's self to thee grant highest place!"

104

Envious wits, what hath been mine offense,
That with such poisonous care my looks you mark,
That to each word, nay sigh of mine, you hark,
As grudging me my sorrow's eloquence?

---

[3] Galen's adoptive sons . . . fault on sickness lay—doctors following the judgments of the ancient physician Galen, and riding their old-fashioned diagnoses like winded nags, blame illness for the change.
  [4] fur—far.
  [1] Aeol's youth—breezes, the children of Aeolus, god of the winds.
  [2] fair disgrace—lovely disorder.

Ah, is it not enough that I am thence,   5
Thence, so far thence, that scarcely any spark
Of comfort dare come to this dungeon dark,
Where rigorous exile locks up all my sense?
But if I by a happy[1] window pass,
If I but stars upon mine armor bear—   10
Sick, thirsty, glad (though but of empty glass),[2]
Your moral notes[3] straight my hid meaning tear
    From out my ribs, and, puffing, prove that I
    Do Stella love; fools, who doth it deny?

Eleventh Song

[handwritten: "It's probably not in orig."]

"Who is it that this dark night   *[handwritten: Stella speaks]*
Underneath my window plaineth?"
It is one who from thy sight
Being, ah, exil'd disdaineth
Every other vulgar light.   5

"Why, alas, and are you he?
Be not yet those fancies changed?"
Dear, when you find change in me,
Though from me you be estranged,
Let my change to ruin be.   10

"Well, in absence this will die;
Leave to see and leave to wonder."
Absence sure will help, if I
Can learn how myself to sunder
From what in my heart doth lie.   15

"But time will these thoughts remove;
Time doth work what no man knoweth."

---

[1] happy—because Stella used to look through it.
[2] Sick . . . empty glass—the associations here are confusing: "sick"
suggests "thirsty" which suggests "empty glass" which suggests "glad"
because of the "happy window" reference just above.
[3] notes—observations.

Time doth as the subject prove;[1]
With time still the affection groweth
In the faithful turtle dove.   20

"What if you new beauties see,
Will not they stir new affection?"
I will think they pictures be,
Image-like, of saint's perfection,
Poorly counterfeiting thee.   25

"But your reason's purest light
Bids you leave such minds to nourish."[2]
Dear, do reason no such spite;
Never doth thy beauty flourish
More than in my reason's sight.   30

"But the wrongs love bears will make
Love at length leave undertaking."
No, the more fools it do shake
In a ground of so firm making
Deeper still they drive the stake.   35

"Peace, I think that some give ear;
Come no more lest I get anger."
Bliss, I will my bliss forbear;
Fearing, sweet, you to endanger;
But my soul shall harbor there.   40

"Well, begone, begone, I say,
Lest that Argus' eyes[3] perceive you."
O, unjustest Fortune's sway,
Which can make me thus to leave you,
And from louts to run away.   45

[1] Time doth as the subject prove—whether time has any effect depends upon the nature of the person involved.

[2] leave such minds to nourish—stop indulging these emotions.

[3] Argus' eyes—Juno set the hundred-eyed monster Argus to guard Jupiter's mistress, Io, who had been transformed by Juno into a cow.

105

Unhappy sight, and hath she vanish'd by
So near, in so good time, so free a place?
Dead glass,[1] dost thou thy object so embrace
As what my heart still sees thou canst not spy?[2]
I swear, by her I love and lack, that I   5
Was not in fault who bent thy dazzling race[3]
Only unto the heaven of Stella's face,
Counting but dust what in the way did lie.
But cease, mine eyes, your tears do witness well
That you, guiltless thereof, your nectar miss'd: 10
Curs'd be the page from whom the bad torch fell;
Curs'd be the night which did your strife resist;
 Curs'd be the coachman which did drive so fast,
 With no worse curse than absence makes me taste.

106

O absent presence! Stella is not here.
False-flattering hope, that with so fair a face
Bare me in hand,[1] that in this orphan[2] place
Stella, I say my Stella, should appear
What sayst thou now? where is that dainty cheer   5
Thou told'st mine eyes should help their famish'd case?
But thou art gone, now that self-felt disgrace[3]
Doth make me most to wish thy comfort near.
But here I do store of fair ladies meet
Who may with charm of conversation sweet   10

[1] dead glass—my eyes.
[2] dost thou thy object . . . thou canst not spy—have you received so strong an impression that my mind can still see her although you (my eyes) cannot?
[3] dazzling race—burning gaze.
[1] bare me in hand—led me by the hand.
[2] orphan—abandoned by her.
[3] self-felt disgrace—inward grief.

Make in my heavy mold[4] new thoughts to grow.
Sure they prevail as much with me as he
   That bad his friend, but then new-maim'd, to be
   Merry with him, and not think of his woe.

107

Stella, since thou so right[1] a princess art
Of all the powers which life bestows on me,
That ere by them aught undertaken be
They first resort unto the sovereign part;
Sweet, for a while give respite to my heart,   5
Which pants as though it still should leap to thee,
And on my thoughts give they lieutenancy[2]
To this great cause, which needs both use and art.[3]
And as a queen, who from her presence sends
Whom she employs, dismiss from thee my wit   10
Till it have wrought what thy own will attends.
On servants' shame oft master's blame doth sit.
   O let not fools in me thy works reprove,
   And scorning say, "See what it is to love!"

108 *See "When in disgrace w/ fortune... opposite bird movement*

When Sorrow, using mine own fire's might,
Melts down his lead into my boiling breast,
Through that dark furnace to my heart oppress'd
There shines a joy from thee my only light;
But soon as thought of thee breeds my delight,   5
And my young soul flutters to thee his nest,
Most rude despair, my daily unbidden guest,

---

[4] mold—earth; therefore, body.
[1] right—true.
[2] on my thoughts give they lieutenancy—deputize my thoughts.
[3] use and art—experience and knowledge.

Clips straight my wings, straight wraps me in his night,
And makes me then bow down my head and say:
"Ah, what doth Phoebus' gold that wretch avail   10
Whom iron doors do keep from use of day?"
So strangely, alas, thy works in me prevail,
    That in my woes for thee thou art my joy,
    And in my joys for thee my only annoy.

The end of Astrophel and Stella.

The New Arcadia

IN BOOK I of the *Old Arcadia*, when the narrator is presenting for the first time Pyrocles and Musidorus, he casually mentions, after having said that at one point during their adventure they had been shipwrecked on the coast of Lydia, "what befell unto them, what valiant acts they did, passing (in one year's space) through the lesser Asia, Syria, and Egypt, how many ladies they defended from wrong, and disinherited persons restored to their right, is a work for a higher style than mine." This remark clearly indicates that the nature and tone of the *Old Arcadia* are low romance and the comic. It indicates as well, however, that the nature and tone of the *New Arcadia* are high romance and the heroic.

Critics have never disagreed that there is a greater thematic and artistic seriousness in the revision of the *Old Arcadia*, but they have never agreed upon an appropriate generic label for the *New Arcadia*—heroic-romance, romantic-epic, epic-pastoral, and all the various possible combinations, double and triple, of these and other terms. An exact label does not matter. It is clear from the beginning in the middle of things, from the kind of additions, and from the serious themes of love and honor which pervade, that Sidney meant the *New Arcadia* to be an epic poem in prose.

The almost ritual question of "love and honor" was to become the staple of heroic drama from Marlowe through Dryden, but the simple citation of this question does not do justice to the *New Arcadia*, where the variations and gradations of characters and actions make the whole alive and exciting. Love appears in full range in all of its positive and negative aspects, and in all kinds and conditions. And the lives of men and women are fully displayed, virtuous and perverted, fortunate and unfortunate. As a result, although set in the world of chivalric romance, a full and vibrant picture of life is rendered.

Why, then, did Sidney stop writing? He stopped not because he went off to war against Spain; rather, the old story of Arcadia was not compatible with the new attitude and tone. The original version centered in part on the foolish Basilius doltishly in love with Pyrocles disguised as an Amazon. This aspect of the story necessarily comes in to Book III of the revision when Basilius attempts to put down the insurrection of Amphialus and his followers; however, this aspect of the story simply does not merge with the action in the tragic-comic world of Book III. Sidney stopped writing, so to speak, when he recalled his own caveat in *The Defence of Poesy*. In the digression on English poetry, he criticized the fact that English plays "be neither right tragedies, nor right comedies, mingling kings and clowns, not because the matter so carrieth it, but thrust in the clown by head and shoulders, to play a part in majestical matters, with neither decency nor discretion, so as neither the admiration and commiseration, nor the right sportfulness, is by their mongrel tragicomedy obtained." Sidney does not deny the possibility of tragicomedy; what he objects to is the awkward mingling, for no reason, of high or low. In short, Sidney realized that having Basilius-in-love take charge of the siege was indeed thrusting in a clown to play a part in majestical matters. Whether or not Sidney ever would have tried to complete this in some way, or have tried a third version, we will never know. Suffice it to say, the *New Arcadia* as he left it has two completed books, a third one longer than either of the first two but incomplete, and no Eclogues.

The *New Arcadia*, however, exists in two printed versions, those of 1590 and 1593 (reprinted in 1598). The version of 1590, the one closest to the manuscript which Sidney left, was published by William Ponsonby, as edited by Sidney's literary executor Fulke Greville. But even this version, by Greville's own admission, is not exactly as Sidney left it:

> The division and summing of the chapters was not of Sir Philip Sidney's doing, but adventured by the overseer of the print for the

more ease of the readers. He therefore submits himself to their judgment, and if his labor answer not the worthiness of the book, desireth pardon for it. As also, if any defect be found in the Eclogues, which although they were Sir Philip Sidney's writing, yet were they not perused by him but left till the work had been finished, that then choice should have been made which should have been taken, and in what manner brought in. This time they have been chosen and disposed of as the overseer thought best.

In 1593, the Countess of Pembroke oversaw a second edition of the *New Arcadia*, which contains with slight changes the three books of 1590, together with the last three books of her manuscript version of the *Old Arcadia*, edited to conform with the new names and geography of the revision and to comply with the notes left by Sidney for changes he desired made in the *Old Arcadia*. Because this second edition appeared again in the collected works of 1598, the version of 1590 tended to be lost from sight, and because the *Old Arcadia* was not printed until this century, ironically, the bastard version of 1593 is the one the world for three centuries celebrated as "Sidney's *Arcadia.*"

Important as 1593 may be for cultural history, then, the 1590 text (STC 22539) has been picked as the copy-text for the present edition for the obvious reason that it most closely follows Sidney's manuscript. The chapter headings provided by Greville, nevertheless, have been retained "for the more ease of the readers," but no Eclogues have been included. The dedication letter to the Countess of Pembroke which was printed in 1590 has been placed in the first section of the present anthology along with the *Old Arcadia* where it properly belongs. Book I has been retained complete in order that comparisons can be made with Book I of the *Old Arcadia*, but Books II and III appear in selections only, with parts cut out in synopsis, yet divided under the appropriate chapter headings as written by Greville. No editor of Sidney wishes to cut any of the *New Arcadia;* however, space is not presently available for the whole work. As a result, that which has been cut from Book II is generally the material reported by the various main characters in the story proper concerning the trials, ordeals, and triumphs of the two Princes before they arrived in Arcadia. Although these stories tend to be rather flat narrative, they do explore through contrast and irony the important themes of love and honor which run through the main story as it develops through the existing three books. The cuts in Book III are of a different nature because the narrative there is uninterrupted by flashbacks; as a result, what has been retained are the most essential and typically illustrative aspects.

THE COUNTESS OF
PEMBROKE'S ARCADIA (1590)

Book I

CHAPTER I

The shepherdish complaints of the absented lovers Strephon and Claius.[1] The second shipwreck of Pyrocles and Musidorus.[2] Their strange saving, interview, and parting.

It was in the time that the Earth begins to put on her new apparel against the approach of her lover, and that the sun running a most even course becomes an indifferent arbiter between the night and the day, when the hopeless shepherd Strephon was come to the sands which lie against the island of Cithera,[3] where, viewing the place with a heavy kind of delight, and sometimes casting his eyes to the isleward, he called his friendly rival the pastor Claius unto him; and, setting first down in his darkened countenance a doleful copy of what he would speak, "O my Claius," said he, "hither we are now come to pay the rent for which we are so called unto by over-busy remembrance; remembrance, restless remembrance, which claims not only this duty of us, but for it will have us forget ourselves.[4] I pray you—

---

[1] Strephon and Claius—Strephon ("writhe") and Claius ("weep") are two gentlemen in the *Old Arcadia*, Fourth Eclogues; they embrace the shepherd's life out of love for the shepherdess Urania.

[2] Pyrocles and Musidorus—cf. *O.A.*, ft. 13, 17

[3] Cithera—the Ionian isle near which Venus rose from the sea; off the coast of Laconia, it is called the home of Aphrodite Urania.

[4] but for it will have us forget ourselves—but will have us forget ourselves in order to perform it.

when we were amid our flock, and that, of other shepherds some
were running after their sheep, [some] strayed beyond their
bounds, some delighting their eyes with seeing them nibble upon
the short and sweet grass, some medicining their sick ewes, some
setting a bell for an ensign of a sheepish squadron, some with
more leisure inventing new games of exercising their bodies and
sporting their wits—did remembrance grant us any holiday,
either for pastime or devotion, nay, either for necessary food or
natural rest, but that still it forced our thoughts to work upon this
place, where we last (alas, that the word 'last' should so long last)
did gaze our eyes upon her ever-flourishing beauty; did it not still
cry within us: 'Ah, you base-minded wretches! are your thoughts
so deeply demired in the trade of ordinary worldlings as, for respect of gain some paltry wool may yield you, to let so much
time pass without knowing perfectly her estate, especially in so
troublesome a season; to leave that shore unsaluted from whence
you may see to the island where she dwelleth; to leave those steps
unkissed wherein Urania[5] printed the farewell of all beauty?'

"Well, then, remembrance commanded, we obeyed, and here
we find that as our remembrance came ever clothed unto us in
the form of this place, so this place gives new heat to the fever
of our languishing remembrance. Yonder, my Claius, Urania
lighted; the very horse methought bewailed to be so disburdened;
and as for thee, poor Claius, when thou wentest to help her down,
I saw reverence and desire so divide thee that thou didst at one
instant both blush and quake, and instead of bearing her wert
ready to fall down thyself. There she sat, vouchsafing my cloak
(then most gorgeous) under her; at yonder rising of the ground
she turned herself, looking back toward her wonted abode, and
because of her parting, bearing much sorrow in her eyes, the
lightsomeness whereof had yet so natural a cheerfulness as it
made even sorrow seem to smile; at that turning she spake unto
us all, opening the cherry of her lips, and, Lord! how greedily
mine ears did feed upon the sweet words she uttered! And here
she laid her hand over thine eyes, when she saw the tears spring-

[5] Urania—an epithet for the celestial Venus, meaning "heavenly."

ing in them, as if she would conceal them from other and yet herself feel some of thy sorrow. But woe is me! yonder, yonder did she put her foot into the boat, at that instant, as it were, dividing her heavenly beauty between the earth and the sea. But when she was embarked did you not mark how the winds whistled, and the seas danced for joy; how the sails did swell with pride, and all because they had Urania? O Urania, blessed be thou, Urania, the sweetest fairness and fairest sweetness!"

With that word his voice brake so with sobbing that he could say no further; and Claius thus answered: "Alas, my Strephon," said he, "what needs this score to reckon up only our losses? What doubt is there but that the light of this place doth call our thoughts to appear at the court of Affection, held by that racking[6] steward Remembrance? As well may sheep forget to fear when they spy wolves, as we can miss such fancies, when we see any place made happy by her treading. Who can choose that saw her but think where she stayed, where she walked, where she turned, where she spoke? But what is all this? Truly no more but, as this place served us to think of those things, so those things serve as places[7] to call to memory more excellent matters.

"No, no, let us think with consideration, and consider with acknowledging, and acknowledge with admiration, and admire with love, and love with joy in the midst of all woes; let us in such sort think, I say, that our poor eyes were so enriched as to behold, and our low hearts so exalted as to love, a maid who is such, that as the greatest thing the world can show is her beauty. Certainly, as her eye-lids are more pleasant to behold than two white kids climbing up a fair tree and browsing on his tenderest branches (and yet are nothing compared to the day-shining stars contained in them), and as her breath is more sweet than a gentle south-west wind which comes creeping over flowery fields and shadowed waters in the extreme heat of summer (and yet is nothing compared to the honey-flowing speech that breath doth carry), no more all that our eyes can see of her—though when

[6] racking—extortionate.
[7] places—subjects or topics, as used in logic.

they have seen her, what else they shall ever see is but dry stubble after clovers-grass[8]—is to be matched with the flock of unspeakable virtues laid up delightfully in that best-builded fold. But, indeed, as we can better consider the sun's beauty by marking how he gilds these waters and mountains than by looking upon his own face (too glorious for our weak eyes), so it may be our conceits, not able to bear her sun-staining excellency, will better weigh it by her works upon some meaner subject employed. And, alas, who can better witness that than we, whose experience is grounded upon feeling? Hath not the only love[9] of her made us, being silly ignorant shepherds, raise up our thoughts above the ordinary level of the world, so as great clerks do not disdain our conference? Hath not the desire to seem worthy in her eyes made us, when others were sleeping, to sit viewing the course of the heavens; when others were running at base,[10] to run over learned writings; when others mark their sheep, we to mark ourselves? Hath not she thrown reason upon our desires, and, as it were, given eyes unto Cupid? Hath in any, but in her, love-fellowship maintained friendship between rivals and beauty taught the beholders chastity?"

He was going on with his praises, but Strephon bade him stay and look, and so they both perceived a thing which floated, drawing nearer and nearer to the bank, but rather by the favorable working of the sea than by any self-industry. They doubted a while what it should be, till it was cast up even hard before them, at which time they fully saw that it was a man. Whereupon, running for pity's sake unto him, they found his hands (as it should appear, constanter friends to his life than his memory) fast gripping upon the edge of a square small coffer which lay all under his breast; else in himself no show of life, so as the board seemed to be but a bier to carry him a-land to his sepulchre. So drew they up a young man of so goodly shape and well-pleasing favor that one would think death had in him

8 clovers-grass—clover.
9 the only love—only the love.
10 running at base—a game in which boys from one side chase and capture boys of the other side.

a lovely countenance, and that, though he were naked, nakedness was to him an apparel.

That sight increased their compassion, and their compassion called up their care, so that, lifting his feet above his head, making a great deal of salt water come out of his mouth, they laid him upon some of their garments, and fell to rub and chafe him, till they brought him to recover both breath, the servant, and warmth, the companion, of living. At length, opening his eyes, he gave a great groan (a doleful note, but a pleasant ditty, for by that they found not only life, but strength of life in him). They therefore continued on their charitable office until, his spirits being well returned, he, without so much as thanking them for their pains, got up, and, looking round about to the uttermost limits of his sight, and crying upon the name of Pyrocles. Nor seeing nor hearing cause of comfort, "What," said he, "and shall Musidorus live after Pyrocles?" There-withal he offered willfully to cast destruction and himself again into the sea: a strange sight to the shepherds to whom it seemed that before, being in appearance dead had yet saved his life, and now coming to his life should be a cause to procure his death; but they ran unto him, and pulling him back (then too feeble for them) by force stickled[11] that unnatural fray.

"I pray you," said he, "honest men, what such right have you in me as not to suffer me to do with myself what I list; and what policy have you to bestow a benefit where it is counted an injury?"

They hearing him speak in Greek, which was their natural language, became the more tender-hearted towards him; and considering by his calling and looking that the loss of some dear friend was great cause of his sorrow, told him they were poor men that were bound, by course of humanity, to prevent so great a mischief, and that they wished him, if opinion of somebody's perishing bred such desperate anguish in him, that he should be comforted by his own proof, who had lately escaped as apparent danger as any might be.

"No, no," said he, "it is not for me to attend so high a bliss-

11 stickled—stopped.

fulness; but since you take care of me, I pray you find means that some bark may be provided, that will go out of the haven, that if it be possible we may find the body far, far too precious a food for fishes." "And for the hire," said he, "I have within this casket, of value, sufficient to content them."

Claius presently went to a fisherman, and having agreed with him, and provided some apparel for the naked stranger, he embarked, and the shepherds with him, and were no sooner gone beyond the mouth of the haven, but that some way into the sea they might discern, as it were, a stain of the water's color, and by times some sparks and smoke mounting thereout. But the young man no sooner saw it, but that, beating his breast, he cried that there was the beginning of his ruin, entreating them to bend their course as near unto it as they could, telling how that smoke was but a small relic of a great fire which had driven both him and his friend rather to commit themselves to the cold mercy of the sea than to abide the hot cruelty of the fire; and that, therefore, though they both had abandoned the ship, that he was, if anywhere, in that course to be met withal. They steered, therefore, as near thitherward as they could; but when they came so near as their eyes were full masters of the object, they saw a sight full of piteous strangeness—a ship, or rather the carcass of the ship, or rather some few bones of the carcass, hulling[12] there, part broken, part burned, part drowned, death having used more than one dart to that destruction. About it floated great store of very rich things, and many chests which might promise no less, and amidst the precious things were a number of dead bodies, which likewise did not testify both elements' violence, but that the chief violence was grown of human inhumanity, for their bodies were full of grisly wounds, and their blood had, as it were, filled the wrinkles of the sea's visage, which it seemed the sea would not wash away, that it might witness it is not always his fault when we condemn his cruelty. In sum, a defeat, where the conquered kept both field and spoil; a shipwreck without storm or ill-footing; and a waste of fire in the midst of water.

[12] hulling—floating with the wind or current.

But a little way off they saw the mast, whose proud height now lay along, like a widow having lost her mate of whom she held her honor; but upon the mast they saw a young man, at least if he were a man, bearing show of about eighteen years of age, who sat as on horse-back, having nothing upon him but his shirt, which, being wrought with blue silk and gold, had a kind of resemblance to the sea, on which the sun, then near his western home, did shoot some of his beams. His hair, which the young men of Greece used to wear very long, was stirred up and down with the wind, which seemed to have a sport to play with it, as the sea had to kiss his feet; himself full of admirable beauty, set forth by the strangeness both of his seat and gesture; for, holding his head up full of unmoved majesty, he held a sword aloft with his fair arm, which often he waved about his crown, as though he would threaten the world in that extremity.

But the fishermen, when they came so near him that it was time to throw out a rope, by which hold they might draw him, their simplicity bred such amazement, and their amazement such a superstition, that (assuredly thinking it was some God begotten between Neptune and Venus that had made all this terrible slaughter) as they went under sail by him, they held up their hands and made their prayers. Which when Musidorus saw, though he were almost as much ravished with joy as with astonishment, he leapt to the mariner, and took the rope out of his hand, and, saying, "Dost thou live, and art well?" (who answered, "Thou canst tell best, since most of my well-being stands in thee,") threw it out; but already the ship was passed beyond Pyrocles, and therefore Musidorus could do no more but persuade the mariners to cast about again, assuring them that he was but a man, although of most divine excellencies, and promising great rewards for their pain.

And now they were already come upon the stays,[13] when one of the sailors descried a galley which came with sails and oars directly in the chase of them, and straight perceived it was

[13] come upon the stays—turning the boat around to windward in the course of tacking.

a well-known pirate, who hunted, not only for goods, but for bodies of men, which he employed either to be his galley-slaves or to sell at the best market; which when the master understood, he commanded forthwith to set on all the canvas they could and fly homeward, leaving in that sort poor Pyrocles, so near to be rescued. But what did not Musidorus say? What did he not offer to persuade them to venture the fight? But fear, standing at the gates of their ears, put back all persuasions; so that he had nothing to accompany Pyrocles but his eyes, nor to succor him but his wishes.

Therefore praying for him, and casting a long look that way, he saw the galley leave the pursuit of them and turn to take up the spoils of the other wreck; and, lastly, he might well see them lift up the young man; and, "Alas!" said he to himself, "dear Pyrocles, shall that body of thine be enchained? Shall those victorious hands of thine be commanded to base offices? Shall virtue become a slave to those that be slaves to viciousness? Alas, better had it been thou hadst ended nobly thy noble days. What death is so evil as unworthy servitude?"

But that opinion soon ceased when he saw the galley setting upon another ship, which held long and strong fight with her; for then he began afresh to fear the life of his friend, and to wish well to the pirates, whom before he hated, lest in their ruin he might perish. But the fishermen made such speed into the haven that they absented his eyes from beholding the issue; where being entered, he could procure neither them nor any other as then to put themselves into the sea; so that, being as full of sorrow for being unable to do anything, as void of counsel how to do anything (besides that sickness grew something upon him), the honest shepherds Strephon and Claius—who, being themselves true friends, did the more perfectly judge the justness of his sorrow—advised him that he should mitigate somewhat of his woe, since he had gotten an amendment in fortune, being come from assured persuasion of his death to have no cause to despair of his life, as one, that had lamented the death of his sheep should after know they were but strayed, would receive pleasure, though readily he knew not where to find them.

CHAPTER 2

The pastors' comforts to the wrecked Musidorus. His passage into Arcadia. The descriptions of Laconia, Arcadia, Kalander's person, house, and entertainment to Musidorus, now called Palladius. His sickness, recovery, and perfections.

"Now, sir," said they, "thus for ourselves it is: we are, in profession, but shepherds, and, in this country of Laconia,[14] little better than strangers, and, therefore, neither in skill nor ability of power greatly to stead you. But what we can present unto you is this: Arcadia, of which country we are, is but a little way hence; and even upon the next confines.

There dwelleth a gentleman, by name Kalander,[15] who vouchsafeth much favor unto us; a man who for his hospitality is so much haunted that no news stir but come to his ears; for his upright dealing so beloved of his neighbors that he hath many ever ready to do him their uttermost service, and, by the great goodwill our Prince bears him, may soon obtain the use of his name and credit, which hath a principal sway, not only in his own Arcadia, but in all these countries of Peloponnesus; and, which is worth all, all these things give him not so much power as his nature gives him will to benefit, so that it seems no music is so sweet to his ear as deserved thanks. To him we will bring you, and there you may recover again your health, without which you cannot be able to make any diligent search for your friend, and, therefore, but in that respect,[16] you must labor for it. Besides, we are sure the comfort of courtesy and ease of wise counsel shall not be wanting."

Musidorus, who (besides he was merely[17] unacquainted in the country) had his wits astonished with sorrow, gave easy consent to that from which he saw no reason to disagree; and, therefore, defraying the mariners with a ring bestowed upon them, they took their journey together through Laconia, Claius and

[14] Laconia—southeast portion of the Peloponnesus, south of Arcadia; a rocky and infertile land, the capital of which is Sparta.
[15] Kalander—"good man"; the Kerxenus of *Old Arcadia*.
[16] but in that respect—if only on that account.
[17] merely—completely.

Strephon by course[18] carrying his chest for him, Musidorus only bearing in his countenance evident marks of a sorrowful mind supported with a weak body; which they perceiving, and knowing that the violence of sorrow is not, at the first, to be striven withal (being like a mighty beast, sooner tamed with following than overthrown by withstanding), they gave way unto it for that day and the next, never troubling him, either with asking questions or finding fault with his melancholy, but rather fitting to his dolor dolorous discourses of their own and other folk's misfortune; which speeches, though they had not a lively entrance to his senses (shut up in sorrow) yet, like one half asleep, he took hold of much of the matters spoken unto him, so as a man may say, ere sorrow was aware, they made his thoughts bear away something else beside his own sorrow, which wrought so in him that at length he grew content to mark their speeches, then to marvel at such wit in shepherds, after to like their company, and lastly to vouchsafe conference; so that the third day after, in the time that the morning did strow roses and violets in the heavenly floor against the coming of the sun, the nightingales, striving one with the other which could in most dainty variety recount their wrong-caused sorrow,[19] made them put off their sleep; and, rising from under a tree, which that night had been their pavilion, they went on their journey, which by-and-by welcomed Musidorus' eyes (wearied with the wasted soil of Laconia) with delightful prospects.

There were hills which garnished their proud heights with stately trees; humble valleys whose base estate seemed comforted with refreshing of silver rivers; meadows enamelled with all sorts of eye-pleasing flowers; thickets which, being lined with most pleasant shade, were witnessed so to by the cheerful deposition[20]

[18] by course—by turns.
[19] wrong-caused sorrow—the nightingale is, according to mythology, Philomela, who was raped by her sister's husband, Tereus, and then mutilated by him so that she could not relate the crime; but Philomela succeeded in communicating the atrocity to her sister, Procne, who then slew her son by Tereus and served him in a meal to his father; ultimately, the gods turned all three into birds.
[20] deposition—testimony.

of many well-tuned birds; each pasture stored with sheep, feeding with sober security, while the pretty lambs, with bleating oratory, craved the dams' comfort. Here a shepherd's boy piping, as though he should never be old; there a young shepherdess knitting, and withal singing, and it seemed that her voice comforted her hands to work, and her hands kept time to her voice's music. As for the houses of the country—for many houses came under their eye—they were all scattered, no two being one by the other, and yet not so far off as that it barred mutual succor, a show, as it were, of an accompanable solitariness, and of a civil wildness.

"I pray you," said Musidorus, then first unsealing his long-silent lips, "what countries be these we pass through, which are so diverse in show, the one wanting no store, the other having no store but of want?"

"The country," answered Claius, "where you were cast ashore, and now are passed through, is Laconia, not so poor by the barrenness of the soil—though in itself not passing fertile—as by a civil war, which, being these two years within the bowels of that estate, between the gentlemen and the peasants—by them named Helots[21]—hath in this sort, as it were, disfigured the face of nature and made it so unhospitable as now you have found it, the towns neither of the one side nor the other willingly opening their gates to strangers, nor strangers willingly entering, for fear of being mistaken.

"But this country, where now you set your foot, is Arcadia; and even hard by is the house of Kalander, whither we lead you. This country being thus decked with peace, and the child of peace, good husbandry, these houses you see so scattered are of men, as we two are, that live upon the commodity of their sheep, and therefore, in the division of the Arcadian estate, are termed shepherds—a happy people, wanting little, because they desire not much."

"What cause, then," said Musidorus, "made you venture to

[21] Helots—the original Achaean inhabitants of Laconia, reduced to slavery by the Spartans, who lived entirely on their labor.

leave this sweet life and put yourself in yonder unpleasant and dangerous realm?"

"Guarded with poverty," answered Strephon, "and guided with love."

"But now," said Claius, "since it hath pleased you to ask anything of us, whose baseness is such as the very knowledge is darkness, give us leave to know something of you and of the young man you so much lament, that at least we may be the better instructed to inform Kalander, and he the better know how to proportion his entertainment."

Musidorous, according to the agreement between Pyrocles and him to alter their names, answered that he called himself Palladius,[22] and his friend Daïphantus.[23] "But, till I have him again," said he, "I am indeed nothing, and therefore my story is of nothing. His entertainment, since so good a man he is, cannot be so low as I account my estate; and, in sum, the sum of all his courtesy may be to help me by some means to seek my friend."

They perceived he was not willing to open himself further, and, therefore, without further questioning, brought him to the house, about which they might see (with fit consideration both of the air, the prospect, and the nature of the ground) all such necessary additions to a great house as might well show Kalander knew that provision is the foundation of hospitality, and thrift the fuel of magnificence. The house itself was built of fair and strong stone, not affecting so much any extraordinary kind of fineness as an honorable representing of a firm stateliness; the lights,[24] doors, and stairs rather directed to the use of the guest than to the eye of the artificer, and yet as the one [was] chiefly heeded, so the other not neglected; each place handsome without curiosity,[25] and homely[26] without loathsomeness; not so dainty as not to be trod on, nor yet slubbered up with good fellow-

---

[22] Palladius—"noble youth."
[23] Daïphantus—"burning brightly."
[24] lights—windows.
[25] curiosity—over-elaboration.
[26] homely—plain.

ship;[27] all more lasting than beautiful, but that the consideration of the exceeding lastingness made the eye believe it was exceeding beautiful; the servants, not so many in number as cleanly in apparel and serviceable in behavior, testifying even in their countenances that their master took as well care to be served, as of them that did serve.

One of them was forthwith ready to welcome the shepherds, as men who, though they were poor, their master greatly favored; and understanding by them that the young man with them was to be much accounted of, for that they had seen tokens of more than common greatness, howsoever now eclipsed with fortune, he ran to his master, who came presently forth, and pleasantly welcoming the shepherds, but especially applying him to Musidorus, Strephon privately told him all what he knew of him, and particularly that he found this stranger was loth to be known.

"No," said Kalander, speaking aloud, "I am no herald to inquire of men's pedigrees; it sufficeth me if I know their virtues; which, if this young man's face be not a false witness, do better apparel his mind than you have done his body." While he was speaking, there came a boy, in show like a merchant's prentice, who, taking Strephon by the sleeve, delivered him a letter, written jointly both to him and Claius from Urania; which they no sooner had read, but that with short leave-taking of Kalander, who quickly guessed and smiled at the matter, and once again, though hastily recommending the young man unto him, they went away, leaving Musidorus even loth to part with them, for the good conversation he had of them, and obligation he accounted himself tied in unto them; and, therefore, they delivering his chest unto him, he opened it, and would have presented them with two very rich jewels, but they absolutely refused them, telling him that they were more than enough rewarded in the knowing of him, and without hearkening unto a reply, like men whose hearts disdained all desires but one, got speedily away, as if the letter had brought wings to make them fly. But by

27 slubbered up with good fellowship—muddied up with the feet of many visitors.

that sight Kalander soon judged that his guest was of no mean calling; and therefore the more respectfully entertaining him, Musidorus found his sickness, which the fight, the sea, and late travel had laid upon him, grow greatly, so that fearing some sudden accident, he delivered the chest to Kalander, which was full of most precious stones, gorgeously and cunningly set in divers manners, desiring him he would keep those trifles, and if he died, he would bestow so much as was needful to find out and redeem a young man naming himself Daïphantus, as then in the hands of Laconian pirates.

But Kalander seeing him faint more and more, with careful speed conveyed him to the most commodious lodging in his house; where, being possessed with an extreme burning fever, he continued some while with no great hope of life; but youth at length got the victory of sickness, so that in six weeks the excellency of his returned beauty was a credible ambassador of his health, to the great joy of Kalander, who, as in this time he had by certain friends of his, that dwelt near the sea in Messenia,[28] set forth a ship and a galley to seek and succor Daïphantus, so at home did he omit nothing which he thought might either profit or gratify Palladius.

For, having found in him (besides his bodily gifts, beyond the degree of admiration) by daily discourses, which he delighted himself to have with him, a mind of most excellent composition, a piercing wit, quite void of ostentation, high-erected thoughts seated in a heart of courtesy, an eloquence as sweet in the uttering as slow to come to the uttering, behavior so noble as gave a majesty to adversity, and all in a man whose age could not be above one-and-twenty years,[29] the good old man was even enamored with a fatherly love towards him, or rather became his servant by the bonds such virtue laid upon him, once, he acknowledged himself so to be, by the badge of diligent attendance.

[28] Messenia—fertile seacoast region of Greece, south of Arcadia and west of Laconia.
[29] one-and-twenty years—cf. the ages in the *Old Arcadia*.

CHAPTER 3

The pictures of Kalander's dainty garden-house. His narration of the Arcadian estate, the King, the Queen, their two daughters, and their guardians, with their qualities, which is the ground of all this story.

But Palladius having gotten his health, and only staying there to be in place where he might hear answer of the ships set forth, Kalander one afternoon led him abroad to a well-arrayed ground he had behind his house, which he thought to show him before his going, as the place himself, more than in any other, delighted. The backside of the house was neither field, garden, nor orchard, or rather it was both field, garden, and orchard; for as soon as the descending of the stairs had delivered them down, they came into a place cunningly set with trees of the most taste-pleasing fruits; but scarcely they had taken that into their consideration, but that they were suddenly stepped into a delicate green; of each side of the green a thicket bend,[30] behind the thickets again new beds of flowers, which being under the trees, the trees were to them a pavilion, and they to the trees a mosaical floor, so that it seemed that Art therein would needs be delightful, by counterfeiting his enemy, Error, and making order in confusion.

In the midst of all the place was a fair pond, whose shaking crystal was a perfect mirror to all the other beauties, so that it bare show of two gardens: one in deed, the other in shadows. And in one of the thickets was a fine fountain made thus: a naked Venus of white marble, wherein the graver had used such cunning that the natural blue veins of the marble were framed in fit places to set forth the beautiful veins of her body. At her breast she had her babe Aeneas, who seemed (having begun to suck) to leave that to look upon her fair eyes, which smiled at the babe's folly, the meanwhile the breast running. Hard by was a house of pleasure built for a summer retiring place, whither Kalander leading him, he found a square room full of delightful pictures made by the most excellent workman of Greece. There

30 thicket bend—grove.

was Diana when Actaeon saw her bathing,[31] in whose cheeks the painter had set such a color as was mixed between shame and disdain; and one of her foolish nymphs, who weeping and withal lowering, one might see the workman meant to set forth tears of anger. In another table was Atalanta,[32] the posture of whose limbs was so lively expressed that, if the eyes were the only judges, as they be the only seers, one would have sworn the very picture had run. Besides many more, as of Helena,[33] Omphale,[34] Iole.[35]

But in none of them all beauty seemed to speak so much as in a large table,[36] which contained a comely old man with a lady of middle, but of excellent, beauty, and more excellent would have been deemed but that there stood between them a young maid, whose wonderfulness took away all beauty from her but that which, it might seem, she gave her back again by her very shadow. And such difference (being known that it did indeed counterfeit a person living) was there between her and all the other, though goddesses, that it seemed the skill of the painter bestowed on the other new beauty, but that the beauty of her bestowed new skill on the painter. Though he thought inquisitiveness an uncomely guest, he could not choose but ask who she was that, bearing show of one being indeed, could with

[31] Diana when Actaeon saw her bathing—Diana was so anrgy when the hunter Actaeon saw her naked that she turned him into a stag, and he was torn to pieces by his own hounds.

[32] Atalanta—a virgin who agreed to marry any youth who could conquer her in a foot race; Hippomenes succeeded by tossing irresistible golden apples, given him by Venus, off to one side, thereby causing Atalanta to slow down in order to pick them up.

[33] Helena—Helen of Troy, the fairest woman in the world, and Paris' prize for choosing Venus as the most beautiful of the goddesses.

[34] Omphale—the Lydian queen who made Hercules dress as a woman and spin wool to prove his love for her.

[35] Iole—a female captive of Hercules whose beauty so aroused Deianira, Hercules' wife, to jealousy, that she smeared her husband's cloak with a love potion given her by the centaur Nessus after Hercules shot him; the ointment actually burned Hercules to death.

[36] table—picture.

natural gifts go beyond the reach of invention.[37] Kalander answered that it was made by Philoclea,[38] the younger daughter of his prince, who also with his wife were contained in that table, the painter meaning to represent the present condition of the young lady, who stood watched by an over-curious eye of her parents; and that he would also have drawn her eldest sister, esteemed her match for beauty, in her shepherdish attire, but that the rude clown her guardian would not suffer it. Neither durst he ask leave of the prince for fear of suspicion.

Palladius perceived that the matter was wrapped up in some secrecy and therefore would for modesty demand no further. But yet his countenance could not but with dumb eloquence desire it, which Kalander perceiving, "Well," said he, "my dear guest, I know your mind, and I will satisfy it. Neither will I do it like a niggardly answerer, going no further than the bounds of the questions, but I will discover unto you as well that wherein my knowledge is common with others as that which by extraordinary means is delivered unto me, knowing so much in you, though not long acquainted, that I shall find your ears faithful treasurers."

So then sitting down in two chairs, and sometimes casting his eye to the picture, he thus spake: "This country, Arcadia, among all the provinces of Greece, hath ever been had in singular reputation, partly for the sweetness of the air, and other natural benefits, but principally for the well-tempered minds of the people, who, finding that the shining title of glory, so much affected by other nations, doth indeed help little to the happiness of life, are the only people which, as by their justice and providence, give neither cause nor hope to their neighbors to annoy them; so are they not stirred with false praise to trouble others' quiet, thinking it a small reward for the wasting of their own lives in ravening that their posterity should long after say they had done so. Even the Muses seem to approve their good determination by choosing this country for their chief repairing

---

[37] invention—creative imagination; artistic skill.
[38] Philoclea—cf. *O.A.*, ft. 6.

place, and by bestowing their perfections so largely here, that the very shepherds have their fancies lifted to so high conceits as the learned of other nations are content both to borrow their names and imitate their cunning.

"Here dwelleth and reigneth this prince whose picture you see, by name Basilius;[39] a prince of sufficient skill to govern so quiet a country, where the good minds of the former princes had set down good laws, and the well bringing up of the people doth serve as a most sure bond to hold them. But to be plain with you, he excels in nothing so much as in the zealous love of his people, wherein he doth not only pass all his own fore-goers, but, as I think, all the princes living. Whereof the cause is that, though he exceed not in the virtues which get admiration —as depth of wisdom, height of courage, and largeness of magnificence—yet is he notable in those which stir affection—as truth of word, meekness, courtesy, mercifulness, and liberality.

"He, being already well stricken in years, married a young princess named Gynecia,[40] daughter to the king of Cyprus,[41] of notable beauty, as by her picture you see; a woman of great wit, and in truth of more princely virtues than her husband; of most unspotted chastity, but of so working[42] a mind, and so vehement spirits, as a man may say it was happy she took a good course, for otherwise it would have been terrible.

"Of these two are brought to the world two daughters, so beyond measure excellent in all the gifts allotted to reasonable creatures, that we may think they were born to show that Nature is no stepmother to that sex, how much soever some men, sharp-witted only in evil speaking, have sought to disgrace them. The elder is named Pamela,[43] by many men not deemed inferior to her sister. For my part, when I marked them both, methought there was (if at least such perfections may receive the word of more) more sweetness in Philoclea, but more majesty in Pamela; methought Philoclea's beauty only persuaded, but so persuaded

[39] Basilius—cf. *O.A.*, ft. 2.
[40] Gynecia—cf. *O.A.*, ft. 3.
[41] Cyprus—cf. *O.A.*, ft. 4.
[42] working—active.
[43] Pamela—cf. *O.A.*, ft. 5.

as all hearts must yield; Pamela's beauty used violence, and such violence as no heart could resist. And it seems that such proportion is between their minds: Philoclea so bashful as though her excellencies had stolen into her before she was aware, so humble that she will put all pride out of countenance, in sum, such proceeding as will stir hope, but teach hope good manners; Pamela of high thoughts, who avoids not pride with not knowing her excellencies, but by making that one of her excellencies to be void of pride [has] her mother's wisdom, greatness, nobility, but (if I can guess aright) knit with a more constant temper.

"Now, then, our Basilius being so publicly happy as to be a prince, and so happy in that happiness as to be a beloved prince, and so in his private blessed as to have so excellent a wife, and so over-excellent children, hath of late taken a course which yet makes him more spoken of than all these blessings. For, having made a journey to Delphos,[44] and safely returned, within short space he brake[45] up his court and retired himself, his wife and children, into a certain forest hereby, which he calleth his desert; wherein, besides an house appointed for stables, and lodgings for certain persons of mean calling, who do all household services, he hath builded two fine lodges; in the one of them himself remains with his younger daughter Philoclea (which was the cause they three were matched together in this picture), without having any other creature living in that lodge with him. Which, though it be strange, yet not so strange as the course he hath taken with the Princess Pamela, whom he hath placed in the other lodge. But how think you accompanied? Truly with none other but one Dametas,[46] the most arrant, doltish clown that I think ever was without the privilege of a bauble,[47] with his wife Miso[48] and daughter Mopsa,[49] in whom no wit can devise anything, wherein they may pleasure her, but to exercise her patience, and

[44] Delphos—cf. *O.A.*, ft. 7.
[45] brake—broke.
[46] Dametas—cf. *O.A.*, ft. 9.
[47] bauble—a small stick topped with a grotesque head wearing ass' ears; the emblem of the court fool.
[48] Miso—cf. *O.A.*, ft. 11.
[49] Mopsa—cf. *O.A.*, ft. 12.

to serve for a foil of her perfections. This loutish clown is such that you never saw so ill-favored a vizar;[50] his behavior such that he is beyond the degree of ridiculous; and for his apparel, even as I could wish him. Miso his wife, so handsome a beldame[51] that only her face and her splay-foot have made her accused for a witch, only one good point she hath, that she observes decorum, having a froward mind in a wretched body. Between these two personages, who never agreed in any humor but in disagreeing, is issued forth mistress Mopsa, a fit woman to participate of both their perfections.

"But because a pleasant fellow of my acquaintance set forth her praises in verse, I will only repeat them and spare mine own tongue, since she goes for a woman. These verses are these, which I have so often caused to be sung that I have them without book:

[*OA3, see above p. 39, was reprinted here*]

"Now truly having made these descriptions unto you, methinks you should imagine that I rather feign some pleasant device than recount a truth that a prince (not banished from his own wits) could possibly make so unworthy a choice. But truly, dear guest, so it is, that princes (whose doing have been often soothed with good success) think nothing so absurd which they cannot make honorable. The beginning of his credit was by the prince's straying out of the way one time he hunted, where, meeting this fellow and asking him the way and so falling into other questions, he found some of his answers (as a dog sure, if he could speak, had wit enough to describe his kennel) not unsensible and all uttered with such rudeness, which he interpreted plainness (though there be great difference between them), that Basilius, conceiving a sudden delight, took him to his court with apparent show of his good opinion, where the flattering courtier had no sooner taken the prince's mind but that there were straight reasons to confirm the prince's doing and shadows

50 vizar—face.
51 beldame—hag.

of virtues found for Dametas. His silence grew wit, bluntness, integrity, his beastly ignorance, virtuous simplicity; and the prince, according to the nature of great persons, in love with that he had done himself, fancied that his weakness with his presence would much be mended. And so, like a creature of his own making, he liked him more and more; and thus, having first given him the office of principal herdman, lastly, since he took this strange determination, he hath in manner put the life of himself and his children into his hands. Which authority, like too great a sail for so small a boat, doth so oversway poor Dametas, that, if before he were a good fool in a chamber, he might be allowed it now in a comedy; so as I doubt me (I fear me indeed) my master will in the end, with his cost, find that his office is not to make men, but to use men as men are, no more than a horse will be taught to hunt, or an ass to manage. But in sooth I am afraid I have given your ears too great a surfeit with the gross discourses of that heavy piece of flesh. But the zealous grief I conceive to see so great an error in my lord hath made me bestow more words than I confess so base a subject deserveth."

CHAPTER 4

The cause of Basilius' discourting. Philanax's dissuasive letter. Basilius' privileged company. Four causes why old men are discoursers. The state, the skill, and exercise of the Arcadian shepherds.

"Thus much now that I have told you is nothing more than in effect any Arcadian knows. But what moved him to this strange solitariness hath been imparted, as I think, but to one person living. Myself can conjecture, and indeed more than conjecture, by this accident that I will tell you. I have an only son, by name Clitophon,[52] who is now absent, preparing for his own marriage, which I mean shortly shall be here celebrated. This son of mine, while the prince kept his court, was of his bed-chamber; now, since the breaking up thereof, returned home; and showed me, among other things he had gathered, the copy

---

[52] Clitophon—"lovely voice."

which he had taken of a letter; which, when the prince had
read, he had laid in a window, presuming nobody durst look
in his writings; but my son not only took a time to read it, but
to copy it. In truth I blamed Clitophon for the curiosity, which
made him break his duty in such a kind, whereby kings' secrets
are subject to be revealed, but, since it was done, I was content
to take so much profit as to know it. Now here is the letter, that
I ever since for my good liking have carried about me, which
before I read unto you, I must tell you from whom it came. It is
a nobleman of this country, named Philanax, appointed by the
prince, regent in this time of his retiring, and most worthy so to
be, for there lives no man whose excellent wit more simply em-
braceth integrity, besides his unfeigned love to his master,
wherein never yet any could make question, saving whether he
loved Basilius or the prince better[53]—a rare temper, while most
men either servilely yield to all appetites, or with an obstinate
austerity, looking to that they fancy good, in effect neglect the
prince's person. This, then, being the man, whom of all other,
and most worthy, the prince chiefly loves, it should seem (for
more than the letter I have not to guess by) that the prince, upon
his return from Delphos (Philanax then lying sick), had written
unto him his determination, rising, as evidently appears, upon
some oracle he had there received, whereunto he wrote this
answer:

Philanax's Letter to Basilius

'Most redoubted and beloved Prince, if as well it had pleased
you at your going to Delphos as now to have used my humble
service, both I should in better season and to better purpose have
spoken, and you (if my speech had prevailed) should have been
at this time as no way more in danger so much more in quietness.
I would then have said that wisdom and virtue be the only
destinies appointed to man to follow, whence we ought to seek
all our knowledge, since they be such guides as cannot fail, which
—besides their inward comfort—do lead so direct a way of pro-

---

[53] loved Basilius or the prince better—loved the man or the rank of
office, a reference to the concept that a prince has two bodies, a personal and
a public.

ceeding as either prosperity must ensue, or, if the wickedness of
the world should oppress it, it can never be said that evil happeneth to him who falls accompanied with virtue. I would then
have said the heavenly powers to be reverenced and not searched
into, and their mercies rather by prayers to be sought than their
hidden counsels by curiosity. These kind of soothsayers (since
they[54] have left us in ourselves sufficient guides) to be nothing
but fancy, wherein there must either be vanity or infallibleness,
and so either not to be respected or not to be prevented. But
since it is weakness too much to remember what should have
been done, and that your commandment stretcheth to know what
is to be done, I do, most dear lord, with humble boldness say
that the manner of your determination doth in no sort better
please me than the cause of your doing. These thirty years you
have so governed this region that neither your subjects have
wanted justice in you nor you obedience in them, and your neighbors have found you so hurtlessly strong that they thought it better to rest in your friendship than make new trial of your enmity.
If this then have proceeded out of the good constitution of your
state and out of a wise providence generally to prevent all those
things which might encumber your happiness, why should you
now seek new courses, since your own ensample comforts you
to continue, and that it is to me most certain (though it please
you not to tell me the very words of the oracle) that yet no
destiny nor influence whatsoever can bring man's wit to a higher
point than wisdom and goodness. Why should you deprive yourself of government for fear of losing your government, like one
that should kill himself for fear of death? Nay rather, if this
oracle be to be accounted of, arm up your courage the more
against it, for who will stick to him that abandons himself? Let
your subjects have you in their eyes; let them see the benefits of
your justice daily more and more; and so must they needs rather
like of present sureties than uncertain changes. Lastly, whether
your time call you to live or die, do both like a prince.

'Now for your second resolution, which is to suffer no
worthy prince to be a suitor to either of your daughters, but

[54] they—the heavenly powers.

while you live to keep them both unmarried and, as it were, to
kill the joy of posterity, which in your time you may enjoy,
moved perchance by a misunderstood oracle. What shall I say, if
the affection of a father to his own children cannot plead sufficiently against such fancies? Once certain it is, the God, which
is God of nature, doth never teach unnaturalness; and even the
same mind hold I touching your banishing them from company
lest I know not what strange loves should follow. Certainly, sir,
in my ladies, your daughters, nature promiseth nothing but goodness, and their education, by your fatherly care, hath been
hitherto such as hath been most fit to restrain all evil, giving their
minds virtuous delights and not grieving them for want of well
ruled liberty. Now to fall to a sudden straitening them, what
can it do but argue suspicion, a thing no more unpleasant than
unsure for the preserving of virtue? Leave woman's minds, the
most untamed that way of any. See whether any cage can please
a bird, or whether a dog grow not fiercer with tying. What doth
jealousy but stir up the mind to think what it is from which they
are restrained? For they are treasurers or things of great delight
which men use to hide for the aptness they have to catch men's
fancies. And the thoughts once awaked to that, harder sure it is
to keep those thoughts from accomplishment than it had been
before to have kept the mind (which being the chief part by this
means is defiled) from thinking.

'Lastly, for the recommending so principal a charge of the
Princess Pamela (whose mind goes beyond the governing of
many thousands such) to such a person as Dametas is, besides
that the thing in itself is strange, it comes of a very evil ground
that ignorance should be the mother of faithfulness. O no, he
cannot be good that knows not why he is good, but stands so
far good as his fortune may keep him unassayed;[55] but coming
once to that, his rude simplicity is either easily changed or easily
deceived; and so grows that to be the last excuse of his fault
which seemed to have been the first foundation of his faith. Thus
far hath your commandment and my zeal drawn me, which I,
like a man in a valley that may discern hills or like a poor pas-

[55] unassayed—untried.

senger that may spy a rock, so humbly submit to your gracious consideration, beseeching you again to stand wholly upon your own virtue as the surest way to maintain you in that you are and to avoid any evil which may be imagined.'

"By the contents of this letter you may perceive that the cause of all hath been the vanity which possesseth many, who, making a perpetual mansion of this poor baiting-place of man's life, are desirous to know the certainty of things to come, wherein there is nothing so certain as our continual uncertainty. But what in particular points the oracle was, in faith I know not; neither (as you may see by one place of Philanax's letter) he himself distinctly knew. But this experience shows us that Basilius' judgment, corrupted with a prince's fortune, hath rather heard than followed the wise (as I take it) counsel of Philanax. For, having lost the stern of his government, with much amazement to the people (among whom many strange bruits[56] are received for current, and with some appearance of danger in respect of the valiant Amphialus[57] his nephew, and much envy in the ambitious number of the nobility against Philanax) to see Philanax so advanced (though, to speak simply, he deserve more than as many of us as there be in Arcadia), the prince himself hath hidden his head, in such sort as I told you, not sticking plainly to confess that he means not, while he breathes, that his daughters shall have any husband, but keep them thus solitary with him; where he gives no other body leave to visit him at any time but a certain priest, who being excellent in poetry, he makes him write out such things as he best likes, he being no less delightful in conversation than needful for devotion, and about twenty specified shepherds, in whom, some for exercises, and some for eclogues, he taketh greater recreation.

"And now you know as much as myself, wherein if I have held you overlong, lay hardly the fault upon my old age, which in the very disposition of it is talkative. Whether it be," said he smiling, "that nature loves to exercise that part most which

56 bruits—rumors.
57 Amphialus—"between two seas."

is least decayed, and that is our tongue; or that, knowledge being the only thing whereof we poor old men can brag, we cannot make it known but by utterance; or that mankind, by all means seeking to eternize himself so much the more as he is near his end, doth it not only by the children that come of him but by speeches and writings recommended to the memory of hearers and readers. And yet thus much I will say for myself: that I have not laid these matters, either so openly or largely, to any as yourself; so much (if I much fail not) do I see in you which makes me both love and trust you."

"Never may he be old," answered Palladius, "that doth not reverence that age whose heaviness, if it weigh down the frail and fleshly balance, it as much lifts up the noble and spiritual part. And well might you have alleged another reason: that their wisdom makes them willing to profit others. And that have I received of you, never to be forgotten but with ungratefulness. But among many strange conceits you told me which have showed effects in your prince, truly even the last, that he should conceive such pleasure in shepherd's discourses, would not seem the least unto me, saving that you told me at the first that this country is notable in those wits, and that indeed myself having been brought not only to this place, but to my life, by Strephon and Claius, in their conference found wits as might better become such shepherds as Homer speaks of that be governors of peoples than such senators who hold their council in a sheepcote."

"For them two," said Kalander, "especially Claius, they are beyond the rest by so much as learning commonly doth add to nature, for, having neglected their wealth in respect of their knowledge, they have not so much impaired the meaner as they bettered the better. Which all notwithstanding, it is a sport to hear how they impute to love, which hath indued[58] their thoughts, say they, with such a strength.

"But certainly, all the people of this country from high to low is given to those sports of the wit, so as you would wonder to hear how soon even children will begin to versify. Once ordinary it is among the meanest sort to make songs and dia-

---

[58] indued—invested with a power or a spiritual quality.

logues in meter, either love whetting their brain or, long peace having begun it, example and emulation amending it. Not so much but the clown Dametas will stumble sometimes upon some songs that might become a better brain; but no sort of people so excellent in that kind as the pastors, for their living standing upon the looking to their beasts, they have ease, the nurse of poetry. Neither are our shepherds such as, I hear, they be in other countries; but they are the very owners of the sheep, to which either themselves look or their children give daily attendance. And then truly it would delight you under some tree or by some river's side, when two or three of them meet together, to hear their rural muse, how prettily it will deliver out, sometimes joys, sometimes lamentations, sometimes challengings one of the other, sometimes under hidden forms uttering such matters as otherwise they durst not deal with. Then they have most commonly one who judgeth the prize to the best doer, of which they are no less glad than great princes are of triumphs. And his part is to set down in writing all that is said, save that it may be his pen with more leisure doth polish the rudeness of an unthought-on song. Now the choice of all, as you may well think, either for goodness of voice or pleasantness of wit, the prince hath, among whom also there are two or three strangers whom, inward melancholies having made weary of the world's eyes, have come to spend their lives among the country people of Arcadia; and their conversation being well approved, the prince vouchsafeth them his presence and, not only by looking on but by great courtesy and liberality, animates the shepherds the more exquisitely to labor for his good liking. So that there is no cause to blame the prince for sometimes hearing them; the blameworthiness is that to hear them he rather goes to solitariness than makes them come to company, as Dametas is, since God forbid but where worthiness is, as truly it is among diverse of that fellowship, any outward lowness should hinder the highest raising, but that he would needs make election of one the baseness of whose mind is such that it sinks a thousand degrees lower than the basest body could carry the most base fortune, which, although it might be answered for the prince that it is rather a trust he hath in his simple plainness than any great advancement, being the chief herdman, yet all honest hearts feel that the trust of their lord goes beyond all advancement. But I am ever too long upon him when he crosseth the way of my speech, and by the shadow of yonder tower, I see it is a fitter time, with our supper, to pay the duties we owe to our stomachs than to break the air with my idle discourses. And more wit I might have learned of Homer, whom even now you mentioned, who never entertained either guests or hosts with long speeches till the mouth of hunger be thoroughly stopped."

So withal he rose, leading Palladius through the garden again to the parlor where they used to sup, Palladius assuring him that he had already been more fed to his liking than he could be by the skillfullest trenchermen of Media.[59]

CHAPTER 5

The sorrow of Kalander for his son Clitophon. The story of Argalus[60] *and Parthenia:*[61] *their perfections, their love, their troubles, he impoisoning, his rare constancy, her strange refusal, their pathologies,*[62] *her flights, his revenge on his rival, the mischiefworker Demagoras,*[63] *then captain of the rebel Helots, who take him, and Clitophon that sought to help him; but both are kept alive by their new captain.*

But being come to the supping-place, one of Kalander's servants rounded in his ear, at which, his color changing, he retired himself into his chamber, commanding his men diligently to wait and attend upon Palladius, and to excuse his absence with some necessary business he had presently to dispatch; which they accordingly did, for some few days forcing themselves to let no change appear, but, though they framed their countenances never so cunningly, Palladius perceived there was some ill-pleasing accident fallen out. Whereupon, being again set alone at supper, he

---

[59] trenchermen of Media—Persian cooks.
[60] Argalus—"grievous."
[61] Parthenia—"virgin."
[62] pathologies—pathos.
[63] Demagoras—"crooked frame."

called to the steward, and desired him to tell him the matter of his sudden alteration; who, after some trifling excuses, in the end confessed unto him that his master had received news that his son, before the day of his near marriage, chanced to be at a battle which was to be fought between the gentlemen of Lacedæmon[64] and the Helots, who, winning the victory, he was there made prisoner, going to deliver a friend of his taken prisoner by the Helots; that the poor young gentleman had offered great ransom for his life, but that the hate those peasants conceived against all gentlemen was such, that every hour he was to look for nothing but some cruel death; which hitherunto had only been delayed by the captain's vehement dealing for him, who seemed to have a heart of more manly pity than the rest; which loss had stricken the old gentleman with such sorrow, as if abundance of tears did not seem sufficiently to witness it, he was alone retired, tearing his beard and hair, and cursing his old age that had not made his grave to stop his ears from such advertisements; but that his faithful servants had written in his name to all his friends, followers, and tenants (Philanax, the governor, refusing to deal in it, as a private cause, but yet giving leave to seek their best redress, so as they wronged not the state of Lacedæmon) of whom there were now gathered upon the frontiers good forces that he was sure would spend their lives by any way to redeem or revenge Clitophon.

"Now sir," said he, "this is my master's nature, though his grief be such as to live is a grief unto him and that even his reason is darkened with sorrow; yet the laws of hospitality, long and holily observed by him, gave still such a sway to his proceeding that he will no way suffer the stranger lodged under his roof to receive, as it were, any infection of his anguish, especially you, toward whom I know not whether his love or admiration be greater."

But Palladius could scarce hear out his tale with patience, so was his heart torn in pieces with compassion of the case, liking of Kalander's noble behavior, kindness for his respect to him-

[64] Lacedæmon—Sparta.

ward, and desire to find some remedy, besides the image of his dearest friend Daiphantus, whom he judged to suffer either a like or worse fortune. Therefore, rising from the board, he desired the steward to tell him particularly the ground and event of this accident, because, by knowledge of many circumstances, there might perhaps some way of help be opened. Whereunto the steward easily in this sort condescended.

"My lord," said he, "when our good King Basilius, with better success than expectation, took to wife, even in his more than decaying years, the fair young Princess Gynecia, there came with her a young lord, cousin-germane to herself, named Argalus, led hither partly with the love and honor of his noble kinswoman, partly with the humor of youth, which ever thinks that good whose goodness he sees not. And in this court he received so good increase of knowledge that, after some years spent, he so manifested a most virtuous mind in all his actions that Arcadia gloried such a plant was transported unto them, being a gentleman indeed most rarely accomplished, excellently learned, but without all vain glory, friendly without factiousness; valiant, so as, for my part, I think the earth hath no man that hath done more heroical acts than he; howsoever now of late the same flies of the two princes of Thessalia[65] and Macedon,[66] and hath long done of our noble Prince Amphialus, who, indeed, in our parts is only accounted likely to match him; but I say, for my part, I think no man, for valor of mind and ability of body, to be preferred, if equalled, to Argalus, and yet so valiant as he never durst do anybody injury. In behavior some will say ever sad, surely sober, and somewhat given to musing but never uncourteous; his word ever led by his thought and followed by his deed; rather liberal than magnificent, though the one wanted not and the other had ever good choice of the receiver. In sum (for I perceive I shall easily take a great draught of his praises, whom both I and all this country love so well) such a man was, and I hope is, Argalus as hardly the nicest[67] eye can find a spot in, if the over-

[65] Thessalia—cf. *O.A.*, ft. 18.
[66] Macedon—cf. *O.A.*, ft. 15.
[67] nicest—most fastidious.

vehement constancy of yet spotless affection may not in hard wrested constructions be counted a spot, which in this manner began that work in him which hath made both him, and itself in him, over all this country famous. My master's son Clitophon— whose loss gives the cause to this discourse, and yet gives me cause to begin with Argalus, since his loss proceeds from Argalus —being a young gentleman, as of great birth, being our king's sister's son, so truly of good nature, and one that can see good and love it, haunted more the company of this worthy Argalus than of any other; so as if there were not a friendship—which is so rare as it is to be doubted whether it be a thing indeed, or but a word—at least there was such a liking and friendliness as hath brought forth the effects which you shall hear.

"About two years since it so fell out that he brought him to a great lady's house, sister to my master, who had with her her only daughter, the fair Parthenia; fair indeed, fame I think itself daring not to call any fairer, if it be not Helen, queen of Corinth,[68] and the two incomparable sisters of Arcadia; and that which made her fairness much the fairer was that it was but a fair embassador of a most fair mind, full of wit, and a wit which delighted more to judge itself than to show itself, her speech being as rare as precious, her silence without sullenness, her modesty without affectation, her shamefastness without ignorance; in sum, one that to praise well one must first set down with himself what it is to be excellent, for so she is.

"I think you think that these perfections meeting could not choose but find one another, and delight in that they found; for likeness of manners is likely in reason to draw liking with affection—men's actions do not always cross with reason. To be short, it did so indeed. They loved, although for a while the fire thereof, hope's wings being cut off, were blown by the bellows of despair, despair, upon this occasion.

"There had been, a good while before, and so continued, a suitor to this same lady, a great nobleman, though of Laconia, yet near neighbor to Parthenia's mother, named Demagoras; a man

[68] Corinth—the neck of land connecting the Peloponnesus with the rest of Greece.

mighty in riches and power, and proud thereof, stubbornly
stout, loving nobody but himself, and, for his own delight's sake,
Parthenia; and, pursuing vehemently his desire, his riches had so
gilded over all his other imperfections that the old lady, though
contrary to my lord her brother's mind, had given her consent,
and, using a mother's authority upon her fair daughter, had made
her yield thereunto, not because she liked her choice, but because her obedient mind had not yet taken upon it to make
choice; and the day of their assurance drew near when my young
lord Clitophon brought this noble Argalus, perchance principally
to see so rare a sight as Parthenia, by all well-judging eyes, was
judged.

"But, though few days were before the time of assurance[69]
appointed, yet Love, that saw he had a great journey to make in
short time, hasted so himself that, before her word could tie her
to Demagoras, her heart hath vowed her to Argalus, with so
grateful a receipt in mutual affection that, if she desired above
all things to have Argalus, Argalus feared nothing but to miss
Parthenia. And now Parthenia had learned both liking and mis-
liking, loving and loathing, and out of passion began to take the
authority of judgment; insomuch, that, when the time came that
Demagoras, full of proud joy, thought to receive the gift of herself, she, with words of resolute refusal, though with tears, showing she was sorry she must refuse, assured her mother she would
first be bedded in her grave than wedded to Demagoras.

"The change was no more strange than unpleasant to the
mother, who, being determinately (lest I should say of a great
lady, willfully) bent to marry her to Demagoras, tried all ways
in which a witty and hard-hearted mother could use upon so
humble a daughter, in whom the only resisting power was love.
But the more she assaulted the more she taught Parthenia to
defend, and the more Parthenia defended the more she made her
mother obstinate in the assault, who at length finding that Argalus, standing between them, was it that most eclipsed her affection from shining upon Demagoras, she sought all means how to
remove him (so much the more as he manifested himself an un-

69 assurance—betrothal.

removable suitor to her daughter) first by employing him in as many dangerous enterprises as ever the evil step-mother Juno recommended to the famous Hercules;[70] but the more his virtue was tried the more pure it grew, while all the things she did to overthrow him did set him up upon the height of honor, enough to have moved her heart, especially to a man every way so worthy as Argalus. But she struggling against all reason because she would have her will and show her authority in matching her with Demagoras, the more virtuous Argalus was, the more she hated him, thinking herself conquered in his conquests and, therefore, still employing him in more and more dangerous attempts. Meanwhile she used all extremities possible upon her fair daughter to make her give over herself to her direction. But it was hard to judge whether he in doing or she in suffering showed greater constancy of affection; for as to Argalus the world sooner wanted occasions than he valor to go through them, so to Parthenia malice sooner ceased than her unchanged patience. Lastly, by treasons Demagoras and she would have made away Argalus; but he with providence and courage so passed over all that the mother took such a spiteful grief at it that her heart brake withal, and she died.

"But then Demagoras, assuring himself that now Parthenia was her own she would never be his, and receiving as much by her own determinate answer, not more desiring his own happiness than envying Argalus, whom he saw with narrow eyes even ready to enjoy the perfection of his desires, strengthening his conceit with all the mischievous counsels which disdained love and envious pride could give unto him, the wicked wretch, taking a time that Argalus was gone to his country to fetch some of his principal friends to honor the marriage, which Parthenia had most joyfully consented unto, the wicked Demagoras, I say, desiring to speak with her, with unmerciful force, her weak arms in vain resisting, rubbed all over her face a most horrible poison, the effect whereof was such that never leper looked more ugly than she did; which done, having his men and horses ready, de-

---

[70] Juno . . . the famous Hercules—Juno persecuted Hercules because he was one of Jupiter's bastards.

parted away in spite of her servants, as ready to revenge as could be in such an unexpected mischief. But the abominableness of this fact being come to my lord Kalander, he made such means, both by our king's intercession and his own, that by the king and senate of Lacedæmon Demagoras was, upon pain of death, banished the country; who, hating the punishment where he should have hated the fault, joined himself with all the powers he could make unto the Helots, lately in rebellion against that state; and they, glad to have a man of such authority among them, made him their general, and under him have committed divers the most outrageous villainies that a base multitude, full of desperate revenge, can imagine.

"But, within a while after this pitiful fact committed upon Parthenia, Argalus returned (poor gentleman!), having her fair image in his heart, and already promising his eyes the uttermost of his felicity, when they, nobody else daring to tell it him, were the first messengers to themselves of their own misfortune. I mean not to move passions with telling you the grief of both when he knew her; for at first he did not, nor at first knowledge could possibly have virtue's aid so ready as not even weakly to lament the loss of such a jewel; so much the more as that skillful men in that art assured it was unrecoverable. But, within a while, truth of love (which still held the first face in his memory), a virtuous constancy, and even a delight to be constant, faith given, and inward worthiness shining through the foulest mists, took so full hold of the noble Argalus that, not only in such comfort which witty arguments may bestow upon adversity, but even with the most abundant kindness that an eye-ravished lover can express, he labored both to drive the extremity of sorrow from her, and to hasten the celebration of their marriage; whereunto he unfeignedly showed himself no less cheerfully earnest than if she had never been disinherited of that goodly portion which nature had so liberally bequeathed unto her, and for that cause deferred his intended revenge upon Demagoras, because he might continually be in her presence, showing more humble serviceableness and joy to content her than ever before.

"But as he gave this rare ensample, not to behoped for of any other but of another Argalus, so, of the other side, she took as strange a course in affection; for, where she desired to enjoy him more than to live, yet did she overthrow both her own desire and his, and in no sort would yield to marry him, with a strange encounter of love's affects and effects, that he, by an affection sprung from excessive beauty, should delight in horrible foulness, and she of a vehement desire to have him should kindly build a resolution never to have him; for truth it is, that so in heart she loved him as she could not find in her heart he should be tied to what was unworthy of his presence.

"Truly, sir, a very good orator might have a fair field to use eloquence in if he did but only repeat the lamentable and truly affectionated speeches while he conjured her by remembrance of her affection and true oaths of his own affection not to make him so unhappy as to think he had not only lost her face but her heart; that her face when it was fairest had been but as a marshall to lodge the love of her in his mind, which now was so well placed it needed no further help of any outward harbinger, beseeching her, even with tears, to know that his love was not so superficial as to go no further than the skin, which yet now to him was most fair since it was hers. How could he be so ungrateful as to love her the less for that which she had only received for his sake? That he never beheld it but therein he saw the loveliness of her love toward him, protesting unto her that he would never take joy of his life if he might not enjoy her for whom principally he was glad he had life. But (as I heard by one that overheard them) she, wringing him by the hand, made no other answer but this:

" 'My lord,' said she, 'God knows I love you. If I were princess of the whole world and had withal all the blessings that ever the world brought forth, I should not make delay to lay myself and them under your feet. Or if I had continued but as I was, though I must confess far unworthy of you, yet would I, with too great joy for my heart to think of, have accepted your vouchsafing me to be yours and with faith and obedience would have supplied all other defects. But first let me be much more miserable than I am ere I match Argalus to such a Parthenia. Live happy, dear

Argalus; I give you full liberty, and I beseech you take it. And I assure you I shall rejoice (whatsoever become of me) to see you so coupled as may be fit both for your honor and satisfaction.'

"With that she burst out in crying and weeping, not able longer to contain herself from blaming her fortune and wishing her own death. But Argalus with a most heavy heart still pursuing his desire, she fixed of mind to avoid further intreaty and to fly all company (which, even of him, grew unpleasant unto her) one night she stole away, but whither as yet is unknown, or indeed what is become of her.

"Argalus sought her long and in many places; at length, despairing to find her, and the more he despaired the more enraged, weary of his life, but first determining to be revenged of Demagoras, he went alone disguised into the chief town held by the Helots, where, coming into his presence, guarded about by many of his soldiers, he could delay his fury no longer for a fitter time, but setting upon him, in despite of a great many that helped him, gave him divers mortal wounds, and himself, no question, had been there presently murdered, but that Demagoras himself desired he might be kept alive, perchance with intention to feed his own eyes with some cruel execution to be laid upon him; but death came sooner than he looked for, yet having had leisure to appoint his successor, a young man not long before delivered out of the prison of the king of Lacedæmon, where he should have suffered death for having slain the king's nephew. But him he named, who at that time was absent making roads upon the Lacedæmonians, but, being returned, the rest of the Helots, for the great liking they conceived of that young man, especially because they had none among themselves to whom the others would yield, were content to follow Demagoras's appointment. And well hath it succeeded with them, he having since done things beyond the hope of the youngest heads, of whom I speak the rather, because he hath hitherto preserved Argalus alive under pretence to have him publicly, and with exquisite torments, executed after the end of these wars, of which they hope for a soon and prosperous issue.

"And he hath likewise hitherto kept my young lord Clitophon alive, who, to redeem his friend, went with certain other noblemen of Laconia, and forces gathered by them, to besiege this young and new successor; but he, issuing out, to the wonder of all men, defeated the Laconians, slew many of the noblemen, and took Clitophon prisoner, whom with much ado he keepeth alive, the Helots being villainously cruel. But he tempereth them so, sometimes by following their humor, sometimes by striving with it, that hitherto he hath saved both their lives, but in different estates: Argalus being kept in a close and hard prison, Clitophon at some liberty. And now, sir, though, to say the truth, we can promise ourselves little of their safeties while they are in the Helots' hands, I have delivered all I understand touching the loss of my lord's son and the cause thereof; which, though it was not necessary to Clitophon's case to be so particularly told, yet the strangeness of it made me think it would not be unpleasant unto you."

CHAPTER 6

Kalander's expedition against the Helots. Their estate. Palladius' stratagem against them, which prevaileth. The Helots' resistance, discomfiture, and re-enforce by the return of their new captain. The combat and interknowledge of Daiphantus and Palladius, and by their means a peace, with the release of Kalander and Clitophon.

Palladius thanked him greatly for it, being even passionately delighted with hearing so strange an accident of a knight so famous over the world as Argalus, with whom he had himself a long desire to meet, so had fame poured a noble emulation in him towards him.

But then, well bethinking himself, he called for armor, desiring them to provide him of horse and guide; and armed all saving the head, he went up to Kalander, whom he found lying upon the ground, having ever since banished both sleep and food, as enemies to the mourning which passion persuaded him was reasonable. But Palladius raised him up, saying unto him: "No more, no more of this, my lord Kalander; let us labor to find before we lament the loss. You know myself miss one, who, though he be not my son, I would disdain the favor of life after him; but, while there is hope left, let not the weakness of sorrow make the strength of it languish; take comfort, and good success will follow."

And with those words, comfort seemed to lighten in his eyes, and that, in his face and gesture, was painted victory. Once Kalander's spirits were so revived withal that, receiving some sustenance, and taking a little rest, he armed himself, and those few of his servants he had left unsent, and so himself guided Palladius to the place upon the frontiers, where already there were assembled between three and four thousand men, all well disposed, for Kalander's sake, to abide any peril; but, like men disused with a long peace, more determinate to do than skillful how to do lusty bodies and brave armors, with such courage as rather grew of despising their enemies, whom they knew not, than of any confidence for anything which in themselves they knew; but neither cunning use of their weapons nor art showed in their marching or encamping. Which Palladius soon perceiving, he desired to understand, as much as could be delivered unto him, the estate of the Helots.

And he was answered by a man well acquainted with the affairs of Laconia, that they were a kind of people who having been of old freemen and possessioners,[71] the Lacedæmonians had conquered them, and laid not only tribute, but bondage upon them, which they had long borne, till of late the Lacedæmonians, through greediness growing more heavy than they could bear, and through contempt less careful how to make them bear, they had with a general consent, rather springing by the generalness of the cause than of any artificial practice, set themselves in arms, and, whetting their courage with revenge, and grounding their resolution upon despair, they had proceeded with unlooked-for success, having already taken divers towns and castles, with the slaughter of many of the gentry; for whom no sex nor age could be accepted for an excuse. And that, although at the first they had fought rather with beastly fury than any soldierly discipline,

---

[71] possessioners—proprietors.

practice had now made them comparable to the best of the Lacedæmonians, and more of late than ever by reason first of Demagoras, a great lord, who had made himself of their party and, since his death, of another captain they had gotten, who had brought up their ignorance and brought down their fury to such a mean of good government and withal led them so valorously that (besides the time wherein Clitophon was taken) they had the better in some other great conflicts, in such wise that the estate of Lacedæmon had sent unto them offering peace with most reasonable and honorable conditions.

Palladius having gotten his general knowledge of the party against whom, as he had already of the party for whom, he was to fight, he went to Kalander, and told him plainly that by plain force there was small appearance of helping Clitophon; but some device was to be taken in hand, wherein no less discretion than valor was to be used.

Whereupon the counsel of the chief men was called, and at last this way Palladius (who, by some experience, but especially by reading histories, was acquainted with stratagems) invented, and was by all the rest approved: that all the men there should dress themselves like the poorest sort of the people in Arcadia, having no banners, but bloody shirts hanged upon long staves, with some bad bagpipes instead of drum and fife; their armor they should, as well as might be, cover, or at least make them look so rustily and ill-favoredly as might well become such wearers; and this the whole number should do, saving two hundred of the best chosen gentlemen for courage and strength, whereof Palladius himself would be one, who should have their arms chained, and be put in carts like prisoners.

This being performed according to the agreement, they marched on towards the town of Cardamila,[72] where Clitophon was captive; and being come, two hours before sunset, within view of the walls, the Helots already descrying their number and beginning to sound the alarum, they sent a cunning fellow—so much the cunninger as that he could mask it under rudeness—who, with such a kind of rhetoric as weeded out all flowers of

---

[72] Cardamila—Cardamyle, a city in Laconia on the Messenian Gulf.

rhetoric, delivered unto the Helots assembled together that they were country people of Arcadia, no less oppressed by their lords, and no less desirous of liberty, than they, and therefore had put themselves in the field, and had already, besides a great number slain, taken nine or ten score gentlemen prisoners, whom they had there well and fast chained. Now, because they had no strong retiring place in Arcadia, and were not yet of number enough to keep the field against their prince's forces, they were come to them for succor, knowing that daily more and more of their quality would flock unto them; but that in the meantime, lest their prince should pursue them, or the Lacedæmonian king and nobility (for the likeness of the cause) fall upon them, they desired that if there were not room enough for them in the town, that yet they might encamp under the walls, and for surety have their prisoners, who were such men as were ever able to make their peace, kept within the town.

The Helots made but a short consultation, being glad that their contagion had spread itself into Arcadia, and making account that if the peace did not fall out between them and their king, that it was the best way to set fire in all the parts of Greece (besides their greediness to have so many gentlemen in their hands, in whose ransoms they already meant to have a share) to which haste of concluding two things well helped. The one, that their captain, with the wisest of them, was at that time absent, about confirming or breaking the peace with the state of Lacedæmon; the second, that over-many good fortunes began to breed a proud recklessness in them. Therefore, sending to view the camp, and finding that by their speech they were Arcadians, with whom they had had no war, never suspecting a private man's credit could have gathered such a force, and that all other tokens witnessed them to be of the lowest calling, besides the chains upon the gentlemen, they granted not only leave for the prisoners, but for some others of the company, and to all that they might harbor under the walls. So opened they the gates, and received in the carts; which being done, and Palladius seeing fit time, he gave the sign, and, shaking off their chains, which were made with such art that, though they seemed most strong and fast, he that wore them might easily loose them, drew their swords, hidden in the carts, and so setting upon the ward,[73] made them to fly either from the place, or from their bodies, and so give entry to all the force of the Arcadians before the Helots could make any head to resist them.

But the Helots, being men hardened against dangers, gathered, as well as they could, together in the marketplace, and thence would have given a shrewd welcome to the Arcadians, but that Palladius, blaming those that were slow, heartening them that were forward, but especially with his own ensample leading them, made such an impression into the squadron of the Helots, that at first the great body of them beginning to shake and stagger, at length every particular body recommended the protection of his life to his feet. Then Kalander cried to go to the prison where he thought his son was; but Palladius wished him (first scouring the streets) to house all the Helots, and make themselves masters of the gates.

But ere that could be accomplished the Helots had gotten new heart, and, with divers sorts of shot, from corners of streets and house-windows, galled them; which courage was come unto them by the return of their captain, who, though he brought not many with him, having dispersed most of his companies to other of his holds, yet, meeting a great number running out of the gate, not yet possessed by the Arcadians, he made them turn face and, with banners displayed, his trumpet give the loudest testimony he could of his return; which once heard, the rest of the Helots, which were otherwise scattered, bent thitherward with a new life of resolution, as if their captain had been a root out of which, as into branches, their courage had sprung. Then began the fight to grow most sharp, and the encounters of more cruel obstinacy, the Arcadians fighting to keep that they had won, the Helots to recover what they had lost; the Arcadians as in an unknown place, having no succor but in their hands, the Helots as in their own place, fighting for their livings, wives, and

[73] ward—guard.

children. There was victory and courage against revenge and despair, safety of both sides being no otherwise to be gotten but by destruction.

At length the left wing of the Arcadians began to lose ground; which Palladius seeing, he straight thrust himself, with his choice band, against the throng that oppressed them, with such an overflowing of valor that the captain of the Helots— whose eyes soon judged of that wherewith themselves were governed—saw that he alone was worth all the rest of the Arcadians, which he so wondered at that it was hard to say whether he more liked his doings or misliked the effects of his doings; but, determining that upon that cast the game lay, and disdaining to fight with any other, sought only to join with him, which mind was no less in Palladius, having easily marked that he was as the first mover of all the other hands. And so, their thoughts meeting in one point, they consented, though not agreed, to try each other's fortune; and so, drawing themselves to be the uttermost of the one side, they began a combat which was so much inferior to the battle in noise and number as it was surpassing it in bravery of fighting and, as it were, delightful terribleness. Their courage was guided with skill, and their skill was armed with courage; neither did their hardiness darken their wit, nor their wit cool their hardiness: both valiant, as men despising death; both confident, as unwonted to be overcome, yet doubtful by their present feeling, and respectful by what they had already seen; their feet steady, their hands diligent, their eyes watchful, and their hearts resolute. The parts either not armed or weakly armed were well known, and, according to the knowledge, should have been sharply visited but that the answer was as quick as the objection. Yet some lighting, the smart bred rage, and the rage bred smart again, till, both sides beginning to wax faint, and rather desirous to die accompanied than hopeful to live victorious, the captain of the Helots, with a blow whose violence grew of fury, not of strength, or of strength proceeding of fury, strake Palladius upon the side of the head that he reeled astonished, and withal the helmet fell off, he remaining bareheaded; but other of the Arcadians were ready to shield him from any harm might rise of that nakedness.

But little needed it; for his chief enemy, instead of pursuing that advantage, kneeled down, offering to deliver the pommel of his sword, in token of yielding, withal speaking aloud unto him, that he thought it more liberty to be his prisoner than any other's general. Palladius, standing upon himself, and misdoubting some craft, and the Helots that were next their captain wavering between looking for some stratagem or fearing treason, "What," said the captain, "hath Palladius forgotten the voice of Daïphantus?"

By that watchword Palladius knew that it was his only friend Pyrocles, whom he had lost upon the sea, and therefore both, most full of wonder so to be met, if they had not been fuller of joy than wonder, caused the retreat to be sounded, Daïphantus by authority, and Palladius by persuasion; to which helped well the little advantage that was of either side, and that, of the Helots' party, their captain's behavior had made as many amazed as saw or heard of it, and, of the Arcadian side, the good old Kalander, striving more than his old age could achieve, was newly taken prisoner. But indeed the chief parter of the fray was the night, which, with her black arms, pulled their malicious sights one from the other. But he that took Kalander meant nothing less than to save him; but only so long as the captain might learn the enemy's secrets, towards whom he led the old gentleman when he caused the retreat to be sounded, looking for no other delivery from that captivity but by the painful taking away of all pain, when whom should he see next to the captain, with good tokens how valiantly he had fought that day against the Arcadians, but his son Clitophon!

But now the captain had caused all the principal Helots to be assembled, as well to deliberate what they had to do as to receive a message from the Arcadians, among whom Palladius' virtue, besides the love Kalander bare him, having gotten principal authority, he had persuaded them to seek rather by parley to recover the father and the son than by the sword, since the goodness of the captain assured him that way to speed, and his value wherewith he was of old acquainted, made him think any other way dangerous. This, therefore, was done in orderly manner, giving them to understand that, as they came but to deliver Clitophon, so offering to leave the footing they already had in the town, to go away without any further hurt, so as they might have the father and the son without ransom delivered. Which conditions being heard and conceived by the Helots, Daïphantus persuaded them without delay to accept them.

"For first," said he, "since the strife is within our own home, if you lose, you lose all that in this life can be dear unto you. If you win, it will be a bloody victory with no profit but the flattering in ourselves that same bad humor of revenge. Besides, it is like to stir Arcadia upon us, which now, by using these persons well, may be brought to some amity. Lastly, but especially, lest the king and nobility of Laconia, with whom now we have made a perfect peace, should hope by occasion of this quarrel to join the Arcadians with them and so break of the profitable agreement already concluded. In sum, as in all deliberations (weighing the profit of the good success with the harm of the evil success), you shall find this way most safe and honorable."

The Helots, as much moved by his authority as persuaded by his reasons, were content therewith. Whereupon Palladius took order that the Arcadians should presently march out of the town, taking with them their prisoners, while the night with mutual diffidence might keep them quiet, and ere day came they might be well on of their way, and so avoid those accidents which in late enemies a look, a word, or a particular man's quarrel might engender.

This being on both sides concluded on, Kalander and Clitophon, who now, with infinite joy, did know each other, came to kiss the hands and feet of Daïphantus; Clitophon telling his father how Daïphantus (not without danger to himself) had preserved him from the furious malice of the Helots; and even that day, going to conclude the peace, lest in his absence he might receive some hurt, he had taken him in his company and given him armor, upon promise he should take the part of the Helots, which he had in this fight performed, little knowing that it was against his father. "But," said Clitophon, "here is he who, as a father, hath new begotten me, and, as a god, hath saved me from many deaths, which already laid hold on me," which Kalander with tears of joy acknowledged, besides his own deliverance, only his benefit.[74]

But Daïphantus, who loved doing well for itself and not for thanks, brake off those ceremonies, desiring to know how Palladius—for so he called Musidorus—was come into that company, and what his present estate was; whereof, receiving a brief declaration of Kalander, he sent him word by Clitophon that he should not as now come unto him, because he held himself not so sure a master of the Helots' minds that he would adventure him in their power who was so well known with an unfriendly acquaintance, but that he desired him to return with Kalander, whither also he, within few days, having dispatched himself of the Helots, would repair. Kalander would needs kiss his hand again for that promise, protesting he would esteem his house more blessed than a temple of the gods if it had once received him. And then, desiring pardon for Argalus, Daïphantus assured them that he would die but he would bring him, though till then kept in close prison indeed for his safety, the Helots being so animated against him as else he could not have lived; and so, taking their leave of him, Kalander, Clitophon, Palladius, and the rest of the Arcadians, swearing that they would no further in any sort molest the Helots, they straightway marched out of the town, carrying both their dead and wounded bodies with them, and by morning were already within the limits of Arcadia.

CHAPTER 7

The articles of peace between the Lacedæmonians and Helots, Daïphantus' departure from the Helots with Argalus to Kalander's house. The offer of a strange lady to Argalus, his refusal, and who she was.

The Helots, of the other side, shutting their gates, gave themselves to bury their dead, to cure their wounds, and rest

[74] only his benefit—his only benefit.

their wearied bodies; till, the next day bestowing the cheerful use of the light upon them, Daïphantus making a general convocation, spake unto them in this manner: "We are first," said he, "to thank the gods that, further than we had either cause to hope or reason to imagine, have delivered us out of this gulf of danger, wherein we were already swallowed. For all being lost (had they had not directed my return so just as they did), it had been too late to recover that which, being had, we could not keep. And had I not happened to know one of the principal men among them, by which means the truce began between us, you may easily conceive what little reason we have to think but that, either by some supply out of Arcadia or from the nobility of this country (who would have made fruits of wisdom grow out of this occasion), we should have had our power turned to ruin, our pride to repentance and sorrow. But now the storm, as it fell out, so it ceased; and the error committed in retaining Clitophon more hardly than his age or quarrel deserved becomes a sharply learned experience to use in other times more moderation.

"Now have I to deliver unto you the conclusion between the kings with the nobility of Lacedæmon and you, which is in all points as yourselves desired, as well for what you would have granted as for the assurance of what is granted. The towns and forts you presently have are still left unto you, to be kept either with or without garrison, so as you alter not the laws of the country and pay such duties as the rest of the Laconians do. Yourselves are made by public decree free men, and so capable both to give and receive voice in election of magistrates. The distinction of names between Helots and Lacedæmonians to be quite taken away, and all indifferently to enjoy both names and privileges of Laconians. Your children to be brought up with theirs in Spartan discipline; and so you, framing yourselves to be good members of that estate, to be hereafter fellows and no longer servants.

"Which conditions you see carry in themselves no more contentation than assurance. For this is not a peace which is made with them, but this is a peace by which you are made of them. Lastly, a forgetfulness decreed of all what is past, they showing themselves glad to have so valiant men as you are joined to them; so that you are to take minds of peace since the cause of war is finished; and as you hated them before like oppressors, so now to love them as brothers, to take care of their estate because it is yours, and to labor by virtuous doing that the posterity may not repent your joining. But now one article only they stood upon, which in the end I with your commissioners have agreed unto: that I should no more tarry here, mistaking perchance my humor, and thinking me as pernicious as I am young, or else it is the King Amiclas'[75] procuring, in respect that it was my ill hap to kill his nephew Euryleon;[76] but howsoever it be, I have condescended."

"But so will not we," cried almost the whole assembly, counseling one another, rather to try the uttermost event, than to lose him by whom they had been victorious. But he, as well with general orations as particular dealing with the men of most credit, made them thoroughly see how necessary it was to prefer such an opportunity before a vain affection; but yet could not prevail till openly he sware that he would, if at any time the Lacedæmonians brake this treaty, come back again and be their captain.

So then, after a few days, settling them in perfect order, he took his leave of them, whose eyes bade him farewell with tears, and mouths with kissing the places where he stepped, and after making temples unto him, as to a demigod, thinking it beyond the degree of humanity to have a wit so far over-going his age, and such dreadful terror proceed from so excellent beauty. But he for his sake obtained free pardon for Argalus, whom also, upon oath never to bear arms against the Helots, he delivered, and taking only with him certain principal jewels of his own, he would have parted alone with Argalus, whose countenance well showed, while Parthenia was lost, he counted not himself delivered, but that the whole multitude would needs guard him into Arcadia. Where again leaving them all to lament his departure, he by inquiry got to the well-known house of Kalander.

There was he received with loving joy of Kalander, with

[75] Amiclas—from the name of a famous Spartan shrine, Amyclæ.
[76] Euryleon—"far-reaching lion."

joyful love of Palladius, with humble though doleful demeanor of Argalus, whom specially both he and Palladius regarded, with grateful serviceableness of Clitophon, and honorable admiration of all. For, being now well viewed to have no hair on his face to witness him a man, who had done acts beyond the degree of a man, and to look with a certain almost bashful kind of modesty, as if he feared the eyes of men, who was unmoved with the sight of the most horrible countenances of death, and as if Nature had mistaken her work to have a Mars' heart in a Cupid's body, all that beheld him (and all that might behold him did behold him) made their eyes quick messengers to their minds that there they had seen the uttermost that in mankind might be seen. The like wonder Palladius had before stirred, but that Daïphantus, as younger and newer come, had gotten now the advantage in the moist and fickle impression of eyesight. But while all men, saving poor Argalus, made the joy of their eyes speak for their hearts towards Daïphantus, Fortune (that belike was bid to that banquet, and meant then to play the good fellow) brought a pleasant adventure among them.

It was that, as they had newly dined, there came into Kalander a messenger, that brought him word a young noble lady, near kinswoman to the fair Helen, queen of Corinth, was come thither, and desired to be lodged in his house. Kalander, most glad of such an occasion, went out, and all his other worthy guests with him, saving only Argalus, who remained in his chamber, desirous that this company were once broken up that he might go in his solitary quest after Parthenia. But when they met this lady, Kalander straight thought he saw his niece Parthenia, and was about in such familiar sort to have spoken unto her, but she, in grave and honorable manner, giving him to understand that he was mistaken, he, half ashamed, excused himself with the exceeding likeness was between them, though, indeed, it seemed that this lady was of the more pure and dainty complexion. She said it might very well be, having been many times taken one for another. But as soon as she was brought into the house, before she would rest her, she desired to speak with Argalus publicly, who she heard was in the house. Argalus came in hastily, and as hastily thought as Kalander had done, with sudden changes of joy into sorrow.

But she, when she had stayed their thoughts with telling them her name and quality, in this sort spake unto him. "My lord Argalus," said she, "being of late left in the court of Queen Helen of Corinth, as chief in her absence, she being upon some occasion gone thence, there came unto me the Lady Parthenia, so disguised, as I think Greece hath nothing so ugly to behold. For my part, it was many days before, with vehement oaths and some good proofs, she could make me think that she was Parthenia. Yet, at last finding certainly it was she, and greatly pitying her misfortune, so much the more as that all mine had ever told me, as now you do, of the great likeness between us, I took the best care I could of her, and of her understood the whole tragical history of her undeserved adventure; and therewithal of that most noble constancy in you my lord Argalus, which whosoever loves not shows himself to be a hater of virtue, and unworthy to live in the society of mankind. But no outward cherishing could salve the inward sore of her mind; but a few days since she died, before her death earnestly desiring and persuading me to think of no husband but of you, as of the only man in the world worthy to be loved. Withal she gave me this ring to deliver you, desiring you, and by the authority of love commanding you, that the affection you bare her you should turn to me, assuring you that nothing can please her soul more than to see you and me matched together. Now, my lord, though this office be not, perchance, suitable to my estate nor sex, who should rather look to be desired, yet an extraordinary desert requires an extraordinary proceeding; and, therefore, I am come, with faithful love built upon your worthiness, to offer myself, and to beseech you to accept the offer, and if these noble gentlemen present will say it is great folly, let them withal say it is great love." And then she stayed, earnestly attending Argalus' answer; who, first making most hearty sighs do such obsequies as he could to Parthenia, thus answered her.

"Madam," said he, "infinitely bound am I unto you for this no more rare than noble courtesy; but more bound for the goodness I perceive you showed to the Lady Parthenia"—with that the tears ran down his eyes, but he followed on—"and as much as so unfortunate a man, fit to be the spectacle of misery, can do you service, determine you have made a purchase of a slave, while I live, never to fail you. But this great matter you propose unto me, wherein I am not so blind as not to see what happiness it should be unto me, excellent lady, know that, if my heart were mine to give, you before all other should have it; but Parthenia's it is, though dead: there I began, there I end all matter of affection. I hope I shall not long tarry after her, with whose beauty if I had only been in love, I should be so with you, who have the same beauty; but it was Parthenia's self I loved, and love, which no likeness can make one, no commandment dissolve, no foulness defile, nor no death finish."

"And shall I receive," said she, "such disgrace as to be refused?"

"Noble lady," said he, "let not that hard word be used to me who know your exceeding worthiness far beyond my desert; but it is only happiness I refuse, since of the only happiness I could and can desire I am refused."

He had scarce spoken those words when she ran to him, and embracing him, "Why, then, Argalus," said she, "take thy Parthenia"; and Parthenia it was indeed. But because sorrow forbade him too soon to believe, she told him the truth, with all circumstances: how being parted alone, meaning to die in some solitary place, as she happened to make her complaint, the Queen Helen of Corinth, who likewise felt her part of miseries, being then walking also alone in that lovely place, heard her, and never left till she had known the whole discourse. Which the noble queen greatly pitying, she sent to her a physician of hers, the most excellent man in the world, in hope he could help her, which in such sort as they saw performed; and she, taking with her of the queen's servants, thought yet to make this trial, whether he would quickly forget his true Parthenia or no. Her speech was confirmed by the Corinthian gentlemen, who before had kept her counsel, and Argalus easily persuaded to what more than ten thousand years of life he desired; and Kalander would needs have the marriage celebrated in his house, principally the longer to hold his dear guests, towards whom he was now, besides his own habit of hospitality, carried with love and duty, and therefore omitted no service that his wit could invent and his power minister.

CHAPTER 8

The adventures first of Musidorus, then of Pyrocles since their shipwreck, to their meeting. The marriage of Argalus and Parthenia.

But no way he saw he could so much pleasure them as by leaving the two friends alone, who being shrunk aside to the banqueting house, where the pictures were, there Palladius recounted unto him that after they had both abandoned the burning ship (and either of them taken something under him the better to support him to the shore), he knew not how, but either with overlaboring in the fight and sudden cold or the too much receiving of salt water, he was past himself; but, yet holding fast (as the nature of dying men is to do) the chest that was under him, he was cast on the sands, where he was taken up by a couple of shepherds, and by them brought to life again, and kept from drowning himself when he despaired of his safety. How after having failed to take him into the fisher boat, he had by the shepherds' persuasion come to this gentleman's house, where being dangerously sick, he had yielded to seek the recovery of health only for that he might the sooner go seek the delivery of Pyrocles, to which purpose Kalander, by some friends of his in Messenia, had already set a ship or two abroad when this accident of Clitophon's taking had so blessedly procured their meeting.

Then did he set forth unto him the noble entertainment and careful cherishing of Kalander towards him, and so, upon occasion of the pictures present, delivered with the frankness of a friend's tongue, as near as he could, word by word what Kalander had told him touching the strange story (with all the particularities belonging) of Arcadia; which did in many sorts so delight Pyrocles to hear that he would needs have much of it again repeated, and was not contented till Kalander himself had answered him divers questions.

But first, at Musidorus' request, though in brief manner, his mind much running upon the strange story of Arcadia, he did declare by what course of adventures he was come to make up their mutual happiness in meeting. "When, cousin," said he, "we had stripped ourselves, and were both leapt into the sea, and swam a little toward the shore, I found by reason of some wounds I had, that I should not be able to get the land, and therefore returned back again to the mast of the ship, where you found me, assuring myself that, if you came alive to the shore, you would seek me; if you were lost, as I thought it as good to perish as to live, so that place as good to perish in as another. There I found my sword among some of the shrouds, wishing (I must confess) if I died, to be found with that in my hand, and, withal, waving it about my head that the sailors by it might have the better glimpse of me. There you missing me, I was taken up by pirates, who, putting me under board prisoner, presently set upon another ship, and, maintaining a long fight, in the end put them all to the sword. Amongst whom I might hear them greatly praise one young man, who fought most valiantly, whom (as love is careful, and misfortune subject to doubtfulness) I thought certainly to be you. And so, holding you as dead, from that time till the time I saw you, in truth I sought nothing more than a noble end, which perchance made me more hardy than otherwise I would have been.

"Trial whereof came within two days after; for the kings of Lacedæmon having set out some galleys, under the charge of one of their nephews, to scour the sea of the pirates, they met with us, where our captain, wanting men, was driven to arm some of his prisoners, with promise of liberty for well fighting, among whom I was one; and, being boarded by the admiral, it was my fortune to kill Euryleon, the king's nephew. But in the end they prevailed, and we were all taken prisoners (I not caring much what became of me, only keeping the name of Daïphantus, according to the resolution you know is between us) but, being laid in the jail of Tenaria,[77] with special hate to me for the death of Euryleon. The popular sort of that town conspired with the Helots, and so by night opened them the gates, where entering and killing all of the gentle and rich faction, for honesty-sake broke open all prisons, and so delivered me; and I, moved with gratefulness, and encouraged with carelessness of life, so behaved myself in some conflicts they had in few days that they, barbarously thinking unsensible wonders of me (and withal so much the better trusting me as they heard I was hated of the king of Lacedæmon), their chief captain being slain (as you know, by the noble Argalus, who helped thereunto by his persuasion), having borne a great affection unto me, and to avoid the dangerous emulation which grew among the chief, who should have the place, and all so affected, as rather to have a stranger than a competitor, they elected me (God wot little proud of that dignity), restoring unto me such things of mine, as being taken first by the pirates and then by the Lacedæmonians, they had gotten in the sack of the town. Now being in it, so good was my success with many victories, that I made a peace for them, to their own liking, the very day that you delivered Clitophon, whom I, with much ado, had preserved. And in my peace the King Amiclas of Lacedæmon would needs have me banished, and deprived of the dignity whereunto I was exalted; which—and you may see how much you are bound to me—for your sake I was content to suffer, a new hope rising in me that you were not dead, and so meaning to travel over the world to seek you; and now here, my dear Musidorus, you have me."

And with that, embracing and kissing each other, they called Kalander, of whom Daïphantus desired to hear the full story, which before he had recounted to Palladius, and to see the letter of Philanax, which he read and well marked. But, within some days after, the marriage between Argalus and the fair Parthenia being to be celebrated, Daïphantus and Palladius selling some of their jewels, furnished themselves of very fair apparel, meaning

77 Tenaria—Tenarus, a Laconian town reputed to be an entrance to the underworld.

to do honor to their loving host, who, as much for their sakes as for the marriage, set forth each thing in most gorgeous manner. But all the cost bestowed did not so much enrich, nor all the fine deckings so much beautify, nor all the dainty devices so much delight, as the fairness of Parthenia, the pearl of all the maids of Mantinea, who as she went to the temple to be married, her eyes themselves seemed a temple, wherein love and beauty were married; her lips, although they were kept close with modest silence, yet, with a pretty kind of natural swelling, they seemed to invite the guests that looked on them; her cheeks blushing, and withal, when she was spoken unto, a little smiling, were like roses, when their leaves are with a little breath stirred; her hair being laid at the full length down her back, bare showed, as if the voward[78] failed, yet that would conquer. Daïphantus, marking her, "O Jupiter!" saith he, speaking to Palladius, "how happens it that beauty is only confined to Arcadia?", but Palladius not greatly attending his speech. Some days were continued in the solemnizing the marriage, with all conceits that might deliver delight to men's fancies.

CHAPTER 9

Pyrocles' inclination to love. His and Musidorus' disputation thereabouts broken off by Kalander.

But such a change was grown in Daïphantus that, as if cheerfulness had been tediousness, and good entertainment were turned to discourtesy, he would ever get himself alone, though almost when he was in company he was alone, so little attention he gave to any that spoke unto him; even the color and figure of his face began to receive some alteration, which he showed little to heed; but every morning, early going abroad, either to the garden or to some woods towards the desert, it seemed his only comfort was to be without a comforter. But long it could not be hid from Palladius, whom true love made ready to mark, and long knowledge able to mark; and, therefore, being now grown weary of his abode in Arcadia, having informed himself fully of the

---

[78] voward—vanguard.

strength and riches of the country, of the nature of the people, and manner of their laws, and seeing the court could not be visited, prohibited to all men but to certain shepherdish people, he greatly desired a speedy return to his own country, after the many mazes of fortune he had trodden. But, perceiving this great alteration in his friend, he thought first to break with him thereof, and then to hasten his return, whereto he found him but smally inclined; whereupon one day taking him alone with certain graces and countenances, as if he were disputing with the trees, he began in this manner to say unto him:

"A mind well trained and long exercised in virtue, my sweet and worthy cousin, doth not easily change any course it once undertakes but upon well grounded and well weighed causes. For being witness to itself of his own inward good, it finds nothing without it of so high a price for which it should be altered. Even the very countenance and behavior of such a man doth show forth images of the same constancy, by maintaining a right harmony betwixt it and the inward good, in yielding itself suitable to the virtuous resolution of the mind. This speech I direct to you, noble friend Pyrocles, the excellency of whose mind and well chosen course in virtue, if I do not sufficiently know (having seen such rare demonstrations of it), it is my weakness and not your unworthiness. But as indeed I know it, and knowing it, must dearly love both it and him that hath it, so must I needs say that, since our late coming into the country, I have marked in you, I will not say an alteration, but a relenting truly and a slacking of the main career you had so notably begun and almost performed; and that in such sort as I cannot find sufficient reason in my great love toward you how to allow it; for (to leave off other secreter arguments which my acquaintance with you makes me easily find) this in effect to any man may be manifest: that whereas you were wont in all places you came to give yourself vehemently to the knowledge of those things which might better your mind, to seek the familiarity of excellent men in learning and soldiery, and lastly to put all these things in practice both by continual wise proceeding and worthy enterprises as occasion fell for them, you now leave all these things undone; you let your mind fall asleep beside your countenance troubled (which surely comes not of virtue, for virtue, like the clear heaven, is without clouds); and, lastly, you subject yourself to solitariness, the sly enemy that doth most separate a man from well doing."

Pyrocles' mind was all this while so fixed upon another devotion that he no more attentively marked his friend's discourse than the child that hath leave to play marks the last part of his lesson or the diligent pilot in a dangerous tempest doth attend the unskillful words of a passenger. Yet, the very sound having imprinted the general point of his speech in his heart, pierced with any mislike of so dearly an esteemed friend and desirous by degrees to bring him to a gentler consideration of him, with a shamefast look (witnessing he rather could not help, than did not know, his fault) answered him to this purpose:

"Excellent Musidorus, in the praise you gave me in the beginning of your speech, I easily acknowledge the force of your good will unto me, for neither could you have thought so well of me if extremity of love had not made your judgment partial, nor you could have loved me so entirely if you had not been apt to make so great (though undeserved) judgments of me; and even so must I say to those imperfections to which, though I have ever through weakness been subject, yet you by the daily mending of your mind have of late been able to look upon them which before you could not discern; so that the change you speak of falls not out by my impairing, but by your bettering. And yet, under the leave of your better judgment, I must needs say thus much, my dear cousin: that I find not myself wholly to be condemned because I do not with continual vehemency follow those knowledges which you call the bettering of my mind, for both the mind itself must, like other things, sometimes be unbent, or else it will be either weakened or broken; and these knowledges, as they are of good use, so are they not all the mind may stretch itself unto. Who knows whether I feed not my mind with higher thoughts? Truly, as I know not all the particularities, so yet I see the bounds of all these knowledges; but the workings of the mind I find much more infinite than can be led unto by the eye, or imagined by any that distract their thoughts without themselves.

And in such contemplation, or as I think more excellent, I enjoy my solitariness; and my solitariness perchance is the nurse of these contemplations. Eagles we see fly alone, and they are but sheep which always herd together. Condemn not therefore my mind sometime to enjoy itself; nor blame not the taking of such times as serve most fit for it. And alas, dear Musidorus, if I be sad, who knows better than you the just causes I have of sadness?"

And here Pyrocles suddenly stopped, like a man unsatisfied in himself, though his wit might well have served to have satisfied another. And so looking with a countenance as though he desired he should know his mind without hearing him speak, and yet desirous to speak, to breathe out some part of his inward evil, sending again new blood to his face, he continued his speech in this manner: "And Lord, dear cousin," said he, "doth not the pleasantness of this place carry in itself sufficient reward for any time lost in it? Do you not see how all things conspire together to make this country a heavenly dwelling? Do you not see the grass, how in color they excel the emeralds, everyone striving to pass his fellow, and yet they are all kept of an equal height? And see you not the rest of these beautiful flowers, each of which would require a man's wit to know and his life to express? Do not these stately trees seem to maintain their flourishing old age with the only happiness of their seat,[79] being clothed with a continual spring because no beauty here should ever fade? Doth not the air breathe health, which the birds (delightful both to ear and eye) do daily solemnize with the sweet consent of their voices? Is not every echo thereof a perfect music? And these fresh and delightful brooks—how slowly they slide away, as loath to leave the company of so many things united in perfection? And with how sweet a murmur they lament their forced departure? Certainly, certainly, cousin, it must needs be that some goddess inhabiteth this region, who is the soul of this soil, for neither is any less than a goddess worthy to be shrined in such a heap of pleasures, nor any less than a goddess could have made it so perfect a plot of the celestial dwellings," and so ended with

[79] the only happiness of their seat—the mere happiness of their situation.

a deep sigh, ruefully casting his eye upon Musidorus, as more desirous of pity than pleading.

But Musidorus had all this while held his look fixed upon Pyrocles' countenance, and with no less loving attention marked how his words proceeded from him. But in both these he perceived such strange diversities, that they rather increased new doubts than gave him ground to settle any judgment; for, besides his eyes sometimes even great with tears, the oft changing of his color, with a kind of shaking unstaidness over all his body, he might see in his countenance some great determination mixed with fear and might perceive in him store of thoughts, rather stirred than digested; his words interrupted continually with sighs (which served as a burden to each sentence) and the tenor of his speech (though of his wonted phrase) not knit together to one constant end, but rather dissolved in itself as the vehemency of the inward passion prevailed; which made Musidorus frame his answer nearest to that humor which should soonest put out the secret. For, having in the beginning of Pyrocles' speech, which defended his solitariness, framed in his mind a reply against it in the praise of honorable action, in showing that such a kind of contemplation is but a glorious title to idleness, that in action a man did not only better himself but benefit others, that the gods would not have delivered a soul into the body, which hath arms and legs, only instruments of doing, but that it were intended the mind should employ them, and that the mind should best know his own good or evil by practice—which knowledge was the only way to increase the one and correct the other—besides many other arguments, which the plentifulness of the matter yielded to the sharpness of his wit. When he found Pyrocles leave that and fall into such an affected praising of the place, he left it likewise and joined with him therein, because he found him in that humor utter more store of passion, and even thus kindly embracing him, he said:

"Your words are such, noble cousin, so sweetly and strongly handled in the praise of solitariness, as they would make me likewise yield myself up into it but that the same words make me know it is more pleasant to enjoy the company of him that can speak such words than by such words to be persuaded to follow solitariness. And even so do I give you leave, sweet Pyrocles, ever to defend solitariness, so long as, to defend it, you ever keep company. But I marvel at the excessive praises you give to this country; in truth it is not unpleasant, but yet if you would return into Macedon, you should see either many heavens or find this no more than earthly. And even Tempe[80] in my Thessalia (where you and I to my great happiness were brought up together) is nothing inferior unto it. But I think you will make me see that the vigor of your wit can show itself in any subject; or else you feed sometimes your solitariness with the conceits of the poets, whose liberal pens can as easily travel over mountains as molehills and so, like well disposed men, set up everything to the highest note, especially when they put such words in the mouths of one of these fantastical mind-infected people that children and musicians call lovers."

This word, lover, did no less pierce poor Pyrocles than the right tune of music toucheth him that is sick of the tarantula.[81] There was not one part of his body that did not feel a sudden motion, while his heart, with panting, seemed to dance to the sound of that word; yet, after some pause (lifting up his eyes a little from the ground and yet not daring to place them in the eyes of Musidorus) armed with the very countenance of the poor prisoner at the bar, whose answer is nothing but guilty, with much ado he brought forth this question: "And alas," said he, "dear cousin, what if I be not so much the poet (the freedom of whose pen can exercise itself in anything) as even that miserable subject of his cunning, whereof you speak?"

"Now the eternal gods forbid," mainly cried out Musidorus, "that ever my ear should be poisoned with so evil news of you. O let me never know that any base affection should get any lordship in your thoughts." But as he was speaking more, Kalander came and broke off their discourse with inviting them to the hunting of a goodly stag, which, being harbored in a wood thereby, he hoped would make them good sport, and drive away

80 Tempe—cf. *O.A.*, ft. 26.
81 tarantula—cf. *O.A.*, ft. 27.

some part of Daïphantus' melancholy. They condescended; and so, going to their lodgings, furnished themselves as liked them, Daïphantus writing a few words, which he left in a sealed letter against their return.

CHAPTER 10

Kalander's hunting. Daïphantus' close departure, and letter. Palladius' care and quest after him, accompanied with Clitophon. His finding and taking on Amphialus' armor. Their encounter with Queen Helen's attendants. Her mistaking Palladius.

Then went they together abroad, the good Kalander entertaining them with pleasant discoursing—how well he loved the sport of hunting when he was a young man; how much, in the comparison thereof, he disdained all chamber delights; that the sun, how great a journey soever he had to make, could never prevent him with earliness,[82] nor the moon, with her sober countenance, dissuade him from watching till midnight for the deer's feeding. "Oh," said he, "you will never live to my age without you keep yourselves in breath with exercise, and in heart with joyfulness. Too much thinking doth consume the spirits; and oft it falls out that, while one thinks too much of his doing, he leaves to do the effect of his thinking." Then spared he not to remember how much Arcadia was changed since his youth, activity and good fellowship being nothing in the price it was then held in, but, according to the nature of the old-growing world, still worse and worse. Then would he tell them stories of such gallants as he had known, and so, with pleasant company, beguiled the time's haste and shortened the way's length, till they came to the side of the wood where the hounds were, in couples, staying their coming, but, with a whining accent, craving liberty, many of them in color and marks so resembling that it showed they were of one kind.

The huntsmen, handsomely attired in their green liveries, as though they were children of summer, with staves in their hands, to beat the guiltless earth when the hounds were at a fault, and

[82] prevent him with earliness—be up before him.

with horns about their necks, to sound an alarm upon a silly[83] fugitive. The hounds were straight uncoupled; and ere long the stag thought it better to trust to the nimbleness of his feet than to the slender fortification of his lodging; but even his feet betrayed him, for howsoever they went, they themselves uttered themselves to the scent of their enemies; who, one taking it of another, and sometimes believing the wind's advertisement, sometimes the view of their faithful counsellors, the huntsmen, with open mouths then denounced war, when the war was already begun; their cry being composed of so well-sorted mouths that any man would perceive therein some kind of proportion, but the skillful woodmen did find a music. Then delight and variety of opinion drew the horsemen sundry ways, yet, cheering their hounds with voice and horn, kept still (as it were) together.

The wood seemed to conspire with them against his own citizens, dispersing their noise through all his quarters, and even the nymph Echo left to bewail the loss of Narcissus and became a hunter.[84] But the stag was in the end so hotly pursued that (leaving his flight) he was driven to make courage of despair, and so turning his head, made the hounds, with change of speech, to testify that he was at bay, as if from hot pursuit of their enemy, they were suddenly come to a parley. But Kalander, by his skill of coasting[85] the country, was amongst the first that came in to the besieged deer, whom, when some of the younger sort would have killed with their swords, he would not suffer, but with a cross-bow sent a death to the poor beast, who with tears[86] showed the unkindness he took of man's cruelty.

But, by the time that the whole company was assembled, and that the stag had bestowed himself liberally among them that had killed him, Daïphantus was missed; for whom Palladius carefully inquiring, no news could be given him but by one that said he

[83] silly—helpless.
[84] the nymph Echo left to bewail the loss of Narcissus—Echo loved Narcissus, who was so enamoured of himself that he fell into a stream while trying to see his reflection more clearly; Echo then pined away in sorrow, until there was nothing left of her except her voice.
[85] coasting—traversing.
[86] with tears—deer were believed to weep when wounded.

thought he was returned home; for that he marked him, in the chief of the hunting, take a byway which might lead to Kalander's house. That answer for the time satisfying, and they having performed all duties, as well for the stag's funeral as the hounds' triumph, they returned, some talking of the fatness of the deer's body, some of the fairness of his head, some of the hounds' cunning, some of their speed, and some of their cry; till, coming home about the time that the candle begins to inherit the sun's office, they found Daïphantus was not to be found. Whereat Palladius greatly marveling, and a day or two passing, while neither search nor inquiry could help him to knowledge, at last he lighted upon the letter which Pyrocles had written before he went a-hunting and left in his study among other of his writings. The letter was directed to Palladius himself, and contained these words:

"My only Friend—Violence of love leads me into such a course, whereof your knowledge may much more vex you than help me; therefore, pardon my concealing it from you, since, if I wrong you, it is in respect I bear you. Return into Thessalia, I pray you, as full of good fortune as I am of desire; and, if I live, I will in short time follow you; if I die, love my memory."

This was all, and this Palladius read twice or thrice over. "Ah," said he, "Pyrocles, what means this alteration? What have I deserved of thee, to be thus banished of thy counsels? Heretofore I have accused the sea, condemned the pirates, and hated my evil fortune that deprived me of thee; but now thyself is the sea which drowns my comfort, thyself is the pirate that robs thyself of me, thy own will becomes my evil fortune." Then turned he his thoughts to all forms of guesses that might light upon the purpose and course of Pyrocles, for he was not so sure, by his words, that it was love, as he was doubtful where the love was. One time he thought some beauty in Laconia had laid hold of his eyes, another time he feared that it might be Parthenia's excellency which had broken the bands of all former resolution. But the more he thought, the more he knew not what to think, armies of objections rising against any accepted opinion.

Then, as careful he was what to do himself, at length determined never to leave seeking him, till his search should be either by meeting accomplished or by death ended. Therefore (for all the unkindness, bearing tender respect that his friend's secret determination should be kept from any suspicion in others) he went to Kalander and told him that he had received a message from his friend, by which he understood he was gone back again into Laconia about some matters greatly importing the poor men whose protection he had undertaken, and that it was, in any sort, fit for him to follow him, but in such private wise as not to be known, and that, therefore, he would as then bid him farewell; arming himself in a black armor, as either a badge or prognostication of his mind, and taking only with him good store of money and a few choice jewels, leaving the greatest number of them and most of his apparel with Kalander; which he did partly to give the more cause to Kalander to expect their return, and so to be the less curiously inquisitive after them, and partly to leave those honorable thanks unto him, for his charge and kindness, which he knew he would no other way receive.

The good old man, having neither reason to dissuade nor hope to persuade, received the things with mind of a keeper, not of an owner; but, before he went, desired he might have the happiness, fully to know what they were, which, he said, he had ever till then delayed, fearing to be any way importune; but now he could not be so much an enemy to his desires as any longer to imprison them in silence. Palladius told him that the matter was not so secret but that so worthy a friend deserved the knowledge and should have it as soon as he might speak with his friend, without whose consent (because their promise bound him otherwise) he could not reveal it; but bade him hold for most assured that, if they lived but a while, he should find that they which bore the names of Daïphantus and Palladius would give him and his cause to think his noble courtesy well employed. Kalander would press him no further, but desiring that he might have leave to go, or at least to send his son and servants with him, Palladius broke off all ceremonies by telling him his case stood so, that his greatest favor should be in making least ado of his parting. Wherewith Kalander, knowing it to be more cumber than courtesy to strive, abstained from further urging him, but not from hearty mourning the loss of so sweet a conversation.

Only Clitophon, by vehement importunity, obtained to go with him, to come again to Daïphantus, whom he named and accounted his lord. And in such private guise departed Palladius, though having a companion to talk withal, yet talking much more with unkindness. And first they went to Mantinea,[87] whereof because Parthenia was there, he suspected there might be some cause of his abode. But, finding there no news of him, he went to Tegaea, Ripa, Enispæ, Stimphalus, and Pheneus, famous for the poisonous Stygian water,[88] and through all the rest of Arcadia, making their eyes, their ears, and their tongues serve almost for nothing but that inquiry. But they could know nothing but that in none of those places he was known. And so went they, making one place succeed to another, in like uncertainty to their search, many times encountering strange adventures worthy to be registered in the rolls of fame; but this may not be omitted.

As they passed in a pleasant valley, of either side of which high hills lifted up their beetlebrows, as if they would overlook the pleasantness of their under-prospect, they were, by the daintiness of the place and the weariness of themselves, invited to light from their horses; and pulling off their bits, that they might something refresh their mouths upon the grass, which plentifully grew, brought up under the care of those well-shading trees, they themselves laid them down hard by the murmuring music of certain waters which spouted out of the side of the hills, and in the bottom of the valley made of many springs a pretty brook, like a commonwealth of many families. But when they

[87] Mantinea—cf. *O.A.*, ft. 24.

[88] Tegaea, Ripa, Enispae, Stimphalus, and Pheneus—supposedly a group of towns in Arcadia, running from south, counterclockwise, to north; but Ripa and Enispae are either fabricated or incorrect—perhaps Dipaea and Elymia. Pheneus has nothing to do with the Styx, which is a real river in Arcadia, believed to have poisonous waters; the town to which the text refers is Nonacris, not far from Pheneus.

had a while hearkened to the persuasion of sleep, they rose and walked onward in that shady place, till Clitophon espied a piece of armor, and not far off another piece; and so the sight of one piece teaching him to look for more, he at length found all, with head-piece and shield, by the device whereof, which was,[89] he straight knew it to be the armor of his cousin, the noble Amphialus. Whereupon, fearing some inconvenience happened unto him, he told both his doubt and his cause of doubt to Palladius, who, considering thereof, thought best to make no longer stay but to follow on, lest, perchance, some violence were offered to so worthy a knight, whom the fame of the world seemed to set in balance with any knight living. Yet, with a sudden conceit,[90] having long borne great honor to the name of Amphialus, Palladius thought best to take that armor, thinking thereby to learn by them that should know that armor some news of Amphialus, and yet not hinder him in the search of Daïphantus too. So he, by the help of Clitophon, quickly put on that armor, whereof there was no one piece wanting, though hacked in some places, betraying some fight not long since passed. It was something too great, but yet served well enough.

And so, getting on their horses, they traveled but a little way when, in opening of the mouth of the valley into a fair field, they met with a coach drawn with four milk-white horses, furnished all in black, with a blackamoor boy upon every horse, they all appareled in white, the coach itself very richly furnished in black and white. But, before they could come so near as to discern what was within, there came running upon them above a dozen horsemen, who cried to them to yield themselves prisoners, or else they should die.

But Palladius, not accustomed to grant over the possession of himself upon so unjust titles, with sword drawn gave them so rude an answer that divers of them never had breath to reply again; for, being well backed by Clitophon, and having an excellent horse under him, when he was over-pressed by some, he

---

[89] The 1590 text indicates that Sidney left a space in his manuscript for the description of Amphialus's device, but never returned to fill it out.

[90] conceit—idea.

avoided them, and, ere the other thought of it, punished in him his fellow's faults; and so, either with cunning or with force, or rather with a cunning force, left none of them either living or able to make his life serve to other's hurt. Which being done, he approached the coach, assuring the black boys they should have no hurt, who were else ready to have run away; and, looking in the coach, he found in the one end a lady of great beauty, and such a beauty as showed forth the beams both of wisdom and good nature, but all as much darkened, as might be, with sorrow; in the other, two ladies who, by their demeanor, showed well they were but her servants, holding before them a picture in which was a goodly gentleman (whom he knew not) painted, having in their faces a certain waiting sorrow, their eyes being infected with their mistress's weeping.

But the chief lady, having not so much as once heard the noise of this conflict (so had sorrow closed up all the entries of her mind, and love tied her senses to that beloved picture), now the shadow of him falling upon the picture made her cast up her eye; and seeing the armor which too well she knew, thinking him to be Amphialus, the lord of her desires, blood coming more freely into her cheeks, as though it would be bold, and yet there growing new again pale for fear, with a pitiful look, like one unjustly condemned, "My lord Amphialus," said she, "you have enough punished me; it is time for cruelty to leave you, and evil fortune, me; if not, I pray you—and, to grant my prayer, fitter time nor place you can have—accomplish the one even now, and finish the other."

With that, sorrow, impatient to be slowly uttered in her often staying speeches, poured itself so fast into tears, that Palladius could not hold her longer in error; but pulling off his helmet, "Madam," said he, "I perceive you mistake me. I am a stranger in these parts, set upon (without any cause given by me) by some of your servants, whom, because I have in just defense evil entreated,[91] I came to make my excuse to you, whom seeing such as I do, I find greater cause why I should crave pardon of you."

[91] evil entreated—evilly treated.

When she saw his face and heard his speech, she looked out of the coach, and seeing her men, some slain, some lying under their dead horses and striving to get from under them, without making more account of the matter, "Truly," said she, "they are well served that durst lift up their arms against that armor." "But, sir knight," said she, "I pray you tell me how come you by this armor? For if it be by the death of him that owned it, then have I more to say unto you." Palladius assured her it was not so, telling her the true manner how he found it. "It is like enough," said she, "for that agrees with the manner he hath lately used." "But I beseech you, sir," said she, "since your prowess hath bereft me of my company, let it yet so far heal the wounds itself hath given as to guard me to the next town."

"How great so ever my business be, fair lady," said he, "it shall willingly yield to so noble a cause. But first even by the favor you bear to the lord of this noble armor, I conjure you to tell me the story of your fortune herein, lest, hereafter, when the image of so excellent a lady in so strange a plight come before mine eyes, I condemn myself of want of consideration in not having demanded thus much. Neither ask I it without protestation that wherein my sword and faith may avail you, they shall bind themselves to your service."

"Your conjuration, fair knight," said she, "is too strong for my poor spirit to disobey, and that shall make me (without any hope, my ruin being but by one irrelievable) to grant your will herein; and to say the truth, a strange niceness were it in me to refrain that from the ears of a person representing so much worthiness, which I am glad even to rocks and woods to utter."

[92] Philoxenus—"love of friend."

on Palladius for Amphialus' armor, whose grief is amplified by meeting his dead friend's dog. Palladius' parting with Helen and Clitophon.

"Know you, then, that my name is Helen, queen by birth, and hitherto possessed of the fair city and territory of Corinth. I can say no more of myself, but beloved of my people—and may justly say beloved, since they are content to bear with my absence and folly. But I being left by my father's death, and accepted by my people in the highest degree that country could receive as soon, or rather before that, my age was ripe for it, my court quickly swarmed full of suitors, some perchance loving my estate, others my person; but [at] once, I know, all of them, howsoever my possessions were in their hearts, my beauty (such as it is) was in their mouths—many strangers of princely and noble blood, and all of mine own country to whom either birth or virtue gave courage to avow so high a desire.

"Among the rest, or rather before the rest, was the lord Philoxenus, son and heir to the virtuous nobleman Timotheus,[93] which Timotheus was a man, both in power, riches, parentage, and (which passed all these) goodness, and (which followed all these) love of the people, beyond any of the great men of my country. Now this son of his, I must say truly not unworthy of such a father, bending himself by all means of serviceableness to me, and setting forth of himself to win my favor, won thus far of me, that in truth I less misliked him than any of the rest, which in some proportion my countenance delivered unto him. Though I must protest it was a very false ambassador, if it delivered at all any affection, whereof my heart was utterly void —I as then esteeming myself born to rule, and thinking foul scorn willingly to submit myself to be ruled.

"But whiles Philoxenus in good sort pursued my favor, and perchance nourished himself with over-much hope because he found I did in some sort acknowledge his value, one time among the rest he brought with him a dear friend of his." With that she looked upon the picture before her, and straight sighed, and straight tears followed, as if the idol of duty ought to be

93 Timotheus—"God-fearing."

honored with such oblations; and then her speech stayed, the tale having brought her to that look, but that look having quite put her out of her tale.

But Palladius greatly pitying so sweet a sorrow in a lady, whom by fame he had already known and honored, besought her for her promise sake to put silence so long unto her moaning till she had recounted the rest of this story. "Why," said she, "this is the picture of Amphialus! What need I say more to you? What ear is so barbarous but hath heard of Amphialus? Who follows deeds of arms, but everywhere finds monument of Amphialus? Who is courteous, noble, liberal, but he that hath the example before his eyes of Amphialus? Where are all heroical parts, but in Amphialus? O Amphialus, I would thou were not so excellent, or I would I thought thee not so excellent, and yet would I not that I would so." With that, she wept again, till he again soliciting the conclusion of her story, "Then must you," said she, "know the story of Amphialus; for his will is my life, his life my history. And indeed, in what can I better employ my lips than in speaking of Amphialus?

"This knight, then, whose figure you see, but whose mind can be painted by nothing but by the true shape of virtue, is brother's son to Basilius, king of Arcadia, and in his childhood esteemed his heir, till Basilius, in his old years marrying a young and a fair lady, had of her those two daughters so famous for their perfection in beauty, which put by their young cousin from that expectation. Whereupon his mother, a woman of a haughty heart, being daughter to the king of Argos,[94] either disdaining, or fearing, that her son should live under the power of Basilius, sent him to that lord Timotheus, between whom and her dead husband there had passed straight bands of mutual hospitality, to be brought up in company with his son Philoxenus.

"A happy resolution for Amphialus, whose excellent nature was by this means trained on with as good education as any prince's son in the world could have, which otherwise it is thought his mother (far unworthy of such a son) would not have given him, the good Timotheus no less loving him than his own

---

[94] Argos—town in the southern Peloponnesus.

son. Well, they grew in years, and shortly occasions fell aptly to try Amphialus; and all occasions were but steps for him to climb fame by. Nothing was so hard but his valor overcame, which yet still he so guided with true virtue that, although no man was in our parts spoken of, but he, for his manhood, yet, as though herein he excelled himself, he was commonly called the courteous Amphialus. An endless thing it were for me to tell how many adventures (terrible to be spoken of) he achieved, what monsters, what giants, what conquest of countries, sometimes using policy, sometimes force, but always virtue, well followed, and but followed by Philoxenus; between whom and him so fast a friendship by education was knit that at last Philoxenus, having no greater matter to employ his friendship in than to win me, therein desired, and had, his uttermost furtherance. To that purpose brought he him to my court, where truly I may justly witness with him[95] that what his wit could conceive (and his wit can conceive as far as the limits of reason stretch) was all directed to the setting forward the suit of his friend Philoxenus. My ears could hear nothing from him but touching the worthiness of Philoxenus and of the great happiness it would be unto me to have such a husband, with many arguments which, God knows, I cannot well remember because I did not much believe. For why should I use many circumstances to come to that where already I am and ever, while I live, must continue?

"In few words, while he pleaded for another, he won me for himself—if, at least," with that she sighed, "he would account it a winning; for his fame had so framed the way to my mind that his presence, so full of beauty, sweetness, and noble conversation, had entered there before he vouchsafed to call for the keys. O Lord, how did my soul hang at his lips while he spoke! O, when he in feeling manner would describe the love of his friend, how well (thought I) doth love between those lips! When he would with daintiest eloquence stir pity in me toward Philoxenus, why sure (said I to myself) Helen, be not afraid; this heart cannot want pity. And when he would extol the deeds

95 witness with him—testify of him.

of Philoxenus, who indeed had but waited of him[96] therein, alas
(thought I), good Philoxenus, how evil doth it become thy
name to be subscribed to his letter. What should I say? Nay,
what should I not say, noble knight, who am not ashamed—nay,
am delighted—thus to express mine own passions?

"Days passed; his eagerness for his friend never decreased;
my affection to him ever increased. At length, in way of ordinary
courtesy, I obtained of him (who suspected no such matter)
this his picture, the only Amphialus, I fear, that I shall ever
enjoy; and, grown bolder, or madder, or bold with madness, I
discovered my affection unto him. But, Lord! I shall never forget how anger and courtesy at one instant appeared in his eyes,
when he heard that motion, how with his blush he taught me
shame. In sum, he left nothing unassayed which might disgrace
himself to grace his friend, in sweet terms making me receive a
most resolute refusal of himself. But when he found that his
presence did far more persuade for himself than his speech could
do for his friend, he left my court; hoping that forgetfulness
(which commonly waits upon absence) would make room for
his friend, to whom he would not utter thus much, I think, for
a kind fear not to grieve him, or perchance (though he cares
little for me) of a certain honorable gratefulness nor yet to discourse so much of my secrets; but as it should seem, meant to
travel into far countries, until his friend's affection either ceased
or prevailed.

"But within a while Philoxenus came to see how onward the
fruits were of his friend's labor, when (as in truth I cared not
much how he took it) he found me sitting, beholding this picture,
I know not with how affectionate countenance, but I am sure
with a most affectionate mind. I straight found jealousy and disdain took hold of him; and yet the froward pain of mine own
heart made me so delight to punish him, whom I esteemed the
chiefest let in my way, that, when he, with humble gesture
and vehement speeches, sued for my favor, I told him that I
would hear him more willingly if he would speak for Amphialus

[96] but waited of him—was excelled only by him.

as well as Amphialus had done for him. He never answered me, but, pale and quaking went straight away, and straight my heart misgave me some evil success;[97] and yet, though I had authority enough to have stayed him (as in these fatal things it falls out that the high working powers make second causes unwittingly accessory to their determinations), I did no further but sent a footman of mine, whose faithfulness to me I well knew, from place to place to follow him and bring me word of his proceedings, which (alas) have brought forth that which I fear I must ever rue.

"For he had traveled scarce a day's journey out of my country but that, not far from his place, he overtook Amphialus, who, by succoring a distressed lady, had been here stayed; and by-and-by called him to fight with him, protesting that one of them two should die. You may easily judge how strange it was to Amphialus, whose heart could accuse itself of no fault but too much affection towards him; which he, refusing to fight with him, would fain have made Philoxenus understand; but, as my servant since told me, the more Amphialus went back, the more he followed, calling him traitor and coward, yet never telling the cause of this strange alteration.

" 'Ah, Philoxenus,' said Amphialus, 'I know I am no traitor, and thou well knowest I am no coward: but I pray thee content thyself with this much, and let this satisfy thee that I love thee, since I bear thus much of thee.' But he, leaving words, drew his sword, and gave Amphialus a great blow or two, which, but for the goodness of his armor, would have slain him; and yet so far did Amphialus contain himself, stepping aside and saying to him, 'Well, Philoxenus, and thus much villainy am I content to put up, not any longer for thy sake (whom I have no cause to love, since thou dost injure me and wilt not tell me the cause) but for thy virtuous father's sake, to whom I am so much bound. I pray thee go away and conquer thy own passion, and thou shalt make me soon yield to be thy servant.

"But he would not attend his words, but still struck so fiercely at Amphialus that in the end (nature prevailing above determination) he was fain to defend himself, and withal to

---

[97] success—result.

offend him, that by an unlucky blow the poor Philoxenus fell
dead at his feet, having had time only to speak some words,
whereby Amphialus knew it was for my sake—which when
Amphialus saw, he forthwith gave such tokens of true-felt sorrow that, as my servant said, no imagination could conceive
greater woe, but that by-and-by an unhappy occasion made
Amphialus pass himself in sorrow: for Philoxenus was but newly
dead, when there comes to the same place the aged and virtuous
Timotheus, who, having heard of his son's sudden and passionate
manner of parting from my court, had followed him as speedily
as he could; but, alas, not so speedily but that he found him
dead before he could overtake him. Though my heart be nothing
but a stage for tragedies, yet, I must confess, it is even unable
to bear the miserable representation therefore, knowing Amphialus and Timotheus as I have done. Alas, what sorrow, what
amazement, what shame was in Amphialus when he saw his dear
foster-father find him the killer of his only son! In my heart,
I know, he wished mountains had lain upon him, to keep him
from that meeting. As for Timotheus, sorrow of his son, and (I
think principally) unkindness of Amphialus, so devoured his
vital spirits that, able to say no more but 'Amphialus, Amphialus,
have I—?' he sank to the earth and presently died.

"But, not my tongue, though daily used to complaints; no,
nor if my heart, which is nothing but sorrow, were turned to
tongues, durst it undertake to show the unspeakableness of his
grief, but (because this serves to make you know my fortune)
he threw away his armor, even this which you have now upon
you, which at the first sight I vainly hoped he had put on again;
and then, as ashamed of the light, he ran into the thickest of the
woods, lamenting, and even crying out so pitifully that my servant, though of a fortune not used to much tenderness, could
not refrain weeping when he told it me. He once overtook him;
but Amphialus, drawing his sword, which was the only part
of his arms (God knows to what purpose) he carried about
him, threatened to kill him if he followed him; and withal bade
him deliver this bitter message, that he well enough found I was
the cause of all this mischief, and that if I were a man he would

go over the world to kill me; but bade me assure myself that, of all creatures in the world, he most hated me. Ah, sir knight (whose ears I think by this time are tired with the rugged ways of these misfortunes), now weigh my cause, if at least you know what love is. For this cause have I left my country, putting in hazard how my people will in time deal by me, adventuring what perils or dishonors might ensue, only to follow him who proclaimeth hate against me, and to bring my neck unto him, if that may redeem my trespass and assuage his fury." "And now, sir," said she, "you have your request, I pray you take pains to guide me to the next town, that there I may gather such of my company again as your valor hath left me."

Palladius willingly condescended; but ere they began to go, there came Clitophon, who, having been something hurt by one of them, had pursued him a good way, at length overtaking him, and ready to kill him, understood they were servants to the fair Queen Helen, and that the cause of this enterprise was for nothing but to make Amphialus prisoner, whom they knew their mistress sought, for she concealed her sorrow, nor cause of her sorrow, from nobody.

But Clitophon, very sorry for this accident, came back to comfort the queen, helping such as were hurt in the best sort that he could, and framing friendly constructions of this rashly-undertaken enmity, when in comes another, till that time unseen, all armed, with his beaver down, who, first looking round about upon the company, as soon as he spied Palladius, he drew his sword, and, making no other prologue, let fly at him. But Palladius, sorry for so much harm as had already happened, sought rather to retire and ward, thinking he might be some one that belonged to the fair queen, whose case in his heart he pitied. Which Clitophon seeing, stepped between them, asking the new-come knight the cause of his quarrel; who answered him that he would kill that thief, who had stolen away his master's armor, if he did not restore it. With that Palladius looked upon him and saw that he of the other side had Palladius' own armor upon him. "Truly," said Palladius, "if I have stolen this armor, you did not buy that; but you shall not fight with me upon such a quarrel. You shall have this armor willingly, which I did only put on to do honor to the owner."

But Clitophon straight knew by his words and voice that it was Ismenus,[98] the faithful and diligent page of Amphialus; and therefore, telling him that he was Clitophon, and willing him to acknowledge his error to the other, who deserved all honor, the young gentleman pulled off his headpiece, and, lighting, went to kiss Palladius' hands, desiring him to pardon his folly, caused by extreme grief, which easily might bring forth anger.

"Sweet gentleman," said Palladius, "you shall only make me this amends that you shall carry this, your lord's armor, from me to him, and tell him, from an unknown knight who admires his worthiness, that he cannot cast a greater mist over his glory than by being unkind to so excellent a princess as this queen is."

Ismenus promised he would as soon as he durst find his master, and with that went to do his duty to the queen, whom, in all these encounters, astonishment made hardy; but as soon as she saw Ismenus (looking to her picture), "Ismenus," said she, "here is my lord; where is yours? Or come you to bring me some sentence of death from him? If it be so, welcome be it. I pray you speak, and speak quickly."

"Alas! madam," said Ismenus, "I have lost my lord!"—with that tears came unto his eyes—"for, as soon as the unhappy combat was concluded with the death both of father and son, my master, casting off his armor, went his way, forbidding me, upon pain of death, to follow him. Yet divers days I followed his steps, till lastly I found him, having newly met with an excellent spaniel belonging to his dead companion Philoxenus. The dog straight fawned on my master for old knowledge,[99] but never was there thing more pitiful than to hear my master blame the dog for loving his master's murderer, renewing afresh his complaints with the dumb counsellor as if they might comfort one another in their miseries. But my lord, having spied me, rose up in such rage that, in truth, I feared he would kill me; yet as then he said only, if I would not displease him, I should not come near

98 Ismenus—"the one who had remained."
99 for old knowledge—because of long acquaintance.

him till he sent for me—too hard[100] a commandment for me to disobey. I yielded, leaving him only waited on by his dog, and, as I think, seeking out the most solitary places that this or any other country can grant him; and I, returning where I had left his armor, found another instead thereof and, disdaining (I must confess) that any should bear the armor of the best knight living, armed myself therein to play the fool, as even now I did."

"Fair Ismenus," said the Queen, "a fitter messenger could hardly be to unfold my tragedy. I see the end; I see my end."

With that, sobbing, she desired to be conducted to the next town, where Palladius left her to be waited on by Clitophon, at Palladius' earnest entreaty, who desired alone to take that melancholy course of seeking his friend; and therefore, changing armors again with Ismenus (who went withal to a castle belonging to his master), he continued his quest for his friend Daïphantus.

CHAPTER 12

Palladius, after long search of Daïphantus, lighteth on an Amazon lady. Her habit, song, and who she was. Objections of the one against women, and love of them. The answers of the other for them both. Their passionate conclusion in relenting kindness.

So, directed he his course to Laconia, as well among the Helots as Spartans. There, indeed, he found his fame flourishing, his monument engraved in marble, and yet more durable in men's memories; but the universal lamenting his absented presence assured him of his present absence. Thence into the Elean province[101] to see whether at the Olympian games (there celebrated) he might in such concourse bless his eyes with so desired an encounter. But that huge and sportful assembly grew to him a tedious loneliness, esteeming nobody found, since Daïphantus was lost. Afterward he passed through Achaia and

100 hard—emphatic.
101 Elean province—a country in the Peloponnesus, west of Arcadia.

Sicyonia to the Corinthians,[102] proud of their two seas, to learn whether by the strait of that isthmus it was possible to know of his passage. But finding every place more dumb than other to his demands, and remembering that it was late-taken love which had wrought this new course, he returned again (after two months' travel in vain) to make fresh search in Arcadia; so much the more, as then first[103] he bethought himself of the picture of Philoclea (in resembling her he had once loved) might perhaps awake again that sleeping passion. And having already passed over the greatest part of Arcadia, one day, coming under the side of the pleasant mountain Menalus,[104] his horse (nothing guilty of his inquisitiveness) with flat tiring taught him that discreet stays make speedy journeys; and therefore, lighting down and unbridling his horse, he himself went to repose himself in a little wood he saw thereby. Where, lying under the protection of a shady tree, with intention to make forgetting sleep comfort a sorrowful memory, he saw a sight which persuaded and obtained of his eyes that they would abide yet a while open. It was the appearing of a lady, who, because she walked with her side toward him, he could not perfectly see her face, but so much he might see of her that was a surety for the rest that all was excellent.

Well might he perceive the hanging of her hair in fairest quantity, in locks, some curled, and some, as it were, forgotten, with such a careless care, and an art so hiding art, that she seemed she would lay them for a pattern whether nature simply, or nature helped by cunning, be the more excellent; the rest whereof was drawn into a coronet of gold richly set with pearl, and so joined all over with gold wires, and covered with feathers of divers colors, that it was not unlike to an helmet, such a glittering show it bore, and so bravely it was held up from the head.

[102] through Achaia and Sicyonia to the Corinthians—he is heading northward along the west coast of the Peloponnesus, then, along the shore of the Gulf of Corinth, which bounds the Peloponnesus on the north and divides it from the rest of Greece.

[103] as then first—as then for the first time.

[104] Menalus—a mountain in west central Arcadia; sacred to Pan.

Upon her body she wore a doublet of sky-color satin, covered with plates of gold and, as it were, nailed with precious stones, that in it she might seem armed. The nether part of her garment was so full of stuff, and cut after such a fashion that, though the length of it reached to the ankles, yet, in her going, one might sometimes discern the small of her leg, which, with the foot, was dressed in a short pair of crimson velvet buskins, in some places open, as the ancient manner was, to show the fairness of the skin. Over all this she wore a certain mantle, made in such manner that, coming under the right arm, and covering most of that side, it had no fastening on the left side, but only upon the top of the shoulder, where the two ends met, and were closed together with a very rich jewel, the device whereof, as he after saw, was this: a Hercules, made in little form, but a distaff set within his hand, as he once was by Omphale's commandment,[105] with a word in Greek, but thus to be interpreted, "Never more valiant." On the same side, on her thigh, she wore a sword, which, as it witnessed her to be an Amazon, or one following that profession, so it seemed but a needless weapon, since her other forces were without withstanding. But this lady walked outright,[106] till he might see her enter into a fine close arbor. It was of trees, whose branches so lovingly interlaced one the other that it could resist the strongest violence of eyesight; but she went into it by a door she opened, which moved him, as warily as he could, to follow her; and by-and-by he might hear her sing this song, with a voice no less beautiful to his ears than her goodliness was full of harmony to his eyes:

[*OA2, see above p. 37, followed here*]

The ditty gave him some suspicion, but the voice gave him almost assurance, who the singer was. And, therefore, boldly thrusting open the door and entering into the arbor, he perceived indeed that it was Pyrocles thus disguised; wherewith, not receiving so much joy to have found him as grief so to have

105 Hercules—cf. *O.A.*, ft. 34.
106 outright—straight onward.

found him, amazedly looking upon him—as Apollo is painted, when he saw Daphne suddenly turned into a laurel[107]—he was not able to bring forth a word. So that Pyrocles, who had as much shame as Musidorus had sorrow, rising to him, would have formed a substantial excuse; but his insinuation[108] being of blushing, and his division[109] of sighs, his whole oration stood upon a short narration, what was the causer of this metamorphosis.

But by that time Musidorus had gathered his spirits together, and, yet casting a ghastful countenance upon him, as if he would conjure some strange spirits, he thus spake unto him: "And is it possible that this is Pyrocles, the only young prince in the world, formed by nature, and framed by education, to the true exercise of virtue? Or is it indeed some Amazon that hath counterfeited the face of my friend, in this sort to vex me? For likelier sure I would have thought it that any outward face might have been disguised than that the face of so excellent a mind could have been thus blemished. O sweet Pyrocles, separate yourself a little (if it be possible) from yourself, and let your own mind look upon your own proceedings. So shall my words be needless, and you best instructed. See with yourself how fit it will be for you in this your tender youth, born so great a prince, and of so rare not only expectation, but proof, desired of your old father and wanted of your native country, now so near your home, to divert your thoughts from the way of goodness, to lose, nay to abuse, your time. Lastly, to overthrow all the excellent things you have done, which have filled the world with your fame, as if you should drown your ship in the long desired haven, or, like an ill player, should mar the last act of his tragedy.

"Remember, (for I know you know it) that if we will be men, the reasonable part of our soul is to have absolute commandment, against which, if any sensual weakness arise, we are to yield all our sound forces to the overthrowing of so unnatural a rebellion, wherein how can we want courage, since we are to deal

---

107 Apollo . . . Daphne—cf. *O.A.*, ft. 29.
108 insinuation—the introduction to a speech.
109 division—the organization of a speech into parts.

against so weak an adversary, that in itself is nothing but weakness? Nay, we are to resolve that, if reason direct it, we must do it, for to say I cannot is childish, and I will not, womanish. And see how extremely every way you endanger your mind, for to take this womanish habit (without you frame your behavior accordingly) is wholly vain. Your behavior can never come kindly from you, but as the mind is proportioned unto it. So that you must resolve, if you will play your part to any purpose, whatsoever peevish affections are in that sex, soften your heart to receive them, the very first down-step to all wickedness. For do not deceive yourself, my dear cousin—there is no man suddenly excellently good or extremely evil, but grows either as he holds himself up in virtue or lets himself slide to viciousness.

"And let us see what power is the author of all these troubles. Forsooth, love; love, a passion, and the basest and fruitlessest of all passions. Fear breedeth wit; anger is the cradle of courage; joy openeth and enableth the heart; sorrow, as it closeth, so it draweth it inward to look to the correcting of itself; and so all generally have power towards some good by the direction of right reason. But this bastard love—for, indeed, the name of love is most unworthily applied to so hateful a humor—as it is engendered betwixt lust and idleness,[110] as the matter it works upon is nothing but a certain base weakness (which some gentle fools call a gentle heart), as his adjoined companions be unquietness, longings, fond comforts, faint discomforts, hopes, jealousies, ungrounded rages, causeless yieldings,[111] so is the highest end it aspires unto, a little pleasure—with much pain before, and great repentance after. But that end, how endless it runs to infinite evils, were fit enough for the matter we speak of, but not for your ears, in whom, indeed, there is so much true disposition to virtue; yet, thus much of his worthy effects in yourself is to be seen, that, besides your breaking laws of hospitality with Kalander, and of friendship with me, it utterly subverts the course of nature in making reason give place to sense, and man to woman. And truly I think hereupon it

[110] it is engendered betwixt lust and idleness—cf. *O.A.*, ft. 33.
[111] companions—Cupid's companions included Pothos (longings), Tyche (uncertainty), Himeros (desire), and Peitho (yielding).

first got the name of love, for, indeed, the true love hath that excellent nature in it that it doth transform the very essence of the lover into the thing loved, uniting, and as it were incorporating, it with a secret and inward working. And herein do these kinds of loves imitate the excellent, for as the love of heaven makes one heavenly, the love of virtue, virtuous, so doth the love of the world make one become worldly; and this effeminate love of a woman doth so womanize a man that, if he yield to it, will not only make him an Amazon, but a launder, a distaff spinner,[112] or whatsoever other vile occupation their idle heads can imagine and their weak hands perform. Therefore (to trouble you no longer with my tedious but loving words) if either you remember what you are, what you have been, or what you must be; if you consider what it is that moved you, or by what cause or creature you are moved; you shall find the cause so small, the effect so dangerous, yourself so unworthy to run into the one or to be driven by the other, that I doubt not I shall quickly have occasion rather to praise you for having conquered it than to give you further counsel how to do it."

But in Pyrocles this speech wrought no more but that he, who before he was espied, was afraid; after being perceived, was ashamed; now being hardly rubbed upon, left both fear and shame, and was moved to anger. But the exceeding good-will he bore to Musidorus striving with it, he thus, partly to satisfy him, but principally to loose the reins to his own motions, made him answer: "Cousin, whatsoever good disposition nature hath bestowed upon me, or howsoever that disposition hath been by bringing up confirmed, this must I confess: that I am not yet come to that degree of wisdom to think light of the sex of whom I have my life, since if I be anything—which your friendship rather finds than I acknowledge—I was, to come to it, born of a woman, and nursed of a woman. And certainly—for this point of your speech doth nearest touch me—it is strange to see the unmanlike cruelty of mankind, who, not content with their tyrannous ambition to have brought the others' virtuous patience under them, like to childish masters, think their masterhood nothing without

[112] a launder, a distaff spinner—cf. *O.A.*, ft. 34.

doing injury to them who, if we will argue by reason, are framed of nature with the same parts of the mind for the exercise of virtue as we are. And for example, even this estate of Amazons (which I now for my greatest honor do seek to counterfeit) doth well witness that, if generally the sweetness of their dispositions did not make them see the vainness of these things which we accept glorious, they neither want valor of mind nor yet doth their fairness take away their force. And truly we men, and praisers of men, should remember that, if we have such excellencies, it is reason to think them excellent creatures, of whom we are—since a kite never brought forth a good flying hawk.

"But to tell you true, as I think it superfluous to use any words of such a subject which is so praised in itself as it needs no praises, so withal I fear lest my conceit (not able to reach unto them) bring forth words which, for their unworthiness, may be a disgrace unto them I so inwardly honor. Let this suffice, that they are capable of virtue, and virtue (ye yourselves say) is to be loved, and I, too, truly. But this I willingly confess: that it likes me much better when I find virtue in a fair lodging than when I am bound to seek it in an ill-favored creature, like a pearl in a dunghill. As for my fault of being an uncivil guest to Kalander, if you could feel what an inward guest myself am host unto, ye would think it very excusable in that I rather perform the duties of an host than the ceremonies of a guest. And for my breaking the laws of friendship with you (which I would rather die than effectually do), truly, I could find in my heart to ask you pardon for it but that your handling of me gives me reason to my former dealing."

And here Pyrocles stayed as to breathe himself, having been transported with a little vehemency because it seemed him Musidorus had over-bitterly glanced against the reputation of womankind. But then quieting his countenance (as well as out of an unquiet mind it might be) he thus proceeded on: "And poor love," said he, "dear cousin, is little beholding unto you, since you are not contented to spoil it of the honor of the highest power of the mind, which notable men have attributed unto it; but ye deject it below all other passions, in truth somewhat strangely; since, if love receive any disgrace, it is by the company of these passions you prefer before it. For those kinds of bitter objections (as that lust, idleness, and a weak heart should be, as it were, the matter and form of love) rather touch me, dear Musidorus, than love. But I am good witness of mine own imperfections, and therefore will not defend myself. But herein, I must say, you deal contrary to yourself; for if I be so weak, then can you not with reason stir me up as ye did by remembrance of my own virtue. Or if indeed I be virtuous, then must ye confess that love hath his working in a virtuous heart. And so no doubt hath it, whatsoever I be, for if we love virtue, in whom shall we love it but in a virtuous creature? (Without your meaning be, I should love this word virtue where I see it written in a book.)[113] Those troublesome effects you say it breeds be not the faults of love but of him that loves, as an unable vessel to bear such a liquor, like evil eyes not able to look on the sun, or like an ill brain soonest overthrown with the best wine. Even that heavenly love you speak of is accompanied in some hearts with hopes, griefs, longings, and despairs. And in that heavenly love, since there are two parts (the one the love itself, the other the excellency of the thing loved), I, not able at the first leap to frame both in me, do now (like a diligent workman) make ready the chief instrument and first part of that great work, which is love itself, which when I have a while practiced in this sort, then you shall see me turn it to greater matters. And thus gently you may (if it please you) think of me. Neither doubt ye, because I wear a woman's apparel, I will be the more womanish, since, I assure you, for all my apparel, there is nothing I desire more than fully to prove myself a man in this enterprise. Much might be said in my defense, much more for love, and most of all for that divine creature which hath joined me and love together. But these disputations are fitter for quiet schools than my troubled brains, which are bent rather in deeds to perform than in words to defend the noble desire which possesseth me."

---

[113] Without . . . book—paraphrased: unless you mean that how should I love virtue merely reading about it?

"O Lord," said Musidorus, "how sharp witted you are to hurt yourself."

"No," answered he, "but it is the hurt you speak of which makes me so sharp witted."

"Even so," said Musidorus, "as every base occupation makes one sharp in that practise and foolish in all the rest."

"Nay, rather," answered Pyrocles, "as each excellent thing, once well learned, serves for a measure of all other knowledges."

"And is that become," said Musidorus, "a measure for other things, which never received measure in itself?"

"It is counted without measure," answered Pyrocles, "because the workings of it are without measure; but otherwise in nature it hath measure, since it hath an end allotted unto it."

"The beginning being so excellent, I would gladly know the end."

"Enjoying," answered Pyrocles, with a great sigh.

"O," said Musidorus, "now set ye forth the baseness of it; since if it end in enjoying, it shows all the rest was nothing."

"Ye mistake me," answered Pyrocles, "I spoke of the end to which it is directed, which end ends not, no sooner than the life."

"Alas, let your own brain disenchant you," said Musidorus.

"My heart is too far possessed," said Pyrocles.

"But the head gives you direction."

"And the heart gives me life," answered Pyrocles.

But Musidorus was so grieved to see his well beloved friend obstinate, as he thought, to his own destruction, that it forced him, with more than accustomed vehemency, to speak these words: "Well, well," said he, "you list to abuse yourself; it was a very white and red virtue[114] which you could pick out of a painterly gloss of a visage. Confess the truth, and ye shall find the utmost was but beauty, a thing which, though it be in as great excellency in yourself as may be in any, yet I am sure you make no further reckoning of it than of an outward fading benefit nature bestowed upon you. And yet such is your want of a true grounded virtue, which must be like itself in all points, that what you wisely account a trifle in yourself, you fondly become a slave

[114] a very white and red virtue—cf. *O.A.*, ft. 38.

unto in another. For my part I now protest I have left nothing unsaid which my wit could make me know or my most entire friendship to you requires of me; I do now beseech you even for the love betwixt us (if this other love have left any in you towards me), and for the remembrance of your old careful father (if you can remember him that forget yourself), lastly, for Pyrocles' own sake (who is now upon the point of falling or rising), to purge yourself of this vile infection; otherwise give me leave to leave of this name of friendship, as an idle title of a thing which cannot be, where virtue is abolished."

The length of these speeches before had not so much cloyed Pyrocles, though he were very unpatient of long deliberations, as the last farewell of him he loved as his own life did wound his soul; thinking himself afflicted, he was the apter to conceive unkindness deeply, insomuch that, shaking his head and delivering some show of tears, he thus uttered his griefs: "Alas," said he, "Prince Musidorus, how cruelly you deal with me; if you seek the victory, take it; if ye list, triumph. Have you all the reason of the world, and with me remain all the imperfections, yet such as I can no more lay from me than the crow can be persuaded by the swan to cast off all his black feathers. But truly you deal with me like a physician that, seeing his patient in a pestilent fever, should chide him instead of ministering help, and bid him be sick no more; or rather like such a friend that, visiting his friend condemned to perpetual prison and loaded with grievous fetters, should will him to shake off his fetters, or he would leave him. I am sick, and sick to the death; I am a prisoner; neither is any redress, but by her to whom I am slave. Now if you list to, leave him that loves you in the highest degree, but remember ever to carry this with you: that you abandon your friend in his greatest extremity."

And herewith the deep wound of his love, being rubbed afresh with this new unkindness, began (as it were) to bleed again in such sort that he was not able to bear it any longer, but, gushing out abundance of tears, and crossing his arms over his woeful heart as if his tears had been out-flowing blood, his arms an over-pressing burden, he sunk down to the ground; which sudden trance went so to the heart of Musidorus that, falling down by him and kissing the weeping eyes of his friend, he besought him not to make account of his speech, which if it had been over vehement, yet was it to be borne withal because it came out of a love much more vehement; that he had not thought fancy could have received so deep a wound, but now finding in him the force of it, he would no further contrary it, but employ all his service to medicine it in such sort as the nature of it required. But even this kindness made Pyrocles the more melt in the former unkindness, which his manlike tears well showed, with a silent look upon Musidorus, as who should say, "And is it possible that Musidorus should threaten to leave me?" And this struck Musidorus' mind and senses so dumb too that, for grief being not able to say anything, they rested with their eyes placed one upon another in such sort as might well paint out the true passion of unkindness to be never aright but betwixt them that most dearly love.

And thus remained they a time, till at length Musidorus, embracing him, said, "And will you thus shake off your friend?"

"It is you that shake me off," said Pyrocles, "being for my unperfectness unworthy of your friendship."

"But this," said Musidorus, "shows you more unperfect—to be cruel to him that submits himself unto you." "But since you are unperfect," said he smiling, "it is reason you be governed by us wise and perfect men. And that authority will I begin to take upon me, with three absolute commandments: the first, that you increase not your evil with further griefs; the second, that you love her with all the powers of your mind; and the last commandment shall be, ye command me to do what service I can towards the attaining of your desires."

Pyrocles' heart was not so oppressed with the mighty passions of love and unkindness but that it yielded to some mirth at this commandment of Musidorus that he should love. So that something clearing his face from his former shows of grief: "Well," said he, "dear cousin, I see by the well choosing of your commandments that you are fitter to be a prince than a counselor; and therefore, I am resolved to employ all my endeavor to obey you, with this condition: that the commandments ye command me to lay upon you shall only be that you continue to love me and look upon my imperfections with more affection than judgment."

"Love you?" said he. "Alas, how can my heart be separated from the true embracing of it,[115] without it[116] burst, by being too full of it?"[117] "But," said he, "let us leave of these flowers of new begun friendship; and now I pray you again tell me—but tell it me fully, omitting no circumstances—the story of your affection's both beginning and proceeding, assuring yourself that there is nothing so great which I will fear to do for you nor nothing so small which I will disdain to do for you. Let me therefore receive a clear understanding, which many times we miss, while those things we account small, as a speech or a look, are omitted, like as a whole sentence may fail of his congruity by wanting one particle. Therefore between friends, all must be laid open, nothing being superfluous nor tedious."

"You shall be obeyed," said Pyrocles; "and here are we in as fit a place for it as may be, for this arbor nobody offers to come into but myself, I using it as my melancholy retiring-place, and therefore that respect is borne unto it; yet if by chance any should come, say that you are a servant sent from the queen of the Amazons to seek me, and then let me alone for the rest." So sat they down, and Pyrocles thus said.

CHAPTER 13

How Pyrocles fell in love with Philoclea. His counsel and course therein. His disguising into Zelmane. Her meeting with Dametas, Basilius, the Queen and her daughters, and their speeches. Her abode there over entreated;[118] and the place thereof described.

"Cousin," said he, "then began the fatal overthrow of all my liberty when, walking among the pictures in Kalander's house,

---

[115] it—love of you.
[116] it—my heart.
[117] it—love of you.
[118] entreated—sketched.

you yourself delivered unto me what you had understood of Philoclea, who, much resembling—though I must say, much surpassing—the lady Zelmane, whom too well I loved, there were mine eyes infected, and at your mouth did I drink my poison. Yet, alas! so sweet was it unto me that I could not be contented till Kalander had made it more and more strong with his declaration. Which, the more I questioned, the more pity I conceived of her unworthy fortune; and when with pity once my heart was made tender, according to the aptness of the humor, it received quickly a cruel impression of that wonderful passion, which to be defined is impossible, because no words reach to the strange nature of it; they only know it which inwardly feel it: it is called love. Yet did I not (poor wretch!) at first know my disease, thinking it only such a wonted kind of desire to see rare sights, and my pity to be no other but the fruits of a gentle nature. But even this arguing with myself came of further thoughts; and the more I argued, the more my thoughts increased. Desirous I was to see the place where she remained, as though the architecture of the lodges would have been much for my learning, but more desirous to see herself, to be judge, forsooth, of the painter's cunning. For thus at the first did I flatter myself, as though my wound had been no deeper. But when within short time I came to the degree of uncertain wishes, and that the wishes grew to unquiet longings; when I could fix my thoughts upon nothing but that within little varying they should end with Philoclea; when each thing I saw seemed to figure out some parts of my passions; when even Parthenia's fair face became a lecture to me of Philoclea's imagined beauty; when I heard no word spoken but that methought it carried the sum of Philoclea's name—then indeed, then I did yield to the burden, finding myself prisoner before I had leisure to arm myself, and that I might well, like the spaniel, gnaw upon the chain that ties him, but I should sooner mar my teeth than procure liberty.

"Yet I take to witness the eternal spring of virtue, that I had never read, heard, nor seen anything, I had never any taste of philosophy nor inward feeling in myself, which for a while I did

not call for my succor. But (alas) what resistance was there when
ere long my very reason was (you will say, corrupted), I must
needs confess, conquered, and that methought even reason did
assure me that all eyes did degenerate from their creation,[119]
which did not honor such beauty? Nothing, in truth, could hold
any plea with it, but the reverent friendship I bore unto you.
For as it went against my heart to break any way from you, so
did I fear more than any assault to break it to you, finding (as it
is indeed) that to a heart fully resolute, counsel is tedious but
reprehension is loathsome; and that there is nothing more terrible
to a guilty heart than the eye of a respected friend. This made
me determine with myself (thinking it a less fault in friendship
to do a thing without your knowledge than against your will) to
take this secret course. Which conceit was most builded up in
me the last day of my parting and speaking with you, when,
upon your speech with me and my but naming love (when else
perchance I would have gone further), I saw your voice and
countenance so change as it assured me my revealing it should
but purchase your grief with my cumber,[120] and (therefore, dear
Musidorus) even ran away from thy well known chiding. For
having written a letter (which I know not whether you found
or no), and taking my chief jewels with me, while you were in
the midst of your sport, I got a time (as I think) unmarked to
steal away, I cared not whither, so I might 'scape you; and so
came I to Ithonia[121] in the province of Messenia, where lying
secret I put this in practice which before I had devised. For remembering by Philanax's letter and Kalander's speech how obstinately Basilius was determined not to marry his daughters, and
therefore fearing lest any public dealing should rather increase
her captivity than further my love, love (the refiner of invention) had put in my head thus to disguise myself, that under that

[119] all eyes did degenerate from their creation—had lost their power to
perceive.
[120] cumber—embarrassment.
[121] Ithonia—Ithome, a fortress-city in the western mountains of Messenia.

mask I might (if it were possible) get access, and what access could bring forth commit to fortune and industry, determining to bear the countenance of an Amazon.

"Therefore, in the closest manner I could, naming myself Zelmane, for that dear lady's sake to whose memory I am so much bound, I caused this apparel to be made, and, bringing it near the lodges, which are hard at hand, by night thus dressed myself, resting till occasion might make me to be found by them whom I sought, which the next morning happened as well as mine own plot could have laid it. For, after I had run over the whole pedigree of my thoughts, I gave myself to sing a little, which, as you know, I ever delighted in, so now especially, whether it be the nature of this clime to stir up poetical fancies, or rather, as I think, of love, whose scope being pleasure will not so much as utter his griefs but in some form of pleasure.

"But I had sung very little, when (as I think, displeased with my bad music) comes master Dametas, with a hedging-bill[122] in his hand, chafing and swearing by the pantaple[123] of Pallas, and such other oaths as his rustical bravery could imagine; and when he saw me, I assure you, my beauty was no more beholding to him than my harmony; for, leaning his hands upon his bill and his chin upon his hands, with the voice of one that playeth Hercules in a play, but never had his fancy in his head, the first word he spoke unto me was—'Am not I Dametas? Why, am not I Dametas?' He needed not name himself, for Kalander's description had set such a note upon him as made him very notable unto me; and therefore, the height of my thoughts would not descend so much as to make him any answer, but continued on my inward discourses; which he, perchance witness of his own unworthiness, and therefore the apter to think himself contemned, took in so heinous manner that, standing upon his tiptoes, and staring as though he would have had a mote pulled out of his eye, 'Why,' said he, 'thou woman, or boy, or both, whatsoever thou be, I tell thee here is no place for thee; get thee gone. I tell thee it is the prince's pleasure; I tell thee it is Dametas' pleasure.'

---

[122] hedging-bill—cf. *O.A.*, ft. 51.
[123] pantaple—cf. *O.A.*, ft. 52.

"I could not choose but smile at him, seeing him look so like an ape that had newly taken a purgation; yet, taking myself with the manner,[124] spoke these words to myself: 'O spirit,' said I, 'of mine, how canst thou receive any mirth in the midst of thine agonies? And thou, mirth, how darest thou enter into a mind so grown of late thy professed enemy?'

" 'Thy spirit!' said Dametas. 'Dost thou think me a spirit? I tell thee I am Basilius' officer, and have charge of him and his daughters.'

" 'O, only pearl,' said I, sobbing, 'that so vile an oyster should keep thee!'

" 'By the combcase of Diana!' swore Dametas, 'this woman is mad. Oysters and pearls! Dost thou think I will buy oysters? I tell thee once again, get thee packing.' And with that lifted up his bill to hit me with the blunt end of it; but, indeed, that put me quite out of my lesson, so that I forgot all Zelmaneship and, drawing out my sword, the baseness of the villain yet made me stay my hand; and he who, as Kalander told me, from his childhood ever feared the blade of a sword, ran backward, with his hands above his head, at least twenty paces, gaping and staring, with the very grace, I think, of the clowns that, by Latona's prayers, were turned into frogs.[125]

"At length, staying, finding himself without the compass of blows, he fell to a fresh scolding, in such mannerly manner as might well show he had passed through the discipline of a tavern; but, seeing me walk up and down, without marking what he said, he went his way, as I perceived after, to Basilius; for within a while he came unto me, bearing, indeed, shows in his countenance of an honest and well-minded gentleman, and, with as much courtesy as Dametas with rudeness, saluting me, 'Fair lady,' said he, 'it is nothing strange that such a solitary place as this should receive solitary persons, but much do I marvel how such a beauty as yours is should be suffered to be thus alone.'

"I, that now knew it was my part to play, looking with a grave majesty upon him, as if I found in myself cause to be rev-

---

[124] taking myself with the manner—catching myself in the act.
[125] by Latona's prayers, were turned into frogs—cf. *O.A.*, ft. 59.

erenced, 'They are never alone,' said I, 'that are accompanied with noble thoughts.' 'But those thoughts,' replied Basilius, 'can in this your loneliness neither warrant you from suspicion in others, nor defend you from melancholy in yourself.'

"I then, showing a mislike that he pressed me so far, 'I seek no better warrant,' said I, 'than my own conscience, nor no greater pleasures than mine own contentation.' 'Yet virtue seeks to satisfy others,' said Basilius. 'Those that be good,' said I; 'and they will be satisfied as long as they see no evil.' 'Yet will the best in this country,' said Basilius, 'suspect so excellent a beauty, being so weakly guarded.' 'Then are the best but stark naught,' answered I; 'for open suspecting others comes of secret condemning themselves; but in my country, whose manners I am in all places to maintain and reverence, the general goodness, which is nourished in our hearts, makes every one think the strength of virtue in another, whereof they find the assured foundation in themselves.'

" 'Excellent lady,' said he, 'you praise so greatly, and yet so wisely, your country, that I must needs desire to know what the nest is out of which such birds do fly.' 'You must first deserve it,' said I, 'before you may obtain it.' 'And by what means,' said Basilius, 'shall I deserve to know your estate?' 'By letting me first know yours,' answered I. 'To obey you,' said he, 'I will do it, although it were so much more reason yours should be known first, as you do deserve in all points to be preferred. Know you, fair lady, that my name is Basilius, unworthily lord of this country; the rest, either fame hath brought to your ears, or, if it please you to make this place happy by your presence, at more leisure you shall understand of me.'

"I that from the beginning assured myself it was he, but would not seem I did so, to keep my gravity the better, making a piece of reverence unto him, 'Mighty prince,' said I, 'let my not knowing you serve for the excuse of my boldness; and the little reverence I do you, impute it to the manner of my country, which is the invincible land of the Amazons; myself, niece to Senicia, queen thereof, lineally descended of the famous Penthe-

silea, slain by the bloody hand of Pyrrhus.[126] I, having in this my
youth determined to make the world see the Amazons' excellencies, as well in private as in public virtue, have passed some
dangerous adventures in divers countries, till the unmerciful sea
deprived me of my company; so that shipwreck casting me not
far hence, uncertain wandering brought me to this place.'

"But Basilius (who now began to taste that which since he
hath swallowed up, as I will tell you) fell to more cunning
entreating my abode than any greedy host would use to well-
paying passengers. I thought nothing could shoot righter at the
mark of my desires; yet had I learned already so much, that it
was against my womanhood to be forward in my own wishes.
And therefore he, to prove whether intercessions in fitter mouths
might better prevail, commanded Dametas to bring forthwith
his wife and daughters thither, three ladies, although of diverse,
yet all of excellent beauty.

"His wife in grave matron-like attire, with countenance and
gesture suitable, and of such fairness, being in the strength of her
age, as, if her daughters had not been by, might with just price
have purchased admiration; but they being there, it was enough
that the most dainty eye would think her a worthy mother of
such children. The fair Pamela, whose noble heart, I find,
doth greatly disdain that the trust of her virtue is reposed in
such a lout's hands as Dametas', had yet, to show an obedience,
taken on a shepherdish apparel, which was but of russet cloth,
cut after their fashion, with a straight body, open-breasted, the
nether part full of plaits, with long and wide sleeves; but, believe
me, she did apparel her apparel, and with the preciousness of her
body made it most sumptuous. Her hair at the full length, wound
about with gold lace, only by the comparison to see how far her
hair doth excel in color; betwixt her breasts, which sweetly
rose up like two fair mountainettes in the pleasant vale of Tempe,
there hung a very rich diamond, set but in a black horn;[127] the
word, I have since read, is this: 'Yet still myself.' And thus

---

[126] Senicia, Penthesilea, Pyrrhus—cf. *O.A.*, fts. 66, 67, 68.
[127] set but in a black horn—encased in nothing better than black horn.

particularly have I described them, because you may know that mine eyes are not so partial but that I marked them too.

"But when the ornament of the earth, the model of heaven, the triumph of nature, the light of beauty, queen of love, young Philoclea, appeared in her nymph-like apparel, so near nakedness as one might well discern part of her perfections, and yet so appareled as did show she kept best store of her beauty to herself, her hair (alas, too poor a word, why should I not rather call them her beams?) drawn up into a net able to take Jupiter when he was in the form of an eagle, her body (O sweet body!) covered with a light taffeta garment so cut as the wrought smock[128] came through it in many places enough to have made your restrained imagination have thought what was under it, with the cast of her black eyes—black indeed, whether nature so made them, that we might be the more able to behold and bear their wonderful shining, or that she, goddess-like, would work this miracle in herself, in giving blackness the price above all beauty—then, I say, indeed methought the lilies grew pale for envy, the roses methought blushed to see sweeter roses in her cheeks, and the apples, methought, fell down from the trees to do homage to the apples of her breast. Then the clouds gave place that the heavens might more freshly smile upon her—at the least the clouds of my thoughts quite vanished, and my sight, then more clear and forcible than ever, was so fixed there that I imagine I stood like a well-wrought image, with some life in show but none in practice.

"And so had I been like enough to have stayed long time, but that Gynecia stepping between my sight and the only Philoclea, the change of object made me recover my senses so that I could with reasonable good manner receive the salutation of her and of the Princess Pamela, doing them yet no further reverence than one prince useth to another. But when I came to the never-enough praised Philoclea, I could not but fall down on my knees, and taking by force her hand, and kissing it, I must confess, with more than womanly ardency, 'Divine lady,' said I, 'let not the world nor these great princes marvel to see me, contrary to my

128 wrought smock—cf. *O.A.,* ft. 70.

manner, do this especial honor unto you, since all, both men and women, do owe this to the perfection of your beauty.' But she, blushing like a fair morning in May at this my singularity, and causing me to rise, 'Noble lady,' said she, 'it is no marvel to see your judgment mistaken in my beauty, since you begin with so great an error as to do more honor unto me than to them, whom I myself owe all service.' 'Rather,' answered I, with a bowed down countenance, 'that shows the power of your beauty, which forced me to do such an error, if it were an error.' 'You are so well acquainted,' said she sweetly, most sweetly smiling, 'with your own beauty, that it makes you easily fall into the discourse of beauty.' 'Beauty in me?' said I, truly sighing; 'alas, if there be any, it is in my eyes, which your blessed presence hath imparted unto them.'

"But then, as I think Basilius willing her so do, 'Well,' said she, 'I must needs confess I have heard that it is a great happiness to be praised of them that are most praiseworthy; and well I find that you are an invincible Amazon, since you will overcome, though in a wrong matter. But if my beauty be anything, then let it obtain thus much of you, that you will remain some while in this company, to ease your own travel and our solitariness.' 'First let me die,' said I, 'before any word spoken by such a mouth should come in vain.' And thus, with some other words of entertaining, was my staying concluded, and I led among them to the lodge—truly a place for pleasantness, not unfit to flatter solitariness, for, it being set upon such an unsensible rising of the ground as you are come to a pretty height before almost you perceive that you ascend, it gives the eye lordship over a good large circuit, which, according to the nature of the country, being diversified between hills and dales, woods and plains, one place more clear, and the other more darksome, it seems a pleasant picture of nature, with lovely lightsomeness and artificial[129] shadows. The lodge is of a yellow stone, built in the form of a star, having round about a garden framed into like points, and beyond the garden ridings[130] cut out, each answering

---

[129] artificial—as skillful as if contrived by an artist.
[130] ridings—riding paths.

the angles of the lodge. At the end of one of them is the other smaller lodge, but of like fashion, where the gracious Pamela liveth, so that the lodge seemeth not unlike a fair comet, whose tail stretcheth itself to a star of less greatness."

CHAPTER 14

The devices of the first banquet to Zelmane.[131] *Her crosses in love, by the love of Basilius and Gynecia. The conclusion between Musidorus and Zelmane.*

"So Gynecia herself bringing me to my lodging, anon after[132] I was invited and brought down to sup with them in the garden, a place not fairer in natural ornaments than artificial inventions, wherein is a banqueting house among certain pleasant trees, whose heads seemed curled with the wrappings about of vine branches. The table was set near to an excellent waterwork, for by the casting of the water in most cunning manner, it makes (with the shining of the sun upon it) a perfect rainbow, not more pleasant to the eye than to the mind so sensibly to see the proof of the heavenly Iris. There were birds also made so finely that they did not only deceive the sight with their figure but the hearing with their songs, which the watery instruments did make their gorge deliver. The table at which we sat was round, which being fast to the floor whereon we sat, and that divided from the rest of the buildings, with turning a vice (which Basilius at first did to make me sport) the table, and we about the table, did all turn round by means of water which ran under and carried it about as a mill. But, alas, what pleasure did it to me to make diverse times the full circle round about, since Philoclea (being also set) was carried still in equal distance from me, and that only my eyes did overtake her, which, when the table was stayed and we began to feed, drank much more eagerly of her beauty than my mouth did of any other liquor. And so was my common sense deceived (being chiefly bent to her) that as I drank the wine and withal stole a look on her, me seemed I tasted her

131 Zelmane—"rare zeal."
132 anon after—soon afterward.

deliciousness. But, alas, the one thirst was much more inflamed than the other quenched. Sometimes my eyes would lay themselves open to receive all the darts she did throw, sometimes close up with admiration, as if with a contrary fancy they would preserve the riches of that sight they had gotten, or cast my lid as curtains over the image of beauty her presence had painted in them. True it is that my reason (now grown a servant to passion) did yet often tell his master that he should more moderately use his delight. But he, that of a rebel had become prince, disdained almost to allow him the place of a counselor; so that my senses' delights being too strong for any other resolution, I did even loose the reins unto them, hoping that (going for a woman) my looks would pass either unmarked or unsuspected.

"Now thus I had, as methought, well played my first act, assuring myself that under that disguisement I should find opportunity to reveal myself to the owner of my heart. But who would think it possible (though I feel it true) that in almost eight weeks' space I have lived here, having no more company but her parents, and I, being familiar, as being a woman, and watchful, as being a lover, yet could never find opportunity to have one minute's leisure of privy conference, the cause whereof is as strange as the effects are to me miserable? And, alas! this it is.

"At the first sight Basilius had of me (I think Cupid having headed his arrows with my misfortune) he was stricken, taking me to be such as I professed, with great affection towards me, which since is grown to such a doting love that (till I was fain to get this place, sometimes to retire unto freely) I was even choked with his tediousness. You never saw fourscore years dance up and down more lively in a young lover: now as fine in his apparel as if he would make me in love with a cloak, and verse for verse with the sharpest witted lover in Arcadia. Do you not think that this is a salad of wormwood,[133] while mine eyes feed upon the ambrosia of Philoclea's beauty?

"But this is not all; no, this is not the worst; for he (good

[133] wormwood—a bitter plant, a common emblem of whatever is bitter to the soul.

man) were easy enough to be dealt with. But (as I think) love and mischief, having made a wager which should have most power in me, have set Gynecia also on such a fire towards me as will never (I fear) be quenched but with my destruction. For she (being a woman of excellent wit and of strong working thoughts) whether she suspected me by my over-vehement shows of affection to Philoclea (which love forced me unwisely to utter while hope of my mask foolishly encouraged me) or that she hath taken some other mark of me that I am not a woman; or what devil it is hath revealed it unto her, I know not. But so it is that all her countenances, words, and gestures are miserable portraitures of a desperate affection. Whereby a man may learn that these avoidings of company do but make the passions more violent when they meet with fit subjects. Truly, it were a notable dumb show of Cupid's kingdom[134] to see my eyes, languishing with over-vehement longing, direct themselves to Philoclea; and Basilius as busy about me as a bee, and indeed as cumbersome, making such suits to me, who neither could if I would nor would if I could, help him; while the terrible wit of Gynecia, carried with the beer[135] of violent love, runs through us all. And so jealous is she of my love to her daughter that I could never yet begin to open my mouth to the unevitable[136] Philoclea, but that her unwished presence gave my tale a conclusion before it had a beginning.

"And surely if I be not deceived, I see such shows of liking and (if I be acquainted with passions) of almost a passionate liking in the heavenly Philoclea towards me that I may hope her ears would not abhor my discourse. And for good Basilius, he thought it best to have lodged us together, but that the eternal hatefulness of my destiny made Gynecia's jealousy stop that and all other my blessings. Yet must I confess that one way her love doth me pleasure, for since it was my foolish fortune, or un-

[134] a notable dumb show of Cupid's kingdom—allegorical processions and pageants dedicated to Cupid; a common device in Renaissance entertainments, but the origins are medieval.
[135] beer—force, impetus.
[136] unevitable—inevitable; the one from whom he cannot keep himself.

fortunate folly, to be known by her, that keeps her from betraying me to Basilius. Thus, my Musidorus, you have my tragedy played unto you by myself, which, I pray the gods, may not indeed prove a tragedy." And there he ended, making a full point of a hearty sigh.

Musidorus recommended to his best discourse all which Pyrocles had told him. But therein he found such intricateness that he could see no way to lead him out of the maze; yet, perceiving his affection so grounded that striving against it did rather anger than heal the wound, and rather call his friendship in question than give place to any friendly counsel, "Well," said he, "dear cousin, since it hath pleased the gods to mingle your other excellencies with this humor of love, yet happy it is that your love is employed upon so rare a woman; for certainly, a noble cause doth ease much a grievous case. But as it stands now, nothing vexeth me as that I cannot see wherein I can be serviceable unto you."

"I desire no greater service of you," answered Pyrocles, "than that you remain secretly in this country, and sometimes come to this place, either late in the night or early in the morning, where you shall have my key to enter, because, as my fortune either amends or impairs, I may declare it unto you, and have your counsel and furtherance; and hereby I will of purpose lead her that is the praise, and yet the stain, of all womankind, that you may have so good a view as to allow my judgment; and as I can get the most convenient time, I will come unto you; for, though by reason of yonder wood you cannot see the lodge, it is hard at hand." "But now," said she, "it is time for me to leave you, and towards evening we will walk out of purpose hitherward; therefore keep yourself close in that time."

But Musidorus, bethinking himself that his horse might happen to betray them, thought it best to return for that day to a village not far off, and, dispatching his horse in some sort, the next day early to come afoot thither, and so to keep that course afterward which Pyrocles very well liked of. "Now farewell, dear cousin," said he, "from me—no more Pyrocles, nor Daiphantus, now but Zelmane; Zelmane is my name, Zelmane is my title, Zelmane is the only hope of my advancement." And with that word going out and seeing that the coast was clear, Zelmane dismissed Musidorus, who departed as full of care to help his friend as before he was to dissuade him.

CHAPTER 15

The labyrinth of Zelmane's love. The ladies' exercises. The challenge of Phalantus[137] in paragon[138] of Artesia's[139] beauty. The description of their persons and affections, and occasion of this challenge. The success thereof abroad.

Zelmane returned to the lodge, where, inflamed by Philoclea, watched by Gynecia, and tired by Basilius, she was like a horse desirous to run and miserably spurred, but so short reined as he cannot stir forward; Zelmane sought occasion to speak with Philoclea, Basilius with Zelmane, and Gynecia hindered them all. If Philoclea happened to sigh, and sigh she did often, as if that sigh were to be waited on, Zelmane sighed also, whereto Basilius and Gynecia soon made up four parts of sorrow.

Their affection increased their conversation, and their conversation increased their affection. The respect born, bred due ceremonies; but the affection shined so through them that the ceremonies seemed not ceremonious. Zelmane's eyes were (like children afore sweetmeat) eager, but fearful of their ill pleasing governors. Time in one instant seeming both short and long unto them: short in the pleasingness of such presence, long in the stay of their desires.

But Zelmane failed not to entice them all many times abroad because she was desirous her friend Musidorus (near whom of purpose she led them) might have full sight of them. Sometimes angling to a little river near hand, which for the moisture it bestowed upon roots of some flourishing trees, was rewarded with their shadow. There would they sit down and pretty wagers be made between Pamela and Philoclea which could soonest

137 Phalantus—"battle line."
138 in paragon of—to compete over.
139 Artesia—"arranger."

beguile silly fishes, while Zelmane protested that the fit prey for them was hearts of princes. She also had an angle in her hand, but the taker was so taken that she had forgotten taking. Basilius in the meantime would be the cook himself of what was so caught, and Gynecia sit still, but with no still pensiveness. Now she [Zelmane] brought them to see a seeled dove, who, the blinder she was, the higher she strove. Another time a kite, which, having a gut cunningly pulled out of her and so let fly, called all the kites in that quarter, who (as oftentimes the world is deceived) thinking her prosperous when indeed she was wounded, made the poor kite find that opinion of riches may well be dangerous.

But these recreations were interrupted by a delight of more gallant show, for one evening, as Basilius returned from having forced his thoughts to please themselves in such conquests, there came a shepherd, who brought him word that a gentleman desired leave to do a message from his lord unto him. Basilius granted, whereupon the gentleman came, and, after the dutiful ceremonies observed in his master's name, told him that he was sent from Phalantus of Corinth to crave license that, as he had done in many other courts, so he might in his presence defy all Arcadian knights in the behalf of his mistress's beauty, who would, besides, herself in person be present, to give evident proof what his lance should affirm. The conditions of his challenge were, that the defendant should bring his mistress's picture, which being set by the image of Artesia (so was the mistress of Phalantus named) who in six courses should have the better of the other, in the judgment of Basilius, with him both the honors and pictures should remain. Basilius, though he had retired himself into that solitary dwelling with intention to avoid, rather than to accept any matters of drawing company, yet because he would entertain Zelmane, that she might not think the time so gainful to him, loss to her, granted him to pitch his tent for three days not far from the lodge, and to proclaim his challenge, that what Arcadian knight—for none else but upon his peril was licensed to come—would defend what he honored against Phalantus, should have the like freedom of access and return.

This obtained and published, Zelmane being desirous to learn what this Phalantus was (having never known him further than by report of his own good, in so much as he was commonly called "the fair man of arms"), Basilius told her that he had had occasion by one very inward with him to know in part the discourse of his life, which was, that he was bastard-brother to the fair Helen, queen of Corinth, and dearly esteemed of her for his exceeding good parts, being honorably courteous, and wronglessly valiant, considerately pleasant in conversation, and an excellent courtier, without unfaithfulness; who, finding his sister's unpersuadable melancholy, through the love of Amphialus, had for a time left her court, and gone into Laconia, where in the war against the Helots he had gotten the reputation of one that both durst and knew. But as it was rather choice than nature that led him to matters of arms, so as soon as the spur of honor ceased, he willingly rested in peaceable delights, being beloved in all companies for his lovely qualities and (as a man may term it) cunning cheerfulness, whereby to the prince and court of Laconia none was more agreeble than Phalantus, and he, not given greatly to struggle with his own disposition, followed the gentle current of it, having a fortune sufficient to content, and he content with a sufficient fortune. But in that court he saw, and was acquainted with, this Artesia, whose beauty he now defends, became her servant, said himself, and, perchance thought himself, her lover.

"But certainly," said Basilius, "many times it falls out that these young companions make themselves believe they love at the first liking of a likely beauty—loving because they will love for want of other business, not because they feel indeed that divine power which makes the heart find a reason in passion—and so (God knows) as inconstantly lean upon the next chance that beauty casts before them. So therefore taking love upon him like a fashion, he courted this lady Artesia, who was as fit to pay him in his own money as might be, for she, thinking she did wrong to her beauty if she were not proud of it, called her disdain of him chastity, and placed her honor in little setting[140]

[140] in little setting—in miniature.

by his honoring her, determining never to marry but him whom she thought worthy of her, and that was one in whom all worthinesses were harbored.

"And to this conceit not only nature had bent her, but the bringing up she received at my sister-in-law, Cecropia,[141] had confirmed her, who, having in her widowhood taken this young Artesia into her charge because her father had been a dear friend of her dead husband's, and taught her to think that there is no wisdom but in including heaven and earth in one's self, and that love, courtesy, gratefulness, friendship, and all other virtues are rather to be taken on, than taken in, one's self. And so good discipline she found of her that, liking the fruits of her own planting, she was content, if so her son could have liked of it, to have wished her in marriage to my nephew Amphialus. But I think that desire hath lost some of his heat since she hath known that such a queen as Helen is doth offer so great a price as a kingdom to buy his favor, for, if I be not deceived in my good sister Cecropia, she thinks no face so beautiful as that which looks under a crown.

"But Artesia indeed liked well of my nephew Amphialus— for I can never deem that love, which in haughty hearts proceeds of a desire only to please and, as it were, peacock themselves. But yet she hath showed vehemency of desire that way (I think because all her desires be vehement) insomuch that she hath both placed her only brother, a fine youth called Ismenus, to be his squire, and herself is content to wait upon my sister, till she may see the uttermost what she may work in Amphialus, who being of a melancholy (though, I must needs say, courteous and noble) mind, seems to love nothing less than love, and of late having through some adventure, or inward miscontentment, withdrawn himself from anybody's knowledge where he is, Artesia the easier condescended to go to the court of Laconia, whither she was sent for by the king's wife, to whom she is somewhat allied. And there, after the war of the Helots, this knight Phalantus (at least, for tongue delight) made himself her servant, and she, so little caring as not to show mislike

[141] Cecropia—"Athenian."

thereof, was content only to be noted to have a notable servant. For truly one in my court nearly acquainted with him, within these few days made me a pleasant description of their love.

"While he with cheerful looks would speak sorrowful words, using the phrase of his affection in so high a style that Mercury[142] would not have wooed Venus with more magnificent eloquence, but else neither in behavior nor action accusing in himself any great trouble in mind whether he sped or no, and she, of the other side, well finding how little it was and not caring for more, yet taught him that often it falleth out but a foolish wittiness to speak more than one thinks. For she made earnest benefit of his jest, forcing him (in respect of his promise) to do her such service as were both cumbersome and costly unto him, while he still thought he went beyond her, because his heart did not commit the idolatry. So that, lastly, she—I think having in mind to make the fame of her beauty an orator for her to Amphialus (persuading herself, perhaps, that it might fall out in him as it doth in some that have delightful meat before them and have no stomach to it, before other folks praise it)—she took the advantage one day upon Phalantus' unconscionable praisings of her and certain castaway vows—how much he would do for her sake—to arrest his word as soon as it was out of his mouth and, by the virtue thereof, to charge him to go with her through all the courts of Greece, and, with the challenge now made, to give her beauty the principality over all other.

"Phalantus was entrapped, and saw round about him, but could not get out. Exceedingly perplexed he was (as he confessed to him that told me the tale) not for doubt he had of himself (for indeed he had little cause, being accounted, with his lance especially, whereupon the challenge is to be tried, as perfect as any that Greece knoweth) but because he feared to offend his sister Helen, and withal (as he said) he could not so much believe his love but that he might think in his heart (whatsoever his mouth affirmed) that both she, my daughters, and the fair Parthenia (wife to a most noble gentleman, my wife's near

[142] Mercury—the god of eloquence.

kinsman) might far better put in their claim for that prerogative. But his promise had bound him prentice, and therefore it was now better with willingness to purchase thanks than with a discontented doing to have the pain and not the reward; and therefore, went on as his faith, rather than love, did lead him.

"And now hath he already passed the courts of Laconia, Elis, Argos, and Corinth; and, as many times it happens that a good pleader makes a bad cause to prevail, so hath his lance brought captives to the triumph of Artesia's beauty such as, though Artesia be among the fairest, yet in that company were to have the pre-eminence; for in those courts many knights that had been in other far countries defended such as they had seen, and liked, in their travel; but their defense had been such as they had forfeited the picture of their ladies to give a forced false testimony to Artesia's excellency. And now lastly is he come hither, where he hath leave to try his fortune. But I assure you, if I thought it not in due and true consideration an injurious service and churlish courtesy to put the danger[143] of so noble a title in the deciding of such a dangerless combat, I would make younger master Phalantus know that your eyes can sharpen a blunt lance and that age, which my grey hairs (only gotten by the loving care of others) make seem more than it is, hath not diminished in me the power to protect an undeniable verity."

With that he bustled up himself as though his heart would fain have walked abroad. Zelmane with an inward smiling gave him outward thanks, desiring him to reserve his force for worthier causes.

CHAPTER 16

Phalantus and Artesia's pompous entrance. The painted master of an eleven conquered beauties.

So, passing their time according to their wont, they waited for the coming of Phalantus, who, the next morning, having already caused his tents to be pitched near to a fair tree hard by the lodge, had upon the tree made a shield to be hanged up,

[143] danger—dominion, control.

which the defendant should strike that would call him to the maintaining his challenge. The impresa[144] in the shield was a heaven full of stars, with a speech signifying that it was "the beauty which gave it the praise."

Himself came in next, after a triumphant chariot made of carnation velvet enriched with purple and pearl, wherein Artesia sat, drawn by four winged horses, with artificial flaming mouths and fiery wings, as if she had newly borrowed them of Phoebus. Before her marched, two after two, certain footmen pleasantly attired, who between them held one picture after another of them that, by Phalantus' well running, had lost the prize in the race of beauty; and, at every pace they stayed, turning the pictures to each side, so leisurely that with perfect judgment they might be discerned.

The first that came in (following the order of the time wherein they had been won) was the picture of Andromana, Queen of Iberia,[145] whom a Laconian knight having sometime, and with special favor, served (though some years since returned home), with more gratefulness than good fortune defended. But therein Fortune had borrowed wit, for indeed she was not comparable to Artesia, not because she was a good deal elder (for time had not yet been able to impoverish her store thereof), but an exceeding red hair with small eyes did, like ill companions, disgrace the other assembly of most commendable beauties.

Next after her was borne the counterfeit of the Princess of Elis, a lady that taught the beholders no other point of beauty but this: that as liking is not always the child of beauty, so whatsoever liketh is beautiful, for in that visage there was neither majesty, grace, favor, nor fairness; yet she wanted not a servant that would have made her fairer than the fair Artesia. But he wrote her praises with his helmet in the dust and left her picture

[144] impresa—chivalric device made up of words and pictures.
[145] Andromana—"lustful" queen of Iberia, the region bordered by the Caucasus Mountains on the north, ancient Albania on the east, Armenia on the south, and Colchis on the west.

to be as true a witness of his overthrow as his running was of her beauty.

After her was the goodly Artaxia, great Queen of Armenia,[146] a lady upon whom nature bestowed and well placed her delightful colors and, withal, had proportioned her without any fault quickly to be discovered by the senses; yet, altogether seemed not to make up that harmony that Cupid delights in; the reason whereof might seem a mannish countenance, which overthrew that lovely sweetness, the noblest power of womankind, far fitter to prevail by parley than by battle.

Of a far contrary consideration was the representation of her that next followed, which was Erona, Queen of Licia,[147] who though of so brown a hair as no man should have injured it to have called it black, and that in the mixture of her cheeks the white did so much overcome the red (though what was, was very pure) that it came near to paleness, and that her face was a thought longer than the exact symmetrians perhaps would allow, yet love played his part so well, in every part, that it caught hold of the judgment before it could judge, making it first love and after acknowledge it fair, for there was a certain delicacy, which in yielding, conquered, and with a pitiful look made one find cause to crave help himself.

After her came two ladies of noble, but not of royal, birth. The former was named Baccha,[148] who though very fair and of a fatness rather to allure than to mislike, yet her breasts over-familiarly laid open, with a mad countenance about her mouth (between simpering and smiling), her head bowed somewhat down, seemed to languish with over-much idleness, with an inviting look cast upward, dissuading with too much persuading, while hope might seem to overcome desire.

[146] Artaxia—from Artuxata, the capital of Armenia, an Asian country south of Iberia and Colchis, north of Mesopotamia, east of Pontus and Cappadochia.
[147] Erona—"loving" (with connotations of error) queen of Licia, a region in southwest Asia Minor, bordering on the Mediterranean.
[148] Baccha—"raving."

The other, whose name was written Leucippe,[149] was of a fine daintiness of beauty, her face carrying in it a sober simplicity, like one that could do much good and meant no hurt, her eyes having in them such a cheerfulness as nature seemed to smile in them, though her mouth and cheeks obeyed that pretty demureness, which the more one marks, the more one would judge the poor soul apt to believe, and therefore the more pity to deceive her.

Next came the Queen of Laconia, one that seemed born in the confines of beauty's kingdom, for all her lineaments were neither perfect possessions thereof nor absent strangers thereto; but she was a queen, and therefore beautiful.

But she that followed, conquered—indeed, with being conquered—and might well have made all the beholders wait upon her triumph, while herself were led captive. It was the excellently-fair Queen Helen, whose jacinth[150] hair, curled by nature, and intercurled by art, like a fine brook through golden sands, had a rope of fair pearls, which, now hiding, now hidden by the hair, did, as it were, play at fast-or-loose each with other, mutually giving and receiving riches. In her face so much beauty and favor expressed as, if Helen had not been known, some would rather have judged it the printer's exercise, to show what he could do, than counterfeiting of any living pattern, for no fault the most fault-finding wit could have found, if it were not that to the rest of the body the face was somewhat too little; but that little was such a spark of beauty as was able to enflame a world of love, for everything was full of a choice fineness, that, if it wanted anything in majesty, it supplied it with increase of pleasure; and, if at the first it strake not admiration, it ravished with delight, and no indifferent soul there was, which if it could resist from subjecting itself to make it his princess, that would not long to have such a playfellow. As for her attire, it was costly and curious, though the look, fixed with more sadness than it seemed nature had bestowed to any that knew her fortune, betrayed that, as she used those ornaments,

149 Leucippe—"white mare."
150 jacinth—reddish-orange.

not for herself, but to prevail with another, so she feared that all would not serve.

Of a far differing, though esteemed equal, beauty was the fair Parthenia, who next waited on Artesia's triumph, though far better she might have sat upon the throne, for in her everything was goodly and stately; yet so, that it might seem that great-mindedness was but the ancient-bearer[151] to humbleness. For her great grey eye, which might seem full of her own beauties, a large, and exceedingly fair forehead, with all the rest of her face and body, cast in the mold of nobleness; was yet so attired[152] as might show the mistress thought it either not to deserve, or not to need, any exquisite decking, having no adorning but cleanliness, and so far from all art that it was full of carelessness, unless that carelessness itself (in spite of itself) grew artificial.

But Basilius could not abstain from praising Parthenia as the perfect picture of a womanly virtue and wifely faithfulness, telling withal Zelmane how he had understood that, when in the court of Laconia her picture (maintained by a certain Sicyonian knight) was lost through want rather of valor than justice, her husband, the famous Argalus, would in a chase have gone and redeemed it with a new trial, but she (more sporting than sorrowing for her undeserved champion) told her husband she desired to be beautiful in nobody's eye but his, and that she would rather mar her face, as evil as ever it was, than that it should be a cause to make Argalus put on armor. Then would Basilius have told Zelmane that which she already knew of the rare trial of their coupled affection, but the next picture made the mouth give place to their eyes.

It was of a young maid, which sat pulling out a thorn out

[151] ancient-bearer—standard-bearer.
[152] For her great grey eye . . . so attired—Because the "great grey eye" phrase is obsolete and because Sidney's syntax breaks down, the following extended paraphrase is offered: as a setting for her big blue eyes, which could have been obsessed with her own beauties (but were not), she had a full (signifying generosity) and fair forehead, which, along with the rest of her face and her body, was cast in the mold of nobleness; yet, her body was so attired, etc.

of a lamb's foot, with her look so attentive upon it as if that little foot could have been the circle of her thoughts; her apparel so poor, as it had nothing but the inside to adorn it; a sheep-hook lying by her with a bottle upon it. But, with all that poverty, beauty played the prince and commanded as many hearts as the greatest queen there did. Her beauty and her estate made her quickly to be known to be the fair shepherdess Urania, whom a rich knight called Lacemon,[153] far in love with her, had unluckily defended.

The last of all in place, because last in the time of her being captive, was Zelmane, daughter to the king Plexirtus,[154] who at the first sight seemed to have some resembling of Philoclea, but with more marking (comparing it to the present Philoclea, who indeed had no paragon but her sister) they might see it was but such a likeness as an unperfect glass doth give—answerable enough in some features and colors but erring in others. But Zelmane sighing, turning to Basilius, "Alas, sir," said she, "here be some pictures which might better become the tombs of their mistresses than the triumph of Artesia."

"It is true, sweetest lady," said Basilius, "some of them be dead, and some other captive. But that hath happened so late as it may be the knights that defended their beauty knew not so much, without we will say (as in some hearts I know it would fall out) that death itself could not blot out the image which love hath engraven in them." "But divers besides these," said Basilius, "hath Phalantus won; but he leaves the rest, carrying only such who, either for greatness of estate or of beauty, may justly glorify the glory of Artesia's triumph."

CHAPTER 17

The overthrow of five Arcadian knights. The young shepherd's pretty challenge. What passions the sixth knight's foil[155] bred in Zelmane. Clitophon hardly over-matched by Phalantus. The

153 Lacemon—"shriek with disgrace."
154 Plexirtus—"striking."
155 foil—failure.

*ill-arrayed and the black knights' contention for priority against
Phalantus. The halting knight's complaint against the black
knight. Phalantus' fall by the ill-furnished knight. The cross
parting of Phalantus with Artesia, and who the victor was.*

Thus talked Basilius with Zelmane, glad to make any matter
subject to speak of with his mistress, while Phalantus in this
pompous manner brought Artesia, with her gentlewomen, into
one tent, by which he had another, where they both waited who
would first strike upon the shield, while Basilius, the judge, appointed sticklers[156] and trumpets, to whom the other should
obey. But none that day appeared, nor the next, till already
it had consumed half his allowance of light, but then there came
in a knight, protesting himself as contrary to him in mind as he
was in apparel, for Phalantus was all in white, having in his bases
and caparison[157] embroidered a waving water, at each side
whereof he had nettings cast over, in which were divers fishes
naturally made, and so prettily,[158] that as the horse stirred, the
fishes seemed to strive and leap in the net. But the other knight,
by name Nestor,[159] by birth an Arcadian, and in affection vowed
to the fair shepherdess, was all in black, with fire burning both
upon his armor and horse. His impresa in his shield was a fire
made of juniper, with this word, "More easy and more sweet."[160]
But this hot knight was cooled with a fall, which at the third
course he received of Phalantus, leaving his picture to keep
company with the other of the same stamp, he going away
remedilessly chafing at his rebuke.

The next was Polycetes,[161] greatly esteemed in Arcadia for
deeds he had done in arms, and much spoken of for the honorable love he had long borne to Gynecia, which Basilius himself

156 sticklers—umpires.
157 bases and caparison—plaited skirt hanging from waist to knee; cloth
covering spread over saddle and harness.
158 naturally made,and so prettily—resembling nature, skillfully.
159 Nestor—"returned home."
160 juniper—a conifer with pungent berries and prickly leaves; used in
medicine and in gin.
161 Polycetes—"full of monsters."

was content not only to suffer, but to be delighted with, he carried it in so honorable and open plainness, setting to his love no other mark than to do her faithful service. But neither her fair picture nor his fair running could warrant him from overthrow, and her from becoming as then the last of Artesia's victories—a thing Gynecia's virtues would little have recked at[162] another time, nor then, if Zelmane had not seen it. But her champion went away as much discomforted as discomfited. Then Telamon for Polixena, and Eurimelon for Elpine, and Leon for Zoana[163] all brave knights, all fair ladies, with their going down, lifted up the balance of his praise for activity, and hers for fairness.

Upon whose loss, as the beholders were talking, there comes into the place where they ran a shepherd stripling—for his height made him more than a boy, and his face would not allow him a man—brown of complexion, whether by nature or by the sun's familiarity, but very lovely withal, for the rest so perfectly proportioned that Nature showed, she doth not like men, who slubber up matters of mean account.[164] And well might his proportion be judged, for he had nothing upon him but a pair of slops,[165] and upon his body a goat-skin, which he cast over his shoulder, doing all things with so pretty grace that it seemed ignorance could not make him do amiss because he had a heart to do well.

Holding in his right hand a long staff, and so coming with a look full of amiable fierceness, as in whom choler could not take away the sweetness, he came towards the king, and, making a reverence which in him was comely, because it was kindly, "My liege lord," said he, "I pray you hear a few words, for my heart will break if I say not my mind to you. I see here the picture of Urania, which (I cannot tell how nor why)

[162] have recked at—have been bothered by
[163] Telamon, "patient," Polixena, "many friends," Eurimelon, "melody," Elpine, "hopeful," Leon, "lion," Zoana, "living."
[164] doth not like men, who slubber up matters of mean account—does not act like men who make a thing crudely, simply because it is lowly or of mean estate.
[165] slops—boots.

these men, when they fall down, they say is not so fair as yonder gay woman. But, pray God, I may never see my old mother alive if I think she be any more match to Urania than a goat is to a fine lamb, or than the dog that keeps our flock at home is like your white greyhound that pulled down the stag last day. And therefore I pray you let me be dressed as they be, and my heart gives me I shall tumble him on the earth, for, indeed, he might as well say that a cowslip is as white as a lily. Or else, I care not, let him come with his great staff and I with this in my hand, and you shall see what I can do to him."

Basilius saw it was the fine shepherd Lalus,[166] whom once he had afore him in pastoral sports, and had greatly delighted in his wit, full of pretty simplicity; and therefore, laughing at his earnestness, he bade him be content, since he saw the pictures of so great queens were fain to follow their champions' fortune. But Lalus, even weeping ripe, went among the rest, longing to see somebody that would revenge Urania's wrong, and praying heartily for everybody that ran against Phalantus, then began to feel poverty, that he could not set himself to that trial.

But by-and-by, even when the sun, like a noble heart, began to show his greatest countenance in his lowest estate, there came in a knight called Phebilus,[167] a gentleman of that country for whom hateful fortune had borrowed the dart of love to make him miserable by the sight of Philoclea. For he had even from her infancy loved her, and was stricken by her before she was able to know what quiver of arrows her eyes carried; but he loved and despaired; and the more he despaired, the more he loved. He saw his own unworthiness and thereby made her excellency have more terrible aspect upon him. He was so secret therein, as not daring to be open, that to no creature he ever spoke of it, but his heart made such silent complaints within itself that, while all his senses were attentive thereto, cunning judges might perceive his mind; so that he was known to love though he denied, or rather was the better known because he denied it. His armor and his attire was of a sea color, his im-

---

166 Lalus—"loquacious"; a shepherd in the *Old Arcadia*
167 Phebilus—"radiant."

presa, the fish called sepia,[168] which being in the net casts a black ink about itself, that in the darkness thereof it may escape. His word was, "Not so." Philoclea's picture with almost an idolatrous magnificence was borne in by him. But straight, jealousy was a harbinger for disdain in Zelmane's heart when she saw any but herself should be avowed a champion for Philoclea; insomuch that she wished his shame, till she saw him shamed. For at the second course he was stricken quite from out of the saddle, so full of grief, and rage withal, that he would fain with the sword have revenged it. But that, being contrary to the order set down, Basilius would not suffer, so that, wishing himself in the bottom of the earth, he went his way, leaving Zelmane no less angry with his loss than she would have been with his victory. For if she thought before a rival's praise would have angered her, her lady's disgrace did make her much more forget what she then thought, while that passion reigned so much the more as she saw a pretty blush in Philoclea's cheeks betray a modest discontentment.

But the night commanded truce for those sports, and Phalantus, though entreated, would not leave Artesia, who in no case would come into the house, having, as it were, sucked of Cecropia's breath a mortal mislike against Basilius. But the night, measured by the short ell[169] of sleep, was soon past over, and the next morning had given the watchful stars leave to take their rest, when a trumpet summoned Basilius to play his judge's part; which he did, taking his wife and daughters with him (Zelmane having locked her door so as they would not trouble her for that time), for already there was a knight in the field ready to prove Helen of Corinth had received great injury, both by the erring judgment of the challenger and the unlucky weakness of her former defender. The new knight was quickly known to be Clitophon (Kalander's son, of Basilius' sister) by his armor, which, all gilt, was so well handled that it showed like a glittering sand and gravel interlaced with silver rivers. His device he had put in the picture of Helen (which he defended):

---

[168] sepia—octopus.
[169] measured by the short ell—measured unfairly.

it was the ermion with a speech that signified, "Rather dead than spotted."[170] But in that armor—since he had parted from Helen (who would no longer his company, finding him to enter into terms of affection) he had performed so honorable actions, still seeking for his two friends by the names of Palladius and Daïphantus—that, though his face were covered, his being was discovered, which yet Basilius (which had brought him up in his court) would not seem to do; but, glad to see trial of him of whom he had heard very well, he commanded the trumpets to sound; to which the two brave knights obeying, they performed their courses, breaking their six staves with so good both skill in the hitting and grace in the manner that it bred some difficulty in the judgment.

But Basilius in the end gave sentence against Clitophon, because Phalantus had broken more staves upon the head,[171] and that once Clitophon had received such a blow that he had lost the reins of his horse, with his head well-nigh touching the crupper[172] of the horse. But Clitophon was so angry with the judgment, wherein he thought he had received wrong, that he omitted his duty to his prince and uncle, and suddenly went his way, still in the quest of them whom, as then he had left by seeking; and so yielded the field to the next comer, who, coming in about two hours after, was no less marked than all the rest before, because he had nothing worth the marking; for he had neither picture nor device, his armor of as old a fashion, besides the rusty poorness, that it might better seem a monument of his grandfather's courage. About his middle he had, instead of bases, a long cloak of silk, which as unhandsomely, as it needs must, became the wearer, so that all that looked on measured his length on the earth already, since he had to meet one who had been victorious of so many gallants. But he went on towards the shield, and with a sober grace struck it; but as he let his

170 ermion—ermine; the beast's pure white coat was an emblem for purity.

171 had broken more staves upon the head—had caused more lances to shatter against his shield.

172 crupper—strap along the back and running under the tail of the horse to keep the saddle from slipping forward.

sword fall upon it, another knight, all in black, came rustling in, who struck the shield almost as soon as he, and so strongly, that he broke the shield in two. The ill-appointed knight, for so the beholders called him, angry with that, as he accounted, insolent injury to himself, hit him such a sound blow that they that looked on said it well became a rude arm. The other answered him again in the same case, so that lances were put to silence, the swords were so busy.

But Phalantus, angry of this defacing his shield, came upon the black knight, and with the pommel of his sword set fire to his eyes, which presently was revenged, not only by the black, but the ill-apparelled knight, who disdained another should enter into his quarrel, so as whoever saw a matachin dance[173] to imitate fighting, this was a fight that did imitate the matachin; for they, being but three that fought, every one had adversaries striking him, who struck the third, and revenging, perhaps, that of him which he had received of the other. But Basilius, rising himself to part them (the sticklers' authority scarcely able to persuade choleric hearers), and part them he did.

But, before he could determine, comes in a fourth, halting on foot, who complained to Basilius, demanding justice on the black knight for having by force taken away the picture of Pamela from him, which in little form he wore in a tablet,[174] and, covered with silk, had fastened it to his helmet, purposing, for want of a bigger, to paragon the little one with Artesia's length, not doubting but in that little quantity the excellency of that would shine through the weakness of the other, as the smallest star doth through the whole element of fire. And, by the way, he had met with this black knight, who had, as he said, robbed him of it. The injury seemed grievous, but, when it came fully to be examined, it was found that the halting knight, meeting the other, asking the cause of his going thitherward, and finding it was to defend Pamela's divine beauty against Artesia's, with a proud jollitie[175] commanded him to leave that quarrel only for

[173] matachin dance—sword dance resembling a three-way duel.
[174] in little form . . . tablet—in miniature on a wood panel.
[175] jollitie—insolent presumption.

him, who was only worthy to enter into it. But the black knight obeying no such commandments, they fell to such a bickering that he got a halting and lost his picture. This understood by Basilius, he told him he was now fitter to look to his own body than another's picture; and so, uncomforted therein, sent him away to learn of Aesculapius[176] that he was not fit for Venus.

But then the question arising who should be the former against Phalantus of the black or the ill-apparelled knight (who now had gotten the reputation of some sturdy lout, he had so well defended himself), of the one side was alleged the having a picture which the other wanted, of the other side the first striking the shield; but the conclusion was that the ill-apparelled knight should have the precedence if he delivered the figure of his mistress to Phalantus, who, asking him for it, "Certainly," said he, "her liveliest picture, if you could see it, is in my heart, and the best comparison I could make of her is of the sun and of all other the heavenly beauties. But because, perhaps, all eyes cannot taste the divinity of her beauty, and would rather be dazzled than taught by the light (if it be not clouded by some meaner thing), know you then, that I defend that same lady whose image Phebilus so feebly lost yesternight, and, instead of another, if you overcome me, you shall have me your slave to carry that image in your mistress's triumph." Phalantus easily agreed to the bargain, which already he made his own.

But, when it came to the trial, the ill-apparelled knight, choosing out the greatest staves in all the store, at the first course gave his head such a remembrance that he lost almost his remembrance, he himself receiving the encounter of Phalantus without any extraordinary motion; and at the second, gave him such a counterbuff that, because Phalantus was so perfect a horseman as not to be driven from the saddle, the saddle with broken girts was driven from the horse, Phalantus remaining angry and amazed, because now, being come almost to the last of his promised enterprise, that disgrace befell him which he had never before known.

But the victory being by the judges given, and the trumpets

176 Aesculapius—the god of medicine.

witnessed, to the ill-apparalled knight, Phalantus' disgrace was ingrieved,[177] in lieu of comfort, by Artesia, who, telling him she never looked for other,[178] bade him seek some other mistress. He, excusing himself, and turning over the fault to fortune, "Then let that be your ill fortune too," said she, "that you have lost me."

"Nay, truly, madam," said Phalantus, "it shall not be so, for I think the loss of such a mistress will prove a great gain"; and so concluded—to the sport of Basilius, to see young folks' love that came in masked with so great pomp go out with so little constancy. But Phalantus, first professing great service to Basilius for his courteous intermitting his solitary course for his sake, would yet conduct Artesia to the castle of Cecropia, whither she desired to go, vowing in himself that neither heart nor mouth-love should ever any more entangle him; and with that resolution he left the company.

Whence all being dismissed—among whom the black knight went away repining at his luck, that had kept him from winning the honor, as he knew he should have done, to the picture of Pamela—the ill-apparelled knight (who was only desired to stay because Basilius meant to show him to Zelmane) pulled off his helmet, and then was known himself to be Zelmane, who that morning, as she told, while the others were busy, had stolen out to the prince's stable, which was a mile off from the lodge, had gotten a horse (they knowing it was Basilius' pleasure she should be obeyed), and, borrowing that homely armor for want of a better, had come upon the spur to redeem Philoclea's picture, which, she said, she could not bear (being one of that little wilderness-company) should be in captivity, if the cunning she had learned in her country of the noble Amazons could withstand it. And under that pretext, fain she would have given a secret passport to her affection, but this act painted at one instant redness in Philoclea's face and paleness in Gynecia's, but brought forth no other countenances but of admiration, no

177 ingrieved—aggravated.
178 she never looked for other—she never expected a different conclusion to the enterprise.

speeches but of commendations—all these few (besides Love)[179] thinking they honored themselves in honoring so accomplished a person as Zelmane, whom daily they sought with some or other sports to delight, for which purpose Basilius had in a house not far off servants who, though they came not uncalled, yet at call were ready.

CHAPTER 18

Musidorus disguised. His song. His love, the cause thereof. His course therein.

And so many days were spent and many ways used, while Zelmane was like one that stood in a tree waiting a good occasion to shoot, and Gynecia a blancher,[180] which kept the dearest deer from her. But the day being come which, according to an appointed course, the shepherds were to assemble and make their pastoral sports afore Basilius, Zelmane, fearing lest many eyes, and coming divers ways, might hap to spy Musidorus, went out to warn him thereof.

But, before she could come to the arbor, she saw, walking from her-ward,[181] a man in shepherdish apparel, who, being in the sight of the lodge, it might seem he was allowed there. A long cloak he had on, but that cast under his right arm, wherein he held a sheep-hook so finely wrought that it gave a bravery to poverty, and his raiments, though they were mean, yet received they handsomeness by the grace of the wearer, though he himself went but a kind of languishing pace, with his eyes somewhat cast up to heaven, as though his fancies strove to mount higher, sometimes thrown down to the ground, as if the earth could not bear the burdens of his sorrows. At length, with a lamentable tune, he sung these few verses:

[179] these few (besides Love)—all in this little "wilderness-company" (in addition, Love).
[180] blancher—hunter's assistant, assigned to divert or drive the quarry.
[181] from her-ward—away from her.

[OA4 reprinted here, see above p. 50]

And having ended, he struck himself on the breast, saying, "O miserable wretch, whither do thy destinies guide thee?" The voice made Zelmane hasten her pace to overtake him, which having done, she plainly perceived that it was her dear friend Musidorus; whereat marvelling not a little, she demanded of him whether the goddess of those woods had such a power to transform everybody; or whether, as in all enterprises else he had done, he meant thus to match her to this new alteration. "Alas!" said Musidorus, "what shall I say, who am loth to say, and yet fain would have said? I find, indeed, that all is but lip wisdom which wants experience. I now (woe is me!) do try what love can do. O Zelmane, who will resist it must either have no wit, or put out his eyes. Can any man resist his creation? Certainly by love we are made, and to love we are made. Beasts only cannot discern beauty; and let them be in the roll of beasts that do not honor it."

The perfect friendship Zelmane bare him, and the great pity she, by good trial, had of such cases, could not keep her from smiling at him, remembering how vehemently he had cried out against the folly of lovers. And therefore, a little to punish him, "Why, how now, dear cousin," said she, "you that were last day so high in pulpit against lovers, are you now become so mean an auditor? Remember that love is a passion, and that a worthy man's reason must ever have the masterhood."

"I recant, I recant," cried Musidorus, and withal falling down prostrate. "O thou celestial, or infernal, spirit of love, or what other heavenly or hellish title thou list to have (for effects of both I find in myself), have compassion of me, and let thy glory be as great in pardoning them that be submitted to thee as in conquering those that were rebellious."

"No, no," said Zelmane, "I see you well enough; you make but an interlude[182] of my mishaps, and do but counterfeit thus, to make me see the deformity of my passions; but take heed that this jest do not one day turn to earnest."

[182] interlude—diverting comedy.

"Now I beseech thee," said Musidorus, taking her fast by the hand, "even for the truth of our friendship, of which, if I be not altogether an unhappy man, thou hast some remembrance, and by those sacred flames which, I know, have likewise nearly touched thee, make no jest of that which hath so earnestly pierced me through, nor let that be light to thee which is to me so burdenous that I am not able to bear it." Musidorus, both in words and behavior, did so lively deliver out his inward grief that Zelmane found, indeed, he was thoroughly wounded; but there rose a new jealousy in her mind, lest it might be with Philoclea, by whom, as Zelmane thought, in right all hearts and eyes should be inherited. And therefore, desirous to be cleared of that doubt, Musidorus shortly, as in haste and full of passionate perplexedness, thus recounted his case unto her.

"The day," said he, "I parted from you, I being in mind to return to a town from whence I came hither, my horse (being before tired) would scarce bear me a mile hence, where, being benighted, the light of a candle I saw a good way off guided me to a young shepherd's house, by name Menalcas,[183] who, seeing me to be a straying stranger, with the right honest hospitality which seems to be harbored in the Arcadian breasts, and though not with curious costliness, yet with cleanly sufficiency, entertained me; and having, by talk with him, found the manner of the country something more in particular than I had by Kalander's report, I agreed to sojourn with him in secret, which he faithfully promised to observe; and so hither to your arbor divers times repaired, and here by your means had the sight—O that it had never been so; nay, O that it might ever be so—of a goddess who, in a definite compass,[184] can set forth infinite beauty."

All this while Zelmane was racked with jealousy. But he went on: "For," said he, "I lying close and, in truth, thinking of you and saying thus to myself, 'O sweet Pyrocles, how art thou bewitched? Where is thy virtue? Where is the use of thy reason? How much am I inferior to thee in the state of the mind?

---

[183] Menalcas—cf. *O.A.*, ft. 72.
[184] definite compass—limited space.

And yet know I that all the heavens cannot bring me to such thralldom.' Scarcely, think I, had I spoken this word when the ladies came forth, at which sight, I think, the very words returned back again to strike my soul; at least, an unmeasurable sting I felt in myself that I had spoken such words."

"At which sight?" said Zelmane, not able to bear him any longer.

"O," said Musidorus, "I know your suspicion. No, no, banish all such fear; it was, it is, and must be Pamela."

"Then all is safe," said Zelmane. "Proceed, dear Musidorus."

"I will not," said he, "impute it to my late solitary life (which yet is prone to affections), nor to the much thinking of you (though that called the consideration of love into my mind, which before I ever neglected), nor to the exaltation[185] of Venus, nor revenge of Cupid—but even to her who is the planet, nay, the goddess, against which the only shield must be my sepulcher.

"When I first saw her, I was presently stricken; and I (like a foolish child that, when anything hits him, will strike himself again upon it) would needs look again, as though I would persuade mine eyes that they were deceived. But, alas! well have I found that Love to a yielding heart is a king, but to a resisting, is a tyrant. The more with arguments I shaked the stake which he had planted in the ground of my heart, the deeper still it sank into it. But what mean I to speak of the causes of my love, which is an impossible to describe as to measure the backside of heaven? Let this word suffice: I love.

"And that you may know I do so, it was I that came in black armor to defend her picture, where I was both prevented and beaten by you. And so I that waited here to do you service have now myself most need of succor."

"But whereupon got you yourself this apparel?" said Zelmane.

"I had forgotten to tell you," said Musidorus, "though that were one principal matter of my speech—so much am I now master of my own mind. But thus it happened: being returned

[185] exaltation—the time when a planet exerts its greatest influence.

to Menalcas' house, full of tormenting desire, after a while
fainting under the weight, my courage stirred up my wit to
seek for some relief before I yielded to perish. At last this came
into my head, that very evening that I had to no purpose last
used my horse and armor. I told Menalcas that I was a Thes-
salian gentleman, who, by mischance having killed a great favorite
of the prince of that country, was pursued so cruelly that in
no place but, either by favor or corruption, they would obtain
my destruction; and that therefore I was determined, till the fury
of my persecutions might be assuaged, to disguise myself among
the shepherds of Arcadia, and, if it were possible, to be one of
them that were allowed the prince's presence; because, if the
worst should fall that I were discovered, yet, having gotten the
acquaintance of the prince, it might happen to move his heart
to protect me.

"Menalcas, being of an honest disposition, pitied my case,
which my face, through my inward torment, made credible; and
so, I giving him largely for it, let me have this raiment, instructing me in all the particularities touching himself, or myself,
which I desired to know; yet not trusting so much to his constancy as that I would lay my life, and life of my life, upon
it, I hired him to go into Thessalia to a friend of mine, and to
deliver him a letter from me, conjuring him to bring me as speedy
an answer as he could, because it imported me greatly to know
whether certain of my friends did yet possess any favor, whose
intercessions I might use for my restitution. He willingly took
my letter, which, being well sealed, indeed contained other
matter. For I wrote to my trusty servant Calodoulus[186] whom
you know, that as soon as he had delivered the letter, he should
keep him prisoner in his house, not suffering him to have conference with anybody till he knew my further pleasure—in all
other respects that he should use him as my brother. And thus
is Menalcas gone, and I here a poor shepherd, more proud of this
estate than of any kingdom; so manifest it is that the highest
point outward things can bring one unto is the contentment of
the mind, with which no estate—without which, all estates—be

[186] Calodoulus—"trusty servant"

miserable. Now have I chosen this day, because, as Menalcas told me, the other shepherds are called to make their sports, and hope that you will, with your credit, find means to get me allowed among them."

"You need not doubt," answered Zelmane, "but that I will be your good mistress; marry, the best way of dealing must be by Dametas, who, since his blunt brain hath perceived some favor the prince doth bear unto me—as without doubt the most servile flattery is lodged most easily in the grossest capacity, for their ordinary conceit draweth a yielding to their greaters, and then have they not wit to learn the right degrees of duty—is much more serviceable unto me than I can find any cause to wish him. And therefore despair not to win him, for every present occasion will catch his senses, and his senses are masters of his silly mind. Only reverence him and reward him, and with that bridle and saddle you shall well ride him."

"O heaven and earth," said Musidorus, "to what a pass are our minds brought that, from the right line of virtue, are wried[187] to these crooked shifts? But, O Love, it is thou that dost it. Thou changest name upon name; thou disguisest our bodies and disfigurest our minds. But indeed thou hast reason, for though the ways be foul, the journey's end is most fair and honorable."

CHAPTER 19

The means of Musidorus' apprenticeage unto Dametas. The preparation and place of the pastorals. The lion's assault on Philoclea, and death by Zelmane. The she-bear's on Pamela, and death by Dorus.[188] The Io pæan[189] of Dametas, and his scape from the bear. The victors' praises. Whence those beasts were sent.

"No more, sweet Musidorus," said Zelmane, "of these philosophies, for here comes the very person of Dametas." And

187 wried—deflected.
188 Dorus—cf. *O.A.*, ft. 79.
189 Io pæan—hymn of thanksgiving for deliverance.

so he did indeed, with a sword by his side, a forest-bill[190] on
his neck, and a chopping knife under his girdle, in which provided
sort he had ever gone since the fear Zelmane had put him in. But
he no sooner saw her, but with head and arms he laid his reverence afore her, enough to have made any man forswear all
courtesy. And then in Basilius' name he did invite her to walk
down to the place where that day they were to have the pastorals.

But when he spied Musidorus to be none of the shepherds
allowed in that place, he would fain have persuaded himself to
utter some anger, but that he durst not; yet, muttering and
champing, as though his cud troubled him, he gave occasion to
Musidorus to come near him, and feign this tale of his own life:
that he was a younger brother of the shepherd Menalcas, by
name Dorus, sent by his father in his tender age to Athens, there
to learn some cunning more than ordinary, that he might be the
better liked of the prince, and that, after his father's death, his
brother Menalcas, lately gone thither to fetch him home, was
also deceased, where, upon his death, he had charged him to seek
the service of Dametas, and to be wholly and ever guided by him,
as one in whose judgment and integrity the prince had singular
confidence. For token whereof, he gave to Dametas a good sum
of gold in ready coin, which Menalcas had bequeathed unto
him, upon condition he should receive this poor Dorus into his
service, that his mind and manner might grow the better by his
daily example.

Dametas, that of all manners of style could best conceive of
golden eloquence, being withal tickled by Musidorus' praises, had
his brain so turned that he became slave to that which he, that
showed to be his servant, offered to give him; yet, for countenance' sake, he seemed very squeamish, in respect of the charge
he had of the Princess Pamela. But such was the secret operation
of the gold, helped with the persuasion of the Amazon Zelmane
(who said it was pity so handsome a young man should be anywhere else than with so good a master), that in the end he
agreed, if that day he behaved himself so to the liking of Basilius

190 forest-bill—a long-handled knife for chopping branches off of trees.

as he might be contented, that then he would receive him into his service.

And thus went they to the lodge, where they found Gynecia and her daughters ready to go to the field, to delight themselves there a while until the shepherds' coming; whither also taking Zelmane with them, as they went Dametas told them of Dorus, and desired he might be accepted there that day instead of his brother Menalcas. As for Basilius, he stayed behind to bring the shepherds, with whom he meant to confer, to breed the better Zelmane's liking, which he only regarded, while the other beautiful band came to the fair field appointed for the shepherdish pastimes.

It was indeed a place of delight, for through the midst of it there ran a sweet brook, which did both hold the eye open with her azure streams, and yet seek to close the eye with the purling noise it made upon the pebble stones it ran over, the field itself being set in some places with roses, and in all the rest constantly preserving a flourishing green; the roses added such a ruddy show unto it as though the field were bashful at his own beauty. About it, as if it had been to enclose a theater, grew such a sort of trees as either excellency of fruit, stateliness of growth, continual greenness, or poetical fancies have made at any time famous; in most part of which there had been framed by art such pleasant arbors that, one tree to tree answering another, they became a gallery aloft from almost round about,[191] which below gave a perfect shadow—a pleasant refuge then from the choleric look of Phoebus.

In this place, while Gynecia walked hard by them, carrying many unquiet contentions about her, the ladies sat them down, inquiring many questions of the shepherd Dorus, who, keeping his eye still upon Pamela, answered with such a trembling voice and abashed countenance, and oftentimes so far from the matter, that it was some sport to the young ladies, thinking it want of education which made him so discountenanced with unwonted presence. But Zelmane, that saw in him the glass of

---

[191] aloft from almost round about—making a roof almost all the way around.

her own misery, taking the hand of Philoclea, and with burning kisses setting it close to her lips, as if it should stand there like a hand in the margin of a book to note some saying worthy to be marked, began to speak these words: "O Love, since thou art so changeable in men's estates, how art thou so constant in their torments?" when suddenly there came out of a wood a monstrous lion, with a she-bear not far from him, of little less fierceness, which (as they guessed) having been hunted in forests far off, were by chance come thither, where before such beasts had never been seen.

Then care, not fear, or fear not for themselves, altered something the countenances of the two lovers; but so, as any man might perceive, was rather an assembling of powers than dismayedness of courage. Philoclea no sooner espied the lion but that, obeying the commandment of fear, she leapt up and ran to the lodge-ward as fast as her delicate legs could carry her, while Dorus drew Pamela behind a tree, where she stood quaking like the partridge on which the hawk is even ready to seize. But the lion, seeing Philoclea run away, bent his race to her-ward, and was ready to seize himself on the prey, when Zelmane, to whom danger then was a cause of dreadlessness (all the composition of her elements being nothing but fiery), with swiftness of desire crossed him, and with force of affection struck him such a blow upon his chine[192] that she opened all his body, wherewith the valiant beast turning upon her with open jaws, she gave him such a thrust through his breast that all the lion could do was with his paw to tear off the mantle and sleeve of Zelmane, with a little scratch, rather than a wound, his death-blow having taken away the effect of his force; but therewithal he fell down, and gave Zelmane leisure to take off his head, to carry it for a present to her lady Philoclea, who all this while, not knowing what was done behind her, kept on her course, like Arethusa when she ran from Alpheus;[193] her light apparel being carried up with the wind, that much of those beauties she would at another time have willingly hidden was present to the sight

192 chine—spine.
193 Arethusa when she ran from Alpheus—cf. *O.A.*, ft. 82.

of the twice wounded Zelmane. Which made Zelmane not follow her over-hastily, lest she should too soon deprive herself of that pleasure; but carrying the lion's head in her hand, did not fully overtake her till they came to the presence of Basilius.

Neither were they long there but that Gynecia came thither also, who had been in such a trance of musing that Zelmane was fighting with the lion before she knew of any lion's coming; but then affection resisting, and the soon ending of the fight preventing all extremity of fear, she marked Zelmane's fighting, and when the lion's head was off, as Zelmane ran after Philoclea, so she could not find in her heart but run after Zelmane; so that it was a new sight fortune had prepared to those woods, to see these great personages thus run one after the other, each carried forward with an inward violence: Philoclea with such fear, that she thought she was still in the lion's mouth; Zelmane with an eager and impatient delight; Gynecia with wings of love, flying they neither knew, nor cared to know, whither. But now being all come before Basilius, amazed with this sight, and fear having such possession in the fair Philoclea that her blood durst not yet to come to her face to take away the name of paleness from her most pure whiteness, Zelmane kneeled down and presented the lion's head unto her.

"Only lady," said she, "here see you the punishment of that unnatural beast, which, contrary to her own kind, would have wronged prince's blood, guided with such traitorous eyes as durst rebel against your beauty."

"Happy am I, and my beauty both," answered the sweet Philoclea, then blushing—for fear had bequeathed his room to his kinsman bashfulness—"that you, excellent Amazon, were there to teach him good manners."

"And even thanks to that beauty," answered Zelmane, "which can give an edge to the bluntest swords."

There Philoclea told her father how it had happened, but as she had turned her eyes in her tale to Zelmane, she perceived some blood upon Zelmane's shoulder, so that starting with the lovely grace of pity, she showed it to her father and mother, who as the nurse sometimes with over-much kissing may forget to give the babe suck, so had they, with too much delighting in beholding and praising Zelmane, left off to mark whether she needed succor. But then they ran both unto her, like a father and mother to an only child, and (though Zelmane assured them it was nothing) would needs see it, Gynecia having skill in surgery, an art in those days much esteemed because it served to virtuous courage, which even ladies would (even with the contempt of courage) seem to cherish. But, looking upon it (which gave more inward bleeding wounds to Zelmane, for she might sometimes feel Philoclea's touch, whiles she helped her mother), she found it was indeed of no great importance; yet, applied she a precious balm unto it, of power to heal a greater grief.

But even then, and not before, they remembered Pamela, and, therefore, Zelmane, thinking of her friend Dorus, was running back to be satisfied, when they might all see Pamela coming between Dorus and Dametas, having in her hand the paw of a bear, which the shepherd Dorus had newly presented unto her, desiring her to accept it, as of such a beast, which, though she deserved death for her presumption, yet was her will to be esteemed, since she could make so sweet a choice. Dametas for his part came piping and dancing, the merriest man in a parish; but when he came so near as he might be heard of Basilius, he would needs break through his ears with this joyful song of their good success:

[*OA5 followed here, see above p. 62*]

Being all now come together, and all desirous to know each other's adventures, Pamela's noble heart would needs gratefully make known the valiant mean of her safety, which, directing her speech to her mother, she did in this manner.

"As soon," said she, "as ye were all run away (and that I hoped to be in safety), there came out of the same woods a foul horrible bear, which, fearing, belike, to deal while the lion was present, as soon as he was gone, came furiously towards the place where I was, and this young shepherd left alone by me. I, truly not guilty of any wisdom (which since they lay to my charge because they say it is the best refuge against that beast, but even pure fear bringing forth that effect of wisdom), fell down flat of my face, needing not counterfeit being dead, for, indeed, I was little better. But this shepherd, having no other weapon but that knife you see, standing before the place where I lay, so behaved himself that the first sight I had, when I thought myself nearer Charon's ferry, was the shepherd showing me his bloody knife in token of victory."

"I pray you," said Zelmane, speaking to Dorus, whose valor she was careful to have manifested, "in what sort, so ill-weaponed, could you achieve this enterprise?"

"Noble lady," said Dorus, "the manner of these beasts' fighting with any man is to stand up upon their hinder feet; and so this did; and being ready to give me a shrewd embracement, I think the god Pan (ever careful of the chief blessings of Arcadia) guided my hand so just to the heart of the beast that neither she could once touch me, nor (which is the only matter in this worthy remembrance) breed any danger to the princess. For my part, I am rather, with all subjected humbleness, to thank her excellencies, since the duty thereunto gave me heart to save myself, than to receive thanks for a deed which was her only inspiring."

And this Dorus spoke, keeping affection as much as he could back from coming into his eyes and gestures. But Zelmane, that had the same character in her heart, could easily discern it, and, therefore, to keep him the longer in speech, desired to understand the conclusion of the matter, and how the honest Dametas was escaped.

"Nay," said Pamela, "none shall take that office from myself, being so much bound to him as I am for my education." And with that word, scorn borrowing the countenance of mirth, somewhat she smiled, and thus spake on: "When," said she, "Dorus made me assuredly perceive that all cause of fear was passed, the truth is, I was ashamed to find myself alone with this shepherd; and therefore, looking about me if I could see anybody, at length we both perceived the gentle Dametas, lying with his breast and head as far as he could thrust himself into a bush, drawing up his legs as close unto him as he could; for, like a man of a very kind nature, soon to take pity of himself, he was fully resolved not to see his own death. And when this shepherd pushed him, bidding him to be good cheer, it was a good while ere we could persuade him that Dorus was not the bear, so that he was fain to pull him out by the heels and show him the beast as dead as he could wish it, which, you may believe me, was a very joyful sight unto him. But then he forgot all courtesy, for he fell upon the beast, giving it many a manful wound, swearing by much it was not well such beasts should be suffered in a commonwealth; and then my governor, as full of joy as before of fear, came dancing and singing before us, as even now you saw him!"

"Well, well," said Basilius, "I have not chosen Dametas for his fighting, nor for his discoursing, but for his plainness and honesty; and therein I know he will not deceive me." But then he told Pamela (not so much because she should know it as because he would tell it) the wonderful act Zelmane had performed, which Gynecia likewise spoke of, both in such extremity of praising as was easy to be seen the constructions of their speech might best be made by the grammar rules of affection. Basilius told with what a gallant grace she ran with the lion's head in her hand, like another Pallas with the spoils of Gorgon;[194] Gynecia swore she saw the face of the young Hercules killing the Nemean lion;[195] and all with a grateful assent confirmed the same praises. Only poor Dorus, though of equal desert, yet not proceeding of equal estate, should have been left forgotten had not Zelmane again, with great admiration, begun to speak of him, asking whether it were the fashion or no in Arcadia that shepherds should perform such valorous enterprises.

This Basilius, having the quick sense of a lover, took as though his mistress had given a secret reprehension that he had not showed more gratefulness to Dorus, and therefore, as nimbly

[194] Pallas with the spoils of Gorgon—cf. *O.A.*, ft. 85.
[195] Hercules killing the Nemean lion—cf. *O.A.*, ft. 86.

as he could, inquired of his estate, adding promise of great rewards, among the rest offering to him, if he would exercise his courage in soldiery, he would commit some charge unto him under his lieutenant Philanax. But Dorus, whose ambition climbed by another stair, having first answered touching his estate, that he was brother to the shepherd Menalcas, who, among other, was wont to resort to the prince's presence, and excused his going to soldiery by the unaptness he found in himself that way, he told Basilius that his brother in his last testament had willed him to serve Dametas, and therefore (for due obedience thereunto) he would think his service greatly rewarded if he might obtain by that mean to live in the sight of his prince, and yet practice his own chosen vocation. Basilius, liking well his goodly shape and handsome manner, charged Dametas to receive him like a son into his house, saying that his valor and Dametas' truth would be good bulwarks against such mischiefs as, he sticked not to say, were threatened to his daughter Pamela.

Dametas, no whit out of countenance with all that had been said (because he had no worse to fall into than his own), accepted Dorus, and withal telling Basilius that some of the shepherds were come, demanded in what place he would see their sports; who first curious to know whether it were not more requisite for Zelmane's hurt to rest than sit up at those pastimes, and she (that felt no wound but one) earnestly desiring to have pastorals, Basilius commanded it should be at the gate of the lodge, where the throne of the prince being (according to the ancient manner), he made Zelmane sit between him and his wife therein, who thought herself between drowning and burning, and the two young ladies of either side the throne, and so prepared their eyes and ears to be delighted by the shepherds.

But before all of them were assembled to begin their sports, there came a fellow who, being out of breath, or seeming so to be, for haste, with humble hastiness told Basilius that his mistress, the lady Cecropia, had sent him to excuse the mischance of her beasts ranging in that dangerous sort, being happened by the folly of the keeper, who, thinking himself able to rule them, had carried them abroad, and so was deceived; whom, yet, if Basilius would punish for it, she was ready to deliver. Basilius made no other answer but that his mistress, if she had any more such beasts, should cause them to be killed; and then he told his wife and Zelmane of it, because they should not fear those woods, as though they harbored such beasts where the like had never been seen.

But Gynecia took a further conceit of it, mistrusting Cecropia because she had heard much of the devilish wickedness of her heart and that particularly she did her best to bring up her son Amphialus (being brother's son to Basilius) to aspire to the crown as next heir male after Basilius, and, therefore, saw no reason, but that she might conjecture it proceeded rather of some mischievous practice than of misfortune. Yet did she only utter her doubt to her daughters, thinking, since the worst was past, she would attend a further occasion, lest overmuch haste might seem to proceed of the ordinary mislike between sisters-in-law. Only they marveled that Basilius looked no further into it, who (good man) thought so much of his late conceived commonwealth that all other matters were but digressions unto him. But the shepherds were ready and, with well handling themselves, called their senses to attend their pastimes.

Book II

CHAPTER I

[After the pastorals, Gynecia, stricken with remorse because of her love for Zelmane, leaves the lodge and wanders into a nearby desert. There she laments her loss of virtue, rehearses her misery, and vows that, since there is no comfort in shame, she will abjure all pity and keep her daughter, Philoclea, from possessing Zelmane, even if she has to kill the girl to do this. As she roams about, Gynecia hears a voice singing a love complaint so mournful that she is drawn toward the sound in her desire to discover the identity of the unhappy singer, who proves to be none other than Zelmane, lamenting her own sad fortunes. At this point, Gynecia, distraught, declares her passion and reveals that she knows the Amazon is a man. Before Zelmane is forced to reply, Basilius passes, absorbed in his own love plaint. When he sees his wife and mistress, he sends Gynecia home, then avows his devotion to Zelmane. She, however, receives the declaration with shows of scorn and leaves, astonished at the intricate difficulties her love and her disguise have involved her in.]

CHAPTER 2

[Zelmane, tired of solitude, seeks the company of Dorus, whom she finds being instructed in the art of shepherding by Dametas. In private, she tells Dorus of her passion and her despair, then invites him to confide his state of mind to her. Dorus describes how, having taken on the guise of a shepherd to pursue his love for Pamela, he had been relegated to the position of an overly forward servant. However, by concealing his love for Pamela beneath the fiction of a passion for Mopsa, Dametas' daughter, he was again permitted to frequent Pamela's company and to discuss amorous matters with her. Of course, Pamela soon realized Dorus' ruse, but she did not discourage it, having found the shepherd witty and attractive. At the end of the chapter, Dorus begins to relate to Zelmane a story he told Pamela in order to prove himself worthy of Mopsa's hand.]

CHAPTER 3

[The story Dorus tells Pamela is the story of his own life: his education, his friendship with Pyrocles, his disaster at sea, his arrival in Arcadia, and his love for the Princess Pamela; but he narrates this account as though it were the tale of another man's fortunes. Afterward, he begs Pamela to plead with Mopsa on his behalf, which she agrees to do; but her modest graciousness, her refusal either to acknowledge Dorus' revelations or reject them, leaves the shepherd helpless. He tells Zelmane that this serene graciousness, Pamela's chief characteristic, brings him close to despair, for, while he would know how to respond to hate or love, he is nonplused by the cold calm of her nobility.]

CHAPTER 4

[Dorus is about to continue his tale, when Dametas comes to inform Zelmane that the king waits upon her at the lodge. Basilius and Gynecia, accompanied by Philoclea and their Amazon guest, drive out for an afternoon ride and a show of falconry which has been prepared for Zelmane's pleasure. On the return trip, Dametas, absorbed in thoughts of a broken vine-press, overturns the carriage, and Gynecia suffers a wrenched shoulder. Once confined to bed, the queen is tortured by jealous fear and, to keep Philoclea away from Zelmane, sends the maiden to spend the night at the lodge of her sister Pamela. While walking through the woods to the other lodge, Philoclea meditates on her love for Zelmane, tormented by its inexplicable ardor and apparent impossibility.]

CHAPTER 5

[Philoclea arrives to find her sister red-eyed from weeping. Pamela finally admits that she is desperately in love with the seemingly unsuitable shepherd, Dorus.]

CHAPTER 6

[When the sisters awake the next morning, Pamela, uneasy because she has treated Dorus with coldness, sends for the shepherd to offer him some encouragement and urge him to continue his tales. Dorus narrates the story of King Evarchus ("good ruler") of Macedon, the father of Pyrocles: how he reformed his country and won the love of his people, and how he married his sister to Dorilaus, a union which resulted in the birth of Musidorus. At the child's birth, soothsayers predicted that Musidorus would perform strange and even godlike deeds. These predictions caused the king of Phrygia, allied with the

king of Lydia, to invade Crete with the intention of killing
Musidorus. However, they were soon defeated by Evarchus, who
rushed to support Dorilaus and, after the war, married Dorilaus'
sister. From this union came a son, Pyrocles, at whose birth there
were signs in the heavens and on earth, portending a heroical
virtue. When Evarchus returned to his own country, he found
the king of Thrace and his brother in rebellion. In the succeed-
ing war, Dorilaus was killed fighting in defense of his friend.]

CHAPTER 7

[Dorus continues his narration, relating the story of Pyrocles'
and Musidorus' upbringing under the care of Evarchus' sister,
their princely education, and the excellence of their youthful
deeds; finally, he describes their shipwreck during a trip intended
to take them to join Evarchus, who was then besieging Byzantium.]

CHAPTER 8

[The story continues. Pyrocles and Musidorus, having been
saved from drowning by their servants Leucippus and Nelsus,
were separated at sea. Pyrocles was washed up on the shore of
Phrygia, seized, and taken to the king, who, morbidly convinced
that things always turn out as badly as possible, sentenced him
to death. Meanwhile, Musidorus, washed from the sea and
succored by a fisherman from Pontus, heard of his cousin's
plight and offered his own life to save Pyrocles'. The king of
Phrygia, more interested in the death of Musidorus, whose birth
had been attended by prophecies which seemed to endanger the
king's regime, agreed to the exchange. But Pyrocles, hiring himself out as the executioner's servant, succeeded in arming his
friend on the scaffold, where they fought side by side in search
of an honorable death. However, a quarrel among the king's
soldiers precipitated a rebellion of the citizens, culminating in
the tyrant's overthrow and Musidorus' election to the throne.

Musidorus then relinquished the kingship to an elderly prince of
the blood.]

CHAPTER 9

[Although Musidorus and Pyrocles believed their servants,
Leucippus and Nelsus, to have drowned at sea, the pair had
actually succeeded in swimming to Pontus, where they were
first accepted by the king, but, with the news that their masters
had helped overthrow the king of Phrygia, they were executed.
To gain revenge, Musidorus and Pyrocles raised an army in
Phrygia, conquered Pontus, and slew the false king on the tomb
of their servants. While in Pontus, the heroes performed various
wonderful adventures, including the destruction of two giants
who had been ravaging the countryside.]

CHAPTER 10

[Dorus relates another adventure: while journeying through
Galacia in the middle of winter, Musidorus and Pyrocles, who
had just left Pontus, encountered a ragged, blind, old man being
guided by his son. The youth was Leonatus, and his father was
the prince of Paphlagonia,[1] who, blindly devoted to a bastard
son, Plexirtus ("striking a blow"), had attempted to murder his
legitimate heir, Leonatus, only to lose both his kingdom and
his eyes at the command of Plexirtus. When, soon after the
old man related his sin, his bastard son arrived to kill Leonatus,
Pyrocles and Musidorus repulsed his soldiers and then, aided by
troops from Pontus and Phrygia, drove Plexirtus from his last
stronghold. Soon after Leonatus was crowned and his father died,
the usurper was forced to surrender and reconcile himself with
Leonatus. Peace of a kind having been restored to Galacia,
Pyrocles and Musidorus departed in search of other adventures,
including the defense of Queen Erona of Lycia against the armies

[1] Paphlagonia—this story is often cited as the source of the Gloucester
plot in *King Lear*.

of the Armenian king. There they met Prince Plangus ("lamentation"), an acquaintance of Pamela.]

CHAPTER I I

Dorus' suit to Pamela interrupted by Mopsa's waking. The sisters' going with Zelmane to wash themselves. The pleasantness of the river. The pleasure Zelmane had in seeing them, uttered in speech and song. She led by a spaniel to know and hurt her noble rival. The parting of that fray.

"I have heard," said Pamela, "that part of the story of Plangus when he passed through this country; therefore, you may, if you list, pass over that war of Erona's quarrel, lest, if you speak too much of war matters, you should wake Mopsa, which might happily² breed a great broil."

He looked and saw that Mopsa indeed sat swallowing of sleep with open mouth, making such a noise withal as nobody could lay the stealing of a nap to her charge. Whereupon, willing to use that occasion, he kneeled down, and, with humble-heartedness and hearty earnestness printed in his graces. "Alas!" said he, "divine lady, who have wrought such miracles in me as to make a prince—none of the basest—to think all principalities base, in respect of the sheephook which may hold him up in your sight, vouchsafe now, at last, to hear in direct words my humble suit, while this dragon sleeps that keeps the golden fruit.³ If in my desire I wish, or in my hopes aspire, or in my imagination feign to myself, anything which may be the least spot to that heavenly virtue which shines in all your doings, I pray the eternal powers that the words I speak may be deadly poisons while they are in my mouth, and that all my hopes, all my desires, all my imaginations may only work their own confusion. But if love, love of you, love of your virtues, only that favor of you which be-

² happily—perhaps.
³ this dragon sleeps that keeps the golden fruit—the many-headed mythological dragon called Ladon, which guarded the golden apples of the Hesperides and never slept until Hercules slew him to steal the fruit.

cometh that gratefulness which cannot misbecome your excellency, O do not———"

He would have said further, but Pamela calling aloud, "Mopsa!", she suddenly started up, staggering and rubbing her eyes, ran first out of the door, and then back to them, before she knew how she went out or why she came in again; till at length, being fully come to her little self, she asked Pamela why she had called her.

"For nothing," said Pamela, "but that ye might hear some tales of your servant's telling; and therefore, now," said she, "Dorus, go on."

But as he (who found no so good sacrifice as obedience) was returning to the story of himself, Philoclea came in, and by-and-by after her, Miso; so as, for that time, they were fain to let Dorus depart. But Pamela, delighted even to preserve in her memory the words of so well a beloved speaker, repeated the whole substance to her sister, till, their sober dinner being come and gone, to recreate themselves something (even tired with the noisomeness of Miso's conversation) they determined to go, while the heat of the day lasted, to bathe themselves (such being the manner of the Arcadian nymphs often to do) in the river of Ladon[4] and take with them a lute, meaning to delight them under some shadow. But they could not stir, but that Miso with her daughter Mopsa was after them. And as it lay in their way to pass by the other lodge, Zelmane out of her window espied them and so stole down after them, which she might the better do because that Gynecia was sick and Basilius, that day being his birthday, according to his manner, was busy about his devotions; and therefore, she went after, hoping to find some time to speak with Philoclea. But not a word could she begin, but that Miso would be one of the audience, so that she was driven to recommend thinking, speaking, and all, to her eyes, who diligently performed her trust, till they came to the river's side, which

[4] Ladon—the name of the above dragon; also the stream by which Syrinx, in flight from Pan, metamorphosed into a reed.

of all the rivers of Greece had the price[5] for excellent pureness and sweetness, insomuch as the very bathing in it was accounted exceeding healthful. It ran upon so fine and delicate a ground as one could not easily judge whether the river not running forth-right, but almost continually winding, as if the lower streams would return to their spring, or that the river had a delight to play with itself, the banks of either side seeming arms of the loving earth that fain would embrace it, and the river a wanton nymph which still would stir from it, either side of the bank being fringed with most beautiful trees, which resisted the sun's darts from over-much piercing the natural coldness of the river. There was the. . . .[6] But among the rest a goodly cypress who, bowing her fair head over the water, it seemed she looked into it and dressed her green locks by that running river. There the princesses determining to bathe themselves, though it was so privileged a place, upon pain of death, as nobody durst presume to come thither, yet for the more surety, they looked round about and could see nothing but a water spaniel, who came down the river, showing that he hunted for a duck, and with a snuffling grace disdaining that his smelling force could not as well prevail through the water as through the air (and therefore waiting with his eye to see whether he could espy the ducks getting up again) but then a little below them failing of his purpose, he got out of the river and, shaking off the water (as great men do their friends) now he had no further cause to use it, inweeded himself so as the ladies lost the further marking his sportfulness, and, inviting Zelmane also to wash herself with them, and she excusing herself with having taken a late cold, they began by piece-meal to take away the eclipsing of their apparel.

Zelmane would have put to her helping hand, but she was taken with such a quivering that she thought it more wisdom to lean herself to a tree and look on while Miso and Mopsa, like a couple of foreswat melters,[7] were getting the pure silver of their bodies out of the ore of their garments. But as the rai-

[5] had the price—was judged best.
[6] There was the—this hiatus is in the 1590 text.
[7] foreswat melters—sweaty furnace-men.

ments went off to receive kisses of the ground, Zelmane envied
the happiness of all, but of the smock was even jealous; and
when that was taken away too, and that Philoclea remained (for
her Zelmane only marked) like a diamond taken from out the
rock, or rather like the sun getting from under a cloud and
showing his naked beams to the full view, then was the beauty
too much for a patient sight, the delight too strong for a staid
conceit; so that Zelmane could not choose but run, to touch,
embrace, and kiss her. But conscience made her come to herself
and leave Philoclea, who blushing, and withal smiling, making
shamefastness pleasant, and pleasure shamefast, tenderly moved
her feet, unwonted to feel the naked ground, till the touch of
the cold water made a pretty kind of shrugging come over her
body, like the twinkling of the fairest among the fixed stars.
But the river itself gave way unto her, so that she was straight
breast high, which was the deepest that thereabout she could be;
and when cold Ladon had once fully embraced them, himself
was no more so cold to those ladies, but, as if his cold complexion
had been heated with love, so seemed he to play about every part
he could touch.

"Ah sweet, now sweetest Ladon," said Zelmane, "why dost
thou not stay thy course to have more full taste of thy happiness? But the reason is manifest: the upper streams make such
haste to have their part of embracing that the nether, though
loathly, must needs give place unto them. O happy Ladon, within
whom she is, upon whom her beauty falls, through whom her
eye pierceth. O happy Ladon, which art now an unperfect mirror of all perfection, canst thou ever forget the blessedness of
this impression? If thou do, then let thy bed be turned from fine
gravel to weeds and mud; if thou do, let some unjust niggards
make weirs[8] to spoil thy beauty; if thou do, let some greater
river fall into thee to take away the name of Ladon. O Ladon,
happy Ladon, rather slide than run by her, lest thou shouldest
make her legs slip from her; and then, O happy Ladon, who
would then call thee, but the most cursed Ladon?" But as the
ladies played them in the water, sometimes striking it with their

[8] weirs—dams.

hands, the water, making lines in his face, seemed to smile at such beating and, with twenty bubbles, not to be content to have the picture of their face in large upon him, but he would in each of those bubbles set forth the miniature of them.

But Zelmane, whose sight was gainsaid by nothing but the transparent veil of Ladon, like a chamber where a great fire is kept (though the fire be at one stay, yet with the continuance continually hath his heat increased) had the coals of her affection so kindled with wonder, and blown with delight, that now all her parts grudged that her eyes should do more homage than they to the princess of them. Insomuch that, taking up the lute, her wit began to be with a divine fury inspired; her voice would in so beloved an occasion second her wit; her hands accorded the lute's music to the voice; her panting heart danced to the music; while, I think, her feet did beat the time; while her body was the room where it should be celebrated; her soul the queen which should be delighted. And so together went the utterance and the invention that one might judge it was Philoclea's beauty which did speedily write it in her eyes; or the sense thereof, which did word by word indite it in her mind, whereto she (but as an organ) did only lend utterance. The song[9] was to this purpose:

[OA62]

What tongue can her perfections tell
In whose each part all pens may dwell?
Her hair fine threads of finest gold
In curled knots man's thought to hold;
But that her forehead says in me   5

[9] song—Ringler points out that Sidney made more corrections and revisions in this romance-blazon (a form as old as the *Song of Songs*, but done here by Sidney with many innovations) than in any of his other works. Furthermore, from the number of transcriptions and reprints of it, as well as references to it, the poem was a favorite among Elizabethans. In the *Old Arcadia*, Pyrocles recalled this song as he observed, toward the end of Book II, the nearly naked Philoclea sleeping. There the song is attributed to the lonely shepherd Philisides (Sidney) who once sang this in tribute to his dark-eyed mistress, Mira.

A whiter beauty you may see
(Whiter indeed; more white than snow,
Which on cold winter's face doth grow)
That doth present those even brows,
Whose equal line their angles bows[10]   10
Like to the moon when after change
Her horned head abroad doth range,
And arches be to heavenly lids,
Whose wink each bold attempt forbids:
For the black stars those spheres contain,   15
The matchless pair, even praise doth stain.
No lamp, whose light by art is got,
No sun, which shines and seeth not,
Can liken them without all peer,
Save one as much as other clear,   20
Which only thus unhappy be,
Because themselves they cannot see.
   Her cheeks with kindly claret[11] spread,
Aurora-like new out of bed,
Or like the fresh queen-apple's[12] side,   25
Blushing at sight of Phoebus' pride.
   Her nose, her chin, pure ivory wears,
No purer than the pretty ears:
So that therein appears some blood,
Like wine and milk that mingled stood,   30
In whose encirclets if ye gaze,
Your eyes may tread a lover's maze;
But with such turns the voice to stray,
No talk untaught[13] can find the way;
The tip no jewel needs to wear: 35
The tip is jewel of the ear.
   But who those ruddy lips can miss?

10 their angles bows—rounds their angles.
11 kindly claret—natural red.
12 queen-apple—an early variety of apple.
13 talk untaught—loose talk.

Which blessed still themselves do kiss:
Rubies, cherries, and roses new,
In worth, in taste, in perfect hue;   40
Which never part but that they show
Of precious pearl the double row,
The second sweetly-fenced ward,
Her heav'nly-dewed tongue to guard;
Whence never word in vain did flow.   45
   Fair under these doth stately grow,
The handle of this precious work,
The neck, in which strange graces lurk—
Such be, I think, the sumptuous towers
Which skill doth make in prince's bowers.   50
So good a say[14] invites the eye,
A little downward to espy
The lively clusters of her breasts
(Of Venus' babe the wanton nests)
Like pommels[15] round of marble clear,   55
Where azur'd veins well mix'd appear,
With dearest tops of porphyry.[16]
   Betwixt these two a way doth lie,
A way more worthy beauty's fame,
Than that which bears the milky name.   60
This leads into the joyous field,
Which only still doth lilies yield
(But lilies such whose native smell
The Indian odors[17] doth excel);
Waist it is call'd, for it doth waste   65
Men's lives, until it be embrac'd.
   There may one see, and yet not see,
Her ribs in white all armed be,
More white than Neptune's foamy face,
When struggling rocks he would embrace.   70

[14] say—sample.
[15] pommels—ornamental balls.
[16] porphyry—a red or purple stone.
[17] Indian odors—exotic spices from the East Indies.

In those delights the wand'ring thought
Might of each side astray be brought,
But that her navel doth unite,
In curious circle, busy sight:
A dainty seal of virgin-wax,   75
Where nothing but impression lacks.
 Her belly then glad sight doth fill,
Justly entitled Cupid's hill,
A hill most fit for such a master,
A spotless mine of alabaster;   80
Like alabaster fair and sleek,
But soft and supple satin like,
In that sweet seat the boy doth sport.
Loath, I must leave his chief resort;
For such a use the world hath gotten,[18] 85
The best things still must be forgotten.
 Yet never shall my song omit
Thighs, for Ovid's song[19] more fit;
Which flanked with two sug'red flanks,
Lift up their stately swelling banks;   90
That Albion clives[20] in whiteness pass,
With haunches smooth as looking glass.
 But bow all knees, now of her knees
My tongue doth tell what fancy sees:
The knots of joy, the gems of love,   95
Whose motion makes all graces move;
Whose bough'd incav'd[21] doth yield such sight,
Like cunning painter shadowing white;
The gart'ring place with childlike sign,
Shows easy print in metal fine.   100
But then again the flesh doth rise
In her brave calves, like crystal skies,

[18] such a use the world hath gotten—the world has come to such a pass.
[19] Ovid's song—for example, Elegy 5 of Book I, which celebrates the unexpected sight of Corinna's naked body.
[20] Albion clives—white cliffs of Dover.
[21] bough'd incav'd—inward-bending curve.

Whose Atlas[22] is a smallest small,
More white than whitest bone of whale.[23]
   Thereout steals out that round clean foot   105
This noble cedar's precious root,
In show and scent pale violets,
Whose step on earth all beauty sets.
   But back unto her back, my muse,
Where Leda's swan[24] his feathers mews,[25]   110
Along whose ridge such bones are met,
Like comfits[26] round in marchpane[27] set.
   Her shoulders be like two white doves,
Perching within square royal roofs,
Which leaded are with silver skin,   115
Passing the hate-spot ermelin.[28]
And thence those arms derived are;
The Phoenix' wings[29] are not so rare
For faultless length and stainless hue.
   Ah woe is me, my woes renew;   120
Now course doth lead me to her hand
(Of my first love the fatal band)
Where whiteness doth forever sit:
Nature herself enamel'd it.
For there with strange compact doth lie   125
Warm snow, moist pearl, soft ivory;
There fall those sapphire-colored brooks,
Which conduitlike with curious crooks,
Sweet islands make in that sweet land.

---

[22] Atlas—the muscles supporting this world of beauty.
[23] whale—in Ringler, "whall," an eye-rhyme; in 1590, "all."
[24] Leda's swan—Jove, who metamorphosed into a swan to carry Leda away with him.
[25] mews—sheds.
[26] comfits—sugared almonds.
[27] marchpane—marzipan, a sugar and almond paste.
[28] hate-spot ermelin—see Bk. I, ft. 170.
[29] Phoenix' wings—a rare mythological bird, only one of which can exist at a time; when it dies, it consumes itself on a funeral pyre, and a new phoenix arises from its ashes.

As for the fingers of the hand,   130
The bloody shafts of Cupid's war,
With amethysts they headed are.
   Thus hath each part his beauty's part,
But how the graces do impart
To all her limbs a special grace   135
(Becoming every time and place),
Which doth even beauty beautify,
And most bewitch the wretched eye.
How all this is but a fair inn
Of fairer guests, which dwell within,   140
Of whose high praise, and praiseful bliss,
Goodness the pen, heaven paper is,
The ink immortal fame doth lend.
As I began, so must I end:
   No tongue can her perfections tell,   145
   In whose each part all tongues may dwell.

But as Zelmane was coming to the latter end of her song, she might see the same water-spaniel, which before had hunted, come and fetch away one of Philoclea's gloves, whose fine proportion showed well what a dainty guest was wont there to be lodged. It was a delight to Zelmane to see that the dog was therewith delighted, and so let him go a little way withal, who quickly carried it out of sight among certain trees and bushes, which were very close together. But by-and-by he came again, and, amongst the raiments (Miso and Mopsa being preparing sheets against their coming out) the dog lighted upon a little book of four or five leaves of paper, and was bearing that away too. But then Zelmane, not knowing what importance it might be of, ran after the dog, who going straight to those bushes, she might see the dog deliver it to a gentleman who secretly lay there. But she hastily coming in, the gentleman rose up, and, with a courteous (though sad) countenance, presented himself unto her. Zelmane's eyes straight willed her mind to mark him, for she thought in her life she had never seen a man of a more goodly presence, in whom strong making took not away delicacy, nor beauty fierceness, being indeed such a right man-like man as Nature, often erring, yet shows she would fain make. But when she had a while, not without admiration, viewed him, she desired him to deliver back the glove and paper because they were the lady Philoclea's, telling him withal that she would not willingly let them know of his close lying in that prohibited place while they were bathing themselves because she knew they would be mortally offended withal.

"Fair lady," answered he, "the worst of the complaint is already passed, since I feel of my fault in myself the punishment. But for these things, I assure you, it was my dog's wanton boldness, not my presumption." With that he gave her back the paper. "But for the glove," said he, "since it is my lady Philoclea's, give me leave to keep it, since my heart cannot persuade itself to part from it. And I pray you tell the lady (lady indeed of all my desires) that owns it that I will direct my life to honor this glove with serving her."

"O villain!" cried out Zelmane, madded with finding an unlooked-for rival, and that he would make her a messenger, "Dispatch," said she, "and deliver it, or, by the life of her that owns it, I will make thy soul, though too base a price, pay for it." And with that drew out her sword, which, Amazon-like, she ever wore about her.

The gentleman retired himself into an open place from among the bushes; and then drawing out his too, he offered to deliver it unto her, saying withal, "God forbid I should use my sword against you, since, if I be not deceived, you are the same famous Amazon that both defended my lady's just title of beauty against the valiant Phalantus, and saved her life in killing the lion; therefore, I am rather to kiss your hands, with acknowledging myself bound to obey you."

But this courtesy was worse than a bastinado[30] to Zelmane, so that again, with rageful eyes, she bade him defend himself, for no less than his life should answer it. "A hard case," said he, "to teach my sword that lesson, which hath ever used to turn itself

---

[30] bastinado—beating.

to a shield in a lady's presence." But Zelmane, hearkening to no more words, began with such witty fury[31] to pursue him with blows and thrusts that nature and virtue commanded the gentleman to look to his safety. Yet still courtesy, that seemed incorporate in his heart, would not be persuaded by danger to offer any offense, but only to stand upon the best defensive guard he could: sometimes going back, being content, in that respect, to take on the figure of cowardice, sometime with strong and well-met wards, sometimes cunning avoidings of his body, and sometimes feigning some blows, which himself pulled back before they needed to be withstood. And so, with play, did he a good while fight against the fight of Zelmane, who, more spited with that courtesy (that one that did nothing should be able to resist her), burned away with choler any motions which might grow out of her own sweet disposition, determining to kill him if he fought no better; and so, redoubling her blows, drove the stranger to no other shift than to ward and go back, at that time seeming the image of innocency against violence.

But at length he found that, both in public and private respects, who stands only upon defense stands upon no defense. For Zelmane, seeming to strike at his head and he, going to ward it, withal stepped back, as he was accustomed, she stopped her blow in the air, and, suddenly turning the point, ran full at his breast, so as he was driven with the pommel of his sword (having no other weapon of defense) to beat it down; but the thrust was so strong that he could not so wholly beat it away, but that it met with his thigh, through which it ran. But Zelmane retiring her sword, and seeing his blood, victorious anger was conquered by the before-conquered pity; and heartily sorry, and even ashamed with herself she was, considering how little he had done who well (she found) could have done more; inasmuch that she said, "Truly I am sorry for your hurt; but yourself gave the cause, both in refusing to deliver the glove, and yet not fighting as I know you could have done." "But," said she, "because I perceive you disdain to fight with a woman, it may be, before a year

31 witty fury—cunning swordsmanship in the service of anger.

come about, you shall meet with a near kinsman of mine, Pyrocles, prince of Macedon; and I give you my word, he, for me, shall maintain this quarrel against you."

"I would," answered Amphialus, "I had many more such hurts to meet and know that worthy prince, whose virtue I love and admire, though my good destiny hath not been to see his person."

But, as they were so speaking, the young ladies came, to whom Mopsa (curious in anything but her own good behavior, having followed and seen Zelmane fighting, had cried what she had seen, while they were drying themselves, and the water, with some drops, seemed to weep that it should part from such bodies. But they, careful of Zelmane (assuring themselves that any Arcadian would bear reverence to them), Pamela with a noble mind, and Philoclea with a loving, hastily hiding the beauties whereof nature was proud and they ashamed, they made quick work to come to save Zelmane.

But already they found them in talk, and Zelmane careful of his wound; but when they saw him, they knew it was their cousin-germane,[32] the famous Amphialus, whom (yet with a sweet-graced bitterness) they blamed for breaking their father's commandment, especially while themselves were in such sort retired. But he craved pardon, protesting unto them that he had only been to seek solitary places by an extreme melancholy that had a good while possessed him, and guided to that place by his spaniel, where, while the dog hunted in the river, he had withdrawn himself to pacify with sleep his over-watched eyes, till a dream waked him, and made him see that whereof he had dreamed, and withal not obscurely signified that he felt the smart of his own doings. But Philoclea (that was even jealous of herself for Zelmane) would needs have her glove, and not without so mighty a lour as that face could yield.

As for Zelmane, when she knew it was Amphialus, "Lord Amphialus," said she, "I have long desired to know you, heretofore (I must confess) with more good-will, but still with honoring your virtue, though I love not your person; and at this time,

[32] cousin-germane—first cousin.

I pray you, let us take care of your wound, upon condition you shall hereafter promise that a more knightly combat shall be performed between us."

Amphialus answered in honorable sort, but with such excusing himself that more and more accused his love to Philoclea, and provoked more hate in Zelmane. But Mopsa had already called certain shepherds not far off (who knew and well observed their limits) to come and help to carry away Amphialus, whose wound suffered him not without danger to strain it; and so, he, leaving himself with them, departed from them, faster bleeding in his heart than at his wound, which, bound up by the sheets wherewith Philoclea had been wrapped, made him thank the wound and bless the sword for that favor.

CHAPTER 12

[The ladies leave the river and spend a pleasant hour at Zelmane's arbor, during which time Zelmane reads Basilius' poetic rendition of his meeting with Plangus and Plangus' lament for Erona. Zelmane then begs Philoclea to narrate the story of Plangus and Erona, a favor which Philoclea is quite pleased to grant.]

CHAPTER 13

Erona, irreligious 'gainst love, must love the base Antiphilus,[33] is loved, pursued, and beleaguered by the great Tiridates.[34] The two Greek princes aid her. They combat with two kings; Antiphilus with Plangus; they conquerors, he prisoner. Erona's hard choice to redeem him. Tiridates slain, Antiphilus delivered, Artaxia chased by the two princes, and her hate to them.

"Of late there reigned a king in Lycia, who had for the blessing of his marriage this only daughter of his, Erona, a princess worthy, for her beauty, as much praise as beauty may be praiseworthy. This princess Erona, being nineteen years of age, seeing the country of Lycia so much devoted to Cupid as that in every

33 Antiphilus—"against love."
34 Tiridates—"to cut in half."

place his naked pictures and images were superstitiously adored, either moved thereunto by the esteeming that could be no god-head which could breed wickedness, or the shamefast considera-tion of such nakedness, procured so much of her father as utterly to pull down and deface all those statues and pictures. Which how terribly he punished—for to that the Lycians impute it—quickly after appeared.

"For she had not lived a year longer when she was stricken with most obstinate love to a young man, but of mean parentage, in her father's court, named Antiphilus: so mean as that he was but the son of her nurse, and by that means (without other desert) became known of her. Now, so evil could she conceal her fire, and so wilfully persevered she in it, that her father offering her the marriage of the great Tiridates, king of Armenia, who desired her more than the joys of heaven, she, for Antiphilus' sake, refused it. Many ways her father sought to withdraw her from it: sometimes persuasions, sometimes threatenings; once hiding Antiphilus, and giving her to understand that he was fled the country; lastly, making a solemn execution to be done of an-other, under the name of Antiphilus, whom he kept in prison. But neither she liked persuasions, nor feared threatenings, nor changed for absence; and when she thought him dead, she sought all means, as well by poison as by knife, to send her soul, at least, to be married in the eternal church with him. This so broke the tender father's heart that, leaving things as he found them, he shortly after died. Then forthwith Erona, being seized of the crown, and arming her will with authority, sought to advance her affection to the holy title of matrimony.

"But before she could accomplish all the solemnities, she was overtaken with a war the king Tiridates made upon her, only for her person, towards whom (for her ruin) Love had kindled his cruel heart indeed cruel and tyrannous for, being far too strong in the field, he spared not man, woman, and child, but (as though there could be found no foil to set forth the extremity of his love, but extremity of hatred) wrote, as it were, the sonnets of his love in the blood, and tuned[35] them in the cries, of her subjects (although his fair sister Artaxia, who would accompany him in the army, sought all means to appease his fury), till, lastly, he besieged Erona in her best city, vowing to win her or lose his life. And now he had brought her to the point either of a woeful consent, or a ruinous denial, when there came thither (following the course which virtue and fortune led them) two excellent young princes, Pyrocles and Musidorus, the one prince of Macedon, the other of Thessalia; two princes, as Plangus said (and he witnessed his saying with sighs and tears) the most accomplished both in body and mind that the sun ever looked upon."

While Philoclea spake these words, "O sweet words," thought Zelmane to herself, "which are not only praise to me, but a praise to praise itself, which out of that mouth issueth."

"These two princes," said Philoclea, "as well to help the weaker, especially being a lady, as to save a Greek people from being ruined by such whom we call and count barbarous, gathering together such of the honestest Lycians as would venture their lives to succor their princess, giving order by a secret message they sent into the city that they should issue with all force at an appointed time, they set upon Tiridates' camp with so well-guided a fierceness, that, being of both sides assaulted, he was like to be overthrown; but that this Plangus, being general of Tiridates' horsemen, especially aided by the two mighty men Eurades and Barzanes,[36] rescued the footmen, even almost defeated, but yet could not bar the princes, with their succors both of men and victual, to enter the city.

"Which when Tiridates found would make the war long (which length seemed to him worse than a languishing consumption), he made a challenge of three princes in his retinue against those two princes and Antiphilus, and that thereupon the quarrel should be decided, with compact that neither side should help his fellow, but of whose side the more overcame, with him the victory should remain. Antiphilus, though Erona chose rather

[35] tuned—set them to music.
[36] Euardes, Barzanes—"well governing," "tower of Zeus."

to bide the brunt of war than venture him, yet could not for shame refuse the offer, especially since the two strangers, that had no interest in it, did willingly accept it; besides that, he saw it like enough that the people, weary of the miseries of war, would rather give him up, if they saw him shrink, than for his sake venture their ruin, considering that the challengers were far of greater worthiness than himself. So it was agreed upon, and against Pyrocles was Euardes, king of Bithynia, Barzanes of Hircania[37] against Musidorus—two men that thought the world scarce able to resist them—and against Antiphilus he placed this same Plangus, being his own cousin-germane, and son to the king of Iberia. Now, so it fell out that Musidorus slew Barzanes, and Pyrocles Eurades, which victory those princes esteemed above all that ever they had; but of the other side Plangus took Antiphilus prisoner; under which color (as if the matter had been equal, though, indeed, it was not, the greater part being overcome of his side) Tiridates continued his war, and to bring Erona to a compelled yielding, sent her word that he would the third morrow after, before the walls of the town, strike off Antiphilus' head, without his suit in that space were granted, adding withal, because he had heard of her desperate affection, that if in the meantime she did herself any hurt, what tortures could be devised should be laid upon Antiphilus.

"Then lo if Cupid be a god, or that the tyranny of our own thoughts seem as a god unto us; but whatsoever it was, then it did set forth the miserableness of his effects, she being drawn to two contraries by one cause: for the love of him commanded her to yield to no other, the love of him commanded her to preserve his life, which knot might well be cut, but untied it could not be. So that Love in her passions, like a right make-bate,[38] whispered to both sides arguments of quarrel.

" 'What,' said he of the one side, 'dost thou love Antiphilus,

[37] Bithynia, Hircania—Bithynia, small country in northwest Asia Minor, bordered by the Black Sea on the north and Phrygia on the south; Hircania, region in Asia, east of Armenia, with the Caspian on the north and Media and Persia on the south.
[38] make-bate—mischief maker.

O Erona? And shall Tiridates enjoy thy body? With what eyes
wilt thou look upon Antiphilus, when he shall know that another possesseth thee? But if thou wilt do it, canst thou do it?
Canst thou force thy heart? Think with thyself, if this man have
thee, thou shalt never have more part of Antiphilus than if he
were dead. But thus much more, that the affection shall be gnaw-
ing, and the remorse still present. Death perhaps will cool the
rage of thy affection, where thus thou shalt ever love and ever
lack. Think this beside: if thou marry Tiridates, Antiphilus is so
excellent a man that long he cannot be from being in some high
place married. Canst thou suffer that, too? If another kill him, he
doth him the wrong; if thou abuse thy body, thou dost him the
wrong. His death is a work of nature, and either now or at another time he shall die. But it shall be thy work, thy shameful
work, which is in thy power to shun, to make him live to see thy
faith falsified and his bed defiled.'

"But when Love had well kindled that part of her thoughts,
then went he to the other side. 'What,' said he, 'O Erona, and
is thy love of Antiphilus come to that point as thou dost now
make it a question whether he shall die or no? O excellent affection, which for too much love will see his head off. Mark well the
reasons of the other side, and thou shalt see, it is but love of
thyself which so disputeth. Thou canst not abide Tiridates: this
is but love of thyself. Thou shalt be ashamed to look upon him
afterward: this is but fear of shame and love of thyself. Thou
shalt want him as much then: this is but love of thyself. He shall
be married: if he be well, why should that grieve thee, but for
love of thyself? No, no, pronounce these words if thou canst:
"Let Antiphilus die." ' Then the images of each side stood before
her understanding. One time she thought she saw Antiphilus
dying; another time she thought Antiphilus saw her by Tiridates
enjoyed. Twenty times calling for a servant to carry message of
yielding, but before he came the mind was altered. She blushed
when she considered the effect of granting; she was pale when
she remembered the fruits of denial. As for weeping, sighing,
wringing her hands, and tearing her hair, were indifferent of both
sides. Easily she would have agreed to have broken all disputa-

tions with her own death, but that the fear of Antiphilus' further torments stayed her.

"At length, even the evening before the day appointed of his death, the determination of yielding prevailed, especially growing upon a message of Antiphilus, who, with all the conjuring terms he could devise, besought her to save his life upon any condition. But she had no sooner sent her messenger to Tiridates but her mind changed, and she went to the two young princes, Pyrocles and Musidorus, and, falling down at their feet, desired them to try some way for her deliverance, showing herself resolved not to over-live Antiphilus, nor yield to Tiridates.

"They, that knew not what she had done in private, prepared that night accordingly; and, as sometimes it falls out that what is inconstancy seems cunning, so did this change, indeed, stand in as good stead as a witty dissimulation, for it made the king as reckless as them diligent, so that, in the dead time of the night, the princes issued out of the town, with whom she would needs go, either to die herself or rescue Antiphilus, having no armor nor weapon, but affection. And I cannot tell you how, by what device (though Plangus at large described it) the conclusion was, the wonderful valor of the two princes so prevailed that Antiphilus was succored and the king slain. Plangus was then the chief man left in the camp; and therefore, seeing no other remedy, conveyed in safety into her country Artaxia, now queen of Armenia, who, with true lamentations, made known to the world that her new greatness did no way comfort her in respect of her brother's loss, whom she studied all means possible to revenge upon every one of the occasioners, having (as she thought) overthrown her brother by a most abominable treason. Insomuch that, being at home, she proclaimed great rewards to any private man, and herself in marriage to any prince, that would destroy Pyrocles and Musidorus. But thus was Antiphilus redeemed, and, though against the consent of all her nobility, married to Erona; in which case the two Greek princes, being called away by another adventure, left them."

CHAPTER 14[39]

[Before Philoclea can proceed with the history of Plangus, who was the cousin of Tiridates and commander of his cavalry, Miso intrudes and demands the right to tell the next story. Her tale involves an old woman who, when Miso was young, tutored her on the proper way to obtain pleasure from men without ever surrendering her heart, proving, by means of a poem, that Love is not the fine Cupid of courtly myth, but an ugly beast begot by Argus upon a cow. After this, the women draw lots to determine who will tell the next tale, and Mopsa wins. She begins to relate the fairy story of the princess who falls in love with a knight whose name she must never ask, for, if she does, he will disappear; but Philoclea halts Mopsa before her climax and asks that the servant save her story for Philoclea's wedding day. Then, upon Zelmane's request, Pamela resumes the story of Plangus.]

CHAPTER 15

[Plangus, son of the king of Iberia, became enamored, in his early manhood, of a married woman. After successfully seducing her, Plangus was discovered by his father, who, influenced by his son's ardent praises of the woman, also fell in love with her. The king then sent his son off to war in order to woo the young man's mistress. When Plangus returned three or four years later, he found that his former *inamorata* was now his stepmother, her first husband having died. The new queen tried to renew her relationship with the young man, but Plangus, out of respect for his father, repulsed her advances. Incensed and fearful, the woman influenced her husband to exile Plangus, who fled to the court of his cousin, Tiridates. At this point in the story, when Pamela has returned to the war between Tiridates and Erona, and is about to reveal the treason of Antiphilus, Basilius enters and invites them to his lodging.]

[39] Chapter 14—this chapter was left out most reluctantly, for the comic, but diverse characterization of Miso and Mopsa through their behavior, language, and stories add to the appreciation of the range of Sidney's art.

CHAPTER 16

[At Basilius' lodge, Zelmane endures once more the tedious passion of both the king and Gynecia, after which the latter, desperate with desire, suffers through the night in great anguish. The following morning, Basilius overhears Zelmane complaining of her own love and, thinking it is himself for whom she yearns, declares his passion to her. Zelmane assumes the cloak of· wounded and indignant virtue and then, softening the blow with sly intent, suggests that the same message might meet with a better reception if carried by Philoclea. Basilius immediately hastens to enlist his daughter's aid, and Philoclea, anxious to obtain private conversation with Zelmane, accepts the assignment, but only after her father promises that she will not be asked to transmit any dishonorable proposals.]

CHAPTER 17

[Philoclea discovers Zelmane leaning over the river Ladon, weeping into its waters, and lamenting her love. For a short while she listens unseen, then broaches her father's plea. Zelmane, however, seizes the opportunity to confess both his devotion to Philoclea herself and his own identity as Pyrocles, prince of Macedon. The maiden realizes then that her passion for the Amazon is neither hopeless nor wrong, and she immediately admits that she loves him. Then, scarcely able to trust herself to virtue, she commits her honor to Pyrocles' safekeeping; they swear a betrothal. And then Philoclea asks Pyrocles to resume the story of his life at the point where Dorus abandoned it.]

CHAPTER 18

[Pyrocles tells Philoclea how, after he and Musidorus had killed Tiridates' ally Euardes, Anaxius ("unworthy"), Euardes' nephew and a famous knight, challenged Pyrocles to private combat in Lycia. While journeying towards this duel, Pyrocles rescued a bound and helpless man who was being jabbed with hairpins by nine furious women. One of the females refused to run away; and she, Dido by name, told Pyrocles that the man he had saved was a renowned lecher called Pamphilus ("all loving"), who had seduced all of these vengeful women and foresaken them afterwards. Pyrocles settled a truce between Dido and Pamphilus and continued on his way to Lycia.]

CHAPTER 19

[In Lycia Pyrocles met Anaxius. The fight was evenly matched and quite brutal, but, before a conclusion could be reached, Pamphilus entered with Dido, birching her before him. Pyrocles immediately broke off his duel in order to rescue the unfortunate lady; and, promising to return, he rode off in pursuit of Pamphilus. At dusk he overtook the pair and rescued Dido, who invited him to pass the night in her father's castle, which was near-by. But she warned him of the old man's niggardliness, a quality which proved dangerous when he, Chremes by name, discovered Pyrocles' identity and formed a plot to sell him to Artaxia, Tiridates' vengeful sister. Pyrocles would surely have been betrayed had not first Musidorus and then the king of Iberia come to his aid. In the ensuing battle, Dido was slain while trying to defend Pyrocles, and Chremes was captured, later to be executed for his treachery.]

CHAPTER 20

[The king of Iberia invited Pyrocles and Musidorus to convalesce at his court, where they discovered that the real ruler was the domineering Queen Andromana ("lustful"), who controlled her husband's mind. Andromana quickly succumbed to a lustful passion for both young heroes and initiated a campaign to seduce them. Pyrocles and Musidorus resisted her advances so steadfastly, however, that she was driven to the desperate measure of having them imprisoned for intriguing against the king. Even this did not weaken their virtuous resolve, and they might have remained in chains forever, if Zelmane, Plexirtus' daughter

and the beloved of Palladius, Andromana's son, had not fallen
in love with Pyrocles. She persuaded Palladius to help the pair
escape.]

CHAPTER 21

[Each year jousts were held in Iberia to commemorate the marriage of the queen, and Iberian knights ordinarily overcame all
challengers. This year, however, during the first three days
of the contest, the knights of Helen of Corinth were more successful. Palladius therefore persuaded Andromana that, if the
honor of Iberia were to be preserved, they should make use of
such renowned champions as the imprisoned Pyrocles and
Musidorus. On the fifth day the cousins, having triumphed in
the field, escaped with Palladius. The queen's soldiers pursued
them into Bythinia, where Palladius was slain in battle with a
knight who had once been a lover of Andromana's. Driven to
despair by her son's death and the continued refusals of Pyrocles
and Musidorus, the queen killed herself with Palladius' dagger.]

CHAPTER 22

[Returning to their travels, the cousins encountered Leucippe,
who had been abandoned by her fiance, Pamphilus, in favor of
Baccha. Unable to assist her in any other way, they conveyed
her to a nunnery where she wished to pass the remainder of
her life. On the following morning, they were overtaken by
Zelmane, who, disguised as the youth Daiphantus, begged to
accompany Pyrocles as his page. At the end of two months'
wanderings, the three adventurers discovered the brothers
Tydeus and Telenor engaged in mortal combat with one another. Pyrocles and Musidorus separated them, but not before
both had been mortally wounded. They attributed their tragedy
to Plexirtus, Zelmane's father, who, jealous of the brothers'
popularity in the realm they had helped him to win, had tricked
them into mutual hatred and distrust.]

CHAPTER 23

[Musidorus and Pyrocles now headed towards Pontus, where Otaves, brother of Barzanes, who had been slain by the cousins, had attacked the king in hope of luring the two heroes into the battle and obtaining revenge upon them. However, Daiphantus fell sick along the road and, hearing that her father, Plexirtus, was in danger of death, grew worse. Just before she died, she confessed both her identity and her love to Pyrocles. Then, as a final boon, she begged him to forgive her father and rescue him and also to sojourn in Greece under the name of Daiphantus, with Musidorus, likewise, adopting the name of Palladius. After this episode, the heroes separated, the one to aid the king of Pontus and the other to assist Plexirtus, who was imprisoned by an ancient knight anxious to avenge an old injustice. Pyrocles freed the father of his lost admirer by slaying a dragon set to devour the old man; and Musidorus, in Pontus, succeeded in defeating Otaves.]

CHAPTER 24

[After receiving homage from all the kings they had succored, Musidorus and Pyrocles left Pontus for Greece. However, their ship was supplied by the untrustworthy Plexirtus, who had commissioned some of the crew to assassinate the cousins. The commander was able to warn them, and, when the attack occurred, it resulted in a lively, chaotic battle, with each man slaying the one next to him, and no man certain of his friends or his foes. When a fire broke out and the ship was threatened with destruction, Musidorus and Pyrocles escaped into the sea, where the latter was captured by pirates. (End of Chapter 24 follows:)]

"But what," said Philoclea, "became of your cousin Musidorus?"

"Lost," said Pyrocles.

"Ah! my Pyrocles," said Philoclea, "I am glad I have taken

you. I perceive you lovers do not always say truly—as though I know not your cousin Dorus, the shepherd!"

"Life of my desires," said Pyrocles, "what is mine, even to my soul, is yours; but the secret of my friend is not mine. But if you know so much, then I may truly say he is lost, since he is no more his own. But, I perceive, your noble sister and you are great friends, and well doth it become you so to be."

"But go forward, dear Pyrocles; I long to hear out till your meeting me, for there to me-ward is the best part of your story."

"Ah, sweet Philoclea," said Pyrocles, "do you think I can think so precious leisure as this well spent in talking? Are your eyes a fit book, think you, to read a tale upon? Is my love quiet enough to be an historian? Dear princess, be gracious unto me."

And then he fain would have remembered to have forgot himself. But she, with a sweetly disobeying grace, desired that her desire (once for ever) might serve, that no spot might disgrace that love which shortly, she hoped, should be to the world warrantable. Fain he would not have heard, till she threatened anger; and then the poor lover durst not, because he durst not.

"Nay, I pray thee, dear Pyrocles," said she, "let me have my story."

"Sweet princess," said he, "give my thoughts a little respite, and if it please you, since this time must so be spoiled, yet it shall suffer the less harm if you vouchsafe to bestow your voice and let me know how the good Queen Erona was betrayed into such danger, and why Plangus sought me. For, indeed, I should pity greatly any mischance fallen to that princess."

"I will," said Philoclea, smiling, "so you give me your word, your hands shall be quiet auditors."

"They shall," said he, "because subject."

Then began she to speak, but with so pretty and delightful a majesty, when she set her countenance to tell the matter, that Pyrocles could not choose but rebel so far as to kiss her. She would have pulled her head away and speak, but while she spoke he kissed, and it seemed he fed upon her words; but she got away.

"How will you have your discourse," said she, "without you let my lips alone?" He yielded, and took her hand.

"On this," said he, "will I revenge my wrong," and so began to make much of that hand, when her tale and his delight were interrupted by Miso, who, taking her time while Basilius' back was turned, came unto them and told Philoclea, she deserved she knew what, for leaving her mother (being evil at ease) to keep company with strangers. But Philoclea telling her that she was there by her father's commandment, she went away muttering that though her back, and her shoulders, and her neck were broken, yet as long as her tongue would wag, it should do her errand to her mother.

CHAPTER 25

Gynecia's divining dream. Her passionate jealousy in actions, speech, and song described. Her troubling Philoclea and Zelmane. The rebels troubling her. Rebels resisted by Zelmane. Zelmane assisted by Dorus. Dorus and Zelmane's five memorable strokes.

So went up Miso to Gynecia, who was at that time miserably vexed with this manner of dream. It seemed unto her to be in a place full of thorns,[40] which so molested her as she could neither abide standing still, nor tread safely going forward. In this case she thought Zelmane, being upon a fair hill delightful to the eye and easy in appearance, called her thither: whither with much anguish being come, Zelmane was vanished, and she found nothing but a dead body like unto her husband, which, seeming at the first with a strange smell to infect her as she was ready likewise within a while to die, the dead body, she thought, took her in his arms and said, "Gynecia, leave all; for here is thy only rest."

With that she awaked, crying very loud, "Zelmane, Zelmane!" But remembering herself and seeing Basilius by (her guilty conscience more suspecting than being suspected), she turned her call and called for Philoclea. Miso forthwith like a

---

[40] thorns—emblematically associated with the pains of love.

valiant shrew (looking at Basilius as though she would speak
though she died for it) told Gynecia that her daughter had been
a whole hour together in secret talk with Zelmane. "And," says
she, "for my part I could not be heard (your daughters are
brought up in such awe) though I told her of your pleasure sufficiently." Gynecia, as if she had heard her last doom pronounced
against her, with a side-look and changed countenance, "O my
Lord," said she, "what mean you to suffer these young folks
together?"

Basilius, that aimed nothing at the mark of her suspicion,
smilingly took her in his arms. "Sweet wife," said he, "I thank
you for your care of your child; but they must be youths of
other mettle than Zelmane that can endanger her."

"Oh, but—" cried Gynecia, and therewith she stayed. For
then indeed she did suffer a right conflict betwixt the force of
love and rage of jealousy. Many times was she about to satisfy
the spite of her mind and tell Basilius how she knew Zelmane
to be far otherwise than the outward appearance. But those
many times were all put back by the manifold objections of her
vehement love. Fain she would have barred her daughter's hap,
but loath she was to cut off her own hope. But now, as if her
life had been set upon a wager of quick rising, as weak as she
was, she got up; though Basilius (with a kindness flowing only
from the fountain of unkindness, being indeed desirous to win
his daughter as much time as might be) was loath to suffer it,
swearing he saw sickness in her face, and therefore was loath
she should adventure the air.

But the great and wretched lady Gynecia, possessed with
those devils of love and jealousy, did rid herself from her tedious
husband and, taking nobody with her, going toward them, "O
jealousy," said she, "the frenzy of wise folks, the well-wishing
spite, and unkind carefulness, the self-punishment for other's
faults and self-misery in other's happiness, the cousin of envy,
daughter of love, and mother of hate how couldest thou so
quietly get thee a seat in the unquiet heart of Gynecia?"
"Gynecia," said she, sighing, "thought wise, and once virtuous.
Alas! it is thy breeder's power which plants thee there; it is the

flaming agony of affection that works the chilling access of thy
fever, in such sort that nature gives place; the growing of my
daughter seems the decay of myself; the blessings of a mother
turn to the curses of a competitor; and the fair face of Philoclea
appears more horrible in my sight than the image of death."
Then remembered she this song, which she thought took a
right measure of her present mind.

[*OA22*]

With two strange fires of equal heat possess'd
The one of love, the other jealousy,
Both still do work, in neither find I rest;
For both, alas, their strengths together tie:
The one aloft doth hold, the other high.
   Love wakes the jealous eye lest thence it moves:
   The jealous eye, the more it looks, it loves.

These fires increase; in these I daily burn:
They feed on me, and with my wings do fly,
My lovely joys to doleful ashes turn;
Their flames mount up, my powers prostrate lie;
They live in force, I quite consumed die.
   One wonder yet far passeth my conceit:
   The fuel small, how be the fires so great?

But her unleisured thoughts ran not over the ten first words;
but going with a pace, not so much too fast for her body as slow
for her mind, she found them together, who, after Miso's departure, had left their tale and determined what to say to
Basilius. But full abashed was poor Philoclea (whose conscience
now began to know cause of blushing) for first salutation, receiving an eye from her mother full of the same disdainful scorn
which Pallas showed to poor Arachne,[41] that durst contend

[41] Pallas showed to poor Arachne—Arachne claimed to be capable of
weaving more beautifully than Pallas could; when she lost a contest with
the goddess, Pallas changed her into a spider—or, in some versions, when
she did not lose.

with her for the prize of well weaving; yet, did the force of love so much rule her that, though for Zelmane's sake she did detest her, yet for Zelmane's sake she used no harder words to her than to bid her go home and accompany her solitary father.

Then began she to display to Zelmane the storehouse of her deadly desires, when suddenly the confused rumor of a mutinous multitude gave just occasion to Zelmane to break off any such conference—for well she found, they were not friendly voices they heard—and to retire with as much diligence as conveniently they could towards the lodge. Yet, before they could win the lodge by twenty paces, they were overtaken by an unruly sort of clowns, and other rebels, which, like a violent flood, were carried, they themselves knew not whither. But, as soon as they came within perfect discerning these ladies, like enraged beasts, without respect of their estates, or pity of their sex, they began to run against them, as right villains, thinking ability to do hurt to be a great advancement; yet, so many as they were, so many almost were their minds, all knit together only in madness. Some cried "Take," some "Kill," some "Save." But even they that cried "Save" ran for company with them that meant to kill. Every one commanded, none obeyed; he only seemed chief captain that was most rageful.

Zelmane, whose virtuous courage was ever awake, drew out her sword, which upon those ill-armed churls giving as many wounds as blows, and as many deaths almost as wounds— lightning courage and thundering smart upon them—kept them at a bay, while the two ladies got themselves into the lodge; out of the which Basilius, having put on an armor long untried, came to prove his authority among his subjects, or, at least, to adventure his life with his dear mistress, to whom he brought a shield, while the ladies tremblingly attended the issue of this dangerous adventure. But Zelmane made them perceive the odds between an eagle and a kite, with such a nimble stayedness, and such an assured nimbleness, that, while one was running back for fear, his fellow had her sword in his guts.

And by-and-by was both her heart and help well increased

by the coming of Dorus, who, having been making of hurdles[42] for his master's sheep, heard the horrible cries of this mad multitude; and having straight represented before the eyes of his careful love the peril wherein the soul of his soul might be, he went to Pamela's lodge, but found her in a cave hard by with Mopsa and Dametas, who at that time would not have opened the entry to his father.

And therefore leaving them there (as in a place safe, both for being strong and unknown), he ran as the noise guided him. But when he saw his friend in such danger among them, anger and contempt, asking no counsel but of courage, made him room among them with no other weapon but his sheephook, and with that overthrowing one of the villains, took away a two-hand sword from him, and withal helped him from ever being ashamed of losing it. Then lifting up his brave head, and flashing terror into their faces, he made arms and legs go complain to the earth how evil their masters had kept them. Yet the multitude still growing, and the killing wearying them—fearing lest in long fight they should be conquered with conquering—they drew back toward the lodge; but drew back in such sort that still their terror went forward like a valiant mastiff, whom when his master pulls back by the tail from the bear (with whom he hath already interchanged a hateful embracement), though his pace be backward, his gesture is forward, his teeth and eyes threatening more in the retiring than they did in the advancing; so guided they themselves homeward, never stepping step backward but that they proved themselves masters of the ground where they stept.

Yet among the rebels there was a dapper fellow, a tailor by occupation, who, fetching his courage only from their going back, began to bow his knees and very fencer-like to draw near to Zelmane. But as he came within her distance, turning his sword very nicely about his crown, Basilius with a side blow strake off his nose. He, being a suitor to a seamster's daughter, and therefore not a little grieved for such a disgrace, stooped

42 hurdles—temporary sheep-pens.

down because he had heard that if it were fresh put to it would
cleave on again. But as his hand was on the ground to bring his
nose to his head, Zelmane, with a blow sent his head to his nose.
That saw a butcher, a butcherly chuff[43] indeed, who that day was
sworn brother to him in a cup of wine, and lifted up a great
lever,[44] calling Zelmane all the vile names of a butcherly eloquence. But she, letting slip the blow of the lever, hit him so surely
on the side of his face that she left nothing but the nether jaw,
where the tongue still wagged, as willing to say more, if his
master's remembrance had served.

"O," said a miller that was half drunk, "see the luck of a
good fellow!" And with that word, ran with a pitchfork at
Dorus; but the nimbleness of the wine carried his head so fast
that it made it over-run his feet, so that he fell withal just between the legs of Dorus, who, setting his foot on his neck
(though he offered two milch kine and four fat hogs for his
life), thrust his sword quite through, from one ear to the other;
which took it very unkindly, to feel such news before they
heard of them—instead of hearing, to be put to such feeling.[45]
But Dorus, leaving the miller to vomit his soul out in wine and
blood, with his two-hand sword strake off another quite by the
waist, who the night before had dreamed he was grown a
couple and, interpreting it he should be married, had bragged
of his dream that morning among his neighbors.

But that blow astonished quite a poor painter, who stood
by with pike in his hands. This painter was to counterfeit the
skirmishing between the Centaurs and Lapiths[46] and had been
very desirous to see some notable wounds, to be able the more
lively to express them; and this morning, being carried by the
stream of this company, the foolish fellow was even delighted
to see the effect of blows. But this last, happening near him, so

---

[43] chuff—churl.
[44] lever—cleaver.
[45] which took it . . . to such feeling—his ears were sorry to have to
feel pain physically, instead of from the reception of sad news.
[46] the skirmishing between the Centaurs and Lapiths—the Centaurs
raped some Lapith women at a wedding to which they were invited by the
Lapiths; this caused a savage war.

amazed him that he stood still, while Dorus (with a turn of his sword) strake off both his hands. And so the painter returned well skilled in wounds, but with never a hand to perform his skill.

CHAPTER 26

Zelmane's confident attempt to appease the mutiny. A bone of division cast by her, and caught by them. Her pacificatory oration. The acceptation and issue of it.

In this manner they recovered the lodge and gave the rebels a face of wood of the outside. But they then (though no more furious, yet more courageous when they saw no resister) went about with pickaxe to the wall, and fire to the gate, to get themselves entrance. Then did the two ladies mix fear with love, especially Philoclea, who ever caught hold of Zelmane, so, by the folly of love, hindering the help which she desired. But Zelmane, seeing no way of defense nor time to deliberate (the number of those villains still increasing, and their madness still increasing with their number), thought it only the means to go beyond their expectation with an unused boldness and with danger to avoid danger, and therefore opened again the gate, and (Dorus and Basilius standing ready for her defense) she issued again among them. The blows she had dealt before, though all in general were hasty, made each of them in particular take breath, before they brought them suddenly over-near her, so that she had time to get up to the judgment seat of the prince, which, according o the guise[47] of that country, was before the gate. There she paused a while, making sign with her hand unto them, and withal speaking aloud, that she had something to say unto them that would please them. But she was answered a while with nothing but shouts and cries and some beginning to throw stones at her, not daring to approach her.

But at length a young farmer (who might do most among the country sort, and was caught in a little affection towards Zelmane), hoping by this kindness to have some good of her,

[47] guise—custom.

desired them, if they were honest men, to hear the woman speak. "Fie, fellows, fie!" said he. "What will all the maids in our town say, if so many tall[48] men shall be afraid to hear a fair wench? I swear unto you by no little ones, I had rather give my team of oxen than we should show ourselves so uncivil wights.[49] Besides, I tell you true, I have heard it of old men counted wisdom, to hear much and say little." His sententious speech so prevailed that the most part began to listen. Then she, with such efficacy of gracefulness and such a quiet magnanimity represented in her face in this uttermost peril, as the more the barbarous people looked, the more it fixed their looks upon her, in this sort began unto them.

"It is no small comfort unto me," said she, "having to speak something unto you for your own behoofs, to find that I have to deal with such a people, who show indeed in themselves the right nature of valor, which, as it leaves no violence unattempted, while the choler is nourished with resistance, so when the subject of their wrath doth of itself unlooked-for offer itself into their hands, it makes them at least take a pause before they determine cruelty. Now then, first, before I come to the principal matter, have I to say unto you that your Prince Basilius himself in person is within this lodge, and was one of the three, who a few of you went about to fight withal." And this she said, not doubting but they knew it well enough, but because she would have them imagine that the prince might think that they did not know it. "By him am I sent unto you, as from a prince to his well approved subjects—nay, as from a father to beloved children—to know what it is that hath bred just quarrel among you, or who they be that have any way wronged you? What it is with which you are displeased, or of which you are desirous? This he requires, and indeed (for he knows your faithfulness) he commands you presently to sit down and to choose among yourselves someone who may relate your griefs or demands unto him."

This, being more than they hoped for from their prince,

[48] tall—brave.
[49] wights—creatures.

assuaged well their fury, and many of them consented (especially the young farmer helping on, who meant to make one of the demands that he might have Zelmane for his wife), but, when they began to talk of their griefs, never bees made such a confused humming: the town dwellers demanding putting down of imposts,[50] the country fellows laying out of commons;[51] some would have the prince keep his court in one place, some in another; all cried to have new counsellors, but when they should think of any new, they liked them as well as any other that they could remember; especially they would have the treasure so looked unto as that he should never need to take any more subsidies.

At length they fell to direct contrarieties. For the artisans, they would have corn and wine set at a lower price and bound to be kept so still; the plowmen, vine-laborers, and farmers would none of that. The countrymen demanded that every man might be free in the chief towns; that could not the burgesses like of. The peasant would have the gentlemen destroyed; the citizens (especially such as cooks, barbers, and those other that lived most on gentlemen) would but have them reformed. And of each side were like divisions, one neighborhood beginning to find fault with another. But no confusion was greater than of particular men's likings and dislikings: one dispraising such a one whom another praised, and demanding such a one to be punished whom the other would have exalted. No less ado was there about choosing him who should be their spokesman. The finer sort of burgesses, as merchants' prentices and clothworkers, because of their riches disdaining the baser occupations, and they, because of their number, as much disdaining them; all they scorning the countrymen's ignorance, and the countrymen suspecting as much their cunning.

So that Zelmane (finding that their united rage was now grown, not only to a dividing, but to a crossing one of another, and that the mislike grown among themselves did well allay the

[50] imposts—customs duties levied on goods.
[51] laying out of commons—return of public lands which had been enclosed for private use.

heat against her) made tokens again unto them (as though she took great care of their well doing and were afraid of their falling out) that she would speak unto them. They now grown jealous one of another (the stay having engendered division, and division having manifested their weakness) were willing enough to hear, the most part striving to show themselves willinger than their fellows; which Zelmane, by the acquaintance she had had with such kind of humors, soon perceiving, with an angerless bravery and an unabashed mildness in this manner spake unto them.

"An unused thing it is, and I think not heretofore seen, O Arcadians, that a woman should give public counsel to men; a stranger, to the country people; and that lastly in such a presence, by a private person, the regal throne should be possessed. But the strangeness of your action makes that used for virtue which your violent necessity imposeth. For certainly, a woman may well speak to such men who have forgotten all manlike government. A stranger may with reason instruct such subjects, that neglect due points of subjection. And is it marvel this place is entered into by another, since your own prince, after thirty years' government, dare not show his face unto his faithful people? Hear, therefore, O Arcadians, and be ashamed. Against whom hath this rage been stirred? Whither have been bent these manful weapons of yours? In this quiet, harmless lodge are harbored no Argians,[52] your ancient enemies, nor Laconians,[53] your now feared neighbors. Here be neither hard landlords nor biting usurers. Here lodge none but such as either you have great cause to love or no cause to hate; here being none, besides your prince, princess, and their children, but myself.

"Is it I, then, O Arcadians, against whom your anger is armed? Am I the mark of your vehement quarrel? If it be so, that innocency shall not be a stop for fury; if it be so, that the law of hospitality, so long and holily observed among you, may not defend a stranger fled to your arms for succor; if in fine it be so, that so many valiant men's courages can be inflamed to

[52] Argians—natives of Argos, a small region east of Arcadia.
[53] Laconians—Spartans.

the mischief of one silly woman—I refuse not, to make my life a sacrifice to your wrath. Exercise in me your indignation; so it go no further, I am content to pay the great favors I have received among you with my life. Not ill deserving I present it here unto you, O Arcadians, if that may satisfy you, rather than you (called over the world the wise and quiet Arcadians) should be so vain as to attempt that alone, which all the rest of your country will abhor, than you should show yourselves so ungrateful as to forget the fruit of so many years peaceable government or so unnatural as not to have with the holy name of your natural prince any fury over-mastered.

"For such a hellish madness, I know, did never enter into your hearts as to attempt anything against his person, which no successor, though never so hateful, will ever leave (for his own sake) unrevenged. Neither can your wonted valor be turned to such baseness as, instead of a prince delivered unto you by so many royal ancestors, to take the tyrannous yoke of your fellow subject, in whom the innate means will bring forth ravenous covetousness, and the newness of his estate, suspectful cruelty. Imagine, what could your enemies more wish unto you than to see your own estate with your own hands undermined. O what would your forefathers say, if they lived at this time and saw their offspring defacing such an excellent principality, which they with so much labor and blood so wisely have established? Do you think them fools that saw you should not enjoy your vines, your cattle—no, not your wives and children—without government, and that there could be no government without a magistrate, and no magistrate without obedience, and no obedience where everyone, upon his own private passion, may interpret the doings of the rulers.

"Let your wits make your present example to you. What sweetness, in good faith, find you in your present condition? What choice of choice find you, if you had lost Basilius? Under whose ensign would you go, if your enemies should invade you? If you cannot agree upon one to speak for you, how will you agree upon one to fight for you? But with this fear of I cannot tell what, one is troubled, and with that passed wrong, another is grieved. And I pray you, did the sun ever bring you a fruitful harvest, but that it was more hot than pleasant? Have any of you children that be not sometimes cumbersome? Have any of you fathers that be not sometime wearish?[54] What, shall we curse the sun, hate our children, or disobey our fathers?"

"But what need I use these words, since I see in your countenances—now virtuously settled—nothing else but love and duty to him by whom for your only sakes the government is embraced. For all what is done, he doth not only pardon you, but thank you, judging the action by the minds and not the minds by the action. Your griefs and desires, whatsoever and whensoever you list, he will consider of, and to his consideration it is reason you should prefer them. So then, to conclude: the uncertainty of his estate made you take arms; now you see him well, with the same love lay them down. If now you end (as I know you will), he will make no other account of this matter but as of a vehement—I must confess over-vehement—affection. The only continuance might prove a wickedness. But it is not so, I see very well; you began with zeal, and will end with reverence."

The action Zelmane used, being beautified by nature and appareled with skill (her gestures being such that, as her words did paint out her mind, so they served as a shadow, to make the pictures more lively and sensible, with the sweet clearness of her voice, rising and falling kindly as the nature of the word and efficacy of the matter required), altogether in such admirable person, whose incomparable valor they had well felt, whose beauty did pierce through the thick dullness of their senses, gave such a way unto her speech through the rugged wilderness of their imaginations, who (besides they were striken in admiration of her, as of more than a human creature) were cold with taking breath and had learned doubts out of leisure, that, instead of roaring cries, there was now heard nothing but a confused muttering, whether her saying were to be followed, betwixt fear to pursue and loathsomeness to leave. Most of them could have

[54] wearish—tiresome.

been content it had never been begun, but how to end it (each afraid of his companion) they knew not, finding it far easier to tie than to loose knots.

But Zelmane, thinking it no evil way in such mutinies to give the mutinous some occasion of such service as they might think in their own judgment would countervail their trespass, withal to take the more assured possession of their minds, which she feared might begin to waver, "Loyal Arcadians," said she, "now do I offer unto you the manifesting of your duties: all those that have taken arms for the prince's safety, let them turn their backs to the gate, with their weapons bent against such as would hurt his sacred person."

"O weak trust of the many-headed multitude, whom inconstancy only doth guide to well-doing; who can set confidence there, where company takes away shame, and each may lay the fault of his fellow?" So said a crafty fellow among them, named Clinias,[55] to himself, when he saw the word no sooner out of Zelmane's mouth but that there were some shouts of joy, with "God save Basilius!" and divers of them with much jollity grown to be his guard, that but little before meant to be his murderers.

CHAPTER 27

[The author narrates the history of Clinias: how he incited the people against Basilius and how, when the insurrection seemed to be losing popular support, he recanted, thereby precipitating a riot in which all but twelve of the insurgents were slain. Then Clinias, brought before Basilius, recites his version of the events, winning the king's favor through judicious flattery. Basilius then takes measures to garrison the principal towns of his realm against further violence.]

CHAPTER 28

The praises of Zelmane's act. Dametas' carol for saving himself and his charge. Basilius' conference with Philanax of the oracle

[55] Clinias—"parasitic."

(the ground of all this story). His wrong construction of it. His courting turned over to tale-telling.

This, Clinias (having his ear one way when his eye was another) had perceived, and therefore hasted away with mind to tell Cecropia that she was to take some speedy resolution, or else it were danger those examinations would both discover and ruin her; and so went his way, leaving that little company with embracements, and praising of Zelmane's excellent proceeding, to show that no decking sets forth anything so much as affection. For as, while she stood at the discretion of those indiscreet rebels, every angry countenance any of them made seemed a knife laid upon their own throats; so unspeakable was now their joy, that they saw (besides her safety and their own) the same wrought, and safely wrought by her means, in whom they had placed all their delights. What examples Greece could ever allege of wit and fortitude were set in the rank of trifles, being compared to this action.

But as they were in the midst of those unfeigned ceremonies, a gittern[56] ill played on, accompanied with a hoarse voice (who seemed to sing maugre[57] the Muses, and to be merry in spite of fortune), made them look the way of the ill-noised song. The song was this:

[*OA25*]

A hateful cure with hate to heal;
A bloody help with blood to save;
A foolish thing with fools to deal;
Let him be bold that bobs[58] will have.
  But who by means of wisdom high
  Hath sav'd his charge? It is even I.

Let other deck their pride with scars,
And of their wounds make brave lame shows;

---

[56] gittern—a medieval guitar.
[57] maugre—in spite of.
[58] bobs—obeisances.

First let them die, then pass the stars,
When rotten fame will tell their blows.
    But eye from blade, and ear from cry,
    Who hath sav'd all? It is even I.

They had soon found it was Dametas, who came with no less
lifted-up countenance than if he had passed over the bellies of all
his enemies, so wise a point he thought he had performed, in
using the natural strength of a cave. But never was it his doing to
come so soon thence till the coast were more assuredly clear, for
it was a rule with him that, after a great storm there ever fall a
few drops before it be fully finished. But Pamela (who had now
experienced how much care doth solicit a lover's heart) used this
occasion of going to her parents and sister, indeed as well for that
cause as being unquiet till her eye might be assured how her
shepherd had gone through the danger. But Basilius, with the
sight of Pamela, of whom almost his head, otherwise occupied,
had left the wonted remembrance, was suddenly stricken into a
devout kind of admiration, remembering the oracle, which, according to the fawning humor of false hope, he interpreted
now his own to his own best, and with the willing blindness of
affection (because his mind ran wholly upon Zelmane), he
thought the gods in their oracles did principally mind her.
    But, as he was deeply thinking of the matter, one of the
shepherds told him that Philanax was already come with a hundred horse in his company. For having by chance rid not far off
the little desert, he had heard of this uproar, and so was come
upon the spur, gathering a company of gentlemen as fast as he
could, to the succor of his master. Basilius was glad of it; but,
not willing to have him, nor any other of the noblemen, see his
mistress, he himself went out of the lodge, and so giving order
unto him of placing garrisons and examining these matters, and
Philanax, with humble earnestness, beginning to entreat him to
leave of his solitary course, which already had been so dangerous unto him, "Well," said Basilius, "it may be ere long I will
condescend unto your desire. In the meantime, take you the best
order you can to keep me safe in my solitariness." "But," said he,

"do you remember how earnestly you wrote unto me that I should not be moved by that oracle's authority, which brought me to this resolution?"

"Full well, sir," answered Philanax, "for though it pleased you not as then to let me know what the oracle's words were, yet—all oracles holding in my conceit, one degree of reputation —it sufficed me to know it was but an oracle which led you from your own course."

"Well," said Basilius, "I will now tell you the words, which before I thought not good to do because when all the events fall out, as some already have done, I may charge you with your incredulity." So he repeated them in this sort:[59]

"Thy elder care shall from thy careful face
By princely mean be stol'n, and yet not lost;
Thy younger shall with nature's bliss embrace
An uncouth love, which nature hateth most;
Both they themselves unto such two shall wed,
Who at thy bier, as at a bar, shall plead
Why thee, a living man, they had made dead.
In thine own seat a foreign state shall sit;
And ere that all these blows thy head do hit,
Thou, with thy wife, adultery shall commit."

"For you, forsooth," said he, "when I told you that some supernatural cause sent me strange visions, which being confirmed with presagious chances, I had gone to Delphos, and there received this answer, you replied to me, that the only supernatural causes were the humors of my body, which bred such melancholy dreams, and that both they framed a mind full of conceits, apt to make presages of things which in themselves were merely changeable; and withal, as I say, you remember what you wrote unto me touching authority of the oracle. But now I have some notable trial of the truth thereof, which hereafter I will more largely communicate unto you. Only now know that the thing I most feared is already performed—I mean that a foreign state

[59] sort—compare with OA 1.

should possess my throne. For that hath been done by Zelmane, but not, as I feared, to my ruin, but to my preservation."

But when he had once named Zelmane, that name was as good as a pulley to make the clock of his praises run on in such sort that, Philanax found, was more exquisite than the only admiration of virtue breedeth, which his faithful heart inwardly repining at made him shrink away as soon as he could to go about the other matters of importance which Basilius had enjoined unto him.

Basilius returned into the lodge, thus by himself construing the oracle: that, in that he said his elder care should by princely mean be stolen away from him and yet not lost, it was now performed, since Zelmane had, as it were, robbed from him the care of his first-begotten child, yet was it not lost, since in his heart the ground of it remained. That his younger should with nature's bliss embrace the love of Zelmane because he had so commanded her for his sake to do, yet should it be with as much hate of nature, for being so hateful an opposite to the jealousy he thought her mother had of him. The sitting in his seat he deemed by her already performed, but that which most comforted him was his interpretation of the adultery, which he thought he should commit with Zelmane, whom afterwards he should have to his wife. The point of his daughters' marriage because it threatened his death withal, he determined to prevent with keeping them unmarried while he lived. But having, as he thought, gotten thus much understanding of the oracle, he determined for three days after to perform certain rites to Apollo; and even then began with his wife and daughters to sing this hymn, by them yearly used.

[There follows the hymn, OA 26, after which Philoclea tells her father that she will continue to woo Zelmane for him and Zelmane asks Basilius to continue the story of Plangus and Erona.]

CHAPTER 29

[Basilius finally tells the story of Antiphilus. After receiving his throne from Musidorus and Pyrocles, the vain husband of

Erona fell prey to courtly sycophants who persuaded him that he
stemmed from a royal line usurped by his wife's family. Consequently, Antiphilus began to hate Erona and to seek another,
concurrent marriage with Artaxia, Tiridates' sister, who hated
both him and his wife. Artaxia pretended interest, and, when
Antiphilus came to make the final arrangements, she imprisoned
both him and Erona. Plangus, who was still at the court of Armenia, became enamoured of Erona; and, since she remained
faithful to her unworthy husband, Plangus sought means to
rescue Antiphilus. In this cause he failed, however, and the luck-
less king was executed. But he did succeed in defeating Artaxia's
forces and saving the life of Erona. In the subsequent bargaining,
it was agreed that, if Pyrocles and Musidorus did not appear
within a year and overcome any two knights of Artaxia's choosing, Erona would be burned at the stake; otherwise, she would
be freed. Plangus began to seek the cousins, but, having inter-
cepted some letters from Plexirtus to Artaxia, his fiancée, he
discovered the assassination plot. Moreover, in Plangus' absence,
Artaxia and Plexirtus besieged the castle in which Erona was
being held for safekeeping. Distraught, Plangus was seeking
Evarchus, to beg his aid, when he encountered Basilius.]

Book III

CHAPTER I

*Dorus' fair and foul weather in his love. His forlorn agonies. His
doubts to write, and Pamela's, to read, his elegy.*

This last day's danger, having made Pamela's love discern
what a loss it should have suffered if Dorus had been destroyed,
bred such tenderness of kindness in her toward him that she
could no longer keep love from looking through her eyes, and
going forth in her words, whom before as a close prisoner she
had to her heart only committed; so as finding not only by his
speeches and letters, but by the pitiful oration of languishing
behavior and the easily deciphered character of a sorrowful face

that despair began now to threaten him destruction, she grew content both to pity him and let him see she pitied him, as well by making her own beautiful beams thaw away the former iciness of her behavior, as by entertaining his discourses, whensoever he did use them, in the third person of Musidorus, to so far a degree that in the end she said that, if she had been the princess whom that disguised prince had virtuously loved, she would have requited his faith with faithful affection, finding in her heart that nothing could so heartily love as virtue; with many mo words to the same sense of noble favor and chaste plainness, which, when at the first it made that expected[1] bliss shine upon Dorus, he was like one frozen with extremity of cold, overhastily brought to a great fire: rather oppressed, than relieved, with such a lightening of felicity.

But after the strength of nature had made him able to feel the sweetness of joyfulness, that again being a child of passion, and never acquainted with mediocrity,[2] could not set bounds upon his happiness, nor be content to give desire a kingdom, but that it must be an unlimited monarchy; so that the ground he stood upon being over-high in happiness and slippery through affection, he could not hold himself from falling into such an error, which with sighs blew all comfort out of his breast, and washed away all cheerfulness of his cheer with tears. For this favor filling him with hope, hope encouraging his desire, and desire considering nothing but opportunity, one time (Mopsa being called away by her mother, and he left alone with Pamela) the sudden occasion called love, and that never stayed to ask reason's leave, but made the too-much loving Dorus take her in his arms, offering to kiss her, and, as it were, to establish a trophy of his victory.

But she, as if she had been ready to drink a wine of excellent taste and color, which suddenly she perceived had poison in it, so did she put him away from her. Looking first unto heaven, as amazed to find herself so beguiled in him, then laying the cruel punishment upon him of angry love and lowering beauty, show-

1 expected—desired.
2 mediocrity—moderation.

ing disdain (and a despising disdain), "Away!" said she, "unworthy man to love, or to be loved. Assure thyself, I hate myself for being so deceived; judge then what I do thee for deceiving me. Let me see thee no more, the only fall of my judgment and stain of my conscience." With that she called Mopsa, not staying for any answer (which was no other but a flood of tears, which she seemed not to mark, much less to pity), and chid her for having so left her alone.

It was not an amazement, it was not a sorrow, but it was even a death, which then laid hold of Dorus; which certainly at that instant would have killed him, but that the fear to tarry longer in her presence, contrary to her commandment, gave him life to carry himself away from her sight, and to run into the woods, where, throwing himself down at the foot of a tree, he did not fall to lamentation, for that proceeded of pitying or grieving for himself, which he did no way, but to curses of his life, as one that detested himself. For, finding himself not only unhappy, but unhappy after being fallen from all happiness, and to be fallen from all happiness, not by any misconceiving, but by his own fault, and his fault to be done to no other but to Pamela, he did not tender his own estate, but despised it, greedily drawing into his mind all conceits which might more and more torment him. And so remained he two days in the woods, disdaining to give his body food or his mind comfort, loving in himself nothing but the love of her.

And indeed that love only strove with the fury of his anguish, telling it that, if it destroyed Dorus, it should also destroy the image of her that lived in Dorus; and when the thought of that was crept in unto him, it began to win of him some compassion to the shrine of the image, and to bewail not for himself (whom he hated) but that so notable a love should perish. Then began he only so far to wish his own good as that Pamela might pardon him the fault, though not the punishment; and the uttermost height he aspired unto was, that after his death she might yet pity his error, and know that it proceeded of love, and not of boldness. That conceit found such friendship in his thoughts that at last he yielded, since he was banished her presence, to seek some means by writing to show his sorrow and testify his repentance. Therefore, getting him the necessary instruments of writing, he thought best to counterfeit his hand (fearing that as already she knew his, she would cast it away as soon as she saw it) and to put it in verse, hoping that would draw her on to read the more, choosing the elegiac as fittest for mourning. But pen did never more quakingly perform his office; never was paper more double moistened with ink and tears; never words more slowly married together, and never the Muses more tired than now with changes and rechanges of his devices, fearing how to end before he had resolved how to begin, mistrusting each word, condemning each sentence. This word was not significant, that word was too plain; this would not be conceived,[3] the other would be ill conceived. Here sorrow was not enough expressed; there he seemed too much for his own sake to be sorry. This sentence rather showed art[4] than passion; that sentence rather foolishly passionate than forcibly moving. At last, marring with mending, and putting out better than he left, he made an end of it. And being ended, and diverse times ready to tear it, till his reason assuring him, the more he studied the worse it grew, he folded it up, devoutly invoking good acceptation unto it. And watching his time, when they were all gone one day to dinner (saving Mopsa) to the other lodge, stole up into Pamela's chamber, and in her standish[5] (which first he kissed and craved of it a safe and friendly keeping) left it there to be seen at her next using her ink (himself returning again to be true prisoner to desperate sorrow), leaving her standish upon her bed's head, to give her the more occasion to mark it, which also fell out.

For she, finding it at her afternoon return in another place than she left it, opened it. But when she saw the letter, her heart gave her from whence it came. And therefore clapping it to again, she went away from it, as if it had been a contagious garment of an infected person, and yet, was not long away but that she wished she had read it, though she were loath to read it.

[3] conceived—understood.
[4] art—artificiality.
[5] standish—a stand containing pens, ink, and writing paper.

"Shall I," said she, "second his boldness so far as to read his presumptuous letters?" "And yet," said she, "he sees me not to grow the bolder thereby. And how can I tell whether they be presumptuous?" The paper came from him, and therefore not worthy to be received, and yet the paper, she thought, was not guilty. At last, she concluded, it were not much amiss to look it over that she might out of his words pick some further quarrel against him. Then she opened it, and threw it away, and took it up again, till (ere she were aware) her eyes would needs read it, containing this matter:

[*OA74 followed here*]

CHAPTER 2

The young ladies met: invited to the country wenches' sports, go thither, there are taken, and thence carried to Amphialus' castle. Their entertainment there. Cecropia's auricular[6] confession of her proud carriage in prosperity, and ambitious practices in adversity. Amphialus' affection[7] in these actions.

What this would have wrought in her, she herself could not tell; for, before her reason could moderate the disputation between favor and faultiness, her sister and Miso called her down to entertain Zelmane, who was come to visit the two sisters, about whom, as about two poles, the sky of beauty was turned; while Gynecia wearied her bed with her melancholy sickness, and made Miso's shrewdness (who, like a sprite set to keep a treasure, barred Zelmane from any further conference) to be the lieutenant of her jealousy, both she and her husband driving Zelmane to such a strait of resolution—either of impossible granting or dangerous refusing—as the best escape she had was, as much as she could, to avoid their company. So as, this day, being the fourth day after the uproar, Basilius being with his sick wife (conferring upon such examinations as Philanax and other of his noblemen

---

[6] auricular—private.
[7] Amphialus' affection—the role of Amphialus' affections.

had made of this late sedition, all touching Cecropia with vehement suspicion of giving either flame or fuel unto it), Zelmane came with her body to find her mind, which was gone long before her and had gotten his seat in Philoclea, who now, with a bashful cheerfulness, as though she were ashamed that she could not choose but be glad, joined with her sister in making much of Zelmane.

And so, as they sat devising how to give more feathers to the wings of time, there came to the lodge-door six maids, all in one livery scarlet petticoats,[8] which were tucked up almost to their knees, the petticoats themselves being in many places garnished with leaves, their legs naked, saving that above the ankles they had little black silk laces, upon which did hang a few silver bells, like which they had a little above their elbows, upon their bare arms. Upon their hair they wore garlands of roses and gilliflowers,[9] and the hair was so dressed as that came again above the garlands, interchanging a mutual covering; so as it was doubtful, whether the hair dressed the garlands, or the garlands dressed the hair. Their breasts liberal to the eye, the face of the foremost of them in excellency fair, and of the rest lovely, if not beautiful; and beautiful would have been, if they had not suffered greedy Phoebus, over-often and hard, to kiss them. Their countenances full of a graceful gravity, so as the gesture matched with the apparel, it might seem a wanton modesty and an enticing soberness. Each of them had an instrument of music in their hands, which, consorting their well-pleasing tunes, did charge each ear with unsensibleness that did not lend itself unto them. The music entering alone into the lodge, the ladies were all desirous to see from whence so pleasant a guest was come, and therefore went out together, where, before they could take the pains to doubt, much less to ask the question of their quality, the fairest of them, with a gay, but yet discreet, demeanor, in this sort spake unto them:

"Most excellent ladies, whose excellencies have power to make cities envy these woods, and solitariness to be accounted

[8] petticoats—skirts.
[9] gilliflowers—clove-scented pinks.

the sweetest company, vouchsafe our message your gracious hearing, which, as it comes from love, so comes it from lovely[10] persons. The maids of all this coast of Arcadia, understanding the often access that certain shepherds of these quarters are allowed to have in this forbidden place, and that their rural sports are not disdained of you, have been stirred up with emulation to them, and affection to you, to bring forth something which might as well breed your contentment; and therefore, hoping that the goodness of their intention and the hurtlessness of their sex shall excuse the breach of the commandment in coming to this place unsent for, they chose out us to invite both your princely parents and yourselves to a place in the woods, about half a mile hence, where they have provided some such sports as they trust your gracious acceptations will interpret to be delightful. We have been at the other lodge, but, finding them there busied in weightier affairs, our trust is, that you yet will not deny the shining of your eyes upon us."

The ladies stood in some doubt whether they should go or not, lest Basilius might be angry withal. But Miso, that had been at none of the pastorals, and had a great desire to lead her old senses abroad to some pleasure, told them plainly they should nor will nor choose, but go thither, and make the honest country people know that they were not so squeamish as folks thought of them. The ladies, glad to be warranted by her authority, with a smiling humbleness obeyed her, Pamela only casting a seeking look whether she could see Dorus (who, poor wretch, wandered half mad for sorrow in the woods, crying for pardon of her who could not hear him), but indeed was grieved for his absence, having given the wound to him through her own heart. But so the three ladies and Miso went with those six nymphs, conquering the length of the way with the force of music, leaving only Mopsa behind, who disgraced weeping with her countenance, because her mother would not suffer her to show her new-scoured face among them; but the place appointed, as they thought, met them half in their way, so well were they pleased with the sweet tunes and pretty conversation of their inviters.

[10] lovely—lovable.

There found they, in the midst of the thickest part of the wood, a little square place, not burdened with trees, but with a board covered and beautified with the pleasantest fruits that sun-burned autumn could deliver unto them. The maids besought the ladies to sit down and taste of the swelling grapes, which seemed great with child of Bacchus, and of the divers colored plums, which gave the eye a pleasant taste before they came to the mouth. The ladies would not show to scorn their provision, but eat and drank a little of their cool wine, which seemed to laugh for joy to come to' such lips.

But after the collation was ended, and that they looked for the coming forth of such devices as were prepared for them, there rushed out of the woods twenty armed men, who round about environed them, and, laying hold of Zelmane before she could draw her sword, and taking it from her, put hoods over the heads of all four, and, so muffled, by force set them on horse-back and carried them away, the sisters in vain crying for succor, while Zelmane's heart was rent in pieces with rage of the injury and disdain of her fortune. But when they had carried them a four or five mile further, they left Miso with a gag in her mouth, and bound hand and foot, so to take her fortune, and brought the three ladies (by that time that the night seemed with her silence to conspire to their treason) to a castle about ten mile off from the lodges, where they were fain to take boat which waited for them. For the castle stood in the midst of a great lake, upon a high rock, where, partly by art, but principally by nature, it was by all men esteemed impregnable.

But at the castle gate their faces were discovered, and there were met with a great number of torches, after whom the sisters knew their aunt-in-law, Cecropia. But that sight increased the deadly terror of the princesses, looking for nothing but death, since they were in the power of the wicked Cecropia, who yet came unto them, making courtesy the outside of mischief, and desiring them not to be discomforted; for they were in a place dedicated to their service. Philoclea, with a look where love shined through the mist of fear, besought her to be good unto them, having never deserved evil of her. But Pamela's high heart disdaining humbleness to injury, "Aunt," said she, "what you have determined of us I pray you do it speedily; for my part, I look for no service where I find violence."

But Cecropia, using no more words with them, conveyed them all three to several lodgings (Zelmane's heart so swelling with spite that she could not bring forth a word), and so left them, first taking from them their knives, because they should do themselves no hurt before she had determined of them; and then, giving such order that they wanted nothing but liberty and comfort, she went to her son, who yet kept his bed because of his wound he had received of Zelmane, and told him whom now he had in his power. Amphialus was but even then returned from far countries, where he had won immortal fame, both of courage and courtesy, when he met with the princesses, and was hurt by Zelmane, so as he was utterly ignorant of all his mother's wicked devices, to which he would never have consented, being—like a rose out of a briar—an excellent son of an evil mother; and now, when he heard of this, was as much amazed as if he had seen the sun fall to the earth, and therefore desired his mother that she would tell him the whole discourse, how all these matters had happened.

"Son," said she, "I will do it willingly, and, since all is done for you, I will hide nothing from you. And howsoever I might be ashamed to tell it strangers, who would think it wickedness, yet what is done for your sake, how evil soever to others, to you is virtue. To begin, then, even with the beginning, this doting fool Basilius that now reigns, having lived unmarried till he was nigh threescore years old, and in all his speeches affirming, and in all his doings assuring, that he never would marry, made all the eyes of the country to be bent upon your father, his only brother, but then younger by thirty years, as upon the undoubted successor, being indeed a man worthy to reign, thinking nothing enough for himself; where this goose, you see, puts down his head before there be anything near to touch him. So that he, holding place and estimation as heir of Arcadia, obtained me of my father the king of Argos, his brother helping to the conclusion with protesting his bachelorly intention, forelse (you may be sure) the king of Argos nor his daughter, would have suffered their royal blood to be stained with the base name of subjection. So that I came into this country as apparent princess thereof, and accordingly was courted and followed of the ladies of this country. My port and pomp did well become a king of Argos' daughter. In my presence their tongues were turned into ears, and their ears were captives unto my tongue; their eyes admired my majesty, and happy was he or she on whom I would suffer the beams thereof to fall. Did I go to church, it seemed the very gods waited for me, their devotions not being solemnized till I was ready. Did I walk abroad to see any delight—nay, my walking was the delight itself, for to it was the concourse,[11] one thrusting upon another, who might show himself most diligent and serviceable towards me. My sleeps were inquired after, and my wakings never unsaluted; the very gate of my house full of principal persons, who were glad if their presents had received a grateful acceptation. And in this felicity wert thou born, the very earth submitting itself unto thee to be trodden on as by his prince; and to that pass had my husband's virtue (by my good help) within short time brought it with a plot we laid, as we should not have needed to have waited the tedious work of a natural end of Basilius, when the heavens, I think envying my great felicity, then stopped thy father's breath, when he breathed nothing but power and sovereignty. Yet did not thy orphancy, or my widowhood, deprive us of the delightful prospect, which the hill of honor doth yield, while expectation of thy succession did bind dependencies unto us.

"But before, my son, thou wert come to the age to feel the sweetness of authority, this beast (whom I can never name with patience) falsely and foolishly married this Gynecia, then a young girl, and brought her to sit above me in all feasts, to turn her shoulder to me-ward in all our solemnities. It is certain it is not so great a spite to be surmounted by strangers as by one's own allies. Think, then, what my mind was, since withal there is no question the fall is greater from the first to the second than from the second to the undermost. The rage did swell in my

---

[11] to it was the concourse—people thronged towards it.

heart, so much the more as it was fain to be suppressed in silence, and disguised with humbleness. But, above all the rest, the grief of griefs was, when with these two daughters, now thy prisoners, she cut off all hope of thy succession. It was a tedious thing to me that my eyes should look lower than anybody's, that, myself being by, another's voice than mine should be more respected. But it was insupportable unto me, to think that not only I, but thou, shouldst spend all thy time in such misery, and that the sun should see my eldest son less than a prince. And though I had been a saint I could not choose, finding the change this change of fortune bred unto me, for now from the multitude of followers, silence grew to be at my gate, and absence in my presence. The guess of my mind could prevail more before than now many of my earnest requests; and thou, my dear son, by the fickle multitude no more than any ordinary person, born of the mud of the people, regarded.

"But I (remembering that in all miseries weeping becomes fools, and practice wise folks) have tried divers means to pull us out of the mire of subjection. And, though many times fortune failed me, yet did I never fail myself. Wild beasts I kept in a cave hard by the lodges, which I caused by night to be fed in the place of their pastorals, I as then living in my house hard by the place; and against the hour they were to meet (having kept the beasts without meat) then let them loose, knowing that they would seek their food there, and devour what they found. But blind Fortune, hating sharpsighted inventions, made them unluckily to be killed. After, I used my servant Clinias to stir a notable tumult of country people; but these louts were too gross instruments for delicate conceits. Now, lastly, finding Philanax's examinations grow dangerous, I thought to play double or quit, and with a sleight I used of my fine-witted wench Artesia, with other maids of mine, would have sent these goodly inheritrixes of Arcadia to have pleaded their cause before Pluto, but that, over-fortunately for them, you made me know the last day how vehemently this childish passion of love doth torment you. Therefore I have brought them unto you, yet wishing rather hate than love in you. For hate often begetteth victory; love commonly is the instrument of subjection. It is true that I would also by the same practice have entrapped the parents, but my maids failed of it, not daring to tarry long about it. But this sufficeth, since, these being taken away, you are the undoubted inheritor, and Basilius will not long overlive this loss."

"Oh, mother," said Amphialus, "speak not of doing them hurt, no more than to mine eyes or my heart, or if I have anything more dear than eyes or heart unto me. Let others find what sweetness they will in ever fearing, because they are ever feared; for my part, I will think myself highly entitled if I may be once by Philoclea accepted for a servant."

"Well," said Cecropia, "I would I had borne you of my mind, as well as of my body; then should you not have sunk under base weaknesses. But since you have tied your thoughts in so willful a knot, it is happy I have brought matters to such a pass as you may both enjoy affection and upon that build your sovereignty."

"Alas," said Amphialus, "my heart would fain yield you thanks for setting me in the way of felicity, but that fear kills them in me before they are fully born. For if Philoclea be displeased, how can I be pleased? If she count it unkindness, shall I give tokens of kindness? Perchance she condemns me of this action, and shall I triumph? Perchance she drowns now the beauties I love with sorrowful tears, and where is then my rejoicing?"

"You have reason," said Cecropia, with a feigned gravity; "I will therefore send her away presently, that her contentment may be recovered."

"No, good mother," said Amphialus, "since she is here, I would not for my life constrain presence, but rather would I die than consent to absence."

"Pretty intricate follies," said Cecropia; "but get you up, and see how you can prevail with her, while I go to the other sister, for after we shall have our hands full to defend ourselves, if Basilius hap to besiege us." But, remembering herself, she turned back, and asked him what he would have done with Zelmane, since now he might be revenged of his hurt.

"Nothing but honorably," answered Amphialus, "having deserved no other of me, especially being, as I hear, greatly cherished of Philoclea; and therefore, I could wish they were lodged together."

"Oh, no," said Cecropia, "company confirms resolutions, and loneliness breeds a weariness of one's thoughts, and so a sooner consenting to reasonable proffers."

CHAPTER 3

Amphialus' addressing him to Philoclea. Her melancholy habit. His humble suit. Her pitiful answer, and his compassionate reply. Their parting with cold comfort.

But Amphialus (taking of his mother Philoclea's knives, which he kept as a relic since she had worn them) got up, and calling for his richest apparel, nothing seemed sumptuous enough for his mistress's eyes, and that which was costly, he feared was not dainty, and though the invention were delicate, he misdoubted the making. As careful he was too of the color, lest if gay, he might seem to glory in his injury and her wrong; if mourning, it might strike some evil presage unto her of her fortune. At length he took a garment more rich than glaring, the ground being black velvet, richly embroidered with great pearl and precious stones, but they set so among certain tufts of cypress, that the cypress was like black clouds through which the stars might yield a dark luster. About his neck he wore a broad and gorgeous collar, whereof the pieces interchangeably answering: the one was of diamonds and pearl, set with a white enamel, so as by the cunning of the workman it seemed like a shining ice; and the other pieces being of rubies and opals, had a fiery glistering, which he thought pictured the two passions of fear and desire, wherein he was enchained. His hurt (not yet fully well) made him a little halt, but he strove to give the best grace he could unto his halting.

And in that sort he went to Philoclea's chamber, whom he found—because her chamber was over-lightsome—sitting of that side of her bed which was from the window, which did cast such a shadow upon her as a good painter would bestow upon Venus, when, under the trees, she bewailed the murther of Adonis; her hands and fingers, as it were, indented one within the other, her shoulder leaning to her bed's head, and over her head a scarf, which did eclipse almost half her eyes, which under it fixed their beams upon the wall by, with so steady a manner as if in that place they might well change, but not mend, their object; and so remained they a good while after his coming in, he not daring to trouble her, nor she perceiving him, till that, a little varying her thoughts something quickening her senses, she heard him as he happened to stir his upper garment, and, perceiving him, rose up with a demeanor where, in the book of beauty, there was nothing to be read but sorrow, for kindness was blotted out, and anger was never there.

But Amphialus, that had intrusted his memory with long and forcible speeches, found it so locked up in amazement that he could pick nothing out of it but the beseeching her to take what was done in good part, and to assure herself there was nothing but honor meant unto her person. But she, making no other answer, but letting her hands fall one from the other, which before were joined, with eyes something cast aside, and a silent sigh, gave him to understand that, considering his doings, she thought his speech as full of incongruity as her answer would be void of purpose; whereupon, he kneeling down and kissing her hand, which she suffered with a countenance witnessing captivity, but not kindness, he besought her to have pity of him, whose love went beyond the bounds of conceit, much more of uttering; that in her hands the balance of his life or death did stand, whereto the least motion of hers would serve to determine, she being indeed the mistress of his life, and he her eternal slave; and with true vehemency besought her that he might hear her speak, whereupon she suffered her sweet breath to turn itself into these kind of words.

"Alas, cousin," said she, "what shall my tongue be able to do, which is informed by the ears one way, and by the eyes another? You call for pity, and use cruelty; you say you love me, and yet do the effects of enmity; you affirm your death is in my hands, but you have brought me to so near a degree to death as, when you will, you may lay death upon me; so that while you say I am mistress of your life, I am not mistress of mine own. You entitle yourself my slave, but I am sure I am yours. If, then, violence, injury, terror, and depriving of that which is more dear than life itself—liberty—be fit orators for affection, you may expect that I will be easily persuaded. But if the nearness of our kindred breed any remorse in you, or there be any such thing in you which you call love toward me, then let not my fortune be disgraced with the name of imprisonment; let not my heart waste itself by being vexed with feeling evil and fearing worse. Let not me be a cause of my parents' woeful destruction, but restore me to myself, and, so doing, I shall account I have received myself of you. And what I say for myself, I say for my dear sister and my friend Zelmane, for I desire no well-being without they may be partakers." With that her tears rained down from her heavenly eyes, and seemed to water the sweet and beautiful flowers of her face.

But Amphialus was like the poor woman who, loving a tame doe she had, above all earthly things, having long played withal and made it feed at her hand and lap, is constrained at length by famine (all her flock being spent, and she fallen into extreme poverty) to kill the deer to sustain her life. Many a pitiful look doth she cast upon it, and many a time doth she draw back her hand before she can give the stroke. For even so Amphialus, by a hunger-starved affection, was compelled to offer this injury, and yet the same affection made him, with a tormenting grief, think unkindness in himself that he could find in his heart any way to restrain her freedom. But at length, neither able to grant nor deny, he thus answered her.

"Dear lady," said he, "I will not say unto you (how justly soever I may do it) that I am neither author nor accessory unto this your withholding; for, since I do not redress it, I am as faulty as if I had begun it. But this I protest unto you—and this protestation of mine, let the heavens hear; and if I lie, let them answer me with a deadly thunderbolt—that in my soul I wish I had never seen the light, or rather, that I had never had a father to beget such a child, than that by my means those eyes should overflow their own beauties, than by my means the sky of your virtue should be overclouded with sorrow. But woe is me, most excellent lady. I find myself most willing to obey you, neither truly do mine ears receive the least word you speak with any less reverence than as absolute and unresistible commandments; but, alas, that tyrant love, which now possesseth the hold of all my life and reason, will no way suffer it. It is love, it is love, not I, which disobey you. What then shall I say, but that I, who am ready to lie under your feet, to venture, nay, to lose my life at your least commandment, I am not the stay of your freedom, but love, love, which ties you in your own knots. It is you yourself that imprison yourself; it is your beauty which makes these castle walls embrace you; it is your own eyes which reflect upon themselves this injury. Then is there no other remedy, but that you some way vouchsafe to satisfy this love's vehemency, which since it grew in yourself, without question you shall find it, far more than I, tractable."

But with these words Philoclea fell to so extreme a quaking, and her lively whiteness did degenerate to so dead a paleness, that Amphialus feared some dangerous trance; so that, taking her hand, and feeling that it—which was wont to be one of the chief firebrands of Cupid—had all the sense of it wrapt up in coldness, he began humbly to beseech her to put away all fear, and to assure herself upon the vow he made thereof unto God and herself that the uttermost forces he would ever employ to conquer her affection should be desire and desert. That promise brought Philoclea again to herself, so that, slowly lifting up her eyes upon him, with a countenance ever courteous, but then languishing, she told him that he should do well to do so, if, indeed, he had ever tasted what true love was; for that where now she did bear him good will, she should, if he took any other way, hate and abhor the very thought of him, offering him withal that, though his mother had taken away her knives, yet the house of death had so many doors as she would easily fly into, if ever she found her honor endangered.

Amphialus, having the cold ashes of care cast upon the coals

of desire, leaving some of his mother's gentlewomen to wait upon
Philoclea, himself, indeed, a prisoner to his prisoner, and making
all his authority to be but a footstool to humbleness, went from
her to his mother; to whom, with words which affection indited,
but amazement uttered, he delivered what had passed between
him and Philoclea, beseeching her to try what her persuasions
could do with her, while he gave orders for all such things as
were necessary against such forces as he looked daily Basilius
would bring before his castle. His mother bade him quiet himself, for she doubted not to take fit times; but that the best way
was, first, to let her own passion a little tire itself.

CHAPTER 4

*Amphialus' warlike preparations. His justification. His fortifica-
tions. His art of men. His love passions, and passionate complaints.*
So they calling Clinias, and some other of their counsel, advised upon their present affairs. First, he dispatched private letters
to all those principal lords and gentlemen of the country whom
he thought either alliance or friendship to himself might draw,
with special motions from the general consideration of duty, not
omitting all such whom either youthful age or youthlike minds
did fill with unlimited desires, besides such whom any discontentment made hungry of change, or an over-spended want made
want a civil war, to each, according to the counsel of his mother,
conforming himself after their humors. To his friends, friendliness; to the ambitious, great expectations; to the displeased, revenge; to the greedy, spoil; wrapping their hopes with such
cunning as they rather seemed given over unto them as partakers
than promises sprung of necessity. Then sent he to his mother's
brother, the king of Argos, but he was as then so over-laid with
war himself as from thence he could attend small succor.

But, because he knew how violently rumors do blow the
sails of popular judgments, and how few there be that can discern between truth and truthlikeness, between shows and substance, he caused a justification of this his action to be written,
whereof were sowed abroad many copies, which, with some

glosses of probability, might hide indeed the foulness of his treason, and from true common-places fetch down most false applications. For, beginning how much the duty which is owed to the country goes beyond all other duties, since in itself it contains them all, and that for the respect thereof, not only all tender respects of kindred, or whatsoever other friendships, are to be laid aside, but that even long-held opinions—rather builded upon a secret of government than any ground of truth—are to be forsaken, he fell by degrees to show, that since the end whereto anything is directed is ever to be of more noble reckoning than the thing thereto directed, that therefore the weal public was more to be regarded than any person or magistrate that thereunto was ordained. The feeling consideration whereof had moved him, though as near of kin to Basilius as could be, yet to set principally before his eyes the good estate of so many thousands, over whom Basilius reigned, rather than so to hoodwink himself with affection as to suffer the realm to run to manifest ruin. The care whereof did kindly appertain to those who, being subaltern magistrates and officers of the crown, were to be employed as from the prince, so for the people; and of all other, especially himself, who being descended of the royal race, and next heir male, nature had no sooner opened his eyes, but that the soil whereupon they did look was to look for at his hands a continual carefulness, which as from his childhood he had ever carried; so now finding that his uncle had not only given over all care of government, but had put it into the hands of Philanax, a man neither in birth comparable to many, nor for his corrupt, proud, and partial dealing, liked of any, but, beside, had set his daughters (in whom the whole estate, as next heirs thereunto, had no less interest than himself) in so unfit and ill-guarded a place, as it was not only dangerous for their persons, but (if they should be conveyed to any foreign country) to the whole commonwealth pernicious; that, therefore, he had brought them into this strong castle of his, which way, if it might seem strange, they were to consider that new necessities require new remedies; but there they should be served and honored as belonged to their greatness, until, by the general assembly of the estates, it should be determined how they should to their best (both private and public) advantage be matched, vowing all faith and duty both to the father and children, never by him to be violated. But if in the meantime, before the estates could be assembled, he were assailed, he would then for his own defense take arms; desiring all, that either tendered the dangerous case of their country or in their hearts loved justice, to defend him in this just action. And if the prince should command them otherwise, yet to know, that therein he was no more to be obeyed than if he should call for poison to hurt himself withal, since all that was done was done for his service, howsoever he might—seduced by Philanax—interpret of it; he protesting that whatsoever he should do for his own defense should be against Philanax, and no way against Basilius.

To this effect, amplified with arguments and examples, and painted with rhetorical colors, did he sow abroad many discourses, which as they prevailed with some of more quick than sound conceit to run his fortune with him, so in many did it breed a coolness to deal violently against him, and a false-minded neutrality to expect the issue.[12] But, besides the ways he used to weaken the adverse party, he omitted nothing for the strengthening of his own; the chief trust whereof, because he wanted men to keep the field, he reposed in the surety of his castle, which at least would win him much time, the mother of many mutations. To that, therefore, he bent his outward and inward eyes, striving to make art strive with nature, to whether of them two that fortification should be most beholding. The seat nature bestowed, but art gave the building, which as his rocky hardness would not yield to undermining force, so to open assaults he took counsel of skill, how to make all approaches, if not impossible, yet difficult, as well at the foot of the castle as round about the lake, to give unquiet lodgings to them whom only enmity would make neighbors. Then omitted he nothing of defense, as well simple defense as that which did defend by offending, fitting instruments of mischief to places whence the mischief might be most liberally bestowed. Neither was his smallest care for victuals, as

12 expect the issue—await the outcome.

well for the providing that which should suffice, both in store and goodness, as in well preserving it, and wary distributing it, both in quantity and quality, spending that first which would keep least.

But wherein he sharpened his wits to the piercingest point was touching his men, knowing them to be the weapon of weapons and masterspring, as it were, which makes all the rest to stir; and that, therefore, in the art of man stood the quintessence and ruling skill of all prosperous government, either peaceable or military. He chose in number as many as without pestering[13] (and so, danger of infection) his victual would seem for two years to maintain; all of able bodies, and some few of able minds to direct, not seeking many commanders, but contenting himself that the multitude should have obeying wills, everyone knowing whom he should command and whom he should obey, the place where, and the matter wherein; distributing each office as near as he could to the disposition of the person that should exercise it, knowing no love, danger, nor discipline can suddenly alter a habit in nature. Therefore would he not employ the still man to a shifting practice,[14] nor the liberal man to be a dispenser of his victuals, nor the kind-hearted man to be a punisher, but would exercise their virtues in sorts where they might be profitable, employing his chief care to know them all particularly and thoroughly, regarding also the constitution of their bodies, some being able better to abide watching, some hunger, some labor, making his benefit of each ability, and not forcing beyond power. Time to everything by just proportion he allotted, and as well in that, as in everything else, no small error winked at, lest greater should be animated. Even of vices he made his profit, making the cowardly Clinias to have care of the watch, which he knew his own fear would make him very wakefully perform.

And before the siege began, he himself caused rumors to be sowed, and libels to be spread against himself, fuller of malice than witty persuasion: partly, to know those that would be apt

[13] pestering—over-crowding.
[14] the still man to a shifting practice—the sedentary man to a course of moving about.

to stumble at such motions, that he might cull them from the faithfuller band; but principally, because in necessity they should not know, when any such thing were in earnest attempted, whether it were, or not, of his own invention. But even then (before the enemy's face came near to breed any terror) did he exercise his men daily in all their charges, as if danger had presently presented his most hideous presence. Himself rather instructing by example than precept, being neither more sparing in travail nor spending in diet than the meanest soldier, his hand and body disdaining no base matters nor shrinking from the heavy.

[The chapter ends with a description of Amphialus' distraction, and his love lamentation.]

CHAPTER 5

Subtle Cecropia visits sad Philoclea. The shameless aunt's shrewd temptations to love and marriage. The modest niece's maidenly resistance.

Cecropia seeing her son's safety depend thereon, though her pride much disdained the name of a desire,[15] took the charge upon her, not doubting the easy conquest of an unexpert virgin, who had already with subtlety and impudency begun to undermine a monarchy. Therefore, weighing Philoclea's resolutions by the counterpease[16] of her own youthful thoughts (which she then called to mind), she doubted not at least to make Philoclea receive the poison, distilled in sweet liquor, which she with little disguising had drunk up thirstily. Therefore, she went softly to Philoclea's chamber and, peeping through the side of the door (then being a little open), she saw Philoclea sitting low upon a cushion, in such a given-over manner that one would have thought silence, solitariness, and melancholy were come there under the ensign of mishap to conquer delight and drive him from his natural seat of beauty. Her tears came dropping down

[15] disdained the name of a desire—resented admitting that she wanted something.

[16] counterpease—counterpoise, a weight used to achieve balance.

like rain in sunshine, and she not taking heed to wipe the tears, they ran down upon her cheeks and lips as upon cherries which the dropping tree bedeweth. In the dressing of her hair and apparel, she might see neither a careful art nor an art of carelessness, but even left to a neglected chance, which yet could no more unperfect her perfections than a die any way could lose his squareness.

Cecropia, stirred with no other pity but for her son, came in, and haling[17] kindness into her countenance, "What ails this sweet lady," said she, "will you mar so good eyes with weeping? Shall tears take away the beauty of that complexion, which the women of Arcadia wish for, and the men long after? Fie of this peevish sadness; in sooth it is untimely for your age. Look upon your own body and see whether it deserves to pine away with sorrow. See whether you will have these hands"—with that she took one of her hands and, kissing it, looked upon it as if she were enamored with it—"fade from their whiteness, which makes one desire to touch them, and their softness, which rebounds again a desire to look on them, and become dry, lean, and yellow, and make everybody wonder at the change and say that, sure, you had used some art before, which now you had left, for if the beauties had been natural, they would never so soon have been blemished. Take a glass and see whether these tears become your eyes; although, I must confess, those eyes are able to make tears comely."

"Alas, Madam," answered Philoclea, "I know not whether my tears become mine eyes, but I am sure mine eyes, thus beteared, become my fortune."

"Your fortune," said Cecropia, "if she could see to attire herself, would put on her best raiments. For I see—and I see it with grief, and, to tell you true, unkindness—you misconstrue everything that only for your sake is attempted. You think you are offended, and are indeed defended; you esteem yourself a prisoner, and are in truth a mistress; you fear hate, and shall find love. And truly, I had a thing to say to you, but it is no matter, since I find you are so obstinately melancholy

17 haling—forcing.

as that you woo his fellowship. I will spare my pains, and hold my peace."

And so stayed indeed, thinking Philoclea would have had a female inquisitiveness of the matter. But she, who rather wished to unknow what she knew than to burden her heart with more hopeless knowledge, only desired her to have pity of her, and if indeed she did mean her no hurt, then to grant her liberty; for else the very grief and fear would prove her unappointed executioners.

"For that," said Cecropia, "believe me upon the faith of a king's daughter, you shall be free so soon as your freedom may be free of mortal danger, being brought hither for no other cause but to prevent such mischiefs as you know not of. But if you think indeed to win me to have care of you, even as of mine own daughter, then lend your ears unto me and let not your mind arm itself with a wilfulness to be flexible to nothing. But if I speak reason, let reason have his due reward—persuasion.

"Then, sweet niece," said she, "I pray you presuppose that now—even in the midst of your agonies, which you paint unto yourself most horrible, wishing with sighs, and praying with vows, for a soon and safe delivery—imagine, niece, I say, that some heavenly spirit should appear unto you and bid you follow him through the door that goes into the garden, assuring you that you should thereby return to your dear mother, and what other delights soever your mind esteems delights. Would you, sweet niece, would you refuse to follow him; and say that, if he led you not through the chief gate, you would not enjoy your over-desired liberty? Would you not drink the wine you thirst for, without it were in such a glass as you especially fancied? Tell me, dear niece—but I will answer for you, because I know your reason and will is such as must needs conclude that such niceness can no more be in you, to disgrace such a mind, than disgracefulness can have any place in so faultless a beauty. Your wisdom would assuredly determine how the mark were hit, not whether the bow were of yew or no, wherein you shot. If this be so, and thus, sure, my dear niece, it is, then, I pray you, imagine that I am that same good angel who, grieving in your grief, and in truth not able to suffer that bitter sighs should be sent forth with so sweet a breath, am come to lead you, not only to your desired and imagined happiness, but to a true and essential happiness; not only to liberty, but to liberty with commandment.

"The way I will show you, which, if it be not the gate builded hitherto in your private choice, yet shall it be a door to bring you through a garden of pleasures as sweet as this life can bring forth; nay, rather, which makes this life to be a life: my son—let it be no blemish to him that I name him my son, who was your father's own nephew, for you know I am no small king's daughter—my son, I say, far passing the nearness of his kindred with the nearness of good will, and striving to match your matchless beauty with a matchless affection, doth by me present unto you the full enjoying of your liberty, so as with this gift you will accept a greater, which is this castle, with all the rest which you know he hath, in honorable quantity; and will confirm his gift, and your receipt of both, with accepting him to be yours. I might say much both for the person and the matter, but who will cry out the sun shines? It is so manifest a profit unto you as the meanest judgment must straight apprehend it; so far is it from the sharpness of yours thereof to be ignorant. Therefore, sweet niece, let your gratefulness be my intercession and your gentleness my eloquence, and let me carry comfort to a heart which greatly needs it."

Philoclea looked upon her and cast down her eye again. "Aunt," said she, "I would I could be so much a mistress of my own mind as to yield to my cousin's virtuous request, for so I construe of it. But my heart is already set"—and staying a while on that word, she brought forth afterwards—"to lead a virgin's life to my death, for such a vow I have in myself devoutly made."

"The heavens prevent such a mischief," said Cecropia. "A vow, quoth you? No, no, my dear niece. Nature, when you were first born, vowed you a woman, and as she made you child of a mother, so to do your best to be mother of a child. She gave you beauty to move love; she gave you wit to know love; she gave you an excellent body to reward love; which kind of liberal rewarding is crowned with unspeakable felicity. For this, as it bindeth the receiver, so it makes happy the bestower; this doth not impoverish but enrich the giver. O the sweet name of a mother! O the comfort of comforts, to see your children grow up, in whom you are, as it were, eternalized. If you could conceive what a heart-tickling joy it is to see your own little ones, with awful love, come running to your lap, and like little models of yourself still carry you about them, you would think unkindness in your own thoughts that ever they did rebel against the mean unto it. But perchance I set this blessedness before your eyes as captains do victory before their soldiers, to which they might come through many pains, griefs, and dangers? No, I am content you shrink from this my counsel, if the way to come unto it be not most of all pleasant."

"I know not," answered the sweet Philoclea, fearing lest silence would offend her sullenness, "what contentment you speak of, but I am sure the best you can make of it, which is marriage, is a burdenous yoke."

"Ah, dear niece," said Cecropia, "how much you are deceived! A yoke indeed we all bear, laid upon us in our creation, which by marriage is not increased but thus far eased, that you have a yoke-fellow to help to draw through the cloddy cumbers of this world. O widow-nights, bear witness with me of the difference! How often, alas, do I embrace the orphan-side of my bed, which was wont to be imprinted by the body of my dear husband, and with tears acknowledge that I now enjoy such a liberty as the banished man hath, who may, if he list, wander over the world but is ever restrained from his most delightful home! That I have now such a liberty as the seeled dove hath, which, being first deprived of eyes, is then by the falconer cast off! For believe me, niece, believe me, man's experience is woman's best eyesight. Have you ever seen a pure rosewater kept in a crystal glass, how fine it looks, how sweet it smells, while that beautiful glass imprisons it? Break the prison and let the water take his own course, doth it not embrace dust and lose all his former sweetness and fairness? Truly so are we if we have not the stay, rather than the restraint, of crystalline marriage. My heart melts to think of the sweet comforts I in that happy time received, when I had never cause to care but the care was doubled, when I never rejoiced, but that I saw my joy shine in another's eyes. What shall I say of the free delight which the heart might embrace without the accusing of the inward conscience of fear of outward shame? And is a solitary life as good as this? Then can one string make as good music as a consort; then can one color set forth a beauty.

"But it may be the general consideration of marriage doth not so much mislike you as the applying of it to him? He is my son; I must confess, I see him with a mother's eyes, which if they do not much deceive me, he is no such one over whom contempt may make any just challenge. He is comely, he is noble, he is rich; but that which in itself should carry all comeliness, nobility, and riches, he loves you; and he loves you, who is beloved of others. Drive not away his affection, sweet lady, and make no other lady hereafter proudly brag that she hath robbed you of so faithful and notable a servant."

Philoclea heard some pieces of her speeches no otherwise than one doth when a tedious prattler cumbers the hearing of a delightful music. For her thoughts had left her ears in that captivity and conveyed themselves to behold, with such eyes as imagination could lend them, the estate of her Zelmane, for whom how well she thought many of those sayings might have been used with a far more grateful acceptation. Therefore, listing not to dispute in a matter whereof herself was resolute, and desired not to inform the other, she only told her that, whilst she was so captived, she could not conceive of any such persuasions (though never so reasonable) any otherwise than as constraints; and, as constraints, must need even in nature abhor them, which, at her liberty, in their own force of reason, might more prevail with her, and so fain would have returned the strength of Cecropia's persuasions, to have procured freedom.

CHAPTER 6

Fresh motives[18] *to Philoclea. Cecropia's new fetch*[19] *to attempt Pamela. Pamela's prayer, and saint-like graces in it. Her aunt's fruitless arguments.*

But neither her witty words in any enemy, nor those words made more than eloquent with passing through such lips, could prevail in Cecropia, no more than her persuasions could win Philoclea to disavow her former vow, or to leave the prisoner Zelmane for the commanding Amphialus. So that both sides being desirous, and neither granters, they broke off conference, Cecropia sucking up more and more spite out of her denial, which yet, for her son's sake, she disguised with a visard of kindness, leaving no office unperformed which might either witness or endear her son's affection.

Whatsoever could be imagined likely to please her was, with liberal diligence, performed: musics at her window, and especially such musics as might (with doleful embassage) call the mind to think of sorrow, and think of it with sweetness; with ditties so sensibly expressing Amphialus' case, that every word seemed to be but a diversifying of the name of Amphialus. Daily presents, as it were oblations to pacify an angry deity, sent unto her: wherein, if the workmanship of the form had striven with the sumptuousness of the matter, as much did the invention in the application contend[20] to have the chief excellency; for they were as so many stories of his disgraces, and her perfections, where the richness did invite the eyes, the fashion did entertain the eyes, and the device did teach the eyes the present misery of the presenter himself, awfully[21] serviceable, which was the more notable, as his authority was manifest. And for the bondage wherein she lived, all means used to make known, that if it were a bondage, it was a bondage only knit in love-knots.

But in heart already understanding no language but one, the

[18] motives—temptations.

[19] fetch—stratagem.

[20] the invention in the application contend—the brilliance of the design contended with the marvelous execution.

[21] awfully—reverently.

music wrought indeed a dolefulness, but it was a dolefulness to be in his power; the ditty intended for Amphialus, she translated to Zelmane; the presents seemed so many tedious clogs of a thralled obligation;[22] and his service, the more diligent it was, the more it did exprobate[23] (as she thought) unto her, her unworthy estate, that even he that did her service, had authority of commanding her, only construing her servitude in his own nature, esteeming it a right, and a right bitter, servitude. So that all their shots (how well soever levelled) being carried awry from the mark by the storm of her mislike, the Prince Amphialus affectionately languished, and Cecropia, spitefully cunning, disdained at the barrenness of their success.

Which willingly Cecropia would have revenged, but that she saw her hurt could not be divided from her son's mischief; wherefore, she bethought herself to attempt Pamela, whose beauty being equal, she hoped, if she might be won, that her son's thoughts would rather rest on a beautiful gratefulness, than still be tormented with a disdaining beauty. Wherefore, giving new courage to her wicked inventions, and using the more industry, because she had missed in this, and taking even precepts[24] of prevailing in Pamela, by her failing in Philoclea, she went to her chamber, and (according to her own ungracious method of a subtle proceeding) stood listening at the door, because that out of the circumstance of her present behavior there might kindly arise a fit beginning of her intended discourse.

And so she might perceive that Pamela did walk up and down, full of deep (though patient) thoughts. For her look and countenance was settled, her pace soft, and almost still of one measure, without any passionate gesture of violent motion. Till at length, as it were, awakening, and strengthening herself, "Well," said she, "yet this is the best, and of this I am sure, that howsoever they wrong me, they cannot over-master God. No darkness blinds his eyes, no jail bars him out. To whom then else should I fly, but to him, for succor?"

22 clogs of a thralled obligation—chains of an unwanted bond.
23 exprobate—cast in her teeth.
24 precepts—mandates, orders.

And therewith kneeling down, even in the same place where she stood, she thus said,[25] "O all-seeing Light, and eternal Life of all things, to whom nothing is either so great, that it may resist, or so small, that it is contemned; look upon my misery with thine eyes of mercy, and let thine infinite power vouchsafe to limit out some proportion of deliverance unto me, as to thee shall seem most convenient. Let not injury, O Lord, triumph over me, and let my faults by thy hands be corrected, and make not mine unjust enemy the minister of thy justice. But yet, my God, if in thy wisdom, this be the aptest chastisement for my inexcusable folly, if this low bondage be fittest for my over-high desires, if the pride of my not-enough-humble heart be thus to be broken, O Lord, I yield unto thy will, and joyfully embrace what sorrow thou wilt have me suffer. Only thus much let me crave of thee (let my craving, O Lord, be accepted of thee, since even that proceeds from thee), let me crave, even by the noblest title which in my greatest affliction I may give myself, that I am thy creature, and by thy goodness (which is thyself), that thou wilt suffer some beam of thy majesty so to shine into my mind, that it may still depend confidently upon thee. Let calamity be the exercise, but not the overthrow, of my virtue; let their power prevail, but prevail not to destruction; let my greatness be their prey; let my pain be the sweetness of their revenge; let them (if so it seem good unto thee) vex me with more and more punishment. But, O Lord, let never their wickedness have such a hand, but that I may carry a pure mind in a pure body." And pausing a while, "And, O most gracious Lord," said she, "what ever become of me, preserve the virtuous Musidorus."

The other part Cecropia might well hear, but this latter prayer for Musidorus, her heart held it as so jewel-like a treasure, that it would scarce trust her own lips withal. But this prayer—sent to heaven from so heavenly a creature, with such a fervent grace as if devotion had borrowed her body to make of itself a most beautiful representation; with her eyes so lifted to the sky-ward, that one would have thought they had begun to fly

---

[25] said—This is the prayer which, much to Milton's disgust, Charles I is reported to have repeated just before his execution.

thitherward, to take their place among their fellow stars; her naked hands raising up their whole length, and as it were kissing one another, as if the right had been the picture of zeal and the left of humbleness, which both united themselves to make their suits more acceptable; lastly, all her senses being rather tokens than instruments of her inward motions—altogether had so strange a working power, that even the hardhearted wickedness of Cecropia, if it found not a love of that goodness, yet it felt an abashment at that goodness; and if she had not a kindly remorse, yet had she an irksome accusation of her own naughtiness, so that she was put from the bias of her fore-intended lesson. For well she found there was no way at that time to take that mind, but with some (at least) image of virtue, and what the figure thereof was, her heart knew not.

Yet did she prodigally spend her uttermost eloquence, leaving no argument unproved, which might with any force invade her excellent judgment: the justness of the request, being but for marriage; the worthiness of the suitor; then her own present fortune, if she would not only have amendment but felicity; besides falsely making her believe, that her sister would think herself happy if now she might have his love which before she contemned; and obliquely touching what danger it should be for her, if her son should accept Philoclea in marriage, and so match the next heir apparent, she being in his power; yet plentifully perjuring, how extremely her son loved her, and excusing the little shows he made of it, with the dutiful respect he bore unto her, and taking upon herself that she restrained him, since she found she could set no limits to his passions. And as she did to Philoclea, so did she to her, with the tribute of gifts, seek to bring her mind into servitude, and all other means, that might either establish a beholdingness, or at the least awake a kindness; doing it so, as by reason of their imprisonment, one sister knew not how the other was wooed, but each might think that only she was sought. But if Philoclea with sweet and humble dealing did avoid their assaults, she with the majesty of virtue did beat them off.

CHAPTER 7

[When Basilius' troops are advancing on the castle, Clinias hides,
while Amphialus, anxious for battle, takes a portion of his men
to a fortress across the lake and then leads them out to meet
the enemy. In the combat, Amphialus slays Agenor, Philanax'
youngest brother, and his comrade, Leontius. Throughout the
fierce and bloody fighting, Amphialus, spurred on by love, mir-
rors valor in all of his actions.]

CHAPTER 8

[Amphialus is winning the battle, when Philanax brings rein-
forcements to Basilius; the king's troops then rally and turn the
tide, slaughtering Amphialus' men as their own soldiers had been
slaughtered. Philanax, discovering his brother's body on the field,
becomes so enraged that he kills Amphialus' young squire, Ismenus, and drives so deeply into the enemy's ranks that he is
captured. After this loss, Basilius' troops begin to waver again,
but a black knight suddenly appears and rallies them with his
courage in combat. Amphialus, observing the havoc wreaked
among his soldiers by this newcomer, engages him in a duel.
But, before either man can deliver a decisive stroke, two of
Amphialus' men dishonorably wound the black knight from behind and urge their captain to retreat to the town, lest Basilius
cut them off.]

CHAPTER 9

[Back in the castle, Amphialus has a song sung to Philoclea, a
song made from the dream he dreamed on the eve of the day
he fell in love with her. In it, he is asked to choose whether
Venus should rule Diana, or vice versa. But he rejects both,
crowning instead a fair nymph named Mira. In retaliation, Venus
and Diana curse him with the burden of an unquenchable love
never to be satisfied. Philoclea remains indifferent, so Amphialus
departs to arrange Philanax' execution. Hearing of this, Philoclea

sends a letter to her captor, begging for Philanax' life. Amphialus, pleased to be addressed by his beloved, frees his prisoner, thanking him for having served as the occasion of so great a boon. Philanax, in reply, urges Amphialus to surrender and ask pardon of Basilius, advice which the desperate lover refuses. Meanwhile, Cecropia continues to woo both Philoclea and Pamela, intending that, if one should yield, the other should be secretly poisoned.]

CHAPTER 10

Pamela's exercise. Cecropia's talk with her of beauty and the use thereof. The aunt's atheism refuted by the niece's divinity.[26]

Cecropia, threatening in herself to run a more ragged race with her, went to her sister Pamela, who that day having wearied herself with reading, and with the height of her heart disdaining to keep company with any of the gentlewomen appointed to attend her, whom she accounted her jailors, was working upon a purse certain roses and lilies, as by the fineness of the work one might see she had borrowed her wits of the sorrow that owned them and lent them wholly to that exercise. For the flowers she had wrought carried such life in them that the cunningest painter might have learned of her needle, which with so pretty a manner made his careers to and fro through the cloth, as if the needle itself would have been loath to have gone from-ward such a mistress but that it hoped to return thence-ward very quickly again; the cloth looking with many eyes upon her, and lovingly embracing the wounds she gave it; the shears also were at hand to behead the silk that was growing too short. And if at any time she put her mouth to bite it off, it seemed that where she had been long in making of a rose with her hand, she would in an instant make roses with her lips; as the lilies seemed to have their whiteness rather of the hand that made them than of the matter whereof they were made; and that they grew there by the suns of her eyes, and were refreshed by the most (in discomfort) comfortable air, which an unawares sigh might bestow upon them. But the colors for the ground were so well chosen, neither

[26] divinity—skill in theology, also holiness.

sullenly dark nor glaringly lightsome, and so well proportioned as that, though much cunning were in it, yet it was but to serve for an ornament of the principal work; that it was not without marvel to see how a mind which could cast a careless semblant upon the greatest conflicts of fortune could command itself to take care for so small matters. Neither had she neglected the dainty dressing of herself, but, as it had been her marriage time to affliction, she rather seemed to remember her own worthiness than the unworthiness of her husband. For well one might perceive she had not rejected the counsel of a glass, and that her hands had pleased themselves in paying the tribute of undeceiving skill to so high perfections of nature.

The sight whereof, so diverse from her sister (who rather suffered sorrow to distress itself in her beauty than that she would bestow any entertainment of so unwelcome a guest), made Cecropia take a sudden assuredness of hope that she should obtain somewhat of Pamela: thinking (according to the squaring out of her own good nature)[27] that beauty carefully set forth would soon prove a sign of an unrefusing harborough.[28] Animated wherewith, she sat down by Pamela, and taking the purse, and with an affected curiosity looking upon the work, "Fully happy is he," said she, "at least if he knew his own happiness, to whom a purse in this manner, and by this hand wrought, is dedicated. In faith he shall have cause to account it, not as a purse for treasure, but as a treasure in itself, worthy to be pursed up in the purse of his own heart."

"And think you so, indeed," said Pamela, half smiling. "I promise you I wrought it but to make some tedious hours believe that I thought not of them; for else I valued it, but even as a very purse."

"It is the right nature," said Cecropia, "of beauty, to work unwitting effects of wonder."

"Truly," said Pamela, "I never thought till now that this outward glass, entitled beauty, which it pleaseth you to lay to

---

[27] according to the squaring out of her own good nature—judging by herself.

[28] harborough—shelter.

my (as I think) unguilty charge, was but a pleasant mixture of natural colors, delightful to the eye, as music is to the ear, without any further consequence, since it is a thing which not only beasts have, but even stones and trees, many of them, do greatly excel in it."

"That other things," answered Cecropia, "have some portion of it takes not away the excellency of it, where indeed it doth excel, since we see that even those beasts, trees, and stones are in the name of beauty only highly praised. But that the beauty of human persons be beyond all other things there is great likelihood of reason, since to them only is given the judgment to discern beauty; and among reasonable wights, as it seems that our sex hath the pre-eminence, so that in that pre-eminence, nature countervails[29] all other liberalities, wherein she may be thought to have dealt more favorably toward mankind. How do men crown, think you, themselves with glory, for having either by force brought others to yield to their mind, or, with long study and premeditated orations, persuaded what they would have persuaded? And see, a fair woman shall not only command without authority, but persuade without speaking. She shall not need to procure attention, for their own eyes will chain their ears unto it. Men venture lives to conquer; she conquers lives without venturing. She is served and obeyed, which is the most notable, not because the laws so command it, but because they become laws to themselves to obey her, not for her parents' sake, but for her own sake. She need not dispute whether to govern by fear or by love, since, without her thinking thereof, their love will bring forth fear, and their fear will fortify their love; and she need not seek offensive or defensive force, since her lips may stand for ten thousand shields, and ten thousand unevitable shot go from her eyes. Beauty, beauty, dear niece, is the crown of the feminine greatness, which gift, on whomsoever the heavens (therein most niggardly) do bestow, without question she is bound to use it to the noble purpose for which it is created, not only winning, but preserving; since that, indeed, is the right hap-

[29] countervails—reciprocates.

piness which is not only in itself happy, but can also derive the happiness to another."

"Certainly, aunt," said Pamela, "I fear me you will make me not only think myself fairer than ever I did, but think my fairness a matter of greater value than heretofore I could imagine it; for I ever, till now, conceived these conquests you spoke of rather to proceed from the weakness of the conquered than from the strength of the conquering power; as they say the cranes overthrow whole battles[30] of pigmies,[31] not so much of their cranish courage as because the other are pigmies, and that we see young babes think babies of wonderful excellency, and yet the babies are but babies. But, since your elder years and abler judgment find beauty to be worthy of so incomparable estimation, certainly, methinks, it ought to be held in dearness, according to the excellency, and (no more than we would do of things which we account precious) ever to suffer it to be defiled."

"Defiled!" said Cecropia; "marry, God forbid that my speech should tend to any such purpose as should deserve so foul a title. My meaning is to join your beauty to love, your youth to delight. For truly, as colors should be as good as nothing if there were no eyes to behold them, so is beauty nothing without the eye of love behold it; and therefore, so far is it from defiling it, that it is the only honoring of it, the only preserving of it. For beauty goes away, devoured by time, but where remains it ever flourishing, but in the heart of a true lover? And such a one (if ever there were any) is my son, whose love is so subjected unto you that, rather than breed any offense unto you, it will not delight itself in beholding you."

"There is no effect of his love," answered Pamela, "better pleaseth me than that. But as I have often answered you so resolutely, I say unto you, that he must get my parents' consent, and then he shall know further of my mind, for, without that, I know I should offend God."

[30] battles—battalions.

[31] cranes . . . pigmies—according to Ovid, the two war constantly; Juno changed a pigmy queen into a crane so she would war with those she ruled.

"O sweet youth," said Cecropia, "how untimely subject it is to devotion! No, no, sweet niece, let us old folks think of such precise[32] considerations; do you enjoy the heaven of your age, whereof you are sure; and like good householders, which spend those things that will not be kept, so do you pleasantly enjoy that which else will bring an over-late repentance when your glass shall accuse you to your face, what a change there is in you. Do you see how the springtime is full of flowers, decking itself with them, and not aspiring to the fruits of autumn? What lesson is that unto you, but that in the April of your age, you should be like April? Let not some of them, for whom already the grave gapeth, and perhaps envy the felicity in you which themselves cannot enjoy, persuade you to lose the hold of occasion, while it may not only be taken, but offers—nay sues—to be taken; which, if it be not now taken, will never hereafter be overtaken. Yourself know how your father hath refused all offers made by the greatest princes about you, and will you suffer your beauty to be hid in the wrinkles of his peevish thoughts?"

"If he be peevish," said Pamela, "yet is he my father, and how beautiful soever I be, I am his daughter; so, as God claims at my hands obedience, and makes me no judge of his imperfections."

These often replies upon conscience in Pamela made Cecropia think that there was no righter way for her than as she had, in her opinion, set her in liking of beauty, with persuasion not to suffer it to be void of purpose, so if she could make her less feeling of those heavenly conceits, that then she might easily wind her to her crooked bias. Therefore, employing the uttermost of her mischievous wit and speaking the more earnestly because she spake as she thought, she thus dealt with her:

"Dear niece, or, rather, dear daughter (if my affection and wish might prevail therein), how much doth it increase, trow you, the earnest desire I have of this blessed match, to see these virtues of yours knit fast with such zeal of devotion—indeed the best bond which the most politic wits have found to hold man's wit in well-doing? For, as children must first by fear be induced

---

[32] precise—over-scrupulous.

to know that which after, when they do know, they are most glad of, so are these bugbears of opinions brought by great clerks into the world, to serve as shewels[33] to keep them from those faults whereto else the vanity of the world, and weakness of senses, might pull them. But in you, niece, whose excellency is such as it need not to be held up by the staff of vulgar opinions, I would not you should love virtue servilely, for fear of I know not what, which you see not, but even for the good effects of virtue which you see. Fear—and indeed foolish fear—and fearful ignorance, was the first inventor of those conceits; for, when they heard it thunder, not knowing the natural cause, they thought there was some angry body above that spake so loud; and ever the less they did perceive, the more they did conceive. Whereof they knew no cause, that grew straight a miracle— foolish folks, not marking that the alterations be but upon particular accidents, the universality being always one. Yesterday was but as today, and tomorrow will tread the same footsteps of his foregoers; so, as it is manifest enough that all things follow but the course of their own nature, saving only man, who, while by the pregnancy of his imagination he strives to things supernatural, meanwhile he loseth his own natural felicity. Be wise, and that wisdom shall be a god unto thee; be contented, and that is thy heaven; for else to think that those powers (if there be such) above are moved, either by the eloquence of our prayers, or in a chafe, by the folly of our actions, carries as much reason as if flies should think that men take great care which of them hums sweetest and which of them flies nimblest."

She would have spoken further, to have enlarged and confirmed her discourse, but Pamela, whose cheeks were dyed in the beautifulest grain of virtuous anger, with eyes which glistered forth beams of disdain, thus interrupted her: "Peace! wicked woman, peace! unworthy to breathe, that dost not acknowledge the breath-giver; most unworthy to have a tongue, which speakest against him through whom thou speakest; keep your affection to yourself, which, like a bemired dog, would defile with fawning. You say yesterday was as today. O foolish woman, and

33 shewels—examples.

most miserably foolish, since wit makes you foolish! What doth that argue, but that there is a constancy in the everlasting governor? Would you have an inconstant God, since we count a man foolish that is inconstant? He is not seen, you say; and would you think him a god who might be seen by so wicked eyes as yours (which yet might see enough if they were not like such who, for sport sake, willingly hoodwink themselves to receive blows the easier)? But, though I speak to you without any hope of fruit in so rotten a heart (and there be nobody else here to judge of my speeches), yet be thou my witness, O captivity, that my ears shall not be willingly guilty of my creator's blasphemy. You say, because we know not the causes of things, therefore fear was the mother of superstition; nay, because we know that each effect hath a cause, that hath engendered a true and lively devotion. For this goodly work of which we are, and in which we live, hath not his being by chance; on which opinion it is beyond marvel by what chance any brain could stumble. For if it be eternal, as you would seem to conceive of it, eternity and chance are things unsufferable together. For that is chanceable which happeneth; and, if it happen, there was a time before it happened when it might not have happened; or else it did not happen, and so, of chanceable, not eternal, as now being, then not being.

"And as absurd it is to think that, if it had a beginning, his beginning was derived from chance, for chance could never make all things of nothing; and if there were substances before, which by chance should meet to make up this work, thereon follows another bottomless pit of absurdities. For then those substances must needs have been from ever, and so eternal; and that eternal causes should bring forth chanceable effects is as sensible as that the sun should be the author of darkness. Again, if it were chanceable, then was it not necessary; whereby you take away all consequents. But we see in all things, in some respect or other, necessity of consequence; therefore, in reason, we must needs know that the causes were necessary. Lastly, chance is variable, or else it is not to be called chance; but we see this work is steady and permanent. If nothing but chance had glued those pieces of this all, the heavy parts would have gone infinitely downward, the light infinitely upward, and so never have met to have made up this goodly body. For, before there was a heaven or an earth, there was neither a heaven to stay the height of the rising, nor an earth which, in respect of the round walls of heaven, should become a center. Lastly, perfect order, perfect beauty, perfect constancy, if these be the children of chance, or fortune the efficient of these, let wisdom be counted the root of wickedness, and eternity the fruit of her inconstancy.

"But you will say it is so by nature; as much as if you said it is so, because it is so. If you mean of many natures conspiring together, as in a popular government, to establish this fair estate, as if the elementish and ethereal parts should in their town-house[34] set down the bounds of each one's office, then consider what follows: that there must needs have been a wisdom which made them concur, for their natures, being absolute contrary, in nature rather would have sought each other's ruin than have served as well-consorted parts to such an inexpressible harmony. For that contrary things should meet to make up a perfection without a force and wisdom above their powers is absolutely impossible—unless you will fly to that hissed-out opinion of chance again. But you may perhaps affirm that one universal nature, which hath been forever, is the knitting together of these many parts to such an excellent unity. If you mean a nature of wisdom, goodness, and providence, which knows what it doth, then say you that which I seek of you, and cannot conclude those blasphemies with which you defiled your mouth and mine ears. But if you mean a nature, as we speak of the fire, which goeth upward it knows not why, and of the nature of the sea, which in ebbing and flowing seems to observe so just a dance and yet understands no music, it is but still the same absurdity superscribed with another title. For this word one being attributed to that which is all is but one mingling of many, and many ones; as in a less matter, when we say one kingdom which contains many cities, or one city which contains many persons; wherein the under-ones, if there be not a superior power

34 town-house—town hall.

and wisdom, cannot by nature regard to any preservation but of themselves; no more we see they do, since the water willingly quenches the fire, and drowns the earth, so far are they from a conspired unity; but that a right heavenly nature indeed, as it were unnaturing them, doth so bridle them.

"Again, it is as absurd in nature that from a unity many contraries should proceed, still kept in a unity, as that from the number of contrarieties a unity should arise. I say still, if you banish both a singularity and plurality of judgment from among them, then (if so earthly a mind can lift itself up so high) do but conceive how a thing whereto you give the highest and most excellent kind of being, which is eternity, can be of the base and vilest degree of being, and next to a not-being, which is so to be as not to enjoy his own being. I will not here call all your senses to witness, which can hear nor see nothing which yields not most evident evidence of the unspeakableness of that wisdom, each thing being directed to an end, and an end of preservation; so proper effects of judgment, as speaking and laughing, are of mankind. But what mad fury can ever so inveigle any conceit[35] as to see our mortal and corruptible selves to have a reason, and that this universality, whereof we are but the least pieces, should be utterly devoid thereof? As if one should say that one's foot might be wise and himself foolish. This heard I once alleged against such a godless mind as yours, who, being driven to acknowledge these beastly absurdities, that our bodies should be better than the whole world if it had the knowledge whereof the other were void, he sought (not able to answer directly) to shift it off in this sort: that, if that reason were true, then must it follow also that the world must have in it a spirit that could write and read too, and be learned, since that was in us so commendable. Wretched fool! not considering that books be but supplies of defects, and so are praised because they help our want, and therefore cannot be incident to the eternal intelligence, which needs no recording of opinions to confirm his knowledge, no more than the sun wants wax to be the fuel of his glorious lightfulness.

[35] inveigle any conceit—deceive any intellect.

"This world, therefore, cannot otherwise consist but by a mind of wisdom which governs it; which, whether you will allow to be the creator thereof, as undoubtedly he is, or the soul and governor thereof, most certain it is that, whether he govern all, or make all, his power is above either his creatures or his government. And if his power be above all things, then, consequently, it must needs be infinite, since there is nothing above it to limit it; for beyond which there is nothing must needs be boundless and infinite. If his power be infinite, then likewise must his knowledge be infinite; for else there should be an infinite proportion of power which he should not know how to use, the unsensibleness whereof I think even you can conceive; and if infinite, then must nothing—no, not the estate of flies, which you, with so unsavory scorn, did jest at—be unknown unto him. For if it were, then there were his knowledge bounded, and so not infinite. If knowledge and power be infinite, then must needs his goodness and justice march in the same rank, for infiniteness of power and knowledge, without like measure of goodness, must necessarily bring forth destruction and ruin, and not ornament and preservation. Since, then, there is a God, and an all-knowing God, so as he sees into the darkest of all natural secrets, which is the heart of man, and sees therein the deepest dissembled thoughts (nay, sees the thoughts before they be thought); since he is just to exercise his might, and mighty to perform his justice; assure thyself, most wicked woman (that hast so plaguily a corrupted mind as thou canst not keep thy sickness to thyself, but must most wickedly infect others) assure thyself, I say (for what I say depends on everlasting and unremovable causes), that the time will come when thou shalt know that power by feeling it, when thou shalt see his wisdom in the manifesting thy ugly shamelessness, and shalt only perceive him to have been a creator in thy destruction."

CHAPTER 11

[Pamela's speech merely increases Cecropia's anger, motivating the vicious woman to urge her son on to further violence. In the meantime, Basilius entrenches his forces around Amphialus' garrison and besieges the castle. Phalantus of Corinth, who finds this policy too restraining, challenges any knight of Amphialus' court to meet him in single combat. Amphialus himself agrees to the duel, and defeats his opponent, sparing his life out of admiration for his courage.]

CHAPTER 12

Philoclea's ill-taking Amphialus' well-meaning. His challenge and conquests continued for love, and his love. Argalus sent for to this challenge. The conjugal happiness of him and his wife. The passions stirred by this message. Their sorrow-sounding farewell. Argalus's defiance. Amphialus' answer. Argalus's furniture. Their combat, bloody to both, deadly to Argalus. Parthenia comes to the end of it, and him. Her and his lamentations. The funerals.

[After Amphialus defeated Phalantus, he was again rebuffed by Philoclea, but Cecropia softens the message,] powdering it with some hope-giving phrases, which were of such joy to Amphialus that he, though against public respect and importunity of dissuaders, presently caused it to be made known to the camp that whatsoever knight would try the like fortune as Phalantus did, he should in like sort be answered; so as divers of the valiantest, partly of themselves, partly at the instigation of Basilius, attempted the combat with him; and according to every one's humor, so were the causes of the challenge grounded: one laying treason to his charge; another preferring himself in the worthiness to serve Philoclea; a third exalting some lady's beauty beyond either of the sisters; a fourth laying disgraces to love itself, naming it the bewitcher of the wit, the rebel to reason, the betrayer of resolution, the defiler of thoughts, the underminer of magnanimity, the flatterer of vice, the slave to weakness, the infection of youth, the madness of age, the curse of life, and reproach of death; a fifth, disdaining to cast at less than at all, would make the cause of his quarrel the causers of love, and proclaim his blasphemies against womankind, that, namely, that sex was the oversight of nature, the disgrace of reasonableness, the obstinate cowards, the slave-born tyrants, the shops of vanities, the gilded weathercocks, in whom conscience is but peevishness, chastity waywardness, and gratefulness a miracle. But all these challenges, how well soever indited, were so well answered that some by death taught others, though past learning themselves, and some by yielding gave themselves the lie for having blasphemed, to the great grief of Basilius, so to see his rebel prevail, and in his own sight to crown himself with deserved honor.

Whereupon, thirsting for revenge, and else not hoping to prevail, the best of his camp being already overthrown, he sent a messenger to Argalus, in whose approved courage and force he had—and had cause to have—great confidence, with a letter, requiring him to take this quarrel in hand, from which he had hitherto spared him in respect of his late marriage. But now his honor and (as he esteemed it) felicity standing upon it, he could no longer forbear to challenge of him his faithful service.

The messenger made speed, and found Argalus at a castle of his own, sitting in a parlor with the fair Parthenia, he reading in a book the stories of Hercules, she by him, as to hear him read; but, while his eyes looked on the book, she looked on his eyes, and sometimes staying him with some pretty question, not so much to be resolved of the doubt as to give him occasion to look upon her. A happy couple, he joying in her, she joying in herself, but in herself because she enjoyed him; both increasing their riches by giving to each other, each making one life double because they made a double life one; where desire never wanted satisfaction, nor satisfaction never bred satiety; he ruling because she would obey, she therein ruling.

But when the messenger came in with letters in his hand and haste in his countenance, though she knew not what to fear, yet she feared because she knew not; but she rose and went aside, while he delivered his letters and message; yet, afar off she looked, now at the messenger, and then at her husband, the same fear which made her loth to have cause of fear yet making her seek cause to nourish her fear. And well she found there was some serious matter, for her husband's countenance figured some resolution between loathsomeness and necessity; and once his eye cast upon her, and finding hers upon him, he blushed, and she blushed because he blushed, and yet straight grew paler because she knew not why he had blushed. But when he had read, and heard, and dispatched away the messenger, like a man in whom honor could not be rocked on[36] sleep by affection, with promise quickly to follow, he came to Parthenia, and, as sorry as might be for parting, and yet more sorry for her sorrow, he gave her the letter to read. She with fearful slowness took it, and with fearful quickness read it, and having read it, "Ah, my Argalus," said she, "and have you made such haste to answer? And are you so soon resolved to leave me?" But he discoursing unto her how much it imported his honor (which, since it was dear to him, he knew it would be dear unto her) her reason, overclouded with sorrow, suffered her not presently to reply, but left the charge thereof to tears and sighs, which he not able to bear, left her alone, and went to give order for his present departure.

By that time he was armed and ready to go she had recovered a little strength of spirit again, and coming out, and seeing him armed, and wanting nothing for his departure but her farewell, she ran to him, took him by the arm, and kneeling down, without regard who either heard her speech or saw her demeanor, "My Argalus! my Argalus!" said she, "do not thus forsake me. Remember, alas! remember that I have interest in you, which I will never yield, shall be thus adventured. Your valor is already sufficiently known, sufficiently have you already done for your country; enow, enow there are besides you to lose less worthy lives. Woe is me! what shall become of me, if you thus abandon me? Then was it time for you to follow these adventures, when you adventured nobody but yourself, and were nobody's but your own. But now, pardon me, that now or never I claim mine own; mine you are, and without me you can undertake no danger. And will you endanger Parthenia? Parthenia shall be in the battle of your fight,[37] Parthenia shall smart in your pain, and your blood must be bled by Parthenia."

"Dear Parthenia," said he, "this is the first time that ever you

---

[36] rocked on—rocked to.
[37] battle of your fight—thick of your fight.

resisted my will; I thank you for it, but persever not in it, and let not the tears of those most beloved eyes be a presage unto me of that which you would not should happen. I shall live, doubt not, for so great a blessing, as you are, was not given unto me so soon to be deprived of it. Look for me, therefore, shortly, and victorious, and prepare a joyful welcome, and I will wish for no other triumph."

She answered not, but stood as it were thunder-stricken with amazement, for true love made obedience stand up against all other passions. But when he took her in his arms, and sought to print his heart in her sweet lips she fell in a swound, so as he was fain to leave her to her gentlewomen; and, carried away by the tyranny of honor, though with many a back-cast look and hearty groan, went to the camp. When understanding the notable victories of Amphialus, he thought to give him some days' respite of rest because he would not have his victory disgraced by the other's weariness. In which days he sought by all means, having leave to parley with him, to dissuade him from his enterprise; and then imparting his mind to Basilius, because he found Amphialus was inflexible, wrote his defiance unto him in this manner:

"RIGHT FAMOUS AMPHIALUS, if my persuasion in reason or prayer in goodwill might prevail with you, you should by better means be like to obtain your desire. You should make many brave enemies become your faithful servants and make your honor fly up to the heaven, being carried up by both the wings of valor and justice, whereof now it wants the latter. But since my suit, nor counsel, can get no place in you, disdain not to receive a mortal challenge, from a man so far inferior unto you in virtue as that I do not so much mislike of the deed as I have the doer in admiration. Prepare therefore yourself, according to the noble manner you have used, and think not lightly of never so weak an arm which strikes with the sword of justice."

To this quickly he received this answer:

"MUCH MORE FAMOUS ARGALUS, I, whom never threatenings could make afraid, am now terrified by your noble courtesy. For well I know from what height of virtue it doth proceed, and what cause I have to doubt such virtue bent to my ruin; but love, which justifieth the injustice you lay unto me, doth also animate me against all dangers, since I come full of him by whom yourself have been (if I be not deceived) sometimes conquered. I will therefore attend your appearance in the isle, carrying this advantage with me, that as it shall be a singular honor if I get the victory, so there can be no dishonor in being overcome by Argalus."

The challenge thus denounced and accepted, Argalus was armed in a white armor, which was all gilded over with knots of woman's hair, which came down from the crest of his headpiece and spread itself in rich quantity over all his armor; his furniture[38] was cut out into the fashion of an eagle, whereof the beak, made into a rich jewel, was fastened to the saddle, the tail covered the crupper of the horse, and the wings served for trappers,[39] which falling of each side, as the horse stirred, the bird seemed to fly. His petrel[40] and reins were embroidered with feathers suitable unto it; upon his right arm he wore a sleeve which his dear Parthenia had made for him to be worn in a joust, in the time that success was ungrateful to their well-deserved love; it was full of bleeding hearts, though never intended to any bloody enterprise. In his shield, as his own device, he had two palm trees[41] near one another, with a word signifying, "In that sort flourishing." His horse was of a fiery sorrel, with black feet, and black list[42] on his back, who with open nostrils breathed war before he could see an enemy; and now up with one leg, and then with another, seemed to complain of Nature that she had made him any whit earthy.

But he had scarcely viewed the ground of the island, and considered the advantages (if any were) thereof, before the castle boat had delivered Amphialus, in all points provided to give a hard entertainment. And then sending each to other their

---

[38] furniture—trappings of the horse.

[39] trappers—defensive coverings hanging down on either side of the horse.

[40] petrel—horse's breastplate.

[41] palm trees—because the date palm is an unisexual tree, two palms symbolize a fruitful marriage.

[42] list—stripe.

squires in honorable manner, to know whether they should attend any further ceremony, the trumpets sounding, the horses with smooth running, the staves with unshaked motion, obediently performed their choleric commandments. But, when they drew near, Argalus' horse, being hot, pressed in with his head, which Amphialus perceiving, knowing if he gave him his side it should be to his disadvantage, pressed in also with him, so as both the horses and men met shoulder to shoulder, so as the horses (hurt as much with the striking as being stricken) tumbled down to the earth, dangerously to their masters, but that they, by strength nimble, and by use skillful, in the falling shunned the harm of the fall, and, without more respite, drew out their swords with a gallant bravery, each striving to show himself the less endamaged, and to make known that they were glad they had now nothing else to trust to but their own virtue.

True it is that Amphialus was the sooner up, but Argalus had his sword out the sooner; and then fell they to the cruelest combat that any present eye had seen; their swords first, like cannons, battering down the walls of their armor, making breaches almost in every place for troops of wounds to enter. Among the rest, Argalus gave a great wound to Amphialus' disarmed face, though part of the force of it Amphialus warded upon his shield, and withal, first casting his eye up to Philoclea's window, as if he had fetched his courage thence, feigning to intend the same sort of blows, turned his sword, and, with a mighty reverse, gave a cruel wound to the right arm of Argalus, the unfaithful armor yielding to the sword's strong-guided sharpness. But, though the blood accused the hurt of Argalus, yet would he in no action of his confess it, but, keeping himself in a lower ward,[43] stood watching with timely thrusts to repair his loss, which quickly he did.

For Amphialus, following his fawning fortune, laid on so thick upon Argalus that his shield had almost fallen piecemeal to the earth, when Argalus coming in with his right foot, and something stooping to come under his armor, thrust him into the belly dangerously, and mortally it would have been, but that,

[43] ward—defensive position.

with the blow before, Amphialus had over-thrown himself so as he fell sideward down, and with falling saved himself from ruin, the sword by that means slipping aside, and not piercing more deeply. Argalus, seeing him fall, threatening with voice and sword, bade him yield. But he striving without answer to rise, Argalus struck with all his might upon his head. But his hurt arm, not able to master so sound a force, let the sword fall so as Amphialus, though astonished with the blow, could arise; which Argalus, considering, ran in to grasp with him, and so closed together, falling so to the ground, now one getting above, and then the other.

At length, both weary of so unlovely embracements, with a dissenting consent got up and went to their swords, but happened each of his enemy's; where Argalus finding his foe's sword garnished in his blood, his heart rose with the same sword to revenge it, and on that blade to ally their bloods together. But his mind was evil waited on by his lamed force, so as he received still more and more wounds, which made all his armor seem to blush that it had defended his master no better. But Amphialus perceiving it, and weighing the small hatefulness of their quarrel with the worthiness of the knight, desired him to take pity of himself. But Argalus, the more repining, the more he found himself in disadvantage, filling his veins with spite instead of blood, and making courage rise against faintness, like a candle, which a little before it goes out gives then the greatest blaze, so did he unite all his force that, casting away the little remnant of his shield, and taking his sword in both hands, he struck such a notable blow that he cleft his shield, armor, and arm almost to the bone.

But then Amphialus forgot all ceremonies, and with cruel blows made more of his blood succeed the rest, till his hand being stayed by his ear, his ear filled with a pitiful cry, the cry guided his sight to an excellent fair lady, who came running as fast as she could, and yet, because she could not so fast as she would, she sent her lamentable voice before her; and being come, and being known to them both to be the beautiful Parthenia, who had that night dreamed she saw her husband in such estate as she then found him, which made her make such haste thither, they both marvelled. But Parthenia ran between them, fear of love making her forget the fear of nature, and then fell down at their feet, determining so to part them till she could get breath to sigh out her doleful speeches; and when her breath (which running had spent, and dismayedness made slow to return) had by sobs gotten into her sorrow-closed breast, for a while she could say nothing but "O wretched eyes of mine, O wailful sight, O day of darkness!"

At length turning her eyes, wherein sorrow swam, to Amphialus, "My lord," said she, "it is said you love; in the power of that love I beseech you to leave of this combat, as even your heart may find comfort in his affection, even for her sake, I crave it; or, if you be mortally determined, be so pitiful unto me as first to kill me, that I may not see the death of Argalus."

Amphialus was about to have answered, when Argalus, vexed with his fortune, but most vexed that she should see him in that fortune, "Ah, Parthenia," said he, "never till now unwelcome unto me, do you come to get my life by request? And cannot Argalus live but by request? Is it a life?" With that he went aside, for fear of hurting her, and would have begun the combat afresh.

But Amphialus, not only conjured by that which held the monarchy of his mind, but even in his noble heart melting with compassion at so passionate a sight, desired him to withhold his hands, for that he should strike one who sought his favor, and would not make resistance. A notable example of the wonderful effects of virtue, where the conqueror sought for friendship of the conquered, and the conquered would not pardon the conqueror, both indeed being of that mind to love each other for accepting, but not for giving mercy, and neither affected to overlive a dishonor; so that Argalus, not so much striving with Amphialus—for if he had had him in the like sort, in like sort he would have dealt with him—as laboring against his own power, which he chiefly despised, set himself forward, stretching his strength to the uttermost. But the first of that strife, blown with his inward rage, boiled out his blood in such abundance that he was driven to rest upon the pommel of his sword; and then each thing beginning to turn round in the dance of death before his eyes, his sight both dazzled and dimmed, till, thinking to sit down, he fell in a swound.

Parthenia and Amphialus both hastily went unto him; Amphialus took off his helmet, and Parthenia laid his head in her lap, tearing off her linen sleeves and partlet[44] to serve about his wounds, to bind which she took off her hair-lace, and would have cut off her fair hair herself but that the squires and judges came in with fitter things for the purpose, while she bewailed herself with so lamentable sweetness as was enough to have taught sorrow to the gladdest thoughts, and have engraved it in the minds of hardest metal.

"O, Parthenia, no more Parthenia," said she, "what art thou? What seest thou? How is thy bliss in a moment fallen! How art thou even now before all ladies the example of perfect happiness, and now the gazing stock of endless misery! O God, what hath been my desert to be thus punished? Or, if such have been my desert, why was I not in myself punished? O wandering life, to what wilderness wouldst thou lead one? But sorrow, I hope thou art sharp enough to save my labor from other remedies. Argalus, Argalus, I will follow thee, I will follow thee!"

But with that Argalus came out of his swound, and, lifting up his languishing eyes, which a painful rest and iron sleep did seek to lock up, seeing her in whom, even dying, he lived, and himself seated in so beloved a place, it seemed a little cheerful blood came up to his cheeks, like a burning coal almost dead, if some breath a little revive it; and forcing up, the best he could, his feeble voice, "My dear, my dear, my better half," said he, "I find I must now leave thee; and by that sweet hand and fair eyes of thine, I swear that death brings nothing with it to grieve me but that I must leave thee, and cannot remain to answer part of thy infinite deserts with being some comfort unto thee. But since so it pleaseth him, whose wisdom and goodness guideth all, put thy confidence in him, and one day we shall blessedly meet again, never to depart; meanwhile, live happily, dear Parthenia, and I

[44] partlet—neckerchief.

persuade myself it will increase the blessedness of my soul, so to see thee. Love well the remembrance of thy loving, and truly loving, Argalus; and let not"—with that word he sighed—"this disgrace of mine make thee one day think thou hadst an unworthy husband." They could scarcely understand the last words, for death began to seize himself of his heart; neither could Parthenia make answer, so full was her breast of anguish. But, while the other sought to staunch his remediless wounds, she with her kisses made him happy, for his last breath was delivered into her mouth.

But when indeed she found his ghost was gone, then sorrow lost the wit of utterance and grew rageful and mad, so that she tore her beautiful face and rent her hair, as though they could serve for nothing since Argalus was gone; till Amphialus, so moved with pity of that sight as that he honored his adversary's death with tears, caused her, with the help of her women that came with her, partly by force to be conveyed into boat, with the dead body of Argalus, from which she could not depart.

And being come of the other side, there she was received by Basilius himself, with all the funeral pomp of military discipline, trailing all their ensigns upon the ground, making his warlike instruments sound doleful notes, and Basilius, with comfort in his mouth and woe in his face, sought to persuade some ease into Parthenia's mind; but all was as easeful to her as the handling of sore wounds, all the honor done being to her but the triumph of her ruin, she finding no comfort but in desperate yielding to sorrow, and rather determined to hate herself, if ever she should find ease thereof. And well might she hear, as she passed through the camp, the great praises spoken of her husband, which all were records of her loss. But the more excellent he was (being, indeed, accounted second to none in all Greece), the more did the breath of those praises bear up the wings of Amphialus' fame, to whom yet, such was his case, that trophy upon trophy still did but build up the monument of his thraldom, he ever finding himself in such favor of Philoclea that she was most absent when he was present with her, and ever sorriest when he had best success; which would have made him renounce all comfort, but that his mother, with diversity of devices, kept up his heart.

But while he allayed thus his outward glory, with inward discomfort, he was like to have been overtaken with a notable treason, the beginning whereof (though merely ridiculous) had like to have brought forth unto him a weeping effect.

CHAPTER 13

[Dametas, inspired by the now proverbial cowardice of Clinias, challenges him to combat, secure in the belief that the offer will be refused. With a show of bravado he arms himself and mounts for the fray. But Amphialus compels Clinias to accept the challenge. When he hears of this, Dametas tries to squirm out of his role as hero, but his friends lead him by the bridle to the ferry. On the island, the two cowards engaged in a farcical battle, and Dametas, by very chance, overcomes his opponent.]

CHAPTER 14

[Clinias, having been so humiliated by Amphialus, begins to plan revenge. He forms an alliance with Artesia, the sister of Ismenus and the unrequited lover of Amphialus. The pair decide to poison Amphialus and open the gates to the enemy, and, in order to protect themselves from Basilius' men, they determine to take Philoclea and Pamela into their confidence. Both sisters refuse complicity, but Pamela, outraged at such ignoble treason, directs Cecropia's suspicion towards the rebels. Cecropia, having uncovered the plot, hangs Clinias; but Artesia is merely confined to her bedroom, Amphialus being reluctant to slay the sister of his beloved Ismenus.]

CHAPTER 15

Proud Anaxius[45] *breaketh through the besiegers. His welcome by Amphialus. The music, and love-song, made to Philoclea. The*

[45] Anaxius—"proud."

sally of Anaxius and his on the Basilians, backed by Amphialus, beaten back by three unknown knights. The retreat of both sides.

But the noise they heard in the camp was occasioned by the famous Prince Anaxius, nephew to the giant Euardes, whom Pyrocles slew; a prince, of body exceeding strong, in arms so skillful and fortunate as no man was thought to excel him, of courage that knew not how to fear—parts worthy praise, if they had not been guided by pride and followed by unjustice. For, by a strange composition of mind, there was no man more tenderly sensible in anything offered to himself, which, in the farthest-fet[46] construction, might be wrested to the name of wrong; no man, that in his own actions could worse distinguish between valor and violence; so proud, as he could not abstain from a Thraso-like boasting,[47] and yet (so unlucky a lodging his virtues had gotten) he would never boast more than he would accomplish; falsely accounting an inflexible anger a courageous constancy; esteeming fear and astonishment righter causes of admiration than love and honor.

This man had four sundry times fought with Amphialus, but Mars had been so unpartial an arbiter that neither side got advantage of the other. But in the end it happened that Anaxius found Amphialus (unknown) in a great danger, and saved his life, whereupon, loving his own benefit, began to favor him, so much the more as, thinking so well of himself, he could not choose but like him, whom he found a match for himself; which at last grew to as much friendship towards him as could by a proud heart be conceived.

So as in this travail (seeking Pyrocles to be revenged of his uncle's death), hearing of this siege, never taking pains to examine the quarrel, like a man whose will was his god, and his hand his law, taking with him his two brothers, men accounted little inferior to himself in martial matters, and two hundred chosen horsemen, with whom he thought himself able to conquer the world, yet commanding the rest of his forces to follow, he him-

[46] farthest-fet—most far-fetched.
[47] Thraso-like boasting—Thraso is the bragging soldier in Terence's *Eunuch.*

self upon such an unexpected suddenness entered in upon the back of Basilius, that many with great unkindness took their death, not knowing why, nor how, they were so murdered. There, if ever, did he make known the wonderfulness of his force. But the valiant and faithful Philanax, with well-governed speed, made such head against him as would have showed how soon courage falls in the ditch which hath not the eye of wisdom, but that Amphialus at the same time issued out, and winning with an abundance of courage one of the sconces[48] which Basilius had builded, made way for his friend Anaxius, with great loss of both sides, but especially of the Basilians, such notable monuments had those two swords especially left of their masters' redoubted worthiness.

There, with the respect fit to his estate, the honor due to his worthiness, and the kindness which accompanies friendship, made fast by interchanged benefits, did Amphialus enforce himself, as much as in a besieged town he could, to make Anaxius know that his succor was not so needful as his presence grateful. For, causing the streets and houses of the town to witness his welcome, making both soldiers and magistrates in their countenances to show their gladness of him, he led him to his mother, whom he besought to entertain him with no less love and kindness than as one who once had saved her son's life, and now came to save both life and honor.

"Tush!" said Anaxius, speaking aloud, looking upon his brothers, "I am only sorry there are not half a dozen kings more about you, that what Anaxius can do might be the better manifested." His brothers smiled, as though he had over-modestly spoken, far underneath the pitch of his power. Then was he disarmed at the earnest request of Amphialus, for Anaxius boiled with desire to issue out upon the enemies, persuading himself that the sun should not be set before he had overthrown them.

And having reposed himself, Amphialus asked him whether he would visit the young princesses. But Anaxius whispered him in the ear: "In truth," said he, "dear friend Amphialus, though I

[48] sconces—small forts erected for protection.

am none of those that love to speak of themselves, I never came
yet in company of ladies but that they fell in love with me. And
I, that in my heart scorn them as a peevish, paltry sex, not worthy
to communicate with my virtues, would not do you the wrong,
since, as I hear, you do debase yourself so much as to affect
them."

The courteous Amphialus could have been angry with him
for those words, but, knowing his humor, suffered him to dance
to his own music, and gave himself to entertain both him and his
brothers with as cheerful a manner as could issue from a mind
whom unlucky love had filled with melancholy. For to Anaxius
he yielded the direction of all. He gave the watchword, and, if
any grace were granted, the means were to be made to Anaxius.
And that night, when supper was ended, wherein Amphialus
would needs himself wait upon him, he caused in boats upon the
lake an excellent music to be ordered, which, though Anaxius
might conceive was for his honor, yet, indeed, he was but the
brick wall[49] to convey it to the ears of the beloved Philoclea.

The music was of cornets, whereof one answering the other
with a sweet emulation, striving for the glory of music, and
striking upon the smooth face of the quiet lake, was then delivered up to the castle walls, which, with a proud reverberation
spreading it into the air, it seemed before the harmony came to
the ear that it had enriched itself in travel, the nature of those
places adding melody to that melodious instrument. And when a
while that instrument had made a brave proclamation to all un-
possessed minds of attention, an excellent consort straight followed of five viols and as many voices, which all being but
orators of their masters' passions, bestowed this song upon her,
that thought upon another matter:

[CS3 *follows here*]

But Anaxius, seeming aweary before it was ended, told
Amphialus that, for his part, he liked no music but the neighing

[49] the brick wall—refers to the wall through which Pyramus and Thisbe
conversed and nourished their love.

of horses, the sound of trumpets, and the cries of yielding persons; and therefore, desired that the next morning they should issue upon the same place where they had entered that day, not doubting to make them quickly aweary of being the besiegers of Anaxius. Amphialus, who had no whit less courage, though nothing blown up with pride, willingly condescended; and so, the next morning, giving false alarm to the other side of the camp (Amphialus, at Anaxius' earnest request, staying within the town to see it guarded), Anaxius and his brethren Lycurgus[50] and Zoilus[51] sallied out with the best chosen men. But Basilius, having been the last day somewhat unprovided, now had better fortified the overthrown sconce, and so well had prepared everything for defense that it was impossible for any valor from within to prevail. Yet things were performed by Anaxius beyond the credit of the credulous, for thrice, valiantly followed by his brothers, did he set up his banner upon the rampier[52] of the enemy, though thrice again by the multitude, and advantage of the place, but especially by the coming of three valiant knights, he were driven down again. Numbers there were that day whose deaths and overthrows were executed by the well-known sword of Anaxius. But the rest, by the length of time and injury of historians, have been wrapped up in dark forgetfulness. Only Tressenius[53] is spoken of because, when all abandoned the place, he only made head to Anaxius, till, having lost one of his legs, yet not lost the heart of fighting, Lycurgus (second brother to Anaxius) cruelly murdered him, Anaxius himself disdaining any further to deal with him.

But so far had Anaxius at the third time prevailed that now the Basilians began to let their courage descend to their feet, Basilius and Philanax in vain striving, with reverence of authority, to bridle the flight of astonishment and to teach fear discretion; so that Amphialus, seeing victory show such a flattering counte-

---

[50] Lycurgus—"furious wolf."
[51] Zoilus—"like an animal."
[52] rampier—rampart.
[53] Tressenius—"fearless."

nance to him, came out with all his force, hoping that day to end the siege.

But that fancy altered quickly by the sudden coming to the other side of three knights, whereof the one was in white armor, the other in green, and the third, by his black armor and device, straight known to be the notable knight, who, the first day, had given fortune so short a stop with his notable deeds, and fighting hand to hand with the deemed-invincible Amphialus. For the very cowards no sooner saw him but, as borrowing some of his spirit, they went like young eagles to the prey, under the wing of their dam. For the three adventurers, not content to keep them from their rampier, leaped down among them and entered into a brave combat with the three valiant brothers. But to whether side fortune would have been partial could not be determined, for the Basilians, lightened with the beams of these strangers' valor, followed so thick that the Amphialians were glad with some haste to retire to the walls-ward, though Anaxius neither reason, fear, nor example, could make him assuage the fury of his fight, until one of the Basilians (unworthy to have his name registered, since he did it cowardly, sideward, when he least looked that way) almost cut off one of his legs, so as he fell down, blaspheming heaven, that all the influences thereof had power to overthrow him; and there death would have seized of his proud heart, but that Amphialus took in hand the black knight, while some of his soldiers conveyed away Anaxius, so requiting life for life unto him.

And, for the love and example of Amphialus, the fight began to enter into a new fit of heat, when Basilius (that thought enough to be done for that day) caused retreat to be sounded, fearing lest his men, following over-earnestly, might be the loss of those excellent knights, whom he desired to know. The knights, as soon as they heard the retreat, though they were eagerly set,[54] knowing that courage without discipline is nearer beastliness than manhood, drew back their swords, though hungry of more blood, especially the black knight, who, knowing Amphialus, could not refrain to tell him that this was the second time he escaped out of

[54] set—engaged.

his hands, but that he would shortly bring him a bill of all the former accounts. Amphialus, seeing it fit to retire also (most of his people being hurt, both in bodies and hearts), withdrew himself, with so well-seated a resolution that it was as far from anger as from dismayedness, answering no other to the black knight's threats but that, when he brought him his account, he should find a good paymaster.

CHAPTER 16

The unknown knights will not be known. The knight of the tomb's show, and challenge accepted by Amphialus. Their fight, with the death of the tomb-knight. Who that knight was. The dying speeches, and the lamentable funerals.

The fight being ceased, and each side withdrawn within their strengths, Basilius sent Philanax to entertain the strange knights, and to bring them unto him, that he might acknowledge what honor was due to their virtue. But they excused themselves, desiring to be known first by their deeds, before their names should excuse their unworthiness; and, though the other replied according as they deserved, yet, finding that unwelcome courtesy is a degree of injury, he suffered them to retire themselves to a tent of their own without the camp, where they kept themselves secret; Philanax himself being called away to another strange knight—strange not only by the unlooked-for-ness of his coming, but by the strange manner of his coming. For he had before him four damosels, and so many behind him, all upon palfreys, and all appareled in mourning weeds; each of them servants of each side, with like liveries of sorrow; himself in an armor all painted over with such a cunning of shadow that it represented a gaping sepulcher; the furniture of his horse was all of cypress branches, wherewith in old time they were wont to dress graves. His bases (which he wore so long as they came almost to his ankle) were embroidered only with black worms, which seemed to crawl up and down, as ready already to devour him. In his shield, for impresa, he had a beautiful child, but having two heads, whereof the one showed that it was already dead, the other alive, but in that case necessarily looking for death. The word was, "No way to be rid from death, but by death."

This Knight of the Tomb—for so the soldiers termed him—sent to Basilius to demand leave to send in a damosel into the town to call out Amphialus, according as before-time some others had done; which being granted (as glad any would undertake the charge, which nobody else in that camp was known willing to do), the damosel went in; and, having with tears sobbed out a brave challenge to Amphialus from the Knight of the Tomb, Amphialus, honorably entertaining the gentlewoman, and desiring to know the knight's name, which the doleful gentlewoman would not discover, accepted the challenge, only desiring the gentlewoman to say thus much to the strange knight from him, that, if his mind were like to his title, there were more cause of affinity than enmity between them. And, therefore, presently, according as he was wont, as soon as he perceived the Knight of the Tomb, with his damosels and judge, was come into the island, he also went over in accustomed manner, and yet, for the courtesy of his nature, desired to speak with him.

But the Knight of the Tomb, with silence, and drawing his horse back, showed no will to hear nor speak, but, with lance on thigh, made him know it was fit for him to go to the other end of the career,[55] whence, waiting the start of the unknown knight, he likewise made his spurs claim haste of his horse. But, when his staff was in his rest,[56] coming down to meet with the knight, now very near him, he perceived the knight had missed his rest; wherefore the courteous Amphialus would not let his lance descend, but with a gallant grace ran over the head of his therein friended enemy; and having stopped his horse, and, with the turning of him, blessed his sight with the window where he thought Philoclea might stand, he perceived the knight had lighted from his horse and thrown away his staff, angry with his misfortune as of having missed his rest, and drawn his sword to make that supply his fellow's fault.

[55] career—the ground over which they would run at one another.
[56] rest—hollow in the tilting-saddle, into which the lance was placed to hold it more steadily.

He also lighted and drew his sword, esteeming victory by advantage rather robbed than purchased; and so, the other coming eagerly toward him, he, with his shield out and sword aloft, with more bravery than anger, drew unto him, and straight made their swords speak for them a pretty while with equal fierceness. But Amphialus, to whom the earth brought forth few matches, having both much more skill to choose the places and more force to work upon the chosen, had already made many windows in his armor for death to come in at, when (the nobleness of his nature abhorring to make the punishment overgo the offense) he stepped a little back, and withal, "Sir knight," said he, "you may easily see that it pleaseth God to favor my cause; employ your valor against them that wish you hurt; for my part, I have not deserved hate of you."

"Thou liest, false traitor!" said the other, with an angry, but weak, voice.

But Amphialus, in whom abused kindness became spiteful rage, "Ah, barbarous wretch!" said he, "only courageous in discourtesy, thou shalt soon see whether thy tongue hath betrayed thy heart, or no"; and with that, redoubling his blows, gave him a great wound upon his neck, and, closing with him, overthrew him, and with the fall thrust him mortally into the body, and with that went to pull off his helmet, with intention to make him give himself the lie for having so said, or to cut off his head.

But the headpiece was no sooner off, but that there fell about the shoulders of the overcome knight the treasure of fair golden hair, which, with the face, soon known by the badge of excellency, witnessed that it was Parthenia, the unfortunately virtuous wife of Argalus; her beauty then, even in despite of the passed sorrow, or coming death, assuring all beholders that it was nothing short of perfection. For her exceeding fair eyes, having with continual weeping gotten a little redness about them; her roundy, sweetly-swelling lips a little trembling, as though they kissed their neighbor death; in her cheeks, the whiteness striving, by little and little, to get upon the rosiness of them; her neck—a neck indeed of alabaster—displaying the wound which, with most dainty blood, labored to drown his own beauties; so as here was a river of purest red, there an island of perfectest white, each giving luster to the other, with the sweet countenance, God knows, full of an unaffected languishing; though these things, to a grossly conceiving sense, might seem disgraces, yet indeed were they but appareling beauty in a new fashion, which all looked upon through the spectacles of pity, did even increase the lines of her natural fairness, so as Amphialus was astonished with grief, compassion, and shame, detesting his fortune that made him unfortunate in victory.

Therefore, putting off his headpiece and gauntlet, kneeling down unto her, and with tears testifying his sorrow, he offered his (by himself accursed) hands to help her, protesting his life and power to be ready to do her honor. But Parthenia, who had inward messengers of the desired death's approach, looking upon him, and straight turning away her feeble sight, as from a delightless object, drawing out her words, which her breath, loath to part from so sweet a body, did faintly deliver, "Sir," said she, "I pray you, if prayers have place in enemies, to let my maids take my body untouched by you; the only honor I now desire by your means is, that I have no honor of you. Argalus made no such bargain with you that the hands which killed him should help me. I have of them—and I do not only pardon you, but thank you for it— the service which I desired. There rests nothing now but that I go live with him, since whose death I have done nothing but die." Then pausing, and a little fainting, and again coming to herself, "Oh, sweet life, welcome," said she; "now feel I the bands untied of the cruel death which so long hath held me. And O life, O death, answer for me, that my thoughts have, not so much as in a dream, tasted any comfort since they were deprived of Argalus. I come, my Argalus, I come! And O God, hide my faults in thy mercies, and grant, as I feel thou dost grant, that, in thy eternal love, we may love each other eternally. And this, O Lord—," but there Atropos[57] cut off her sentence; for with that, casting up both eyes and hands to the skies, the noble soul departed, one might well assure himself, to heaven, which left the body in so heavenly a demeanor.

[57] Atropos—of the three Fates, the one who cuts the thread of life.

But Amphialus, with a heart oppressed with grief, because of her request, withdrew himself; but the judges, as full of pity, had been all this while disarming her, and her gentlewomen, with lamentable cries, laboring to stanch the remediless wounds; and a while she was dead before they perceived it, death being able to divide the soul, but not the beauty, from that body. But when the infallible tokens of death assured them of their loss, one of the women would have killed herself, but that the squire of Amphialus, perceiving it, by force held her. Others that had as strong passions, though weaker resolution, fell to cast dust upon their heads, to tear their garments, all falling upon, and crying upon, their sweet mistress, as if their cries could persuade the soul to leave the celestial happiness, to come again into the elements of sorrow; one time calling to remembrance her virtue, chasteness, sweetness, goodness to them; another time accursing themselves, that they had obeyed her, they having been deceived by her words, who assured them that it was revealed unto her that she should have her heart's desire in the battle against Amphialus, which they wrongly understood. Then kissing her cold hands and feet, weary of the world since she was gone who was their world, the very heavens seemed with a cloudy countenance to lower at the loss, and fame itself, though by nature glad to tell rare accidents, yet could not choose but deliver it in lamentable accents, and in such sort went it quickly all over the camp; and, as if the air had been infected with sorrow, no heart was so hard but was subject to that contagion; the rareness of the accident matching together the rarely matched together—pity with admiration.

Basilius himself came forth, and brought forth the fair Gynecia with him, who was gone into the camp under color of visiting her husband and hearing of her daughters; but, indeed, Zelmane was the saint to which her pilgrimage was intended; cursing, envying, blessing, and, in her heart, kissing, the walls which imprisoned her. But both they, with Philanax and the rest of the principal nobility, went out to make honor triumph over death, conveying that excellent body, whereto Basilius himself would needs bend his shoulder, to a church a mile from the

camp, where the valiant Argalus lay intombed, recommending
to that sepulcher the blessed relics of faithful and virtuous love,
giving order for the making of marble images to represent them,
and each way enriching the tomb; upon which Basilius himself
caused this epitaph to be written:[58]

[*The Epitaph*

> His being was in her alone,
> And he not being, she was none.
> They joy'd one joy, one grief they griev'd,
> One love they lov'd, one life they liv'd.
> The hand was one, one was the sword
> That did his death, her death afford.
> As all the rest, so now the stone
> That tombs the two is justly one.
> >   Argalus and Parthenia.]

CHAPTER 17

*The remorse of Amphialus for his last deed, and lasting destiny.
His reverent respect in love. His mother's ghosty[59] counsel to a
rape.*

Then, with eyes full of tears, and mouths full of her praises,
returned they to the camp, with more and more hate against
Amphialus, who, poor gentleman, had therefor greater portion
of woe than any of them. For that courteous heart, which would
have grieved but to have heard the like adventure, was rent with
remembering himself to be the author, so that his wisdom could
not so far temper his passion but that he took his sword, counted
the best in the world, which with much blood he had once conquered of a mighty giant, and brake it into many pieces (which
afterwards he had good cause to repent), saying that neither it
was worthy to serve the noble exercise of chivalry, nor any other

[58] epitaph to be written—the epitaph did not appear in 1590, but was
supplied by the Countess of Pembroke in 1593.
[59] ghosty—demoniac.

worthy to feel that sword, which had stricken so excellent a lady; and withal, banishing all cheerfulness of his countenance, he returned home, where he got him to his bed, not so much to rest his restless mind as to avoid all company, the sight whereof was tedious unto him. And then melancholy, only rich in unfortunate remembrances, brought before him all the mishaps with which his life had wrestled, taking this not only as a confirming of the former, but a presage of following misery.

[His pangs of guilt are compounded by the pangs of love; still, he rejects his mother's advice of rape.]

CHAPTER 18

[In answer to a new challenge, Amphialus takes the field in black clothes, fashioned to resemble rags, and artificially rusted armor. On the island he meets the black knight, whose dress and countenance so reflect his own that Amphialus seeks to establish a friendship between them. But, when he falsely believes that they are rivals in love for Philoclea, he begins to unleash all his pent-up rage on the new-comer. When both the black knight and Amphialus were stripped of their weapons and armor, and scarred all over with wounds, the fierce battle is interrupted by Anaxius' brothers, who, fearing for Amphialus' life, ignore the rules of chivalry and attack the black knight. However, before they can reach him, the other two unknown knights intercept their charge. Cecropia, fearing the outcome of a general melee, sends a company of soldiers to the island, but these are routed by Basilius' men. However, they do succeed in carrying off the wounded and unconscious Amphialus. Philanax and two knights rescue the black knight, who, when his wounds have begun to heal, departs for a secret castle where he can convalesce incognito.]

CHAPTER 19

[Amphialus' wounds are not mortal, but he refuses to cooperate with the surgeons' efforts to restore his health, even going so far as to re-open his wounds. Cecropia, meanwhile, enjoys complete control of the town, and she vows that the sisters will either gratify her son's desires or suffer death for their intransigency. She also attempts to halt the siege by threatening Basilius with the death of his daughters and Zelmane. Kalander counsels the king to lift the siege, but Philanax argues strongly that the safest course is to maintain it. While he is still talking, (actual text follows:)] when Gynecia came running in, amazed for her daughter Pamela, but mad for Zelmane, and, falling at Basilius' feet, besought him to make no delay, using such gestures of compassion, instead of stopped words, that Basilius, otherwise enough tender-minded, easily granted to raise the siege, which he saw dangerous to his daughters, but, indeed, more careful for Zelmane, by whose besieged person the poor old man was straitly[60] besieged. So as, to rid him of the famine of his mind, he went in speed away, discharging his soldiers, only leaving the authority, as before, in Philanax' hands; he himself went with Gynecia to a strong castle of his, where he took counsel how first to deliver Zelmane, whom he called the poor stranger, as though only law of hospitality moved him, and for that purpose sent divers messengers to traffic with Cecropia.

CHAPTER 20

The sweet resistance of the true sisters to the sour assaults of their false aunt. The whipping of Philoclea and Pamela. The patience of both and passions for their lovers.

Cecropia, by this means rid of the present danger of the siege, desiring Zoilus and Lycurgus to take the care, till their brother recovered, of revictualling and furnishing the city, both with men and what else wanted, against any new occasion should urge them; she herself, disdaining to hearken to Basilius without he would grant his daughter in marriage to her son, which by no means he would be brought unto, bent all the sharpness of her malicious wit, how to bring a comfortable grant to her son, whereupon she well found no less than his life depended. There-

---

[60] straitly—closely.

fore, for a while she attempted all means of eloquent praying and flattering persuasion, mingling sometimes gifts, sometimes threatenings, as she had cause to hope that either open force or undermining would best win the castle of their resolution. And ever as much as she did to Philoclea, so much did she to Pamela, though in manner sometimes differing, as she found fit to level at the one's noble height and the other's sweet lowliness. For, though she knew her son's heart had wholly given itself to Philoclea, yet, seeing the equal gifts in Pamela, she hoped a fair grant would recover the sorrow of a fair refusal, cruelly intending the present empoisoning the one as soon as the other's affection were purchased.

But in vain was all her vain oratory employed. Pamela's determination was built upon so brave a rock that no shot of hers could reach unto it; and Philoclea, though humbly seated, was so environed with sweet rivers of clear virtue as could neither be battered nor undermined; her witty persuasions had wise answers; her eloquence recompensed with sweetness; her threatenings repelled with disdain in the one and patience in the other; her gifts either not accepted, or accepted to obey, but not to bind.

So as Cecropia, in nature violent; cruel, because ambitious; hateful, for old rooted grudge to their mother; and now spiteful because she could not prevail with girls, as she counted them; lastly, drawn on by her love to her son, and held up by a tyrannical authority, forthwith followed the bias of her own crooked disposition, and doubling and redoubling her threatenings, fell to confirm some of her threatened effects; first, withdrawing all comfort, both of servants and service from them. But that those excellent ladies had been used unto, even at home, and then found in themselves how much good the hardness of education doth to the resistance of misery. Then dishonorably using them, both in diet and lodging, by a contempt to pull down their thoughts to yielding. But as before the consideration of a prison had disgraced all ornaments, so now the same consideration made them attend all diseasefulness.[61] Then still, as she found those not prevail, would she go forward with giving them terrors, some-

---

[61] attend all diseasefulness—put up with any discomfort.

times with noises of horror, sometimes with sudden frightings in the night, when the solitary darkness thereof might easier astonish the disarmed senses. But, to all, virtue and love resisted, strengthened one by the other, when each found itself over-vehemently assaulted. Cecropia still sweetening her fiercenesses with fair promises, if they would promise fair; that feeling evil, and seeing a way far better, their minds might the sooner be mollified. But they, that could not taste her behavior when it was pleasing, indeed could worse now, when they had lost all taste by her injuries.

She, resolving all extremities rather than fail of conquest, pursued on her rugged way, letting no day pass without new and new perplexing the poor ladies' minds, and troubling their bodies; and still swelling the more she was stopped, and growing hot with her own doings, at length abominable rage carried her to absolute tyrannies; so that taking with her certain old women (of wicked dispositions, and apt for envy's sake to be cruel to youth and beauty), with a countenance empoisoned with malice, flew to the sweet Philoclea, as if so many kites should come about a white dove, and matching violent gestures with mischievous threatenings, she having a rod in her hand (like a fury that should carry wood to the burning of Diana's temple)[62] fell to scourge that most beautiful body, love in vain holding the shield of beauty against her blind cruelty. The sun drew clouds up to hide his face from so pitiful a sight; and the very stone walls did yield drops of sweat for agony of such a mischief; each senseless thing had sense of pity; only they that had sense were senseless. Virtue rarely found her worldly weakness more than by the oppression of that day; and weeping Cupid told his weeping mother, that he was sorry he was not deaf, as well as blind, that he might never know so lamentable a work. Philoclea, with tearful eyes and sobbing breast (as soon as her weariness, rather than compassion, gave her respite) kneeled down to Cecropia, and making pity in

[62] like a fury that should carry wood to the burning of Diana's temple —furies torment damned souls; this one (Cecropia) torments an innocent virgin, who is likened to the Ephesian temple of Diana, the goddess of chastity, which was sacriligeously burned by Herostratus.

her face honorable, and torment delightful, besought her, since she hated her (for what cause she took God to witness she knew not), that she would at once take away her life, and not please herself with the tormenting of a poor gentlewoman.

"If," said she, "the common course of humanity cannot move you, nor the having me in your own walls cannot claim pity; nor womanly mercy, nor near alliance, nor remembrance (how miserable soever now) that I am a prince's daughter; yet let the love you have often told me your son bears me, so much procure, that for his sake, one death may be thought enough for me; I have not lived so many years but that one death may be able to conclude them; neither have my faults, I hope, been so many, but that one death may satisfy them. It is no great suit to an enemy, when but death is desired. I crave but that; and as for the granting your request, know for certain you lose your labors, being every day further-off-minded from becoming his wife, who useth me like a slave." But that, instead of getting grace, renewed again Cecropia's fury; so that (excellent creature) she was newly again tormented by those hellish monsters, Cecropia using no other words, but that she was a proud and ungrateful wench, and that she would teach her to know her own good, since of herself she would not conceive it.

So that with silence and patience (like a fair gorgeous armor hammered upon by an ill-favored smith) she abode their pitiless dealing with her; till, rather reserving her for more, than meaning to end, they left her to an uncomfortable leisure, to consider with herself her fortune; both helpless herself, being a prisoner, and hopeless, since Zelmane was a prisoner—who therein only was short of the bottom of misery, that she knew not how unworthily her angel by these devils was abused; but wanted (God wot) no stings of grief, when those words did but strike upon her heart, that Philoclea was a captive, and she not able to succor her. For well she knew the confidence Philoclea had in her, and well she knew Philoclea had cause to have confidence: and all trodden underfoot by the wheel of senseless fortune. Yet if there be that imperious power in the soul, as it can deliver knowledge to another, without bodily organs, so vehement were the workings of their spirits, as one met with other, though themselves perceived it not, but only thought it to be the doubling of their own loving fancies. And that was the only worldly thing whereon Philoclea rested her mind, that she knew she should die beloved of Zelmane, and should die rather than be false to Zelmane. And so this most dainty nymph, easing the pain of her mind with thinking of another's pain, and almost forgetting the pain of her body through the pain of her mind, she wasted, even longing for the conclusion of her tedious tragedy.

But for a while she was unvisited, Cecropia employing her time in using the like cruelty upon Pamela, her heart growing not only to desire the fruit of punishing them, but even to delight in the punishing them. But if ever the beams of perfection shined through the clouds of affliction, if ever virtue took a body to show his (else inconceivable) beauty, it was in Pamela. For when reason taught her there was no resistance (for to just resistance first her heart was inclined), then with so heavenly a quietness, and so graceful a calmness, did she suffer the divers kinds of torments they used to her, that while they vexed her fair body, it seemed that she rather directed than obeyed the vexation. And when Cecropia ended, and asked whether her heart would yield, she a little smiled, but such a smiling as showed no love, and yet could not but be lovely. And then, "Beastly woman," said she, "follow on, do what thou wilt, and canst, upon me, for I know thy power is not unlimited. Thou mayst well wrack this silly body, but me thou canst never overthrow. For my part, I will not do thee the pleasure to desire death of thee, but assure thyself, both my life and death shall triumph with honor, laying shame upon thy detestable tyranny."

And so, in effect, conquering their doing with her suffering, while Cecropia tried as many sorts of pains as might rather vex them than spoil them (for that she would not do while she were in any hope to win either of them for her son), Pamela remained almost as much content with trial in herself, what virtue could do, as grieved with the misery wherein she found herself plunged, only sometimes her thoughts softened in her, when with open wings they flew to Musidorus. For then she would think with herself, how grievously Musidorus would take this her misery; and she, that wept not for herself, wept yet Musidorus' tears, which he would weep for her. For gentle love did easlier yield to lamentation than the constancy of virtue would else admit. Then would she remember the case wherein she had left her poor shepherd, and she, that wished death for herself, feared death for him; and she that condemned in herself the feebleness of sorrow, yet thought it great reason to be sorry for his sorrow; and she that long had prayed for the virtuous joining themselves together, now thinking to die herself, heartily prayed that long time their fortunes might be separated. "Live long, my Musidorus," would she say, "and let my name live in thy mouth, in thy heart my memory. Live long, that thou mayst love long the chaste love of thy dead Pamela." Then would she wish to herself that no other woman might ever possess his heart; and yet scarcely the wish was made a wish, when herself would find fault with it, as being too unjust, that so excellent a man should be banished from the comfort of life. Then would she fortify her resolution with bethinking the worst, taking the counsel of virtue and comfort of love.

CHAPTER 21

Cecropia's indurate tyrannies. Her device with the death of one to threaten another. Philoclea threatened, persisteth. The execution done in sight of Philoclea and Zelmane. Philoclea's sorrow for her sister.

So these diamonds of the world—whom Nature had made to be preciously set in the eyes of her creatures, to be the chief works of her workmanship, the chief ornaments of the world, and princesses of felicity—by rebellious injury were brought to the uttermost distress that an enemy's heart could wish or a woman's spite invent; Cecropia daily in one or other sort punishing them, still with her evil torments giving them fear of worse, making the fear itself the sorriest torment of all, that, in the end, weary of their bodies, they should be content to bestow them at her appointment.

But as in labor, the more one doth exercise it, the more by the doing one is enabled to do, strength growing upon the work, so as what at first would have seemed impossible, after grows easy: so these princesses, second to none, and far from any second, only to be matched by themselves, with the use of suffering their minds got the habit of suffering, so as all fears and terrors were to them but summons to a battle, whereof they knew before hand they would be victorious, and which in the suffering was painful, being suffered, was a trophy to itself, whereby Cecropia found herself still farther off; for where at first she might perchance have persuaded them to have visited her son, and have given him some comfort in his sickness (drawing near to the confines of death's kingdom), now they protested that they would never otherwise speak to him than as to the enemy, of most unjust cruelty towards them, that any time or place could ever make them know.

This made the poison swell in her cankered breast, perceiving that (as in water) the more she grasped, the less she held; but yet now, having run so long the way of rigor, it was too late in reason, and too contrary to her passion, to return to a course of meekness. And, therefore, taking counsel of one of her old associates (who so far excelled in wickedness as that she had not only lost all feeling of conscience, but had gotten a very glory in evil), in the end they determined that beating, and other such sharp dealing, did not so much pull down a woman's heart as it bred anger, and that nothing was more enemy to yielding than anger, making their tender hearts take on the armor of obstinacy —for thus did their wicked minds, blind to the light of virtue, and owly-eyed in the night of wickedness, interpret it—and that, therefore, that was no more to be tried. And for fear of death, which, no question, would do most with them, they had been so often threatened as they began to be familiarly acquainted with it, and learned to esteem threatening words to be but words. Therefore the last, but best, way now was, that the one seeing indeed the other's death should perceive there was no dallying meant; and then there was no doubt that a woman's soul would do much rather than leave so beautiful a body.

This being concluded, Cecropia went to Philoclea, and told her that now she was to come to the last part of the play; for her part, though she found her hard-hearted obstinacy such that neither the sweetness of loving means nor the force of hard means could prevail with her, yet, before she would pass to a further degree of extremity, she had sought to win her sister, in hope that her son might be with time satisfied with the love of so fair a lady; but, finding her also rather more than less willful, she was now minded that one of their deaths should serve for an example to the other, that despising worthy folks was more hurtful to the despiser than the despised; that yet, because her son especially affected her, and that in her own self she was more inclinable to pity her than she had deserved, she would begin with her sister, who that afternoon should have her head cut off before her face; if in the meantime one of them did not pull out their ill-wrought stitches of unkindness, she bad her look for no other, nor longer time, than she told her.

There was no assault given to the sweet Philoclea's mind that entered so far as this; for where, to all pains and dangers of herself, foresight, with his lieutenant, resolution, had made ready defense, now with the love she bare her sister, she was driven to a stay before she determined; but long she stayed not, before this reason did shine unto her, that since in herself she preferred death before such a base servitude, love did teach her to wish the same to her sister.

Therefore, crossing her arms, and looking sideward upon the ground, "Do what you will," said she, "with us; for my part, heaven shall melt before I be removed. But, if you will follow my counsel, for your own sake—for, as for prayers for my sake, I have felt how little they prevail—let my death first serve for example to win her, who perchance is not so resolved against Amphialus, and so shall you not only justly punish me (who indeed do hate both you and your son), but, if that may move you, you shall do more virtuously in preserving one most worthy of life, and killing another most desirous of death; lastly, in winning her, instead of a peevish unhappy creature, that I am, you shall bless your son with the most excellent woman in all praiseworthy things, that the world holdeth."

But Cecropia (who had already set down to herself what she would do) with bitter both terms and countenance, told her that she should not need to woo death over-eagerly, for, if her sister going before her did not teach her wit, herself should quickly follow. For, since they were not to be gotten, there was no way for her son's quiet but to know that they were past getting. And so, since no intreating, nor threatening, might prevail, she bad her prepare her eyes for a new play, which she should see within few hours in the hall of that castle.

A place indeed over-fit for so unfit a matter; for being so stately made that the bottom of it being even with the ground, the roof reached as high as any part of the castle, at either end it had convenient lodgings. In the one end was, one story from the ground, Philoclea's abode; in the other, of even height, Pamela's; and Zelmane's, in a chamber above her; but all so vaulted of strong and thickly-built stone as one could no way hear the other. Each of these chambers had a little window to look into the hall, but, because the sisters should not have so much comfort as to look out to one another, there was, of the outsides, curtains drawn, which they could not reach with their hands, so barring the reach of their sight.

But when the hour came that the tragedy should begin, the curtains were withdrawn from before the windows of Zelmane and of Philoclea, a sufficient challenge to call their eyes to defend themselves in such an encounter. And by-and-by came in at one end of the hall, with about a dozen armed soldiers, a lady, led by a couple, with her hands bound before her, from above her eyes to her lips muffled with a fair kerchief, but from her mouth to the shoulders all bare; and so was led on to a scaffold raised a good deal from the floor, and all covered with crimson velvet. But neither Zelmane nor Philoclea needed to be told who she was, for the apparel she wore made them too well assured that it was the admirable Pamela; whereunto, the rare whiteness of her naked neck gave sufficient testimony to their astonished senses. But the fair lady being come to the scaffold, and then made to kneel down, and so left by her unkind supporters, as it seemed that she was about to speak somewhat (whereunto Philoclea, poor soul, earnestly listened, according to her speech even minded to frame her mind, her heart never till then almost wavering to save her sister's life), before the unfortunate lady could pronounce three words, the executioner cut off the one's speech and the other's attention with making his sword do his cruel office upon that beautiful neck. Yet the pitiless sword had such pity of so precious an object, that at first it did but hit flat-long. But little availed that, since the lady falling down astonished withal, the cruel villain forced the sword with another blow to divorce the fair marriage of the head and body.

And this was done so in an instant that the very act did overrun Philoclea's sorrow, sorrow not being able so quickly to thunderbolt her heart through her senses, but first only oppressed her with a storm of amazement; but when her eyes saw that they did see, as condemning themselves to have seen it, they became weary of their own power of seeing, and her soul then drinking up woe with great draughts, she fell down to deadly trances; but her waiting jailers, with cruel pity, brought loathed life unto her, which yet many times took his leave as though he would indeed depart; but, when he was stayed by force, he kept with him deadly sorrow, which thus exercised her mourning speech: "Pamela! my sister, my sister Pamela! woe is me for thee! I would I had died for thee! Pamela, never more shall I see thee, never more shall I enjoy thy sweet company and wise counsel! Alas, thou art gone to beautify heaven, and hast thou left me here, who have nothing good in me but that I did ever love thee, and ever will lament thee? Let this day be noted of all virtuous folks for most unfortunate. Let it never be mentioned, but among curses; and cursed be they that did this mischief, and most accursed be mine eyes that beheld it. Sweet Pamela! that head is stricken off, where only wisdom might be spoken withal. That body is destroyed, which was the living book of virtue. Dear Pamela, how hast thou left me to all wretchedness and misery? Yet while thou livedst, in thee I breathed, of thee I hoped. O Pamela, how much did I for thy excellency honor thee, more than my mother, and love thee more than myself? Never more shall I lie with thee; never more shall we bathe in the pleasant river together; never more shall I see thee in thy shepherd apparel. But thou art gone, and where am I? Pamela is dead; and live I? My God!"

And with that she fell again in a swoon, so as it was a great while before they could bring her to herself again. But being come to herself, "Alas," said she, "unkind women, since you have given me so many deaths, torment me not now with life. For God's sake, let me go, and excuse your hands of more blood. Let me follow my Pamela, whom ever I sought to follow. Alas, Pamela, they will not let me come to thee. But if they keep promise, I shall tread thine own steps after thee. For to what am I born (miserable soul) but to be most unhappy in myself, and yet more unhappy in others? But O! that a thousand more miseries had happened unto me, so thou hadst not died, Pamela, my sister Pamela!"

And so, like lamentable Philomela, complained she the horrible wrong done to her sister, which, if it stirred not in the wickedly-closed minds of her tormentors a pity of her sorrow, yet bred it a weariness of her sorrow, so as, only leaving one to prevent any harm she should do herself, the rest went away, consulting again with Cecropia, how to make profit of this their late bloody act.

CHAPTER 22

Cecropia's policy to use Zelmane's intercession. Zelmane's self-conflict. Her motion to Philoclea rather to dissemble than die. Philoclea's resolution rather to die than dissemble. At sight of Philoclea's head Zelmane's ecstasies, desperate designs, and comfortless complaints.

In the end, that woman that used most to keep company with Zelmane told Cecropia that she found, by many most sensible proofs in Zelmane, that there was never woman so loved another as she loved Philoclea, which was the cause that she, further than the commandment of Cecropia, had caused Zelmane's curtains to be also drawn; because, having the same spectacle that Philoclea had, she might stand in the greater fear for her whom she loved so well, and that indeed she had hit the needle in that device; for never saw she creature so astonished as Zelmane, exceedingly sorry for Pamela, but exceedingly exceeding that exceedingness in fear for Philoclea. Therefore her advice was, she should cause Zelmane to come and speak with Philoclea; for, there being such vehemency of friendship between them, it was both likely to move Zelmane to persuade and Philoclea to be persuaded. Cecropia liked well of the counsel, and gave order to the same woman to go deal therein with Zelmane, and to assure her with oath that Cecropia was determined Philoclea should pass the same way that Pamela had done, without she did yield to satisfy the extremity of her son's affection, which the woman did, adding thereunto many (as she thought) good reasons to make Zelmane think Amphialus a fit match for Philoclea.

But Zelmane (who had from time to time understood the cruel dealing they had used to the sisters, and now had her own eyes wounded with the sight of one's death) was so confused withal (her courage still rebelling against her wit, desiring still with force to do impossible matters) that as her desire was stopped with power, so her conceit was darkened with a mist of desire. For blind love and invincible valor still would cry out, that it could not be Philoclea should be in so miserable estate, and she not relieve her; and so while she haled her wit to her courage, she drew it from his own limits. But now Philoclea's death (a word able to marshal all his thoughts in order) being come to so short a point either with small delay to be suffered, or by the giving herself to another to be prevented, she was driven to think, and to desire some leisure of thinking, which the woman granted for that night unto her. A night that was not half so black, as her mind, not half so silent, as was fit for her musing thoughts. At last, he that would fain have desperately lost a thousand lives for her sake, could not find in his heart, that she should lose any life for her own sake; and he that despised his own death in respect of honor, yet could well-nigh dispense with honor itself in respect of Philoclea's death; for once the thought could not enter into his heart, nor the breath issue out of his mouth, which could consent to Philoclea's death for any bargain. Then, how to prevent the next degree to death (which was her being possessed by another) was the point of his mind's labor; and in that he found no other way, but that Philoclea should pretend a yielding unto Cecropia's request; and so by speaking with Amphialus, and making fair (but delaying) promises, procure liberty for Zelmane, who only wished but to come by a sword, not doubting then to destroy them all, and deliver Philoclea; so little did both the men and their forces seem in her eyes, looking down upon them from the high top of affection's tower.

With that mind, therefore, (but first well bound) she was brought to Philoclea, having already plotted out in her conceit, how she would deal with her; so came she with heart and eyes, which did each sacrifice either to love upon the altar of sorrow. And there had she the pleasing displeasing sight of Philoclea, Philoclea, whom already the extreme sense of sorrow had brought to a dullness therein, her face not without tokens that beauty had been by many miseries cruelly battered, and yet showed it most the perfection of the beauty, which could remain unoverthrown by such enemies. But when Zelmane was set down by her, the women gone away (because she might be the better persuaded when nobody was by, that had heard her say she would not be persuaded) then began first the eyes to speak and the hearts to cry out: sorrow a while would needs speak his own language without using their tongues to be his interpreters. At last Zelmane brake silence, but spoke with the only eloquence of amazement; for all her long methodized oration was inherited only by such kind of speeches, "Dear lady, in extreme necessities we must not—but alas, unfortunate wretch that I am, that I live to see this day. And I take heaven and earth to witness, that nothing—" and with that her breast swelled so with spite and grief, that her breath had not leisure to turn herself into words.

But the sweet Philoclea, that had already died in Pamela, and of the other side had the heaviness of her heart something quickened in the most beloved sight of Zelmane, guessed somewhat at Zelmane's mind; and therefore, spoke unto her in this sort.

"My Pyrocles," said she, "I know this exceeding comfort of your presence is not brought unto me for any goodwill that is owed unto me, but (as I suppose) to make you persuade me to save my life with the ransom of mine honor. Although nobody should be so unfit a pleader in that cause as your self, yet perchance you would have me live."

"Your honor! God forbid," said Zelmane, "that ever, for any cause, I should yield to any touch of it. But a while to pretend some affection, till time, or my liberty, might work something for your service. This, if my astonished senses would give me leave, I would fain have persuaded you."

"To what purpose, my Pyrocles?" said Philoclea. "Of a miserable time, what gain is there? Hath Pamela's example wrought no more in me? Is a captive life so much worth? Can ever it go out of these lips that I love any other but Pyrocles? Shall my tongue be so false a traitor to my heart as to say I love any other but Pyrocles? And why should I do all this? To live? O Pamela, sister Pamela, why should I live? Only for thy sake, Pyrocles, I would live; but to thee I know too well I shall not live; and if not to thee, hath thy love so base alloy, my Pyrocles, as to wish me to live? For dissimulation, my Pyrocles, my simplicity is such that I have hardly been able to keep a straight way; what shall I do in a crooked? But in this case there is no mean of dissimulation, not for the cunningest; present answer is required, and present performance upon the answer. Art thou so terrible, O death? No, my Pyrocles; and for that I do thank thee, and in my soul thank thee; for I confess the love of thee is herein my chiefest virtue. Trouble me not, therefore, dear Pyrocles, nor double not my death by tormenting my resolution; since I cannot live with thee, I will die for thee. Only remember me, dear Pyrocles, and love the remembrance of me; and if I may crave so much of thee, let me be thy last love, for though I be not worthy of thee (who indeed art the worthiest creature living), yet remember that my love was a worthy love."

But Pyrocles was so overcome with sorrow (which wisdom

and virtue made just in so excellent a lady's case, full of so excellent kindness) that words were ashamed to come forth, knowing how weak they were to express his mind and her merit; and
therefore, so stayed in a deadly silence, forsaken of hope and for-
saking comfort, till the appointed guardians came in, to see the
fruits of Zelmane's labor. And then Zelmane, warned by their
presence, fell again to persuade, though scarcely herself could tell
what, but in sum, desirous of delays. But Philoclea sweetly continuing constant, and in the end punishing her importunity with
silence, Zelmane was fain to end. Yet craving another time's conference, she obtained it and divers others, till at the last Cecropia
found it was to no purpose, and therefore determined to follow
her own way; Zelmane yet still desirous to win, by any means,
respite, even wasted with sorrow and uncertain whether in worse
case in her presence or absence, being able to do nothing for
Philoclea's succor but by submitting the greatest courage of the
earth to fall at the feet of Cecropia, and crave stay of their
sentence till the uttermost was seen what her persuasions might
do.

Cecropia seemed much to be moved by her importunity, so
as divers days were won of painful life to the excellent Philoclea;
while Zelmane suffered some hope to cherish her mind, especially
trusting upon the help of Musidorus, who, she knew, would not
be idle in this matter; till one morning a noise awaked Zelmane,
from whose over-watchful mind the tired body had stolen a little
sleep, and straight, with the first opening of her eyes, care taking
his wonted place, she ran to the window which looked into the
hall—for that way the noise guided her—and there might she
see, the curtain being left open ever since the last execution,
seven or eight persons in a cluster upon the scaffold, who by-and-
by retiring themselves, nothing was to be seen thereupon but a
basin of gold, pitifully enameled with blood, and, in the midst of
it, the head of the most beautiful Philoclea.

The horribleness of the mischief was such as Pyrocles could
not at first believe his own senses, but bent his woeful eyes to
discern it better, where too well he might see it was Philoclea's
self, having no veil, but beauty, over the face, which still appeared

to be alive; so did those eyes shine, even as they were wont—and they were wont more than any other—and sometimes, as they moved, it might well make the beholder think that death therein had borrowed her beauty, and not they any way disgraced by death, so sweet and piercing a grace they carried with them.

It was not a pity, it was not an amazement, it was not a sorrow, which then laid hold on Pyrocles, but a wild fury of desperate agony, so that he cried out, "O tyrant heaven! traitor earth! blind providence! no justice! How is this done? How is this suffered? Hath this world a government? If it have, let it pour out all his mischiefs upon me, and see whether it have power to make me more wretched than I am. Did she excel for this? Have I prayed for this? Abominable hand that did it, detestable devil that commanded it, cursed light that beheld it; and, if the light be cursed, what are then mine eyes that have seen it? And have I seen Philoclea dead, and do I live? And have I lived, not to help her, but to talk of her? And stand I still talking?"

And with that, carried with the madness of anguish, not having a readier way to kill himself, he ran as hard as ever he could, with his head, against the wall, with intention to brain himself, but the haste to do it made the doing the slower. For, as he came to give the blow, his foot tripped, so as it came not with the full force, yet forcible enough to strike him down, and withal to deprive him of his sense, so that he lay a while, comforted by the hurt in that he felt not his discomfort.

And when he came again to himself, he heard, or he thought he heard, a voice which cried, "Revenge! Revenge!" whether indeed it were his good angel, which used that voice to stay him from unnatural murdering of himself, or that his wandering spirits lighted upon that conceit, and by their weakness, subject to apprehensions, supposed they heard it. But that indeed, helped with virtue and her valiant servant anger, stopped him from present destroying himself; yielding in reason and manhood first to destroy man, woman, and child, that were any way of kin to them that were accessory to this cruelty; then to raze the castle, and to build a sumptuous monument for her sister, and a most sumptuous for herself, and then himself to die upon her tomb. This determining in himself to do, and to seek all means how, for that purpose, to get out of prison, he was content a while to bear the thirst of death; and yet went he again to the window, to kiss the beloved head with his eyes, but there saw he nothing but the scaffold, all covered over with scarlet, and nothing but solitary silence to mourn this mischief. But then, sorrow having dispersed itself from his heart in all his noble parts, it proclaimed his authority, in cries and tears, and with a more gentle dolefulness could pour out his inward evil.

"Alas," said he, "and is that head taken away, too, so soon from mine eyes? What, mine eyes, perhaps they envy the excellency of your sorrow? Indeed, there is nothing now left to become the eyes of all mankind, but tears; and woe be to me, if any exceed me in woefulness. I do conjure you all, my senses, to accept no object, but of sorrow. Be ashamed, nay, abhor, to think of comfort. Unhappy eyes, you have seen too much, that ever the light should be welcome to you. Unhappy ears, you shall never hear the music of music in her voice. Unhappy heart, that hast lived to feel these pangs. Thou hast done thy worst, world, and cursed be thou, and cursed art thou, since to thine own self thou hast done the worst thou couldest do. Exiled beauty, let only now thy beauty be blubbered faces. Widowed music, let now thy tunes be roarings and lamentations. Orphan virtue, get thee wings, and fly after her into heaven; here is no dwelling place for thee. Why lived I, alas? Alas, why loved I? To die wretched, and to be the example of the heavens' hate? And hate, and spare not, for your worst blow is stricken.

"Sweet Philoclea, thou art gone, and hast carried with thee my love, and hast thy love in me; and I, wretched man! do live. I live, to die continually, till thy revenge do give me leave to die; and then die I will, my Philoclea; my heart willingly makes this promise to itself. Surely he did not look upon thee that gave the cruel blow, for no eye could have abidden to see such beauty overthrown by such mischief. Alas, why should they divide such a head from such a body? No other body is worthy of that head; no other head is worthy of that body. O yet, if I had taken my last leave, if I might have taken a holy kiss from that dying mouth—. Where art thou, hope, which promisest never to leave a man while he liveth? Tell me, what canst thou hope for? Nay, tell me, what is there which I would willingly hope after? Wishing power (which is accounted infinite), what now is left to wish for? She is gone, and gone with her all my hope, all my wishing. Love, be ashamed to be called love; cruel hate, unspeakable hate, is victorious over thee. Who is there now left that can justify thy tyranny and give reason to thy passion?

"O cruel divorce of the sweetest marriage that ever was in nature! Philoclea is dead; and dead is with her all goodness, all sweetness, all excellency! Philoclea is dead; and yet life is not ashamed to continue upon the earth! Philoclea is dead! O deadly word, which containeth in itself the uttermost of all misfortunes; but happy word, when thou shalt be said of me; and long it shall not be, before it be said!"

CHAPTER 23

A lady's kind comforts to Pyrocles' comfortless unkindness. His hardly knowing her. Her unmasking of Cecropia's fruitless sophistry. Their medley of solace and sorrow.

Then stopping his words with sighs, drowning his sighs in tears, and drying again his tears in rage, he would sit a while in a wandering muse, which represented nothing but vexations unto him; then throwing himself sometimes upon the floor, and sometimes upon the bed, then up again, till walking was wearisome and rest loathsome; and so, neither suffering food nor sleep to help his afflicted nature, all that day and night he did nothing but weep "Philoclea," sigh "Philoclea," and cry out "Philoclea"; till, as it happened, at that time upon his bed, toward the dawning of the day, he heard one stir in his chamber, by the motion of garments, and he, with an angry voice, asked who was there.

"A poor gentlewoman," answered the party, "that wishes long life unto you."

"And I soon death to you," said he, "for the horrible curse you have given me."

"Certainly," said she, "an unkind answer, and far unworthy the excellency of your mind, but not unsuitable to the rest of your behavior. For most part of this night I have heard you her skill, when she made them; you shall find many their superiors, (being let into your chamber, you never perceiving it, so was your mind estranged from your senses) and have heard nothing of Zelmane, in Zelmane, nothing but weak wailings, fitter for some nurse of a village than so famous a creature as you are."

"O God," cried out Pyrocles, "that thou wert a man that useth these words unto me! I tell thee I am sorry, I tell thee I will be sorry, in despite of thee and all them that would have me joyful."

"And yet," replied she, "perchance Philoclea is not dead, whom you so much bemoan."

"I would we were both dead on that condition," said Pyrocles.

"See the folly of your passion," said she; "as though you should be nearer to her, you being dead, and she alive, than she being dead, and you alive. And, if she be dead, was she not born to die? What, then, do you cry out for? Not for her, who must have died one time or other, but for some few years; so as it is time and this world that seem so lovely things, and not Philoclea, unto you."

"O noble sisters," cried Pyrocles, "now you be gone, who were the only exalters of all womankind, what is left in that sex but babbling and busyness?"

"And truly," said she, "I will yet a little longer trouble you."

"Nay, I pray you do," said Pyrocles, "for I wish for nothing in my short life but mischiefs and cumbers, and I am content you shall be one of them."

"In truth," said she, "you would think yourself a greatly privileged person if, since the strongest building and lastingest monarchies are subject to end, only your Philoclea (because she is yours) should be exempted. But, indeed, you bemoan yourself, who have lost a friend; you cannot her, who hath in one act both preserved her honor and left the miseries of this world."

"O woman's philosophy, childish folly," said Pyrocles; "as,

though, if I do bemoan myself, I have not reason so to do, having lost more than any monarchy—nay, than my life—can be worth unto me."

"Alas!" said she, "comfort yourself; Nature did not forget and perchance such as, when your eyes shall look abroad, yourself will like better."

But that speech put all good manners out of the conceit of Pyrocles, in so much that, leaping out of his bed, he ran to have stricken her; but, coming near her, the morning then winning the field of darkness, he saw, or he thought he saw, indeed, the very face of Philoclea; the same sweetness, the same grace, the same beauty; with which, carried into a divine astonishment, he fell down at her feet.

"Most blessed angel," said he, "well hast thou done to take that shape, since thou wouldest submit thyself to mortal sense; for a more angelical form could not have been created for thee. Alas! even by that excellent beauty, so beloved of me, let it be lawful for me to ask of thee, what is the cause that she, that heavenly creature whose form you have taken, should by the heavens be destined to so unripe an end? Why should injustice so prevail? Why was she seen to the world, so soon to be ravished from us? Why was she not suffered to live, to teach the world perfection?"

"Do not deceive thyself," answered she; "I am no angel: I am Philoclea, the same Philoclea, so truly loving you, so truly beloved of you."

"If it be so," said he, "that you are indeed the soul of Philoclea, you have done well to keep your own figure, for no heaven could have given you a better. Then, alas! why have you taken the pains to leave your blissful seat to come to this place, most wretched to me, who am wretchedness itself, and not rather obtain for me that I might come where you are, there eternally to behold, and eternally to love, your beauties? You know (I know) that I desire nothing but death, which I only stay to be justly revenged of your unjust murderers."

"Dear Pyrocles," said she, "I am thy Philoclea, and, as yet, living, not murdered, as you supposed, and therefore to be comforted"; and with that gave him her hand.

But the sweet touch of that hand seemed to his estrayed powers[63] so heavenly a thing that it rather for a while confirmed him in his former belief; till she, with vehement protestations (and desire that it might be so, helping to persuade that it was so) brought him to yield, yet doubtfully to yield, to this height of all comfort, that Philoclea lived; which witnessing with the tears of joy, "Alas!" said he, "how shall I believe mine eyes any more? Or do you yet but appear thus unto me, to stay me from some desperate end? For, alas! I saw the excellent Pamela beheaded; I saw your head—the head, indeed, and chief part of all nature's works—standing in a dish of gold—too mean a shrine, God wot, for such a relic. How can this be, my only dear, and you live? Or, if this be not so, how can I believe mine own senses? And, if I cannot believe them, why should I now believe these blessed tidings they bring me?"

"The truth is," said she, "my Pyrocles, that neither I, as you find, nor yet my dear sister, is dead, although the mischievously subtle Cecropia used sleights to make either of us think so of other. For, having in vain attempted the farthest of her wicked eloquence, to make either of us yield to her son, and seeing that neither it, accompanied with great flatteries and rich presents, could get any ground of us, nor yet the violent way she fell into of cruelty, tormenting our bodies, could prevail with us, at last she made either of us think the other dead, and so hoped to have wrested our minds to the forgetting of virtue; and first she gave to mine eyes the miserable spectacle of my sister's (as I thought) death; but, indeed, not my sister—it was only Artesia, she who so cunningly brought us to this misery. Truly I am sorry for the poor gentlewoman, though justly she be punished for her double falsehood; but Artesia, muffled so as you could not easily discern her, and in my sister's apparel, which they had taken from her under color of giving her other, did they execute; and when I, for thy sake especially, dear Pyrocles, could by no force nor fear be won, they essayed the like with my sister, by bringing me

---

[63] estrayed powers—confused faculties.

down under the scaffold, and, making me thrust my head up through a hole they had made therein, they did put about my poor neck a dish of gold, whereout they had beaten the bottom, so as having set blood in it, you saw how I played the part of death—God knows, even willing to have done it in earnest— and so had they set me, that I reached but on tiptoes to the ground, so as scarcely I could breathe, much less speak. And truly, if they had kept me there any whit longer, they had strangled me, instead of beheading me; but then they took me away, and, seeking to see their issue of this practice, they found my noble sister, for the dear love she vouchsafeth to bear me, so grieved withal that she willed them to do their uttermost cruelty unto her; for she vowed never to receive sustenance of them that had been the causers of my murder; and, finding both of us even given over, not like to live many hours longer, and my sister Pamela rather worse than myself—the strength of her heart worse bearing those indignities—the good woman Cecropia, with the same pity as folks keep fowl, when they are not fat enough for their eating, made us know her deceit, and let us come one to another—with what joy you can well imagine, who, I know, feel the like, saving that we only thought ourselves reserved to miseries, and therefore fitter for condoling than congratulating.

"For my part, I am fully persuaded it is but with a little respite, to have a more feeling sense of the torments she prepares for us. True it is, that one of my guardians would have me to believe that this proceeds of my gentle cousin Amphialus, who, having heard some inkling that we were evil entreated,[64] had called his mother to his bedside, from whence he never rose since his last combat, and besought and charged her, upon all the love she bare him, to use us with all kindness, vowing, with all the imprecations he could imagine, that if ever he understood for his sake that I received further hurt than the want of my liberty, he would not live an hour longer. And the good woman swore to me that he would kill his mother, if he knew how I had been dealt with; but that Cecropia keeps him from understanding things how they pass, only having heard a whispering, and myself

[64] evil entreated—cruelly treated.

named, he had (of abundance, forsooth, of honorable love) given this charge for us. Whereupon this enlargement of mine was grown. For my part, I know too well their cunning (who leave no money unoffered that may buy mine honor) to believe any word they say, but, my dear Pyrocles, even look for the worst, and prepare myself for the same. Yet I must confess, I was content to rob from death, and borrow of my misery the sweet comfort of seeing my sweet sister, and most sweet comfort of thee, my Pyrocles.

"And so, having leave, I came stealing into your chamber, where (O Lord) what a joy it was unto me, to hear you solemnize the funerals of the poor Philoclea! That I myself might live to hear my death bewailed! And by whom? By my dear Pyrocles. That I saw death was not strong enough to divide thy love from me! O my Pyrocles, I am too well paid for my pains I have suffered. Joyful is my woe for so noble a cause; and welcome be all miseries, since to thee I am so welcome. Alas! how I pitied to hear thy pity of me; and yet a great while I could not find in my heart to interrupt thee, but often had even pleasure to weep with thee; and so kindly came forth thy lamentations that they enforced me to lament too, as if, indeed, I had been a looker-on to see poor Philoclea die. Till at last I spake with you, to try whether I could remove thee from sorrow, till I had almost procured myself a beating."

And with that she prettily smiled, which, mingled with her tears, one could not tell whether it were a mourning pleasure or a delightful sorrow, but like when a few April drops are scattered by a gentle zephyrus among fine-colored flowers. But Pyrocles, who had felt (with so small distance of time) in himself the overthrow both of hope and despair, knew not to what key he should tune his mind, either of joy or sorrow. But finding perfect reason in neither, suffered himself to be carried by the tide of his imagination, and his imaginations to be raised even by the sway, which hearing or seeing might give unto them. He saw her alive; he was glad to see her alive. He saw her weep; he was sorry to see her weep. He heard her comfortable speeches, nothing more gladsome; he heard her prognosticating her own destruction, nothing more doleful. But when he had a little taken breath from the panting motion of such contrariety in passions, he fell to consider with her of her present estate, both comforting her, that certainly the worst of this storm was past, since already they had done the worst which man's wit could imagine; and that if they had determined to have killed her, they would have now done it; and also earnestly counseling her, and enabling his counsels with vehement prayers, that she would so far second the hopes of Amphialus as that she might but procure him liberty, promising then as much to her as the liberality of loving courage durst promise to himself.

CHAPTER 24

Amphialus excuseth. The princesses accuse. Cecropia seeking their death findeth her own. Amphialus's death-pangs and self-killing. The woeful knowledge of it.

But who would lively describe the manner of these speeches should paint out the lightsome colors of affection, shaded with the deepest shadows of sorrow, finding then between hope and fear a kind of sweetness in tears; till Philoclea, content to receive a kiss, and but a kiss of Pyrocles, sealed up his moving lips, and closed them up in comfort, and herself, for the passage was left between them open, went to her sister, with whom she had stayed but a while, fortifying one another, while Philoclea tempered Pamela's just disdain, and Pamela ennobled Philoclea's sweet humbleness, when Amphialus came unto them, who never since he had heard Philoclea named could be quiet in himself, although none of them about him (fearing more his mother's violence than his power) would discover what had passed; and many messages he sent to know her estate, which brought answer back, according as it pleased Cecropia to indite them, till his heart, full of unfortunate affliction, more and more misgiving him, having impatiently borne the delay of the night's unfitness, this morning he got up, and, though full of wounds (which not without danger could suffer such exercise), he appareled himself, and, with a countenance that showed strength in nothing but in grief, he came where the sisters were, and weakly kneeling down, he besought them to pardon him, if they had not been used in that castle according to their worthiness and his duty, beginning to excuse small matters, poor gentleman, not knowing in what sort they had been handled.

But Pamela's high heart, having conceived mortal hate for the injury offered to her and her sister, could scarcely abide his sight, much less hear out his excuses, but interrupted him with these words: "Traitor," said she, "to thine own blood, and false to the profession of so much love as thou hast vowed! Do not defile our ears with thy excuses, but pursue on thy cruelty, that thou and thy godly mother have used towards us; for my part, assure thyself—and do so I answer for my sister, whose mind I know—I do not more desire mine own safety than thy destruction."

Amazed with this speech, he turned his eye, full of humble sorrowfulness, to Philoclea: "And is this, most excellent lady, your doom of me also?"

She, sweet lady, sat weeping; for, as her most noble kinsman, she had ever favored him, and loved his love, though she could not be in love with his person; and now, partly unkindness of his wrong, partly pity of his case, made her sweet mind yield some tears before she could answer, and her answer was no other but that she had the same cause as her sister had. He replied no further, but delivering from his heart two or three untaught sighs, rose, and, with most low reverence, went out of their chamber, and straight, by threatening torture, learned of one of the women in what terrible manner those princesses had been used. But when he heard it, crying out, "O God!" and then not able to say any more, for his speech went back to rebound woe upon his heart, he needed no judge to go upon him, for no man could ever think any other worthy of greater punishment than he thought himself.

Full, therefore, of the horriblest despair which a most guilty conscience could breed, with wild looks promising some terrible issue, understanding his mother was on the top of the leads,[65]

---

[65] leads—the roof-top walk.

he caught one of his servant's swords from him, and none of them daring to stay him, he went up, carried by fury instead of strength, where she was at that time musing how to go through with this matter, and resolving to make much of her nieces in show and secretly to impoison them, thinking, since they were not to be won, her son's love would no otherwise be mitigated.

But when she saw him come in with a sword drawn, and a look more terrible than the sword, she straight was stricken with the guiltiness of her own conscience; yet, the well-known humbleness of her son somewhat animated her, till he, coming nearer her, and crying to her, "Thou damnable creature! only fit to bring forth such a monster of unhappiness as I am!" she, fearing he would have stricken her, though indeed he meant it not, but only intended to kill himself in her presence, went back so far, till, ere she were aware, she overthrew herself from over the leads, to receive her death's kiss at the ground; and yet was she not so happy as presently to die, but that she had time, with hellish agony, to see her son's mischief, whom she loved so well, before her end; when she confessed, with most desperate but not repenting mind, the purpose she had to impoison the princesses, and would then have had them murthered. But everybody seeing, and glad to see, her end, had left obedience to her tyranny.

And, if it could be, her ruin increased woe in the noble heart of Amphialus, who, when he saw her fall, had his own rage stayed a little with the suddenness of her destruction. "And I was not enough miserable before," said he, "but that before my end I must be the death of my mother? Who, how wicked soever, yet I would she had received her punishment by some other. O Amphialus! wretched Amphialus! Thou hast lived to be the death of thy most dear companion and friend Philoxenus, and of his father, thy most careful foster-father; thou hast lived to kill a lady with thine own hands, and so excellent and virtuous a lady as the fair Parthenia was; thou hast lived to see thy faithful Ismenus slain in succoring thee, and thou not able to defend him; thou hast lived to show thyself such a coward as that one unknown knight could overcome thee in thy lady's presence; thou hast lived to bear arms against thy rightful prince, thine own uncle; thou hast lived to be accounted, and justly accounted, a traitor, by the most excellent persons that this world holdeth; thou hast lived to be the death of her that gave thee life. But, ah, wretched Amphialus! thou hast lived for thy sake, and by thy authority, to have Philoclea tormented: O heavens! in Amphialus' castle, where Amphialus commanded—tormented! Tormented! Torment of my soul! Philoclea tormented! And thou hast had such comfort in thy life as to live all this while! Perchance this hand, used only to mischievous acts, thinks it were too good a deed to kill me; or else, filthy hand, only worthy to kill women, thou art afraid to strike a man. Fear not, cowardly hand, for thou shalt kill but a cowardly traitor; and do it gladly, for thou shalt kill him whom Philoclea hateth."

With that, furiously he tore open his doublet, and setting the pommel of the sword to the ground and the point to his breast, he fell upon it. But the sword, more merciful than he to himself, with the slipping of the pommel the point swerved, and razed him but upon the side; yet with the fall, his other wounds opened so as he bled in such extremity that Charon's boat might very well be carried in that flood, which yet he sought to hasten by this means.

As he opened his doublet and fell, there fell out Philoclea's knives, which Cecropia at the first had taken from her and delivered to her son, and he had ever worn them next his heart as the only relic he had of his saint; now, seeing them by him (his sword being so, as weakness could not well draw it out from his doublet), he took the knives, and pulling one of them out, and many times kissing it, and then, first with the passions of kindness and unkindness melting in tears, "O dear knives, you are come in a good time to revenge the wrong I have done you all this while in keeping you from her blessed side, and wearing you without your mistress' leave. Alas! be witness with me yet before I die—and well you may, for you have lain next my heart—that, by my consent, your excellent mistress should have had as much honor as this poor place could have brought forth for so high an excellency; and now I am condemned to die by her mouth. Alas! other, far other, hope would my desire often have given me, but other event it hath pleased her to lay upon me. Ah, Philoclea"—with that his tears gushed out as though they would strive to overflow his blood—"I would yet thou knewest how I love thee. Unworthy I am, unhappy I am, false I am; but to thee, alas! I am not false. But what a traitor am I, any way to excuse him, whom she condemneth! Since there is nothing left me wherein I may do her service, but in punishing him who hath so offended her, dear knife, then do your noble mistress' commandment."

With that he stabbed himself into divers places of his breast and throat, until those wounds, with the old freshly bleeding, brought him to the senseless gate of death. By which time, his servants having with fear of his fury abstained a while from coming unto him, one of them, preferring dutiful affection before fearful duty, came in, and there found him swimming in his own blood, there giving a pitiful spectacle, where the conquest was the conqueror's overthrow, and self-ruin the only triumph of a battle fought between him and himself. The time full of danger, the person full of worthiness, the manner full of horror, did greatly astonish all the beholders, so as by-and-by all the town was full of it, and then of all ages came running up to see the beloved body, everybody thinking their safety bled in his wounds, and their honor died in his destruction.

CHAPTER 25

Anaxius' rages for the death; Queen Helen's coming for the cure of Amphialus. Her complaints over him. Her passport and safe conduct to carry him to her surgeon. The people's sorrow, set down in a song.

But when it came, and quickly it came, to the ears of his proud friend Anaxius (who by that time was grown well of his wound, but never had come abroad, disdaining to abase himself to the company of any other but of Amphialus), he was exceedingly vexed, either with kindness, or (if a proud heart be not capable thereof) with disdain, that he who had the honor to be called the friend of Anaxius should come to such an unexpected ruin. Therefore, then, coming abroad with a face red in anger and engrained[66] in pride, with lids raised up and eyes levelling from top to the toe of them that met him, treading as though he thought to make the earth shake under him, with his hand upon his sword, short speeches and disdainful answers, giving straight order to his two brothers to go take the oath of obedience, in his name, of all the soldiers and citizens in the town, and, withal, to swear them to revenge the death of Amphialus upon Basilius, he himself went to see him, calling for all the surgeons and physicians there, spending some time in viewing the body, and threatening them all to be hanged if they did not heal him. But they, taking view of his wounds, and falling down at Anaxius' feet, assured him that they were mortal, and no possible means to keep him above two days alive; and he stood partly in doubt to kill or save them, between his own fury and their humbleness; but vowing with his own hands to kill the two sisters, as causers of his friend's death, when his brothers came to him and told him they had done his commandment, in having received the oath of allegiance, with no great difficulty, the most part terrified by their valor and force of their servants, and many that had been forward actors in the rebellion willing to do anything rather than come under the subjection of Basilius again, and such few as durst gainsay being cut off by present slaughter.

But, withal, as the chief matter of their coming to him, they told Anaxius that the fair Queen Helen was come, with an honorable retinue, to the town, humbly desiring leave to see Amphialus, whom she had sought in many places of the world; and, lastly, being returned into her own country, she heard together of the late siege, and of his combat with the strange knight who had dangerously hurt him; whereupon, full of loving care, which she was content even to publish to the world, how ungratefully soever he dealt with her, she had gotten leave of Basilius to come by his frontiers to carry away Amphialus with her to the excellentest surgeon then known, whom she had in her county, but so old as not able to travel, but had given her sovereign anointments to preserve his body withal, till he might be brought unto him; and that Basilius had granted leave, either

[66] engrained—dyed crimson.

natural kindness prevailing over all the offenses done, or rather glad to make any passage which might lead him out of his country and from his daughters. This discourse Lycurgus understanding of Helen, delivered to his brother, with her vehement desire to see the body, and take her last farewell of him. Anaxius, though he were fallen out with all womankind, in respect of the hate he bore the sisters, whom he accounted murderers of Amphialus, yet, at his brother's request, granted her leave; and she, poor lady, with grievous expectation and languishing desire, carried her faint legs to the place where he lay, either not breathing, or in all appearance breathing but death.

In which piteous plight when she saw him, though sorrow had set before her mind the pitifullest conceit thereof that it could paint, yet the present sight went beyond all former apprehensions, so that beginning to kneel by the body, her sight ran from her service rather than abide such a sight, and she fell in a swound upon him, as if she could not choose but die of his wounds. But when her breath, aweary to be closed up in woe, broke the prison of her fair lips and brought memory, with his servant senses, to his natural office, she yet made the breath convey these doleful words with it.

"Alas!" said she, "Amphialus, what strange diseases be these, that, having sought thee so long, I should be now sorry to find thee! That these eyes should look upon Amphialus and be grieved withal! That I should have thee in my power without glory, and embrace thee without comfort! How often have I blest the means that might bring me near thee! Now, woe worth[67] the cause that brings me so near thee! Often, alas! often hast thou disdained my tears, but now, my dear Amphialus, receive them; these eyes can serve for nothing else but weep for thee: since thou wouldst never vouchsafe them thy comfort, yet disdain not them thy sorrow. I would they had been more dear unto thee, for then hadst thou lived. Woe is me that thy noble heart could love who hated thee, and hate who loved thee! Alas! why should not my faith to thee cover my other defects, who only sought to make

[67] woe worth—how unfortunate.

my crown thy foot-stool, myself thy servant? That was all my ambition, and, alas! thou disdainedst it to serve them by whom thy incomparable self wert disdained. Yet, O Philoclea, wheresoever you are, pardon me if I speak in the bitterness of my soul, excellent may you be in all other things, and excellent sure you are since he loved you, your want of pity, where the fault only was infiniteness of desert, cannot be excused. I would, O God! I would that you had granted his deserved suit of marrying you, and that I had been your serving-maid, to have made my estate the foil of your felicity, so he had lived. How many weary steps have I trodden after thee, while my only complaint was that thou wert unkind! Alas! I would now thou wert to be unkind. Alas! why wouldst thou not command my service in persuading Philoclea to love thee? Who could, or (if every one could) who would, have recounted thy perfections so well as I? Who, with such kindly passions, could have stirred pity for thee as I, who should have delivered not only the words but the tears I had of thee, and so shouldst thou have exercised thy disdain in me, and yet used my service for thee?"

With that the body moving somewhat, and giving a groan full of death's music, she fell upon his face and kissed him, and withal cried out: "O miserable I, that have only favor by misery!" And then would she have returned to a fresh career of complaints, when an aged and wise gentleman came to her and besought her to remember what was fit for her greatness, wisdom, and honor; and withal, that it was fitter to show her love in carrying the body to her excellent surgeon, first applying such excellent medicines as she had received of him for that purpose, rather than only show herself a woman-lover in fruitless lamentations. She was straight warned with the obedience of an overthrown mind, and, therefore, leaving some surgeons of her own to dress the body, went herself to Anaxius, and humbling herself to him, as low as his own pride could wish, besought him that, since the surgeons there had utterly given him over, that he would let her carry him away in her litter with her, since the worst he could have should be to die, and to die in her arms that loved him above all things; and where he should have such monuments erected over him as were fit for her love and his worthiness; beseeching him withal, since she was in a country of enemies, where she trusted more to Anaxius' valor than Basilius' promise, that he would convey them safely out of those territories. Her reasons something moved him, but nothing thoroughly persuaded him but the last request of his help, which he straight promised, warranting all security as long as that sword had his master alive. She as happy therein as unhappiness could be, having received as small comfort of her own surgeons as of the others, caused yet the body to be easily conveyed into the litter, all the people then beginning to roar and cry, as though never till then they had lost their lord; and if the terror of Anaxius had not kept them under, they would have mutinied rather than suffered his body to be carried away.

But Anaxius himself riding before the litter, with the choice men of that place, they were afraid even to cry, though they were ready to cry for fear, but because that they might do, everybody forced (even with harming themselves) to do honor to him, some throwing themselves upon the ground, some tearing their clothes and casting dust upon their heads, and some even wounding themselves and sprinkling their own blood in the air. Among the rest, one accounted good in that kind, and made the better by the true feeling of sorrow, roared out a song of lamentation, which (as well as might be) was gathered up in this form:

[*OA75 was placed here*]

CHAPTER 26

The public grief amplified. Anaxius' death-threatening to the princesses. Their resoluteness in it. His return and stop. Zelmane's brave challenge unto him scorned by him. His love to Pamela scorned by her. His brothers' brave loves have as mean success.

The general consort of all such numbers' mourning performed so the natural times of sorrow, that even to them (if any such were) that felt not the loss, yet others' grief taught them grief, having before their compassionate sense so passionate a spectacle of a young man of great beauty, beautified with great honor, honored by great honor, made of inestimable valor, by the noble using of it, to lie there languishing under the arrest of death, and a death where the manner could be no comfort to the discomfortableness of the matter. But when the body was carried through the gate, and the people (saving such as were appointed) not suffered to go further, then was such an universal cry, as if they had all had but one life, and all received but one blow.

Which so moved Anaxius to consider the loss of his friend that, his mind apter to revenge than tenderness, he presently giving order to his brother to keep the prisoners safe, and unvisited, till his return from conveying Helen, he sent a messenger to the sisters to tell them this courteous message: that at his return, with his own hands, he would cut off their heads and send them for tokens to their father.

This message was brought unto the sisters as they sat at that time together with Zelmane, conferring how to carry themselves, having heard of the death of Amphialus; and, as no expectation of death is so painful as where the resolution is hindered by the intermixing of hopes, so did this new alarm, though not remove, yet move somewhat the constancy of their minds, which were so unconstantly dealt with. But, within a while, the excellent Pamela had brought her mind again to his old acquaintance, and then, as careful for her sister, whom most dearly she loved, "Sister," said she, "you see how many acts our tragedy hath. Fortune is not yet aweary of vexing us. But what? A ship is not counted strong for biding one storm. It is but the same trumpet of death, which now perhaps gives the last sound. And let us make that profit of our former miseries, that in them we learned to die willingly."

"Truly," said Philoclea, "dear sister, I was so beaten with the evils of life that, though I had not virtue enough to despise the sweetness of it, yet my weakness bred that strength to be weary of the pains of it. Only I must confess that little hope, which by these late accidents was awaked in me, was at the first angry withal. But even in the darkness of that horror, I see a light of comfort appear; and how can I tread amiss, that see Pamela's steps? I would only (O that my wish might take place) that my school-mistress might live to see me say my lesson truly."

"Were that a life, my Philoclea?" asked Pamela. "No, no," said she, "let it come and put on his worst face; for at the worst it is but a bugbear. Joy is it to me to see you so well resolved; and since the world will not have us, let it lose us. Only"—with that she stayed a little and sighed—"only, my Philoclea"—then she bowed down and whispered in her ear—"only Musidorus, my shepherd, comes between me and death, and makes me think I should not die, because I know he would not I should die."

With that Philoclea sighed also, saying no more, but looking upon Zelmane, who was walking up and down the chamber, having heard this message from Anaxius and, having in times past heard of his nature, thought him like enough to perform it, which winded her again into the former maze of perplexity. Yet debating with herself of the manner how to prevent it, she continued her musing humor, little saying, or indeed, little finding in her heart to say, in a case of such extremity, where preemptorily death was threatened. And so stayed they, having yet that comfort, that they might tarry together; Pamela nobly, Philoclea sweetly, and Zelmane sadly and desperately, none of them entertaining sleep, which they thought should shortly begin, never to awake.

But Anaxius came home, having safely conducted Helen; and safely he might well do it, for, though many of Basilius' knights would have attempted something upon Anaxius, by that means to deliver the ladies, yet Philanax, having received his master's commandment, and knowing his word was given, would not consent unto it; and the Black Knight, who by then was able to carry abroad his wounds, did not know thereof, but was bringing forces, by force to deliver his lady. So as Anaxius, interpreting it rather fear than faith, and making even chance an argument of his virtue, returned; and, as soon as he was returned, with a felon heart calling his brothers up with him, he

went into the chamber where they were all three together, with
full intention to kill the sisters with his own hands, and send
their heads for tokens to their father; though his brothers, who
were otherwise inclined, dissuaded him; but his reverence[68]
stayed their persuasions. But when he was come into the chamber,
with the very words of choleric threatening climbing up his
throat, his eyes first lighted upon Pamela, who, hearing he was
coming, and looking for death, thought she would keep her own
majesty in welcoming it, but the beams thereof so struck his eyes,
with such a counterbuff upon his pride, that, if his anger could
not so quickly love, nor his pride so easily honor, yet both were
forced to find a worthiness. Which, while it bred a pause in
him, Zelmane, who had ready in her mind both what and how to
say, stept out unto him, and with a resolute staidness, void either
of anger, kindness, disdain, or humbleness, spake in this sort.

"Anaxius," said she, "if fame have not been over-partial to
thee, thou art a man of exceeding valor. Therefore, I do call thee
even before that virtue, and will make it the judge between us.
And now I do affirm, that to the eternal blot of all the fair acts
that thou hast done, thou doest weakly in seeking without danger
to revenge his death, whose life with danger thou mightest perhaps have preserved; thou doest cowardly in going about by
the death of these excellent ladies, to prevent the just punishment that hereafter they, by the powers which they, better
than their father, or any other, could make, might lay upon
thee, and doest most basely, in once presenting thyself as an
executioner, a vile office upon men, and in a just cause—beyond the degree of any vile word in so unjust a cause, and
upon ladies, and such ladies. And therefore, as a hangman, I say,
thou art unworthy to be counted a knight, or to be admitted into
the company of knights. Neither for what I say will I allege
other reasons of wisdom or justice to prove my speech, because
I know thou doest disdain to be tied to their rules; but even in
thine own virtue, thereof thou so much gloriest, I will make my
trial, and therefore defy thee, by the death of one of us two,
to prove, or disprove, these reproaches. Choose thee what arms

[68] his reverence—reverence for him.

thou likest; I only demand that these ladies, whom I defend, may in liberty see the combat."

When Zelmane began her speech, the excellency of her beauty and grace made him a little content to hear. Besides that, a new lesson he had read in Pamela had already taught him some regard; but when she entered into bravery of speech, he thought at first a mad and railing humor possessed her, till, finding the speeches hold well together, and at length come to flat challenge of combat, he stood leaning back with his body and head, sometimes with bent brows looking upon the one side of her, sometimes of the other, beyond marvel marveling that he, who had never heard such speeches from any knight, should be thus rebuffed by a woman, and that marvel made him hear out her speech, which ended, he turned his head to his brother Zoilus and said nothing, but only lifting up his eyes, smiled.

But Zelmane finding his mind, "Anaxius," said she, "perchance thou disdainest to answer me, because, as a woman, thou thinkest me not fit to be fought withal; but I tell thee that I have been trained up in martial matters with so good success that I have many times overcome better knights than thyself, and am well known to be equal in feats of arms to the famous Pyrocles, who slew thy valiant uncle, the giant Euardes."

The remembrance of his uncle's death something nettled him, so as he answered thus.

"Indeed," said he, "any woman may be as valiant as that coward and traitorly boy, who slew my uncle traitorously, and after ran from me in the plain field. Five thousand such could not have overcome Euardes, but by falsehood; but I sought him all over Asia, following him still from one of his cony-holes[69] to another, till, coming into this country, I heard of my friend's being besieged, and so came to blow away the wretches that troubled him. But wheresoever the miserable boy fly, heaven nor hell shall keep his heart from being torn by these hands."

"Thou liest in thy throat!" said Zelmane; "that boy, wherever he went, did so noble act as thy heart, as proud as it is, dares not think of, much less perform. But, to please thee the better with

[69] cony-holes—rabbit holes.

my presence, I tell thee, no creature can be nearer of kin to him than myself; and so well we love, that he would not be sorrier for his own death than for mine—I being begotten by his father of an Amazon lady. And therefore, thou canst not devise to revenge thyself more upon him than by killing me, which, if thou darest do manfully, do it; otherwise, if thou harm these incomparable ladies, or myself, without daring to fight with me, I protest before these knights, and before heaven and earth, that will reveal thy shame, that thou art the beggarliest, dastardly villain that dishonoreth the earth with his steps; and if thou lettest me overlive them, so will I blaze[70] thee."

But all this could not move Anaxius, but that he only said, "Evil should it become the terror of the world to fight, much less to scold, with thee." "But," said he, "for the death of these same"—pointing to the princesses—"of my grace, I give them life"; and withal, going to Pamela, and offering to take her by the chin, "And as for you, minion," said he, "yield but gently to my will, and you shall not only live, but live so happily—"

He would have said further, when Pamela, displeased both with words, matter, and manner, putting him away with her fair hand, "Proud beast!" said she, "yet thou playest worse thy comedy than thy tragedy. For my part, assure thyself, since my destiny is such that at each moment my life and death stand in equal balance, I had rather have thee, and think thee far fitter, to be my hangman than my husband."

Pride and anger would fain have cruelly revenged so bitter an answer, but already Cupid had begun to make it his sport to pull his plumes, so that, unused to a way of courtesy, and put out of his bias of pride, he hastily went away, grumbling to himself, between threatening and wishing, leaving his brothers with them, the elder of whom, Lycurgus, liked Philoclea, and Zoilus would needs love Zelmane, or at least entertain themselves with making them believe so. Lycurgus more braggard, and near his brother's humor, began with setting forth their blood, their deeds, how many they had despised of most excellent women, how much they were bound to them that would seek

---

[70] blaze—proclaim.

that of them; in sum, in all his speeches more like the bestower than the desirer of felicity, whom it was an excellent pastime (to those that would delight in the play of virtue) to see with what a witty ignorance she would not understand; and how, acknowledging his perfections, she would make that one of his perfections not to be injurious to ladies. But when he knew not how to reply, then would he fall to touching and toying, still viewing his graces in no glass but self-liking, to which Philoclea's shamefastness and humbleness were as stong resisters as choler and disdain; for, though she yielded not, he thought she was to be overcome, and that thought a while stayed him from further violence. But Zelmane had eye to his behavior and set in her memory, upon the score of revenge, while she herself was no less attempted by Zoilus, who, less full of brags, was forwardest in offering (indeed) dishonorable violence.

CHAPTER 27

Zelmane's persuasions to temporize, and refer them to Basilius. Anaxius' embassage to treat the marriage. Basilius' recourse to a new oracle, and his negative thereon. The flattering relation of his Mercury.[71] *The brothers' course to resist force without, and use force within.*

But when, after their fruitless labors, they had gone away, called by their brother, who began to be perplexed between new-conceived desires, and disdain to be disdained, Zelmane, who with most assured quietness of judgment looked into their present estate, earnestly persuaded the two sisters that, to avoid the mischiefs of proud outrage, they would only so far suit their behavior to their estates as they might win time, which as it could not bring them to worse case than they were, so it might bring forth unexpected relief.

"And why," said Pamela, "shall we any longer flatter adversity? Why should we delight to make ourselves any longer balls to injurious Fortune, since our own kin are content traitorously to abuse us? Certainly, in mishap it may be some comfort

[71] Mercury—messenger.

to us that we are lighted in these fellows' hands, who yet will keep us from having cause of being miserable by our friends' means. Nothing grieves me more than that you, noble lady Zelmane, to whom the world might have made us able to do honor, should receive only hurt by the contagion of our misery. As for me and my sister, undoubtedly it becomes our birth to think of dying nobly, while we have done or suffered nothing which might make our soul ashamed at the parture from these bodies. Hope is the fawning traitor of the mind, while under color of friendship, it robs it of his chief force of resolution."

"Virtuous and fair lady," said Zelmane, "what you say is true; and that truth may well make up a part in the harmony of your noble thoughts. But yet the time (which ought always to be one) is not tuned for it; while that may bring forth any good, do not bar yourself thereof; for then would be the time to die nobly, when you cannot live nobly." Then so earnestly she persuaded with them both to refer themselves to their father's consent (in obtaining whereof they knew some while would be spent) and by that means to temper the minds of their proud wooers, that in the end Pamela yielded to her, because she spoke reason, and Philoclea yielded to her reason, because she spoke it.

And so, when they were again solicited in that little-pleasing petition, Pamela forced herself to make answer to Anaxius that, if her father gave his consent, she would make herself believe that such was the heavenly determination, since she had no means to avoid it. Anaxius, who was the most frank promiser to himself of success, nothing doubted of Basilius' consent, but rather assured himself he would be his orator in that matter; and therefore, he chose out an officious servant (whom he esteemed very wise because he never found him but just of his opinion), and willed him to be his ambassador to Basilius, and to make him know that, if he meant to have his daughter both safe and happy, and desired himself to have such a son-in-law as would not only protect him in his quiet course, but, if he listed to accept it, would give him the monarchy of the world, that then he should receive Anaxius, who never before knew what it was to pray anything. That, if he did not, he would make him know that the power of Anaxius was in everything beyond his will, and yet his will not to be resisted by any other power.

His servant, with smiling and cast-up look, desired God to make his memory able to contain the treasure of that wise speech; and therefore, besought him to repeat it again, that by the oftener hearing it, his mind might be the better acquainted with the divineness thereof; and that being graciously granted, he then doubted not by carrying with him in his conceit the grace where with Anaxius spoke it, to persuade rocky minds to their own harm; so little doubted he to win Basilius to that which he thought would make him think the heavens opened, when he heard but the proffer thereof. Anaxius gravely allowed the probability of his conjecture, and therefore sent him away, promising him he should have the bringing up of his second son by Pamela.

The messenger with speed performed his lord's command-ment to Basilius, who by nature quiet, and by superstition made doubtful, was loath to take any matter of arms in hand, wherein already he had found so slow success, though Philanax vehe-mently urged him thereunto, making him see that his retiring back did encourage injuries. But Basilius, betwixt the fear of Anaxius' might, the passion of his love, and jealousy of his estate, was so perplexed, that, not able to determine, he took the com-mon course of men, to fly only then to devotion, when they want resolution; so, detaining the messenger with delays, he deferred the directing of his course to the counsel of Apollo, which, because himself at that time could not well go to require,[72] he intrusted the matter to his best trusted Philanax, who, as one in whom obedience was sufficient reason unto him, went with diligence to Delphos, where, being entered into the secret place of the temple, and having performed the sacrifices usual, the spirit that possessed the prophesying woman with a sacred fury attended not his demand, but, as if it would argue him of in-credulity, told him, not in dark wonted speeches, but plainly to be understood, what he came for, and that he should return to Basilius and will him to deny his daughters to Anaxius and his

---

[72] require—inquire.

brothers, for that they were reserved for such as were better beloved of the gods. That he should not doubt, for they should return unto him safely and speedily, and that he should keep on his solitary course, till both Philanax and Basilius fully agreed in the understanding of the former prophecy, withal commanding Philanax from thenceforward to give tribute, but not oblation, to human wisdom.

Philanax, then finding that reason cannot show itself more reasonable than to leave reasoning in things above reason, returns to his lord, and, like one that preferred truth before the maintaining of an opinion, hid nothing from him; nor from thenceforth durst any more dissuade him from that which he found by the celestial providence directed; but he himself looking to repair the government as much as in so broken an estate by civil dissension he might, and fortifying with notable art both the lodges so as they were almost made unapproachable, he left Basilius to bemoan the absence of his daughters, and to bewail the imprisonment of Zelmane; yet, wholly given holily to obey the oracle, he gave a resolute negative unto the messenger of Anaxius, who all this while had waited for it, yet in good terms desiring him to show himself, in respect of his birth and profession, so princely a knight as, without forcing him to seek the way of force, to deliver in noble sort those ladies unto him, and so should the injury have been in Amphialus and the benefit in him.

The messenger went back with this answer, yet having ever used to sugar anything which his master was to receive, he told him that, when Basilius first understood his desires, he did overreach so far all his most hopeful expectations, that he thought it were too great a boldness to hearken to such a man, in whom the heavens had such interest, without asking the god's counsel, and therefore had sent his principal counsellor to Delphos, who, although he kept the matter never so secret, yet his diligence, inspired by Anaxius' privilege over all worldly things, had found out the secret, which was that he should not presume to marry his daughters to one who already was enrolled among the demigods, and yet much less he should dare the attempting to take them out of his hands.

Anaxius, who till then had made fortune his creator, and force his god, now began to find another wisdom to be above, that judged so rightly of him; and where in this time of his servant's waiting for Basilius' resolution, he and his brothers had courted their ladies, as whom they vouchsafed to have for their wives, he resolved now to dally no longer in delays, but to make violence his orator, since he had found persuasions had gotten nothing but answers.[73] Which intention he opened to his brothers, who, having all this while wanted nothing to take that way, but his authority, gave spurs to his running and (unworthy men), neither feeling virtue in themselves nor tendering it in others, they were headlong to make that evil consort of love and force, when Anaxius had word that from the tower there were descried some companies of armed men marching towards the town; wherefore, he gave present order to his servants and soldiers to go to the gates and walls, leaving none within but himself and his brothers: his thoughts then so full of their intended prey that Mars' loudest trumpet could scarcely have awaked him.

CHAPTER 28

Zoilus the messenger, and first offerer, of force is forced to fly and die. Lycurgus pointed to kill, is fought withal, foiled, and killed. Anaxius the revenger with Pyrocles the punisher brave, and bravely combatted.

But, while he was directing what he would have done, his youngest brother Zoilus, glad that he had the commission, went in the name of Anaxius to tell the sisters, that, since he had answer from their father, that he and his brother Lycurgus should have them in what sort it pleased them, that they would now grant them no longer time, but presently to determine whether they thought it more honorable comfort to be compelled or persuaded. Pamela made him answer that, in a matter whereon the whole state of her life depended, and wherein she had ever answered, she would not lead, but follow her parents'

[73] answers—refusals.

pleasure, she thought it reason she should, either by letter or particular messenger, understand something from themselves, and not have their belief bound to the report of their partial servants; and therefore, as to their words, she and her sister had ever a simple and true resolution, so against their unjust force God, they hoped, would either arm their lives or take away their lives.

"Well, ladies," said he, "I will leave my brothers, who by-and-by will come unto you, to be their own ambassadors; for my part, I must now do myself service." And with that, turning up his mustachios, and marching as if he would begin a pavan,[74] he went toward Zelmane; but Zelmane having had, all this while of the messenger's being with Basilius, much to do to keep those excellent ladies from seeking by the passport of death to escape those base dangers whereunto they found themselves subject, still hoping that Musidorus would find some means to deliver them, and therefore, had often, both by her own example and comfortable reasons, persuaded them to overpass many insolent indignities of their proud suitors, who thought it was a sufficient favor not to do the uttermost injury, now come again to the strait she most feared for them, either of death or dishonor, if heroical courage would have let her, she had been beyond herself amazed; but that yet held up her wit to attend the uttermost occasion, which even then brought his hairy forehead[75] unto her; for Zoilus, smacking his lips as for the prologue of a kiss, and something advancing himself, "Darling," said he, "let thy heart be full of joy, and let thy fair eyes be of council with it; for this day thou shalt have Zoilus, whom many have longed for; but none shall have him, but Zelmane. And O, how much glory I have to think what a race will be between us. The world, by the heavens, the world will be too little for them."

And with that, he would have put his arm about her neck, but she, withdrawing herself from him, "My lord," said she, "much good may your thoughts do you, but that I may not

[74] pavan—pavan, a grave, slow, stately dance.
[75] his hairy forehead—Occasion was typically pictured as having a long forelock in front and a bald head behind; man must grasp the long hair as Occasion rushes by.

dissemble with you, my nativity being cast by one that never failed in any of his prognostications, I have been assured that I should never be apt to bear children. But since you will honor me with so high favor, I must only desire that I may perform a vow which I made among my countrywomen, the famous Amazons, that I would never marry none, but such one as was able to withstand me in arms. Therefore, before I make mine own desire serviceable to yours, you must vouchsafe to lend me armor and weapons, that at least, with a blow or two of the sword, I may not find myself perjured to myself."

But Zoilus (but laughing with a hearty loudness) went by force to embrace her; making no other answer, but since she had a mind to try his knighthood, she should quickly know what a man of arms he was, and so, without reverence to the ladies, began to struggle with her. But in Zelmane then disdain became wisdom, and anger gave occasion. For abiding no longer abode in the matter, she that had not put off, though she had disguised, Pyrocles, being far fuller of strong nimbleness, tripped up his feet, so that he fell down at hers, and, withal, meaning to pursue what she had begun, pulled out his sword, which he wore about him; but, before she could strike him withal, he got up and ran to a fair chamber, where he had left his two brethren preparing themselves to come down to their mistresses. But she followed at his heels, and even as he came to throw himself into their arms for succor, she hit him with his own sword such a blow upon the waist, that she almost cut him asunder, once she sundered his soul from his body, sending it to Proserpina[76] an angry goddess against ravishers.

But Anaxius, seeing before his eyes the miserable end of his brother, fuller of despite than wrath, and yet fuller of wrath than sorrow, looking with a woeful eye upon his brother Lycurgus, "Brother," said he, "chastise this vile creature, while I go down and take order lest further mischief arise"; and so went down to the ladies, whom he visited, doubting there had been some further practice than yet he conceived; but, finding them only strong in

[76] Proserpina—the queen of hell, a very stern goddess, who hates ravishers because she herself was carried off to the underworld by Pluto.

patience, he went and locked a great iron gate, by which only anybody might mount to that part of the castle, rather to conceal the shame of his brother, slain by a woman, than for doubt of any other annoyance, and then went up to receive some comfort of the execution he was sure his brother had done of Zelmane.

But Zelmane no sooner saw those brothers, of whom reason assured her she was to expect revenge, but that she leaped to a target,[77] as one that well knew the first mark of valor to be defense. And then, accepting the opportunity of Anaxius' going away, she waited not the pleasure of Lycurgus, but, without any words (which she ever thought vain when resolution took the place of persuasion), gave her own heart the contentment to be the assailer. Lycurgus, who was in the disposition of his nature hazardous, and by the lucky passing through many dangers grown confident in himself, went toward her, rather as to spoil than to fight, so far from fear that his assuredness disdained to hope.

But when her sword made demonstrations above all flattery of arguments, and that he found she pressed so upon him as showed that her courage sprang not from blind despair, but was guarded both with cunning and strength, self-love then first in him divided itself from vainglory, and made him find that the world of worthiness had not his whole globe comprised in his breast, but that it was necessary to have strong resistance against so strong assailing. And so between them, for a few blows, Mars himself might have been delighted to look on; but Zelmane, who knew that, in her case, slowness of victory was little better than ruin, with the bellows of hate blew the fire of courage, and he, striking a main blow at her head, she warded it with the shield, but so warded that the shield was cut in two pieces while it protected her; and, withal, she ran in to him, and thrusting at his breast, which he put by with his target, as he was lifting up his sword to strike again, she let fall the piece of her shield, and with her left hand catching his sword of the inside of the pommel, with nimble and strong sleight she had gotten his sword out of his hand before his sense could convey to his imagination what was

[77] target—shield.

to be doubted. And, having now two swords against one shield, meaning not foolishly to be ungrateful to good fortune, while he was no more amazed with his being unweaponed than with the suddenness thereof, she gave him such a wound upon his head, in despite of the shield's over-weak resistance, that withal he fell to the ground, astonished with pain, and aghast with fear.

But seeing Zelmane ready to conclude her victory in his death, bowing up his head to her, with a countenance that had forgotten all pride, "Enough, excellent lady," said he, "the honor is yours, whereof you shall want the best witness, if you kill me. As you have taken from men the glory of manhood, return so now again to your own sex for mercy. I will redeem my life of you with no small services, for I will undertake to make my brother obey all your commandments. Grant life, I beseech you, for your own honor, and for the person's sake that you love best."

Zelmane repressed a while her great heart, either disdaining to be cruel or pitiful, and therefore not cruel. And now the image of human condition began to be an orator unto her of compassion, when she saw, as he lifted up his arms with a suppliant's grace, about one of them, unhappily, tied a garter with a jewel, which (given to Pyrocles by his aunt of Thessalia, and greatly esteemed by him) he had presented to Philoclea, and with inward rage promising extreme hatred, had seen Lycurgus with a proud force, and not without some hurt unto her, pull away from Philoclea, because at entreaty she would not give it him. But the sight of that was like a cipher signifying all the injuries which Philoclea had of him suffered, and that remembrance, feeding upon wrath, trod down all conceits of mercy. And therefore saying no more but, "No, villain, die! It is Philoclea that sends thee this token for thy love."

With that she made her sword drink the blood of his heart, though he, wresting his body, and with a countenance prepared to excuse, would fain have delayed the receiving of death's ambassadors.

But neither that stayed Zelmane's hand, nor yet Anaxius' cry unto her, who, having made fast the iron gate, even then came to the top of the stairs, when, contrary to all his imaginations, he saw his brother lie at Zelmane's mercy; therefore, crying, promising, and threatening to her to hold her hand, the last groan of his brother was the only answer he could get to his unrespected eloquence. But then pity would fain have drawn tears, which fury, in their spring, dried; and anger would fain have spoken, but that disdain sealed up his lips; but in his heart he blasphemed heaven, that it could have such a power over him; no less ashamed of the victory he should have of her than of his brother's overthrow, and no more spited that it was yet unrevenged than that the revenge should be no greater than a woman's destruction; therefore, with no speech, but such a groaning cry as often is the language of sorrowful anger, he came running at Zelmane, use of fighting then serving instead of patient consideration what to do. Guided wherewith, though he did not with knowledge, yet did he according to knowledge, pressing upon Zelmane in such a well-defended manner that, in all the combats that ever she had fought, she had never more need of quick senses and ready virtue. For being one of the greatest men of stature then living, as he did fully answer that stature in greatness of might, so did he exceed both in greatness of courage, which, with a countenance formed by the nature both of his mind and body to an almost horrible fierceness, was able to have carried fear to any mind that was not privy to itself of a true and constant worthiness. But Pyrocles, whose soul might well be separated from his body, but never alienated from the remembering what was comely, if at the first he did a little apprehend the dangerousness of his adversary, whom once before he had something tried, and now perfectly saw, as the very picture of forcible fury, yet was that apprehension quickly stayed in him, rather strengthening than weakening his virtue by that wrestling, like wine growing the stronger by being moved.[78] So that they both, prepared in hearts and able in hands, did honor solitariness there with such a combat as might have demanded, as a right of fortune, whole armies of beholders.

---

[78] wine growing the stronger by being moved—refers to fermentation, which is an excitation.

But no beholders needed there, where manhood blew the trumpet, and satisfaction did whet as much as glory. There was strength against nimbleness, rage against resolution, fury against virtue, confidence against courage, pride against nobleness; love, in both, breeding mutual hatred, and desire of revenging the injury of his brothers' slaughter, to Anaxius, being like Philoclea's captivity to Pyrocles. Who had seen the one, would have thought nothing could have resisted; who had marked the other, would have marvelled that the other had so long resisted. But like two contrary tides, either of which are able to carry worlds of ships and men upon them, with such swiftness as nothing seems able to withstand them, yet, meeting one another, with mingling their watery forces, and struggling together, it is long to say whether stream gets the victory; so between these, if Pallas[79] had been there, she could scarcely have told whether she had nursed better in the feats of arms. The Irish greyhound against the English mastiff, the sword-fish against the whale, the rhinoceros against the elephant, might be models, and but models, of this combat. Anaxius was better armed defensively, for, beside a strong casque bravely covered, wherewith he covered his head, he had a huge shield, such, perchance, as Achilles showed to the pale walls of Troy, wherewithal that body was covered. But Pyrocles, utterly unarmed for defense, to offend had the advantage; for in either hand he had a sword, and with both hands nimbly performed that office. And according as they were diversely furnished, so did they differ in the manner of fighting; for Anaxius most by warding, and Pyrocles oftenest by avoiding, resisted the adversary's assault. Both hasty to end, yet both often staying for advantage. Time, distance, and motion, custom made them so perfect in that, as if they had been fellow counsellors, and not enemies, each knew the other's mind, and knew how to prevent it; so as their strength failed them sooner than their skill, and yet their breath failed them sooner than their strength. And breathless indeed they grew before either could complain of any loss of blood.

[79] Pallas—goddess of warfare, and of the wise use of arms.

CHAPTER 29

The combatants' first breathing, re-encounter, and————

So consenting, by the mediation of necessity, to a breathing time of truce, being withdrawn a little one from the other, Anaxius stood leaning upon his sword, with his grim eye so settled upon Zelmane as is wont to be the look of an earnest thought. Which Zelmane marking, and, according to the Pyroclean nature, fuller of gay bravery in the midst than in the beginning, of danger, "What is it," said she, "Anaxius, that thou so deeply musest on? Doth thy brothers' example make thee think of thy fault past, or of thy coming punishment?"

"I think," said he, "what spiteful god it should be who, envying my glory, hath brought me to such a wayward case that neither thy death can be a revenge, nor thy overthrow a victory."

"Thou doest well indeed" said Zelmane, "to impute thy case to the heavenly providence, which will have thy pride find itself, even in that whereof thou art most proud, punished by the weak sex which thou most contemnest."

But then, having sufficiently rested themselves, they renewed again their combat, far more terribly than before, like nimble vaulters, who at the first and second leap do but stir and, as it were, awake the fiery and airy parts, which after, in the other leaps, they do with more excellency exercise. For in this pausing, each had brought to his thoughts the manner of the other's fighting, and the advantages which by that, and by the quality of their weapons, they might work themselves, and so again repeated the lesson they had said before, more perfectly, by the using of it.

Anaxius oftener used blows, his huge force (as it were) more delighting therein, and the large protection of his shield animating him unto it. Pyrocles, of a more fine and deliver[80] strength, watching his time when to give fit thrusts, as, with the quick obeying of his body to his eye's quick commandment, he shunned any harm Anaxius could do to him, so would he soon have made an end of Anaxius if he had not found him a man of wonderful,

[80] deliver—nimble.

and almost matchless, excellency in matters of arms. Pyrocles used divers feignings to bring Anaxius on into some inconvenience. But Anaxius, keeping a sound manner of fighting, never offered but seeing fair cause, and then followed it with well-governed violence.

Thus spent they a great time, striving to do, and, with striving to do, wearying themselves more than with the very doing. Anaxius, finding Zelmane so near unto him that with little motion he might reach her, knitting all his strength together, at that time mainly foined[81] at her face. But Zelmane, strongly putting it by with her right-hand sword, coming in with her left foot and hand, would have given him a sharp visitation to his right side, but that he was fain to leap away. Whereat ashamed, as having never done so much before in his life———

[81] mainly foined—stabbed fiercely.